RUNNING with the LEGENDS

Michael Sandrock
Sports Editor, *Colorado Daily*

Human Kinetics

Library of Congress Cataloging-in-Publication Data

Sandrock, Mike, 1958-
    Running with the legends / Mike Sandrock.
        p.   cm.
    Includes index.
    ISBN 0-87322-493-0
    1. Runners (Sports)--Biography.   I. Title.
    GV1061.14.S36   1996
    796.42'092'2--dc20
    [B]   96-3790
                                                      CIP

ISBN: 0-87322-493-0

On the cover: A pack of runners, including some legends, out for a training run on the outskirts of Boulder, Colorado. From left to right, in front, Frank Shorter, Priscilla Welch, Rosa Mota, and Lorraine Moller.

Developmental Editor: Julie Rhoda; **Assistant Editors:** Susan Moore and Sandra Merz Bott; **Editorial Assistant:** Jennifer J. Hemphill; **Copyeditors:** David Frattini and Michael Ryder; **Proofreader:** Jim Burns; **Indexer:** Joan Griffitts; **Typesetters and Layout Artists:** Angie Snyder and Julie Overholt; **Text Designer:** Judy Henderson; **Photo Editor:** Boyd LaFoon; **Cover Designer:** Jack Davis; **Photographer** (cover): Tim DeFrisco; **Photographers** (interior): United States Olympic Committee, Archive Photos/Popperfoto, Express Newspapers, AFP, Photo Run/Victah Sailer, Thomas Lydon, Takashi Ito, and Boston Marathon/Robert Sacchetti; **Printer:** Versa Press

Human Kinetics books are available at special discounts for bulk purchase. Special editions or book excerpts can also be created to specification. For details, contact the Special Sales Manager at Human Kinetics.

Printed in the United States of America   10   9   8   7   6   5   4   3   2

Human Kinetics
Web site: http://www.humankinetics.com

United States: Human Kinetics
P.O. Box 5076
Champaign, IL 61825-5076
1-800-747-4457
e-mail: humank@hkusa.com

Canada: Human Kinetics, Box 24040
Windsor, ON N8Y 4Y9
1-800-465-7301 (in Canada only)
e-mail: humank@hkcanada.com

Europe: Human Kinetics,
P.O. Box IW14
Leeds LS16 6TR, United Kingdom
(44) 1132 781708
e-mail: humank@hkeurope.com

Australia: Human Kinetics
57A Price Avenue
Lower Mitcham, South Australia 5062
(08) 277 1555
e-mail: humank@hkaustralia.com

New Zealand: Human Kinetics
P.O. Box 105-231, Auckland 1
(09) 523 3462
e-mail: humank@hknewz.com

For Emil Zatopek
Men like you should run for 1,000 years.

Dedication

Contents

Foreword   vii

Acknowledgments   x

Credits   xi

Introduction   xii

1   Emil Zatopek   1

"No, no … I was not very talented. My basic speed was low. Only with willpower was I able to reach this world-best standard in long-distance running."

2   Hezekiah Kipchoge "Kip" Keino   37

"I run because I enjoy running.… There is nothing special about me. There will soon be many in Kenya as good as me."

3   Priscilla Welch   67

"The further I got into training for health and fitness, which it was in the beginning, the better it got. The fitter I got, the more I wanted to pursue it. It was just like holding a carrot in front of a horse."

4   Bill Rodgers   97

"I became a runner because it suited my personality. It suited me as an individual."

5   Frank Shorter   133

" With victory in hand, running at maximum effort becomes very difficult. Without some company in the difficult miles, the body's mission becomes lonely and dark."

6   Lasse Viren   171

"I just had to get to the line first. My coach said, 'Get to the front with 600 meters left, and stay there.' I did."

7   Alberto Juantorena   203

*"The medal is not for yourself. It couldn't be done without the
support and help of my people, runners, and coaches."*

8   Grete Waitz   223

*"Whatever moves the other runners made, I knew I could re-
spond.... I felt if I had to, I could fly."*

9   Steve Jones   241

*"In running you can't say you want to be the best. You just have to
work very hard, really. You're only a hamstring injury away from
oblivion."*

10   Lorraine Moller   269

*"When I was growing up I wasn't inspired to be a marathoner. It
wasn't even in a little girl's vocabulary."*

11   Sebastian Coe   289

*"I was now running for the tape, the mental agony of knowing I
had hit my limit, of not knowing what was happening behind me. I
was not to know they were fading, too. The anxiety over the last 20
meters was unbearable, it showed in my face as I crossed the line."*

12   Ingrid Kristiansen   325

*When I am training and competing, I really concentrate, but during
the rest of the day, I don't want to think about running. I think too
many runners today are too serious about their running."*

13   Toshihiko Seko   345

"The marathon is my only girlfriend. I give her everything I have."

14   Robert de Castella   369

*"Running well is a matter of having the patience to persevere when
you are tired and not expecting instant results. The only secret is
that it is consistent, often monotonous, boring, hard work. And it's
tiring."*

15   Juma Ikangaa   403

"I don't train to beat another runner. We are out there together, competing with the marathon, and I train to run the marathon as fast as I can."

16   Joan Benoit Samuelson   421

"Every time I fail I assume I will be a stronger person for it. I keep on running figuratively and literally, despite a limp that gets more noticeable with each passing season, because for me there has always been a place to go and a terrible urgency to get there."

17   Said Aouita   445

"I do everything I can to win."

18   Rosa Mota   467

"I was motivated to win (the Boston Marathon) not only for myself, but for the Portuguese people of Boston. They were with me all the way and made winning this race the nicest moment of my life."

19   Arturo Barrios   491

"I train for good luck."

20   Uta Pippig   519

"I'm more relaxed for training . . . more mentally strong, so I can train much harder. I have the mentality that I can train like a man, and it helps me a lot. So we'll go for fast times and if it works, OK. If not, then we tried."

21   Noureddine Morceli   549

"To really prove yourself in athletics nowadays, you have to stay 10 to 15 years. That's what I intend to do."

Index   569
About the Author   575

Foreword

The best, most knowing, observation about running a world record came from the 1500-meter 1960 Olympic champion, Herb Elliott of Australia. "You have to have the sheer arrogance to believe you can run your distance faster than anyone else who ever lived," he said, "and then you have to have the humility to actually go out and do it."

Arrogance and humility. In this book, Michael Sandrock identifies greatness in fifty years of distance runners. His choices all have that essential mix of confidence and acceptance. His profiles of them are full of explanatory fire. And his effect upon this ex-Olympic marathoner was to force me to realize how my perspective has changed with regard to my discipline's "legends."

Keep in mind that when you actually race the men and women herein, you don't want to hear about their being the stuff of legend. You want flesh and blood, preferably flesh coated with a slothful six or seven percent body fat and blood running a little low on hemoglobin. You want to see an arm action start to labor, a back stiffen. You want mortality, not legend.

But when Abebe Bikila is running off one shoulder and Ron Clarke off the other, you cannot deny that you would never be competing against runners such as these if you had not once worshipped them. Their stories ignite and shape our young strainings.

Years before I became a marathoner, I read of Zatopek, the strange Czech who was the only man ever to win the 5,000 meters, the 10,000 meters, and marathon in a single Olympics (1952) and who grimaced as he ran. He seemed somehow more honest for acknowledging the pain that others hid—the pain that had overwhelmed me as a high school sophomore in 1959 running cross-country in Oregon.

I memorized his pioneering interval workouts and his almost goofy experiments in training. Years later, when I met him at a dinner before the New York City Marathon, he confirmed my favorite story: He *had* done his laundry by putting it in the bathtub, adding soap and water, and running on it with combat boots for two hours.

"I run and run, soft and squishy, easy rhythm, thinking of other things," he said, "and Dana [his wife] comes home and there is yelling. Soapsuds down the hall! Soapsuds in the kitchen! But even she admit no one ever got shirts so white!"

That creative eccentricity was shared by my coach at the University of Oregon, Bill Bowerman, whose experiments with shoe soles led to his bonding shut several of his wife Barbara's, waffle irons—and led, too, to the great success of the Nike shoe company.

Now *there* was a legend. Bowerman was the guide or teacher who appears in every mythic narrative at Oregon about coming of age. His main lesson was, in the words of the oracle, "Know thyself." He tailored our training to the peculiarities of our talents. When he made me take extra days of rest between workouts, I improved so much it was an epiphany. Soon I was an international-class competitor.

My perspective had to change. I had to see myself, at worst, as a man among equals. By the late '60s and '70s, as I raced Frank Shorter and Bill Rodgers, placing fourth behind Frank in the 1972 Munich Olympic Marathon, I was hardly worshipful. I was antilegend. So, it turned out, were they. When Rodgers learned that I'd been told I wasn't officer material in the Army because I was thought not to have the requisite drive to bend other men to my will, he practically hugged me in recognition—and solidarity.

And when a research psychologist once described the finest distance runners as "emotionally stable to the point of aloofness," I thought of Shorter. He and Rodgers were and are compulsively, heroically dutiful *to their own chosen way*. To many other ways they are blissfully aloof. Together, they inspired America in its great running boom. And having done that, they seemed tinged by faint embarrassment. Perhaps they just didn't want it to look like they had *ordered* everyone into the streets.

In fact, not one of the runners in this book has had a hard time being himself or herself. We honor them all according to how well they honored their own individuality. This brings us, without question, to Joan Benoit.

In March, 1983, the Friday before the World Cross-Country Championships in Gateshead, England, Benoit took me on a 10-mile run. She picked it up until I was using everything I had to stay with her. Then, up a long English hill in the rain, she became the first woman ever to run away from me. Her face (I saw when she let me catch up on the downhill) was filled with a crazed, remorseless joy.

A few weeks later Benoit would run her 2:23 world best at Boston, but it was her face, that exultation in the repeated spending of herself, in coming so deathly close to her limits, that was the real revelation to me, to her dismayed mother, and, far more important, to women everywhere. No athlete was ever tougher than Joan Benoit, and no one more defining in her cycle of injury, recovery, victory, and injury—of love and loving too much.

I'd written about runners for *Sports Illustrated* for 10 years by then, but my perspective was still largely that of a competitor. I didn't care to speculate about the wider meaning of my subjects, about *why* a Shorter or a Steve Prefontaine won the hearts of so many spectators. That was for the spectators to know. I cared more about evocative detail, about the image of an opal-pale Rodgers, caught at 4:00 A.M. in the refrigerator's light after a 30-mile day, eating mayonnaise with a tablespoon from the jar, asking with perfect quizzicallity, "Do I run so much to eat like this, or do I eat like this to run so much?"

But the revelation of Benoit was so important for all those women trying to make real the potential they could feel calling them from their genes—but not from their society—that I finally took a broader view. Even as Benoit won the first women's Olympic marathon in 1984, I knew she was a legend. My perspective shifted again, and I tried to see such rare creatures as exemplars of the humanly possible, templates for the generations.

All of this is a tortured way of saying that Michael Sandrock has written a book from a vantage that spans the entire sweep of my journey. Here is compelling inspiration, ferocious racing, vital history, fascinating personality, and essential training lore. Each champion is placed where he or she came in the long relay of performances that led to today's records. This is a book worthy of its subjects—and all in perspective.

—*Kenny Moore*

Thanks to my family for their support; Clint Talbott and the other *Colorado Daily* editors for giving me time to write; David Morrill for doing research; Mary Mabwa for making ugali and other meals to keep my strength up; my training partner Dave Smith for waiting; Julie Rhoda for her work as developmental editor at Human Kinetics; and, especially to all the runners who patiently answered my questions.

Acknowledgments

Credits

Tables on pages 185, 264, 316, 333, 334, 502, and 565 adapted, by permission, from E. zur Megede and R. Hymans, 1991, *Progression of World Best Performances and Official IAAF Records* (St. Louis: International Athletic Foundation).

Selected material in chapter 1 reprinted, by permission, from R. Clark and N. Harris, 1967, *The Lonely Breed* (London: Pelham Books).

Selected material in chapter 1 reprinted, by permission, from B. Lenton, 1983, *Off the Record* (Canberra, Australia: Canberra).

Selected material in chapter 2 reprinted, by permission, from F. Noronha, 1970, *Kipchoge of Kenya* (Nairobi, Kenya: Elimu Publishers).

Selected material in chapter 4 reprinted, by permission, from B. Rodgers, 1980, *Marathoning* (New York: Simon and Schuster).

Selected material in chapters 8 and 14 reprinted, by permission, from B. Foster and C. Temple, 1978, *Brendan Foster* (London: Heinemann).

Selected material in chapter 8 reprinted, by permission, from G. Waitz and G. Averbuch, 1986, *World Class* (New York: Warner Books).

Selected material in chapter 11 reprinted, by permission, from S. Coe and D. Miller, 1981, *Running Free* (New York: St. Martin's Press).

Selected material in chapter 14 reprinted, by permission, from B. Lenton, 1983, *Through the Tape* (Canberra, Australia: Canberra).

"What interests me are great souls, and great souls alone," French essayist and novelist Albert Camus wrote in his journals. So it is with running: Those who interest us most are the "great souls" of the sport, those runners who have captivated and inspired us by the way they train, race, and live.

This book is an attempt to capture a bit of what makes these 14 men and 7 women the legends of running they are. There is no formula for how many wins, records, or medals a runner must earn to qualify as "a legend." Rather, the sobriquet is reserved for those who carry a mystique that transcends the finish line, making them much more than champion athletes. Runners are the Don Quixotes of the world, forever flailing at windmills, sometimes laughed at, rarely understood. The athletes in this book have donned armor, mounted their loyal steeds, and done great battle on the road and track.

The idea for this book came one holiday season, when I was back home in Chicago at a race with my brother and a cousin. We were discussing training, as all runners do. My brother said he was tired because he had run twelve 400-meter intervals the day before.

"Why so many?" I asked. "The most Rob de Castella ever does is eight, and he's a 2:07 marathoner."

"Really? What else does he do?" my brother asked.

Soon the other runners in my family were asking questions. When talk turned to Emil Zatopek, my oldest nephew (a high school runner) leaned forward and eagerly soaked in stories of this giant of a runner, just as I had when I first heard mysterious tales about him years ago. Later my brother said, "You know, you should transcribe your interviews with those runners." Ted Miller of Human Kinetics then suggested taking it a step further by focusing on the training, racing, thinking, and coaching of these elite runners, some of the greatest of modern history.

One day the University of Colorado women's cross-country team was out training. As the runners passed through campus, Frank Shorter jogged by, warming up for an interval session, as he had for the past 25 years.

"Good luck at nationals," Frank said as he passed the team.

"That's Frank Shorter!" said the coach.

"Wow, Frank Shorter," said one girl. "Isn't he the guy who does the TV commentating?"

Yes, Shorter does TV work. But he also has done a whole lot more in his career, and when I heard that a runner in Shorter's own town did not know his story, I knew I had to finish up this book. (The runner had not even been born when Shorter won his first Olympic medal in 1972.)

Those of you who love running and love talking about it know who the runners in this book are; for you, I wanted to provide some insight into what made them tick, how their backgrounds shaped their running, how they trained, how they ate, and how they rested. And my goal for newcomers to running and younger runners was to pass along the training and racing stories and the methods of these legends, to provide some knowledge of a glorious running heritage replete with heroes and heroines, victory and defeat, and the tales of some extraordinary men and women.

Two books that influenced me were Kenny Moore's *Best Efforts* and Ron Clarke's *The Lonely Breed*, in which Clarke writes of 21 runners from the past. I wanted to also write about 21 runners, adding to what Clarke wrote. The runners whom I have chosen to write about comprise only a partial list of legends. I started with the runners I knew, then added others, like Noureddine Morceli, Joan Benoit Samuelson, and Kip Keino, who indisputably rank among the all-time greats.

These runners are like diamonds. Look at them from different angles, and you see reflected different facets of their personalities, ambitions, and motivations. Writing about them is a subjective endeavor, and others who know these runners would no doubt come up with different profiles. There are many other runners who deserve to be included: Sweden's great pair of milers, Gunder Hägg and Arne Andersson; the original Flying Finns, Hannes Kolehmainen, Ville Ritola, Paavo Nurmi; milers Glenn Cunningham, Herb Elliott, Peter Snell, Jim Ryun, and Eamonn Coghlan; Ron Clarke, Carlos Lopes, Gelindo Bordin, Alberto Salazar, Vladimir Kuts, and Gordon Pirie. Each has a unique story worth retelling. Pirie, for instance, used to run until he'd be so tired he couldn't stand up anymore. After lying down in a ditch and sleeping for a while, he would get up and continue running. These are the kind of stories we love hearing, which can motivate us when our commitment to training wavers.

Several years ago I interviewed mythologist Joseph Campbell. When I asked what the best experience of his life was, Campbell, author of *The Masks of God* and the *Power of Myth*, replied that it was being on the track team at Columbia, where he had been a middle-distance runner in the mid-1920s. It struck me that Campbell, a man who had studied nearly every society and culture in his travels around the world, valued his track days so highly. Many of us feel the same way about our own running.

Once when I was injured from overtraining (yes, it happens to nonelites and elites alike), I tried bicycling. It was a difficult chore, as I had to fight traffic and walk the bike up steep hills. When I was healthy again and could run with the training group once more, I thought, "How lucky that we were born runners, and not bicyclists, swimmers, or—perish the thought!—football players." It was then that I started paying attention to the way the great runners trained, to see how they did it. I found out that there really is a "joy of running" that most of us feel and that I hope comes through in the lives of these runners. These legendary athletes are perhaps at the top of running's pyramid, but it is the common runners who make up its base and who are the foundation of our sport.

As Dieter Hogen says about training, this book was both fun and hard work. I talked with many of the runners who train in Boulder, a city that if allowed to enter the Olympics would win more medals than most countries. I also went to the small town of Myrskerlä in the middle of Finland, to visit with Lasse Viren; to Tanzania to visit with Juma Ikangaa and Filbert Bayi; to Czechoslovakia, when it was splitting into the Czech and Slovakian Republics, to pay my respects to Emil Zatopek; to Mexico City to see where Arturo Barrios trained; and to Havana, Cuba, to meet Alberto Juantorena.

The diverse countries and backgrounds of the athletes in this book show how universal running is. This point was brought home when I went to Belgrade, the capital of Yugoslavia. Even during the height of the war in neighboring Bosnia, Dejan Nikolic persisted in putting on the Belgrade Marathon. Because of the war runners had to fly into Sofia or Budapest and then take a 10-hour bus ride into Belgrade. Supplies were scarce, but despite the difficulties, Nikolic insisted that the marathon must continue because, he said, he wanted "to show the world that runners have so much in common." And, at the race, runners from the split-up Yugoslavia ran together: Serbs, Croats, and Muslims, some of them wearing shirts that read "Mir" (peace). One Serbian I met was running from Banja Luka to Athens to lend support to the peace process. People like that have a spirit that makes you proud to be a runner.

I had a similar thought in Coban, a city in the Guatemalan highlands where another unsung race director, Juan Reyes, puts on the largest race in Guatemala, with Mayans, Kenyans, South, Central, and North Americans, and Europeans in the field. As in Belgrade, running is what brings together these people from around the world, showing how minor the differences between us really are.

At races such as Coban, I see many motivated, hungry runners who will never have the chance to realize their running potential as the athletes in this book did. I recall running a marathon in Cameroon, West Africa. Hearing a strange sound near 20 miles, I looked over my shoulder and saw that a local runner had caught up to me. He was running in plastic sandals, one with a broken strap that slapped on the road with each step. His feet were bloody from hitting the asphalt. It was hot and I was reduced to doing the "marathon shuffle." After offering some encouraging words and a pat on the back, my newfound Cameroonian friend ran off after the leaders. I struggled on, following his bloody trail to the finish. At the end (can there be any better feeling than finishing a marathon after hitting the wall early on?), I grabbed him and the runner from the Soviet Union who had won the race, and in a hot, sweaty embrace, we hobbled off together. A friendship and understanding were born that day that crossed the national borders that separated us. It didn't matter if we were black or white, communist or capitalist—all we knew was that we were tired, thirsty, and sore marathoners. In other words, brothers.

If the runners in this book were good solely at training, they would be interesting, but only up to a point. As you'll notice, however, many of them have a social conscience. There is something about running that knocks down the "Berlin Walls" of race, religion, custom, and language that divide us, reminding us—as Alberto Juantorena says—that we all have "not four eyes, but two."

In this book I have tried to set down some of their stories and give an appreciation of what it takes to be a champion. Running with these athletes showed me that the simple pleasures in life really are the greatest ones. I feel a little frustration, because it is hard to capture in words the feelings of camaraderie and satisfaction that come from doing a solid 10-mile run with friends and then going to breakfast and having good conversation afterward. Small things like this are the stuff of which runners of all levels are made.

There are hundreds of talented people out there who have never reached their potential—I have come across many of them, and I am sure you have, too. Only a special few have the drive, motivation, and dedication to train for years toward one goal. As I write this, I look out the window and see several lean, shirtless guys running hard up Four Mile Canyon west of town, and I'm glad. Running is like going to a spring:

each of us drinks our fill, and new runners come, pushing aside those in front. Those of us running now, I hope this book shows, are running on the shoulders of giants. It should make us proud to know we are part of a running lineage that stretches back from the original Olympic Games in 776 BC to this very moment. When you run a set of 400-meter intervals, think to yourself that you are doing the same workout as Nurmi, Zatopek, Shorter, Viren, Barrios, Kristiansen, Aouita, and many of the other legends. They may run the intervals a little (or a lot) faster, but they are all part of the same running community that we are.

It is good to see newer runners like Marc Davis, who, when talking about Noureddine Morceli, winks and says, "Oh, yes, Noureddine is one of the best ever. But he can be beaten." This is the attitude I hope you'll take away with you: to recognize these legends of running and yet strive to surpass them. And I hope someone reading this years from now will make a list of 21 new runners, people like Moses Kiptanui and Haile Gebrselassie, and write another book to further expand stories of the greats of running.

When Henry Rono was a young boy, Kipchoge Keino gave a talk in a stadium near Eldoret, Kenya. Rono did not go in. Instead he climbed a tree and watched the Olympian Keino talk to the crowd. Up in the tree Rono vowed he would one day be as great a runner as Kipchoge. This book is a way for you to climb a tree, peer down at these runners, and perhaps make a vow yourself.

Rob de Castella once remarked in introducing me to a friend that "Sandrock's a 2:17 marathoner; he just hasn't done it yet." Though I continue thinking I may break 2:20 one day, I know, unfortunately, it is unlikely I'll ever run that fast. This book is my attempt to compensate for it. Hope you like it.

Emil Zatopek

The Immortal Czech

Born September 22, 1922, Czechoslovakia

Eighteen world records

Olympic gold, 10,000; silver, 5,000, 1948

Olympic gold, 5,000, 10,000, and marathon, 1952

Emil Zatopek leans out of the second-story window of his modest home on a quiet street in a residential section of north Prague. "Be right down," he yells. A minute later, the iron door set in the stone wall swings open, and a wide-shouldered, moon-faced man holds out his hand.

"Hello. I am Zatopek."

You suddenly feel as if you have been transported back to the 1952 Helsinki Olympics, for these are the same words that Zatopek, then at the peak of his running career, used to introduce himself to Jim Peters, the marathon world-record holder from England, at the start of the Olympic Marathon. It would be the race that capped one of the greatest performances in Olympic history: Zatopek winning the marathon after taking gold medals in the 5,000- and 10,000-meter races earlier in the week. He set Olympic records in all three races and a world record for a marathon loop course in his first attempt at the distance.

Immediately after crossing the finish line in Helsinki Stadium, Zatopek was hailed as one of the best distance runners ever. In the years to come, his reputation would grow to near-legendary proportions as the stories about this great runner and lover of life were circulated and embellished. In the ensuing decades, the tales of the "Human Locomotive" went beyond history and entered the rarefied air reserved for myth and fables. More than just a superb athlete, Zatopek became a folk hero for runners around the world.

Zatopek was a runner who smashed barriers, changing forever the way runners trained. His revolutionary ideas on mileage and interval training helped open the door to the modern era of distance running. He did not just shatter the old ways of thinking—he ran through the limitations runners had placed on themselves. Zatopek is sometimes credited with being the "father of interval training," and runners following in his footsteps built upon his sturdy foundation. Mention the name "Zatopek," and invariably runners' eyes will light up as they become eager to tell their own inspirational stories of Emil the Great, passed down from veteran runners to newcomers. These stories, some so fantastic that they must seem apocryphal when first heard, are an integral part of the running heritage, part of the common language that binds runners of all ages and origins. As long as there are runners, tales will be told of Zatopek.

And how pleasing it is to discover that the stories not only are true, but in fact just touch the surface of this man called, for good reason, the "Immortal Czech." He is bursting with such energy and goodwill that anyone who meets him—friends, strangers, opponents, or teammates—loves him. During a 12-year international career, Zatopek set 18 official world records, the third most in track and field history after the great

Finnish champion Paavo Nurmi (22) and Sweden's Werner Hardmo (22). Although his records are substantial, Zatopek was much more than an accumulator of fast times. He personifies the iron will that running champions have all possessed. Everything about the man is unique: his attitude toward his competitors, his training methods, his integrity, and his friendships. In addition, of course, there was his shocking form while running: his head rolled to one side, his arms clawed across his chest, and his face was fixed in a grimace that reflected all the pain and struggle of being a runner. "He runs like a man who's just been stabbed in the heart," one contemporary coach said. The five Olympic medals, four gold and one silver won in the 1948 and 1952 games, along with all the world records, are more than enough for Emil to be considered one of the greatest runners of all time. Emil Zatopek, however, most deserves special recognition in the annals of sport because his approach to running and to life carries lessons for us all, lessons that will never go out of style.

A Merry Man

We walk up the narrow path, through a garden bursting with flowers, into the warm, cozy house. The walls are lined with pictures of Emil laughing with friends, running on the track, and posing with his wife, Dana, as the golden couple of the 1952 Olympics. When English runner Gordon Pirie, who set world records in the 3,000 meters (1954) and 5,000 meters (1956), visited the house in the early 1950s, he called it "the merriest and gayest home I've been in." It remains that way. It is a clean, well-lighted place, and books, paintings, and photographs crowd the walls with the mementos of a lifetime of friendships. Sitting in his third-floor study, beneath an icon of St. Barbara (the patron saint of miners), Emil reflects on 70 years of triumph and struggle. After spending several days with him, you realize that, when the trumpets sound to announce the Day of Judgment, and runners have to select one person to represent all of us at that final reckoning, surely we will choose Emil to present our lives before the Great Timekeeper; he will smile, gesticulate, and, in the end, win.

"Emil is always busy," says Dana, as she prepares a simple meal of tomatoes, bread, soup, and beer. "People come from everywhere to see him." Mostly, young runners make pilgrimages from around the globe to pay their respects to this most determined—and the most human—of all runners; they find in him something that can help them in their own race through life.

"What will you have?" Emil asks in good English, one of seven languages in which he is fluent. He opens two bottles of Staropranen, a strong Czechoslovakian beer. "I'm not supposed to have a beer, but. . ."

But Emil Zatopek has earned the right to drink a beer. His life has been full of sound and fury, signifying meaning, beginning from his modest origins in northern Moravia, an industrial land of coal mines and steel factories. He was born of peasant parents on September 22, 1922, in Zlin. "It is a heavy industrial center, like maybe, Ohio," says Zatopek. "We were eight children, but now we are only three. The three youngest brothers are still here today." Despite a large family of modest means, Zatopek says he had a pleasant childhood. "It was very happy. To visit school was wonderful! No responsibilities," recalls Emil, who remained a lover of learning his entire life.

Moravia in the 1920s and 1930s, like many parts of the world, was economically depressed. Emil described his life during that time: "The problem was after the school, what to do? I finished elementary school when I was 15, and at the time, in 1937, it was like the Depression. It was a problem to find work." The Buta shoe factory, headquartered in Toronto, was the main employer in Zlin. "After the social revolution, the factory was nationalized, which was normal." With a large pool of unemployed laborers in Moravia and not many jobs, the shoe factory could afford to be selective in its hiring.

> This Buta concern would choose from many, many thousands of young boys and girls each year. Out of everyone who wanted work, they picked only one hundred. They hired those people after giving us psychological and medical tests. But I was lucky; they choose me. . . . It was a chance to work in the factory, to study in evening school, and . . . just to have a chance in life.

He worked all day in the shoe factory, which is still active. "I was apprenticed, and we lived in an apprentice home. During the day we worked in the factory, in the evening it was an industrial school." Zatopek worked in the factory for several years, and he did not take part in organized sports. When he was 19, he had his first chance to run. "I was in my last year in this apprentice home, and a race sponsored by the factory was organized across the city. I was obliged to take part. I wanted not to run." To get out of competing, Zatopek told his boss that he was sick and that his knee hurt. But after examining him, the factory doctor said Emil was healthy, and he was signed up to run.

"But then, ahh, once I was entered, I tried to win. I came in second." Emil might have forgotten the race and fallen back into factory life like so many others if not for the encouragement of a top Czech runner who recognized Emil's talent. "Uphill from the factory in the city was a very good track and field club, with good runners. And one, our national record holder for 1,500 meters, invited me to join the club."

"Come on boy, you are good," the older runner told Zatopek. "Would you come tomorrow to the stadium? You can practice with us, and you will get a tracksuit and running shoes. You will be an athlete."

Emil was honored to receive this recognition. To be an athlete was to be somebody special, to escape from the factory's dull routine, and he eagerly seized the offer.

> Because he was very popular, oohh, of course, the next day, I came. And this runner was my coach. It was necessary to know what it means, warming up, what to do, and how to practice. It was useful for me.

The invitation to the athletic club launched Zatopek's career, and the apprentice shoe maker found a home in the track stadium, surrounded by friends. In 1941, in the midst of the grim days of World War II, the track club provided more than an opportunity for Zatopek to train. The Nazi army, claiming its need to protect German-speaking Czechs, had invaded Czechoslovakia in 1939 and overrun the country in one week.

> It was during the war, and for me, being in the club was a great pleasure. Because it was a sad time, not a very favorable time. It was not allowed to dance, maybe. It was not possible to buy chocolate, maybe.

"It was very *triste,* very sad," Zatopek says, looking out the window. "But in the stadium, oh," he continues, his voice rising. "It was very nice. We young boys had not only training but pleasure, too. To run. To jump. To have fun." Emil seized the opportunity to run and pursued it with all his vast discipline and intelligence. He remained with the Zlin club throughout World War II, but after a year of learning the rudiments of training from the others, he sought new and better ways to train. "After the next year, I was independent," a trait that was to be the hallmark of his running career.

"Simple" Training

Emil's determination to improve soon produced results. Because he did not have a chance to travel to other countries during the war, Zatopek competed only in Czechoslovakia for the next five years. His first track race was a 3,000-meter event, and he ran 9:12, three seconds behind the winner. Zatopek's performance was mentioned in the local newspaper, and Emil carried the newspaper clipping—"A good performance by Zatopek"—in his wallet for years. From the start of his running career, the inquisitive Zatopek was always thinking of ways to improve, always asking questions of others and of himself. He investigated new ways of improving his speed and strength. "My training," he says, "was very simple and very primitive."

The training was unbelievably difficult. Zatopek brought to distance running an unheard-of capacity for unremitting, unending hard work, though always guided by reason. The basis of his training was "speed and stamina. It's very primitive," he explains with a laugh. "Speed, by running short distance, maybe 100 meters." He moves his hands to one side, "and stamina, not to have rest during the training," he says, swinging his hands to the other side. "100 meters fast," his voice rises, "and 100 meters easy," his voice lowers. "100 meters fast," his voice rises again, "100 meters easy," he says, lowering his voice again. "This way, I was able to run faster than by using the former training methods. Why should I practice running slow? I already know how to run slow. I must learn how to run fast." That was the essence of his training: running fast intervals for speed and repeating them many times for endurance. A "simple" yet powerful idea.

The other runners in the club were shocked by Zatopek's radical training.

"That's crazy," they told him. "What are you doing? You are not a sprinter."

"That's true," Emil replied. "But if I run 100 meters say, 30 times, that is three kilometers and no longer a sprint."

"It won't work," the doubters told him.

"We will see," responded Zatopek. "If I can get better, why not?"

First the Czechs, then the world did see, as he continued to improve by pursuing his belief that to improve your speed during races, you must first run fast while training. Zatopek brought training into the modern era, showing just how much a runner could handle, and paved the way for runners like Vladimir Kuts and Ron Clarke. Zatopek is the bridge between the first wave of great runners, exemplified by Paavo Nurmi and the other Finns, and the modern era.

Zatopek took a few ideas from Nurmi, the most famous runner to that time, and recast them to match his iron will and endurance. Emil believed that whatever Nurmi or the others had done, he could do more of it. "I read in a small book that Paavo Nurmi was able during one hour to run 4 × 400 meters in his best time. I said, 'Ohh, oh, OK then, I will try to run six times, my best time.'" Zatopek also built on the interval training used by German Woldemar Gerschler, coach of Rudolph Harbig, who set the 800-meter world record of 1:46.6 in 1939.

Zatopek completed the toughest workouts the world had ever seen. He ran his own training at the stadium, because the other club runners were not convinced that his strange notions would lead anywhere except to exhaustion. One observer who recalls as a boy watching Zatopek train in Prague's stadium describes him as circling the track endlessly, at times looking "as though he would fall over dead from exhaustion. He just kept going and going around, with his tongue hanging out like [basketball star] Michael Jordan."

The "speed and stamina" workouts began producing results, and Emil soon won races throughout Czechoslovakia. "I was getting better and better," says Zatopek, who was developing into what New Zealand coach Arthur Lydiard called "a superbly conditioned athlete who knew how to train to run a range of distances."

Going International

When the war ended, Emil was accepted into the Czech military academy in Prague for officer training. There he joined the Buka Military Sports Club, a boon to his running career because the club gave him the opportunity to compete in national military meets and to travel to represent Czechoslovakia in international competitions. Being in the army was an ideal situation, because to his amazement, Zatopek discovered that his superiors *wanted* him to run.

> I was obliged to fulfill this military service, and I found it wonderful. It was nice that in our country, after the war, there was created a military sporting club. . . . And young boys coming to military service had time for training, a tracksuit for training, a stadium for training, and good food. And I esteemed it, because in peaceful times, being in the military is the same as being a civilian, and you can have the sporting living style. Even today, I think the army is the best [for training], if there is not war. In peacetime, the army has the chance to produce good sportsmen.

Zatopek was the best of these sportsmen, though he laughs at that idea. "No, no, no, no. I was not very talented. My basic speed was low. Only with willpower, Eee, ahhhh"—here his face scrunches up into the agonizing Zatopek grimace and a low, grumbling sound comes from somewhere deep within his chest—"was I able to reach this world best standard in long-distance running."

Others began to recognize that Zatopek could be one of the world's best in 1946, when he entered his first international race, the 5,000 meters in the European Championships in Oslo, Norway. It is reported that when he first saw Finland's 10,000-meter world-record holder, Viljo Heino, at the meet, Emil approached him and knelt down, touching Heino's legs in deference to the latest of the Flying Finns. Zatopek's own reliable legs carried him to a 14:25.8 fifth-place finish while England's Sydney Wooderson won.

Zatopek's first international victory came in the inter-Allied meet in Berlin in 1946, where he won the 5,000 meters after bicycling through the Russian lines. Being able to run with the best in Europe was the encouragement he needed to increase his training, because Zatopek saw that he was not far from the top-level competitors. He decided to train through the winter of 1946-47, which meant running through the cold and snow. That was not a problem for Zatopek; he started bounding through the deep snow, leaping with giant strides while wearing his Czech army-issue military boots. Rather than hindering his training, Zatopek says the boots were actually a big help.

> From the point of view of today's runners, the shoes we had were very primitive. Nowadays, there are many shoe factories, very good shoe factories, but there were not at the time. The military boots were not good for technique; they weren't the best for taking off, but they were very safe on the terrain I preferred to run in, woods and forests.

"Oh yes, the boots were very natural, because to run in woods or in a field can also be a risk," Zatopek says, standing and making a running motion with his feet. "Wearing running shoes on stones, oohh!" he says, stomping down his foot. "Also, running shoes are very expensive. But military boots keep this part very safe," he says, grabbing his ankle. "And if there is a stone or something, it doesn't matter; beem, bim," he says, stomping across the floor in imitation of the way he used to stomp through the woods that winter, gradually getting stronger.

"And if the military boots were finished, I change them for another, no problem. Where is a soldier going to find 600 crowns, or 1,000 crowns, for new running shoes? I took them and changed them for another!" he exclaims, as if he still cannot quite believe what a great system that was. "No problem."

Wearing the military boots, Emil began running repeat 400s in the woods, continually increasing the number of repetitions as he got more fit and his capacity to endure hard work also increased. The boot training, while cumbersome, developed his leg muscles. "Maybe wearing heavy boots in training and light shoes in competition was good; when you change, whoosh," he says, his hands flying off into the air. "It was very practical. It belongs to that age." Emil also belongs to that age, but at the same time to the new, post-World War II era that was dawning.

Aided by the unbearable lightness of his competition shoes, Zatopek pulled a shocker in his first 5,000-meter race of 1947, clocking 14:08.2, the second-fastest 5,000 of all time. He then outsprinted Heino over 5,000 meters in Helsinki to win in 14:15.2. Zatopek ended 1947 undefeated and was ranked first in the world in the 5,000; he also ran 8:08.8 for 3,000 meters.

1948 London Olympics

After another winter of boot-training, Zatopek entered the Olympic year of 1948 in even better shape. This was to be the first Olympic Games held since 1936 in Berlin, as the 1940 (Helsinki) and 1944 Games (London) were canceled because of the war. The first 10,000-meter race of Zatopek's career came in May in Budapest, where he ran 30:28.4. Most observers figured Zatopek to run the 5,000 meters at London, but he decided to double. "I was the Czech record holder for 2,000 meters, 3,000 meters, 5,000 meters, and . . ." he pauses, "and I thought about the Olympics in London, and I decided to run the 10,000 and 5,000."

Though he had run 29:27 in Prague Stadium in June (just 1.6 seconds from Heino's record), Zatopek was not considered to have much of a chance in the 10,000. He was up against Heino, the latest (and the last until Lasse Viren, as it turned out) of the great Finnish runners. News moved more slowly in those days, and most of the fans who packed into Wembley Stadium for the opening of the Olympic Games did not realize that Zatopek had run the distance before. "Yes, maybe I was not the favorite for 10,000 meters, because there was world-record holder Viljo Heino of Finland," Zatopek says, with a laugh. "But he was used to practicing near the Arctic Circle, and in London it was a tropical gale, and Heino was unhappy with this climate."

Zatopek devised a plan that shows his intelligence in plotting his training and racing. A teammate was placed in the stands with two shirts—one red, the other white. Zatopek was to look up at him after each lap, and if the 400-meter split was faster than world-record pace, the white shirt would be held up. If the pace slipped over 71 seconds a lap, the red shirt would show, and Emil would know to run faster.

The first eight laps of the 25-lap 10,000-meter race were on record pace, and Zatopek settled in at the back of the pack after seeing the white shirt each time around. But on the ninth lap, the red shirt came up, signaling Emil to move. He did so quickly, slipping up near the leaders. On the next lap, he took the lead from Heino. The Finn would not give up without a spirited fight, however, and he surged past Zatopek. When the red shirt came up on the next lap, Emil charged again. This time Heino could not respond, and Zatopek took a big lead, pressing the pace as hard as he could.

"Where's Heino?" Emil yelled to an official at one point.

"Heino is out," the official answered. The world-record holder had pulled out with seven laps to go, unable to handle Zatopek's constant pressure.

Despite a miscount of the laps by officials, Zatopek ran to the gold medal unchallenged, finishing in a new Olympic record of 29:59.6. He won by a margin of 47 seconds over Alain Mimoun, an Algerian who was competing for France. It was a convincing win and the first gold medal ever for Czechoslovakia, but there was not time for Zatopek to rest on his laurels. His heat of the 5,000 was the next day.

Still full of adrenaline after his 10,000-meter win, Zatopek joined Eric Ahlden of Sweden in taking off from the field in the 5,000-meter preliminary heat, the two running to an insurmountable lead. At the bell, Ahlden began sprinting. Zatopek was running in second, in absolutely no danger of not qualifying for the final, in which a field of well-rested runners would be competing. He could have almost walked the last lap and still been one of the four qualifiers for the finals. But Emil let his emotions overrule his reason. Instead of saving his reserves, Zatopek suddenly began a mad sprint of his own. The crowd gasped in disbelief as Emil went after Ahlden, eating into the lead and nearly catching him at the tape. Zatopek's time in the preliminary was 14:31.6. Gaston Reiff of Belgium, the prerace favorite, won his heat in over 15 minutes.

The 5,000-meter final came two days later. The hot weather was gone and so was Zatopek's stay-back-and-wait strategy that he had used in the 10,000. Emil led for the first 9 laps of the 12-1/2-lap 5,000, which was run in a downpour. Reiff then went ahead with 1,500 meters to go, and Holland's Willi Slykhuis also passed Zatopek, who was soon nearly a straightaway behind Reiff. Worn out from his previous racing, Zatopek could not mount a charge, and with 300 meters to go, he was 30 meters behind. The race looked to be over.

But then, ignoring the rain, Zatopek summoned up his tremendous willpower, lowered his head, and unleashed a furious, primeval sprint. The leaders came back to him as if they were running in slow motion, and Zatopek quickly passed Slykhuis. Reiff still had a 20-meter lead heading into the final straightaway, but incredibly, Zatopek was chasing him down. The crowd was on its feet cheering, and the fans' syncopated cries of "Zat-o-pek, Zat-o-pek" were enough to warn the laboring Reiff. He looked back just in time to see the terrifying image of the "Czech Locomotive" bearing down on him. Mounting a last-ditch sprint of his own, Reiff finished just a step ahead of Zatopek.

"I was beaten by Gaston Reiff." The name rolls off Emil's tongue. He pauses and looks out the window, remembering. Reiff was one of Emil's great rivals. The year after London, Reiff set the world record in the 3,000 meters (7:58.8), breaking Gunder Hägg's mark. Reiff had great speed—just enough, it turned out, to hold off a tired Zatopek in that 1948 London 5,000.

Fans honored Zatopek for his silver medal as much as for his 10,000-meter gold, for that finish showed the world what he was made of and presaged the Olympic 5,000-meter final four years later, in which Zatopek would show an even more phenomenal sprint. What impressed people about Zatopek's finish was that the sprint did not come out of Zatopek's natural speed; indeed, he ran with elbows wide and head tilted, while Reiff was a more classic-looking runner. Rather, the wild sprint seemed to explode out of the exhausted Zatopek, bubbling up from some deep wellspring of will and determination.

Setting Records

Zatopek, by now a lieutenant in the army, returned to Prague a national hero. That fall, he married Dana Ignevona, who had finished seventh in the javelin throw in London. *Sport* magazine reported that Zatopek had promised himself "he would never marry until he met a girl who shared his passion for track and field." He found such a person in Dana.

With two Olympic medals in hand, Zatopek was now ready for a world record. He got his first in the 10,000 meters early in the 1949 track season, running 29:28.2 on June 11 on the track in Ostrava. Zatopek did it on his own, as second-place finisher Frantisek Zanta was nearly 3 minutes behind. "It was in 1949, the year after the Olympics in London, in the army championships. I won the 10,000 meters, no problem." His voice rises as he says, matter-of-factly, "Without adversaries, it was a very easy race for me." But the clock was not so easy. "And the commentator," his voice rises again. "Oh, oh, wonderful, wonderful, he is working hard. I understood after the sixth kilometer that I was strong, because he says, 'After six kilometers, Zatopek is running in better time than Viljo Heino for world record.' Oh, really?" Zatopek laughs. "And the young people yell, 'We want world record.' And I started to run [he jumps out of his chair, pumping his arms vigorously], and I ran world record. The world record was 29:35.4, and I ran 29:28.2," knocking 7.2 seconds off Heino's mark, which had stood since 1944. Heino had been the fifth Finn since 1921 to hold the record in an unbroken streak. Zatopek, with this win in Ostrava, became the first non-Finn since Frenchman Jean Bouin's 30:58 in 1911 to hold the 10,000-meter record.

The Finnish people wanted their champion to have a chance for revenge, and Heino, with the weight of his country and the ghosts of champions past on his back, vowed to reclaim the record. His attempt came on September 1, 1949, in Kouvola, Finland, and he succeeded, taking exactly one second off Zatopek's record.

When the news reached Prague, Zatopek's army superiors called in their young star.

"Emil, you must run again," they told him.

"Allow me three weeks without military duty," Zatopek replied. "Free time for me to practice more. Two weeks very intensive training, and one week easier, easier, easier until I try for the record."

In addition to working harder than anybody else, Zatopek's determination was guided by intelligence. He did not just train hard all the time; he knew the importance of rest while preparing for his world-record assault. "It was good preparation," he said of his two weeks of workouts that included 40 × 400 meters with 200-meter jog intervals.

The preparation was so good that on October 22, once more on the track in Ostrava, he reclaimed the 10,000-meter record by running 29:21.2, finishing more than 3 minutes ahead of the next finisher, Ladislav Klominek. Despite several further attempts, Heino would never regain the record.

The records increased Zatopek's motivation to train, which was the overriding concern in his life. Once, when he was heading out the door to go training, Dana stopped him, saying she wanted him to do the laundry. Showing the wisdom of Solomon, Emil did both, running in place in the bathtub atop the laundry, for two hours.

Offers to race came in, and Emil was happy to oblige. He loved to travel, especially to Finland, which had long produced the best runners and the best track fans. "Finland is wonderful for the long-distance runner," says Zatopek.

His next visit to Finland came in 1950 when he ran 14:06 in Helsinki. He was then invited to race in Turku on August 4. "Turku, it is the city of Paavo Nurmi. He was born in Turku and so I was happy to go there.

It had a nice track, cinder, but of high quality," says Zatopek. The Urheilupuisto Sports Ground was full for the evening meeting, and Zatopek did not disappoint. "And I ran 29 minutes and 2 seconds," he said, far in front of Finn Paavo Ukkonen (31:56).

That 29:02.6 was a world record by 18.6 seconds, the biggest drop in the 10,000 meters since Nurmi's 30:40.2 in 1921 took 18.6 seconds off Frenchman Bouin's record. Afterwards, Zatopek went out of the stadium for his cooldown. His warm-up suit was on the infield of the track, where he had dropped it when he stripped down for the start of the race. But because the field events were taking place, Zatopek could not go back to retrieve his suit. He waited until a lull in the jumps, then he ran out onto the track. The crowd spotted him and the stadium erupted with cheers. The fans gave Zatopek a long standing ovation, for the track-savvy Finns understood what they had just seen. All the Finns, including Heino who also was there watching, cheered the amazing Czech, embracing him as one of their own.

"Oh, it was wonderful," recalls Zatopek. "I waited to get my tracksuit, and the cheers when I ran for it . . . Ooh, oh, bravo." He claps his hands together, smiling. Tears begin welling up in his eyes. "What to say?"

Let the ovation of that packed stadium in Turku ring forever as praise for Zatopek's feats. But he was not through with the 1950 season. Still to come were the European Championships in Brussels, which at the time was the most important meet in the world after the Olympics. But Zatopek became sick from eating a spoiled goose before the competition, and he was hospitalized with food poisoning. The doctors advised him not to try to race in his weakened condition. But Zatopek refused to stay in bed and miss the meet. Despite not having trained for two weeks, he won the 10,000 (29:12) and 5,000 (14:03), the second-fastest times ever recorded for those distances. In the 5,000, he got his revenge on Reiff, soundly beating the Belgian over the last lap and stunning the hometown crowd, which had been counting on a win from their Olympic gold medalist. Such outstanding races after a forced rest came to be known as the "Zatopek phenomenon," and they illustrate the critical role rest and recovery play in getting the most from training.

While he was in Finland in 1950, Zatopek tried to visit Nurmi, whom he admired more than anyone in the world. A peace agreement between the Soviet Union and members of NATO had been signed in Stockholm that year, and Emil and the chief of the Czech delegation decided to see Nurmi to sign a symbolic "peace accord" of their own. Says Zatopek, "There was a shop he owned, and we came there and asked would it be possible to speak with Paavo Nurmi?"

"It is not possible," they were told. "He is not present. He will come this afternoon at about 2 o'clock. What do you wish?"

"Here is Emil Zatopek, world-record holder. Perhaps Paavo Nurmi will sign this peace agreement?" At 2 o'clock that afternoon, Zatopek and the Czech official returned, asking, "Is Paavo Nurmi there?"

"No, he is not. He will not be here all day," they were told. Zatopek was not surprised that Nurmi did not want to see him.

> Paavo Nurmi was famous, but I never spoke with him. It's no wonder, because he was not only good in running, but also in constructing houses. He was chief of a construction company. It was a capitalist system, and I was a representative of another system . . . a socialist, anticapitalistic system. It was like an "anti-Nurmi system." Sportsmen were sometimes used for propaganda, so it was no wonder he would not be able to sign the [peace] contract.

Zatopek was the antithesis of Nurmi in another way. Nurmi was the paradigm of the silent Finn, said to be quiet and unsmiling, often carrying a stopwatch in his hand while training and racing. While both men came from modest backgrounds, Zatopek was the opposite type—gregarious, open, friendly, with a personality forged by an exuberant love of life. Where Nurmi ran with a watch and ignored his competitors, Zatopek ran with his heart, always holding a hand out to other runners, and his foes usually became his friends.

In 1951, Zatopek tried some longer distances. He was constantly pushing himself in workouts, and always thinking of new ways to train. According to Fred Wilt in *How They Train*, his main workout in 1951 was 20 × 200 meters, followed by 40 × 400 meters, then another 20 × 200 meters, all with 200-meter jog intervals. It is hard to know exactly how fast Zatopek was running his intervals, because he never timed them. Zatopek's philosophy of training, says Wilt,

> was to work as hard as possible so that a race seemed comparatively easy. He felt that strength and energy only increase through continual testing. Zatopek had no fear of becoming "burned out." He had such unbelievable willpower that he could impose any burden of training he preferred upon himself . . . . Before Zatopek, nobody realized it was humanly possible to train this hard. Emil is truly the originator of modern intensive training.

Zatopek set a world record for the 1-hour run on September 15 at the Czech army championships in Prague's Strahov Stadium. After an opening 10,000 meters of 31:05, Zatopek, pushing the pace by himself over the second part of the race, broke Heino's record by covering 19,558 meters in the hour. He also set the 20-kilometer record by clocking 1:01:15.8. His second 10,000 was 30:10.8. Zatopek had a new idea after that race. Because he had felt good the entire way, he decided to become the first person to run 20 kilometers in under an hour, an unheard-of proposition.

"It was a pre-Olympic year, and I announced a race for new record," says Zatopek. "I dreamed about the world record." So, just two weeks after his record run, Emil was lining up for another hour run on the track. This time, it was at his favorite track at Houstka Stadium. "It is a stadium in the woods, not far from Prague. There are high trees around track, no dust, and maybe also more oxygen."

The conditions were perfect, and so was Zatopek. He went through the first 10,000 meters in 29:53 and came back in 29:58. At the time, only five other people besides Zatopek had broken 30 minutes for 10,000 meters, and here he had done it twice, with no rest interval. He passed 20 kilometers in a remarkable 59:51, then ran another 52 meters before the gun was fired to signal the end of the hour. Zatopek also set a 10-mile record of 48:12.0 along the way, setting three world records in one race. Zatopek's pulse was taken before and after the run. Just before the race, it was 58 beats per minute; immediately afterwards, it was 168. Four minutes later it was down to 108; another 6 minutes dropped it to 98, and 3 hours later, it was 52.

"This I think was my best race; it was the best distance for me. It suited me," says Zatopek. Others agree. Said Australian great Ron Clarke about Zatopek's record 20-kilometer/hour race, "That was probably the best performance ever, when 'Zatu' ran two consecutive 10,000-meter splits [nearly] faster than any individual had run one."

If Zatopek's career had ended there on the Houstka track, it would already have been full enough for Emil to be listed among the top distance runners in history. But the best was to come the following year at Helsinki, in a performance that lifted Zatopek from the rank of Olympic champions to legendary status.

A Perfect Olympics

Zatopek started 1952 inauspiciously. He fell ill in the spring and did not run spectacular times during the early summer, though he was always thinking and dreaming about the Olympics.

Zatopek almost did not go to Helsinki. One of his friends and teammates was a 1,500-meter runner whose position on the team was endangered because his father had fallen into disfavor with Czech authorities. Zatopek, the star of the Olympic squad, was told to go ahead and fly to Helsinki, and that this runner would follow later. But Zatopek did not budge, saying he would not get on the plane unless his teammate was with him. After that, the runner was allowed to travel with the team.

The first sign that these games were to be special came at the lighting of the Olympic flame. The runner who carried the flame into the stadium was none other than Nurmi himself. The Finns went wild at seeing their hero's return to running; he was balding now, but he retained his impeccable form. Fans and athletes alike jumped to their feet and rushed forward to watch Nurmi circle the track.

Zatopek remained loose and relaxed. In his book *The Four-Minute Mile*, Roger Bannister relates the story of a reporter from Australia who "burst into Zatopek's room at midnight" the night before the 10,000 meters.

> We should have thrown him out angrily, and blamed our failure the following day on his disturbing our non-existent sleep. But Zatopek gave him a 20-minute interview. Then when he found the reporter hadn't a bed for the night he offered him half his own.

The 10,000 meters came early in the Olympics, and it looked as if the runners were going to have to battle the rain as well as their opponents. "It was very interesting," recalls Zatopek. "Opening ceremony. Heavy rain. Representatives were marching," he says, getting up and marching in place to demonstrate. "But the next day, for the 10,000 meters, fine weather. Next day after, rain. Then 5,000 final, sunny weather. But, then it was nice weather till marathon. Raining days, but never in long-distance races." He laughs, "Maybe good." The running gods had smiled on the distance runners, and Emil smiled back.

Zatopek's reputation preceded him onto the track, which he says was nice. "It wasn't a cinder track. Cinder is black. This was red, like a tennis court. It was a good surface." He laughs, "It was a nice track. And in the 10,000 meters, there was an advantage for me. I came to Helsinki as Olympic Champion and world-record holder." When officials yelled out the names of the 32 runners at the starting line, they filled up the first, then the second row, before finally calling out, "Zatopek, Czechoslovakia," putting him in the third row.

> And my adversaries [said], "Oh, oh, Zatopek, please oh, oh, please come on in front." They let me come in the first place in the start

position. It was good sporting. After this, Ready, boom, I went into leading, and they line behind me. Everybody knew me then, and nobody tried to disturb me.

Zatopek was passed early, but he took the lead after eight laps, was quickly passed by Pirie, but just as quickly passed him back. He went through 5,000 meters in 14:43.

It was then down to a two-man race between Zatopek and Mimoun. The runners being lapped by Zatopek would hear his distinctive, heavy breathing and move out of the way. "Because I was . . . huh, huh, huh, huh," he pants in imitation of how he was running, then laughs his great, deep, hearty laugh. "Runners hearing me gave me the chance to go inside. They let me by."

Weaving his way through the lapped runners, Zatopek finished with a 64-second last lap, breaking his Olympic record with a time of 29:17.0, 15 seconds up on Mimoun. Aleksandr Anufriyev of the Soviet Union took the bronze with 29:48.2.

After his win, Zatopek had two-days rest until his heat of the 5,000 meters. Emil, made wise by his experience in the preliminaries of the London 5,000, took it easier this time. He conserved energy by running well within himself, at times dropping back and urging fellow competitors on in their own languages. On the last lap he looked around and held up five fingers, signaling that the leaders were all assured of a spot in the final. John Dixler, an Englishman who won the bronze medal in the steeplechase in the 1952 Helsinki Olympics, remembers,

> One thing people forget about Emil is that at any meet, such as the Olympics, he was the focal point for all the other runners. Emil could be in a room, in the middle of Swedes, Englishmen, Germans, Russians, Hungarians, Czechoslovakians, and all conversation bounced off of him, because he was a linguist. Russians and Americans would be talking, with Emil doing the translation. And on top of that, everything he did he did with dignity. He was a real gentleman.

For perhaps the first time, runners from around the world could exchange ideas.

And Zatopek, adds Dixler, was one of the first to talk about the hard work he did. While some runners played down the amount of work they did, Zatopek was open and honest about his training, and willing to talk with anyone about it.

After two days of rest, the 5,000-meter final came on July 24. Despite his easy win in the 10,000, running from the front, the ever-thinking Zatopek knew he would have to change his strategy for the shorter race.

"OK, 5,000," he said, "it was very different. Basically, I was not the favorite." Emil begins checking off the list of runners in what was to be the deepest field in history. It was the race everyone in Helsinki was waiting for. The three medalists from the 10,000 meters were in it, along with an excellent field of strong, fast runners. By 1952, enough time had passed since the war for a new influx of runners to make their appearance.

"Chris Chataway, oh, very fast runner. Gaston Reiff, Olympic champion from London, also faster than me. Schade, who had the best timing for 5,000 meters in 1952. Alain Mimoun, oh," here Emil's voice rises, "he was always satisfied with second place, but it was possible he could also try to be the Olympic champion. But, what to do in such a situation?"

It would have made sense for Zatopek to try to run the kick out of the fresher runners, who most assumed would be faster than him in a sprint finish. But knowing the strength of England's Chataway and West Germany's Schade, Zatopek did not think that he would be able to run away from them early as he did with the runners in the 10,000. He also did not want to wait until the last straightaway to make his move, because of their superior finishing speed. He decided to try to break away with one lap to go. "It would be nonsense to try to leave [the field], because against these fast runners, it would not be possible. I say, 'No, I will stay in the field and I will see, and I will try on the last lap.'" He enunciates "last lap" with an air of finality; this is where the showdown will come, where the runners' mettle will be tested in what would be called the greatest distance race in Olympic history.

Chataway, who two years later would help pace Roger Bannister through the first sub-4-minute mile, led with a 65.8-second opening lap. Then Schade, who had set an Olympic record of 14:15.4 in his preliminary heat, took the lead, followed by Reiff, with Emil tucked in behind. Nearing the halfway mark, Zatopek, wanting to take his turn in the lead, moved up alongside Schade, saying, "Come on Herbert, run a few laps with me." The surprised Schade looked over at Zatopek, then accelerated to pull ahead. One by one the other competitors fell off the pace until six were left—Schade, Reiff, Zatopek, Chataway, Pirie, and Mimoun.

The lead changed hands until Schade regained the lead with five laps remaining. He then was passed by Pirie. Pirie was, in turn, quickly passed by the other five runners, and the pack went through 4,000 meters in 11:24.8. One-half lap later, Reiff, the defending Olympic champion, unexpectedly dropped out. Emil's plan seemed to be working, as he took the lead at the bell and began his drive to the tape.

> Four-hundred meters to sprint. For me, it was very easy, because every day 40 × 400 meters I ran in training. I thought they will not be keen enough to follow me. . . . To sprint 400 meters for

most runners, it is very difficult, because maybe if you try, you will be in 200 meters full of fatigue.

It was a good plan on paper. However, Zatopek had not counted on the endurance and finishing strength of the others. Only Pirie dropped back. "My fantasy was also wrong. Because I started the last lap," Zatopek says, his voice rising with each word. "Boom! And I started to sprint . . ." his voice goes yet higher, "and they were *twice* as fast as me! Until 300 meters [to go], Chataway, Schade, Mimoun, all three in front, ohh oh," Emil says, his voice dropping. The earlier pace had not been quick enough to run the kick out of the others, and now they were charging for home, with Zatopek seemingly out of contention several meters behind in fourth place. The gold, indeed, any medal, looked to be out of his grasp. As he watched his three opponents powering away from him down the backstraight, Zatopek thought, "And you see, gold medal, silver medal, bronze medal; for me, potato. What to do?"

He did not have to do anything, really. Emil could have come in fourth, taken his 10,000-meter gold medal home, and still have been acknowledged as one of the top runners in the world. But that would never do for the indomitable Zatopek. In one of the truly great moments in track history, he gathered himself, drawing on the countless hours spent training in the dark forests, and he began another sprint. Now he really had a reason to grimace—and the next 30 seconds will forever define Zatopek. Those who saw the finish will never forget it.

"What to do? But to give up? Never! Nah, no, no! I must run and arh!" The words come tumbling out in a nearly inarticulate cry, like that of some trapped wild animal. "I must run, ahh!" He speaks ferociously, his round face expanding. Zatopek growls and viciously bares his teeth, rising from his chair, bursting with energy; he is powerful, strong, and in his prime again, ready to battle all comers. Even 40 years after this 1952 Olympic 5,000, his countenance is so fearful that a visitor cowers against the wall. Emil pauses and after a few moments is back to normal. He asks again, "What to do? I must run!" he growls, his face suddenly twisting into the Zatopek grimace.

Nearing the final turn, he caught the three leaders. "And 200 meters before the tape," his voice drops, "oh, what I saw; they were more and more tired, full of fatigue." His voice rises, and his eyes sparkle as he remembers the moment. "I start again. Ah, once more! And nobody has had reserve." But even with this supreme effort, Zatopek, though passing Mimoun, was not able to take the lead.

No, only Mimoun was tired. But then they [Chataway and Schade] were tired, too. They were full of fatigue. I thought they will stay behind, and I will run in first position to the tape. But no, then they started *the more fast* sprint. Oh, they sprinted. But it is very dangerous, because an absolute sprint, it is a race without recovery. Without recovery; 200 meters, and it's enough.

Swinging wide out of the final turn, Zatopek forced himself past Schade and Chataway into the lead, "summoning up the courage of the angels," in the words of Bill Squires. The inexperienced and faltering Chataway (he was just 22) bumped the inside rail and fell in a heap on the side of the track. Mimoun moved into second, followed by Schade. Zatopek, arms akimbo, head rolling from side to side, powered to the finish, winning in 14:06.6. His last 200 meters had taken just 28.3 seconds, the last lap 57.9. "It was surprise for many experts; it was a surprise also for me. But it (the final 200 meters) was not very difficult; for me it was short distance." Mimoun finished second behind Zatopek in an Olympic final for the third time, in 14:07.4, and Schade got the bronze, 1.2 seconds behind. Chataway returned to the race after his fall and finished fifth.

Chataway and teammate Roger Bannister, who finished fourth in the 1,500-meter, are two of the many people Zatopek made an impression on in Helsinki. "What makes a man superhuman?" Chataway asked in *The Four-Minute Mile*. Bannister wonders, "How can Zatopek do it? He has the prospect of three gold medals in a week, and a fourth for his wife, who may win the javelin event."

"Zatopek isn't human in his achievement," Chataway replies, "yet he's as intelligent as any other athlete running."

A Medal for a Medal

The crowd knew it had seen something special. More than 70,000 fans saw that race, but Dana almost did not. The women's javelin final was set for 3:30 in the afternoon, 10 minutes before the 5,000 final. "Dana was unhappy. Oh, oh," Zatopek says in a loud voice, imitating his wife, bringing his hands to his head. "Oh," his voice rises,

> I cannot go. If you run, I can't watch you. Oh, it was horrible. But there was good luck for Dana, because before the javelin was the hammer throw, and a Hungarian thrower, Csermak, threw a new world record.

Because of the delay while the Hungarian's throw was measured, Dana was able to watch the 5,000. But as the race neared its exciting climax, Dana became too nervous to watch, and she learned of her husband's come-from-behind victory when a Soviet coach yelled out "Dana, Emil wins 5,000 meters in new record!"

At the 5,000-meter victory ceremony in the stadium, Dana and other javelin throwers passed by. Emil explains that Dana came up to him saying, "Oh you won *prima*, where is your gold medal? Give it to me. I'll bring it for good luck." On her first throw, Dana set a new Olympic record, and when the toss held up for the gold medal in the javelin, Dana turned a cartwheel on the infield grass. Emil told her that "My gold medal brings you a world record. I inspired you, and in your enthusiasm you threw two meters more than ever!"

"You mean," replied Dana, "that in the javelin throw, the principle is enthusiasm? If so, you can try and inspire some other girl, and see if she throws an Olympic record."

Emil and Dana were the Golden Couple of Helsinki, and the story of their gold medals was the highlight of the Olympics. "For journalists, it was good material, and they could write about my inspiration for Dana, and Dana's gold medal."

Running to the Flame

Zatopek would need all the inspiration he could find if he were to earn the family's fourth gold medal of the Games, because three days later he would be running 42 kilometers for the first time against the fastest marathoner in the world. Jim Peters of England, who had run a world record 2:20:42 at the Windsor-to-Chiswick British AAA Championship in June 1952, was the clear favorite. But the Olympics are not a time trial; they are a race. The following year Peters would become the first person to break the 2:20 barrier with his 2:18:40 in the Chiswick race, but he was destined to be another in the list of fast runners who failed to produce in championship meets.

Peters, known for being a front-runner, had retired from competition after finishing eighth in the London Olympic 10,000, where he was lapped by Zatopek. Peters had promised his wife he would give up running to concentrate on his job. But running was in his blood, and Peters made a comeback in 1950, doing 20-mile runs on the sly, without telling his wife. He talked with Paavo Nurmi, who told Peters he had trained up to 18 times a week. While working full-time, Peters sometimes ran three times a day. Peters's world record six weeks before Helsinki gave him confidence heading into the Olympics.

Zatopek was not without confidence of his own, however, because of his outstanding 20-kilometer/hour run a year earlier. The head coach of the Czech team questioned the wisdom of Zatopek running the marathon, but like a chess master, Emil was always thinking of how to get the most out of his running.

> To race without experience in the marathon is a great risk. But I was keen enough also to run the marathon because I thought I had a chance. The [20-kilometer] race one year before the Olympics, it was for me a control. What are my chances in the races over 10,000 meters? I saw that they are better.

Zatopek's biggest concern was not Peters or the distance, but rather the surface. His races had almost all been on the track. "I was not used to running on this highway."

Zatopek had never met Peters, the favorite. He read the newspaper the morning of the race and noted Peters's race number. The gregarious Emil searched out the Englishman near the starting line and introduced himself, saying, "Hello, I am Zatopek, Czechoslovakia. You are Peters?" Peters, who would eventually set three more marathon world records in his career, was not interested in making small talk, however, and kept to himself.

The 67 runners in the 1952 Olympic Marathon started out with three laps around the Helsinki track. Peters, seemingly fearful of Zatopek's speed, went out hard and soon built up a 20-second lead. But by 15 kilometers, Zatopek and Sweden's Gustaf Jansson had pulled alongside Peters. Zatopek's plan was to stay with Peters for as long as possible, but he was concerned about the pace.

"The pace, Jim, it is too fast?" asked Zatopek.

"No, Emil," replied Peters. "The pace, it is too slow."

Hearing this, the surprised Zatopek took off, urging Peters to come with him. But the Englishman could not keep up. "I was the favorite and I was confident. Emil had already won the 5,000 and 10,000 meters, and people said there was no way he could beat me after four hard races," Peters told *Athletics Weekly*. "When he came up to me and asked if the pace was right, I said it was too slow just to kid him, but he got away from me. Then I got a cramp for the first time ever at 13 miles." Peters eventually dropped out at 21 miles while running in fourth place. He teetered and fell in a heap on the side of the road, quickly surrounded by anxious officials and spectators. The pace had indeed been too fast.

After dropping Peters, Zatopek and Jansson ran together. Emil was still feeling strong when he and Jansson rounded the halfway post on a road in the countryside outside Helsinki and started for home. But he was now in uncharted territory and running into the wind.

At 21 kilometers I had this, oh, this vision; 21 kilometers more, whhooh, what will it be like? Of course, the organizers tried to make it more easy. They organized this refreshing station that had everything: chocolate, mineral water, and oh, everything possible. And coming to the 26th kilometer, at this refreshment station, they gave a half lemon to Jansson. He took it, and they gave another half lemon to me.

Zatopek shakes his head, waving his hands in front of him. "Oh, I said, no, no, no. I don't take it, because I had no experience. I was not used during the training to eat or drink something. Training, training, training, and I did not ever take refreshments. But . . . ," he laughs, smacking his lips, "we ran together, but then," patting his stomach.

I thought, I'm idiot; there was lemon, and I don't take. But oh, to run back for half a lemon, it would also be stupid. No, I said, I have to go ahead. And I will see. I will be better than Jansson; at the next refreshment station, I will take two or three lemons! But, I don't know, 500 or 600 meters more later, Jansson was tired. What to do? I decide, no, no, no lemon, nothing. It was also stupid. I was afraid to take something.

One report says that Zatopek was also afraid he would have to pay for anything he took from the aid station, and he did not have money to do so.

Running alone now, Zatopek fought his mounting fatigue while building a minute lead on Jansson. But he was tiring, pushing his body farther than it had ever gone before. He pulled his red race singlet up on his chest to try and cool down, and began doubting that he could finish. "I looked ahead, and I can see nothing of the city. I want to quit, yes, but how to get back to town? I am 20 kilometers away, so I say I must run back," he told the *Los Angeles Times*. "So I run. The only thing I can see ahead is a very high tower with a flame on top, the Olympic flame. So I decide I must run to the flame."

The crowds lining the road thickened as Emil neared the city, urging him on. Smiling now, he ran into the stadium and a standing ovation to claim his third gold medal, clocking 2:23:03.2, the fastest time on an out-and-back course. Argentina's Reinaldo Gorno was second, more than two minutes back, while Jansson ended up third. "It was a most nice victory, because the spectators, mostly Finnish people, were so enthusiastic."

Zatopek had done it. Opening and closing the Olympic Games with gold medals, with another sandwiched in between, all in Olympic-record times. "Zatopek's '52 Olympics rates as one of the greatest performances in history, and it's unlikely to ever be duplicated," says Frank Shorter. "To do that well in three events in the Olympics was as much a mental domination of his opponents as a physical one. It was one of the greatest examples of combining psychological and physical tactics."

Now it was time for the Olympics to end, and the crowd was once again on its feet for the closing ceremonies. "At this time, they cheered 'Zatopek, Zatopek, Bye-bye Zatopek.' It was a little sad, that it was . . . ," Emil pauses, searching for the right words, ". . . that it belonged to history. And I knew there could be no repetition. It is possible only once." He pauses again for a long time. With a soft, sad laugh, he looks out the window, saying, "It is possible only once. Then, on the fifth of August, we return home. All the team."

What is most important about Helsinki is not his three gold medals, says Zatopek, but rather that "the atmosphere of those Olympic Games was something special," unlike the politicized games to come. "The Olympic Games at Moscow (in 1980), for example, maybe are not very fair. During the pole vaulting, if a Russian was jumping, it would be quiet. But if it were Polish, 'aie, aie, aie,' all this big crowd tried to disturb the adversary."

It was not like that in Helsinki. Though he had crushed the best Finnish runners and snatched away Heino's world records, Zatopek was saluted wherever he went in Helsinki. "Finland was famous for its long-distance running, and of course they expected more success. But they stood and cheered for me in the 10,000 and 5,000 meters; again Zatopek, Oh, bravo," He claps his hands. "And in the marathon, oh, it was wonderful. They called me 'satu pekka'." "Zatopek" sounded like the Finnish words "satu pekka," which translates from Finnish as "fairy-tale Peter," or the "fairy-tale guy." That was the story of Emil and Dana—the fairy-tale couple of Helsinki.

> The Helsinki Olympics were for us the best. But not only because we were successful. But, also because Finland is another country. People visit Paris to see the Tour d'Effiel, or the Tower Bridge in London. But in Finland, people come to see the beauty of the nature. Woods, lakes, wonderful country, which invites to sporting activities. And that time, there were no problems with a boycott of the Games, or doping, or commercial difficulties. Maybe the most important characteristic of the sports movement is when people have fair play. At Helsinki, it was very proper, very clean, very nice.

"And very sportive and fair. And no mistakes," Zatopek says, his voice trailing off. After a pause, he adds softly, "It was perfect. A perfect Olympics."

More World Records

Zatopek's season was not over. He was in peak form and wanted to take advantage of his fitness. On October 26, he returned to the tree-lined Houstka Stadium in the Stara Boleslav forest for a run at the 30-kilometer record. He got it, clocking 1:35:23.8 to break Russian Yakov Moskachenkov's year-old mark by 3-1/2 minutes. Running far in front of the field, Emil comfortably went through 3,000 meters in 9:27.4, 5,000 meters in 15:48, 10,000 meters in 31:44, and 10 miles in 50:59.8. He passed 15 miles in 1:16:26.4, also a world record, and 25 kilometers in 1:19:11.8, yet another record. Zatopek now had the world record in every track distance exceeding 10,000 meters.

In 1953, Zatopek worked on lowering his 10,000-meter record. He was sick part of the season, but he was able to beat the powerful newcomer from Russia, Vladimir Kuts, over 5,000 meters. On November 1, he once again returned to the forest track and ran 10,000 meters in 29:01.6, knocking one second off his record. He went through 6 miles in 28.08.4, also a record.

In 1954, Zatopek was now 32 and competing for the Dukas Sporting Club. Once more his military superiors called him in.

"Emil," his voice grows low and gruff, imitating an officer. "You have world record 10,000, 15,000, 20,000, 30,000, but no 5,000. 5,000 is Olympic event." The record was 13:58, by Gunder Hägg from Sweden. "Can you get it?"

"Please, allow me to practice in the woods, in the forest, on soft terrain," Zatopek told them, as he had previously when asked to make a record attempt. "Three weeks. I need three weeks. Two weeks very intense productivity, third week, less and less, and then to try for the record."

With time off from his military duties, Zatopek did the hardest training of his life, perhaps the hardest training ever. "I ran every day 100 × 400 meters. In the woods, 400 meters," he whistles, saying "arrhh," and making a face. "Then 150 meters jogging for recovery," he pants, with his tongue hanging out. "50 times in the morning and 50 times in the afternoon. Every day for two weeks. Oh, it was a lot of work." One hundred by 400 meters every day for two weeks—with warm-up and warmdown he was running over 30 miles per day.

After a week of recovery, Zatopek flew to Paris, where he would embark on an incredible two days of racing. First, in Colombes Stadium outside of Paris against some overmatched Yugoslavian and French runners, Zatopek tackled Hägg's historic 5,000-meter record, which had stood for 12 years. Needing to average less than 2:47.6 per kilometer, Zatopek went through the first 2,000 meters in 5:34.1, hitting 1,000-meter splits of 2:47.1 and 2:47.0. But after splits of 8:23.5 at 3,000 meters (2:49.4) and 11:13.4 at 4,000 meters (2:49.9), he was three seconds off Hägg's record pace. But a final kilometer of 2:43.8 brought Zatopek home in 13:57.2, one second under Hägg's record.

After that effort, Emil flew immediately to Belgium, where the very next day he became the first person to break the 29-minute barrier in the 10,000 meters, running 28:54.2 in Brussels's Heysel Stadium. He went through 5,000 meters in 14:27.4, and, running alone, came back in 14:26.8. Second place ended up nearly two minutes behind. Afterwards, the distance was measured as 10,001 meters.

> I was able to change this quantity of training into quality of running. But nowadays, it is not good to recommend young sportsmen to do this. Fifty kilometers a day, huh? Right. Only to get more and more tired. Nowadays, training is oriented toward quality, not quantity of kilometers.

Zatopek's huge training volume, combined with interval training, was followed by runners in the years to come. He changed the notions of how much work a runner could handle. Vladimir Kuts, the Russian who was to follow Zatopek as the world's top distance runner, based his training on Zatopek's for several years, using it as the foundation of his training that would later lead to Olympic gold. No one could do Zatopek's training exactly, and Kuts eventually began reducing his mileage and number of intervals, adding more long-tempo runs.

By the 1954 European Championships in Bern, Switzerland, Emil was a lieutenant colonel in the army and anxious to show some of these upstart runners, like the Soviet Union's Kuts and Aleksandr Anufriyev, Kovacs of Hungary, and Chataway and Pirie of England that he was still the best. Zatopek repeated as European 10,000-meter champ, dominating the race and winning in 28:58, far ahead of Jozsef Kovacs in second place. But in the 5,000, Kuts took Zatopek's world record by running 13:56.6. Chataway was second and Zatopek third, with a time of 14:10.2. However, he ended the year with a 13:57 5,000, tantalizing close to regaining the record for which he had worked so hard.

Amateur Rules

Zatopek never made much money from his records and wins. He competed at a time when, because of amateur rules, runners were unable to take money. The great Swedish runners, Gunder Hägg and Arne Andersson, were banned for being "professionals," as was Paavo Nurmi before the 1932 Olympics. Zatopek says that he had to be careful not to be disqualified. "Paavo Nurmi, for example, won [the Olympics] in 1920, 1924, 1928. He was the favorite in 1932, but he was declared a professional."

> It was a danger for me, also. In 1947, I won Cross d'Algier and the winner was supposed to get a prize worth 12,000 francs. Oh, but amateur rules say you can only take 250 dollars, and it was eight times more. It was a great risk to take it. If caught, you could be disqualified. And it would be very bad to be disqualified, and to return home, and have people say, "Why do you blame us? Why do you shame our country? You are not good enough to represent us." What to do? I took only 300 francs, to get something for my girlfriend—it was '47, and there was another girl, not Dana.

Instead of taking the money, Zatopek made a proposal to the race officials. "Please," he told them, "here is my friend, Chapel from Belgium. He was ninth and has no chance to get something. He can choose something and he will not be disqualified. If he was disqualified, it would make him more famous." Officials gave him the prize.

On another occasion, Zatopek won a race in Germany and was awarded a moped. "But it was also over this amateur limit, and I cannot take it. I had to be very careful." To accept any prize at all, Zatopek first had to get permission from the Czechoslovakia Ministry of Foreign Trade. Sometimes, race directors agreed to send his prize, or money, but it usually never got to him. Zatopek does not know whether the prizes were never sent, or, as is more likely, were sent and kept by government officials.

"It was possible also to misuse these amateur rules," Zatopek says, telling of Heino's response when threatened with disqualification. "Viljo Heino said, 'Oh, is there a problem that I got money? Of course I got money. Do you mean, if I come to a competition, I have to sleep under the bridge?'" Emil's voice raises, "'I need money. I received money to have a hotel, to eat. It's not possible without money, try it yourself,'" his voice gets higher and louder, "'to live without a penny or a cent!' And Heino was not disqualified."

1956 Melbourne Olympics

By 1956 Zatopek had been an international competitor for a decade, and his time at the top was catching up to him. "In the Melbourne Olympics, I was in a very bad situation. There were new training methods, to strengthen muscles, but I didn't want to make weightlifting like many sportsmen." In order to keep pace with runners like Kuts, who had become a good friend, Zatopek decided to try some new techniques of his own invention. "Before Melbourne, I tried to strengthen my muscles. I took Dana on my shoulders, and I ran with her." Carrying his wife on his back, however, was too much even for Zatopek.

"Oh, it was, I don't know. A stone or something. I felt a pain here [points to stomach]. It was a hernia. Hernia," he says softly, his voice trailing off, his mind moving back to other times, other places. After a pause, he begins again. "Before the Olympics, I hesitated what to do. But it was worse and worse. And then, in September, it was necessary to go for an operation."

"Do not run for two months," doctors warned him.

"You are funny," Zatopek replied. "Because in two months, the Olympics will be over."

But Zatopek was unable to train, and the world lost its chance to see him battle Kuts in the 5,000 and 10,000 meters, where the Russian won both races over Pirie of England. Says Zatopek, "I tried to run as soon as possible. Many days, I tried to jog, but it was no good training. I came to Melbourne only to take part in the marathon."

Zatopek's good friend Mimoun was there. He had spent his career chasing Zatopek to the tape. "He was second in the London Olympics, second in the 1950 European Championships in Brussels in the 10,000 and 5,000, and he was second in Helsinki. He was always second," Zatopek says with a laugh. With Emil injured, Mimoun now had his chance. But the Algerian was so accustomed to running behind Zatopek that he did not believe that the hernia had prevented Emil from training. His strategy, as so many times before, was to stick with Zatopek until he was dropped. "In Melbourne, after the start, he ran with me."

"Alain, I am not good," Zatopek told Mimoun. "Don't stay with me. It's useless."

Still, Mimoun hesitated.

"Go on ahead," Zatopek urged his friend again. "You need to follow good runners, not me." Mimoun finally took off and won, in a time three minutes slower than Zatopek's 1952 Helsinki marathon win. After eight years of trying, Mimoun had finally beaten Zatopek.

"Oh, it was great," says Zatopek, his face lighting up with pleasure. After crossing the line in first, Mimoun waited for Zatopek to finish. "He stood there on the track until I came in," in sixth place. "Alain, you are really a hero," Zatopek told him. "Always second, and in your last competition, you are Olympic champion. Congratulations."

Mimoun was the toast of France.

Oh, he was so happy. And the president, Pompideau, invited him for a visit. You are the "golden boy," Pompideau told him. You gave the glory to all of France. Because no one else representing France won a gold medal. Only Mimoun. And later he was named director of local institute of physical training and sport, near Toulouse.

Forged Friendships

Mimoun was just one of Zatopek's many friends. There is a special bond that builds up between great rivals, something forged through the countless hours of training that only they can understand, Zatopek says. Something that is more important than records and medals.

> I value those friendships. Maybe it is also nice, the friendship I have with our neighbor, Antony, when we go out to fish. But that is only one kind of friendship, because we have the chance to see each other every day. But in such an Olympic struggle, ah, it is not so easy. With all their energy, everybody tries to do their best. This struggle, it stays very in your mind. And it produces great respect among adversaries. It is this quality I esteem, not only by winning to get congratulations, but also by losing. It is a chance to think, "What is the reason why I was not good enough?" What to do in training, in living standard. It is really what I have high esteem for, this friendship in sport.

Others esteemed their friendship with Emil as well, as runners continued to visit him through the years after he stopped competing in 1957. "Many of my rivals stay in contact. If Gaston Reiff had a chance to visit Czechoslovakia, always he visited our house. If I go to Paris, always I visit the house of Alain Mimoun. What this is teaching is to esteem adversaries, to esteem the quality of this sporting fellowship." Zatopek pours another beer, looks out the window, and is silent for a long time.

One of the visitors to Zatopek's home was Ron Clarke, the Australian who was the first man to break 28 minutes for 10,000 meters. Clarke came to race in Prague at Zatopek's invitation in the summer of 1966, the peak of Clarke's own career. Clarke had by then set several distance records, but, unlike Emil, had never won a gold medal in the Olympics or the British Commonwealth Games. He was known for making his opponents work during a race. Clarke holds great respect for Zatopek. He told Brian Lenton in *Off the Record* about the special regard with which "Zatu," as Clarke called Zatopek, was treated in Prague. On the morning Clarke was to leave Prague after a two-day visit, the 44-year-old Zatopek took him to the Houtseka track. They did a 10-mile run during which "Emil kept apologizing every now and then for not being good enough, yet it was one of the hardest training runs I had on the tour." They then returned to Prague for some last-minute shopping.

"It was a peak hour and Emil just nonchalantly parked the car in the main street," Clarke said. "There was no one else parked there." When they came out, a policeman was writing a ticket. "When we got closer the officer's eyes lit up and he excitedly said, 'Emil!' He immediately tore the ticket up and turned the book around, and Zatu autographed it.

> Emil then did a U-turn in front of the traffic with drivers getting upset and honking their horns. We drove some distance up the street to find another store and Zatu casually parked the car again. This time when he stopped a policeman was blowing his whistle and angrily waving him on. So Zatu waves back and leaves the car where he shouldn't. The policeman goes bright red and sprints about 40 yards towards us continually blowing his whistle. Emil stops and turns around, and as soon as the officer recognizes who it is, the same thing happens again. His facial expression changes, he pumps Zatopek by the hand and both engage in animated conversation.

After shopping for an hour, Clarke and Zatopek came back outside to discover that the car was gone.

> The policeman had actually got in the car and driven it some distance up the street and was standing beside it in a parking zone. On seeing Emil appear, he drove it back, warmly shook hands again and away we went. I reckon that is the greatest idolization I've ever seen of any sportsman in any city and that was really the way they felt about Zatopek.

In his book *The Lonely Breed*, Clarke gives this insight into Zatopek:

> Up until 1966, I had always been disappointed that I had never met Emil Zatopek. I had been told such wonderful stories of his personality. I had purchased the books on his life, I had met and talked with contemporary Australian athletes of his time, who were all overwhelming in their praise of the mighty Czech. But when I had the opportunity to meet him, I was amazed. No one man at any time has ever made more impression than Emil Zatopek did upon me during those two days in July.

His enthusiasm, his friendliness, his love of life, shone through every movement. There is not and never was, a greater man than Emil Zatopek. In his running career, he pursued training methods more bold and severe than anyone else had attempted. But never did he think of training as torture. Instead, he was fully absorbed with the constant balance between the tiredness of the body and its limitations, for the gathering of strength for future races. Everybody knows of his magnificent performances, but it would not be an overstatement to say that the personality of the man was even greater. In fact, to acknowledge that he was a unique figure in the history of distance running would be doing him an injustice. Much more simply, and more of the truth, Emil Zatopek himself is unique.

After shopping, Zatopek drove Clarke to the airport. "Zatu" took Clarke through customs and came onto the plane to say goodbye. He gave Clarke a small package, telling him, "Look after this; you deserve it." Once the plane was in the air, Clarke opened the package. In it was Zatopek's 10,000-meter gold medal from the Helsinki Olympics, inscribed to Clarke.

"Zatu" Retires

After the Melbourne Olympics, Zatopek competed one more year. He was back in good shape after recovering from the hernia operation, but after winning a cross-country race in Spain in 1957, he retired. Zatopek remained with his military sports club, coaching and teaching physical education in the army. He enjoyed his status as one of the most famous and respected runners in Czechoslovakia.

But in 1968 the idolization in his country changed. That year, the Czech people challenged Soviet rule in what came to be known as the Prague Spring. For a brief time there was a thawing of the authoritarian state, with more freedoms allowed. A true democrat, Zatopek was among those who supported the reforms. Along with Czech intellectuals and leaders from all fields, he and Dana signed the "Manifesto of 2000 Words," a document heralding the Czech people's determination to break free from the rigidity of Soviet rule. "I will explain this Prague Spring," says Zatopek.

At that time it was not allowed to travel to visit foreign countries. Only diplomats and sports persons were allowed. It was a great privilege, but in traveling, we had the chance to see progress, in science and in many areas. And returning home, we were back in a country where time was stopped. No progress; nothing. Then [in 1968] many people tried to fight for more progress, more democracy, for the country not to be so closed, and *retard*. And I was very keen for it. With new leaders, it could be useful to move this stagnation.

The Soviets, however, were not ready to see their empire disintegrate.

Zatopek was one of the Manifesto signers who suffered the consequences when the Prague Spring's bloom faded. Despite his golden past and status as Czechoslovakia's greatest sports hero, Zatopek became a persona non grata. He was expelled from the Communist Party and lost his rank as colonel in the Czech army. He could no longer travel to sports events. To the rest of the world, it appeared Zatopek had "dropped off the face of the earth."

I was kicked out of the army. I could not work in Prague, but only outside of the city, doing only manual work. Only once every two weeks could I come home, in the wintertime. And we tried not to heat the house, only in the bedroom.

After he fell out of favor, it was forbidden to talk about Zatopek in other Eastern Bloc countries, says Dieter Hogen, a coach in East Germany at the time. Says Dixler, "When all the problems came in 1968, Emil never changed his mind, never became a turncoat. He kept his integrity, and that really makes him different."

Authorities in the Soviet-installed Czech government sent Zatopek to the countryside for "geological research," which involved boring for water, uranium, and minerals. Zatopek did not complain. Instead, he made the best of the situation. "I liked it and found it very interesting. Because the earth is nice not only from above, but from inside." The work, he said, was good for "producing muscle; I ate more, and had more static power. I was obliged to work until I retired at pension age, 60."

After retirement, Zatopek was still out of favor with the government. For many years, the International Amateur Athletic Federation (IAAF) tried to honor him, but their requests for Zatopek to come and receive his award were rebuffed. Finally, in the late 1980s, IAAF president Primo Nebiolo traveled to Prague, where he met Zatopek and gave him his award.

Zatopek was rediscovered by the world in 1989, after the Velvet Revolution. This time, the Czech people were successful in throwing off the Soviet yoke. The tide of change swept through eastern Europe, and now

Zatopek was again free to speak and travel. Even when he was hidden away behind the Iron Curtain, Zatopek never gave up his principles. "We were trying to be more free, and the development in our country was going in this direction, towards more democracy." What does it mean to be free? Perhaps no better example exists than Zatopek's gold-medal gift to Ron Clarke. To work unceasingly for years, running thousands of miles, stomping through the woods doing hundreds of quarter-mile intervals a week to get yourself in better shape than anyone in history; to dedicate your entire life and your entire being to winning the gold medal; and then, having won it, to give the gold medal away. That is freedom.

To Know All the Life

Now in his 70s, Zatopek still has his modest house, full of warmth, and his memories of his many world records and his many adventures and friends. He is not a wealthy man; he and Dana live on a small government pension.

> No, becoming rich never was my dream. For me it was best to have time for training, tracksuit for training, running shoes for training, stadium for training, all the nature and good food— that was enough. Maybe every competition, if I run, I got something [pointing to some of his trophies]. It was something, only symbolic. Sometimes I would get a vase, which is nice and useful for flowers. But we are not selfish.

Zatopek has always focused on the nonmaterial aspects of life, something he learned from his humble upbringing and from what he saw in his travels around the world.

> It is not the best style to be very rich. The best style is not to be far away from the misery, and not to fall into the misery. To know what is high living standard, and poor living standard. To know all the life, it is the best. To have millions, millions, people are stupid. Because they don't know what is misery. But in a simple living style, you can see everything. But it is not good really to fall into the misery. For me, it is useless and not good. To be far away, to be very near, and to see what it is to have everything, and to see what it is to have nothing.

The pursuit of money has hurt championship meets like the Olympics, he says, because some athletes skip the meets in order to get a big payday. "In the Olympic Games, there are only medals, a symbol. It is a

Emil Zatopek relaxes at home in his garden.

danger when athletes prefer not to represent their country, but want to take the money." To keep the Olympics in their preeminent role, the games must change with the times, Zatopek believes. "Oh yes. The Olympics are very important, and adding new sports like triathlon is good."

Zatopek, who has great sensitivity for the less fortunate of the world, insists that those becoming wealthy from sport must give something back.

There is much misery in the world. It is also very *triste* maybe, when small children in undeveloped countries die from hunger; it is best to try to help all those. The sporting life is not just for those who are good. I'd prefer it if a sponsor gives maybe one million for a swimming pool. This is useful for sportsmen and for schoolboys. Today, young boys and girls are not as active. By organizing competitions and training, you can grow in ability and health and disposition and have a healthy life. Or, we can live without productivity and training, and we'll go down.

With his intelligence, sensitivity, and empathy for the suffering of others, Zatopek would have made a fine politician, in the mold, perhaps, of one of Plato's philosopher kings. "Oh, pardon," laughs Emil at such a thought. "I remember [learning that] once in ancient Greece, a sportsman from one small state won the Olympiad. Oh, they were so, so happy. They choose him as leader of the state. But after only one year," Emil laughs again, "he was kicked out. The economy collapses," he says, whistling, "goes down. It is nice if someone understands, maybe the discus throw, but it doesn't mean he understands society and the economy."

Emil is one who does understand history, society, and politics, and that is why he was aghast at the breakup of Czechoslovakia into the Czech and Slovak Republics and the rise of nationalism in Eastern Europe in the 1990s.

"There is such a bloody history because the Slovak nations are never together, always. . . ," he makes a shooting noise, holding out his hands as if carrying a gun.

Everyone wants to be separate. This is disintegration. It is not modern. It is stupid. I admire Switzerland, where people are speaking French, Italian, German, and are all together. Or the United States, where people are from different origins, but nobody tries to be sovereign.

Zatopek visited the United States in 1992, at the invitation of medical doctors at Stanford University who wanted to help him with a pinched nerve in his leg. "We have only nice memories now. No more activities, no more practicing or running," Emil explains. "I have had trouble with my leg. And I'm not able to run. It was a virus that came in 1987, affecting the nerves. I'm not able to make this movement," he says, lifting his good leg up and down.

The American doctors looked at Emil and decided against having him undergo an operation. But he is still a vital, strong man. Evening comes, and we walk out of the house into the lush garden, where he grabs a handful of berries growing on the plentiful bushes, munching on them like a hungry animal. "Ah, how sweet these are," he says. Then Zatopek picks up a huge piece of lumber, at least 10-feet long, carries it across the lawn, and heaves it onto the woodpile. As he tosses the lumber, he grunts and breaks into the most famous expression in running history, the Zatopek, half-twisted grimace of agony, pain, and determination. It is the grimace that carried him to 18 world records and 4 gold medals. And here, reveling in the evening breeze, among his and Dana's flowers and plants, he is still bursting with energy. His handshake is strong and firm, and as I walk through the iron gate and take a last look back, Emil's grimace seems to be there, floating in the gathering darkness like the Cheshire Cat's smile, an apt symbol for all who struggle.

That grimace is also the best metaphor for Czechoslovakia. While the rest of the world was going full steam ahead into the 21st century, Czechoslovakia regressed, metamorphosing into a Kafkaesque world of secret police, intolerance, and totalitarianism. Emil the Convoluted, the pictures of him in his prime seem to say, was the image of the troubled, twisted Czech soul—a country slapped together in 1920 and cut in half in 1993.

There have been lots of talented runners. But Zatopek has had more than a talent for running; he also has what Russian novelist Boris Pasternak calls "a talent for life." Emil has an exuberant personality bursting with a zest for living and a love of humanity that squeezed all he could out of life, an approach that makes him an immortal example for all of us, runners or not. Throughout his long, fruitful life and athletic career, Emil Zatopek has been beaten, but never defeated.

Zatopek can no longer run in his favorite forests where he used to tromp and bound in his military boots, but the trails are still there, along with the track in the woods where he set so many records. Now, they are full of Czech runners, trying to get into shape to compete in the New World Order. Hooking up with one, we talk, and I mention how full of agony Zatopek looked in his races.

"Don't let those photos of Emil fool you," he says at the end of the run. "I think he is the only happy man in Czechoslovakia."

2

Hezekiah Kipchoge "Kip" Keino

Kenya's Flying Cop

Born January 17, 1940, Kenya

World records: 3,000 and 5,000 meters

Olympic gold, 1,500, 1968, and steeplechase, 1972

Olympic silver, 5,000, 1968, and 1,500, 1972

The leopard crouched and tensed on the tree branch when it saw the little Kalenjin boy walking near the river. The 6-foot long, powerful animal pounced, but before it could grab its meal the boy's father jumped between them, pulling out his *rotwetabchok*, a double-edged Kenyan sword. Fending off its advances with his robe, he coolly dispatched the leopard, the fourth he had killed in his life.

It was just one of the close calls in the early life of the boy, Hezekiah Kipchoge Keino, who would go on to become the most famous man in the newly independent countries of sub-Saharan Africa. There were all sorts of adventures for Keino growing up in the "bush" in the Rift Valley village of Kapchemoiywo, Kenya: fending off poisonous snakes; roaming the hills as a shepherd; sleeping in a tree to escape beatings from a mean uncle. He survived those trials with a tenacity that was to mark his running, helping him put in the training needed to become one of the most versatile and important champions in track and field.

Through his athletic exploits, Kipchoge (a Swahili word meaning "born near the store for maize") would become a "roving ambassador" who brought pride and self-esteem not just to Kenya, but to all the nascent countries of Africa. Following in the strides of Ethiopian marathon great Abebe Bikila, Keino represented Kenya with a dignity that was a credit to his young country and made him a national treasure.

Keino is a member of the Nandis, a subgroup of the Kalenjins, one of roughly 42 ethnic groups in Kenya. The country's borders were dreamed up during the 1880s when the European powers carved up Africa like it was giant jigsaw puzzle. Germany governed Kenya first, then lost the colony after World War I to the English. When Kip was born in 1940, England still ruled the land, and his early life coincided with the struggle for independence.

Kip was not an overnight running success; when he was 16, he ran only 5:49 for the mile, and he did not start running seriously until he was 20. There were other talented Kenyan runners, but it was Keino who had the drive to put in the years of training needed to develop his slim body, with its long legs and graceful stride, into the best in the world, reaching a rarefied level only a few have attained.

In running to two Olympic and four Commonwealth gold medals, "Kenya's Flying Policeman" became the progenitor of African running, for his medals inspired spirit and enthusiasm in the continent's young nations. He brought crowds to their feet around the world when he was the most traveled runner in track, flying around the globe to take on the best in the world including Ron Clarke and Jim Ryun. "I run because I enjoy running," Keino said. When asked to explain his motivation, Kenya could not have found a better spokesman: Articulate, handsome and humble, he had a deep love for his country, and it showed. Keino was charismatic, patient with fans and reporters, quick-witted, and above all, shone with an effusive joy of running that was evident in his races and which drew the attention and admiration of thousands around the world.

A Young Goatherder

Keino was born January 17, 1940, in the small village of Kipsamo in the Nandi Hills, one of six children. When he was four, his family moved to Kapchemoiywo, where his mother died shortly afterwards during childbirth. In Kenyan society, children of a widower are sent to live with their grandparents, so Kip and his siblings moved back to Kipsamo to be with their grandmother.

His early years were typical of young males in traditional Kenyan society; walking, running, playing in the fields, and doing chores around the farm. The Nandi are renowned as cattle herders, and when he was 10, Kip moved to his uncle's house in a neighboring village to tend goats. He did not go to school like some of the other young boys, instead spending all day in the hills watching the goats.

But living with his uncle was not good, because he would drink at night, then shout at and beat Kip. His uncle's beatings were especially bad when he caught Kip sneaking off to school. Fed up and scared, Kip finally decided to run away. Slinging a calabash full of milk around his neck, he took off on the 16-mile journey back to his father's home. The elder Keino was happy to see his son, who pleaded with his father to send him to school. But Kip's father said no, he must return to his uncle. Keino's biographer, Francis Noronha, reports in *Keino of Kenya* how the elder Keino brought his son back to his uncle's homestead. Standing on a high point in the Nandi Hills near the home, he put his hand on Kip's shoulder and "pointed with his stick to a hill two miles south."

> Do you see that hill, *werei*? That is Ketparak, where our great Laibon, Samoei Arap Koitelal, was killed by the European, Kipkororor. [The German General Meinertzhagen was called "Kipkororor" or "Ostrich feather," because of the two feathers he wore in his helmet. He killed the Nandi leader Samoei on October 19, 1905.] The Laibon tried to stop our land from being taken away. He was a great warrior and united the Nandi when I was not much older than you. He was a great leader. He did not go to school!

And Kip did not either. He continued on as his uncle's goat-herder, but when the beatings continued, Kip's father and his uncle argued, and Kip went back to his father's home for good. He still dreamed of attending school, and finally, after another year of pestering, his father paid the school fees and bought the school uniform. At last, Kip, now 12 years old, was a student.

Once enrolled at the Kaptumo Intermediate School, he studied diligently and was popular with the many friends he made. In 1953, he ran his first race ever, a cross-country competition. He beat most of the older runners and finished fourth. His prize was a bar of soap.

Kip ran a 440-yard race later in the year, and there were many other "unofficial" races through the schoolyard, Noronha tells us. He writes that "the little boy would take on boys twice his size and more often than not beat them in races round the school playground." Kip was happy in school and did well during the next several years, but when he was getting ready to start the fifth grade, there were tuition increases that his father was unable to pay, and Kip's school days were over.

It was time for Kip to earn his own way in the world. The Nandi, like many societies, have formal rituals and ceremonies to mark the passage from childhood to adulthood. Kip went through the tough circumcision ritual, in which the child is symbolically left behind.

Searching for a Profession

At 16, he was now a Nandi man, and Kip built a hut and grew a garden, selling the vegetables to buy clothes. But a man needs a job, so he walked 40 miles to a town where he could catch a train. He found work on a farm and would come back to Kipsamu for visits on the weekends. On one journey home, he was attacked by robbers. Fortunately, Kip was faster than the bandits and able to run away, but the incident convinced him to quit his farm job and try to find work closer to home.

Back in Kipsamu, Kip and his friends raced each other on the crude track they made on his father's farm. The elder Keino sometimes joined the boys, telling them how he had won two races when he was 45 years old. According to the elder Keino as reported by Noronha, "There was no one who could jump over the rocks and burn the ground as fast as I could, and I finished the race while the others were still struggling."

Kip, still 16, drawing motivation from his father's past racing and his own early love of running, went to watch some district competitions at the town of Kapsabet. There he was inspired by seeing Kenya's best runners, including policeman Arere Anentia. Watching Anentia fueled Kip's determination to become a good runner himself. Kip was still searching for an identity, and he thought he might have found it in running. Returning to the farm, he and his friends raced around on their homemade track, taking the names of their favorite runners. Kip's nickname was invariably "Anentia."

In 1957, Keino finished fifth in his first three-mile race, and his reputation as a decent runner began growing. After some more local races, 18-year-old Kip decided in 1958 to enter a marathon. He led at halfway and was still in second at 21 miles. Feeling thirsty, Kip drank a soda and got sick to his stomach, and had to sit down and wait for the "sagwagon" to take him to the finish.

Still looking for a suitable job, Kip decided his future was in the army or police force. But he was still too young to have much luck enlisting in either. He had shown up whenever recruits were solicited, to no avail. He was once again turned down in July 1958 when 18 recruits were selected for the national police force. A despondent Kip sat outside the police station ready to return home, still jobless, when, in one of those quirks of fortune on which lives turn, only 17 recruits turned up. Based in part on his reputation as a good athlete, Kip was tapped to fill the missing recruit's spot and given 30 minutes to catch the bus bringing recruits to the regional police headquarters in Eldoret. That bus ride was the start of a journey that would take Keino around the globe many times and make him one of the most famous athletes in the world.

Becoming a police recruit gave Keino self-confidence, along with a little money. With his first paycheck, he bought a Bible. At Eldoret, Kip prayed that he would prove himself a worthy Nandi in his training and racing. His prayers were answered, as Kip soon showed that he was the best runner in his class. His first competition as a police recruit was a cross-country race, in which Kip took third behind his hero, Arere Anentia, a police corporal.

Keino settled down to the rigorous schedule of police training, which involved some form of physical activity every day. He ran three to five days a week and played soccer and volleyball on his off days. He gradually became stronger under this schedule, and a year after joining the police he ran a 4:38 mile and a 16:17 three-mile in a police track meet. It was one of the few races Kip ran that year, as he and the other recruits were on patrol around the colony. These were the years of rebellion against British rule, and the countryside was full of Mau Mau fighters, struggling for independence for Kenya.

Keino for a time guarded Mau Mau leader Jomo Kenyatta, who in 1964 would become the first president of independent Kenya. Kip spent three years with the police General Services Unit, running a few races, but mostly spending his time in the countryside, engaged in police work such as chasing cattle thieves.

Becoming the Best in Kenya

Kip did his police field work well, but it soon became apparent that his real skill was in running. Athletic competition is intense between the different branches of the Kenyan government. The police, army, and prison meets are hard-fought affairs, with the heads of each organization trying to boost their image by beating the others. Kip's talent was recognized by police officials, and in order to develop his athletic skills, 20-year-old Keino was sent to Kiganjo for training. He immediately drew attention there by winning an 11-mile cross-country race by seven minutes. He continued with his three-day-a-week training until he graduated from the police academy. It was then time for Keino to be assigned to a permanent position.

Kip wanted a job near Eldoret, in order to be near his family. Kenyan officials, however, told him he must stay at Kiganjo, where he would become a physical education teacher. Despite his protests, Kip was stationed at Kiganjo. The chief inspector there, Michael Wade, "can thus be given credit" for what Noronha calls "the most decisive action in the development of Kipchoge's athletic career." Keino for the first time had a somewhat systematic training schedule. Wade gave Kip some structure to his week, advising him to run easy distance mixed with sprints.

Keino got faster with this regular training. In 1961, he defeated his hero Anentia in a three-mile race at a police meet. Flushed with that success, Keino invited his father to come and watch his next race, a steeplechase against a team from the Kenyan army. Kip was confident he would win again, but things did not turn out as he expected. Halfway through the race, he fell in the water jump and finished fourth, disappointed at having let his father down. He would not run another steeplechase in an important meet until 1972 at the Munich Olympics.

Using "sprint" workouts of his own invention, Keino improved to 14:08.9 (three-mile) and 4:17 (one mile) by the time of the 1962 Kenya Championships. Running against the top athletes in the country, he won the three-mile and, along with Pius Talam, made the team for the East Africa Championships to be held in neighboring Tanzania. There he set a Kenyan three-mile record of 13:46.8. Suddenly, Kip Keino was the best runner in Kenya, and he showed it by winning the selection race for the 1962 Perth Commonwealth Games three-mile in 13:55.5.

Kenya's national coach, overseeing the team being sent to Kenya's first-ever international championship, was Archie Evans, Colony Sports

Officer. Evans was a British coach who "must be credited with much of the spadework that paved the way to Kenya's future progress in athletics," writes Noronha. Evans might have done the spadework, but he did not believe much in speedwork, and he and Keino "did not see eye to eye on the kind of training Kip needed." Noronha writes, "As a relative newcomer to the team, Kip found it difficult to press his point and, in any case, his natural diffidence and desire to avoid unpleasantness led him to accept and do whatever he was told to do."

Keino soon became aware of the need for speedwork, when members of Kenya's 1962 Commonwealth team went to prepare in Australia. At their training camp in Perth, Keino was required to follow the training program laid out by Evans. Keino developed some aches and pains from overtraining that forced him to take some days off. He went to the stadium where he watched foreign athletes work out and for the first time began to develop ideas on what interval training was all about.

In one of the several pre-Commonwealth races set up before the Games began, Keino had the first of what would be many races against Australian star Ron Clarke. In his first race outside of Africa, Keino placed third behind Clarke with an 8:52.2 two-mile. At the Commonwealth Games, Keino ran a 4:07 mile, failing to qualify for the final.

He did however qualify in the three-mile, and in the final he gave the world its first glimpse of African front running. In what was to become an East African trademark, Keino went out incredibly fast from the start. He was over a straightaway ahead of the field at halfway, and at the bell the young Kenyan still had a commanding 40-yard lead. On the last lap, however, he was passed, then passed again, again, and yet again, finding no speed to match the finishing kicks of veterans like New Zealand Olympic 5,000-meter champ Murray Halberg and even Clarke, who was not known for his kick. Keino's final lap of 70 seconds was far off Halberg's 53.9 and left him with a 13:50.4, 11th-place finish. While Kip's bid for his country's first medal had fallen short on the last lap, his teammates came through with two gold and silver medals and one bronze.

Training for the Olympics

Keino was busy after Perth, getting married, buying some land near Kipsamu, and starting a farm before resuming his police duties. He also suffered his first injury, one that would severely hinder his buildup for the 1964 Tokyo Olympics. In early 1963, he was using some oxen to tow trees he was using to fence off his 14 acres. Something startled one of the oxen, which kicked Kip's left knee, resulting in a severe dislocation. The knee pained him the whole year. Kip was able to run only a few races in 1963 and was beaten in the East African Championships. It was not until early 1964 that he was able to run consistently again.

Despite the year off, Keino had his sights set high for the Olympics, and in this he received advice from American Mal Whitfield, the 1948 and 1952 Olympic 800-meter gold medalist who spent his postathletic career in East Africa developing sports programs. Whitfield did not give Keino a training program, but did give him insight on what it takes to be a champion. Whitfield was based in Nairobi, and Keino listened eagerly to the American whenever the pair's paths crossed.

"I gave him advice; I didn't coach him and neither did anyone else," Whitfield says. "There is a difference between philosophy and coaching. Unless you are seeing a lot of someone, spending time with them day in and day out, you are not coaching. Saying a few things is not coaching; it's giving assistance and friendship. That's what I did."

Keino would ask Whitfield questions, and Whitfield would tell the young runner about his own racing and training experiences. " We talked about how to become a good athlete, what it takes to be good, how to go about motivating yourself, things like that. I was not out there every day." As he did with all the runners and coaches he talked with, Keino, who remained a self-coached athlete his entire career, took what he thought was important and assimilated it into his own training, Whitfield says.

Keino based his running schedule on his police training in Kiganjo, going for "road work" five mornings a week. Two or three afternoons a week he ran intervals, and sometimes he worked out three times a day, still taking a few days off a week. The countryside around the town was perfect for training, with miles of quiet roads and rolling hills. The question haunting Kip since the last lap of the Perth three-mile was how he could get faster at the end of his races, and he worked on this through short intervals.

In 1964, Kip ran an early-season three-mile in 13:47.2 and a 4:06.6 mile at the Kenya championships. That was a Kenyan and East African record, but not beneath the Olympic qualifying standard. Keino next lowered his mile personal best to 4:03.3 at the Kenyan Olympic trials— still not fast enough to get him into the Olympics, and Keino was left off the team selected to go to Tokyo. Noronha says Keino was battling two obstacles in his attempt to reach the Olympic standard in 1964: first, a lack of competition in East Africa to push him, and second, a "psychological barrier" of there never having been a sub-four-minute mile run by an African.

With only a little over two weeks left before the Olympics, Keino took a last stab at making the qualifying standard. This time he had two pacemakers who led him through the half in under two minutes; a sprint on the last lap brought him through the tape in 4:01.5, fast enough to earn him a place on the team. "Kip had crossed a major hurdle," writes Noronha, "but he had no illusions even at this stage," because Ron Clarke's three-mile record of 13:07.6 was nearly 40 seconds faster than Keino's best time.

President Kenyatta sent off Kenya's first-ever Olympic team with a stirring speech, saying, "We want to show that our model of *Harambee* [pulling together] can be applied to sport, that people of all creeds and colors can pull together. We want Kenya to be an example to the rest of the world."

The enthusiastic but still-inexperienced Keino went to Tokyo for his Olympic baptism in heats of both 5,000 and 1,500 meters. Clarke had the fastest time in the 5,000-meter heat and lined up for the final as the clear favorite, while Keino had set a personal record of 13:49.6 in his heat. The day before the 5,000 final, Kip won his 1,500 quarter-final heat in 3:45.8, saying he felt good for the start of the longer race.

The 5,000 was one of the best races of the 1964 Olympics. Clarke took the lead on the third lap and surged, worried about the kick of Frenchman Michel Jazy. But the pack stuck right with Clarke, including Jazy, Keino, Bob Schul, and Bill Dellinger of the United States, Germany's Harald Norpoth, and Dutov of the Soviet Union.

With a little over a lap to go, Dutov took the lead, followed by Jazy, who on paper had the fastest kick in the field. But in a sprint finish, Schul was a surprise winner in 13:48.8, followed by Norpoth and Dellinger. Jazy placed fourth, 0.6 seconds ahead of Keino in fifth. Although he finished just out of a medal, Keino had beaten top runners like Clarke. Keino then missed qualifying for the 1,500-meter final in a photo-finish semifinal, but he took pride in Wilson Kiprugut's 800-meter bronze medal, Kenya's first Olympic medal. Kenyatta's wish had been fulfilled.

Keino's performance at Tokyo earned him the notice of race directors. His first invitation came from Brazil for the São Silvestre seven-miler through the streets of São Paulo at midnight on New Year's Eve. The race is known for its good fields, hills, and thousands of fans lining the course who are extremely tough on foreign runners. Keino took a large lead over Belgian star Gaston Roelants and looked to be cruising in for an easy win. But going around a corner near the end of the race, Kip found two police motorcycles blocking the road. Unable to stop in time, he ran into the motorcycles and crashed to the ground. He got up to finish eleventh, but his knee was hurt, forcing him to cancel the other races on the tour and to take a break from training.

When he began running again early in 1965, Keino continued tinkering with his training. He was continually watching and talking with the other elite runners he met at races, eager to pick up new ways to train. Mostly he improved on the kinds of intervals he ran. He also continued to get encouragement to pursue his dream of an Olympic medal from Mal Whitfield, who plays down his role in Keino's development. "Kipchoge was a natural," Whitfield said.

> He did what he was born to do. He grew up in a good traditional society, with natural living. He didn't dissipate his energy, but stayed focused on who and what he wanted to become. He was a competitor in his whole lifestyle. You must understand the African lifestyle; first of all, they are disciplined. Secondly, they have a family tradition. . . . He came from a concerned family, and was concerned with others within his community.

That tradition kept Keino connected to his homeland and his family as he traveled the globe almost continuously from 1965 through 1968. Whenever Keino returned from one of his triumphant tours abroad, an elderly Nandi woman always met him at the airport in Nairobi, where she presented him with a calabash of milk in a traditional Nandi ritual.

"Tradition gave Kipchoge a complete personality, and is something people don't write about or learn about when talking about the success of African runners. You learn about living through those traditions," says Whitfield, who spent 35 years in Africa. After he became a star in 1965, Keino took his success in stride, Whitfield says.

> He wasn't cocky after he won; he was just a natural, and he was always humble. He also was always very observant. I would say he believed in us and liked us, because we had the experience, and Kipchoge wanted to become a champion. I just happened to be there.

In spite of Whitfield's modesty, Keino could not have found a better person from whom to get advice than Whitfield. Called "one of the greatest competitors of all time and the best doubler among middle-distance runners of his day" by *Track & Field News*, Whitfield won gold medals in the 1948 and 1952 Olympic Games and went undefeated in championship races from 1948-54, despite taking time off to fight as a tail gunner during the Korean War. Whitfield set three world records in his career, along with three indoor world records. After his running was finished, the U.S. government sent Whitfield to Kenya, where he attended many local track meets, holding coaching courses for army and police coaches and student teachers. "The coaches were the ones who delivered the message (about training), and they are the ones who made all the difference."

What made Keino special, even from the start of his international career, says Whitfield, was that "Kip could run anything: 1,500, mile, 3,000, 5,000, and 10,000." At the start of 1965, Keino was still an unknown—but that would change after he went to Europe for a series of races that summer.

Trotting the Globe

Keino trained harder than he ever had in 1965. The training became more difficult, with two interval sessions a day some days, centering on repeats of 220, 440, and 880 yards, with four-minute recoveries in between.

His new training had its first test later in 1965 at the World Games in Helsinki, where the showcase race was the Michel Jazy/Ron Clarke matchup in the 5,000 meters. Kip showed he would be a factor as well by running a 4:05.5/13:53, high altitude, mile/three-mile double at the Kenyan championships. Still, he was not thought to be in the league of Jazy and Clarke, and the full house at Helsinki's Olympic Stadium was shocked when Keino closely followed Clarke and Jazy until the bell lap. He passed Clarke and was just beaten out at the end by Jazy, 13:27.6 to 13:28.2. Keino had not only beaten Ron Clarke again, but had shown for the first time that he could summon up a sprint at the end of an international race.

Then it was on to Turku, Finland, for Keino and teammate Wilson Kiprugut, who had won the 800-meter gold at the World Games and taken the silver in the 400 meters. For Keino, it was another race against Clarke, who had already set three world records in 1965, and who would go on to set an incredible 12 world records in 44 days on his 1965 European tour. The 5,000 meters at Turku was a ballyhooed race that increased interest in the sport worldwide, billed as the graceful Kenyan versus the hard-running, record-setting Aussie.

A 61-second first lap set the tone of the race. This was one of those races where two runners tried to hammer the other into the ground from the start. There were no tactics, no attempt to outsmart the other. It was simply a matter of each man running as hard as he could, hoping not to be the first to drop back. Keino was able to hang with Clarke despite the Aussie's series of surges, and outkicked him on the last lap to win in 13:26.2, just 0.4 seconds off Clarke's world record.

Keino's next race on his 1965 tour showed how difficult it can be for foreigners racing in Europe. It was another publicized match against Clarke in Stockholm, with newspapers speculating that the 5,000-meter record was sure to fall. Keino again let Clarke set the early pace, then took the lead on the last lap. Keino sprinted in to break the tape, looking to have beaten Clarke again.

However, it turns out that race officials had strung two finishing tapes across the track. The first, the one Keino broke, was put up at three miles in case the record for that distance was broken. Clarke had heard the announcement about the two tapes beforehand; Keino had not. When Kip slowed after breaking the tape, Clarke continued sprinting down the track and broke the second tape, finishing in 13:26.4.

A disappointed Keino returned home, where he earned some satisfaction from winning two gold medals in the first-ever All-African Games, held in the Congo. Then it was back to Scandinavia for another European tour. Keino showed his strength by crushing Gaston Roelants over 5,000 meters, 13:29.4 to 13:45.8.

Keino was getting faster as the summer went on, gaining more and more confidence with each race in Europe. His next race was over 3,000 meters in the Olympia Stadium in Halsingborg, Sweden, on the evening of August 25. Keino had only the clock for competition, as his 59.5 first lap left the field racing for second place. Keino did not let up, clocking splits of 62.0, 62.5, 61.0, 62.0, 63.0; a last lap of 60.1 and last 200 meters of 29.4 brought him home in 7:39.5—a new world record, breaking Siegfried Herrmann's old mark by a whopping 6.4 seconds. His 1,500 splits were 3:49.5 and 3:50.0.

A Star Is Born

Keino was thereafter mobbed wherever he went in Europe. It was not just his world record or his wins, but also his dignified bearing; he had the presence of a star. People flocked to be near him, and there could not have been a better or more charming representative of Kenya than Keino. "Kip was totally unguarded," says Marty Liquori. "Kenyans are very trusting people, and Kip came across as a very nice guy, almost a saintly guy."

Kip next showcased his abilities in London at the Morley Mile. It was a race, some papers wrote, that "will never be forgotten." Keino "made his attack at just the right place" after reaching the bell in 2:58.2, 0.4 seconds up on East German Jurgen May. He powered home with a 56-second last lap to win in 3:54.2, just 0.6 seconds off Michel Jazy's world record. Josef Odlozil was second, (3:55.6), followed by Great Britain's Alan Simpson (3:55.7), and May (3:56.0). All four set national records, and Keino became the first nonwhite runner under the magic four-minute barrier.

Keino had brought something startling to running, with one writer, Noronha, saying it was "a revolution in athletics, for Keino runs with primeval joy and strength, with full-blooded zest almost replacing tactics." Liquori says, "Keino had the biggest impact on the mile, because he was the one who really changed the way people were running. He came in at a time when even pacing was thought to be the best way to run."

Tactics in the mile traditionally involved a fast last quarter. But, says Liquori, "Keino did his kick in the second lap. He took the focus on running evenly and shifted it, saying you can run fast in other laps. He was the first to do that and the most successful."

"When Keino first came on the scene, he was the most flamboyant of the early Kenyan runners," says Frank Shorter. "He certainly had the most talent, and he had the best sense of competition." Reporters rushed to interview the colorful Keino, who stood out in his green vest and orange cap, asking him about Kalenjin customs, spreading rumors of how the secret of his success was that he drank cow's blood. It is true that occasionally Keino, like other Nandi, drank cow's milk mixed with cow's blood, but it was only on special occasions. No matter. Over and over again, "Kip had to describe, in great detail, how the blood was drawn, the different kinds of arrows used, how complete silence had to be observed while the steadiest person with a bow and arrow aimed for the pressure point," Noronha writes. "The blood that was collected had to be stirred with milk immediately if they did not want it to coagulate."

People kept trying to get insight into what made this magnificent athlete tick; was it the diet, the blood, or the altitude? Keino would only smile and say, "There is nothing special about me. There will soon be many in Kenya as good as me." Noronha believes that Keino's real secret, if there was one, was "natural ability improved by practice and determination, and heightened by a simple but deeply religious conviction in the power of prayer."

Keino caused some consternation in the press when, after just missing the world record at the Morley Mile, he told reporters he was not really a miler; he only ran the race to increase his speed. Speculation was rife that the two best middle-distance runners in the world—Jazy of France, world-record holder in the mile and two-mile, and Keino, the 3,000-meter record holder—would meet. Both were in top shape, and a new record would undoubtedly result when the pair hooked up. Unfortunately, Keino left Europe without ever racing Jazy. Keino returned home a hero for Kenya. A road in the coastal city of Mombassa was named after him for the prestige he had brought Kenya.

Ethiopia: From Bikila to Gebrselassie

One African country with the depth of runners equal to Kenya is Ethiopia. And just as Kip Keino is the father of Kenyan running, so is Abebe Bikila, the great two-time Olympic marathon gold medalist, remembered as the father of Ethiopian runners.

It was Bikila, born in 1927, who gave the world its first glimpse of a new kind of runner at the 1960 Rome Olympic Marathon. Running barefoot, Bikila stayed with the pack at the start at the Capitol, passing 5 kilometers in 15:35 and 10 kilometers in a fast 31:07. By 25 kilometers, passed in 1:20:47, the race was down to Rhadi Ben Abdesselem of Morocco and Bikila. The two dueled through 40 kilometers, until Bikila pulled away to win by 25 seconds, in 2:15:16.2, just inside the world record. Bikila's winning time was nearly 10 minutes faster than Alain Mimoun's at the 1956 Games.

In 1964 Bikila's dominance was overwhelming, as he beat second-placer Basil Heatly of Great Britain by over four minutes, with Japan's Kokichi Tsuburaya third. Australia's Ron Clarke led through 5 kilometers in 15:06, with Bikila trailing by 13 seconds. He moved up with Clarke, together passing 10 kilometers in 30:14. Bikila pressed the pace, and by 25 kilometers he was in the clear, going on to finish in 2:12:11.2, another gold medal and another world record.

The sleek, powerful Bikila, a member of Emperor Haile Selassie's imperial guard, was famous throughout the world, and his wins were recognized as the start of a new era of African running. Bikila was the first of the modern marathoners, says Frank Shorter. "Abebe planted the idea that the marathon could be raced in a different way. Up until then, people would save themselves, waiting to see who would drop. He helped change the tactics."

Bikila was one of the inspirations for Shorter's own marathon tactics. "You look and see what people had done in the past. Abebe made me realize that the marathon could be raced in a new way, almost as an extension of a track race, though he wasn't a track runner."

It is appropriate that when Shorter left the awards stand after receiving his gold medal in 1972, he shook hands with Bikila, who was sitting nearby in a wheelchair. The Ethiopian had been in a car accident in 1969 that left him paralyzed, and he died in 1973.

Bikila's spirit lives on in the Ethiopian runners who have followed him. Mamo Wolde won the 1968 Olympic Marathon gold medal and the bronze in 1972. Wolde was followed by the ageless Miruts Yifter, who won the 1980 Olympic 5,000 and 10,000 meters, then Kebede Balcha, marathon silver medalist at the 1983 World Championships. Belayneh Densimo set the marathon world record in 1988, and Deratu Tulu won the 1992 women's Olympic 10,000-meter crown and the 1995 World Cross-Country Championships.

Yet, the fastest Ethiopian of all is Haile Gebrselassie, who began running in 1988 at the age of 15. He first attracted notice by winning the 5,000 and 10,000 meters at the 1992 World Junior Championships. The following year he took the 10,000-meter title at the World Championships. He set the 5,000-meter world record (12:56.96) in 1994.

That was all just a prelude to his 1995 season, one of the best ever by a distance runner. It started with Gebrselassie placing only fourth at the World Cross-Country Championships, after the Ethiopian team had spent two nights in airports and had taken an eight-hour bus ride, arriving the morning of the race.

That loss fueled Gebrselassie's motivation, and in May he broke Kenyan Moses Kiptanui's 2-mile record, running 8:07.46. He then set the 10,000-meter record (26:43.53). Kiptanui ended up taking back his 5,000 record later that year.

Gebrselassie defended his 10,000-meter title at the 1995 Göteborg World Championships, winning in 27:12.95, with an astounding 25.1-second last 200 meters. He then went to Zurich to reclaim his 5,000-meter record with a vengeance. Running by himself after 3,000 meters, Gebrselassie averaged 60.1 seconds for each of his last four laps, finishing in 12:44.39.

"It makes you want to quit," said Mark Plaatjes, 1993 World Championships Marathon gold medalist. Gebrselassie's records continue his rivalry with the Kenyans. In the 1992 World Junior 10,000 meters, he was punched by Kenyan Josephat Machuka, who was angry that Gebrselassie had not led. In the 1993 World Championships he was accused by Kenyan Moses Tanui of stepping on his heel and pulling off Tanui's shoe. Tanui confronted Gebrselassie after the race, angrily waving his shoe in his face. Those incidents have been forgotten, Gebrselassie says, and the track world awaits more spectacular races between the Ethiopians and the Kenyans.

On the Road Again

Keino was not done with 1965 yet. After resting for a short time, he packed his colorful green vest and orange cap, a souvenir of the Tokyo Olympics, and went Down Under. He had taken to throwing the cap off during his last-lap sprints in races—now, it was his trademark, and fans would jump to their feet in excitement when they saw Kip toss off the hat.

Keino's cap next came off in New Zealand, where he soloed to a world record in the 5,000 meters, breaking Clarke's mark by running 13:24.6. After opening splits of 63.8 and 62.7, Keino already had a huge lead. Running alone, he went through the mile in 4:16.0, followed by a second mile of 4:17.8. Knowing he was under world-record pace, he pressed even harder, and though he slowed to a 4:24.5 final mile, he dug down to run his last lap in 63.5, passing three miles in 12:58.5 on his way to his second world record. Clarke sent a telegram of congratulations that concluded, "Looking forward to meeting you in Melbourne."

Keino's next race was a 3:56.9 mile, again by himself. He then was twice edged by East German Jurgen May, nicknamed "The Toiler" for his awkward running style, over a mile, running 3:54.9 and 3:54.4. Keino then flew to Australia, where, again running by himself, he clocked a 8:25.6 two-mile, second best ever.

Keino was in good form for his 5,000-meter showdown with Clarke in Melbourne. The matchup was nearly a bust, as Keino almost did not make it to the starting line. He arrived at the stadium early and went to a room beneath the stadium to relax. When he got up to start his warm-up, he found that the door was locked from the outside. After a tense 15-minute wait, Keino was rescued and made it to the starting line just before the gun sounded.

Perhaps shaken by the close call, Kip dropped back at the start, as Clarke took an immediate lead. With 1,200 meters to go, Clarke had built a comfortable lead and looked to be cruising in for the win. But Keino closed the gap over the next two laps and at the bell he accelerated, going on for a 13:40.6 to 13:47.2 victory. His tour Down Under finished, Kip returned to his farm for a well-deserved rest, ending an amazing year that saw the unknown Keino blossom into the freshest, biggest star in running, breaking two world records and just missing the mile record, foreshadowing Kenya's future dominance as a running powerhouse.

Race invitations for Keino poured into the Kenyan Amateur Athletic Association, which then told Kip which races to run. Early in 1966, Keino went to Los Angeles for his first indoor meet. Again, he turned to Mal Whitfield for advice. Whitfield told him of his experiences running indoors and how it differed from outdoor running, because the tight turns required a different kind of stride and different tactics.

It *was* different, Keino found out. In his first race in Los Angeles, Keino passed the half in 1:58.4 and was leading at three quarters. But U.S. star Jim Grelle, the former two-mile world-record holder, passed him near the end, finishing in 4:00.9, less than a second ahead of Keino.

Keino liked the closeness of the indoor race, where the crowd sits right on the track. After his narrow mile loss, he decided to attempt a double by running the two-mile later in the meet, in order to give the capacity crowd its money's worth. This time he stayed behind until near the end; then off came his orange cap as Kip sprinted by Gaston Roelants and went after Jerry Lawson, who was in the lead. On the last lap, he pulled away for a 8:42.6 win. Some observers called it the best indoor mile/two mile double ever—not a bad start for someone running his first race on the boards. To top off the evening, Keino appropriately enough received the Whitfield Award, awarded to a champion who kept in mind the needs of the less fortunate.

Keino was now the attraction for U.S. media, which normally ignore track and field. They took to the likable Kenyan, their eyes open to the new way and feeling of running. They were especially interested in Kip's cap and how he tossed it off to show he was ready to sprint away from his opponents. Reporters tried to find some mystical significance to the hat. When one asked Kip if it brought him luck, Noronha reports that Keino replied,"No. Sometimes I win and sometimes I don't. The cap has nothing to do with winning. The race is in God's hands."

Racing Well in 1966

Keino had another great year in 1966, racing and beating the best all over the world. His physical abilities were only a part of that success, says Shorter. Keino was also a masterful tactician.

> Kip had what the best runners all have—the instinct to psyche out your opponent in whatever way you can, the same ability Peter Snell and Herb Elliott had. It's how you act, what you do, the personality you establish so you have the opposition more worried about what you are doing than about what they are doing.

Keino's ability to run fast from the start, or wait and kick his opponents down, made the other racers fear him, Shorter says.

In a sense, he was creating a situation where they are all looking to see when you are going to go. It was sort of like, "OK, when is he going to run off and beat me?" He was like (Sebastian) Coe and (Noureddine) Morceli in that, only Keino was very visual in the way he did it.

Keino was called the "Kenyan Gazelle" and "Kenya's Flying Cop" by the press. His hectic schedule continued after his 4:03.9 win in the Wanamaker Mile at the end of January, 1966. He flew back to Kenya, then returned to Los Angeles less than two weeks later for the *Los Angeles Times* indoor meet, where he would race Clarke. A tired Keino placed fifth, and flew back to Kenya the next day to begin his preparations for the Commonwealth Games.

After a month break, his first real rest in a year and a half, Keino resumed training. He put great emphasis on honing his last-lap kick, and his first test on how the training was going came in May 1966 when he returned to the United States for his first race against Jim Ryun, the young American miling prodigy.

Keino had at first turned down the invitation to race Ryun, because he had not had time to build up his training and he knew he wasn't in top shape. But U.S. and Kenyan officials insisted he go, to popularize the race, and finally, against his better judgment, Kip relented. Kip was right, as Ryun decisively beat him in their two-mile meeting, sitting behind until the last lap, then blasting away to win in 8:25.2. Keino was amazed at Ryun's end-of-the-race sprint, one he would run into like a brick wall in their future meetings.

Keino's busy life continued. He flew across the Atlantic for races in East and West Germany, where he was beaten by Harald Norpoth and Jurgen "The Toiler" May. May had become one of Keino's good friends, and Kip invited him and a few other top runners to the first-ever international track meet in Kenya, set for July in Nairobi in conjunction with the Kenyan national championships. It was at these races that the world saw the effects altitude would have on the upcoming Mexico City Olympics.

May, who trained with the scientific backing of the East German sport system, came to Nairobi less than 24 hours before his race to lessen the effects of altitude. But that seemingly didn't help—May finished third, collapsing after he crossed the line, Noronha reports. New Zealander Bill Baillie was lapped for the first time in his career and finished seventh, afterwards saying he felt like he "wanted to lie down and die." Keino felt fine, and his 4:00.9/13:35.2 mile/three-mile double showed he was rounding into good form for the 1966 Commonwealth Games in Kingston, Jamaica, where once again his race against Clarke was being eagerly anticipated. One writer compared it to the Roger Bannister-John Landy Mile of the Century at the 1954 Vancouver Empire Games.

Before the Keino/Clarke three-mile showcase at Kingston, Clarke first had the little matter of the six-mile to take care of. Most considered the race a formality for Clarke to pick up the gold. Despite his world records, Clarke had never won a championship gold, and this time he was heavily favored. But Keino's teammate, little-known Naftali Temu, beat Clarke in the six-mile.

In the three-mile, Clarke's teammate Kerry O'Brien went out very fast in an attempt to entice Keino and the other three Kenyans in the race into running the early laps too fast. But the by-now savvy Keino stayed behind, and when Clarke took the lead with 880 yards to go, Keino was right there shadowing him, and easily sprinted away for a gold medal and new Commonwealth record of 12:57.4. Three days later Keino won his heat of the mile in another Commonwealth Games record of 3:57.4; after two days rest, he won another gold with a 3:55.3 victory.

On the way back to Kenya, Keino stopped in London long enough to crush a good field at the Emsley Carr Mile in 3:53.4, winning by over half a straightaway. It was the second fastest mile ever run, from a runner who did not even consider himself a miler! Keino still maintained he ran the mile only to pick up speed for the longer distances, which he considered his true calling. The great time in the Emsley Carr mile with no competition prompted much speculation that Jim Ryun's mile record was as good as gone as soon as the two best middle-distance runners in the world hooked up. That matchup was soon to come and would present Keino with the most difficult challenge of his career.

Keino was now one of the most famous athletes in the world. He fed on the fans' enthusiasm, giving them exciting races against top runners from all countries. Keino raced the best on their tracks, and beat them. "People really feared him when he was running," says Shorter. "He was a mystery. There was an aura of invincibility about him."

Grateful Kenyan police officials gave him a vacation when he returned from London, which he spent on his farm, catching up with his wife and two daughters. When he returned to his job at the police academy in Kiganjo, there was an invitation to race Jim Ryun in the United States vs. Commonwealth track meet in July 1966 in the Coliseum in Los Angeles. Kip, having just resumed training, declined, but was eventually convinced to go after he ran a 3:55.2 mile at a 6,000-foot altitude in Nyeri.

Ryun and Keino's first meeting over 1,500 meters lived up to its prerace billing. After a pedestrian opening lap of 60.9, Keino moved to the front and put in an amazing 56.0 for the second lap. The third lap was passed in 2:39.2 with Kip still in the lead and feeling strong. It appeared that Keino might have Ryun's number this time. Then, like a Kansas whirlwind, Ryun unleashed a fierce kick, taking only 53.9 seconds to cover the final 400 meters to finish in 3:33.1, breaking Herb Elliott's world record by 2.6 seconds. Kip was second in a good 3:37.2, but had no answer for Ryun's kick.

However, he did have Clarke's number, beating the Australian the following day in a 13:36.8 5,000-meter win. Keino was a bit upset at having raced Ryun when he knew he was not ready, and some observers wondered if Keino was not being forced to overrace because of overzealous Kenyan officials. Noronha writes that Peter Snell said earlier, "I think a big enemy for world-ranking African athletes like Keino is their generous nature and the readiness to run anywhere any time."

The irrepressible Keino shook off his defeat and got ready for a rematch with Ryun in August at the Emsley Carr mile, where Keino had clocked his solo 3:53.4 the year before. It was a cold and windy day, and Keino changed his strategy, letting Ryun take the lead on the third lap. On the backstretch of the last lap, Keino made his move to pass Ryun, but the tall American responded with his typical strong kick, running the last 440 yards in 53.8.

It was Ryun's second convincing win over Keino in little over a month; Keino had lost to Ryun running from the front and had now lost running from behind. There did not seem to be any way to beat the American.

Yet Keino, who was continually plotting new ways to improve his training and racing, began thinking of ways he could beat his rival with the incredible finishing kick.

At a meet in Kenya, Keino ran a great quadruple, winning the mile (3:58.8); 880 (1:49.0); three-mile (14:06.0); and running a leg of the victorious mile relay team. Then he was back in London for the Morley mile, running "as he liked, in his natural unfettered style, like a man running for the sheer pleasure of it," writes Noronha. A fast first lap of 56.0 dropped the field, and Kip finished in 3:53.8, nearly seven seconds ahead of England's Alan Simpson in second.

Simpson then came to Kenya for some races at Keino's invitation. Racing against international runners had helped Keino develop, and he wanted to encourage young Kenyan runners by showing them an international track meet and giving them a chance to run against foreign athletes. On a bumpy track at Kisumu, 3,720 feet above sea level, Simpson stayed with Keino for two laps, after which Kip easily dropped him on his way to a 3:53.1 win, a personal best. He completed the double by clocking 13:31.6 in the 5,000 meters.

Training for Mexico City

Keino's dream remained an Olympic gold medal, and he began planning for the Mexico Olympic Games early in 1967. He was not sure what races he was going to run, but he knew he would have to beat Ryun to get a gold medal.

In order to avoid overdoing it as he had the past two years, Keino turned down several overseas invitations. He decided to build slowly up to a peak that would coincide with the October 1968 Olympics. He began running longer intervals and more hill repeats.

Some reports about Keino misunderstood his training as being "light by modern standards," or wrote that he did it on "talent." Keino's training, however, was very hard, providing the example for the great Kenyan runners who have followed him. It may have seemed light because Keino was a very smart runner, resting on the weekend and doing his hard workouts during the week. Nearly every day he did "exercises" as part of his warm-up. A typical week for Keino when building up for the 1968 Olympics included:

Sunday:	No running.
Monday:	A.M., easy 45-minute jog; noon, hour run; P.M., 10 × 440 yards in 63 seconds, with a 2-minute recovery.
Tuesday:	A.M., easy 45-minute jog; noon, hour run; P.M., 6 × 880 yards in 2:10, with a 3-5 minute recovery.
Wednesday:	A.M., 45-minute jog; noon, hour run; P.M., short intervals such as 220-yard repeats.
Thursday:	A.M., 45-minute jog; noon, hour run; P.M., 100-yard sprints on grass.
Friday:	A.M., 45-minute jog; noon, hour run; P.M., 4 × 80-yard sprints with a 330-yard float after the sprint.
Saturday:	Eight miles easy.

Keino had a combination of stamina and speed unmatched for his day. Martin Keino, Kip's son, says his father "used to train three times a day, five days a week. He never ran on Sunday, and he worked very hard, doing workouts like 25 × 200, with the last one in 22 seconds."

This is the kind of training on which the foundation for Olympic success was laid. Keino's only race from the spring of 1968 to July was in the Ivory Coast. His first major competition of the year came at Oslo, when he hooked up with rival Clarke over 5,000 meters. The race was going along smoothly when, all at once, Keino got stomach cramps and collapsed. He was also sick for his next race, and doctors could find no explanation for his illness. After another 5,000-meter loss to Clarke and a defeat over 1,500 meters, Keino flew to Leningrad for his first visit to the Soviet Union.

The trip did not start off well, as his bag containing all his gear was stolen from the side of the track while he warmed up; Keino had to run in a hastily borrowed pair of shoes. He still won the 5,000 meters and the next day, despite getting bad blisters from the undersized shoes, ran 28:06.4 in the 10,000 meters, the third fastest ever. Keino was now a threat for yet another race at the Olympics.

After heading home, Keino had a month of training before he would leave with the other members of the Kenyan team for the Olympics. He put all his energy into training so that he could beat the seemingly unbeatable Ryun.

Keino had learned from his defeats by the American not to race the best runner in the world without being in top shape. Keino honed his training to peak level at the Olympics. "It was important for Kipchoge to be at top strength," said Whitfield. At a training camp at 8,000-foot Thompson's Fall, Keino ran with the other Kenyan Olympians up "Agony Hill," a very steep hill still used by Kenyan runners. The training was good, with workouts three times a day, and when he left for Mexico City, Kip was certain he was in the best shape of his life.

However, it looked as if the years of hard work, planning, and training might be for naught; when Keino arrived in Mexico City, he again experienced the mysterious stomach pains that had plagued him during his European races in July. The doctor of the West German team examined Kip, telling him he needed to go to a hospital for X-rays.

But instead of going into the hospital, Keino planned for a Zatopek-like Olympics, trying to triple in the 1,500-, 5,000-, and 10,000-meter races. When he lined up for the 10,000 meters on October 13, Keino knew he was not in top physical shape. Two days before the 10,000, Kip had been wracked by pain, which he later discovered resulted from a gallbladder infection.

The pain went away, and somehow, Keino summoned up the courage to start. His strategy was to stay close until the last lap, when he thought his finishing kick could carry him to the gold. The race went smoothly until, suddenly, with three laps to go, Keino became dizzy, slowed to a jog, and collapsed. When officials tried to put him on a stretcher, he bolted up and sprinted around the track, even though he was officially out of the race. He jogged in, cheering on teammate Naftali Temu, who won Kenya's first Olympic gold medal ever in a sprint finish over Mamo Wolde of Ethiopia. Ron Clarke, bitter at having to run the Olympics at high altitude, finished far back, with his last lap taking an agonizing 93 seconds.

Despite his collapse and illness, Keino refused to withdraw from the Olympics, and two days later he won his 5,000-meter heat. After two more days of rest, he was lined up for the final of the 5,000 meters, where he faced a strong field including Clarke and Mohamed Gammoudi of Tunisia. Keino hung behind and in the final straightaway looked to be in position to run in for the win, but it was Gammoudi who pulled away for a 14:05.0 to 14:05.2 win over Keino, with Temu taking the bronze.

With a fit and rested Ryun waiting in the 1,500 meters, it looked as if Keino would have to be satisfied with his silver medal. Keino's yeoman Olympics continued as he and Ryun both won their heats of the 1,500 to qualify for the finals. Afterwards, Keino suffered more stomach cramps.

Before the 1,500 final, Kenyan coach Charles Mukora and the head of the Kenyan team had a meeting with Keino, telling him that they "didn't expect him to compete in view of the circumstances and the danger to his health," Noronha writes.

Keino's reply was that he "would rather die on the track fighting for his country than on a hospital bed." End of discussion. He was more interested in finalizing his race strategy than talking about withdrawing. He and the other Kenyans knew he had little chance of outkicking Ryun; that left only one option, as the world was to see the next day.

Mexico City's Stadio Olimpico was at a feverish pitch when the 1,500-meter finalists walked to the starting line. Keino was competing in his sixth race in eight days, with a painful gallbladder infection, while Ryun was fresh and in the best shape of his life. After wishing each other "good luck," Ryun, Keino, and the other starters were brought to the line.

Could Ryun, who had not lost a mile or 1,500 since 1965, stem the East African tide that had dominated the Mexico City Olympics? Would Keino, who had never beaten Ryun, have any strength left to battle his rival with the great kick?

Keino's strategy was evident from the moment the gun went off—get far enough ahead so that Ryun would not be in range to unleash his kick. Teammate Ben Jipcho towed Kip through splits of 56.0 and 1:53.3, fast enough in the rarefied air of Mexico City to plunge the fittest athlete into oxygen debt. Keino took over from Jipcho and on the third lap increased his lead over Ryun, who had moved near the front of the trailing pack. Kip was so far ahead that it appeared as if he were running by himself. Ryun finally began to sprint, passing East German Bodo Tummler. It was a valiant attempt by the American, but Keino's lead was too much; Ryun could get no closer than three seconds as Keino won the gold with an Olympic record 3:34.9. It was Keino's fastest time ever, and he had another reason to celebrate when he found out his third daughter was born the same day as his 1,500 victory. She was named, appropriately enough, Olympia. "It was the best race he ever ran," says Whitfield.

Marty Liquori, then just 18, had reached the finals of the epic 1968 Olympic 1,500 meters.

> I think everybody knew what Keino was going to do, but we didn't know Jipcho would be the one [to take it out very fast]. Ryun wasn't going to take the bait. In fairness to Jim [Ryun], it was a great race for somebody from sea level to run that fast.

Keino's win over Ryun cemented his reputation as one of the top runners ever. He was able to summon up the guts to beat Ryun, when no one would have disparaged a second-place finish, and it was more than a victory for Keino, or for Kenya—it was a gold medal for all of Africa.

"Mexico City really was the African Olympics," said Shorter of the Africans grabbing 8 of the 12 medals in the steeplechase and the 1,500, 5,000, and 10,000 meters. Amos Biwott in the steeplechase, Naftali Temu in the 10,000 meters, and Keino in the 1,500 gave Kenya three glorious gold medals. Ever since, great runners from the Rift Valley have flooded through that door opened by Keino.

There were stupendous performances in Mexico City—Bob Beamon's, 29-foot, 2-1/2 inch long jump leap, Lee Evans's 400-meter record, which stood for 22 years, and Keino's stirring victory over Jim Ryun in the 1,500 meters are the three that have stood the test of time as some of the greatest ever. Without the gallbladder infection, Whitfield says Keino would have won all three golds at Mexico City. "Look what he did running at less than half strength."

Continuing on Top

Keino took a break in the winter of 1968 and had a good year in 1969, not losing a race, as fans continued coming to see the man who had displayed such courage in Mexico City. After the Olympics, writes Sebastian Coe in *The Olympians*, Keino "remained for another four years the most versatile and talented middle- and long-distance runner in the world."

Keino's next major race was at the 1970 Commonwealth Games in Edinburgh, Scotland, where Kip faced another, different kind of test of his courage in a troubling incident that once again showed Keino's commitment to running for his country. Keino received a death threat and was urged not to run. Philip Ndoo was Keino's roommate at a dormitory at Edinburgh University where the Commonwealth athletes were housed. Here is how Ndoo tells the story in *The African Revolution*:

> I could tell something was wrong because his seemingly perpetual smile was missing. With sunken eyes and a pale face, he said in Swahili, "*Wanataka kuhua mimi*," [They want to kill me]. I interpreted this to mean that he was upset perhaps because the officials wanted him to run in another event—like the 10,000 meters in addition to the 1,500 and 5,000 which he had entered already. Then he added that he had received an unsigned letter telling him that he would be shot if he competed in the 5,000 meters.

The logical thing would have been for Keino to withdraw. But he was adamant about winning gold for Kenya, despite the great risk to himself. He ran the 1,500 and the 5,000 meters, and won gold medals in both.

Keino's travels continued in 1971 with races in Europe and Israel. He clocked 1:47.0 for 800 meters, was edged by Finland's Pekka Vasala over 1,500 meters, and ran 3:54.4 to win the mile in the United States vs. Africa meet in North Carolina. He capped his year with a 3:36.8 win in the African Championships, then took a break to get ready for his third Olympic Games.

In January 1972, Kip competed in some indoor races in the United States, running a 3:59.4 mile and losing a tactical race to Ryun, 4:07.3 to 4:06.8. Keino planned a 1,500/5,000-meter double at the Munich Olympics, but the two finals were scheduled within 30 minutes of each other. With 55 minutes between them, Paavo Nurmi had won both races in the 1924 Paris Olympics, but 30 minutes was not enough time. The world thus lost the chance for a Kip Keino-Lasse Viren matchup in the 5,000.

Wanting to run two events in Munich, Keino chose the steeplechase over the 10,000 meters, making up his mind after running an 8:25.0 steeple in May in Japan. It was a smart decision, as Keino won the gold medal in the steeplechase. He did not show great hurdling form when going over the barriers, but was able to steadily run away from Ben Jipcho and the rest of the field. He looked over his shoulder once after the last barrier, and, seeing that his lead was safe, strode across the line to win with a time of 8:23.6, less than two seconds off the world record held by Kerry O'Brien of Australia.

Keino was the favorite to repeat in the 1,500 meters. Seven quarterfinal heats were scheduled, and mile world-record holder Jim Ryun (3:51.1), eager for his rematch with Keino, drew the same heat as the Kenyan. In a strange occurrence, U.S. track authorities submitted Ryun's best 1,500-meter time to Olympic officials as 3:52.8. That's a great mile time, but slow for a 1,500; somehow, officials forgot to put it down as a mile time. So Ryun and Keino had an earlier-than-planned meeting. They both ran in the back of the pack for the first lap of their heat. On the second lap, Keino went wide and easily slid to the front of the large pack, while Ryun inexplicably remained in the back, staying on the rail and running inside another competitor.

Half a lap later, the American was boxed in, and when Billy Fordjur of Ghana collided with Ryun, the American crashed to the track and lay there for several seconds. Ryun got up slowly and shook his head as if trying to awaken from a bad dream. He started jogging down the track, then began running hard to the applause of the crowd, but it was a futile effort. A sub-55-second last 400 meters could not get him close to the field, which had drawn too far ahead, and the Olympic career of perhaps the most talented miler ever ended on this sour note. Ironically, with the fall, Ryun's time in the heat was within a second of the 3:52.8 that had been submitted.

Keino did not know his rival was out until he crossed the line, winning his heat. He stood and greeted Ryun at the finish, saying, "I'm sorry, Jim." But Keino could not spend much time bemoaning Ryun's fate. He had others to worry about, including young talents Rod Dixon of New Zealand, Brendan Foster of Great Britain, and Finland's Pekka Vasala, who was faster than Keino over 800 meters with a 1:44.5 to his credit three weeks before Munich. Keino himself had run a fine 1:46.4 800 meters not long before the Olympics.

At the gun, Foster went straight into the lead, saying he "wanted to be able to see clearly when Keino made his break, as I was sure he would, so that I could try to follow." That turned out to be the plan of all the runners in the field, as everyone ran with an eye on the Kenyan star. Foster led through a 61.4-second first lap, waiting for Keino to come by. Just before the second lap, Keino glided to the front and the pack moved right with him. Dixon was right on Keino's back, with Vasala a step behind.

Without a Ryun to fear, Keino perhaps waited too long to pick up the pace. Keino's next 400 was a very fast 55.1 seconds, but it was not enough to drop Vasala, the ramrod Finn. Keino continued accelerating at the bell and pushed the pace down the backstraight. He still had the lead around the final curve, but into the homestretch Vasala moved up on his shoulder. Keino looked over at Vasala once, then began his final sprint.

Vasala summoned up his kick as well, and the Finn moved next to Keino. For several meters they ran smoothly side by side, their arms and legs in perfect synchronization. The crowd expected Keino to pull out another gold medal, but it was the Finn who drew away in the last 50 meters to win by a stride in 3:36. It was a hard-earned victory for Vasala, as he was forced to cover the last two laps in 1:48.8 to beat Keino. It was Kip's second Olympic silver medal to go along with his two golds.

A National Treasure

Keino ran only a few races in 1973. Along with Ryun, he entered the professional ranks with the short-lived International Track Association. He never broke four minutes for the mile again, and retired in 1974, receiving the "Order of the Burning Spear," the highest civilian honor awarded in Kenya. He was called "a great son of Africa" by President Kenyatta.

Keino worked with the Kenyan Track Federation for many years, and was a national coach until 1989. Some of his children attended college in the United States. He did not push them into athletics. Youngest sons Bob and Martin, however, took a liking to running and developed into top collegiate runners. Martin won PAC-10 titles in the three events in 1993 and capped his college career by winning the 1994 NCAA Cross-Country Championships. He has the same slim build as his father, the same long and graceful stride. "I heard many stories about my father when I was growing up. He could do anything from 800 to 10,000 meters. He doubled and tripled in the Olympics and was still able to win; that is what separates him from the others."

Keino proved his mettle by being at his best in championship races, and Martin says his father did it through his training. The stories about Keino's boundless natural talent have some truth, for Keino was indeed very talented, blessed with a very fluid running form. Nevertheless, his legacy is that hard work and determination can make a runner a champion, says Martin.

© Photo Run/Victah Sailer

Kip Keino battles Marty Liquori at the 1994 Miami Mile Legends race.

"When my father started out, he wasn't so good. He realized he could be good after he got some international experience and was fifth in the (1964) Olympics. That's when he increased his training and that's when he got good."

"People sometimes say runners like my father and other Kenyan runners win because they are talented," that there must be some secret to Keino's and the Kenyans's success, such as genetics or a different body type. Not so, says Martin. "There's no secret. All there is is hard work, just training very hard. That's how my father did it, and that's how the others are doing it."

Beyond his wins, Keino carried with him into every race a zest for running that made him a crowd favorite wherever he went around the world. And he went everywhere, bringing Kenya into the world consciousness. He encouraged young runners and opened the floodgates for the top Kenyan runners who would dominate the sport in the 1980s and '90s.

Running His Orphanage

When he finally laid down his spikes, Keino continued giving to his country, founding and directing an orphanage that has helped thousands of children. "Even after he retired, Kipchoge did a lot of work with the orphanage, and that's a rarity," says Whitfield.

The scores of children Keino and wife Phyllis take care of at their orphanage come from all around Kenya, and they have never turned a child away from their doors. "They're all my children. I don't know any different," Keino told *Sports Illustrated* after he and Phyllis were named the magazine's Sportsman and Sportswoman of the Year in 1987. The first orphans the Keinos took in were three children Kip found wandering around, eating dirt while on police patrol in the mid-1960s.

Recalling the beatings his uncle used to give him when he was a child, Keino said, "I suppose my upbringing contributed a bit to my outlook. Don't make others suffer. Try to assist them if you can." In 1994, a new building was finished that allowed the Keinos to care for even more children.

"My parents have always helped out," explains Martin. His father also owns a store in Eldoret called the Kip Keino Sports Shop. Keino was nominated to run for office, but was not interested in going into politics—he is a humanitarian, not a politician.

Kenyans from all walks of life still look up to Keino, often stopping in at Eldoret to ask for advice. Keino still travels to masters miles around the world, where he remains a fan favorite. Among those fans is Arthur Lydiard, who said, "One of the athletes I admired most was Kip Keino, who was a real gentleman, highly intelligent, and a brilliant runner, so versatile. He was one of the founders of the great Kenyan distance-running history."

In his 11-year international career Keino established himself as a pioneer, roving ambassador, and sports hero for Africa. And now when he stops atop the hill where his father once pointed out where the Kenyan leader Koitelal died fighting for independence, Keino can smile, knowing that he, too, was a Nandi warrior who did his duty for his country.

3

It's Never Too Late To Start

Born November 22, 1944, England

Masters world records: 10K, 15K, and 10 miles

Masters world records: marathon and half-marathon

The nurse shakes her head as she opens the door of Priscilla Welch's hospital room on the second floor of Boulder Community Hospital. It's so chock full of flowers that people can barely get through the door. There are flowers on the walls, flowers on the tables, and flowers on the floor. Even the receptionist has a flower in her hair.

"We've never had a patient with so many friends," the nurse says of the constant stream of the elite and not-so-elite of running who visit Welch, the top masters runner in the world. At 48, she had won races—both open and masters—all around the world, finished sixth in the inaugural women's Olympic Marathon, been masters runner of the year several times, and set a basketful of records. Now, in the late fall of 1992, she was facing the biggest competition of her life, this one against breast cancer. Welch was in the hospital recovering from a mastectomy and the visitors poured in, coming to lend support to a woman whose heart and spunk had showed thousands of nonathletic people, women and men, that they, too, could "just do it" at any age and at any stage of their life.

In becoming the best female masters runner ever, Welch also became a spokeswoman for "older" women who were taking up exercise for the first time. They could point to the effervescent, attractive Welch, an ex-smoker who didn't start running until she was 35. Once she started, however, there was no holding her back—within four years after starting jogging a mile a day, she was an Olympic marathoner and British record holder. And three years after that, at age 42, she ran a 2:26:51 marathon in London and also won the *open* division of the New York City Marathon. In her races, seminars, and print and television ads, Welch was the role model for women who thought sport had passed them by or, in many cases, who had never had the chance to do anything athletic at all.

Welch's journey from a 35-year-old navy ensign who smoked a pack a day to an Olympic marathoner is one of the most inspiring in sport. While some elite runners often seem to be on another plane, having been stars and turning in fast times since they were young, Welch was different; she didn't run in grade school, high school, or college. Perhaps that's why she's so approachable and friendly—she was a sedentary person who overcame years of bad habits to become one of the best runners in the world.

Then, still at the peak of her career and seemingly in perfect health, Welch received the shocking news that she had cancer. It knocked her down, but not out. She picked herself up and dusted herself off, armed with a new attitude and new message to pass along to runners around the world. "It changed me enormously. I had my head so firmly planted in the sand. Now I see how flimsy life is," Welch said. "I hope it has made me a little more compassionate to others."

Welch battled and overcame the cancer with the same great determination, work ethic, and sense of humor she used in climbing to the top of the running world. And in doing so, she become a heroine whose appeal transcended running. The gospel she had been spreading in races around the world—that "anybody can become a runner if she really wants to"—changed after her bout with cancer to, "Life is fragile. Take care of yourself so it will last as long as possible." As she passed her 50th birthday, having survived the cancer, Priscilla began training and racing again, not worrying whether she could make it to the top once more. If Welch does make it back, it wouldn't surprise her many friends and legions of fans—after what she has accomplished, nothing Priscilla Welch does is surprising.

Giving Running a Go

When Priscilla Jane Mayes was 35, becoming an Olympic marathoner was as farfetched an idea as going for a stroll on the moon. She was in the British navy, assigned to NATO forces in Oslo, Norway. She had become bored with the military, but "couldn't see a way out of it." At least not until she met David Welch, a rough-and-tumble sergeant in the British army who was also stationed in Oslo.

"He convinced me that it was time to go out into the big, bad world and see what I could make of myself," Welch says. Priscilla's life before Dave was similar to that of many single women in the military: smoking cigarettes, eating too much, and hanging out nearly every night in Oslo bars. The only exercise she got was walking between offices at NATO headquarters, or walking to the store to buy another pack of cigarettes. Welch had "never done anything athletic and didn't even know anyone who had." She was, to be honest about it, a couch potato.

How did Welch become a champion runner?

"I simply decided to give running a go."

Priscilla didn't have the opportunity to give running a go when she was a child growing up in the English countryside near the town of Bedfordshire. Like millions of women through the centuries, her role was narrowly defined and her options limited; becoming an athlete simply wasn't something women did.

"Priscilla had a typical English childhood," says her brother. "She was no different than any of the other children in the area, though she was always full of energy as a child. When our mom would ask where Cilla was, she'd always be off on a bicycle somewhere."

Although it was only four decades ago, Priscilla grew up in a time light-years away in terms of opportunities for women. She attended school until she was 15, working part-time as a typist to save up money. Her parents did not have money to support her, so at 16 Priscilla left home, buying a one-way train ticket to an aunt's house hoping that she would take her in. Priscilla did not get along with her cousin, though, and the aunt said it was not such a good idea for Priscilla to stay.

Welch next went to the town of Exeter in southwest England and knocked on the door of another aunt, one who didn't have any children. This time she was taken in. "I didn't have two ha'pennies to rub together, but I gave her something for room and board," says Priscilla. She enrolled in secretarial college and, after graduating, got a job with a stockbroker's firm. Office work quickly became too sedate for the outgoing Welch, who received some advice from her aunt and uncle. "They had both been in the military and thought it would be a good idea for me to join as well."

At 17, Welch enlisted in the British Royal Naval Service. She began smoking, because it was the "thing to do" in the military. "Everyone else did it. I hadn't then found my own identity. I never drank to excess, but I used to party a lot." She weighed 140 pounds, not overweight, but not fit, either. Priscilla's life might have continued down the traditional military career path to eventual retirement if she hadn't met Master Sergeant David Welch of the British army.

The pair have been inseparable since the day they met. Dave, from southeast of London, is the kind of guy Arnold Schwarzenegger would come to for advice, sort of a John Wayne of running. He had many adventures while serving in the British army and was honored for his work helping victims of a terrorist bus bombing. Dave played rugby and ran track when he was young and kept a lifelong enthusiasm for athletics, an enthusiasm he passed along to Priscilla.

Dave and Priscilla hit it off from the start. "She was always laughing and joking, and I liked that," Dave says. They lived together for a year before getting married. Soon after, Priscilla quit the military and struck out on her own. "I couldn't see living a life that was all work and no play. I thought there's got to be more to life than this. The first six years I enjoyed the work. It was good company, lots of travel (to Indonesia, Malta, and around Europe) and great pay."

Because she didn't have a Norwegian work visa, the only job Priscilla could find out of the military was cleaning houses. "I was miserable and ready to try anything new." That "anything new" was running. Dave had joined the local track club in Oslo and Priscilla tagged along to some of his meets, immediately being attracted to the sport. She didn't start running right away, however. For a year, she sat in the stands watching others compete.

The Welches had a friend, a major in the U.S. Marines, whose wife was Peggy O'Rourke, a former long-jump champion. Priscilla was impressed by Peggy's interest in staying fit and by how good she looked, and in 1978, Peggy and Priscilla started running together. First it was one mile, then two, then three miles. "It was fun, so I kept doing it," Welch explains.

On Norwegian Independence Day, Priscilla ran in her first race, a 10K featuring some good runners along with several international cross-country skiers. "I thought Peggy would do pretty well, and that Cilla would come somewhere in the back," recalls Dave. After the race, Dave asked Priscilla how she did.

"I came in second," Priscilla said.

"No," said Dave. "Where did you *really* come in?"

"Second, Dave," Priscilla proudly replied. "I came second."

Dave still didn't believe his wife, so the next day he looked up the results in the newspaper, which in a misprint listed Priscilla 246th. When she saw the mistake, Priscilla angrily phoned up the paper asking that they print the correct results. Despite the snafu, Priscilla was encouraged by seeing her name in print, and she increased her running. She hadn't been particularly good at school and didn't have a lot of self-confidence when she was young. So once she found something she was good at, Priscilla grabbed hold of her new sport with all her enormous energy and never let go. "Running was exciting, and the more I ran the better I got. It was a fun time, and all so new."

Priscilla's First Marathon

In August 1978, Dave, a 2:46 marathoner, went to run in the Stockholm Marathon. When he and Priscilla arrived in Stockholm, all the camping parks were full, so Dave pulled the car over at the first piece of grass he found that was big enough to pitch a tent and set up camp. It was on a traffic median in the middle of Stockholm, and they slept with cars whizzing by on both sides. The day before the race, Priscilla decided to jump into the marathon, though she was averaging just four miles a day. Despite the low mileage and the accommodations, Priscilla went on to finish ninth in 3:26.

"Cilla told me after the race that she reckoned she could take an hour off that time," Dave says. "She didn't realize that if she did, it would be a world record. I thought it was a flippant comment."

There have been other women who've run 3:30 marathons without much training, but that's where it usually ends. What made Priscilla different was her drive to pursue her running as far as it would take her, no matter how much work was involved. Priscilla thrived on hard work. "Cilla really took to the running," says Dave. "We thought that if she could do 3:26 with no training, then she'd be able to run three hours with some training."

Priscilla ran shorter races around Oslo, continually improving until she was "ruling the roost in her age group," said Dave. That summer, she ran a 3,000 meters on the track in Oslo with the younger women, since there was no one in her age group to compete against. "I was watching her run," says Dave, "and a man standing behind me said 'You know, David, Priscilla could be a good marathoner.'" The man was Johan Kaggestad, coach of Grete Waitz and Ingrid Kristiansen. "He takes credit for Priscilla's becoming a marathoner," Dave laughs.

Shetland Sojourn

A key development in Welch's life came in July 1981, when she and Dave moved to the Shetland Islands, where he was to be stationed for the next two years. "For my sins in Norway I got posted in the Shetland Islands as an administrative officer," Dave jokes.

The islands are about 200 miles west of Norway and 200 miles from the coast of Scotland. The Shetlands, Dave jokes again, are "a piece of volcanic rock that protrudes from the ocean, with a peat bog on top, 180,000 sheep and 18,000 alcoholics. It's not the ideal running environment."

But it was that very isolation of the Shetlands that spurred Priscilla's running. Because there wasn't a whole lot to do there, Dave started a running club. Here Priscilla started her serious training, building a base that would propel her to the top of women's marathoning. It was not easy training, because of the poor weather conditions.

"There was several inches of ice on the roads all winter," says Dave, so he and the runners he was coaching ran in rubber boots with nails pounded through them. Priscilla got stronger and stronger through Dave's insistence on building a base. That turned out to be good strategy, since they couldn't run fast in the bad conditions. She was putting in roughly 50 miles a week.

"One afternoon we ran down to the store," recalls Dave.

It was exactly three miles, and it took us 39 minutes, because of the ice and the wind. Training there was a tremendous experience for getting strong. You had to literally poke your head out of the window, to see whether you could do the workout or not. . . . The average winter temperature was 33 degrees (Fahrenheit), with 25 to 150 mile-per-hour winds. Ice was everywhere on the roads. There are no road lights at all in the Shetlands, just one-lane roads, twisting, with a bad surface. When you walk out of the front door of your house, it's complete blackness. There is no moonlight, and you can't see anything. It's like closing your eyes.

Often Priscilla and Dave ran wearing miner's headlamps to light their way through the dark, rainy nights.

The Welches got through those days with the good sense of humor they bring to everything they do. There were only two races on the island, one a 22-mile charity event from Lerwick to Sumbrugh. The unique aspect of the charity fund-raiser is that entrants can get through the race any way they want: running, walking, riding a horse, sitting atop a car. The Welches were living in a little village, in which also lived an elderly woman in her 70s who suffered from agoraphobia, a fear of open spaces. "We decided to put her in a wheelchair and push her from the capital for the race," Dave says. They borrowed a wheelchair, and Priscilla dressed up as a nurse.

The three careened down main street to the finish, where everyone in town had turned out. "It was the little old lady they had come to see." At the finish, the locals took the woman out of the wheelchair and carried her around town in celebration.

"Dave and Priscilla always maintain a sense of humor as a counter-balance" to their training, says friend Paul Christman. It was that fun-loving attitude combined with nonstop, extremely hard work for nearly a decade that made Priscilla into a world-class marathoner.

Welch attributes her success to enjoying her training when she started running seriously in the Shetlands.

Most of all, I began to like what I was doing. I was unemployed, and at the time I was very miserable. I started to like it once I got over the embarrassment. The further I got into training for health and fitness, which it was in the beginning, the better it got. And the fitter I got, the more I wanted to pursue it. It was just like holding a carrot in front of a horse. We were both miserable in the Shetlands. We thought the two years would go quickly, but it didn't. It was like going back in time. We were both left to ourselves, so we ran. It kept us sane. It kept us strong.

The Welches trained with the Dunrossness Athletic Club—a group, founded by Dave, of dedicated runners who helped each other train through the long winters. Dave had applied for and received a grant for the running club that allowed club members to travel to the continent for races, mostly in Scotland. In 1981, Priscilla and some men from the running club went to the first-ever London Marathon. Beforehand, Dave told Priscilla she was ready to run 3 hours, and she did, clocking 2:59:29 to finish 23rd.

Priscilla and seven male runners next went to the 1982 Glasgow Marathon. There, she continued her steady improvement and won her first marathon, clocking 2:46:41. "That was all off running distance," says Dave. "All the distance work Cilla was doing was building up her aerobic base."

It wasn't until 1982 that Priscilla began incorporating speedwork into her training. Dave brought her along slowly during the next year, gradually adding more intervals to her already solid base "until all of a sudden, boom, my times seemed to improve quickly."

Knowing What Makes Her Tick

Dave Welch has been a good athlete his whole life. As a freshman in high school, he lettered in rugby, lacrosse, cricket, and track and field. After joining the British army, he played soccer, rugby, and ran track while stationed in Germany. He ran 52 seconds for 400 meters, despite "never training properly. Our basework was six months of rugby and beer drinking." Dave was always the coach of whatever sport he was playing. His commanders would inform him that the Army track championships were in six weeks and ask him to get the team ready.

During those days, Dave Welch "made every mistake in the book." He'd get his men into great shape and win early competitions, but they would be tired and overtrained by the time the championships came along. "I didn't know anything about peaking," he said. Just like Peter Coe and Dieter Hogen, Dave kept reading and talking to other coaches, eventually learning enough to become certified by the British Amateur Athletic Board.

Britain has a three-tiered coaching system: assistant, club, and senior coach. Coaches first are qualified in general track and field events. After a year of coaching, they are able to specialize. Dave's specialties are middle-distance to long-distance races as well as marathons and ultramarathons. "British athletics turned around when they started the coaching program," says Dave, who scored nearly 100 percent on his coaching exams. The comment on his certification card reads "an excellent coach."

Dave, steeped in the English club system, is indeed an excellent coach, says Priscilla. His greatest gift is an understanding of what makes runners tick.

> Dave knows people. He's perceptive and knowledgeable about so much. Before my marathon in London (in 1981), he told me I could run three hours, and I ran 2:59. I had to walk near the end, and I was thinking "Dave said I could do three hours," and so I believed I could. He's that way not only with me, but with other people as well.

Once Dave discovered Priscilla's talent for running, he mined it like an English coal worker. And Priscilla, once shown the way, took the brakes off and ran at full speed. The Welches don't do anything in half-measure, and with the confidence of having run a marathon in less than three hours, there was no looking back.

Welch returned to the London Marathon in April of 1983 and ran 2:39. "You can't rush marathon training," Dave says. "The aerobic system takes time to build, and to develop it properly, you have to do distance work. You need to have a foundation to run the marathon."

Priscilla and Dave left the Shetlands in July of 1983, moving to London, where Priscilla continued training and Dave began a new post. Later that year, Welch went to Holland, where she won the Enschede Marathon in 2:36, another personal record and a time that put her among the top in the world. "I was surprised and pleased," said Dave. "A lot of people might be just as talented as Cilla, but they don't have a proper strategy."

Training: "Sheer Damn Perseverance"

The strategy was, above all, taking a patient approach to running.

> I saw my times improving, and the more I did well, the more I wanted to see what was over the next ridge. I was very conscious of how old I was, and that there was so much to do before time ran out. It was like an exciting game. I didn't start out wanting to be an international athlete, but the more I did the better I got. With Dave's training, you don't expect success in six months; it takes a long-term commitment in whatever you are doing to reap any benefits.

Says Dave,

> I always tell coaches that Cilla went two years running marathons in the 2:55-3:10 range, yo-yoing back and forth. People don't know

about that. It was just sheer damn perseverance by Priscilla. Once she got through the barrier, she kept improving, from 2:59 to 2:56 to 2:36 to 2:32 to 2:29 to 2:26. It was the process of all those marathons she did that got her stronger and stronger. They gave her the base strength to produce the times she did later on. I tell people to this day that what you do is directly proportional to the amount and quality of your base training. And by quality, I don't mean speed.

Rather, quality in base training means aerobic work.

It was Priscilla's background as a country girl that helped give her the discipline to carry on with Dave's difficult training. "She wasn't subjected to that many diversions," says Dave. "She found something she really loved, and kept doing it."

From the beginning, all of Priscilla's training was done in terms of effort. One of the biggest mistakes runners can make is judging their runs in minutes per mile, says Dave. "We think of it rather in terms of the development of energy systems by duration and intensity, with feedback mechanisms built into the program." That's the core of his coaching philosophy, with refinements added over the years.

The one constant is that it is "absolutely a mistake" to time all an athlete's runs. "What's important is running at the right heartrate intensity for the right length of time." That's the approach that allowed Welch to get more out of her running than nearly any other road racer. All of her training in the early years was done in what Dave calls "stage one," or the base-building phase. Priscilla would do three long runs a week: two between 70 to 80 percent of her maximum heartrate, and the third, a longer one, at 60 percent.

"Bloody hell, I hate these things," Dave says, when looking at a weekly training schedule he's been asked to fill in. That's because under his training, it's hard to give a typical week; it depends on what stage of training the athlete is in. Building a strong base is the fundamental tenet of Dave's training philosophy, based on the ideas of New Zealand coach Arthur Lydiard. "I don't think there's a successful coach alive who hasn't been influenced by Lydiard and his idea of the development of aerobic capacity," Dave says. "Lydiard's influence is of prime importance in the sport."

Welch divides training into three phases. Stage one is the aerobic conditioning phase, that typically would last three months. Stage two is when Priscilla did her anaerobic capacity/aerobic capacity work, followed by stage three, the peaking phase.

Both elite and non-elite runners make two major mistakes, says Welch. One is that "they don't develop the aerobic system," which means fat-burning capacities aren't being used. Another mistake is that "they won't let themselves take weeks off. Take three weeks off, drink beer, eat ice cream, and gain 10 pounds. Let your body be a normal human being again. It terrifies people to do that." When a runner rests, says Welch, echoing what Dieter Hogen advises, "the body recovers and gets stronger. When you get back to training, you lose the weight quickly."

Muscle biopsy tests show Priscilla has 70 percent slow-twitch muscle fibers. Her personal best for 10K is 32:14, and she would have liked to have seen what she could have done if she had concentrated on the 10K. But she is a marathoner, which meant she has concentrated on building strength, not speed. A typical week during phase one, aerobic conditioning, leading up to a marathon, was:

Sunday:	A.M., 30 minutes running in water plus flexibility drills; P.M., 2-1/2 hours at 60-70 percent MHR.
Monday:	A.M., 45 minutes at 70-80 percent maximum heartrate (MHR); P.M., 30 minutes easy.
Tuesday:	A.M., 1-1/2 hours at 70-80 percent MHR on hilly course; P.M., 30 minutes plus flexibility drills.
Wednesday:	A.M., 10 × 100 meters with 300-meter jog with coordination drills; P.M., 30 minutes easy/flexibility drills.
Thursday:	A.M., 1-1/2 hours at 70-80 percent with 20 minutes at 90 percent MHR; P.M., 50 minutes.
Friday:	A.M., 45 minutes at 70-80 percent MHR on treadmill; P.M., 30 minutes easy. ("Make friends with a jogger," Priscilla advises.)
Saturday:	A.M., maximum aerobic pace test; P.M., five miles at 80 percent MHR with coordination drills.

A Bite of the Big Apple

Priscilla's breakthrough came in November 1983, when she entered the New York City Marathon. She had been training for five years by then, and she and Dave saved up money for a running magazine's holiday group tour in New York, not expecting much in terms of her race. Priscilla started out conservatively, but once the race got going, her competitive urges took over. She was trying to beat a British runner who was expected to do well. Priscilla passed that runner early on, but because of the crowded field, didn't realize it. She kept going after that runner, finally getting "the shock of her life," Dave says, when she finished third, in 2:32:32, a half minute behind second placer Laura Fogli of Italy. Dave won a contest among runners on the tour by predicting before the race that Priscilla was going to run 2:32:31, just one second off her actual time. "I had been running with her and knew she was in shape, but it was a big surprise," he said.

Priscilla got another surprise the following day after she and Dave went to see race director Fred Lebow: "Well, the prize money for your place is $9,000, and we'll pay for your fare from England." This astounded Dave, who didn't even know there was any prize money. "I'm thinking about this," says Dave, "and as we walked down the road, I said to Priscilla, 'Do you realize how much we won?'"

"What do you mean? There's no prize money in this race."

"You heard what Fred said," said Dave.

"No, I wasn't listening."

"We just won $9,000 and all our expenses."

Priscilla started shaking and turned as white as if she had seen the ghost of Mary Tudor. Not only had she won prize money for the first time in her life, her time was also the fastest of the year by a British woman, which should have earned her a spot on the British Olympic team going to Los Angeles. But Welch was so new that nobody knew her, and British selectors wanted her to run another marathon. It was after New York that the Welches started mapping out Priscilla's career. "We were running innocent until then. There was nothing planned before that, just put your head down and go. I was just running for the enjoyment of running. After that, we tried to put the icing on the cake."

Welch went to Osaka in February and placed sixth in 2:36, despite developing "horrendous" blisters that were so big that the Japanese took photos of them. That still was not good enough to get her named to the British Olympic team. After returning to London for more training, Priscilla placed second in the 1984 London Marathon in May in

2:30:06 on a windy day. The selectors finally agreed that yes, perhaps Priscilla Welch was for real.

"After London, we decided to drop everything and come to the States to train. And that," says Priscilla, "was a whole different ballgame." Her sponsor, Nike, said it would send her to a training camp at either Portland, Oregon, or in Colorado. They chose Boulder to try altitude training for the first time.

When she arrived in the United States with her new status as an elite marathoner, Priscilla wondered, "What was going to happen now?"

"It was a case of loving what I was doing and the challenge of it," she explains. "I think there must be a little bit of talent there, but talent doesn't take you a long way. I'm lucky I found something I liked to do. And thank heaven I was lucky to find someone who promoted it; there's not many like that." There also aren't many like Priscilla, as she would show in the Olympics and in scores of races to follow.

1984 Los Angeles Olympics

The Welches went about their Olympic preparations very carefully. Priscilla's mileage for the five weeks after London was 56, 109, 78, 75, and 56. Then came two easy weeks, followed by weeks of 73, 84, 87, 125, 90, 90, 110, 90, and 52, topped off by a taper week of 26 miles. Welch did a lot of "aerobic capacity work" between London and Los Angeles, training to increase her maximum oxygen uptake (VO_2 max). Dave had her doing "flat-out runs for nine miles" and track sessions of 1,000-meter intervals.

Once certain that Priscilla would be on the Olympic team and running in Los Angeles in the middle of the summer, Dave went about preparing for the expected hot weather with his typical thoroughness. He rang up the British Olympic Federation, asking for the hottest temperature ever on the date the marathon was scheduled to be run. "94 degrees, they told me. Right, we'll train for that."

Priscilla trained in a plastic suit to acclimatize to the heat. The British press had a field day with the Welches' heat training, writing pejorative articles about Priscilla's being bundled up in sweats and running during the hottest part of the day. Priscilla didn't care what they wrote; she was aiming to place high in that inaugural Olympic Marathon, which is still considered the strongest women's marathon field ever gathered. Ingrid Kristiansen, Grete Waitz, Joan Benoit, Lorraine Moller, Lisa Martin—all the best women runners in history were there, except Katarin Dorre of East Germany, which had boycotted the Games.

It was 68 degrees (F) at the start of the women's marathon, and Priscilla was shivering, having adapted to hot-weather running. During the race, the temperature climbed to 80 degrees. "It was not hot enough," asserts Dave. "That was the problem. We would have loved 90 degrees. 100 would have been marvelous."

Priscilla stayed with the pack when Joan Benoit made her break. "I didn't have much experience," says Welch, "and I was with the group, thinking, 'I'm still with the biggies.'"

After the main pack split up, Welch was running alone in sixth place, trying to push the pace as hard as she could. She came up on Laura Fogli, who had stopped at an aid station. The Italian tucked in behind Welch as she went by. After towing Fogli along for a bit, Priscilla turned and said over her shoulder, "Oh no you don't, young lady!" She then took off, looking to lock up fifth place.

But Lorraine Moller passed her in the last few miles, and Welch finished sixth, in 2:28:54—another personal best and a new British record. In hindsight, Welch says she could have done even better. "If I had the confidence at that time to run my own race, I would have gone with Joanie and not thought, 'Ooops, I'm with the big names,'" she says. "And who knows what would have happened. That's what I say to people today. Talk to your body, and if you're ready to make a commitment, have a go at it."

Not long after the Olympic Games, the Welches decided to move to the United States so she could try the road-racing circuit. Dave quit his job managing the Cobra chain of running stores in London, and the pair took all their savings and flew over the ocean. Priscilla says their idea was, "We'll come to the States and experience road running here. If we're broke, we'll go back and sweep the roads. We were prepared to take the gamble. If you like it, pursue it."

The gamble paid off, as Welch was an instant success and was to be a fixture on the roads for the rest of the decade, getting faster as she got older. She passed her 40th birthday in November 1984 without missing a beat, saying, "I don't think 40, and I certainly don't feel 40. I don't even think 40 is old. It's only early middle age. I think 80 is old."

The road racing circuit then was very strong, with Lisa Martin, Lynn Williams, Betty Springs, Joan Benoit, Lynn Jennings, and Grete Waitz, among others, all racing well. At first there was a bit of jealousy from other masters runners, whose response when Priscilla showed up was usually, "Oh my god, *she's* here," says Dave. "There was almost a little rift, but that healed quickly." After doing well in the open races and dominating the masters circuit in 1985, Priscilla trained and raced even harder in 1986.

"We started to go a little crazy," Dave says, and so he had Priscilla take a break. "We just stopped racing and built up from scratch. Cilla was having a terrible time, so we said OK, we're going to do nothing but aerobic training. And for eight weeks we did that. We went from a 6:25 mile pace at 145 beats a minute to a 5:47 mile pace at 145 beats a minute, just by running between 70 and 80 percent of her maximum heartrate."

1987 London Marathon

The break in 1986 helped, because Priscilla came back for the best year of her life in 1987. She geared her training during the winter of 1986-87 toward the London Marathon, doing her basework of 100 miles a week in New Zealand. In February, she flew from New Zealand to Japan, where she ran a 2:38 marathon.

"How do you feel?" Dave asked when she finished.

"Like I could go a lot farther, but not any faster," Priscilla replied.

That's when Dave knew Priscilla had enough endurance and was ready to start speedwork. "For nine or ten weeks we did a combination of endurance and speed. Dave gave me a schedule and I followed it to an absolute T," says Priscilla. Her training program was typically outlined on sheets of paper. When the endurance phase was finished, Dave gave Priscilla another training sheet for the speed workouts; the key session was 1,000-meter intervals. After her marathon in Japan, Welch's training for London went well, with weekly mileage ranging from 75 to a high of 116. Her longest run was 2 hours, 40 minutes.

London is a special marathon for Welch, partly because at the 25-mile mark the course goes near the military offices where she used to work. Priscilla knew she was fit when she arrived in London. "I never know how I'll feel in a race until it starts," she says. But London was different. While warming up along the Thames River, she felt "light as a feather, like I was floating along. I knew I would do something good."

That "something good" was the masters world record of 2:26:51, as Welch finished second to Ingrid Kristiansen. "It's very difficult to peak, and that was one of the times I did it," she says. "I only did it two or three times in my career." And Welch's time was almost *exactly* an hour off the time she'd run in her first marathon eight years before, just as she had once predicted. "That was the target Cilla set, and she made up her mind she'd do it," says Dave.

After London, Welch hit the roads, continuing her streak of winning every masters race during the summer, all the while aiming to hit another peak at New York. Most people would be happy with a masters win at New York. Not Welch. She was aiming to beat all the elite runners, no matter what their age. She ran 100-mile weeks until the middle of the summer while racing on the weekends. Welch's London run had given her "a glimmer of hope" that she could win New York, and she went back up to altitude for some of her best training ever. She ran well in shorter races, clocking 53:51 for 10 miles after going through 6 miles in 31:50. It was another world over-40 best. After tapering in October, Welch was ready for showtime in New York City.

1987 New York Marathon

It's one of the most remarkable performances in running, or indeed any sport, as Welch showed that with proper preparation and careful attention to diet, sleep, and training, older runners could beat elite runners half their age. "Priscilla never let chronological age be a barrier. She took a chance in New York and it worked," says Paul Christman.

The chance the 42-year-old Welch took was going out hard and fast. She dropped former world-record holder Allison Roe of New Zealand by three miles, then concentrated on getting to the eight-mile mark, where the men's and women's fields merged, as fast as she could. "The men seemed to be having a lot more fun than me," Priscilla said. "They were waving at the cameras." But that didn't distract Welch, who said, "I had blinders on. I was totally focused on my race."

After merging into the men's field, Welch kept reeling off 5:30 miles. She was at the halfway mark in 1:12:17, already two minutes up on Belgian Ria van Landeghem in second place. Though Welch slowed during the second half of the race, her lead was too big for Frenchwoman Francoise Bonnet to make up, and Priscilla won in 2:30:17, picking up $30,000. Bonnet was a minute behind.

Priscilla hit the media spotlight and became the inspiration for women taking their own first steps toward fitness. "I don't know how you're supposed to feel at 40, but I don't think I've grown up properly yet," Welch said afterwards. When asked the secret of her great performances at London and New York in 1987, Welch said they "came about through the training. It's a long haul, and you have to pay your dues."

Monitoring Her Progress

Those dues, as is true with every top runner, involve vast amounts of hard work. Dave is a demanding taskmaster, and Priscilla is one of the few who could handle his workload. "I do the running, Dave does the thinking," Priscilla says. Dave is well-versed in training techniques from around the globe and not averse to experimenting with them on his wife. "Dave saw in Cilla not just the characteristics of a great runner, but also a talent that was far from developed. With a patient, disciplined, but extensive program over time, Dave was able to turn her into one of the foremost marathoners of her time," says Paul Christman.

The key was that Priscilla believed totally in the training program Dave handed her on those sheets of paper. There was no doubt in her mind that Dave wasn't giving her the *exact* workouts she needed to make up for lost time. Priscilla was known for her extremely long track workouts. For 10 years she trained as hard as any of the elite runners in Boulder, men or women. When Rob de Castella and other international runners would show up at the track about 9 on a Tuesday morning, Priscilla would already be working out. Deek and his group would do their warm-up, run their track session, and then warm down, and when they left the track to go home, Priscilla would still be out there running around the track, with Dave in the middle of the infield blowing a whistle to let her know when to start the next interval.

Echoing Steve Jones' and Steve Ovett's words, what Priscilla showed through the years is that training is "bloody hard work, and you need to be committed," says Dave. For Dave, being committed means having a high tolerance for pain, and he had no patience for those without commitment. Many were the runners who ran into the wrath of Dave Welch. One day 2:14 marathoner Steve Benson bumped into Dave as he was leaving the track after a workout.

"What did you do today?" Dave asked.

"Twelve 200s in 32," Benson said.

"You call *that* a workout?" exploded Dave. "Get your butt back out there and do it again, and do it faster!"

Benson did another set of 200s, and they were faster than his first set. Afterwards he said, "I was tired and didn't think I could do that."

Priscilla says the hardest workout she ever did was 3 sets of 5 × 1000 meters. "That's something we worked up to." One of her favorite workouts was a track session of 400 meters on, 200 off; or, a lap of 4 meters per second, followed by a lap of 5 meters per second, "so there'd be a subtle change of pace, and we could feel that change," says Dave. "Theoretically, you don't have to go to the track, as long as you train for the correct intensity for the proper length of time for the right energy system. You can do it on the road, the track, or hills. A track is a convenience for a coach; it's a good meeting point." Running on the track suited Priscilla's personality, and she usually did intervals on her own, saying, "I think it's good to be able to drive yourself."

Dave Welch's careful study of how to run efficiently extended to what pace to run during different parts of a race. "The fastest way to get from point A to point B is a constant pace," he explains. "So we really work this out and really try to be as economical as we can." "Economy" was one of the central tenets of Priscilla's training. Like Ingrid Kristiansen, she and Dave tried to be on the cutting edge of new technology, being one of the first to own a couple of treadmills they could "play with."

The question Dave was always considering was,

> How do we develop good economy? We put a heart rate monitor on and go on the treadmill at a constant pace, say 7-minute miles. And we just run normally as we always run, looking at our heartrate. Say we run those 7-minute miles at 150 beats a minute. Great. Now, let's start playing with body form. Let's start relaxing the shoulders. And we really relax the shoulders, and all a sudden the 150 is down to 145. OK. Let's make sure we don't cross over the middle with our arms. So we just relax the arms, and all a sudden we're under 140. But we're still running the same 7-minute miles, because the treadmill hasn't slowed down. Try to cut down your pace a bit and give it a little more cadence, a little more leg-speed, and a little less stride. Relax the shoulders, relax the arms, and you can just watch that heartrate go down on the monitor.

Priscilla often used the treadmill with her heart monitor on and experimented with her form. It was part of her daily training routine, along with doing "stomach crunches" and other exercises. Training permeated every part of her life and included more than the actual running. Just as for many top runners (though not all), everything Priscilla did, from sleep to diet to shopping to socializing, was dependent on how it affected her training.

Welch, who started using a heartrate monitor in 1985, wore it on her recovery days to make sure she really would have an easy day in advance of a quality session.

> What I was doing in the past was running my easy days too fast and not letting the body rest a bit, and then getting on the track and not putting in the times and the effort. And I was not fresh enough to enjoy what I was doing. That's initially how I came to wear the heartrate monitor.

She then progressed to wearing it during the hard workouts, to try to do the intervals at a higher heartrate so she could run faster repeats on the track. Heartrate monitors can help runners properly develop their aerobic base, which Welch considers the most important part of a training program, because it helps the body develop the capacity to burn fats.

"Most runners don't do that properly at all, and that's why most of us stay at one level for years on end. One of the things you can do with a heartrate monitor is program the monitor to between 70 and 80 percent of your maximum heartrate, so that it beeps at you when you go out of the range. It's like having a coach on your arm. The way to do this is to do all your running between 70 and 80 percent of your maximum heartrate, even if it means walking up a hill."

"The first time I used one," says Dave, "I was in pretty good shape. I went out for a run, and the heartrate monitor started beeping at me going up a big hill. I had to stop and walk and this big, fat jogger came past me. I felt so stupid. But I had to condition myself to do it." Welch measures progress through what he calls a "maximum aerobic pace test."

Calculate 80 percent of your maximum. For Priscilla, that is 145 beats per minute. She'll go down to the track and run five miles with her heartrate at a steady 145 beats per minute. And we time each mile. What you're going to notice if you do this test every week or every 10 days or every two weeks is that you're going to progress if you stay within the zone all the time.

Collen Cannon, the world's best female short-course triathlete for several years, followed Dave's system. One summer Dave gave her a maximum aerobic pace test, which she ran at 8:23 per mile. What that meant was that Cannon was not developed aerobically, even though she was running well at the shorter distances, said Welch. "If she had trained to do a half-marathon, she would have bonked for sure. And within 8 weeks, she was down to under 6 minutes per mile from 8:23."

Priscilla's Preachings

Priscilla says that older runners have to "be very watchful to take extra recovery time. There are ways to get around that, products you can drink immediately after your quality workouts to help you recover quicker."

The Dave Welch Method

Developing an aerobic base, or "aerobic conditioning," is one of the energy systems all athletes need to work on, Dave says. The others are anaerobic conditioning, aerobic capacity, and anaerobic capacity. Says Welch, "They are all achieved by working at different lengths of time at different intensities."

Anyone wishing to train properly must know their maximum heartrate, which is sometimes hard to figure out. When Dave was asked how to do it, he wrote down six different formulas. "And there's more," he said. "But do you know the best one? It's the 'Dave Welch Method.' It's magnificent. You find the biggest hill possible and run up it as hard as you possibly can. When you're about 50 meters from the top, you run *absolutely* eyeballs flat-out. Now, when you are just about totally exhausted, just before you hit the concrete, you check your pulse. And whatever that reads, you take 80 percent of it."

Judicious use of a heartrate monitor was one way Priscilla kept from overtraining, which meant she did not get injured. And that was the key to staying world class in her 40s, she says. "Staying healthy; that's the number one thing. And also, you have to work harder at the quality workouts than a younger person."

Dave's advice to young runners is:

- Make sure you develop your aerobic system properly.
- Try to run with a group. If you don't belong to a club, join one.

I always say this to people. Running clubs are great places. In England, the running club is the hub of your whole social life. It's the hub of your whole damn life. We find in England that wherever we go, we're with our running club. You go out on Saturday night, and everyone meets in a pub at a certain time. And even if you don't go there, they'll find you somewhere. Someone will find you. It really is a great social meeting. And you're also mixing with people who have the same interests as well. If you don't want to join a club, then just find some buddies. There's strength in numbers.

Priscilla had success with a sugar-drink called Cyomex. "Keep your fluid intake up. We found that extra aids and energy drinks are so far advanced now than before, that they are worth taking. Just take a drink that tastes OK," she advises.

I've actually had to pull up short on two marathons by taking the drinks that were given, which are mixed too strongly. I've literally ended walking for five minutes because of that. If you are going to do a marathon, decide what drink you are going to use way ahead of time, and use it in your long training runs. That's really important.

Priscilla never mixed up her drinks in advance—"It's got to be fresh," she says.

Priscilla has long preached the importance of following a healthful diet. She paid strict attention to her diet, but did give herself one "sin day" per week while trying to be good the other six days.

I firmly believe that when I was 18, 20, or 24, I could get away with eating garbage. A lot of young athletes will [dismiss] the idea, but many come around to our way of thinking when they approach 28 or 30. Because the body changes. I could say you can get away with eating garbage if you are 18 or 20, because you can process it. Some of the big shots eat a lot of garbage, and eat it in front of you. And they'll say, "you're wrong." If you want to keep putting in the performances you were putting in when you were in your early 20s, you'll notice a difference if you're eating junk. And these runners wonder why their performances have gone bad. I think we've lost a lot of good athletes that way, people who haven't been too particular about their diet.

To get the best out of themselves, runners need to

put real supreme gas in there. When you've got a new engine, you don't have to tickle the engine to get it to work, do you? You expect it to run well. And when you're a youngster, you expect to run well. But when you're older . . . You know what a vintage car is like; you have to flick open the hood a little bit more and tickle it and replace parts. It's the same with the body, roughly. You can't stop the exterior aging. . . . It's because of health and fitness, and what I eat, and exercise especially, that inside I feel really young. And when I go to competitions the young girls don't look upon me as a granny. Except if you are Uta Pippig. One day I was out training, and she said to me, "Heh, Cilla, you could be my mother." Gee, thanks Uta.

Running helps Welch take aging in stride. "It's a lovely feeling when you're healthy and eating well. You can do things that make you feel younger outside, too. . . . I won't trade this feeling I have inside me, and that's through eating well."

Despite her emphasis on proper nutrition, Welch isn't what she terms "a goody-goody." Meals at her house typically are steamed vegetables, low-fat chicken or fish, and rice or pasta, along with lots of salads. There have been, however, days when she's "really rebelled."

She and Dave follow basic rules about nutrition. "We all know that a high carbohydrate diet balanced with protein and fats in a 70-20-10, or 70-15-15, or 60-20-20 ratio, is best." The main point is to stay "in the ballpark" with your diet, Dave says. Priscilla eats meat, as long as it is a low-fat cut, and Dave believes vegetarianism isn't a good idea for runners. He cites a study that found that the common denominator in women runners with amenorreah wasn't low body weight, but rather following a vegetarian diet.

There are a couple of no-nos for Dave's athletes,

Particularly those who are marathoners and rely on very good fatty acid metabolism. One of the things that will break down fatty acid metabolism and conversion of fatty acids are hydrogenated fats. So if you are eating margarine thinking you are being healthy, you're probably on the wrong track, because that's one of the worst things you can eat. Partially hydrogenated fats are like being partially pregnant.

Hydrogenated fats, adds Priscilla, "sit on your hips; that type of fat is difficult to burn off. That's why you see a lot of people with thick hips and thick legs." Another "food" the Welches avoid is carbonated drinks. "Too much phosphoric acid will destroy calcium in the muscle tissue," said Dave. He once did a study to find out why marathon runners who can run 2:10 one year find themselves struggling to break 2:20 two years later. He found that they often had poor diets and drank a lot of "fizzy" drinks. The good news, Dave says, is that alcohol is OK, in moderation. He calls it "the fifth food group." A couple of glasses of wine with dinner aids your metabolism, helping you digest your food more efficiently, he says.

Priscilla looks very carefully at ingredients when shopping at the grocery store.

It's tough with the hydrogenated and partially hydrogenated fats, because nearly all the cookies on the shelf contain them. All that stuff is there winking at you from the shelf, and you have to put it back because hydrogenated fats are listed on the packet. It's tough to refuse.

But being disciplined—in diet, training, and overall lifestyle—was key to Welch's success.

Massage was another important part of Welch's training. She used it to get rid of lactic acid and treat muscle strains. Dave is a neuromuscular therapist with a thriving business of his own. He's known for being able to get deep down into sore muscles. How deep he goes "really depends on what type of injury it is," Dave says. "A lot of time a strained muscle will be merely a muscle that is contracted through overuse. With careful manipulation, that's not a problem."

But massage isn't recommended for muscle tears, says Welch. "As a basic rule of thumb, I wouldn't recommend deep-tissue therapy for an acute muscle strain." Massage, while very beneficial, can be used improperly. Sometimes deep massage is called for; other times more gentle work does the trick. It all depends on the muscle that is being worked on and how deep it is.

Battling Burnout

Priscilla took a "rest" year in 1990 and did not run any marathons. She was planning on running New York, but was forced to skip it because of injury. "After 10 years of tough marathon training, it was time to give the body a rest," she said. "I really was tired, and I needed to recoup. I needed to go back to 60 to 70 miles per week."

She concentrated on shorter road races, and her masters competitors wished she had run the marathon, because Welch crushed the fields by huge margins. She was named *Runner's World* masters women's runner of year, as she had been in 1985 and 1986, making her the oldest person, man or woman, to lead the year-end rankings.

Welch won the masters division in nine of the ten races she competed in during 1990. She won masters races at the 8K championships in 26:59; the Azalea Trail 10K (34:13); Crescent City Classic (34:28); Nike Women's 8K (26:56); L'eggs 10K (34:48); Bolder Boulder 10K (35:41); Cascade Run-Off 15K (52:06); Philadelphia Half-Marathon (1:13:22); and the Tufts 10K (34:02).

After winning Tufts, Welch returned to England to train, renting a room from an elderly widow in Bishop's Castle, Shropshire, near the Welsh border. She was in top shape, as shown by the fact that at 46, her half-marathon time was remarkably just 15 seconds off her personal best set five years earlier. At the end of the summer Welch began pointing toward the Los Angeles Marathon, saying, "I'll see it blooming next year."

But instead of blooming, Welch wilted. By 1991, she had been running at a high, hard level for more than a decade, and was getting more and more tired, something she attributed to "a bit of burnout." She likened herself to the Energizer bunny that keeps going and going and going. "For the past 10 or 12 years, I really loved what I was doing. But I started taking a bit of a nose-dive in my performances, which was unusual."

Maybe, Welch says, she should have rested a few times

> I've been trying to push it too far, but when you get to be 47 you start to think that time's not all before you, that you're not getting any younger, and there's a last-minute panic trying to cram everything in before the Big Curtain comes down. If you like what you are doing and have a talent for doing it, I say pursue it; otherwise you're going to be disappointed.

Symptoms of burnout Welch experienced in 1991 ranged from "normal moodiness to an inability to keep appointments on time, if I made them at all. There's a general lethargy, just not wanting to do things."

Priscilla can pinpoint the exact day she started feeling tired. Before the 1991 Falmouth road race, track sessions were going "perfectly." At Falmouth, however, she dropped out after two miles. Disappointed, she took a week off, then came back home and went for a track session. "We did the workout we had done the previous week, which had gone superbly," Dave says. "Cilla was doing 1,000-meter intervals, and this time they were 15 seconds slower than they had been a week before. So, it happened real suddenly. No matter how hard we tried, it just wouldn't come back."

Dave immediately decided that Priscilla had to "detrain" completely. That's one of the lessons they've learned along the way.

> Every so often, if you find your times slowing down, if you find your strength leaving you a little bit, don't try to push through it. Totally detrain. Take five weeks off. Don't do any running, don't do anything. Just pig out on everything you've been denying yourself.

The burnout was "an accumulation of all the years," Priscilla said.

> And it creeps up on you slowly. And not having had it before, you don't recognize what's going on. It's weird. To come out of it, I got the hankering for running, so I started running. But I felt so slow.

Though she can't be certain, Priscilla thinks that cancer was already affecting her at this time, and was part of the reason she wasn't training and racing well. "I remember talking with (TV commentator) Tony

Reavis and saying, 'Something just doesn't feel right.' I was always very much aware of my body, and I attributed it [burnout] to the change of life."

Priscilla came back slowly during the winter of 1991-92, running just basework. She went undefeated in masters races in the first half of 1992. Then, in June, during a routine self-examination, she made the discovery that changed her life. Since 1981, Priscilla had had a fibrocystic nodule, the size of a frozen pea, on her left breast. She had regular mammograms, but this day, she discovered something new—a lump under her breast that felt different from the nodule. She knew at once it was something "sinister, but I kept hoping it would go away. I kept saying to myself, 'Well, I think I've got something here, but you never know.'" She went to see her doctor, who gave her a mammogram and told her to come back in six months. She continued training and racing but was struggling. "I just didn't have that energy I had before." At the end of October, she went back to the doctor, who discussed estrogen treatment with her.

"By the way," Welch said. "Could you look at this lump?"

Four days later, we received the results. Dave picked up the results, and when I saw him, he didn't say anything. But I looked at him, and I just knew. It was like being hit in the belly. Really, I already knew, but I let it hit me for a couple of minutes; "I have cancer."

Ten days later, on November 19, 1992, Welch was on the operating table for an 8-1/2-hour mastectomy. "The team was very good," she said. "They all came in before the surgery and told me what they were going to do. I was very sore from the surgery, especially my abdomen, where they took the skin from to reconstruct my breasts.

Life Goes On

Priscilla's been upfront and honest about how cancer has affected her, and what women in similar situations can do. Welch thinks the cancer may have come from the difficult training she did for so many years, "abusing my immune system and not resting much over a period of 10 to 13 years, training and racing hard for a long time. Keeping the immune system healthy and the body chemically balanced while running and racing is so important," she told journalist Kathy Ellwood. "Resting isn't poppycock. It's for real. Otherwise, your immune system gets out of whack. The defending forces get confused and bam! you have something serious on your hands."

© Photo Run/Errol Anderson

Priscilla Welch was undefeated in masters races in the first half of 1992.

Doctors told Welch the cancer could have been there for as many as three years before it was found, and that experts don't know what caused it.

I was aware of something going on in my body. But it could take 15 to 20 years to show up. It could be hormonal changes, where I had an imbalance for a long time, and pollution can upset the genes. At about 44 or 45, if you're experiencing lots of tiredness, do further checking and testing. It could be something sinister, and you could catch it earlier than I did.

Going through two surgeries and being on chemo for six months was very tough mentally for Welch. For years, she had been extremely fastidious about not doing anything bad for her body, and now here she was ingesting chemicals. "I was learning about a whole new world. But I just didn't want to know."

Doctors gave her information about different ways to take the chemicals and asked her to choose one, but she "didn't want to read any of that. I threw everything into a corner. " It wasn't until the day before chemotherapy treatment was to start that she picked one. One of the options was an experimental drug, but Priscilla, not wanting to be a guinea pig, chose the conventional treatment. "I wasn't really brave. Not really; I didn't want to go to the deep blue sky, so I said, 'Let's get on with it.' It felt like the battery slowly draining out, de-energizing. It felt good to make a decision on my own."

Welch, always the fighter, vowed to come back. To maintain fitness, she swam, ran, or biked once a day, though she was tired from the chemotherapy. "I felt that I had run a marathon and a half all the time; that was the type of fatigue it was. I was cranky and sleepy, so I concentrated on a normal life at home, resting often."

To keep her mind off the treatments, Welch went to travel school and became a travel agent. The chemotherapy ended May 12, and then she had corrective surgery. She continued taking Tamoxifen and started building up her running again. "I just have to start from scratch, pay my dues, and see what happens," Priscilla said. She got back into training because she wanted to end her career on a positive note and "not the negative of having to stop because of breast cancer. I think you can bounce back; you can come back as a better person."

The irrepressible Priscilla did bounce back. In her first race after the cancer surgery, she ran a 5K in 19:28, still with a low white blood cell count. "Frank (Shorter) was very concerned. After he finished, he ran back to see how I was doing." She also began helping coach some of Dave's runners. It was her first experience coaching, and she took to it. "Cilla was a bee in a bonnet. It was a lot of fun," said Dave. Priscilla was aiming to be back in top form by November 22, 1994, her 50th birthday. "I don't want anyone to say that breast cancer, a disease, finished Priscilla Welch's racing. I want a good year next year, and then we'll see. One year at a time, right?"

That's the attitude that has fueled Welch's training ever since she took her first steps back in Oslo 16 years earlier. One step at a time was her attitude back then, and one step at a time was the attitude she took in coming back from cancer.

"I look at my disease as a friend to me," Welch told journalist Katy Williams.

> It forced me to take a proper rest, after 10 or 11 years at the top. I had to have the disease in order to stop. And all those years of

going full-speed, I thought I was above all things like cancer. I thought I would live forever. I wasn't ever afraid of the cancer, but I was annoyed. It was an interruption, because I was turning 48 and time was getting on for my running. But I heeded the message. And now that I've come out the other end, I can help other ladies go through the same thing.

"Do We Slow Down?"

Welch says she plans on running the rest of her life,

> at whatever level it is at the moment. I'm trying to convince myself I can get there. But now I'm focusing on masters, whereas before it was the open. It's getting a lot harder because there's a lot of little jackrabbits in there. The masters division is getting more and more interesting.

As she neared 50, Welch asked, "Do we slow down? People are asking me that, and they all seem to be so negative."

Welch's response is that she doesn't know, because she and a few other women are the first to push the envelope of masters running. Joy Smith of England and Sweden's Evy Palm were two other top masters runners, as was the amazing Carla Buerskens of Holland, who's won the Honolulu Marathon open division six times.

Priscilla has learned that

> Time doesn't stand still, and you don't stand still. Things change within yourself, within your life, and within your sport. Stay hungry and excited about what you are doing. It won't be forever and ever, because there will be a time you want to bail out, because you want to do other things. I may want to take up another challenge, use my brains and not my feet. Heaven forbid my brain starts working!

Of course, Welch did use her brains in her comeback. She started slowly, wanting to first get her basic fitness back. She will likely never get back to her previous standard again, but Priscilla continues trying. She is being careful, because "it's harder to recover from an injury, and it's twice as hard mentally as well."

The two main differences between training in your 40s and 50s and when you are 20, says Welch, are how much harder a 40-year-old has to work to maintain speed and how much more important it is to listen to and monitor your body

Priscilla now keeps a closer watch on the way her body feels.

> Dave used to set me out a training schedule, boom, boom, boom,
> boom, and I used to follow it religiously, unless I was crawling
> on the floor with tiredness. . . [Now] if I'm a little bit pooped,
> well, I just don't do the second training session, and I'm not put-
> ting in as many miles as I used to at altitude. I think you have to
> be really sensible about monitoring that. I'm focusing more now
> on being healthy, while trying to get fit and very competitive as
> well.

Welch tries to set an example for others with breast cancer. Her message is that breast cancer patients should exercise for health and fitness. "You don't even have to run; just do something to keep the body
healthy, keep the mind healthy. That way if something does come along,
you're able to cope with it."

In September 1994, Welch ran 38:50 at the Tower Bridge 10K in London, giving her hope of running some good times after she turned 50 in
November. Now that she has hit that milestone, Welch has returned to
her running roots. No longer among the elite, she's having fun meeting
and training with the "regular" runners Dave coaches.

> It's been a tremendous experience to get back to where I was in
> the beginning. I didn't think I would meet so many nice people,
> and I'm really enjoying running with them. They have such in-
> teresting jobs. We get together after our Saturday run and have
> coffee and muffins. There are many interesting stories out there.

Welch won the Foundation Citrus 10K in 39:08 as a 50-year-old, then
was the second master in the 1995 Bolder Boulder. She says her plan is
to run as fast as she's able. "Then," she says, "maybe I'll retire." To that,
fans around the world who know Priscilla say, "We'll believe it when
we see it."

Welch shows no sign of retiring, and she retains her competitive
spirit. She wants to set over-50 records, if she can remain healthy. That
was a problem in 1995, as Priscilla's chemotherapy affected her right
hand, which had been broken when she fell while running on a trail,
and her right foot, which had suffered several stress fractures over the
years. "The chemicals went right to the old injuries."

Welch wasn't able to train like she wanted during the summer of
1995, but as she neared 51, her foot started feeling better. "I'm getting
hungry to do better and be competitive again. I'll just see how the body
goes. It's a fun time for me right now." In October, Welch ran a 5K in
18:03, saying, "All's not lost. I'm going on from here. I want to get fit

and healthy again; then I'll have to make a decision on whether I want to devote everything to running. I'm still trying to come to terms with where I am right now."

No matter how fast she ends up running, Priscilla will remain a role model for women of all ages, as she continues speaking about her extraordinary journey to becoming an elite marathoner.

What I tell women is that anybody can become a runner if she really wants to. If you want to become the best runner you can be, start now. That's all I did. Don't spend the rest of your life wondering if you could do it, because it doesn't matter how old you are. I'm living proof of that.

4

King of the Roads

Born December 23, 1947, United States

World record: 25,000 meters (track)

Four-time winner Boston and New York City Marathons

35 marathons under 2:15

It was a cold February morning in 1973 as Amby Burfoot warmed up for a pre-Boston Marathon 20-mile race over the famed course. While getting ready to start, Burfoot, a top U.S. marathoner, saw a scraggly figure also warming up near the starting line in Hopkinton. The runner was wearing torn blue jeans, a hooded sweatshirt, also badly worn and torn, and had long blond hair reaching down his back. He looked like a homeless man who had accidentally wandered onto the race course.

All at once, Burfoot gave a start when he recognized the scraggly runner—it was none other than Bill Rodgers, his former college roommate at Wesleyan University, whom none of the other runners had heard from in several years. It is no wonder they had not, because Rodgers had not run a race since graduating nearly three years earlier. But here he was lined up to race again, and Burfoot greeted Rodgers warmly, thinking his friend was running only for recreation. "I said, 'Gee, Bill, it's great to see that you are still jogging. It's good for your health and keeps you fit,' and all that stuff."

Rodgers, however, was anything but a jogger. He was getting serious about his running, as Burfoot was to discover. "The race was over the first 20 miles of the Boston course, so it cut off the hills, meaning runners could always run a blazing fast time," said Burfoot.

> The gun goes off and the next thing I know, we pass 10 miles in 50 minutes, and there's a runner next to me—it's Bill Rodgers. It was his first race in God knows how long, and he ran 1:47 something for 20 miles. I was surprised as could be. He was just cruising at 5-minute pace.

That Hopkinton 20-miler was the start of a comeback that was to take Rodgers all the way to the top of the road-running world. Rodgers had been a talented high-school runner who fell away from the sport after a lackluster college career. Rodgers drifted about, searching for himself. His main goal: to stay out of the Vietnam War, then at its height. He ended up smoking, drinking gin and vodka, and hanging out in bars as a release from his grunt job as an orderly pushing corpses around a Boston hospital. Like many young Americans in the late 1960s and early 1970s, Rodgers was searching for some meaning in life, and he discovered it—or, rather, rediscovered it—in running.

Rodgers ended up third behind Burfoot in that 20-mile race, showing that he had the potential to go farther and faster. However, despite his natural talent for long-distance running evident that day, Rodgers was not an instant success on the roads. He took his knocks when he first moved up to the marathon, but each time he raced the 26.2-mile distance he learned something new. Whenever he was knocked down, he picked himself back up, dusted himself off, and did it better the next time. He ended up doing it so well that he became the best marathoner in the world, winning the Boston and New York City Marathons four times each, and in a six-month period becoming the only person to win marathon's "Triple Crown"—Boston, New York City, and Fukuoka. In his long career, Rodgers ran 56 marathons, most against top fields. He won 21 of those, and 35 times—more than anyone in history—he ran under 2:15.

Just as important as Rodgers's many wins was the spirited competition he carried on with Frank Shorter. In going head-to-head with Shorter, the best marathoner of the 1970s, Rodgers became the populist blue-collar star of the running boom, the undisputed "King of the Roads" between 1977 and 1982. Rodgers was a nonconformist who protested the Vietnam War and spoke out against what he saw as mismanagement in sport. He picked up the running torch lit by Shorter and spread it around the world in following in Frank's footsteps as one of the most competitive and consistent marathoners ever. That rivalry gave the sport a new hero and a reason for mainstream media to follow distance running. In running past Shorter, Rodgers carried road racing into a new era of professionalism, one from which there has been no turning back.

The Kid From Newington

There was not much in Rodgers's suburban Connecticut upbringing that suggested he would become a star athlete. He is hewn from the distinctive, self-reliant New England background that has characterized the area since the pilgrims first ventured to the New World. Rodgers had a very active childhood, often going camping and hunting with his brother, Charlie.

> We were always moving. We'd go out and play in the woods, and I always had a lot of energy. I liked going for hikes with the neighborhood kids. We'd go looking for butterflies, and sometimes it would get competitive, and I'd run and swoop them from under the noses of my friends.

His first "official" run came in 1963, when he ran around the block at his home in Newington.

Rodgers went to Newington High School, where he joined the track team, running a 5:10 mile as a sophomore. His coach at Newington High was Frank O'Rourke, who trained Rodgers and the other runners on his team with the interval training popular in the mid-1960s. Rodgers prospered under O'Rourke's close supervision to become one of the fastest runners in the region. His high school bests were 2:07 for 880 yards, 4:28.8 in the mile, and 9:36 for 2 miles. His mother, a homemaker, and his father, a mechanical engineering teacher at a technical college in Hartford, encouraged his running, but they did not push him into it.

In the mid-1960s, there were no external rewards for running—running was its own reward. Rodgers's motivation was not to win races, prizes, or money, but rather to just "enjoy the feeling of running, of moving along the way I did when I ran, and it's something that stayed with me."

Charlie Rodgers is a year older than Bill. He was also on the track team at Newington High School, "but Billy was far superior. Literally, he just loved to run." High school running in 1963 "was like amateur hour," Charlie says. The track the Rodgers brothers started running on was not much more than a dirt path around the football field. Even in high school, Rodgers showed the spark that was to make him one of the best in the world. "The coach would send us off on a long run— which then might be three miles—and Bill would be far more into it than me or the other guys," Charlie says.

> I'd take off and go to my girlfriend's house, but Bill would go run for an hour. He'd take off on a run and jump over things, like trash cans. It was fun for him while for the rest of us, it was a lot of hard work. We'd be croaking out there, and Bill would go out and do more. He just loved it.

The Rodgers were a tight-knit family that stuck together. Says Charlie, "Bill was quite a bit like my father, a nice guy who worked hard." The elder Rodgers would not look for instant success, and neither did Bill. Charlie recalls, I can remember going to our coach and asking him, "Can I be as good as Bill?" He just laughed, and said, "Well, you can try." The real truth was that Bill was far superior.

Indeed, Rodgers was superior to any young runner in Connecticut, winning the state meet and placing sixth in the New England championships. Even in high school, Rodgers showed that rare combination of perseverance and ability that only champion athletes have.

"I first saw Bill run when my brother, Gary, was a junior," recalls Amby Burfoot, who as executive editor of *Runner's World* is now one of the most influential people in the sport. Burfoot was a freshman at Wesleyan University in Middletown, Connecticut, and would go to high-school cross-country meets "and root for my brother to beat the kid from Newington."

Most of the time, it was the kid from Newington who crossed the line first. Rodgers won nearly all his races from 880 yards through 2 miles, and even in high school, says Burfoot, what was noticeable about

Rodgers was that "he ran with a relaxed, flowing stride, and he seemed to have the ability to go out there and hammer people in the middle of the race and not leave it to the end." That strategy was to be key for Rodgers during his marathon career; he would run hard from 6 to 20 miles to get away from the field, then "relax" the rest of the course.

Running "was the only area of my life where I was successful," says Rodgers.

> If you have something you do well, like playing the piano, for instance, you concentrate on it. That's why I liked running; it suited me physically and psychologically. In my high school days, I found I couldn't defeat the other runners with speed, but I could on the distance side.

Rodgers did not always win by huge margins in high school, but he was always "right up there battling with the best." Rodgers called himself "a part-time runner in high school." He had a "part-time" attitude toward running in college as well when he went to Wesleyan, an excellent academic school that attracted good runners, despite not offering athletic scholarships. Together Burfoot and Jeff Galloway, another future Olympian, recruited Rodgers when he was a senior in high school to come to Wesleyan.

A Mentor at Wesleyan

Rodgers agreed to their pitch, and in the fall of 1966 he packed up his bags and went to Wesleyan, which had, Burfoot says, developed "into a completely spontaneous assembly of truly natural runners." Burfoot and Galloway were the best, but there were some other excellent runners as well. "Jeff and I were truly dedicated and intent on becoming good runners. The rest had ability but were more interested in architecture or literature. So even though Bill Rodgers had beaten everybody in high school, there were half a dozen guys faster than him" when he arrived on campus.

Rodgers was not a great student at Wesleyan, and without a tough coach staying on top of him, as coach O'Rourke did in high school, Rodgers did not become a great college runner either, though he showed in races that he had the potential. Rodgers became lax in his training; he would run the required workouts with the team, but he would sleep in on the weekends and miss runs, unless Burfoot woke him up and dragged him out of bed.

Even though Rodgers was not serious about running in college, he was impressed that Burfoot was. In Burfoot, Rodgers found someone he could look up to and who could keep him motivated. "We introduced Bill to a different kind of training. In high school, he had the strong interval training," whereas at Wesleyan, Burfoot's idea of a good workout was "doing a steady 10-miler. Better yet, doing two steady 10-milers back to back." Burfoot was a mature runner, disciplined in his training, and Rodgers saw something to admire in that style.

In 1968, Burfoot was one of the best runners in the U.S., clocking 8:44 for two miles indoor and winning the Boston Marathon in 2:22:17. At 21, he was the youngest runner to win the race. Rodgers, then a sophomore at Wesleyan and rooming with Burfoot, saw how Burfoot trained leading up to Boston and how that training resulted in his win. Burfoot's Boston victory was the race that inspired Rodgers. The biggest lesson he took away from his days rooming with Burfoot, Rodgers writes in *Marathoning*, was that Amby "knew what he wanted."

> The Boston Marathon was his solitary goal. He put everything he had into it. Intercollegiate track meets were not very important. . . . He used them as speed work. . . . He used them as stepping stones to the marathon. He refused to let them become anything he would have to expend any psychological energy on. He geared everything psychologically and physiologically for the Boston Marathon.

In addition to the physical part of training, Rodgers got something more intangible from Burfoot: a connection back to the roots of U.S. running. Through Burfoot, Rodgers was able to tap into the wisdom of John J. Kelly, one of the original, elite U.S. runners who was also Burfoot's high-school coach. Kelly was a two-time Olympian and eight-time national marathon champion who had run the Boston Marathon over 30 times. But Kelly was more than a top runner, says Burfoot: "He was Thoreauvian, an organic gardener, a fan of Jack Kerouac [author of *On the Road* and one of the founders of the Beat Movement]," a free spirit who achieved his success "not by running quarter-mile intervals, but by going out on runs through the woods."

> He taught us that the essence of running was picking apples, jumping in water, and that kind of stuff. We didn't learn about anaerobic thresholds—simply the joy of running. That was in the Jim Ryun era; there were not many good coaches, but Kelly was one. He was just an inspiration to us.

Burfoot did not realize during his Wesleyan days with Rodgers that his roommate would go on to become a great marathoner. How could anyone know who has the talent and dedication needed to become a champion? "In all honesty, I never say 'yes' when I'm asked. The answer is that I realized he had talent. We'd go out on runs, and I had to work hard, concentrate on every stride; Bill would float along, with that vacant look in his eyes." It is a look runner Bruce Gomez described as being "like a kid on a playground, a wild-eyed look of wonder."

That "vacant look" belied a drive to excel that would not surface until he graduated and taken a hiatus from running. Rodgers may have been more talented than Burfoot, but he did not work as hard.

> In college, Bill was still in the process of finding himself. He'd miss workouts and wouldn't run on the weekends. Bill was a party boy in college; he liked to 'sow his wild oats' on the weekends, going out drinking and dancing, normal activities. He didn't have the marathon bug. He didn't have the focus he developed later.

Burfoot and Rodgers came up with a compromise; Burfoot would run the first 15 miles of his Sunday 25-mile run by himself, then come back through campus and pick up Rodgers, who would run the last 10 miles with him. "It was great for me; I looked forward to the company," says Burfoot. Only one time did Rodgers run the entire 25 miles with Burfoot, and he showed his marathon potential by keeping up with Burfoot until Amby surged away from him in the last mile.

After leaving Wesleyan in the spring of 1970 with a degree in sociology, Rodgers disappeared from the running scene. "Nobody knew what had become of Bill after graduation," says Burfoot. After December 1969, Rodgers quit running entirely, and he began smoking, drinking, and hanging out in bars. He had run 8:58 for two miles in an indoor race at Wesleyan, and he thought that was as far as he was going to go in running. "There was a lot going on in politics, with Vietnam, the draft, and student strikes," Rodgers says. "It was absolute chaos. I thought when I graduated that it was time to retire. And I went cold turkey."

Always in the Back of Your Head

At the height of the Vietnam War, in 1969—the year after the Tet Offensive—all Americans between 18 through 25 were required to make themselves available for the draft. Rodgers registered with the Selective Service as a conscientious objector, and after a year, was one of thousands of people granted a 4-F deferment during the course of the war. One of the requirements Rodgers had to fulfill was to work full-time, but he had trouble landing a job. Rodgers moved with a friend to Boston after graduation, and he finally found work at Peter Brent Hospital delivering mail and transporting dead bodies. Rodgers's life from 1970-1971

Amby Burfoot

Amby Burfoot was a good athlete who liked to play baseball and basketball when he was a teen. He took John Kelly's love of running and added to it an interest in the emerging scientific research into running. "I was interested in pulse rate and anaerobic threshold," he says, "I just threw myself into it whole-heartedly."

Burfoot ran his first marathon as a freshman at Wesleyan, finishing 25th at Boston in 2:35. He placed sixth in the NCAA cross-country championships his junior and senior years, and won the Boston Marathon the spring of his senior year. While running at a top level, Burfoot kept a New England sense of fair play about him. During one collegiate race, Burfoot was running neck-and-neck with another runner. As they neared the finish, the runner took a wrong turn. Burfoot magnanimously stopped and yelled to his foe, who got back on course and proceeded to outkick Burfoot.

Burfoot followed up his Boston victory by winning the steeplechase in the New England championships in May, thinking, "I'm in distinctly better shape than in my Boston win." The steeplechase victory came with a high price, however; the next day Burfoot woke up with a pulled gluteus muscle, an injury that ruined his excellent chance at making the 1968 Olympic marathon team. Burfoot went to the Olympic trials in 7,500-foot Alamosa, Colorado. He was in great shape, but was forced to drop out at 19 miles when his injury acted up.

Kenny Moore and George Young were by far the two best runners in the field, but the third and final spot was wide open. Ron Dawes, not the most talented man there, ran the smartest race to finish third. Burfoot showed he could have had that spot on the Olympic team that winter, when, after recovering from the pulled muscle, he won the Fukuoka Marathon in 2:14:28.8, less than a second off Buddy Edelen's American reord. Rodgers says he viewed Burfoot as a "reincarnation" of two-time Olympic champ Abebe Bikila.

After college, Burfoot became an elementary school teacher. Teaching, as Rodgers was to discover a few years later, was not conducive to becoming a good marathoner. "I've found that every September I'd be in 49-minute, 10-mile shape, and every

June, after the school year was over, I'd be in 56-minute, 10-mile shape," Burfoot said. "School took that much out of me." Burfoot continued training at a national-class level until 1976, when he placed tenth in the U.S. Olympic Marathon Trials. He then retired and turned his attention to journalism.

reads like a Charles Bukowski novel, filled with menial work, low-life bars full of cigarette smoke and dim lights, late nights, gin, and beer. During these years, Rodgers was living in "essential poverty in some dumpy apartment," says Charlie.

It is understandable that Rodgers would have quit training when he left Wesleyan, says his brother.

It wasn't a big thing [to quit], because there wasn't much logic to continuing running. Even in high school, you were some kind of fruitcake if you ran, like you were naked in the wind. Nobody else did it; there were no cheerleaders or anything like that. So to drop out of it was no problem.

But, Bill concedes, "Once you are a runner, it's always there in the back of your head."

I remember watching Frank Shorter in the [1972 Munich Olympic] marathon. But I wasn't thinking that I'd end up in the Olympics. It was so far away from that, and something I couldn't conceive of. But I had always watched the Olympics and always loved track.

What Rodgers wanted to do with his life, he realized, was pursue running. "I can recall being down in Provincetown [Massachusetts], sitting there smoking and thinking, 'This can't be it. This just can't be it. There has to be something more to life than drinking and smoking.' That's what drove me out of it." Rodgers took the first steps back by jogging laps around the track at the Boston YMCA. After several months, he ventured outside and began running around the pond in the Fens, a park area in Boston, gradually working his way up to consistent 10-mile runs at a 7-minutes-per-mile pace. After his bicycle was stolen, he also ran the mile and a half to and from work.

In what turned out to be a fortuitous event, Rodgers and a coworker were fired in 1972 for trying to organize a union at the hospital. Free from his mundane hospital work and unable to find another job, Rodgers started thinking about running the Boston Marathon. "When I was fired, I had time on my hands. And it was gnawing at me psychologically to do something positive with my life."

Rodgers was now able to do nothing but train and sleep, and he soon boosted his mileage to 15 miles a day at a 7-minute-per-mile pace. He did that for a year until his return to competition in February of 1973 at the Hopkinton 20-miler. His 1:47:37 over 20 miles in his first race in more than three years showed Rodgers that he could be good again if he kept on training.

"Why did I get seriously involved in running?" Rodgers asks in his book *Marathoning*. "I can't put my finger on one specific thing. I became a runner because it suited my personality. It suited me as an individual. There may be a lot of different reasons, but, somehow, they all came together." Rodgers continued racing locally, placing second in a 30K race and taking first in a 12-mile race in 59:17, his first road race win. "Billy started getting better and was cleaning the clocks of everybody," Charlie said. Bill joined the Boston Athletic Association [BAA] and eyed the Boston Marathon, the race he had heard about since he was a kid. Because he was a BAA member and was running well, Rodgers was given a low number and allowed to start at the front of the 1973 Boston Marathon.

1973 Boston Marathon

Rodgers went into his first Boston Marathon feeling confident and came out of it humbled. It was hot, and he had only a cup of yogurt for breakfast. Rodgers made several other mistakes: he started too fast and drank too much water, forcing him to stop at seven miles. He resumed running, then stopped again at 20 miles; he started running again, and finally dropped out for good at 21 miles. It was an ignominious start to Rodgers's marathoning career, and he wondered what he was doing wrong in his training. "Think back to 1973-74; people didn't know how to train for a marathon," says Charlie, "and Bill was confused as to why he was dying in races."

"I had learned what it means to pace yourself in a marathon," Rodgers says of his DNF at Boston. He was discouraged but not ready to give up on the marathon. Rodgers did not think he could train through the cold Boston winters, so he and his wife, Ellen, loaded up their car and drove to California in an attempt to find a warm-weather training locale. But Rodgers is a New Englander at heart, and he stayed only a few days in California before moving back to Connecticut.

After taking some time off, Rodgers was soon back training up to 120 miles a week. He ran his second marathon in October, 1973, the Bay State Marathon in Framingham, Massachusetts. A little bit wiser, Rodgers's goal this time was to finish the race and to feel good doing it. He did that, winning in 2:28:18. Some people, like Rodgers, may be born marathoners, but there is a lot of learning that goes into it as well, and this was another learning experience. Rodgers discovered that he could run a marathon and finish strong, as long as he ran within his limits.

A Young Scholar of the Marathon

Rodgers was improving rapidly, but he still needed to earn his bread, so he took a job at the Fernald School in Waltham, Massachusetts, working with mentally-challenged men. This made an impression on him, Rodgers writes, because he was seeing firsthand men who "were largely forgotten by society, shunted off to the side by their families." Rodgers's training did not seem as difficult anymore.

Another key change in Rodgers's running came when he joined the Greater Boston Track Club [GBTC], organized by Jack McDonald for runners who had graduated from college and who wanted to keep training. The coaches, who worked for no pay, were Bill Squires and Bob Sevene. With the GBTC Rodgers began training on the track, running "moderate" interval and road workouts with long rests. He did not get caught up in trying to win the track workouts; rather, he would be in the back of the pack, while up front, "some guys would be sprinting their brains out." The GBTC was "more of a track club than a distance club," McDonald says. "It was a full-fledged track team." Just as at Wesleyan, Rodgers, called "Will" by his GBTC teammates, fell in with a group of hard-working, fun-loving runners. "We had a great bunch of guys," says McDonald. "We'd meet at the track for workouts once a week. Billy was wearing our shirt on weekdays and the BAA shirt weekends at races." Rodgers transferred out of the BAA in the spring of 1974 and began competing for the GBTC.

In April, Rodgers was back at the Boston Marathon. With a solid year of training under his belt, he wanted not just to finish but to run under 2:20, a time that marked a marathoner as a national-class runner. Rodgers placed 14th with a time of 2:19:34, despite having to walk for 2 minutes up Heartbreak Hill. Another marathon, another learning experience. Rodgers learned this time that he had not done enough speed work to handle the 5-minute-per-mile pace he ran for the first 10 miles and that he needed to drink more water, as he did not take any until after 10 miles. "Some people say the marathon does not begin until 20 miles," Rodgers writes.

> That's when you hit the wall. The real truth is that the first few miles are the most important ones of the race. People who make mistakes in the early miles by going out too hard or by not taking enough water are the ones who aren't going to win the race, or, perhaps, even finish it.

Rodgers had finished and broken the 2:20 barrier. Now, he was a marathoner. But he was not satisfied; he believed he could run much faster. With time off from teaching at Fernald during the summer, he was able to increase his mileage; he aimed to win the New York Marathon that fall. It was the last year the race was run entirely in Central Park, and after starting out with the leaders, Rodgers once again cramped up, finishing fifth with a time of 2:35:59. He was *still* "being educated," as he puts it. The lesson this time: that he needed regular runs of over 15 miles in his training program. He just did not have the strength or endurance to stay with the leaders.

Rodgers was so disappointed after his first New York race that he even considered quitting the marathon. The failures, however, had a good side—they helped him understand that running well in the marathon would not be easy. He knew from bitter experience what it took to drop out and not succeed in the marathon—now, he was prepared to succeed.

Renewed Motivation

Rodgers, looking to further his teaching career, was accepted to graduate school at Boston College in special education. He continued running consistent 120-mile weeks through the winter of 1974-75, aiming again for Boston in April; one week he ran 200 miles (the only time in his career). With good health, renewed motivation, and serious runners to train with at the GBTC, Rodgers was ready to see how far his running could take him. "I was lucky that I always had good coaches and good training partners," Rodgers said. Those training partners included Randy Thomas, Tom Fleming, and Bob Hodge, all talented and as eager to succeed as Rodgers.

Early in 1975 Rodgers ran in the trials race that would select the U.S. team competing in the International Cross-Country Championships in Morocco. The trials, held in Gainesville, Florida, provided Rodgers with his first race against Olympic gold medalist Frank Shorter. Though hampered by a cold, Rodgers placed third, good enough to make the U.S. team. Then came his breakthrough race at the International Cross-Country Championships. Rodgers and Shorter ran together in the early going, but when Shorter dropped back because of a stitch, Rodgers kept going all the way to the front. "He was totally unknown, and that took a certain amount of audacity," says Charlie. "He just felt good and took the lead."

The flat course suited his style, and Rodgers flew through the 12K in one of the best races of his career. It was a race that showed Rodgers's fierce drive to win, as he broke away from the main pack along with Great Britain's Ian Stewart and Spain's Mario Haro. The pace didn't feel that fast, and Rodgers led Stewart and Haro until getting outkicked in the final 100 meters. No one thought he would be up there, but there he was, beating Shorter, Emiel Puttemans, John Walker, and many other of the world's best distance runners.

"Winning the bronze was very exciting for me," says Rodgers. "I knew I was fit, but I had no idea I'd have a chance to get a medal. Afterwards, I went on a seven-mile warmdown and knew I was in very good shape."

1975 Boston Marathon

The top international runners now knew Rodgers was a competitor, but he was still unknown to most when he lined up at Boston a month after the cross-country championships. Rodgers wore a hand-lettered GBTC T-shirt and floppy white gloves. With a favorable wind at his back, Rodgers blasted the early miles. "We used to call Bill 'feather shoes' because of his light stride," says McDonald. "We knew Bill was going to do well when we felt that southwest wind."

Charlie was on the press truck watching the race. He remembered his brother going out too fast and struggling in the year before. So he was worried when he saw the early splits and realized Bill was on an American-record pace.

"Billy, slow down! Are you nuts?" Charlie yelled from the press truck. But Rodgers was not nuts; just determined. After first dropping Ron Hill and then Jerome Drayton, Rodgers was running by himself. (He became "furious" and ran harder when he heard a spectator cheering for the Canadian Drayton.) Rodgers was looking for a breakthrough in the marathon, and despite stopping twice to tie his shoes and another time to get a drink of water, he got far more than he expected when he finished in 2:09:55 to break Frank Shorter's American record. "After that win I vowed never to question him again," says Charlie.

I wasn't aware of what kind of shape he was in at the time. I'm convinced he would have broken 2:09 that year if there had been any competition. Bill was just floating along. When things were going well like that, he could run almost effortlessly.

Rodgers knew he was running well, but he did not know how well.

I was just focused on the race. Jock Semple [head of the BAA] was on the bus talking to me. I saw a friend near the finish I hadn't seen for a while, and I waved to him. I didn't have any idea [of how big the win would be]. It was just another race I was trying to do well in.

McDonald speaks of Rodgers's victory in reverent tones. "For me as a sports fan, Billy's win in '75 is right up there with Carleton Fisk's home run that won Game 6 of the World Series. It's up there with the top things I've seen in sports, seeing your buddy run and set the record." McDonald and other GBTC members ran along the course to cheer Rodgers on, and at the finish in the Prudential Plaza, McDonald climbed a tree to see Rodgers cross the line. "It was 'Beamonesque' [referring to Bob Beamon's 29-foot, 2-1/2-inch long jump in the 1968 Olympics]. Billy's win was that kind of achievement."

Charlie says his brother was running under 5-minute miles so smoothly that the win "looked like a lark." Says Bill, "I had improved my fitness a big chunk. It was great fun, and winning Boston changed my life." He was now in demand, and as the man who had broken Shorter's record, he received invitations to races around the world. Shorter knew who Rodgers was, of course, and says, "I wasn't concerned that Bill broke my American record. He ran a very good race at Boston. I was more concerned with my own training." Shorter knew he would get his chance to run against Rodgers the following year at the Olympic trials and, perhaps, the Olympics.

1976 Montreal Olympics

Rodgers's '75 Boston win made him one of the favorites for the 1976 Olympics, and he went about preparing for the Montreal Games aiming to earn a medal. Shorter was getting ready out in Colorado as well, and two of the best marathoners ever had their first meeting over the distance in June at the U.S. Olympic trials in Eugene. Rodgers (who had placed third at Fukuoka in 2:11:26 in December, 1975), however, was not at his best; he was suffering from a foot injury, but he still matched strides with Shorter, who was in the best shape of his life. Shorter says it was one of the few times in his career when he peaked, and he and Rodgers ran side by side through 24 miles. Rodgers then fell off the pace after getting a stomach cramp, finishing second in 2:11:58.

"I was obviously struggling more than Frank was," says Rodgers. "I got a side-ache and had a neuroma on the bottom of my foot. It had been sensitive and sore for some months before the trials." Rodgers had been aiming for the 10,000 meters as well as the marathon, but after injuring his foot, he decided in the spring not to compete in the 10,000 in the Olympics, even if he made the team. Rodgers recalls, "I stopped doing speedwork and didn't realize it would hurt me for the marathon if I stopped it for a month. I kept going, doing high mileage, and did the usual cutdown before the race."

Rodgers's taper for the Olympic trials started four days before the race, as was his custom. "I tend to run better if I put in very high mileage the week *before* I start my four-day countdown," Rodgers wrote in *The Runner*. If Rodgers was racing in a marathon on Sunday, his "countdown" started on Wednesday.

> The mileage in my double workouts goes from 13-and-10 to 10-and-8 on Wednesday, 8-and-6 on Thursday, and 3-and-3 on Friday. I run these at about a 7-minute-per-mile pace. Then I do just one 3-mile jog Saturday morning. A few times I have not run the day before a marathon, but I find that even a brief layoff is bad for me.

Rodgers says he did not follow his instincts leading up to the Olympic trials.

> I noted in my diary four or five things I did wrong in preparation for the race: like needing more 25-30 mile training runs, doing more speedwork and drinking more fluids during a race. Unfortunately, I forgot all that at the Olympics. I've gotten into trouble by not giving my body proper attention as a major marathon neared.

Montreal was supposed to be Rodgers's glory day, when he and Shorter duked it out for the gold. When the gun went off, Rodgers ran at the front with Shorter and Jerome Drayton of Canada. As the rain began falling, he gradually drifted to the back of the lead pack, before falling out of contention entirely.

> I never felt good. I was pushing it hard and forcing the pace, because that was the way I'd won before, going to the front and forcing it, forcing it, forcing it. Maybe I felt nervous; certainly I

was a bit dehydrated. It was very humid, and I had lost my anaerobic fitness.

Rodgers felt this strain because he had stopped his speedwork. It was enough to do him in. A disconsolate Rodgers finished in 40th place in 2:25:14, and reporters asked if his career was over. Rodgers was bothered that he did not get much help from U.S. team officials before or after the race, but he was pleasantly surprised when Shorter came up and gave him some extra tickets to the opening ceremonies.

"All of us who didn't go to Montreal watched it on TV," said McDonald. "We were disappointed." GBTC coach Sevene thinks Rodgers would have had a medal if he had not been injured. "Billy had a bad foot but he didn't use it as an excuse. He went into the Olympics looking to medal, and ran with the leaders for as long as he could."

Rodgers came out of Montreal, "pretty beat up." He raced Shorter at Falmouth several weeks later, where "Frank just killed me. It was a sign that he was fitter than me. I just needed sharpening, so I did some shorter races."

Rodgers's Revenge

The defining characteristic of Rodgers's career was the way he always rebounded from a poor race. Behind his quiet demeanor, Rodgers had deep within him a relentless drive and determination to succeed. Burfoot is a keen observer of running, and even he says of Rodgers's ferociousness that he "never saw any of it [in Rodgers] in college, and I don't pretend to understand it. It always mystifies me. Bill was particularly devastating after a bad race; you didn't want to run against him then."

Montreal was a *very* bad race, and Rodgers followed it with a *very* good race at the 1976 New York City Marathon, which he began thinking about as soon as he finished his Olympic run. Shorter would be at New York along with other international runners, and a few days after his Olympic Marathon disappointment, while out on a training run with Sevene, Rodgers vowed he would get him. "Billy said, 'I'm going to take Frank out.' He was on a vendetta," Sevene recalls.

> It was nothing against Frank personally, but rather what Frank represented as the best runner in the world. Billy had full intention of being the best in the world, and he knew he'd have to beat Frank to do that.

After his loss to Shorter at Falmouth, Rodgers trained with renewed determination and with an emphasis on speedwork, doing sessions such as 12 × 400 meters in 62-63 seconds. When he and Shorter hooked up in New York just two months after Montreal, the entire nation was watching. Five of the nine fastest marathoners in history were there. Shorter was the marathoner everyone knew, whether they were runners or not, and his rematch with Rodgers grabbed the spotlight.

Rodgers ran best when he had the most confidence in his training, and at New York "I was in the best shape of my life. I knew I was tough," he later wrote. "I felt good from start to finish." He had run between 130 and 150 miles a week for the two months preceding the race, his most ever. Pekka Paivaiventa of Finland led the first 10 miles; Rodgers took over from Chris Stewart of Britain at halfway and ran in unchallenged, beating Shorter by three minutes. "Frank had probably lost some of his focus and fitness, while I had gotten mine back." Rodgers had gotten his redemption and staked his claim as Shorter's equal by running away from the field to a 2:10:09 course-record win, just 14 seconds off his American record and the eighth fastest ever.

Avocation or Vocation

New York was the start of a superb stretch by Rodgers. But to continue climbing to the top level, Rodgers had to change his work situation. He had trained for the Olympics while teaching full-time and it was not easy. He would get up at 5 AM to get a run in before work, braving the cold, ice, and snow. He was, says Charlie, "risking his life" running on the snowy streets, sliding on the ice and dodging cars. He would also train again in the afternoon, something his coworkers could not understand. One morning, the school principal called Rodgers into her office, sternly lecturing him, "Mr. Rodgers, you have to decide which is more important, your vocation or your avocation."

The frustrated Rodgers wanted to make his avocation his vocation, so he hit upon a plan—he opened the Bill Rodgers Running Center with Charlie in November 1977 so that he could run at more convenient hours. The original store was in a building in Cleveland Circle on the Boston Marathon course. (After the building was torn down to make room for condominiums, the store reopened in a new spot in Quincy Market, near the waterfront.)

Hampered by a knee injury, Rodgers dropped out of Boston in 1977, saying the marathon can "always humble you." But he rebounded to win New York in 2:11:28, 2-1/2 minutes up on Jerome Drayton. In December, he won Fukuoka in 2:10:55, and was ranked number one in the world.

In 1978, Rodgers got his biggest scare at Boston, as American Jeff Wells nearly caught him at the tape. But Rodgers held on for the two-second win, 2:10:13 to 2:10:15. This is when Rodgers began dominating the roads. During 1977 and most of 1978, he won 50 of the 55 "serious" road races he entered. He also set the world record for 25K on the track (1:14:12) and U.S. track records over 15 (43:39.8) and 20 kilometers (58:15) and the hour run.

The next runner to take a shot at Rodgers—in 1978—was Garry Bjorklund, the U.S. 10,000-meter Olympian. Bjorklund (BJ) had his best year in 1978, winning 10 major road races, and he came to New York in the fall gunning for Rodgers. He had placed fifth there in 1977 after battling with Rodgers for 20 miles. Some of the experts believed Bjorklund would get him. "Garry Bjorklund may be the hottest runner of all. The fact that he hasn't run a lot of marathons this year may work to his advantage," Joe Henderson wrote in *The Runner*. Ex-mile great Marty Liquori wrote, "It's only a matter of time before Bjorklund tags him. Bjorklund runs some fast times, which will get even faster when he has more experience."

Others, however, stuck with Rodgers. "I can't see anybody touching Bill right now," wrote Tommy Leonard, founder of the Falmouth road race and owner of the Eliot Lounge in Boston. "He just toys with fields. He plays with them. It's almost a joke." Added Bob Hersh of *Track & Field News*, "Over the last several years, Rodgers has been the most consistent marathoner in the world. Despite his lapse at the last Olympics, he has shown he can win big marathons."

New York was now one of the biggest marathons in the world, and Bjorklund gave an all-out effort to beat Rodgers. Bjorklund was good, but no matter how fast BJ ran on this hot day, Rodgers was always right there. Rodgers followed BJ until getting away from him on the Queensboro Bridge and going for the 2:12:12 win, his third consecutive victory at New York.

The Frank and Billy Show

Rodgers's most significant races perhaps, though not always the most competitive, were with Frank Shorter, and their duel propelled distance running to a new level. The Rodgers/Shorter competitions transcended running to become one of sports' greatest rivalries, on a level with Johnny Unitas and Bart Starr in football, Larry Bird and Magic Johnson in basketball, Muhammad Ali and Joe Frazier in boxing, and Bjorn Borg and John McEnroe in tennis. The Shorter/Rodgers rivalry kept running in the nation's consciousness and helped spur the phenomenal growth of road racing in the 1970s and early 1980s.

Shorter was slowed by injuries in 1977, but there were some great battles when both were in top form. "In the early stages, when I was first racing Frank, there were a whole bunch of American runners chasing him," Rodgers says. "He got me at the cross-country trials [in 1975] and I got him at the championships, and we flip-flopped after that."

Burfoot, a contemporary to the stars of the running boom, places Shorter and Rodgers among the best ever. "What was important was that both are such commanding presences. One of Bill's brilliant, brilliant things was that he returned every phone call from every journalist, meaning he was written up by every paper big and small." Amby recalls being at Rodgers's house:

> He'd get a call from a small paper I'd never even heard of, and Bill would spend a half hour with the guy. He'd answer the same inane questions over and over again. He was just a public relations genius, not because he was witty—Frank was more quotable—but Frank didn't return his phone calls.

Adds Charlie Rodgers, "Frank and Billy were great. It was something the media could focus on. It was a great period of time, and they were important because they brought more runners into racing." Shorter had the better competitive record in championship races, but Rodgers won more races at the time when the boom was really happening. Adds Burfoot, "They didn't have too many races when both were in shape, and their clothing businesses were also competing. They are different personalities, but each wanted to be the best he possibly could be and beat the other guy."

The period from 1976-1982 was "fun," Shorter says. "We were both trying to win. There was such tremendous interest in the 1976 New York race, coming off the Olympics. But we didn't really race that much." "Rodgers," the always-astute Shorter says, "was very smooth from the waist down. He ran up on his toes, and it looked like he was overstriding, but it really worked. He was out there training hard; he built a good foundation and had a good career."

The rivalry may have been real, but the personal animosity between he and Rodgers was overplayed by the media, says Shorter. The two were often portrayed as not liking each other in the buildup to races.

> We were two individuals who both wanted to be the best in the U.S., and being the best in the U.S. at that time pretty much meant you were the best in the world. I just happened to win the Olympics, and Bill won Boston and New York.

Garry Bjorklund

Many have called Garry Bjorklund (BJ), a tough-as-nails outdoorsman from Duluth, Minnesota, one of the most talented U.S. runners. As a high-schooler, BJ ran a 4:05 mile and he and Mike Slack went through the half-mile in 1:57 at his high-school state championship mile. BJ had a great college career at Minnesota and made the 1976 U.S. Olympic Team by beating Rodgers in the 10,000-meter trials race, despite losing a shoe halfway through. BJ was a runner feared by everyone, fast and strong.

Given different circumstances, he may have had a career as great as Rodgers and Shorter. A 27:46 10,000-meter runner on the track, many say he could have run even faster.

"Billy was the man, and I was one of the guys who wanted to dethrone the king. It's to his credit that I had so many opportunities to try, and never did."

> It [losing to Rodgers] doesn't bother me, because there was nobody in America, not even Steve Prefontaine, who I had greater respect for than Bill Rodgers. I took my hardest shots at the guy and couldn't break him. He was always ready.

The race where Bjorklund took his best shot at Rodgers was the 1979 Bloomsday 12K in Spokane, Washington.

> I was fit there, and that race was "The Hunt for Bill Rodgers." I actually threw everything I could at him. I ran the flats hard, the uphill hard, the downhill hard . . . . We came up . . . a 600- or 700-yard steep hill, and I was hammering. I knew Billy was laboring so I kept going as hard as I could. I didn't care anything about the end of the race; all I wanted to do was drop Billy. But as soon as we reached the top of the hill, Billy surged, and in a block he was gone. I couldn't see him anymore. That sticks in my mind. He had me shaking my head after that. And everytime he beat me I became more resolved. I would test him and could never find a flaw. He was a real, real student of the sport. He could tell you everybody who was running well, from the young kids to the older guys.

Bjorklund adds, "I introduced my wife to Billy, and afterwards she just couldn't believe he was the king of the roads. She thought he was just a mild-mannered schoolteacher from suburban Boston. And he was—until he laced on his shoes."

If there was antagonism between them, says Shorter, it was "irritation at constantly being asked" about the other. "Bill beat me like a drum. I never thought of it as personal rivalry but one from an athletic standpoint." It was different on the business level, however, as both headed up sportswear companies trying to carve out their niche in the apparel market.

The one thing that bothered Rodgers during those years was how hard it was to get out from Shorter's shadow. "Many people feel that Frank, simply because he won the gold medal in 1972, is inevitably number 1," Rodgers wrote. "No matter what I or any other marathoner has done since 1972, Frank is number 1."

Despite the rivalry, Rodgers and Shorter got along better than observers might expect. "When I won the bronze medal [at the '75 Cross Country Championships], I was surprised when Frank came up and shook my hand and congratulated me," says Rodgers. "When we were business rivals, we were not as friendly, perhaps, and I said some negative things I sort of regret now."

Because of the business and athletic rivalry between Rodgers and Shorter, and the media attention surrounding them, interest in running increased. The world was fascinated by the rivalry and their presence in a race guaranteed national exposure. Perhaps without Shorter and Rodgers for TV to focus on, long-distance running could have remained like soccer, internationally popular, but a backwater sport in the United States. "They had some flat-out wars," says Sevene. "Billy has a light touch and was a tremendous downhill runner; Frank was a great uphill runner. Both were two fast 10,000-meter guys who ran the marathon, and they were both beautiful runners." "What Bill and Frank did was promote running, and it boomed," said McDonald. Watching Shorter and Rodgers run along the roads like sleek racehorses, people got the urge to run themselves, and running clubs sprang up around the country.

Says Shorter, "Bill was very gifted, and was unusual in that he's probably gotten the fastest marathon times off the slowest track times of anyone. It was incredible, and I was always fascinated by that." Rodgers, like Rob de Castella, most likely would have improved on his track personal bests (13:42.0 for 5,000 meters and 28:04.4 for 10,000 meters) if he had not been concentrating on the roads. "Bill was able to run a lot of races at a high level," Shorter said.

> I can think of only three runners who were able to do that: Bill, Juma Ikangaa, and [U.S. marathoner] Doug Kurtis. Bill found the formula that allowed him to recover quickly. For a 6-year period, from when he started to run well in '75, until 1981, he raced a lot at the 2:11 level. He'd run 2:11, 2:10, 2:11, 2:12.

Shorter points to New York in 1994, won by Mexican German Silva in 2:11:21, and says, "After looking at that race, you realize how good Bill's times really were."

Rodgers became running's biggest hero, the wide-eyed marathon champion. He was seen as the opposite of Shorter; he was, Burfoot said,

> A regular guy who just loves to run. Frank and Bill were both absolutely essential to the running boom, in completely different ways. Frank's biggest imprint was winning the Olympics. Frank was the Olympian in every sense, more regal, king of the land. Bill clearly was the boy next door. Everyone who has known Bill says that; he may have been king of the roads, but he was not regal, not chilly. Frank was regal in every way. Frank got us on the map, with his reach of medals, but Billy was the guy who passed it on. He must have signed 10,000 autographs.

Dedication and Perseverance

The reason Rodgers was able to stay on top for so long was that from 1975 until after he turned 40, he seldom was injured. When Rodgers did get small injuries, he took care of them before they knocked him out. Charlie got an idea of how his brother kept minor injuries from developing into major problems when he saw him before the 1978 Boston Marathon.

> I remember going to visit Bill one day at his apartment. It was 11 in the morning, and he answered the door in his bathrobe. He was injured and was staying in bed the whole day. He did that quite often to eliminate the injury. He had enough sense to back off when he needed to, and also was able to take on a lot of work. If I ever did what he did, I'd be dead from sheer exhaustion.

What set Rodgers apart from other elite runners, his brother says, is that "he really wanted to compete," thriving on head-to-head competition. "I just didn't have the psychology for it. But Billy was very capable of banging with anyone. He always respected the competition; he respected the other runners and saw everyone he was racing against as being capable of beating him." He was always friendly to his competition after races, never aloof."

Bill always liked to run, says Charlie.

> Obviously, he had something different in his mind to train the way he did. He had the ability to push himself as hard as anyone. He was dedicated and persevered, and was very smart about things. He had the sense not to go overboard in his training.

In track sessions with the GBTC

> other runners would be beating the hell out of themselves, and Bill would be at the back of the pack. Bill did his homework. He had the capability to run over 175 miles a week if he needed to, but wouldn't completely thrash himself in track workouts like some people.

One of the runners at the front of the pack was Alberto Salazar. He was a high school star in Massachusetts who came and ran with the GBTC. He was called "The Rookie" at GBTC practices and would succeed Rodgers as the world's top marathoner, winning New York three consecutive years, starting in 1980 after Rodgers's four consecutive wins.

A runner who saw Rodgers's competitiveness up close was Benji Durden, a 2:09:59 marathoner who made the 1980 U.S. Olympic team that boycotted Moscow. Durden was on the losing end of many battles with Rodgers, and he says that "Billy was a little intimidating when he was racing. He was a nice guy, except when he was racing. In a race, he became an animal and would do anything to beat you." Durden got a first-hand look at that in the Wheeling 20K in 1979. Midway through the race, Durden made a break and got a 100-meter lead.

> It was a nasty day, raining hard and windy. Billy caught up to me, looked over, and surged. I responded, then Billy surged again, and I responded again. This went on for three miles. Finally, he looked over at me and growled. Just growled, "Arrghhh!" and put on another surge, getting away from me with a mile to go. It had just pissed him off that I made him work so hard. Billy just never gave up.

Durden says that Rodgers's tenacity is what made him one of the greats.

It takes a lot more than ability to run fast; it takes the ability to keep coming back and keep coming back. There were several races where Bill could have packed it in when he was running against fast guys, and no one would have said anything about it. But he never let that happen.

The Professional

Rodgers's appeal changed the prize structure of running. He was the star attraction on the nascent road-race circuit, and races begged to have him in their events. Because Rodgers did not like to say "no," he kept making his fee higher and higher, and, to his surprise, the races kept paying it. When he came onto the scene in 1975, elite runners might get a first-class airline ticket that they would cash in for a coach ticket, says Durden. "They'd make a few hundred bucks here, a few hundred there."

Things changed with Rodgers. At his peak, he was making up to $20,000 for a marathon, and $3,000 to $10,000 to show up for a road race. "It was a whole new ball game. In a sense, Billy was the first true professional road racer," says Durden. That money given to Rodgers, Shorter, and a few others did not filter down as much as runners hoped it might, so the leading road racers formed the Association of Road Racing Athletes. "We didn't begrudge Billy," says Durden. "It's hard to begrudge Billy." It was not that Rodgers was getting too much money; it was that the rest were not getting enough. For example, when Rodgers won New York in 1978, he received $10,000 to show up and $10,000 to win. Durden placed fifth; he received nothing to show up, and $3,000 for fifth, even though he had been promised a lot more than that. For months afterwards, the airline and hotel he used at New York kept sending him bills, asking for payment. "Race directors would often do whatever they could get away with," Durden says.

Rodgers was the Steve Prefontaine of road racing, rebelling against the system when he did not agree with the way athletes were treated. On runs, he would sometimes smack his palm with his fist, and say, "We have to crush the AAU!" [The AAU, which changed its name to The Athletics Congress (TAC) and now to USA Track & Field, is the governing board of running in the United States.] The more he talked about it, the faster the pace got, Durden says, until he and his training partners would be virtually racing. Rodgers gave something back to running by sponsoring athletes himself. He received a grant from TAC, which he broke into smaller pieces, paying leading runners such as Durden to wear his athletic gear.

During his peak years, when he was the winningest road racer in the world, Rodgers became a hero to young runners. Typical is the response of Mark Coogan, 1995 Pan American Games silver medalist in the marathon.

> Bill was "the man" when I was growing up in Massachusetts. Anyone who has ever met Billy knows he's a real nice guy, and always helpful for younger runners. . . . Billy is a class act. . . . He was just so positive when we used to run together. Before I ran Boston, he took time out to tell me about the course and to be careful, that the race is a little different from the way you think it would be.

While some top runners were aloof, Rodgers would spend hours after races answering questions and encouraging just about every one of the thousands of people who asked him for advice over the years.

1979 Boston Marathon

Rodgers's competitive urge was seen again at Boston in 1979. In December of 1978, he had returned to Fukuoka to defend his title, but he lost to Toshihiko Seko in that young runner's breakthrough race. Fukuoka was still considered the most prestigious marathon outside of the Olympics, and Rodgers had wanted to win it again. He was slowed by the flu and finished sixth with a time of 2:12:51. As was his trademark, he looked to rebound with a good race at Boston in April.

The week before Boston, Rodgers amazingly ran 121 miles, including 20 miles the Thursday before the Monday race. It was cold this year, and Rodgers showed up at the starting line wearing big white gloves (with his BR logo emblazoned on them) and a thick blue stocking cap, complete with a Snoopy patch—the kind a sixth-grader wears! Ellen had given Bill the hat when he left the house that morning, after she saw that it was raining. The hat was appropriate for Rodgers, a Snoopy kind of guy: lovable, cuddly, with big eyes, and that wide-eyed stare.

When the runners lined up, Rodgers was the only one wearing a cap; maybe the others should have followed his lead. The field was stacked, and this year, there would be no early breakaway and easy win. Toshihiko Seko was back after having beaten Rodgers three months earlier in Fukuoka. That was on Seko's home turf; now they were in Billy's country. Boston, wrote one journalist, was "Bill's town, its people his supporters, its streets, from Commonwealth Avenue to the suburbs, his playground."

Boston was indeed Rodgers's race. He lived near the course, trained on it, opened his store on it, saw Burfoot win it. Boston was in his blood.

If ever a runner and a course were made for each other, it was Billy and Boston. The net-downhill of Boston suited his running style perfectly. He liked to bust a race open with a mid-race surge, and at Boston, Rodgers could do that on the downhills, before Heartbreak Hill.

Several other good runners besides Seko were trying to crash Mr. Rodgers's neighborhood. Garry Bjorklund, New Zealander Kevin Ryan, and Jerome Drayton were all gunning for Rodgers. It was raining hard, and Rodgers was content to sit in the pack and let others lead through 10 miles. Tom Fleming, a guy who Rodgers said talked about running a 2:06 marathon someday, was running like he was going to do it this time. The leaders went through 10 miles in a very fast 47:55 and were on a near-record pace at the Natick checkpoint (10.5 miles). Fleming was 40 seconds up on the chase pack; Ryan and Don Kardong gradually fell back, but the dangerous Bjorklund and the impassive Seko were both running strongly behind Fleming. Rodgers was just biding his time, he told Marc Bloom afterwards: "I held back in the early stages because of the cold. I know the course; the final miles are not hard. The tough part is hanging together when everyone kills themselves the first 20."

It did not look like Bjorklund was killing himself, as he passed Fleming at 15-1/2 miles and assumed the lead. He was looking good, and Rodgers was worried as he ran along with Seko. "Oh, oh. There are 10 miles to go and number one, my stomach hurts; number two, Bjorklund looks good out there, and number three, here is Seko, whose presence reminds me of my loss to him in Fukuoka," Rodgers would write later in *The Runner.*

Nearing 20 miles, Rodgers and Seko passed BJ, who yelled out to Rodgers, "Go for 2:08." Rodgers was concerned about the win, not the time. It was hard to read Seko's face, and Rodgers could not see whether Seko was feeling good or not. But the way Rodgers ran the final six miles of the race, it did not matter how good Seko was feeling—nobody was going to beat Rodgers this day. Rodgers got a little gap on Seko, thinking, "Give me an inch, and I'll take a mile."

Heartbreak Hill, it is said, picked up its name from the 1936 race, when Tarzan Brown dropped Johnny Kelly on it. Rodgers pushed it up the first hill, and after another mile had a safe lead on Seko. He got stronger over the last few miles. "I was scared of someone coming up on me like last year," Rodgers said. "I didn't want it taken away. I could taste the third win. Seko was falling back, so I got a chance to savor it."

Savor it he did, drinking in the applause of the crowds, taking off his Snoopy cap and waving it to his admiring fans. As he neared the finish, the announcer said, "Here he comes, the greatest distance runner in the history of the world." A bit of Boston hyperbole perhaps, but on this day, who was going to argue the point? Rodgers ran in to smash his own American record by 28 seconds, clocking 2:09:27. Seko was second in 2:10:12, followed by Hodge, who dropped his personal best from 2:28 to 2:12:30, Fleming (2:12:56), and Bjorklund (2:13:14). Shorter, who had assisted in the birth of his first son just before flying to Boston, finished in 2:21:56.

Boston is considered by many to be the world's top marathon. Only five Americans, besides Rodgers, had won Boston since 1943, and this homegrown, all-American hero was the catalyst the running movement needed when Shorter was felled by injuries. After his win in 1979, Rodgers was invited to the White House by U.S. President Jimmy Carter, and Rodgers said of his Boston win, "I've had a streak, and I'm into my prime years, but it ain't going to last forever."

His career did last long enough for Rodgers to mark his spot among the greatest marathoners ever. He earned the respect of his opponents—Seko, Shorter, Bjorklund and others—through his competitiveness on the race course and his agreeableness off it. "In his day, you could throw a brick wall at Billy and he'd come through it and wouldn't even have dust on him," says Bjorklund.

Olympic Preparation

Rodgers had another battle in New York that fall, as he went for his fourth consecutive title. This time it was 2:10 marathoner Kirk Pfeffer who took off from the start. Rodgers was back in the pack in the early going, then slowly began moving up and picking off the runners ahead of him. He passed Shorter at halfway, with Pfeffer far out in front. Though Rodgers had to push hard to even get Pfeffer in sight by 20 miles, he was not worried. "The marathon is a bizarre event, and as a coach I hate it," says Sevene.

> For most runners, the marathon is like rolling dice. But for Billy it wasn't. He knew exactly what he was doing out there. You have to sometimes let the others get out of sight in a race, and be confident in your training. Billy had confidence in his training.

Rodgers went by Pfeffer at 23 miles and ran in for the 2:11:42 win. The prize for the first New York City Marathon, won by fireman Gary Muhrcke, was a carton of soda. This year, thanks in large part to the publicity from Rodgers's wins, the prize was $10,000.

That New York victory gave Rodgers the number one world ranking again in 1979. And once again, his pre-Olympic year wins made him a favorite for the Olympics. Rodgers was 31; Seko was 22, and a match for a gold medal in the 1980 Moscow Olympics seemed likely. Rodgers knew who his main competitors were going to be in Moscow, and he raced them all in the two years leading up to 1980. Cierpinski, Mosieyv, Seko, Bjorklund, Drayton, Shorter—he had raced all the medal contenders and beaten them all, says Sevene. "Billy had a book on them, and, once he raced them, he knew how to beat them." Referring to his dream to win the gold in Moscow, Rodgers said, "There's only one thing missing. If I get that, I'll retire. Happily."

But Rodgers and Seko were denied their chance for a rubber match at Moscow when the U.S. boycotted the games. An angry Rodgers lashed out at U.S. President Carter, calling him a hypocrite for mixing politics and sport. It is hard for those who do not train and do not know how much training it takes to get to the top level to appreciate Rodgers's anger. Rodgers would gladly have traded a couple of his Boston and New York City wins for an Olympic medal, and not getting the chance to even try for it in 1980 was a great disappointment. "All Bill ever wanted was a medal," says Sevene.

> He wasn't greedy. It didn't matter what color it was: gold, silver, or bronze. As long as it was a medal, even a bronze, it would have been enough. People don't understand that the only thing Billy doesn't have is a medal. Like Frank [Shorter] and Joanie [Benoit], the Olympics are what drove him. And I think Billy would have won the gold medal.

Rodgers was the most outspoken of the athletes denied a chance to compete for a medal, saying, "Suddenly, we're using the Olympics to fight the Russians. I'm willing to sacrifice if I think there is a real need to sacrifice. None of the athletes is for what's happening in Afghanistan," he told Colman McCarthy. "But don't play games with people as Carter is doing, just to get votes. It's got nothing to do with national security." What bothered Rodgers the most was

> no one stood up for us—not the running magazines, not the sportswriters, and not even our own Olympic Committee. All the people on the committee who voted to support Carter should lose their jobs and be banned from sports. Just like they ban athletes who take drugs, we should ban officials.

Running a 20-miler with Sevene the day after Carter's Olympic boycott was announced, Rodgers wondered if he would be able to keep going. "Bill knew that 1980 was to have been his Olympics," says Sevene.

I feel he could have medaled in 1976, but '80 was to have been his Olympics, and it was taken away. He said, "You know Sev, I don't know how I'm going to hang on until '84." It was a question of keeping that mental edge for another four years. He realized his moment was gone. He was ranked No. 1 in the world, he had beaten Cierpinski and the others, he knew the course in Moscow cold, he knew the weather. He was prepared, and had left no stone unturned.

The Roads Scholar

With his Olympic dream taken away, Rodgers turned to racing around the world. And the more Rodgers won, the more popular he became. He won Boston in 1980 in 2:12:11; but Rodgers did not get invited to the White House this time. He stayed on the road through the 1980s, cementing his claim as the king of the roads.

Rodgers's rivalry with Shorter was renewed after Frank recovered from ankle surgery and returned to racing form. Their next battle came at the 1981 Middletown Orange Classic, held in Frank's hometown. Shorter was invited first, then two months before the race, officials told Shorter they had invited Rodgers, ranked number one in the world for the third year. It was a classic confrontation, making the cover of running magazines. Shorter hung on to beat Rodgers this time, but overall Rodgers won more of their races.

In 1982, Bill clocked 2:11:08 in Melbourne, running the second half of the race in 1:04:30. He had a hectic schedule during the early 1980s, sometimes racing 10 or 12 weeks in a row. "You don't want to turn down the money. That's always been my problem," he told Eric Olson.

> I don't think there's another road runner in the country who does the promotional work I do, who has the schedule I have. In fact, one of my greatest dreams is to get [top road racers] Rod Dixon and Herb Lindsay and a few others out there doing everything I do, on my schedule, and then we'd be even.

Rodgers began going to Arizona for his winter training, and it paid off. In January 1983, he ran 28:15 in a 10K road race, and then he won the Orange Bowl Marathon in 2:15:08 one week later. In April, he placed 10th at Boston in 2:11:59. He told Olson he earned about $600,000 in 1983, half from endorsements and half from races and clinics. But he was still driven to make the Olympic team, and so he cut back racing in

1984 in an attempt to make the U.S. squad. He explained his motivation to go for the Olympics again: "What I really like is when people tell me, 'Good try.' That's what it comes down to for every runner. To try. Even when you bomb out, the important thing is to keep trying."

Rodgers, by now 36, placed eighth at the 1984 Olympic Trials Marathon. His best years were past, but in the 1986 Boston Marathon, Rodgers placed fourth in 2:13:26, 33 seconds ahead of a young Mexican named Arturo Barrios.

Training: The Right Recipe

To reach the top, Rodgers trained like the U.S. Postal Service: neither rain, nor heat, nor cold, nor the snow in Boston prevented him from putting in his appointed 20 miles a day. The key to his longevity is that he never lost the drive to put in consistent training year after year. He didn't expect instant success in his training or racing; he was content to slowly build up his strength.

"Bill had the talent, and at some point, he decided to go for it," says Burfoot. "If Bill and I ran 140-mile training weeks, Bill had the ability to run 140-mile weeks without thinking about it. I had to think about it so much, and that was another stress in addition to running the miles."

Says Rodgers, "I built my training up very gradually, and was never a high mileage runner in high school or college. . . It's something I learned from Amby Burfoot. And once I was successful at it, I just kept trying to enjoy it as much as I could," which is why he was able to run so many world-class marathons. "To some extent the fact that I was not an intense runner in high school may have helped me in later years as a marathoner," Rodgers wrote in *The Runner*.

> You can't burn the candle all the time. If you put in long miles as a teenager, how are you going to do it for 20 years after that? There seems to be a pattern of top high school runners fading away after college and not performing up to expectations, especially in the long-distance events.

Rodgers was able to run consistent high mileage without serious injury. "I'm just lucky in terms of the biomechanics," he says. "I've never had a broken bone or a sprained ankle." Rodgers does have a short left leg, and he compensated for it by swinging his arm like he is stirring a cake. In 1977, a podiatrist recommended orthotics, but Rodgers never got them.

What fueled his training is that, like all great runners, Rodgers had "a dream," says Sevene. "It sounds corny, but they all had this dream." Rodgers, like Shorter, was good in college, but not "out of this world.

Billy's claim to fame was breaking 9 minutes as a junior. Then, when he was 26 years old, he became one of the best. He was able to formulate his dream, and he went out and accomplished it."

Rodgers was able to do that because he had a smart approach to training and racing. There are many motivated, talented people who never make it to the top. Often, they are over-motivated. "A lot of runners do training they shouldn't be doing," says Sevene. "Billy knew *exactly* what he needed to do." What he needed was years of 110-140 mile weeks, featuring long, steady runs interspersed with solid, though not spectacular, track workouts.

Rodgers's training plan evolved gradually. After being exposed to interval training in high school, Rodgers next learned from Burfoot in college. "Then, being the student he was, he evolved into studying himself," says Sevene.

> He hooked up with Bill Squires and learned more about interval training. He learned how to run downhill, he learned how to run uphill. It was a combination of things that made him great. He never got hurt; the guy's amazing that way. He was very bright in his training. He didn't train too much, and he didn't train too little. And Billy could go out and crank out miles by himself.

Rodgers usually did four hard sessions a week—two "moderate" speed workouts, a race, and a long run. But, he says, "Most of the training wasn't that hard, just steady."

> It wasn't 7:20 pace, but it wasn't 5:20 pace either. My training stayed pretty much the same my whole career. Lots and lots of weeks of 120 miles, or 100 miles, or 109 miles. It wasn't all that intense, and was all geared for the marathon. Intervals were 66-, 67-, 68-second pace on the track. And I raced heavily to prepare for the marathon. I always thought of myself as a marathoner, so the shorter races were part of marathon preparation for me.

Rodgers's intervals with Squires and the GBTC were what physiologist Jack Daniels now calls "slow intervals," Sevene says. They included up to seven or eight miles of intervals, such as 9:25 two-miles and 4:40 miles. There were also "ladders" with a short rest, and one-half miles and mile repeats.

In 1980, Rodgers began getting "muscular therapy treatments"—deep-muscle massage—something he said was "very valuable. I also did light weights, and some stretching after runs." A typical week for Rodgers leading up to a major marathon included:

Sunday:	A.M., 19-21 mile run, 6:30-mile pace; P.M., 5-6 miles.
Monday:	A.M., 11-12 miles; P.M., 6-7 miles.
Tuesday:	A.M., 10 miles; P.M., hill repeats or track.
Wednesday:	Same as Monday.
Thursday:	A.M., 10 miles; P.M., intervals on track.
Friday:	Same as Monday.
Saturday:	A.M., race; P.M., 5-6 miles.

Rodgers says "Greg Meyer and Randy Thomas introduced me to hill repeats in 1978-79, which were of big benefit. I couldn't challenge Greg on the track or on the hills. The only place I was ahead of him was on the long runs." Rodgers trained in New England because that was where he was the most comfortable. He did not train at altitude "because I was not so aware of the value of it when I was young. It's effective, but tricky to get used to."

Rodgers was not only "King of the Roads"—he also was known at his peak as a "King of the Junk Food." Most of that reputation was an exaggeration fostered by the national media eager to latch on to any story about "those crazy runners," such as Rodgers's late-night forays to the refrigerator to gobble down pizza and mayonnaise. Rodgers basically ate a balanced diet, loaded very heavily with complex carbohydrates. But runners do tell amazing stories of what Rodgers would eat before a race. Pablo Vigil ran with Rodgers on the 1978 world cross-country team that competed in Scotland. "What struck me most about Bill was that he would stop at every corner bakery and buy the gooiest pastries he could find, the kind with green frosting on them," said Vigil. "He could eat *anything*."

It is true that Rodgers ate a lot of sugar, mainly because he was running so many miles. "I craved sweets," he said. But he did eat a good diet otherwise—

one reason, he believes, that he missed only *three* days of training because of sickness or injury his entire career. Rodgers says that if he had been eating a nutrient-poor diet, he would have been sick or injured much more often.

Masters Star

Rodgers's career got new life when he and Shorter turned 40 in 1987; and they have kept a generation running along with them. Their races brought new life into the masters circuit, and the pair remained as popular as ever. New, younger runners were winning the open races, but none have become as popular as the dynamic duo. Rodgers was faster than Shorter as a masters competitor, and even in 1994, he was still running fast. "The s.o.b. isn't slowing down," said Sevene. "I was at a race where he ran a 1:08 half-marathon. He can still crank it."

Rodgers certainly did not lose his great competitive fire when he turned 40. In 1989, he raced Durden at the Frostbite 5-miler in Great Falls, Montana. Once again, Durden and Rodgers were running shoulder to shoulder. "With a mile to go, he surged and beat me. Even then, he wanted it more than me, and he got it," says Durden.

One of the most visible of the masters races Rodgers competed in was the Alamo "Alumni Run" race series, which pitted runners from different schools against each other. Shorter and Rodgers had been at the same college race back in the fall of 1965 during a practice cross-country meet at Yale University. Neither knew the other at the time, and neither could have imagined they would go on to become two of the best-known runners ever. Rodgers was a freshman at the time, and he won the junior varsity race, while Shorter ran in the varsity race, which was won by Amby Burfoot.

"From my own travels, I can tell you Billy is still such a huge draw. He and Frank are almost like folk heroes," says Sevene.

> They dominated for years, and the television coverage at New York gave them both exposure. They were the best in the world; Frank had the gold and silver medal, and Billy was ranked No. 1 in the world for several years in a row, and their personalities still carry importance at races even now.

The pair actually raced more as masters runners than they did during their open days. Rodgers won most of the masters races between the two, as Shorter was concentrating on his biking and his duathlon

© Photo Run/Victah Sailer

Bill Rodgers ran as a masters runner at the 1991
TAC Cross-Country Championships.

career. Rodgers set the masters 10-mile record in 1990, clocking 49:03, and he also ran 29:48 for 10K and 2:18:18 in the marathon.

After turning 40, Rodgers began getting plantar fasciitis, one reason he concentrated on shorter road races over the marathon. He was planning on competing in the 100th running of the Boston Marathon on April 15, 1996. "I don't feel quite so smooth when I'm running now, like I'm always running uphill or against a headwind," Rodgers said in an interview before one masters race. "But I get inspired by progress, which is why I like running. You can always improve through your efforts." Even in 1994, he ran 24:43 for five miles at age 46. "Given all the miles he's put in, it's astounding Bill still has the will to compete," says Charlie. "I guess it's just the nature of the beast."

Rodgers sees problems with track in the 1990s, because it is not marketed in the United States well enough. "It needs to reach more people, and more beginners. We have great athletes, but our sport has to compete with all the other sports." He says it's important to avoid golf's "Palmer-Nicklaus" syndrome, where "old-timers"—like he and Shorter—get all the publicity.

Rodgers learned a lot in his 30 years of running, and he says, "My advice to young runners is to concentrate on track and cross-country."

> Take the gradual approach. Then, when you are in your 20s, experiment with longer road races. Just take a low-key approach. You can't tell in one year or two years what you are going to do. And stretch, because a little bit goes a long way.

Through all the runs, wins, disappointments, and pressures, "It's still fun," Rodgers told Olson.

> In some ways it's still exactly the same as it was the first day I went out for cross-country, although I don't think people believe me when I say that. But it's true. It's just like the beginning. I just love to run.

5

The Man Who Invented Running

Born October 31, 1947, West Germany (United States)

Olympic gold, marathon, 1972

Olympic silver, marathon, 1976

Four consecutive wins at the Fukuoka Marathon

On September 10, 1972, a skinny Yale graduate with a drooping mustache ran onto the track in Munich's Olympic Stadium and invented running. Frank Shorter's marathon win that warm fall day was clinched when he broke away from the two fastest marathoners ever, world-record holder Derek Clayton of Australia and Ron Hill of Britain, along with the rest of the pack at 15 kilometers in Munich's English Gardens. That breakaway started Shorter on his way to the gold medal—and also started a generation on a fitness boom that would make running into a worldwide, mass-participation sport.

After 10 years of running, thousands of miles of training, and 2 years of meticulous planning, it took Shorter just those 2 hours, 12 minutes, and 20 seconds to change running history by "inventing running," a phrase *Outside* magazine coined in a cover story about Shorter. As the first long-distance running star for the baby-boom generation, Shorter was on many magazine covers after his Olympic win. For the first time, ABC-TV had televised the marathon nearly in its entirety, and Shorter's victory, the first by an American since Johnny Hayes in 1908, caught the attention of the United States and the world. The thoughtful, aristocratic-looking Shorter became the spokesman for a nation awakening to the importance of exercise, leading millions of people into the promised land of fitness.

Shorter was a reluctant leader; he was a runner, not a prophet, but in becoming the best marathoner of the decade, he also became the best spokesman for a generation looking to add something to its life.

John Jerome wrote of Shorter that

> This unknown and unchosen star of the event turned out to be personable, articulate, penetratingly intelligent about running, and not about to be shoved into any standard media-jock package. . . . There was something about all those miles, all those minutes of TV coverage through the streets of Munich, something about that silken, light-footed stride and flying hair that lodged forever in our consciousness. Running. Somehow it looked . . . glorious.

Before Shorter, long-distance running in America was part of society's fringe element, along with such esoteric pursuits as martial arts. It was confined to gym classes, and running on the roads was seen as something done only by boxers getting ready for a prize fight. On those rare occasions when the media portrayed marathoners they appeared to be gaunt, emaciated people with strange names who ran millions of miles in foreign countries. The perception of runners in America was that they turned to running because they could not make it in any of the "manly" sports like football or baseball. Shorter showed the world that not only were marathoners athletes—they were very good ones at that.

Shorter also brought something new to the marathon, a way of racing that changed how elite runners approached the distance. He was not content to run a steady pace and outlast his opponents. Instead, he used his speed and an aggressive attitude to make the marathon a race over its entire 26.2-mile distance.

"My strategy was to incorporate track-racing strategy into what had before been more a race of attrition," Shorter said of his Munich win. As his career continued beyond into the 1980s, Shorter brought running into professional light in the United States, which, in turn, opened the way for the growth of running and road races throughout the world. Shorter's victory roused millions of Americans brought up on baseball and football from their sofas and into the streets. These people needed their own races to run in, along with shoes, shorts, and clothing; Shorter's win blossomed into the myriad running-related industries that continue to expand.

"I think Frank's win was crucial," says Kenny Moore, the fourth-place finisher in the 1972 Olympic Marathon and a long-time track writer for *Sports Illustrated*.

> We're talking about a social movement. It was something that . . . was growing, the idea that you could train at any age, that almost anyone could run a marathon if they ran slow enough, and were patient and drank enough liquid along the way.

Running did not become a public movement until after Shorter's victory, says Moore.

> It did not have a spokesman yet. It was still a private thing, where you snuck off to run in old sweats. Then Frank won, and it started to build, and then Bill Rodgers came and there was the great rivalry between Frank and Billy. It was not just Frank winning, but was his persona of an American winning. He took the mystique out of running, and made it a public thing. . . . Then you had Bob Anderson starting a little magazine [what would become *Runner's World*] that said running is the meaning of life.

Shorter's win, coupled with a burgeoning interest in health, meant that during the mid-1970s and early 1980s, new races sprung up like wildflowers after a summer storm—the Chicago Distance Classic, Peachtree 10K, Bolder Boulder, Cascade Run-Off, the Bix 7-Miler, and the Lilac Bloomsday 12K, along with marathons in many major cities, including New York, London, Paris, Mexico City, Rio, and Stockholm.

All that was needed to legitimize a race was Shorter's presence. As Grete Waitz was also to be, Shorter was the star attraction, patiently explaining to nascent runners the basic principles of his sport. His ideas were appealing precisely because they were very basic: go out and run for a minimum of 30 minutes at least 3 days a week, at a pace where you are able to still carry on a conversation. Then, when you want to start racing, begin running some intervals. That was Shorter's message. Rousseau would have liked its simplicity; perhaps Emerson would have written about it.

Shorter was smart, talented, and able to articulate what made marathoners tick. Mainstream media discovered running, and Shorter was featured on the cover of *Life* magazine. Beneath the photo of Shorter running in for the gold was the caption, "The Haywire Olympics; what went wrong?" The murder of 11 Israeli athletes by Palestinian terrorists had darkened the Olympics, and Shorter's win one was one of the few positive stories to come out of the Games.

When the 24-year-old Shorter ran through the tunnel and onto the Olympic track that September afternoon in 1972, he had no idea of the ramifications of his victory. All he wanted to know was why the crowd was whistling (the European way of booing) and soon after, who the heck was that pasty-skinned guy who'd run on the track in front of him, stealing his glory.

Born To Run

Frank Shorter's becoming a runner was as inevitable as water flowing down a mountainside. He had a natural inclination for it, almost a genetic predisposition to go off to the woods and enjoy long runs by himself, as he discovered as a 12-year-old in his hometown of Middletown, New York. However, Shorter's Olympic journey began, ironically enough, on those same streets of Munich where he ran to victory in 1972. He was born there, the son of Katherine and Samuel Shorter, a United States Army doctor stationed in Germany. In 1949, two years after Frank was born, the Shorters moved to West Virginia, where Samuel had taken a job as a doctor for a coal-mining company. "It was a rough life," Shorter says in his book, *Olympic Gold*. He recalls asking why his father carried a gun with him on his trips into the Appalachian hills. "For snakes," his father replied. Later, Frank was to understand that he meant two-legged snakes.

When Frank was four years old, the Shorters moved to Middletown, New York, where Frank's parents had grown up and met. Here they raised their six boys and five girls. Frank, the second youngest, was a good student, and athletically inclined. His great interests as a child included singing and skiing, which he indulged in with his father. He had a typical all-American childhood, spending his summer afternoons and evenings playing outside with the neighborhood kids. He liked all the sports kids in America play: football, swimming, and baseball; he played first base on his little league team (even leading the league in home runs one year).

Shorter's athletic talent surfaced early. At the annual "Field Day" at the Choir School of St. John the Divine in New York City, when Frank was in the sixth grade, he won the running events and the overall school field day multi-event championship, beating the older eighth graders. His prize was a copy of *Famous American Athletes of Today*. Frank had no inkling that he would grow up to be one of the most famous American athletes of tomorrow.

Shorter also had a great love of books, and would spend hours in his room reading or in his mother's studio watching her paint. As the mother of a full household, Katherine Shorter never had enough time to pursue her art. Frank learned from this, and from his father's sometimes all-night work sessions, to become "selfish" about managing time for himself; he has never had much patience for people who waste his time.

Shorter left St. John the Divine to attend seventh grade at a Middletown public school, where his gym class played flag football. Shorter, an all-around athlete with good reflexes and coordination, excelled at it. But the games sometimes degenerated into real tackling, and after one particularly rough game, Shorter asked his gym teacher if he could run *around* the football fields instead of playing football *on* them. The teacher, not knowing what force he was unleashing upon the world, agreed, and thus were the first steps toward an Olympic gold medal taken.

Shorter took to running so much that he sometimes ran the two miles to and from his home to school, wearing low-top, white Keds. "I liked the feeling the first time I ran, and I enjoyed the idea of being a bit unusual," he said. Shorter's heroes as a youth, however, were skiers, and his dream was to become an Olympic skier, not an Olympic runner. He especially liked the French ski racers, both men and women, such as Jean-Claude Killy, Guy Perillat, and sisters Christine and Marielle Goitschel. "I wanted to be a ski racer, and I had read that skiers trained by running in the off-season, so I thought I'd do it, too."

After finishing ninth grade in the Middletown public schools, Shorter's parents enrolled him at Mt. Hermon prep school in Western

Massachusetts. Shorter tried out for the football team at Mt. Hermon and was good enough to become the starting halfback, but he quit the team when his leg was cut during a pileup.

Mt. Hermon has a strong academic tradition, and Shorter studied the basics of a liberal education there. The school also has a long athletic history, including its status as the host of the annual Pie Run, the oldest race in the United States. It has been going on for more than 100 years, and the name comes from the pies given to any boy finishing the 4.55-mile cross-country course in less than 33 minutes. Shorter went out for the race on a whim, figuring he was in good enough shape from skiing and football to finish. To his surprise, not only did he finish, but he placed 12th. The only boys beating him were from the cross-country team.

The spring of his sophomore year, Shorter went out for the track team, but he did not like it. He instead spent that semester playing first base on the Mt. Hermon baseball team. The following year, he went out for cross-country. Shorter was not good at the fast running required in interval training, but endurance running came naturally to him. He was an immediate success as a harrier, becoming one of the top runners in the area.

Later, in the fall of 1964, Shorter was glued to the TV watching U.S. distance runners surprise the rest of the world at the Tokyo Olympics. Bob Schul and Bill Dellinger took first and third in the 5,000 meters, and Billy Mills used a fantastic last-lap sprint to beat favored Ron Clarke of Australia and win the 10,000 meters.

"I was inspired by Mills and Schul in '64," Shorter says. "The 53-second last lap Schul ran, with mud flying everywhere on the cinder track, stood out in my mind." Shorter says Dellinger would have won if he had started his kick earlier, a lesson Shorter remembered in races to come. He ended up having a solid career at Mt. Hermon, running a 9:38 two-mile and setting several school records, capped by the New England two-mile prep title in 1965.

Shorter was accepted at Yale, one of the top universities in the U.S. Yale does not offer athletic scholarships, preferring its athletes to instead concentrate on academics. Shorter studied as a pre-medical and psychology major, and he received good grades while running four years on the track and cross-country teams. He was fortunate enough to fall under the tutelage of Bob Geigengack, Yale's longtime track coach. Geigengack, a U.S. Olympic coach, favored a very moderate, long-term approach to training. One of the problems with collegiate distance running in the United States is that college coaches feel pressure to get their athletes to score as many points in meets as possible, because the coaches' salaries and bonuses are usually tied to how well their teams do at conference and national meets. Overworked runners often leave college—and even high school—frustrated and burned-out, with no interest in continuing to train. The careers of many runners end after college at age 22 or 23, a time when runners in Europe are just beginning to develop. Geigengack, however, was one of those rare coaches who sacrificed points at meets to help his athletes' development.

Running complemented Shorter's challenging studies at Yale. "I used to like running after studying or taking tests," he says. "Running was a good release and was the way I relieved stress."

Shorter never went over 50 miles a week in training until midway through his senior year at Yale. One reason is that he had so many other interests, especially skiing. During college, Shorter often took off on weekends for trips to Vermont ski areas. Without pressure from Geigengack to score points immediately in cross-country and indoor and outdoor track, Shorter was free to develop at his own pace. Like Arturo Barrios, former 10,000-meter world-record holder, Shorter had a great post-collegiate career in part because he was undertrained during his university years. He always had the motivation to train and the desire to be good; he just did not know how fast or how far he could run. Geigengack gave him a clue one June day at the end of his junior year, when Shorter stopped in his office just before leaving for the start of summer vacation.

"Coach, how good can I be?" Shorter asked.

Geigengack had long believed that Shorter's smooth stride and efficient running form would make him an ideal marathoner, and he thought, "Good enough to win the Olympic Marathon." But he did not tell Frank that. Instead, he said, "Go on to New Mexico, get your mileage up, and I'll see you in the fall."

That's what Shorter did. His father had taken a job in Taos, a small town of 7,000 in northern New Mexico, famous for its colony of artists and intellectuals. Shorter spent the summer of 1968 in Taos. Though he was raised on the east coast, Shorter has a western-United States mentality: the west that shaped America; the west of independent men and women; the west of vast open spaces, of possibilities limited only by a person's dreams. That summer, Shorter's dream became the Olympics, and he ran more than he ever had before, going on long runs through the sagebrush, gullies, and cliffs that dot the landscape in the Rio Grande valley outside Taos. It was on those solitary runs that Shorter began building his strength and a marathon mentality.

Meeting the Entomologist

Because the 1968 Olympics were being held in Mexico City, the U.S. Olympic Marathon Trials was scheduled in 7,500-foot Alamosa, an hour's drive from Taos. Because it was so close, Shorter decided to give the marathon a try, driving up with his younger brother, Chris. The night before the race, Shorter stopped by the hotel room where top U.S. star, Amby Burfoot, was staying. "Do you have any shoes I can borrow?" Shorter asked. Burfoot gave Shorter a pair of his shoes, which were a size and one-half too small for Frank, and they ended up blistering his feet the next day when Shorter ran one loop of the race before stopping. It was his first marathon attempt, and he came away from it not only with respect for the distance, but also with the belief that perhaps he could run a good marathon one day. Burfoot stopped not long after Shorter did, and the pair stood and watched George Young, Kenny Moore, and Ron Daws make the team.

After putting in roughly 70 miles a week all summer in Taos, Frank returned to Yale for an excellent senior year. He won all but one of his cross-country races in the fall and placed 19th at the NCAA Cross-Country Championships. Once again, he was glued to the TV, watching the Mexico City Olympic track races, admiring Amos Biwott in the steeplechase, Kip Keino in the 1,500 meters, and Naftali Temu in the 10,000. "Maybe in four years, I'll be there on the Olympic track," Shorter thought. He increased his mileage during the Connecticut winter and had his best indoor track season, finishing second in the indoor NCAA three-mile championships. Shorter eyed the outdoor season with optimism, looking to finish his collegiate career on an up note.

A key development in Shorter's career came when Geigengack took the Yale track team to the University of Florida in March of 1969. Shorter had not gone on the trip his first three years of college, because he was off touring with a university singing group called "The Bachelors," which specialized in old, big-band era songs.

Shorter ran a 4:08 mile and 8:52 two-mile double in a dual meet against Florida, but more significantly, he also met Jack Bacheler, one of the best U.S. long-distance runners. The 6-foot, 6-inch, 165-pound Bacheler, a doctoral student in entomology, was one of the few people Shorter looked up to—literally and figuratively. Bacheler and Shorter hit it off immediately. During that week, Bacheler passed along his ideas on training, and he also gave Frank a dose of confidence. Bacheler advised Shorter to boost his mileage, and Shorter did, running 90 miles a week in April and May. In June, he won his first major title, the NCAA six-mile, and he placed second in the three-mile.

"It was a very important race for me because Geigengack would always take anyone who ran well in the NCAA meet to the AAU championships," says Shorter. In the 1969 AAU championships, two weeks after the NCAAs, Shorter finished fourth (the third American) in the six-mile competition. "Kenny Moore just outkicked me for third," Shorter recalls. Bacheler won, but because of his studies, he turned down a spot on the U.S. team going to Europe. Shorter took his place and went on his first international trip, where in London he ran 29:14 in his first 10,000 meters.

Post-Collegiate Running Woes

Shorter returned from Europe with some international experience under his belt but without any visible means of support. Without a European-type club system to help them, most collegiate runners stopped training after their eligibility ended, and they got jobs. A degree from Yale was the blueprint for the American Dream; young graduates were supposed to become doctors, accountants, or lawyers, to get a house in the suburbs with a white picket fence, and to climb the corporate ladder. But Shorter could not stop running, because he knew he had not come close to realizing his potential.

There was something inside Shorter that drove him to find a way to continue training. Because there was no path to follow, he blazed his own. It took courage to pursue something as obscure as running, especially for a graduate of a prestigious school like Yale, while society said, "get a job." What kept Shorter going was the motivation from Geigengack, Bacheler, and others. At the end of his days at Yale, Geigengack called him into his office and told Frank he could be the best runner in the nation. That was the motivation Shorter needed. He had not put in a lot of miles in college, and he had the determination to give running a shot. He just needed to find a place to live and a way to pay the rent.

After returning from Europe, Shorter drifted between Gainesville and Taos. Then he packed his bags and went to live in Albuquerque to start medical school, but it was not to his liking. The way doctors were trained emphasized mountains of memorization, the kind of learning Charles Dickens criticized in *Hard Times* as "facts, facts, nothing but hard facts." The creative, somewhat whimsical Shorter did not fancy that stifling environment, and he left medical school after three months. Uncertain of his future, knowing only that he was going to continue running, Shorter moved back to Taos and worked construction jobs, all the while increasing his mileage until he was hitting 140 miles a week.

The countryside around Taos is some of the most beautiful in the U.S.; there is something in it that has attracted intellectuals from D.H. Lawrence to R.C. Gorman. It is also a lonely land, with long dirt roads that wind through canyons and mesas. It has long forged endurance runners among the Native Americans; it was here that Pueblo Indians ran from village to village in 1680, announcing the revolt that kicked the Spanish out of New Mexico for 30 years. The Indian runners would cover 80 miles a night. Shorter knew those stories and ran like a Native American, skimming across the sagebrush, a kind of new Runner of the Purple Sage. The locals saw the shirtless Frank running through the countryside, all brown from the sun, and they paid him no attention. The artist colony in town had inured them to eccentrics.

It was not all pleasant in Taos, however. One evening, on his standard 10-mile loop outside of town, Shorter came across a group of local hoods, called *pachucos*, trying to drag a woman into their car. Shorter ran by the car and yelled at the thugs, "I've got your license-plate number!" The *pachucos* let the woman go and gave chase to Shorter, who took refuge in a store. But the incident did not end there. The *pachucos* killed the Shorters' family dogs and put sugar in their cars' gas tanks. For several days, Samuel Shorter rode shotgun in a car, covering Frank's backside when he ran.

After five months of running in Taos, Frank said good-bye to his family in March of 1970 and packed up his bags for Florida. Gainesville, with Bacheler and the Florida Track Club, had the best group of runners in the United States. Shorter was still searching for a model on how to approach his post-collegiate career, and he found one in Bacheler, someone as smart and hardworking as he. Shorter considered Bacheler his equal, intellectually and athletically. Bacheler taught Shorter two things: the importance of high mileage and how to enjoy hard training. Shorter, Bacheler, and the rest of the Florida Track Club dominated running in the U.S. during the next three years.

Those salad days in Florida were difficult. There were no stipends, no free shoes, no contracts. Shorter had to fend for himself on little money, supported in part by his wife, Louise, whom he had met skiing on Taos Mountain. Running was Shorter's life; all he did was sleep, eat, and train. When he got to Gainesville, Shorter was "cocky," thinking, "I'm going to run all these miles and get real good, and the times are going to plummet. Then I realized that I was going to have to take an attitude where I pace myself in training," Shorter told John Parker in *The Frank Shorter Story*. "Even though I'm training hard, there's a pace that goes over the whole season. It's learning to pace yourself and to take things in perspective—different races, different days, and how you're going to be on those days. And not to expect everything."

Training with Bacheler, Parker, and the Florida Track Club was key for his development, and Shorter still advises people wanting to make it as elite runners to find the best runners possible and run with them, just as he did. "Frank and that constellation of guys in Florida fed off each other and inspired each other to possibilities," says Kenny Moore.

Shorter did not change his workouts much after college; he just got faster and better at them. Occasionally, he and Bacheler would hook up for interval sessions, but they often did their workouts separately. Bacheler liked to be out the door by 7 AM, while Shorter's "morning" run would invariably come sometime closer to 11 AM. It was more of a brunch run than a morning run.

Cold War Running

In the summer of 1970, Shorter experienced a breakthrough , when he won the 10,000 meters in the USSR-U.S. dual meet in Leningrad by a big margin, getting him featured on the cover of *Sports Illustrated*. "I didn't realize at the time what a big deal it was [to be on the cover]," Shorter said. Later that summer, he won another 10,000-meter event in Oslo, beating Ron Clarke in what was to be the Australian great's last race. In the preceding weeks, Clarke had run a 10,000-meter event in Edinburgh in 28:13, clocked 13:32 for a 5,000, then raced against Belgian Emiel Puttemans, who, like Shorter, was at the start of a fine career. Though Clarke was tired by the time he hooked up with Shorter, nobody expected the young American to defeat the Australian star. But Shorter did, beating Clarke at his own game—making an early surge to the front and pressing the pace. Clarke hung with Shorter for two miles, until Frank started steadily pulling away. Clarke never dropped out of a race, and he did not this time, although he was tempted to quit. Seeing that he had no chance of catching Shorter, Clarke did pack it in on the final few laps of the last race of his career, finishing sixth, 27 seconds behind Shorter's 28:33. It was a symbolic changing of the guard. Clarke, a multi-world-record holder who was the most consistent runner of the 1960s, was a link back to the 1950s, having raced against stars such as miler John Landy. Now, Clarke had been soundly beaten by the up-and-coming American who was to become the star of the 1970s. Shorter had Clarke's doggedness and ability to put in a mid-race surge. He was faster than Clarke over the shorter distances, and he was developing a good kick on top of it.

Traveling the European track circuit and "paying his dues" was another key for Shorter's development. What is needed to be a champion, Shorter believes, is sometimes putting yourself at risk in races.

You have to go out there and find out who the best people are. It's really that simple, and nothing more complicated than that. We went overseas, and we had meets in which we had to peak as if everyone in the world was there, because they *were* there.

In the fall of 1970, Shorter went to Chicago and demolished the field by winning the AAU National Cross-Country Championships, the first of his five straight cross-country titles. A month later, he won the São Silvestre race in São Paulo, Brazil. Always analytical, Shorter decided he needed to live at a high altitude to get the most out of his training. He did some research and discovered that Boulder, Colorado, was the only city in the United States above 5,000 feet that had an indoor track. (Of course it helped that Louise was in Boulder attending the University of Colorado.) Shorter went there that winter and liked it; in February 1971, he set his first American record, clocking 8:22.2 for two miles.

He then went back to Gainesville, where he enrolled in the University of Florida law school. Parker tells us Shorter "was becoming famous for one workout which consisted of 15 fast quarters [62-63] with lung-searing short rests" of less than a 50-yard jog. Besides all the great training, there was another benefit to living in Florida: "That was when I started thinking seriously about the marathon. I remember starting to talk about it on training runs. I did not envision running it especially well, although my training and body type seemed to be suited to it," Shorter said. He would get his chance at the marathon that spring at the trials race for the Pan-American Games.

Although he is best known for his Olympic Marathon medals, Shorter always considered himself first and foremost a track runner. He did not change his basic training when he decided to try the marathon, but he did increase his mileage. Before heading to Eugene for the trials, Shorter ran a fast three miles at the Kennedy Games in Berkeley, clocking 13:31. Before tackling the marathon the following day, Shorter said that anything under 2:20 would be the encouragement he needed to pursue the distance. He got the encouragement he needed and qualified for the Pan-American team by running 2:17 and finishing second to his good friend Kenny Moore. Turning to Moore around the 20-mile mark, Shorter said, in one of running's great lines, "Why couldn't Pheidippides have died at 20 miles?" (Pheidippides is the Greek messenger who reportedly ran from the battle of Marathon to Athens to bring news of the Greek defeat of the Persians. After saying, "Rejoice, we have conquered," he keeled over, dead.) Shorter, who had never run over 20 miles "was in unchartered territory and feeling bad." The last five miles were a struggle.

1971 Pan-American Games—Planting the Seeds

Cali, the second largest city in Colombia, sits in a fertile green valley. Locals have a saying, "The land is so fertile that if you drop a coin in the soil, a money tree will spring up." Shorter won gold medals there in the 10,000 meters and the marathon in very hot conditions; these victories planted the seed for an Olympic medal the following year.

The extremely hot weather in Cali did not bother Shorter; he liked the heat as much as he disliked the rain. In the Pan-American Games Marathon, he started out with the leaders and was feeling fine until five miles, when he began feeling the need to make a pit stop. He kept it in check, but by mile 16, running in the lead with Moore and two Colombian runners (including 1971 Boston Marathon winner Alvaro Mejia), Shorter had to jump in a ditch to relieve himself. While down in the ditch he was passed by a Mexican runner, and when he started running again, Shorter had given up any thoughts of winning. He was thinking he might finish third and get a medal.

After lightening his load, he began clicking off 4:50 miles and, within 20 minutes, could see the leaders. Frank ran as quietly as he could up behind Moore, then yelled out, "Yoo hoo, I'm back!" Not only was Frank back—he was back and gone, putting in a surge that only Moore could go with. At 20 miles, a heat stroke forced Moore out of the race, leaving Shorter to run in for the 2:22:40 win. It was not that difficult, Shorter thought, and from the moment he crossed the finish line in Cali the marathon was his event.

Two gold medals in hand, Frank went back to Gainesville for another semester of law school. Training went well, even though he was living in a broken-down trailer on the edge of town. Those were good days for U.S. distance runners. Says New Zealander Dick Quax, who was making his first trip to the U.S. after breaking 4 minutes for the mile,

> It was an exciting time. . . . There was a real feeling in the United States at the time that they had some good runners coming along. Besides Frank, there were others like Jack Bacheler, Steve Prefontaine, and a lot of very aggressive, very good runners.

Three months after returning from Cali, Shorter was lined up in the Japanese port city of Fukuoka, on the southern-most island of Kyushu. There he would be running against the Japanese national record holder, Akio Usami, a veteran who, in 1969, placed second in 2:11:27 to Derek Clayton's epic 2:08:33.6 world-best run, a mark that stood for 14 years. That time had broken Clayton's own record of 2:09:36.4, set on the same

Fukuoka course where Shorter was racing this windy December day in 1971. Using what he calls his "pull-ahead and press strategy," Shorter ran away from Usami after the turnaround to win in 2:12:51. That was good enough to earn him the number one ranking in the marathon for the year—but it did not do much for his job prospects. There was not much demand for young men with 2 percent body fat who could run 5-minute miles for 26.2 miles. "There was no support of runners at that time," Shorter says.

An Experiment of Three

Frank ran some good indoor races during the winter of 1971-1972, as fast as 8:26 for two miles. With the 1972 Olympic trials looming, Shorter went to 8,000-foot Vail, Colorado, to train, along with buddies Bacheler and Jeff Galloway. They lived solely for training for six weeks, doing some great workouts.

Vail was still undiscovered by the rest of the world, a small ersatz European village surrounded by the 14,000-foot peaks of the Gore Mountain Range and the endless dirt trails of the White River National Forest. It is a beautiful spot, and Shorter made the most of his time there. The majority of his runs were done in Vail valley, flat enough to allow for training runs at a 6-minute pace, even at the high altitude. Shorter, Bacheler, and Galloway put in three runs a day for up to 170 miles a week, which Shorter says is comparable to 200 miles a week at sea level. Vail, says Shorter, was "our laboratory, and we were the experiment." The three runners were "exhilarated with the challenge of riding the line between intensity and excess," and Shorter always felt "in control," he writes in *Olympic Gold*. "Never did I feel I was overdoing it, and still I was convinced that nobody else in the world could have been training that hard. Whether that was true or not, it was one thing that motivated me." Everything revolved around running; a typical day was an 8-mile run in the morning, 4 miles at noon, and intervals in the afternoon for another 11 miles.

According to Kenny Moore,

> When you ask what makes someone great, for Frank it was being attuned to his own strength, understanding what kind of workout increases his racing ability. Frank was perfectly in tune. He had a recuperative rate far, far better than most of us. He could run a 20-miler, get a good night's sleep, and run hard the next day.

That pace would even catch up with Olympians like Moore, but for Shorter, "It was the best thing for him. All of us were in a struggle to find out what worked best for ourselves."

Shorter found that the Vail experiment worked best for him. In June, he was second at the AAU 10,000-meter National Championships with a personal record 28:08, just behind Greg Fredrick's 28:06. Shorter did not go to Europe early in the summer of 1972; instead, he stayed in the States to get ready for the Olympic trials in Eugene.

Shorter won the trials for 10,000 meters in 28:18, and Galloway earned his trip to Munich by placing second. As was to become his trademark in marathons, Shorter used a hard surge in the middle of the trials marathon to kill off the other runners; only Moore was able to go with him. "Frank looked over like he'd like to get rid of me, too," recalls Moore. But Shorter had done 22 miles of Moore's 35-miler just before the trials, and so "probably did not think he could get rid of me," Moore says. "It was a warm day and I started to get a cramp over Franklin Boulevard. Shorter slowed and offered to carry me in." At the finish on the University of Oregon's Hayward Field track, Moore tried to grab Shorter's hand, but Shorter slapped it away. Moore was surprised, but Shorter later explained how he and Bacheler had been reprimanded by officials for intentional tying at the AAU 6-mile championships in 1970. "I still remember the crowd up and yelling, and him hitting my hand," Moore says. The two tied in 2:16:51. Bacheler and Galloway placed third and fourth. The pair came into the finish together, and Galloway let his friend and training partner step over the line first to earn his ticket to Munich.

After the Olympic trials, Shorter went to Europe for a training camp and a series of track races, against Lasse Viren and the other top Europeans. Moore spent three weeks before Munich in the U.S. pre-Olympic training camp in Oslo with Shorter. One day, U.S. coach Bill Bowerman had his distance runners doing 1,200-meter repeats. Says Moore,

Bowerman was timing us and would say, "OK, run this one in 3:21.6," not giving us any splits along the way. The next one might be 3:30, then a 3:14. He was mixing them up, and we hit them all within a second. That was always important to Frank, that sense of knowing what he was doing out there. And it was so much fun to run with him, because he was so smooth.

In Oslo, Shorter ran another workout of 4 × 880 yards with a 220 jog recovery, averaging 2:02.

In a practice meet in Oslo, Shorter also ran 7:51 for 3,000 meters, beating milers such as Rod Dixon. The shocked New Zealander shook his head after the race, saying "I can't believe I got beat by a bloody marathoner." Francesco Arese, an Italian miler, said to Shorter in French, their common language, *"Tu gagnera le marathon"* ("You will win the marathon"). Shorter used those words to build his confidence for his Olympic races.

Munich Olympics

Shorter was in top shape as the Olympics got underway in September, 1972, and he set an American record of 27:58 in his preliminary heat for the 10,000 meters. In the finals, Englishman Dave Bedford took the race out in just under 60 seconds for the first 400 meters before eventually fading. The field was packed in tight as they circled the track below world-record pace. Shorter was running near Viren when Viren tumbled to the track on the 12th lap. The Finn then sprang back up immediately and rejoined the leaders. With two miles remaining, Frank was one of the five runners who had broken away from the pack. With just two laps to go, Shorter was still with Viren, Puttemans, Gammoudi, and Haro. Shorter was a marathoner, and here he was running with the leaders in history's fastest 10,000-meter race. "At that point I was just hanging on. I was just happy to be there."

Shorter could not match the finishing speed of Viren and Puttemans when they accelerated, and he finished fifth in 27:51.4, breaking his American record. The race confirmed Shorter's belief that he was faster—much faster—than anyone he would be lining up against in the marathon a week later. As Shorter was soon to show, speed was going to become a crucial element for anyone wanting to win major marathons.

With the emergence of African athletes in the 1968 Mexico City Olympics, track was becoming a true international sport. The Olympics were also a growing international media event, with the most press credentials in history issued for Munich. Eight Palestinian terrorists took advantage of this world stage in a shocking manner on September 5. It began with a knock on the dorm room of the Israeli athletes. An Israeli wrestler opened the door, saw the terrorists, and tried to hold the door shut. The terrorists shot and killed him and another athlete, then took nine others hostage.

"It was an incredible day, sad day," said Shorter. He and Kenny Moore stood on the balcony of their room and watched the helicopters flying around. Rumors about what was happening spread, and Shorter turned to Moore and said, "It's not over yet." He was right. During a battle at the Munich airport, a policeman, two terrorists, and all nine hostages were killed.

International Olympic Committee (IOC) officials pondered whether to cancel the Olympics entirely, but it decided after a 34-hour delay to hold a memorial service for the Israelis in the Olympic Stadium and to let the games continue. "We went through stages on what to do," said Shorter. "My first response was, 'Nothing is worth the loss of human life.' Then I thought that by stopping the games we'd be doing exactly what the terrorists wanted."

When the marathoners lined up on the track for the start of their race, Shorter was still unknown to the general public, despite his fast track times and American records. The U.S. networks would not broadcast a race unless there was a good chance an American would do well in it. ABC took a chance at Munich and centered its marathon coverage on Shorter, because of his Fukuoka win the year before. The competitors included Derek Clayton, the strong Australian world-record holder. Ron Hill was another favorite; he had run 2:09:28 to win the Edinburgh Commonwealth Games gold medal in 1970; he had also won Boston in 1970 in a course record 2:10:30.

Perhaps the personalities of Hill and Clayton prevented them from winning. Some runners, like Shorter, are clutch performers, able to relax, concentrate, and get the most out of themselves when it counts. Others let the pressure get to them. When the tragedy of the slain Israeli athletes unfolded, Shorter, though shaken by the killings, remained confident in his training. Hill, however, thought the delay would ruin his chances—and because he thought so, it did. Shorter saw this when the two had dinner one night before the race. "He was ranting and raving about how he needed to run on the day planned for," Shorter recalls. "I said, 'Ron, you've been training for four years. One more day isn't going to make a difference.' And I said to myself right then that he was not going to be a factor."

The colorful Englishman came to the starting line wearing a space-age racing outfit, made out of thin, metallic material, and he wore the thinnest shoes Shorter had ever seen. Hill even cut the tongue out to save weight. Hill, a chemist by trade, is a bit of a fanatic about running. He has the world's longest streak of consecutive days run. Through 1995, his streak was up over 30 years and included days when he hobbled a mile on crutches.

Shorter had an advantage over his competitors in addition to his superior track speed. Though he had been ranked number one in the world the previous year, only Usami and Moore had experienced first-hand Shorter's ability to break open a marathon with a mid-race surge. The others, to their surprise, would soon see it, and would not be ready to respond.

The marathon started with two laps on the track before heading out into the streets. Shorter led with a 72-second first lap before an Argentine runner took the lead. The runners poured outside the stadium, where Shorter was cut off by a TV truck, forcing him to drop 30 feet behind the leaders. After pounding on the back of the truck, Shorter caught up to the pack and stayed in the middle of it in the early miles, monitoring his pace. He felt good and remained confident in his fitness, even when the powerful Clayton took the lead.

Just as with Hill, there is something in Shorter's makeup that set him apart from Clayton. A story that gives an idea of Clayton's personality is one he tells when speaking at prerace clinics. Clayton relates how during a race, he missed his drink at an aid station. A Japanese competitor running alongside graciously offered Clayton his own bottle. After taking some of the drink, Clayton began to hand it back to the Japanese runner. Suddenly, he changed his mind. Instead of giving it back to the Japanese runner, Clayton turned and threw the bottle off to the side of the road. Clayton was proud of that, and of the fact that he trained so hard that he would sometimes be "pissing blood." Lots of runners train hard, but only the select few are able to put it together when it counts.

The leaders passed 5K in 15:19. Erich Segal, one of Shorter's professors at Yale and author of *Love Story*, had been hired to do TV commentating because he had run some marathons. At 8 miles, Segal said, "Frank Shorter looks like he always looks, not haggard, up on his toes." One of Shorter's talents was his almost preternatural ability to judge pace. Just past 9 miles, Shorter felt the leaders slowing, but rather than be prudent and slow with them to stay with the pack, he kept running at his same pace, letting his momentum carry him into the lead. He kept going and no one went with him. "I knew that I was faster on the track and faster in the mile than the others, and figured I would surprise them," Shorter explains.

> I did not think they could run anaerobically off a good, hard pace. I raced on the track, and knew Hill and Clayton did not. My strength was to go into debt and not to have a steady pace. If they had gone with me, I would have tried it again. Their mistake, really, was not finding out how I ran. I read magazines and knew everything about those guys.

The exact timing of his break was not planned beforehand. "It's not that intellectual. It's more instinctive," Shorter says.

> I think you just do it. . . . When someone makes that jump, you just react instinctively. If your reaction in the Olympics is such

that you even think about whether you're going to go, it's too late. It's like practicing starts.

When he broke away, Shorter just tried to run as fast as he could without going over the edge.

You have your own strategy and what you do is go out and use it, and structure the situation so everyone else is forced to use your strategy . . . it really is a control issue. You are trying in whatever way to control what is going on in the race. To employ those kinds of tactics, you have to have the physical capabilities to be right up there with everyone else. In other words, you don't trick anyone. If there are five people of equal abilities, it is just who can compete in the situation in such a way that makes everyone pursue the event at that moment in the way that most suits you. . . . I don't think you rehearse it. I think it's more an instinctive thing. Every individual differs on how to do it. At that point, I was still a mystery.

Shorter kept pressing the pace, and it was soon too late for Clayton and the others. Shorter built his lead to over a minute by halfway, and journalists in the press truck helped Frank by telling him how far in front he was. Shorter began figuring that the others would have to run sub-5 minute miles to catch him. Though he was hurting, Shorter continued running hard, not relaxing until he reached the stadium.

"Frank knew how to pace himself perfectly," says Moore.

Once he got the lead he never backed off. He knew exactly how hard a push to make. That self-knowledge in training and racing, and what to do in given workouts, is all in the same category. Frank was enormously gifted, with a certain rationality about himself.

For most runners, says Moore, goals tend to interfere with a clear-eyed assessment of what they can do.

"By God I'm going to run this pace," they say. Frank had a rational judgment of what he could do. If he had a cold, or was busy in law school, he was always able to make a judgment not to kill himself and stay healthy.

Johnny Hayes was not the first one in the stadium when he won the Olympic Marathon for the U.S. in 1908, and neither was Shorter when he entered the stadium for his final lap in 1972. Hayes actually crossed the line second, but the winner, Italian Dorando Pietri, was disqualified for getting help from officials on the track. (Pietri had collapsed several times in the stadium and had to be helped up. He finished in 2:54:46 but Hayes won the gold with his 2:55.18.4. That is the first "noteworthy performance" in the marathon record book counted by the IAAF. The U.S. also took the bronze in 1908, with Joseph Forshaw clocking 2:57:10, while Pietri was awarded a "special medal" for nearly dying in the race.)

Shorter ran through the tunnel and into the Olympic Stadium expecting the cheers of the crowd, but those cheers had been given out a few minutes earlier to a young German impostor who ran onto the track, fooling officials and fans. The cheers for the impostor quickly turned to whistles when the crowd discovered the first man on the track was not the winner and had not run the 42 kilometers. Anyone who watched the race on TV will never forget the strident voice of ABC commentator Segal, yelling

> That's not Frank! That's not Frank. It's an impostor! Get that guy off the track! How can this can happen in the Olympic Games? It's bush league, get rid of that guy; there is Frank Shorter; that's Frank; come on, Frank, you won it. I wonder what Frank Shorter is thinking.

The baffled Shorter was thinking, "I know I'm American, but this is ridiculous," referring to what he thought was the crowd's anti-American sentiment. Shorter had not seen the impostor, dressed in shorts and a T-shirt, steal his applause by taking a lap around the track. Shorter finished in 2:12:20, and his win broke the streak of three consecutive Olympic Marathon wins by Ethiopians—Abebe Bikila in 1960 and 1964 and Mamo Wolde in 1968—and just missed Bikila's Olympic record. Karel Lismont of Belgium was second, followed by Wolde and Kenny Moore.

After the Munich games, things would change drastically, but when Shorter won the Olympics, running was still an amateur sport. Athletes trained hard in order to win the race, with no thought of what was to come, says Shorter.

> Part of the ability to win big races is that you truly are thinking only up to the finish line, and not worried about what's going to happen. At that time, it was less of a problem, because there was not all the money afterwards, and you did not have to have all the pressure wondering what was going to happen and what the consequences were going to be. What I notice about the Olympics now, part of the human interest aspect of it, implied or overt, is the kind of loss of future income that comes from a failure or for not winning. It's so apparent now. The Olympics are seen as

an opportunity to get financial security; at Munich, that was not how the Olympics were viewed. The goal was to be the best in the world on that particular day.

And on that day in Munich, Shorter was indeed the best in the world. Immediately upon crossing the line, Shorter put his hands on his head and shook it, as if to say, "It is over." But in reality, a new era was just starting for Shorter and for running. He was the Olympic champion, the best marathoner in the world. That was good for his motivation and reputation, and it got him to any race he wanted to go; it did not, however, help to feed him and Louise. The problem the triumphant Shorter faced upon returning home was how to support himself in a way that would allow him to keep on training.

Training was not a problem immediately after Munich because Shorter was too busy to do much running. He went to Middletown for a parade and "Frank Shorter Day," and he was presented with a key to the town. He gave out scores of interviews, including one to *Life* magazine. All the publicity made Shorter a household name. Americans love sports heroes, and Shorter received acclaim as the best marathoner in the world.

A Farewell to the Old Era

The most immediate benefit coming from Shorter's win was that it legitimized his running. Now, when asked what he did, Frank could say "I'm a marathon runner" and not get pelted with tomatoes and laughed out of town. Munich made him respectable in society's eyes. "There was a purpose behind it now, something to be gained," he said. "The victory took the stamp of eccentricity off me. I was a real athlete. My running had been looked upon as a diversion before."

Law school in Florida, to which he returned that fall, was the real diversion. Shorter went back not because he especially wanted to be a lawyer, but because being in school gave him time to train. Shorter was the best in the world, and he proved it again by defending his Fukuoka Marathon title in December 1972, the second consecutive win at what was then the top marathon in the world outside of the Olympics.

With no pressure on him, Shorter went to Fukuoka, deciding that he would go for the world record if the conditions were right. Unfortunately they were not, and the runners had to head into a stiff wind for both the first six and final six miles. Shorter still took a shot at Clayton's record. Leaving the field behind, Shorter passed the turnaround cone in 1:03:36, feeling great. But he had to run by himself the second half,

American Marathoning Tradition

The United States did have a couple of good marathoners after Johnny Hayes; two Americans set marathon world records. In 1925, Albert Michelsen became the first person to break 2:30 when he ran 2:29:01 in Port Chester, breaking the great Hannes Kolehmainen's record set at the 1920 Antwerp Olympic Games. (Clarence DeMar, the bronze medalist in the 1924 Games who would go on to win the Boston Marathon several times, was second in that race.)

In 1963, Leonard "Buddy" Edelen ran a 2:14:28 world best at the Windsor-to-Chiswick Polytechnic race, a course on which six world records have been set.

slowing his pace. He still ran 2:10:30, a new U.S. record and the third-fastest ever, behind Clayton and Ron Hill. Without the wind, and with some competition, Shorter believes he would have been near 2:09 or below.

But 2:10:30 would be the fastest Shorter ever ran. He never raced on a fast course when he was fit and the conditions were just right. "To set the record, you need a perfect day, and you have to have planned perfectly." Frank never got that perfect day, at Rotterdam or Boston. But it does not bother him. "There's serendipity involved," Shorter wrote. "I needed to extend myself [at Fukuoka] and discovered that with victory in hand, running at maximum effort becomes very difficult. Without some company in the difficult miles, the body's mission becomes lonely and dark."

Shorter's first TV guest appearance came in February, when he appeared on Johnny Carson's *Tonight Show*, the most popular talk show in the United States. Kenyan great Kip Keino was in the audience, having come to Los Angeles to compete in a meet. When Carson pointed him out, Keino climbed up on stage with Shorter. That was the first indication, Shorter says, that the repercussions of his gold medal were to be far-reaching, and of the big role TV would have in spreading the gospel of running. "People had started to come up to me and say that they'd seen the telecast of the Olympic Marathon and that they, too, were now running."

Shorter's Fukuoka wins made him a cult figure in Japan. People would cheer him as he ran down the streets by yelling out, "Shorter-san, Shorter-san." In 1973, he won the Mainichi Marathon in Japan. Early on, he had to make a pit stop behind a building, where he was caught with his pants down by a giggling course marshal, who took his photograph. Shorter pulled up his shorts, grabbed the camera and smashed it on to the ground. He lost a minute to the pack, but within two miles he had caught the leader, John Vitale of the U.S., and went on to a 2:12:03 win. Apologetic officials gave him the film. What Shorter learned from that race, he writes, was "how suddenly aggressive I could become, not unlike the aggression all runners suddenly feel when their concentration and peace of mind are broken by a threatening dog or motorist."

In 1974, Shorter went to Europe for his last semester of law school in Cambridge, England, and Warsaw, Poland. He was able to run some track races while studying there. Turning the corner into 1975, Shorter was fitter than ever, and he got ready to defend his Olympic title.

He nearly did not get the chance, however. Shorter was called to testify before a presidential commission about the archaic amateur rules under which athletes were forced to compete. Shorter was blunt in telling the commission that under-the-table payments were made to top runners. Eastern Bloc nations asked the IAAF to investigate the testimony. For a while, there were rumors that Shorter would be declared a professional and be unable to run in Montreal.

With his law degree in hand, Shorter went to work for a Boulder law firm headed by Joe French and Bob Stone. Both were longtime runners and gave Shorter the flexibility to work and train. French, an easygoing man with a shrewd mind, helped Shorter "clarify" his statements so that the AAU could report back to the IAAF that Frank was indeed still an "amateur." (Stone later helped Shorter set up the "TAC Trust" that allowed runners for the first time to openly get paid.) What Shorter would run up against in Montreal was an athlete who was indeed a professional, and who had the full backing of his government behind him. Shorter, meanwhile, continued training the best way he knew—by himself.

Shorter On Training

Garry Bjorklund says about Shorter that, "It's not uncommon to come across a cross-country runner; it's not uncommon to come across a track runner; and it's not uncommon to come across a road runner. But to find that mix of all three [in one person] is special." Shorter is a natural-born runner, but it was his training that made him into something special.

Running at its core, says Shorter, is really pretty basic; if you train well and hard over a period of years and avoid injury, you are going to get better. Throughout his career, Shorter considered himself a track runner, and he trained like a track runner, adding a long run to his weekly schedule as he moved up to the marathon. His philosophy of training was very basic when he was the best marathoner in the world:

> I've always had a simple view of training for distance running: two hard interval sessions a week and one long run—20 miles or two hours, whichever comes first. Every other run is aerobic, and you do as much of that for volume as you can handle. Do this for two or three years, and you'll get good.

It sounds easy, but it is hard to follow for years. Shorter followed that program for so many years that, even counting time off for injuries that came after Montreal, he still averaged 17 miles a day, every day, for the entire decade of the 1970s.

Except for Sundays, Shorter ran 7-10 miles every morning, with a workout or recovery run in the afternoon, for a total of between 16 and 20 miles a day. His long run was his standard 10-mile loop, run twice. He would run the first loop at a 6-minute pace, and the second often at close to a 5-minute pace or faster. He was strong enough to follow this with intervals the next day. Shorter was always able to gauge his body well enough to train just below his limit, red-lining it in a sense, so that he could do as much as possible without overdoing it. "It doesn't do any good to train 30 miles a day and get injured."

Shorter needed 10 hours sleep a night when training at a high level, and if he did not get it, his training suffered. Shorter's ritual before going out for one of his twice-daily training runs was taping his feet. He had weak arches, and he was amazed his feet held up for as long as they did. He was well-known in the University of Colorado training rooms, where he would sometimes go for taping, seemingly using as much tape as the football team's offensive line.

Shorter's weekly training schedule included:

Sunday:	Long run; 2 hours or 20 miles, whichever came first. It was usually 20 miles.
Monday:	A.M., 7-10 miles easy; P.M., 3 miles of 400- or 800-meter repeats. 20 miles total.
Tuesday:	Two easy runs. Total 16-20 miles.

Wednesday:	A.M., 7-10 miles easy; P.M., 400-meter intervals or a ladder consisting of 1 × 1600, 1 × 1200, 1 × 800, 2 × 400, 4 × 200 (meters).
Thursday:	Two easy runs.
Friday:	Two easy runs.
Saturday:	Race. Shorter would still get in 14-18 miles. Or, if not racing, 16 × 200 meters averaging 28.5 with a 200 jog.

Shorter was methodical in his training and differentiated in extremes between his hard days and his easy days. "What really separated Frank from the other good runners was his mental edge, in workouts and in races," sometime training partner Pablo Vigil said. Shorter ran his intervals hard from the first repeat; there was no easing into a hard session, or saving himself for the last 400. His recovery between each repeat was short and quick. Shorter would finish his interval sessions exhausted, feeling like he could not do another repeat.

Shorter always knew what pace he was running, down to within a half-second for 400 meters. As he finished a 400 during an interval workout, he could say, "That was 66.5," without looking at his watch, and be right within a tenth of a second.

Shorter would also run with a variety of people, recalls Louise Shorter.

His sense of fair play was very evident. When he'd train with Pre, Jack [Bacheler], or Marty [Liquori], it was never cutthroat. I never heard Frank say he hated someone, and he never got up by putting someone else down. He was always excellent at analyzing what he was good at and what his opponents were good at, and he'd devise a training program to help him beat them.

On his easy days, Shorter went very easy, running with people of all abilities, being careful not to get caught up running with those who wanted to drop him to prove something. When running with a group, according to Shorter, "You go as slow as the slowest person you're running with. If someone doesn't like that, they should find another group." Shorter was always good about giving advice to the young runners who flocked to him for tips, and he would take time to help the local prep runners. "He'd come and run with the team, and give them talks. He's a great guy," said Boulder High School coach Andy Aiken.

Many runners never discover what a recovery day means. When young runners went with Shorter, they were often surprised how slowly they would go, and how joggers would pass them. They kept expecting the pace to pick up, but it never did.

There was no training through races for Shorter. Like de Castella, when he showed up at a start line, he gave it everything he had. "I remember a cross-country race," says Bjorklund, "where I had Frank beat. Then he came back on me in the last 100 meters and somehow pulled it out. Only the champions have that." Adds Vigil, "Frank ran his intervals like he was racing; he just would not give up."

Another key to a long career, Shorter says, is that "You train best where you are the happiest." A good training situation leads to consistency, which is crucial to reaching your potential. Shorter trained most of his competitive career at altitude for two reasons: He liked living in the mountains, and he wanted to do everything possible to give himself an advantage over his competitors. That idea came from Geigengack, his coach at Yale who was an assistant Olympic coach at the 1968 Lake Tahoe Olympic track trials where Shorter saw how many of the altitude-trained athletes ran personal bests.

Many people know what it takes to be a good or even great runner. But the point comes when theory is merely words floating in the ozone: You have to lace up the shoes and go out the door. Shorter was never one who needed a push to get out and run. He would train with others, but he did the bulk of his running by himself. Louise recalls days when he was bedridden with the flu or a fever, and nevertheless would still go out the door and train. "Getting sick never stopped Frank from training," she said.

Shorter was always consistent. One dark and cold Colorado winter night, when the temperature was far below zero, he arrived home after skiing all day in Taos, and driving for six hours home over ice-laden highways. It was nearly 11 p.m., yet he put on his shoes, took a drink of water, and went out the door for a 10-mile run, his second of the day.

Another time, Shorter took Steve Prefontaine skiing at Taos. Afterwards, they went out for a 10-miler in a harsh blizzard, with wind and snow blowing in their faces. When Prefontaine remarked how tough the conditions were, Shorter replied, "No one in the world is training as hard as we are right now."

1975: Rounding the Corner

In February 1975, Shorter had his first race against Bill Rodgers at the World Cross-Country trials in Gainesville, beating him by 30 seconds in the start of what would become one of running's biggest rivalries. At the World Cross-Country Championships in Rabat, Morocco, Rodgers turned the tables, finishing third, while Shorter was 20th. Early in the race, Shorter passed Emiel Puttemans, "the Belgian Gardener," who was slowed by a cramp. "Too bad," Shorter said as he ran past. Near the end of the race, Puttemans re-passed Frank, saying as he went by, "Too bad."

The World Cross-Country Championships were also the first time Shorter faced Waldemar Cierpinski of East Germany. Frank did not know him at the time, but he certainly would a year and one-half later at the 1976 Olympics.

Shorter liked cross-country running. One of his favorite races was the Cinque Mulini, in Milan, Italy, that goes through five barns. One year at that race, Shorter was in a dogfight with another runner. After passing through one of the five barns, Shorter grabbed the door as he went by, closing it on the other runner.

Shorter was, says Moore "wonderful in cross-country. He always knew how to run within himself. Frank was the 'Great Picker-Offer,' because if someone went out too hard early and was ahead of him, he'd get them." Shorter showed his versatility by winning his five consecutive national cross-country titles.

In the spring of 1975, Shorter was racing even faster than he had before Munich. He and Louise packed up all their belongings and moved from Florida to Colorado. The move meant Shorter trained very little for a month. Then he was asked by Prefontaine to race in Oregon. "I hadn't been planning on running, but when Lasse Viren pulled out, Pre called me up and asked me to run. I said sure," Shorter says. Shorter, Prefontaine, and other top U.S. runners had "a spirit of being willing to go anywhere, at anytime, to race anyone." A year earlier at Hayward, Shorter, not expecting much, ran 12:51.8 for three miles, pushing Prefontaine to an American record of 12:51.4. Shorter had a 10-yard lead with 220 yards to go before Prefontaine ran him down.

Shorter and Prefontaine were good friends, often talking about their careers and the need to make changes in the way their sport was run. Prefontaine, who had placed fourth in the 5,000 meters behind Viren in the Munich Olympics, was training as hard as Shorter. But tragedy struck when Prefontaine, age 24, was tragically killed in a car accident. Shorter was the last person to see Prefontaine. "We went to a party that night, and Steve dropped me off. We talked, then said good-bye and he drove off." Prefontaine remains almost a cult figure for young American runners, who admire his rebelliousness and hard racing.

In Europe during the summer of 1975, Shorter ran a 10,000-meter race against Brendan Foster in London's Crystal Palace. When the pacemaker was unable to set a fast enough pace, Shorter took over the lead for two miles before Foster went by and grabbed a 10-meter lead. But Shorter came back on him, running the final 400 in 57 seconds and coming hard on Foster down the final straightaway. Shorter finished in 27:46.0 just behind Foster.

"Brendan, if the race was three yards longer, I would have caught you," Shorter told Foster afterwards.

"But Frank, I beat you," Foster replied.

"I've always remembered that," Shorter says. "That's it. You can't rationalize performance."

That race was one of the deepest 10,000 meters in history, with five runners under 28 minutes. Off that race, Brendan Foster was ranked number one in the world for 10,000 meters; Shorter was number two.

"I can distinctly remember coming down the last straightaway. I was gaining, but I knew I was not going to catch Brendan. Just then, I was already trying to think of what to do to beat him next time." Shorter worked on his strategy by judiciously using his training log, which he began keeping in 1970. His detailed log was on white, lined notebook paper. Shorter ran best when he had the most faith in his training schedule, and he used his log "for psychological reinforcement. Numbers don't lie. You always seem to remember your workouts as being a little better than they were. It's good to go back and review what you do."

After returning from his race against Foster, Shorter ran a workout of 10 × 400 meters in 62 seconds. "You do that, and you know you are in shape. It's as much for psychological reinforcement. You can't talk yourself into shape. Either you can do it or you can't."

Shorter was known for his streaks of never missing a day of running during the 1970s. Shorter says he has what he calls "a runner's personality," having a need to exercise and do "obligatory" runs. "You can be compulsive until your first big orthopedic injury. Once you have that, you begin to think more."

To find out how good a runner is, ask the competition what they think of him, says Shorter. The Europeans, Africans, and South Americans respected Shorter, and they knew he would be extremely difficult to beat in any race.

How they view you and what they think about you gives a good indication of what a runner's potential is. If someone is not considered a threat, then he probably won't be a threat. I've always been flattered that [New Zealander] Jack Foster, in his book, said I was the only person he never really thought he could beat. I took that as the ultimate compliment from a peer, whether it was true or not.

That psychological edge over opponents "is not something you do consciously. That's just the way things evolve." For Shorter, the psychological advantage over his competitors evolved out of his training. He trained in such a way that he could win from the front, with a mid-race surge, or with a kick. Even during his peak marathon years he was always working on his speed.

Shorter remained the top U.S. runner heading into the Montreal Olympics. In addition to his fast 10,000 against Foster, he clocked 13:29.6 for 5,000 meters. He had won Fukuoka again in 1974 and 1975, and was dominant on the roads.

During the winter of 1975-1976, he ran up to 170 miles a week to get ready for the U.S. Olympic trials, intending to double, as he did in Munich. The trials were again held in Eugene, and Shorter won a great 10,000 meters. Four runners were in the front: Shorter, Rodgers, Garry Bjorklund, and Craig Virgin. When Bjorklund lost his left shoe at four miles, the track-savvy crowd at Eugene's Hayward Field began chanting "BJ, BJ." Bjorklund caught Rodgers in the last 100 meters to make the team in third place, while Shorter pulled away from Virgin with a 60-second last lap to win it in 27:55.6.

Shorter says he really peaked only three times in his long career: the Munich and Montreal Olympic Games, and the 1976 Olympic Marathon Trials race. In the marathon trials, Shorter and Rodgers dropped the rest of the field at eight miles. Running together, they decided to conserve their strength and finish in a tie. But at 24 miles, Rodgers dropped back, and Shorter went on for the win. "My race was the Olympic Trials," Shorter said.

Montreal Olympics

Shorter decided to concentrate on the marathon and not run the Olympic 10,000 meters. He came to Montreal as prepared as he could be, despite a sore ankle that bothered him after the trials. But even the most careful preparation can go for naught, as Shorter experienced when the soles of his custom-made shoes came unglued and began flapping about while he was warming up for the marathon. When the other runners were called to the track for the start, Shorter had to continue waiting inside the stadium for a new pair of shoes to arrive. Top U.S. runner Steve Flanagan, who was staying at Shorter's house in Boulder while Frank was in Montreal, had sent a backup pair via express mail.

But it was five minutes until the start of the Olympic Marathon, and Shorter still did not have any shoes. Frank, however, did not worry. The attitude he carried throughout his career was that things would somehow work out. And they did, as the shoes showed up, and Shorter put them on and dashed out onto the track where the others were waiting.

Unlike at Munich, Shorter was the heavy favorite in Montreal, and when the race started, the others waited to see when he was going to go. Frank had considered making an early break. But once out on the track, waiting for the gun to start the marathon, he looked up in the sky and saw a soft rain beginning to fall out of the Canadian sky. Rain was not good for Shorter, and he had a change of plans; he decided to hold back and see how the race developed.

Shorter used his reputation to his advantage, controlling the race from the back. The other competitors, keying off Shorter, wondered when he was going to take off. There are two ways to run the marathon, Shorter says:

> The lets-see-if-we-can-go-out-hard strategy, vs. the I-know-I-can-come-from-behind strategy. If you're going for the gold, you run in the first group; if you're going for a medal, you run in the second group. Someone from the lead pack will win, with the others coming from behind. The gold medal comes from the front. You have to be there.

Shorter stayed in the front group in the early going. One of those watching Shorter was Lasse Viren. Having won the Olympic 5,000 and 10,000 meters for the second time, the Finn was going for his third gold of the games. He had been told by his coach to do everything Shorter did, a strategy that was obvious to Frank. "I hid from Lasse," he explains. Shorter made a game out of it, sometimes dropping back in the large pack and watching Viren look anxiously around for him. "Lasse was never a factor in the marathon. He was too depleted."

When Shorter's break finally came, at 21 kilometers, the move seemed planned out, but once again, Shorter says it simply felt like the best time to surge. "When you are really successful you have an aura about you that makes opponents not only a little bit wary of you, but makes them a little bit afraid of you, and consider you a threat," said Shorter. The other runners at Montreal watched him and waited for him to make the move they all knew was coming. It was a question of when it would happen and if they would be fit enough to respond to it.

Once committed, Shorter pushed the pace as hard as he could without going over the edge, just as he did in Munich. For a mile, it seemed to be working, as Shorter opened up a gap and looked to be on his way to repeating. But then a white-vested figure separated himself from the trailing pack and appeared in the rain behind Shorter. Soon, he was running next to Shorter. Frank looked over but did not know who it was. "I thought it was Carlos Lopes," he said. It was instead Waldemar Cierpinski of East Germany, and he and Shorter continued through the rain, drawing away from the pack. Rodgers fell back, as did Canada's Jerome Drayton. No one was going to catch Shorter and Cierpinski, and it was now a two-man race for the gold.

"If you have a weak spot, the marathon will let you know," Shorter says. His weak spot was the rain, as the marathon was reminding him by the 30-kilometer mark. "Evidence shows that body temperatures can indeed fall during marathons run under inclement conditions, and athletes like Shorter are particularly prone to this hypothermia because of their low body fat and muscle contents," one researcher wrote.

Shorter was so focused that he did not pay any attention to the rain once the race started. But his stride was noticeably tighter, and Shorter could not respond when Cierpinski counter-surged, eventually opening up a minute lead. Shorter bore down and tried to make a run for Cierpinski, but the East German was too strong this day. Shorter ran in for his silver medal. In the stadium, Cierpinski ran an extra lap around the track, and Shorter was waiting to greet him at the finish. "I did everything right. The strategy was right; there was nothing wrong with the strategy," Shorter said. "And actually there was nothing wrong with the timing, when I went, or anything like that. I just did not beat one guy." Typical was the response of one fan, who said, "Cierpinski beat him, but that's OK. He's still Frank."

And being Frank means having a unique spot in track annals, says Kenny Moore, who missed making a third Olympic team because he got sick just before the trials.

> Shorter is up there among the very best. If it had been a warm day in Montreal, Frank would be a double Olympic champion. Frank was ready to run 2:08 or 2:07 there. He was doing beautiful training beforehand. His long runs and his rhythm runs were at 4:48, 4:50 pace. Not to take anything away from Cierpinski, but it was unfortunate for Frank that it was raining. I've never seen him run any braver than he did in Montreal.

What Shorter did not know at the time was that he was running the Olympic Marathon on a broken ankle, something that affected him as much as the rain. "I think it was really more a factor that my foot was broken. I think my conditioning was a little off. Between the Olympic Trials and the Games I was not really able to train that well because of my ankle."

Shorter broke it in February on the indoor track at the University of Colorado. The eight-lap to a mile indoor track at UC's venerable Balch Fieldhouse was built in 1937 and was not in the best of shape; Shorter thinks he broke his ankle running around its turns. The pain started as slight bursa, which Shorter ran through.

With the wisdom of hindsight, Shorter says he should have taken time off in the spring of 1976, but he was the defending Olympic champ, in great shape and trying to increase his fitness before the Olympics. So he kept on running. "I can stand abuse better than just about anybody. I wish the injury had been acute; I wish it had happened all at once so I could not run, then I would have had the operation right then, and I wouldn't have had the deterioration I have now," he later told journalist Eric Olson in *The Runner*.

When asked after the Montreal Marathon if he would keep going for a third Olympic medal, Shorter replied, "If I can get in a situation that will allow me to keep on training."

A New Era In Running

Shorter created that situation by pioneering a breakthrough for elite runners. It took him until 1979, but after much negotiation, he was able set up the first commercial endorsement approved by the International Olympic Committee (IOC), with Hilton Hotels. Shorter forever changed the landscape of running when he signed a two-year deal with Hilton to do TV commercials. It was a move as important in running history as his gold medal. For the first time, after nearly 100 years of solitude, a long-distance runner could openly get paid and not be banned, as happened to Paavo Nurmi.

In an announcement at the opulent Waldorf-Astoria hotel, Hilton explained that it was paying $25,000, not to Shorter directly, but to the AAU and to Shorter. A Hilton spokesman said Shorter was chosen because of his "special appeal" and because "He is the mature athlete/ businessman, the highest example of physical fitness," *The Runner* reported. Quipped Shorter, "I have probably run through more airports than anyone in the country."

Shorter acknowledged his role in the development of the sport and wears history's crown with great dignity. He was the spokesman for the sport in the years after Montreal, featured in races that drew people out to exercise for the first time. Men and women, who had not been seen in shorts in years, flocked to the roads, discussing anaerobic thresholds, intervals, and fartlek training. The running boom that started after Munich picked up steam after Shorter's silver medal. According to Don Kardong, fourth-place finisher in the Montreal Olympic Marathon, it was a combination of Shorter's wins and the new insights into the benefits of exercise being publicized at the time. Says Shorter, "Running is the kind of sport where, once it becomes part of your daily routine, there's very little attrition. That's what sets the running boom apart from other booms."

Shorter was forced to take time off in 1977 when his ankle worsened. The break from running did not help. Finally, in the spring of 1978, Shorter had Dr. Stan James, an orthopedic surgeon in Eugene, operate on his ankle. Shorter's choice was either have the operation or perhaps never run again. Shorter's rehabilitation included working out on an exercycle on the University of Colorado campus for 90 minutes, getting his pulse up to 140. He would peddle away with his leg in a cast, while students and runners passed by, saying hello to the master.

Shorter does not wonder whether he could have avoided the injury if he had changed his training earlier, and perhaps started cross training while he was still healthy. No, Shorter says, it is not in "obligatory" runners' personalities to back off of training until they must. After two months of cycling, Shorter was able to train again, and he started his comeback. "Right now," he told Eric Olson in 1978, "I'm like I was when I was in high school, just plugging along trying to run better, watching people run past me and telling myself, 'OK, next time I'll be a little closer, and maybe one day I'll be in front.'"

Many doubted he would ever be back in front. The word going around track circles was that Frank was finished. Shorter himself had doubts while waiting for his ankle to heal. "There was no way I could cope with that [not being able to run]," he told Olson. "Trying to intellectualize your way through such a period is like trying to intellectualize your way to a 3:49 mile. You can't."

But the same drive that took Shorter around the football field in gym class back in seventh grade was still there, and, in the summer of 1978, he began jogging again at a 10-minute-mile pace. He gradually resumed his training and, by the fall, was able to run 48 minutes in a 10-mile race, fast enough to get him thinking about the 1980 Moscow Olympics.

The silver lining in Shorter's injury cloud was that being unable to run left him with time to start on the path of running entrepreneur. He started a chain of running stores and a clothing line, and he also got into TV commentating; he felt that he could go to Moscow in 1980 with NBC if he did not make the team. He told Olson,

> What was always in the back of my mind, was finding the means to train, compete, and still live. I did not sit down and one day decide I wanted to be a success in business. I started that first store so I'd have a job that would allow me time to train and so some of the other runners around here (including Mary Decker and Herb Lindsay) would have jobs. Probably if I hadn't been injured, none of these businesses would have worked out as well, and I wouldn't be doing TV at all. But looking back, if I'd had the choice, I'd rather have been able to run.

Shorter ran the 1980 Olympic Trials, his fourth, finishing over 2:20 in 74th place. He continued competing, but he knew his best days were past. He still was able to pick races to run well in, however. Shorter and Rodgers met in 1980 at a 10K in Denver, their only race at altitude. Shorter won in 29:07 to set the Colorado state record.

In 1981, Shorter beat Rodgers again at the Orange Classic in Middletown, New York. "Frank was a real artist at peaking," says Rodgers. "He was very, very careful in his racing. I remember going to his hometown, on a 100-degree day. I was pretty confident I could beat Frank, and I could not. You just never could count him out."

Shorter knew his competitive days as a world-class runner were over after the 1982 Orange Classic. He won and beat Rod Dixon that day, and Shorter calls that his last race as an elite runner. He was 34, and injuries prevented him from doing the level of training he needed to stay competitive. "I gradually started slowing down," Shorter says, "but the Walter Mitty in me never left until I was 39."

Shorter kept going to races and giving clinics, and he continued making an impact on people. Even Joan Benoit Samuelson, winner of the 1984 women's Olympic gold medal, wrote in her autobiography, *Running Tide*, "There's still a little starstruck voice inside me that says 'Frank Shorter!' every time I see him, because I remember his amazing 1972 Olympic Marathon victory and all the gritty duels he ran with Bill Rodgers."

Shorter began doing more television work in the 1980s. Shorter brings the same meticulous preparation to his TV work as he used to bring to his racing. He studies meet results from around the world to keep on top of the scene. "I like going to the events, and it gives me a reason to be there," he explains. "I'm not a passive observer."

He's an astute analyst, often able to handicap a race based on the runners' forms. "Unfortunately, I'm best at predicting my own times. And I can't predict a 27:50 10K for myself anymore. Sometimes it really drives me nuts and makes me very depressed."

Masters Running

Because Shorter and Bill Rodgers both turned 40 in the same year, Frank began racing again, once more carrying a generation along with him. Shorter's first race as a master came at the New York City Marathon on November 1, 1987, one day after turning 40. He was hoping for the masters title, but his legs tightened up, and he had to drop out. Rodgers's and Shorter's first race against each other as masters was the Charlotte Observer 10K the following January in a special masters 10K event. Shorter led early, along with

Frank Shorter's first race as a master: New York City Marathon, 1987.

Barry Brown (another former Florida Track Club member who ran an American marathon masters record of 2:15). Rodgers came back to beat Shorter, 30:49 to 31:10. Shorter tried to maintain 100-mile weeks of training through the summer of 1988, but began getting minor injuries.

Later in 1988, Shorter went to Seoul, South Korea, as an NBC commentator for the Olympic Games. "I did not run a step for the two weeks I was there," Shorter said. "I spent two weeks riding the stationary bicycle in my hotel room. When I got back, I decided if I was going to be spending all this time on the bike, I needed to get back my biking skills."

Shorter has always had the ability to learn from others. With coaching from lawyer Bob Stone and Category 1 rider Michael Tess, Shorter became proficient enough on the bicycle to beat "bicycling guru" John Howard in the 1989 World Biathlon Championships in a highly publicized race. Shorter cut back on his running, and, for the next two years, was the top masters in the now-defunct Coors Light biathlon series. Biathlons, also called duathlons, comprise a 5K run, followed by a 30K bicycle segment, and another 5K run. The duathlons gave him new life because Shorter was beginning to fall apart.

"I don't get hurt cycling. I'm a runner, and what makes me better is intervals on the track." But he bicycles to get aerobic training between his hard days. "It takes just enough stress off," to allow him to keep racing injury-free. Bicycling, says Shorter, has made him stronger, and less injury-prone "I'm a good example of a compulsive trainer," he says. "It's my personality. That's why I got into cross training."

Through the 1990s, Shorter was juggling a variety of interests and responsibilities. He continues to train 70 miles a week of running and another 20-40 miles a day bicycling, often on a turbo-bicycle in his clean, well-lighted house at the base of Flagstaff Mountain. "I feel that's a nice [training] level for me."

Like Bill Rodgers, Shorter is worried about the future of track in the United States, saying that more interest in running has to be created before it can be built upon. "If a television producer isn't reading about road racing and track and field and feeling it is a hot item, he will not make an effort to put it on television." This is where newspapers can come into play, says Shorter. "The print medium is much more powerful than people give it credit for. Probably every male in the country reads the sports section first thing in the morning."

For those who decide they want to be the best they can in running, Shorter's advice is to model yourself after the best runners, such as Noureddine Morceli, Uta Pippig, or Arturo Barrios. "Go knock on Arturo Barrios' door. If I was a young runner today, I'd go and hang around with the top guys like Arturo, and see what he is doing."

Passing Along the Torch

Shorter still passes along his advice to runners at race clinics. He says most people training for fitness should do aerobic runs at a pace where you can carry on a conversation. Whatever the aerobic activity, Shorter says beginning runners should aim to get the pulse rate up to 110-120 beats per minute.

If you do that for two months you'll get in shape. The better shape you want to be in, the more you do. Then once you are doing it a year and you find you want to beat the guy down the street, you start interval training.

He recommends doing a fartlek workout once a week on a standard course. "Run it with the same effort; jog out the door, do the same workout with the same recovery, so if you do it faster, you know you are in better shape." Once you are ready to try a marathon, Shorter has these 10 tips for you:

• **Rest Before the Race:** No training during the final two weeks leading up to the race will have any effect on performance on race day. So, scale back your training by 60 percent during this time.

• **Sleep Well:** Do a reasonably hard training session the day before you travel, and jog very easily for only about 30 minutes the day you arrive. Do not take a nap, and go to bed at your normal time.

• **Don't Change Your Habits:** Do not change any eating or sleeping habits before the race. Do not eat any new or different food. In the three days before the race, decrease your protein intake by 50 percent, and increase complex carbohydrate intake by 50 percent.

• **Drink in Moderation:** If you drink coffee, tea, or alcoholic beverages, it is fine to drink them in the days before the race. Just be sure to drink them all in moderation, because too much caffeine or alcohol can lead to dehydration.

• **Drink During the Marathon:** Drink at every aid station during the race. If you wait until you are thirsty, it will be too late, because you will already be dehydrated. If you have not practiced drinking replacement drinks, water is best.

- **Do Not Wear Sunscreen:** It will inhibit your body's ability to dissipate heat.

- **Eat a Light Breakfast:** If you normally eat before you train, eat 50 percent of your normal breakfast at least 2-1/2 hours before you race. If not, just drink some water.

- **Practice Wearing a Hat**: So you can wear one if it will be sunny.

- **Do Not Run on Race Day**: Unless you find yourself becoming too nervous; if you do need to run, just jog easily for 15 minutes.

- **Start at an Easy Pace:** In the first 5 kilometers, find a very comfortable pace and then back off 40 percent from that effort. This will make the last 10 kilometers of the marathon much easier to bear.

Just as it does in Bill Rodgers, the willingness to train hard still burns inside Shorter. He can be seen down at the University of Colorado track once or twice a week, with stars such as Barrios, Steve Jones, Mark Coogan, and Mark Plaatjes. One day, he was talking to triathlete Scott Molina and duathlete Kenny Souza.

"Do you guys ever hurt in your glutes?" Shorter asked.

"Sure," replied Molina.

"Good," said Shorter. "So do I. I know I'm training well when I get the right injuries."

"Frank gives advice to many people, and he still trains *very* hard," says marathoner Uta Pippig. The difference now is that while the elites are running their 400-meter intervals in 63 seconds, or faster, Shorter's dozen 400 meters are now at 70 seconds, "the same pace I was running as a sophomore at Yale. The effort is the same; I'm just running them slower." He continues doing the same interval workouts he ran in his prime, but now he needs two or three days rest, instead of one, or none, between hard runs. "The ability to recover goes away as you age. What I've found is that my recovery is slower, and I can't do the pounding."

"I am never going to run 13:20 [5K] again, or 27:45 [10K], or 2:11 [marathon] again. It's just not going to happen. So, I need other motivation to keep training." One source of motivation is to make up "equivalent" goals, such as running 10 kilometers in 32 minutes or bicycling 30 kilometers in 45 minutes. But in the end, says Shorter, "You can create all the equivalents you want, but I'll tell you what—nothing beats winning."

Frank Shorter should know. He certainly did enough of it in his career.

6

The Olympian

Born July 22, 1949, Finland

World records: 2-mile, 5,000, and 10,000 meters

Olympic gold, 5,000 and 10,000, 1972

Olympic gold, 5,000 and 10,000, 1976

One warm night during a Finnish summer in the early 1960s, the image of Paavo Nurmi appeared to a skinny Finnish child in the small village of Myrskylä. Nurmi, the greatest of the Flying Finns who dominated the early days of international track, reappeared during the following years, urging this young son of a trucking worker to reclaim the glory that once was Finnish distance running but had disappeared in the preceding 30 years. To be a champion, or not to be—that was the question Lasse Viren pondered; he chose to be a runner and, in doing so, became the fastest Flying Finn of all.

A combination of circumstances, motivation, and talent put Viren in a position to reclaim the lost legacy of the Flying Finns, and it is a grand legacy with such names as Paavo Nurmi, Hannes Kolehmainen, Ville Ritola, Albin Stenroos, Lauri Lehtinen, Volmari Iso-Hollo, and Viljo Heino.

From Kolehmainen's first world record in 1910 through the 1930s, Finns were synonymous with excellence in distance running, winning 24 Olympic gold medals in the distance races and setting a plethora of records. Silent Finns gliding across the track with their impeccable, classic form, earning medals, setting records, and winning races—those are the stories Viren, and all Finnish youngsters, grew up listening to. There is an aura about the Flying Finns, a mystique that makes them special in the annals of running: how could a small country, having only recently won its independence from the Russian Empire, so completely dominate the Olympics?

But there was something rotten in the state of Finnish athletics by the time the 1960s rolled around. The last Finnish world record had been set by Heino back in 1939, and from their unprecedented sweep of all three medals in the 10,000 meters at the 1936 Berlin Olympics—led by the "Golden Officer" Ilmari Salminen—until 1972, Finland earned only one distance medal, a bronze in the 1956 Melbourne Olympic Marathon by Veikko Karvonen. Once-proud Finland had been relegated to the also-rans of nations, fortunate to get even one runner into the finals of a championship race.

Viren was blessed with the talent to reclaim the distance running crown for Finland, but talent is not enough. It would take years of sacrifice, dedication, supremely hard training, and smart racing strategy to return Finland to the top of the running world. Ask fans who is the greatest runner ever, and you will get a variety of responses; ask track experts, and you will get another answer. But ask the athletes themselves, and the name Viren is always near the top of the list.

"Lasse was the most talented runner ever," says Mexican coach and ex-elite runner Rodolfo Gomez. "Lasse Viren and Miruts Yifter are the two finest 10,000-meter runners whose feet ever touched the track," adds former U.S. star Garry Bjorklund.

What made Viren great was not only the three world records he set; others also set records. It was not his overall win-loss record; he lost many times, sometimes even in small races in Finland. Rather, Viren ranks among the best ever because he is the model of the athlete able to plan out a career well enough to peak for one competition—the Olympics. More than anything, Viren loved the competition and the challenge of racing and beating the best in the world.

Perhaps more than any runner, you can not understand Lasse Viren without understanding his homeland, the beautiful, silent, northern land of Finland, forged out of retreating glaciers and invading armies. Out of this land of midnight sun, clear lakes, and rolling pine forests came a long-legged and smooth-striding boy whose destiny was written in the ice of the Finnish winters—to recapture the lost glory of the Flying Finns. Because he kept to himself, Viren remains an enigma to many who do not know him. It was not that he was an arrogant person; Viren is known by those close to him as friendly and fun-loving. Rather, his aloofness was more a matter of being accountable only to himself, to his country, and to the memory of the great Finnish runners who had run down the same lonely road before him. "When you look at why Lasse became Lasse, you have to look at the history, the heritage and the culture of Finland," says Eino Romppanen, a long-time friend of Viren's. "From the time they are kids, Finnish youth are ingrained with the idea that Finns are great athletes, and so we have that mentality. There is something Finns have that makes them think they can overcome incredible odds."

That "something" is *sisu*, the most Finnish of words that is also the most difficult to define for outsiders, but which best explains Viren's and the Finnish character. It is the ability to persevere under the most adverse conditions, when others would have quit; it is the something Viren had that made him special. "Let me say this," explains Viren. "*Sisu* is working really hard for something you want to do and not giving up. That's the main point, never giving up." Never giving up is a fitting summary for Viren's career and epic Olympic races, and with no other runner does one word so readily sum up his personality.

"*Sisu* is a very old word we have in Finnish history," Eino adds. "It means to believe in yourself and have the guts to do it, and have the resistance and the craziness to endure. But we don't like to talk about it so much."

Finland displayed its gutsiness in the Winter War of 1939, when a few Finns on skis, dressed in white for camouflage, held the huge Soviet army to a standoff. Finns still talk about the war as if it happened yesterday. "The Russians invaded Finland, but they never conquered us," Eino boasts. How did this country of five million hold off the Soviet empire? "That's *sisu*," he says. The world came to know it at that time as "cold will," or "pure will."

The war destroyed Finland's running prowess, as the cream of the Finnish runners were sent off to fight, and Finland's running cupboard was not replenished until the early 1970s, with Viren's glorious wins. Says Garry Bjorklund, "*Sisu* is guts, and you know when someone has it. And Lasse had it." Eino agrees, and after thinking for a bit his eyes light up. "*Sisu*. I'll show you *sisu*." He runs to get the famous photograph of Viren crossing the line in front of a grimacing Dick Quax in the Montreal Olympic 5,000-meter final. Holding up the photo, he says, "This is *sisu*."

The Sporting Mentality

Lasse's first exposure to sports came when his parents strapped cross-country skis on him as a baby. "In Finland, you start skiing when you start walking," Eino explains. "If you are born in the wintertime, by the next winter you have already started skiing. The mentality is different here." It is an approach that honors the sporting life, with most young Finns playing ice hockey, cross-country skiing, and running. The Scandinavian countries are sports powerhouses, as evidenced by the 1994 Winter Olympics in which Norway grabbed the most medals of any country.

"In America, for example, sports have a 'big-bully' mentality. For instance, if you find a person who is good at running, he is usually small and wimpy; he runs away from other kids and is called a wimp," says Eino.

> In Finland, we look at him as being an athlete who is good at running. If you look at Finland, Sweden and Norway, there is great interest in sport, with the attitude of having a healthy body and healthy mind. That is the Scandinavian heritage. We love all games, and they are an important part of childhood.

Viren grew up with this sporting mentality, and his father encouraged him. After dabbling in a variety of sports, Viren became interested in running in part because a top Finnish runner named Pertti Sariomaa was from Myrskylä, and Viren would often see him out on the roads training and hear about his races.

Viren was a good runner from the time he started at age 16, and though he was good at other sports as well, running quickly became his favorite. In the back of his mind he had the idea that he "wanted to be like Paavo Nurmi and bring the gold back to Finland."

In Nurmi, perhaps the most enigmatic and prolific runner ever, Viren found a worthy hero. His presence is still pervasive in Finland. Pick up a 10-mark bill, and there is Nurmi's tight-lipped visage looking out at you. Viren's Nurmi-inspired golden journey began at Myrskylä's cinder track where he competed in local races. In Finland, nearly every small village has an outdoor track that remains covered in snow most of the year. When the snow melts, the track meets start and continue all summer.

Viren says he took to running because there was not much else to do in Myrskylä except sports. Indeed, when Viren was growing up, the village had a church, a bank, and no streetlights. Nearby is a small, peaceful lake, and in the winter the area is covered with ice and snow. A person has to be very motivated to run in such conditions, and Viren was. After training with Myrskylä's local sports club, Myrskylän Myrsky, Viren first drew notice in 1965 by racing 3,000 meters in 9:33.8. Running in the summer and cross-country skiing in the winter, by 1967 Viren had improved his 3,000-meter time to 8:32.8, the Finnish under-18 record. He also ran 5,000 meters in 14:59.4, becoming the first Finn under 18-years old to break 15 minutes.

Encouraged by his family and by club members in Myrskylä, Viren started training harder, and, in 1969, set a Finnish junior national 5,000-meter record of 14:17.0. He next won the national 5,000-meter title in 13:55 and also ran 8:05.2 for 3,000 meters. Viren was good from the start and much better than the other Finns his age; even as a teen he was able to push himself harder than anyone he was racing against.

Haikkola's Hero

Thinking it would help him get to the next level, Viren accepted a scholarship to Brigham Young University in Provo, Utah, arriving there in November, 1969. But the training at BYU did not suit Viren (who missed his family), and, after running some lackluster track races in the spring of 1970, he returned to Finland after the semester ended. In his first race back in Helsinki, Viren ran only 14:51 for 5,000 meters. At this time he asked Rolf Haikkola to be his coach. Viren began increasing his mileage, up to 100 miles per week. Later in 1970, he improved to 13:43 for 5,000 meters and 29:15.8 in the 10,000 meters—fast enough to get Viren thinking about the Olympics.

Haikkola was a kind of father-figure coach, much like Bill Bowerman was for runners in Eugene, Oregon. Like several other Finnish coaches,

Haikkola had been influenced by Arthur Lydiard, the famed New Zealand coach of Olympic winners Peter Snell and Murray Halberg. Lydiard came to Finland for a two-year coaching stint in March of 1967. His ideas of building up aerobic strength through long-distance running in the winter, even for 800-meter runners, followed by anaerobic work in the spring and summer, had become popular. Lydiard, whose wife was Finnish, had first visited Finland in 1961. When he came for his second visit in 1967, he was blunt in his assessment of the poor state of Finnish running. Martti Hannus, author of *The Flying Finns*, tells us that on his first day in Finland, Lydiard, then nearly 50, sent members of the Finnish national team on a 30-kilometer run. The venerable coach went with them—and beat all of the runners back except one, vividly illustrating just how far Finnish distance running had fallen. Lydiard, never one to mince words, told the Finns why they had fallen from the top echelons of racing—they had gotten lazy. The solution he offered was high mileage and hard work.

Lydiard said in *Athletic Weekly* that

> When I started running, there were no books or magazines about it. I looked at Paavo Nurmi and the rest of the great Finnish runners before the war, and I realized that what set them up, apart from the others of the day, was that they did high mileage. The problem was that young Finns had lost their toughness. I thought everyone would be out skiing, but they were all indoors watching it on television. The runners did not train in the winter. True, it was cold, but they had to train all year if they were going to get anywhere. Eventually, the press made a big thing of it because I was challenging their national pride by saying they had no guts, and it started to happen.

One of those listening to Lydiard was Haikkola, a former 14:14 5,000-meter runner. There were several other coaches with emerging young runners, the best of the new Finns being Juha Väätäinen, a sprinter who moved up to longer races in 1970. Viren was showing great promise, but, before he burst onto the international scene and added his name to the storied list of Finnish greats, it was Väätäinen who first lit the Finnish running rebirth with double golds in the 5,000 meters and 10,000 meters at the 1971 European Championships in Helsinki.

Viren was there as well, but little notice was paid to the country boy's 17th-place finish in the 10,000 meters and seventh in the 5,000 meters (though he was just a few seconds from a medal), because all of Finland was rejoicing at the country's return to distance-running prominence. Väätäinen won the 10,000 on a last-lap sprint and then came back to take the 5,000. Viren was with the leaders with a lap to go in the 5,000, but he could not match the medalists' finishing kicks.

Viren, who had been hired as a policeman in Myrskylä, showed his potential a week after the European Championships, running 13:29.8 for 5,000 meters (breaking Väätäinen's Finnish record). At the end of the 1971 track season, Viren and Haikkola sat down and set up a one-year plan of attack for the Olympic games, something they would do two other times during the next decade. Viren had decent finishing speed, but they knew he would have to get faster over the last lap if he wanted to win the major championships. One of Viren's workouts, designed to develop the ability to withstand higher levels of lactic acid and to hone his kick, was running 5,000 meters along the grass infield of a track, alternating sprinting 100 meters and floating 100 meters.

Haikkola was a firm believer in high-altitude training, thus, Viren and a teammate went to Kenya to lay the foundation for the 1972 Olympic Games. All they did was run, eat, sleep, and run some more to get ready for Munich. A typical day included a morning run of 1-1/2 hours, then breakfast and a nap, followed by another run in the middle of the day, then more eating and sleeping before an evening run. Viren followed this Spartan regime for three months, running as much as 200 miles a week, laying the base for the next summer's racing that would stun the world. "You can't even measure the amount of mileage they did," said Eino. "They were running every possible moment." Viren also took good care of his body, getting regular massages and taking saunas, another part of his Finnish heritage. The sauna relaxed his muscles and helped his recovery, says Viren. "I took saunas after hard runs whenever I could, but not before a race."

Viren returned to the Finnish countryside early in 1972 and spent the late winter piling on more miles, with little speedwork. That was the traditional Finnish way, pioneered by Paavo Nurmi and Hannes Kolehmainen. Running just off his winter basework, Viren ran a 28:39 10,000 meters in the spring of 1972, then at the beginning of June hit 5,000 meters in 13:37 and 13:33—solid times, but not enough to impress the top runners. Viren remained on the periphery of the track scene outside of Finland as everyone was talking about Dave Bedford, the colorful British runner known for his high mileage training weeks, beer drinking, black socks, and shockingly fast paces.

However, later that summer the track world began paying attention to Viren after he ran 5,000 meters in 13:19.0—a Finnish record—during a meet against Spain and Great Britain in Helsinki. His last two kilometers were 2:39 and 2:30, respectively, and it was the third-fastest 5,000 ever. One month later in Oulu, Viren ran 7:43.2 for 3,000 meters, breaking the Finnish record by 10 seconds. To top off his Olympic preparations, Viren went to the Bislett Games and ran 27:52.4, just inside Väätäinen's Finnish record from 1971. Viren did it with what was to become his trademark—negative splits. He ran a medium-paced first 5,000 (14:00.2) followed by a faster second 5,000 (13:52.2). It was after that race at Bislett that Viren decided to run the 10,000 in Munich.

Olympic Peaking

Because the Olympic games did not start until September, most of the top international runners who would be racing in Munich were in Europe at various training camps, where the "rumor mill was working overtime," Frank Shorter writes in *Olympic Gold*. "We'd learn of the performances of the distance runners competing in pre-Olympic meets. But readiness is something else. Who was really fit? Who was injured? Who'd peaked too soon?"

Not Viren, whom Shorter first saw during the Bislett Games, where the American ran the 3,000 meters and watched Viren in the 10,000. "And what a runner!" Shorter writes of Viren.

> He had a very smooth stride that essentially did not change as he accelerated in the final laps. Unlike most distance runners, he did not switch to a sprinter's gait in a furious drive to the finish. Somehow he was able to maintain his form . . . and simply run faster. It was all in the rpms—his leg rate quickened, which made his speed deceptive. It was something to see.

All the world would get to see Viren's silky form in Munich, but first there were a few more races to hone his peak and to plant the seed in his opponents' minds that he would be difficult—if not impossible—to beat. Shorter, who would be facing Viren in the 10,000 meters, certainly realized that. "The man was ready, all right. I told myself, 'The only thing you can do is stay as close to him as possible, because he's going to win.'"

The insightful Shorter realized Viren was great before the rest of the world did. Bedford was still looked to as being one of the favorites for the 10,000 meters. That changed, however, when the Englishman was crushed during Viren's two-mile run in Sweden on August 14, 1972. Some of the best runners in the world showed up for the race in Stockholm's International Stadium, including: Anders Garderud, who would win the gold in the Munich steeplechase; Britain's Bedford and

Ian Stewart; Emiel Puttemans of Belgium, the two-mile record holder (8:17.8); and the up-and-coming New Zealand star, Dick Quax. Remembering Väätäinen's surprise wins in the European championships the year before, the others moaned when they saw Viren in the field. "Oh, no, not another young Finn!"

Bedford took the lead, as was his wont, completing the first lap in 60.5 seconds. The half-mile split was 2:03 and the mile split, 4:09.4. Running with his light, relaxed stride, Viren stayed right on Bedford's shoulder. He took the lead and gradually quickened the pace, running his second mile in 4:04.6, capped by a 60-second last lap; he finished in 8:14.0, knocking 3.8 seconds off Puttemans's world record. The Belgian was second, also under his record, while Bedford was far back, nearly 100 meters behind.

"My 2-mile world record is one of my favorite races," says Viren. This dominating win by Viren was such a blow to Bedford's confidence that he considered pulling out of the Olympics entirely. When Bedford next hooked up with Viren in the 10,000 meters in Munich, his two-mile loss weighed heavily on his mind and influenced his strategy. That is exactly what Viren wanted it to do, says Shorter.

> Lasse's way to psyche out his opposition was to very carefully plan a series of races leading up to the Olympics that would then show very fast times. After breaking the 2-mile world record within a month of the Munich games, he ran a 10,000 meter time trial in 27:45 by himself. Then he ran 5,000 meters, again by himself, close to the world record. . . . So by the time the Olympics came around, everybody knew he was in great shape based on these performances, and it was almost as if they were waiting for him to go. That is how Lasse did it.

Munich 10,000 Meters

At the 1972 Olympic Games, heats were run in the 10,000 meters for the first time since 1920. Viren's heat on September 1 included Frank Shorter, whose plan was to do whatever Viren did; Mario Haro of Spain; and Tunisia's Mohamed Gammoudi, the 5,000-meter gold medalist from the 1968 Mexico City Olympics and 10,000-meter silver medalist in Tokyo in 1964. Viren finished fourth in his heat in 28:04, while Shorter (27:58.2, a new U.S. record), Gammoudi, and Haro all dipped below 28 minutes, as did Puttemans (27:53.4) and Bedford (27:53.6) in their heats—both broke the Olympic record.

Those were impressive times; only a handful of people in history had ever run a sub-28 minute 10,000 meters. It was a sign of how competitive distance running was becoming that five runners broke the 28-minute barrier in the preliminary heats.

After two days of rest, it was time for the final. Fifteen of the best 10,000-meter runners lined up, with the long-legged Finn the center of attention. "Everyone was looking at Viren," says Shorter. "Everyone thought he was the favorite in the 10,000—and he ran that way." When the gun went off, it was Bedford, as expected, who took the lead. Stung by his loss in the two-mile a month earlier, and lacking confidence in his kick, the Englishman took it upon himself to try to run away from the field, hitting his first lap in 59.9 seconds—faster than the opening lap in the 1,500-meter final three days later. The quick start did not faze Viren. His meticulous preparations had prepared him for just such a crazy pace, as he had gone out in 59 seconds on his way to a 13:32 5,000-meter win earlier in the year. Bedford kept up the speed, passing 800 meters in 2:04.6 and 2,000 meters in 5:18.8.

How fast was it? So fast that the runner in last place at 2,000 meters, Juan Martinez of Mexico, was running at *27:10* speed, far below world record pace. Despite the fast pace, most of the field remained in contact, cruising along the track in single file, with Viren in fifth place. Suddenly, on the backstraight of the 12th lap, Puttemans, in fourth, slowed, causing Viren, who was running just behind him, to slow as well. Gammoudi ran up on Viren and clipped his foot, and both runners tumbled to the track. For an instant, Viren lay on the infield grass while the rest of the field and the gold medal pulled away. Then he quickly shot back up and went after the pack, which had gained 50 meters on him. The other runners had failed to take advantage of Viren's mishap by picking up the pace, and in just over a lap, Viren had rejoined the field.

Gammoudi, however, lay on the infield quite a bit longer. When he got to his feet, he ran only another 600 meters before dropping out. Says Shorter,

> I've always thought the responses of the two men reflected on their character. Gammoudi, though an Olympic champion, seemed the type of person who didn't think he could win unless everything went according to plan. Viren was going to win *no matter what*.

The attitude that winning the Olympics was all that mattered was the central theme of Viren's career.

After rejoining the leaders, Viren settled in behind Haro and the tiny Ethiopian Miruts Yifter, who was loping along in second place. The pack passed the halfway mark in 13:43.9. Viren's kilometer splits were 2:36.9, 2:41.9 (5:18.8), 2:47.6 (8:06.4), 2:49.2 (10:55.6), and 2:48.3 going through 5,000 meters. After halfway, Viren briefly took the lead before dropping back, as one by one Bedford and other runners peeled off the back of the pack. Soon, five were left— Shorter, Haro, Puttemans, Yifter, and Viren—who moved into the lead for good with exactly two laps to go, beginning a long drive to the tape. After leading the other four runners for 200 meters, Viren pressed the pace and broke up the trailing runners.

"Everybody expected Lasse to go, and when he went, he went decisively, and it was with 600 meters to go. He just ran away from everyone," says Shorter, who was dropped along with Haro. That long surge to the tape was the way Viren and Haikkola planned to deflect the leg speed of Yifter, nicknamed "the Shifter" because of his great kick. They thought that the only way to beat a fast finisher was with a long kick. (A contrast with Viren's strategy was seen when Craig Virgin tried to beat Yifter at the World Cup 10,000 by slowing down the pace, actually coming to a complete halt and moving to lane two to make Yifter take the lead. Yifter simply sat on the American and outkicked him on the last lap.)

After Viren's surge, Puttemans and Yifter gamely tried to hang on, but at the bell lap Viren was already clear, and he stayed clear over the last lap to win in 27:38.4, 1.0 second up on Ron Clarke's world record and 1.2 seconds ahead of Puttemans. The small-town policeman had done it— the Olympic gold was returned to Finland and a Flying Finn was back, faster than ever. Yifter got the bronze (27:41.0), followed by Haro in fourth (27:48.2), and then Shorter (27:51.4), who said, "I ran 2:07 for my last 800 meters and still lost 10 seconds to Viren," whose last two laps took only 1:56.2. "And he didn't even go until the last 600."

Viren had run negative splits once again, and his five fastest kilometers, the first four plus the last one, were run in 13:25. His 1,000-meter splits for his second 5,000 meters were 2:51.9 (16:35.8), 2:52.0 (19:27.8), 2:50.0 (22:17.8), 2:51.4 (25:09.2), and an incredible 2:29.0 for his last kilometer, 11 seconds faster than Ron Clarke had run for the last 1,000 meters in his record run. Clarke had held the record since 1963; he set the 10,000-meter mark three times, the last being his 27:39.4 at the 1965 Bislett Games.

Not only had Viren reached the starting line at Munich in great shape, but he also had outsmarted his opponents. According to Shorter,

In retrospect, you look at someone like Yifter and you have to believe Viren even caught him off guard. Yifter probably could have been closer if he had not hesitated [when Viren made his break]. You have to react. As we've seen, Yifter is so good, it could have been closer at the end.

The Munich 10,000 meters was immediately recognized as one of the best races ever. "Among all the Olympic victories of Finnish distance running, this one was the most unbelievable, the most unforgettable, and certainly the most coolly-executed," writes Matti Hannus in *The Flying Finns*. How did Viren do it? Simple, says Eino: "When Lasse was down and then got back up again? That was *sisu*."

Munich 5,000 Meters

On September 7, four days after the thrilling 10,000 meters, the 5,000-meter heats were held. The competition, as in the 10,000, was stiff, and several notable runners were eliminated in the preliminary heats including Kenya's Ben Jipcho, who was still feeling the effects of his second place in the steeplechase three days earlier. Puttemans set a new Olympic record by running 13:31.8 to win his heat ahead of Steve Prefontaine (13:32.6) of the United States and West German, Harald Norpoth (13:33.4), while Väätäinen's 13:32.8 win in his heat showed that Viren was not the only Finn running well. The tone of the 5,000-meter final was further set when Yifter did not make the start of his heat. It seems he went to the wrong gate to get into the Olympic Stadium, and, because of tightened security in the aftermath of the Israeli killings, he was not allowed through. We will never know if Yifter would have gotten a medal, though his bronze in the 10,000 meters shows he was certainly capable of doing so.

Viren was loose as he got ready for the final. Not only because he now had his gold medal from the 10,000, but also because with such a stacked field as he was lining up against, he was not expected to win. Viren would need all his strength and wits in this 5,000-meter final, his fourth race of the Munich games. Prefontaine and Ian Stewart both said before the final that they would run the last mile in 4 minutes if they had to, in order to take the sting out of Viren's kick.

Viren was lined up fourth from the curb, and, at the gun, immediately dropped to last place, where he stayed most of the early going. The first laps were slow, with Britain's Ian McCafferty taking the field through a 69-second first 400 meters. Harald Norpoth of West Germany, the 5,000-meter silver medalist from the 1964 Olympics and perhaps one of the skinniest runners ever, then took over leading the large pack, which spilled out into lane 2. If it appeared to spectators that the runners were jogging, it was because they were. The pace was decent for a college meet, but slow enough to play right into Viren's hands—and feet. He hugged the curb at the back of the pack, letting the other runners spend extra energy running out in the second lane. When Seradov of the Soviet Union took over, pushing the pace to 65 seconds, Viren was running well within himself in tenth place. "Lasse showed that you can control a race by running on the inside in the pack," notes Shorter.

Prefontaine ran at the outside of the first lane, staying in position to match any move, with Bedford alongside of him. Viren and Väätäinen moved up behind them. With eight laps to go, Viren took the lead by quickly passing the entire field within 50 meters. The other runners bunched up behind him, sensing that this might be the move. It was not, as Viren was only stretching his legs. After going to the front, he slowed the pace back down to 68.6 seconds before allowing Bedford to take the lead.

After another 69-second lap, Javiar Alvarez of Spain took over. The other runners tucked in behind Alvarez, and the pace remained slow. The entire field was still in contention, watching Viren and waiting for the real racing to begin. The wily Viren continued to hang back, letting the more excitable runners spend extra energy jostling for position out in the second lane. Because Stewart and Prefontaine had discussed publicly their strategy for the 5,000 meters, Viren knew exactly how the race would unfold, and he was able to plan accordingly. He was confident no one would be able to hold his speed at the end of the race.

With five laps to go, Viren moved up to third behind Alvarez and McCafferty, with Puttemans right on his heels. That lap took 66.5 seconds. Prefontaine, the brash young American, then made good on his prerace promise, surging strongly to the front with four laps to go. He looked strong and was running with a surfeit of energy. Viren was eighth, but immediately moved up on the outside of the bunched pack of runners as Prefontaine toured the lap in 65 seconds.

Viren then moved up on Prefontaine's shoulder, ready to take the lead, but Prefontaine stayed in front, running the next lap in 62.5 seconds. That was enough to finally split open the field, as only four runners were able to hang with Prefontaine: Viren, Gammoudi, Stewart, and Puttemans. Heading up the straightaway, Viren glanced once over his right shoulder, then took the lead with *exactly* two laps to go, Puttemans still directly behind him. It looked like it might be a repeat of the 10,000 with Viren staying in front and pushing the pace to the tape. But Prefontaine would have none of that. On the backstraight, he accelerated and retook the lead, running the penultimate lap in 61 seconds. Prefontaine had promised "a pure guts race at the end"—and the American ran his heart out.

Exactly as the bell sounded for the last lap, Viren passed Prefontaine, with Gammoudi third. Puttemans and Stewart dropped back, and Viren led around the curve. With 300 meters to go, Prefontaine accelerated yet again, and he and Gammoudi both passed Viren. But their final sprint came too early, because, with 200 meters left, Viren repassed Prefontaine, and, coming off the last turn into the finishing straight-away, Viren easily and smoothly passed Gammoudi and pulled away to win by one second in an Olympic record of 13:26.4. Viren, 23, had his double Olympic golds. His last 200 meters had been run in 28 seconds and the last 400 in 56. As in the 10,000, his last two laps took just 1:56, and Viren ran his last mile in 4:01.2. Once again, in a classic race, Viren showcased his superb race tactics and unparalleled finishing drive.

"Lasse's victory in the 10,000, which then carried over to the 5,000, was that he could win at his will, whenever he decided to go. Everyone just hung around and waited for him to go," says Shorter.

Gammoudi took the silver, and Stewart's furious kick nipped Prefontaine at the tape for the bronze, 0.2 seconds behind Gammoudi. Bedford faded to 12th in 13:43.2, one spot ahead of Väätäinen in 13:53.8. Viren's wins set off night-long celebrations in Finland, complete with dancing in the streets. Viren was the fourth runner to win the two track-distance races in the same Olympics, joining Kolehmainen (1912), Emil Zatopek (1952), and Vladimir Kuts of the Soviet Union (1956) in that exclusive club. The blue and white Finnish flag was flying on victory laps again, the Finnish national anthem, *Maamme laulu* (Song of Our Land) was playing, and the glory of the Flying Finns was restored.

Four days after his Olympic 5,000-meter win, on September 14, Viren thrilled a hometown crowd in Helsinki by breaking another of Ron Clarke's world records, this time the 5,000-meter mark, running 13:16.4 to beat Bedford by 14 seconds. Bedford led the first 1,000 meters in 2:36.6; Viren took over at 3,000 meters and easily pulled away, running his last kilometer in 2:33.8. The ghosts of Finns past must have been happy to see the 5,000-meter record being brought back to Finland; Finns had held the record for an incredible 30 consecutive years, from when the IAAF began keeping track of world records in 1912 through 1942. The first official IAAF mark belongs to Kolehmainen, who was the first person to break 15 minutes with his 14:36.6 edging out Frenchman Jean Bouin in the 1912 Stockholm Olympic Games. Then came Nurmi's two world records in 1922 (14:35.4) and 1924 (14:28.2), followed by Lauri Lehtinen (14:17.0), and, finally, Taisto Mäki in 1939 (14:08.8). Mäki's record stood until Gunder Hägg of Sweden broke the 14-minute bar-rier three years later with his 13:58.2. Now the 5,000-meter record was back in Finnish hands, and Viren was not done bringing glory back to Finland.

5,000 Meters World Record Progression

15:20.0	Charles Bennett (GBR)	Paris	July 22, 1900
15:13.5	Johan Svanberg (SWE)	Stockholm	August 8, 1907
15:01.2	Arthur Robertson (GBR)	Stockholm	September 13, 1908
14:36.6	Hannes Kolehmainen (FIN)	Stockholm	July 10, 1912
14:35.4	Paavo Nurmi (FIN)	Stockholm	September 12, 1922
14:28.2	Paavo Nurmi (FIN)	Helsinki	June 19, 1924
14:17.0	Lauri Lehtinen (FIN)	Helsinki	June 19, 1932
14:08.8	Taisto Mäki (FIN)	Helsinki	June 16, 1939
13:58.2	Gunder Hägg (SWE)	Göteborg	September 20, 1942
13:57.2	Emil Zatopek (TCH)	Columbes	May 30, 1954
13:56.6	Vladimir Kuts (URS)	Bern	August 29, 1954
13:51.6	Christopher Chataway (GBR)	London	October 13, 1954
13:51.2	Vladimir Kuts (URS)	Prague	October 23, 1954
13:50.8	Sándor Iharos (HUN)	Budapest	September 10, 1955
13:46.8	Vladimir Kuts (URS)	Belgrade	September 18, 1955
13:40.6	Sándor Iharos (HUN)	Budapest	October 23, 1955
13:36.8	Gordon Pirie (GBR)	Bergen	June 19, 1956
13:35.0	Vladimir Kuts (URS)	Rome	October 13, 1957
13:34.8	Ronald Clarke (AUS)	Hobart	January 16, 1965
13:33.6	Ronald Clarke (AUS)	Aucklund	February 1, 1965
13:25.8	Ronald Clarke (AUS)	Los Angeles	June 4, 1965
13:24.2	Kipchoge Keino (KEN)	Aucklund	November 30, 1965
13:16.6	Ronald Clarke (AUS)	Stockholm	July 5, 1966
13:16.4	Lasse Viren (FIN)	Helsinki	September 14, 1972
13:13.0	Emiel Puttemans (BEL)	Brussels	September 20, 1972
13:12.9	Dick Quax (NZL)	Stockholm	July 5, 1977
13:08.4	Henry Rono (KEN)	Berkeley	April 8, 1978

Electronically timed records

13:06.20	Henry Rono (KEN)	Knarvik	September 13, 1981
13:00.41	David Moorcraft (GBR)	Oslo	July 7, 1982
13:00.40	Said Auoita (MOR)	Oslo	July 27, 1985
12:58.39	Said Auoita (MOR)	Rome	July 22, 1987
12:56.96	Haile Gebrselassie (ETH)	Hengelo	June 4, 1994
12:55.30	Moses Kiptanui (KEN)	Rome	June 8, 1995
12:44.39	Haile Gebrselassie (ETH)	Zurich	August 16, 1995

Paavo Nurmi

Finland's two greatest runners, Lasse Viren and Paavo Nurmi, never met. They had agreed to a visit on October 2, 1973. However, the meeting never came about, as Nurmi died that very day. Viren was one of the pallbearers, along with Nurmi's running-rival-turned-friend Ville Ritola.

Nurmi won gold medals at the 1920 Antwerp Olympics in the 10,000-meter and cross-country races and a silver in the 5,000. In 1924 at the Paris Olympics, Nurmi won the 1,500, 5,000, cross-country, and 3,000-meter team race. He capped his Olympic career in 1928 at Amsterdam with a gold in the 10,000 and silvers in the 5,000 and steeplechase.

Nurmi and Ritola did not get along when they were the best two distance runners in the world during the 1920s, mostly because Ritola won the 10,000-meter gold at the 1924 Paris Olympics after Finnish officials refused to let Nurmi enter the race. It is one of running's great stories: Nurmi never forgave the officials, and it is said that during the 10,000-meter final, Nurmi went to the practice track outside the Olympic Stadium and ran a 10,000-meter time trial by himself. Carrying a stopwatch in his right hand, as was his trademark during races, Nurmi ran 40 seconds faster than Ritola's winning time. He was so furious and angry that it's said he ran under 30 minutes. (Nurmi's best was his 30:06.2 in 1924, and the 30-minute barrier was not officially broken until Finn Taisto Mäki did it 11 years later.) In the 5,000 meters, Nurmi narrowly beat Ritola.

Nurmi was a runner far ahead of his time and was, from his early days, driven to run. He came from a poor background and as a child walked—or ran—everywhere. As a teenager, he gave up eating meat to help his running. Once, it is said, he ran 40 miles from a small town to his home in Turku on the southwest coast of Finland. His wife heard a faint scratching on their back door. Thinking it was a neighborhood dog, she opened the door. There was Paavo, slumped in a heap on the doorstep, so exhausted from his run that he could not open the door.

While preparing for the 1924 Olympics, Nurmi was informed that the Olympic schedule had been released, showing that the 5,000 would be held just 50 minutes after the 1,500 meters.

To see if he would be able to run both events, Nurmi held an "Olympic test" on June 19, 1924 in Helsinki's Eläintarla Sportsground.

In a remarkable demonstration of his ability Nurmi broke the 7-year-old 1,500-meter world record, running 3:52.6. He opened with a 57.3 first 400, then passed the 800 meters in 2:01.0. After another lap of 65.0, a final 300 meters of 46.6 gave him the record.

Then 50 minutes later, Nurmi ran a 5,000 meters. He hit 65 for the first lap, his first kilometer in 2:48.6, and 1,000 meters in 4:14.8. Lapping all the other runners in the race, Nurmi went on to finish in 14:28.2, breaking his own world record by 7.2 seconds.

Battling Injuries

Viren did not train much the winter after his great year in 1972 that had included three world records and two Olympic gold medals. It would not be possible to keep that peak for another year, and Viren returned to the ranks of mere mortals in 1973, clocking good, but not awesome,' times of 13:28 and 28:17. In 1974, he began gearing up for the European Championships in Rome. But the high mileage Viren put in during 1972 had caused leg problems that continued to bother him.

Viren recovered enough to go to the European Championships in decent shape, and he was expected to win. But he was a distant seventh in the 10,000 meters with a time of 28:29.2, run in very hot conditions. He came back to take the bronze behind Brendan Foster in the 5,000 meters, running 13:24.6.

Early in 1975, Viren had an operation on his left thigh, and, after recuperating, he came back that summer to run 13:34 and 28:11. Because of his ability to win big races and run fast times, some question why he did not run world records between the Olympics. The Olympics, however, meant everything to Viren; he prepared and peaked for them. There was not a lucrative road-race circuit to make money on during Viren's competitive years. One of the few international road races was the San Blas Half-Marathon in Puerto Rico. U.S. runner Pablo Vigil went there to race in 1975, where he finished fourth, ahead of Viren. When he returned to the States from San Blas, Vigil told Frank Shorter about the results.

"Frank, I beat the Olympic champion," Vigil boasted.

"That's good," replied Shorter, "but everybody has beaten Lasse at one time or another. But nobody beats him at the Olympics." According to Eino,

> People don't really know Lasse's career. Nine times he ran under 28 minutes [for 10,000 meters], one of the most ever. He was popular and went to hundreds of races. It wasn't important to him to win the smaller meets, because when the time came, he would be ready. When he was getting ready for championship meets, he was running 140-180 miles a week. Naturally, you don't have a lot of leg speed doing that.

Just as they had before the Munich games, in 1975 Viren and Haikkola planned his training a year in advance in order to peak at the Montreal Olympics. This is what others were trying to do, but none could do it like Lasse. Roger Bannister, the great English miler, was one of the few who was able to peak as well as Viren, gearing all his training to one supreme effort.

Viren's training for the Montreal Olympics started in the fall of 1975, when he went to Thompson Falls, Kenya, for the hardest training he had ever done. At an altitude of over 7,000 feet, Viren ran up to 180 miles a week. He was training to defend his Munich 5,000-meter and 10,000-meter gold medals, of course. But secretly, he had another goal in mind that no one outside of his coach and training partners were privy to—the Olympic Marathon, where Viren wanted to challenge Shorter, the defending champ.

The high mileage training paid off, as Viren set a world road best for 25K (1:14.21) in the spring of 1976. After some average races, topped by a 5,000 in 13:44, Viren took a break to get over a sinus infection. When he came back, he showed he was in Olympic shape by running a 27:43.1 10,000 meters at the World Games in Helsinki. Viren was letting his opponents know that anyone wanting to claim his gold medals would have to go through him. Hannus reports of one of Viren's last training sessions done at midnight on the Helsinki track 12 days before the Montreal 10,000: 20 × 200 meters in 28 seconds.

That "Olympic Magic?"

Viren was selected to carry the Finnish flag in the opening ceremonies at Montreal's new Olympic Stadium. He was an appropriate choice, because he had revived the Finnish distance-running spirit, and youth throughout the country were once again out training, hoping to emulate their newest hero. Viren's mystique was by now so great that the other 15 runners in the Olympic 10,000-meter finals "handed" him the race before they even started, says Garry Bjorklund, who made the United States team by nipping Bill Rodgers in the Olympic trials. Bjorklund remembers the tension of waiting to race in the finals.

> As they prepare you to go out on the track, you walk through a labyrinth of tunnels. You don't actually see the track until they lead you out. We sat in a room beneath the stadium, where they checked our spikes and numbers, and we could hear the pulsing of the crowds outside, reverberating. We could feel the Olympics, but not see them.

The finalists waited anxiously in the room. Then, five minutes before they were to go out on the track,

> we realized we were all thinking exactly the same thing—Lasse Viren wasn't there. Just then, in walks Viren, like the imperial king. Officials checked his hip numbers and his spikes, and then he sat down, all by himself. He put his elbows on his knees and just slowly looked around at everyone in the room, one by one, as if to say, "I'm here guys." And the race was over then. I've never seen a presence like that.

The 10,000 meters was Viren's race from the start. There was no Bedford to take the race out fast this time, as he was sidelined by one of his numerous injuries. The only runner who worried Viren was Foster, who had beaten Lasse in the 1974 European Championships and at a 1975 track race in Nice. Carlos Lopes of Portugal, who had been eliminated in the heats in Munich, took the lead after two miles and towed the field past the 5,000-meter mark in a leisurely 14:09, a pace that, as in the Munich Olympics, played directly into Viren's plans. "Carlos did all the work, and that 14:09 felt so good," said Bjorklund. "After 5,000 meters, I thought, 'OK, there's going to be a change here, to 63.' Sure as shooting, we ran a 63. Then there was a 66, and then a 65, 66, 65, 66, that just blew everybody away."

Lopes continued forcing the pace in an attempt to shake Viren, and he succeeded in losing everyone except Viren and Foster, who was attempting to become the first British runner to win a gold in the Olympic 5,000 meters, 10,000 meters, or marathon. Foster finally dropped back, while Viren stuck right behind Lopes. "What a machine Viren is," Bjorklund recalls thinking as he watched the Finn move away from the pack. "It looked like he was out for a Sunday stroll. There was absolutely no doubt in anybody's mind about what was going to happen."

Lopes accelerated on each lap in an attempt to get away from Viren, but to no avail. The Finn followed easily behind, looking down to avoid stepping on Lopes's heels. Nearing the bell lap, Viren took the lead and, his stride not changing, passed Lopes, who was unable to respond. Viren ran in for a 27:40.38 win and his third Olympic gold medal. His second 5,000 meters took only 13:31. Viren held up his shoes on his victory lap—he says it is because of a blister, others say it was a plug for his sponsor, Asics—and two young Finns ran with him, waving a large blue and white Finnish flag. Viren had done it again. He had, said Foster, "that certain Olympic magic about him."

Viren did not have much time to enjoy his win, because a star-studded field was well-rested and waiting for him to show up at the starting line for the 5,000. This one would be anything but a stroll in the park. There was one day's rest before the three heats of the 5,000, and Viren qualified by placing fourth in his heat, three seconds behind Dick Quax's 13:31. Lopes pulled out of the final due to a leg injury suffered in the 10,000, but there were plenty of other dangerous runners: Quax and Rod Dixon had not run the 10,000, nor had Ian Stewart or Klaus-Peter Hildenbrand. And then there was Foster, who won his 5,000 heat in 13:20.4, breaking Viren's Olympic record. All were faster than Viren in an open 1,500 meters, and the accepted thought was that in a sprint finish, there was no way Viren would be able to match their speed.

Viren and Haikkola worked on a strategy they thought might give Viren the win. Eino remembers,

> Lasse and Rolf decided they wanted Lasse to run all out from far out. . . . Do that precisely, with a little twist: every lap, he'll run two seconds faster. His ability to change speed so well, without it being noticed, could work to his advantage.

In the classic Montreal 5,000-meter final, Foster took the early lead, passing 2,000 meters in 5:26.4, before Viren passed him and Hildenbrand. "The whole group was running almost anaerobic; they had all fallen into his trap. He actually challenged them using their strength. It was like the best chess match you'll ever see. They were outmatched mentally as well as physically," said Eino. Viren dropped back in the pack, satisfied that the pace was quick enough. As the laps unfolded and the runners stayed together, it became clear that the race was going to come down to a sprint finish. And a betting man would say there was no way Viren could outkick this field of 1,500-meter runners.

Then, with exactly a lap and one-half to go, Viren put in a surge that brought him to the lead. Before the race, Haikkola had picked that spot to break the field. "Lasse had the ability to change speed without showing effort," says Eino.

First Dixon sprinted, but he could not pass Viren. Next came Hildenbrand, also to no avail. Then, around the turn, Quax went wide, out into the third lane. With a wild look in his eyes, Quax sprinted for all he was worth, but he, too, could not pass Viren, who dug deep for a last 400 meters of 55.4 to hold off the others and win his fourth gold medal. Viren's time for his last 1,500 meters of the 5,000 would have placed him *fourth* in the Montreal 1,500 final.

Viren played down the sprinting ability of the kickers in the race. "I just had to get to the line first," he understated. "My coach said, 'Get to the front with 600 meters left, and stay there.' I did" he told Foster, who summed up the race like this: Quax hoped he could win; Dixon thought he could win; but Viren knew he would win.

Shorter says Dixon might have been in the best shape of all the finalists. But when the New Zealander said before the race, "I'm going to run a world record, and if Lasse passes me, I'll trip him," Shorter knew that Dixon wouldn't win. He knew that mentally Lasse had gotten him.

"Great champions know how to win, and winning is understanding your opponents and outsmarting them. If you have three people who are equally good, it is who runs the smartest, who is trained mentally, who wins," says Eino. "That's what Lasse did in Montreal." He had completely spent himself to the extent he was vomiting afterwards, but he had done it again, and somewhere, Nurmi was watching, clutching his stop watch and smiling.

Viren showed once again that he could never be counted out of an Olympic final. "That is the race that really stands out," says Jaakko Tuominen, a Finnish 400-meter intermediate hurdler. "That's where Lasse ran the toughest. There were still seven guys left on the last lap, and I thought he had no chance. He kept to the inside and let the others fight each other."

Viren always had a plan and followed that plan, no matter what the others in the race were doing. Even in the last laps of the 5,000, with Quax, Foster, and Dixon sitting on his shoulder and breathing down his neck, he did not worry. He kept going faster and faster, took the best shots the others could muster, and came away with the win.

In addition to his talent, Viren also had supreme confidence that he would win. One of the recurring motifs of the careers of Viren and other top runners is that to be the best, you have to believe 100 percent that you are the best; otherwise, you will worry about the other people in the race. That is the attitude Nurmi, Shorter, Zatopek, Coe, and many champions have. They carry images of themselves as being excellent runners, and thus live up to these expectations. Viren is a prime example of how important a role the unconscious plays in who we are and how we act. He truly believed that he was going to beat everyone in his Olympic races; there was not any doubt in his mind.

Says Bjorklund,

> I've never seen a running machine like that. His form was absolutely perfect. There wasn't an ounce of wasted movement with Viren. He ran from the belly, from the belly button. The thing that amazes me about him was how fast he was at the end of the race. He just kept cranking it out and cranking it out. Lasse didn't care about the time; he would cha cha with anyone. He was simply out there competing against the best there were.

Viren's legacy to running, says Shorter, is the way he changed racing tactics.

> He was the first to transform the 5,000 and 10,000 into a protracted sprint. That is how he felt he was his best. Because until Lasse, nobody ever went that early. He created his own tactic, that no one else had trained for, but he had. So all of a sudden, you get to the Olympics and you are faced with 60-second 400s with a mile to go. Until then, the 10,000 meters was a last-lap sprint that started typically at 300 meters to go.
>
> Viren was different. He went into the Olympic games and trained to run 1:56 for the last 800 of the 10,000, and ran 4:01 for the last mile of the 5,000. He trained to do it differently. And people couldn't respond. However he got in a position to do that, he did. What happens is the change in the psychological process in the race. There you are in the Olympic games, and somebody is running 60-second pace in the 5,000 meters and there are still four laps to go. And you've never done this before.

But the indomitable Viren was not finished running at Montreal. The very next day, just 18 hours after his 5,000-meter win that capped 30 kilometers of track racing against the best runners in the world, he was lined up in the Olympic Stadium one more time for the start of the marathon, trying boldly—rashly, some said—to repeat the untouchable triple crown of distance running done only by Emil Zatopek in 1952.

It was Viren's first attempt at the marathon, and he was looking to key off Shorter. The American knew this, and during the early part of the race he hid from Viren behind other runners in the large pack, getting a kick out of watching Viren looking around anxiously for him. Shorter would then suddenly pop out next to Viren, enjoying his game of hide-and-seek.

Viren had his own game to worry about. He ran with the leaders until Shorter made his break at 21 kilometers, despite having his glycogen stores depleted from his hard racing, and he ran in to finish an admirable fifth in 2:13:10.8. "Viren's win in the 10,000 and then the 5,000, when he ran down some of the best milers in the world, and then came back to run the marathon, is the most impressive performance in Olympic history," says Bjorklund.

When he ran his last lap on the track at the finish of the marathon, spectators saw that Viren's graceful stride was stiff for the first time, and that he was grimacing coming around the track. The marathon showed that even Viren was mortal, after all, and also showed that "Lasse just had guts," says Jaakko Tuominen.

Before returning home, Viren went to the United States to race. He ran several races, and he stopped with his wife to stay with Shorter in Boulder. But the Virens cut short their visit; it was nothing personal against Shorter, with whom he remained friends. He was just homesick. "Lasse likes being at home," says Shorter. "He came here to see what it is like, and he decided he didn't like it." Even a town of 80,000, like Boulder was at the time (small by U.S. standards), was a metropolis compared to Myrskylä.

Soon, Viren was back in his village, working as a policeman and relaxing after what were being called his "near-miraculous" Montreal wins. The Finnish people once again embraced Viren's wins with wild celebrations, and the 2,000 villagers of Myrskylä donated land and built a large sauna on the lake for him. He took a break from training, and spent the winter visiting with his family and enjoying his favorite hobby of moose hunting. Viren liked nothing better than coming back to the friendly confines of Myrskylä. "Among his own people, Lasse is extremely nice and very considerate," Eino says. "But as a typical Finn, you have to earn his trust. Once you are in his circle, then you're taken care of. You have to prove yourself first. In Finland, it's not what you say, but what you do." And Viren had proved himself.

Suspicions of Blood Doping

After the Montreal Olympics, however, the question of "blood doping" followed Viren around like an angry crowd of mosquitoes in a marshy Finnish swamp. Blood doping, legal in the 1970s but banned in 1985, is the process of withdrawing some of an athlete's blood, storing it, and then returning it after the body has naturally replenished its diminished supply of red blood cells. Those cells carry oxygen through the body on a compound called hemoglobin, and a greater supply of red blood cells means more oxygen-carrying capacity; it thus produces the ability to race farther and faster. (This is also the principle behind training at altitude.) Blood doping is controversial because it gives those who use the process an unfair advantage. It is also dangerous, having resulted in the deaths of several young bicyclists in the past decade, when those cyclists' blood became so thick with red blood cells that it could not flow through their arteries.

Rumors swirled after Viren's Montreal wins that he had used this technique. The speculation was fueled in part by Viren's oft-repeated quip at a press conference that his secret was "reindeer milk." Viren did drink a lot of milk while training, but it was not reindeer milk. British rival Brendan Foster writes of Viren, "His ability to change his form drastically from race to race had given rise to all kinds of allegations about his methods, none of which I believed." Unlike U.S. stars Carl Lewis and Butch Reynolds two decades later, Viren chose not to defend himself against accusations in the media. He is a quiet man among people he does not know, taciturn even by Finnish standards, and he never had much to do with journalists.

A German publication offered Viren one million dollars for the "exclusive" story on the truth of the blood-doping charges. Viren agreed to tell his side of the story. He told the publisher, "The story will say that I didn't blood dope."

"Then we won't have a story," the publisher said, withdrawing the magazine's offer when he found out Viren was denying the charges.

Viren did not care what the international media said, according to Eino.

> He did what he wanted to do. He wanted his golds; his goal was to do what Paavo Nurmi did. Maybe he should have brought a lawsuit against ABC-TV, but he comes from a small country, and wasn't used to that sort of thing.

Viren says two things bother him most about the accusations: because people were saying he had done it anyway, he could have taken the million dollars from the magazine, and, if blood doping does work, what could he have done if he had tried it?

"I thought he should have come out and denied it categorically," writes Foster in his book *Brendan Foster*. "He did not have to convince me, though, because I feel certain in my own mind that Lasse Viren is simply a remarkable athlete, who needed no such aids as blood doping, even if it did work, to assist him."

Foster points out that blood doping's effects work over a short time, yet Viren "was running brilliantly" when setting a world record for a road 20K in May 1976, and then ran the year's fastest 10,000 meters in June, with the Olympics still three months away. Viren had "a brilliant knack of getting ready on the day that matters and also a tremendous strength of character, which is such that even if he finishes last in a race that is not important, then he genuinely does not worry."

Adds Foster in his book,

> Anyone who is in the public eye but retains a deliberately low profile is bound to be the subject of speculation and rumor. The blood-doping stories were probably given more credence in Montreal because of accusations made by frustrated losers, who could not understand how the man could be so successful. . . . Jealousy was one of the factors behind those stories.

Most have opinions on it, but the fact remains, says 1972 Olympic Marathon gold medalist Frank Shorter, that Viren was the master of peaking. "Lasse did exactly what you are supposed to do," says Shorter. "However he did it, he created the ability to race in a way that other people felt they could not duplicate." Unfortunately, the rumors caused some to question Viren's fantastic achievements. Perhaps *sisu* is what Viren meant when he told reporters his secret was "reindeer milk." Was it blood doping, or was it rather talent, training, and the ineffable *sisu*? The question is still debated among track fans, but the one person who knows for certain, Viren himself, says he did not blood dope.

1980 Moscow Olympics

Viren did not get the chance to prove himself the year after the Olympics, as disaster struck later that winter. While hunting with friends, Viren stepped into a hole and tore ligaments in his ankle. Unable to run, he missed his traditional winter basework and had a poor year in 1977. In 1978, he came back to run a 13:33 5,000 and a 28:11.8 10,000. In 1979, he was back near 28 minutes for 10,000 meters, hitting 28:04 in the fall of 1979. Then it was time, once more, to start his Olympic buildup.

In 1979, Viren quit his job as a policeman and was hired by a Finnish bank to develop a youth training program. He went to Brazil in December for his traditional six weeks of high mileage on a three-times-a-day training schedule. Viren broke up the training by traveling to Puerto Rico in February for the San Blas Half-Marathon. Viren had some fun there, as he liked to do when he was among athletes at road races. Says Bill Rodgers, "I have a lot of respect for Lasse. He was a real character. It wasn't just all work for him."

After returning to Finland for a short break, Viren went back to South America for high-altitude training in Bogota, Colombia, from March 30 to May 2, but suffered a groin injury in the spring and missed valuable training. With the Olympics nearing, he did his favorite workout of 50 × 100 meters all-out. As had become a tradition, Viren climbed over the fence at the track in Helsinki to do this session, as a kind of mental stimulus. Climbing the fence instead of walking through the gate was symbolic of getting over the problems he had faced. Because of the high mileage he did, Viren had several injuries during his career, but he never let the injuries linger. Viren immediately would have surgery when hurt, rather than try to run through an injury. Though it meant missing training at times, that approach let Viren compete in three Olympic Games.

When the Moscow Olympics started, Viren was back trying to mine gold once again. But there was a new opponent this time—stifling heat, the great nemesis of runners from the north. Viren ran just 28:45 in his heat, not fast enough to qualify. He would have missed the 10,000 meters final if Ireland's John Treacy had not collapsed from the heat, opening up a spot for Viren.

In the final, it looked as if Viren's Olympic magic was back. It came down to a thrilling five-man race featuring Finland vs. Ethiopia, with Viren and teammate Kaarlo Maaninka battling Yifter, Mohammad Kedir, and a third Ethiopian. Viren and the Ethiopians exchanged the lead over the last mile. Back and forth they went, with a grimacing Viren and Maaninka going to the front near the end, with Yifter right behind. As in Munich and Montreal, Viren was ahead at the bell with 400 meters to go, just as he had been in his four Olympic victories, and the spectators in Lenin Stadium stood in awed expectation of seeing Viren pull out another win.

Kedir passed Viren, and on the first turn of the last lap, Viren gathered himself and moved up onto Kedir's shoulder, ready to once again start his drive to the tape. Could Viren possibly pull out an Olympic 10,000-meter three-peat? For a magical instant, it did appear that he could, as it looked as if he were going past Kedir, back into the lead. This time, however, it was not to be. When Viren accelerated on the last lap, the others accelerated more. Just as Viren was passing Kedir, Yifter went by them both like a rocket. Then Kedir, the other Ethiopian, and Maaninka all followed Yifter past Viren, who ended up fifth with a time of 27:50.5. He did not win, but his many fans called it one of his best races. It truly was an amazing performance; Viren showed his greatness by running his heart out. He wanted to bow out gracefully from the Olympic state, and he certainly had.

Each of Viren's Olympic runs had its own personality, and this loss showed Viren's dignity and his racing smarts. "That race was the only time the Ethiopians had a good strategy," says Eino, explaining that, unlike the other Olympic races in which Viren was allowed to run rhythmically from the front, this time the Ethiopians constantly went into the lead and slowed down the pace.

"The Ethiopians realized that the only way to win was to have two guys interrupt his run, to run in front and then slow down." By running in front and changing the pace, they broke Viren's stride and did not let him run his race. Viren had never lost an Olympic track final, but he was as gracious in defeat as he was in victory. He had shown the world how to be an Olympic winner; now, he showed us how to lose.

As soon as he finished, Viren embraced Maaninka, who had chased Yifter in for the silver medal, and held up his teammate's arm. He then shook hands with Yifter, a good friend of Viren's with whom he had battled many times through the years. Viren and Maaninka walked slowly past officials lined-up, forming a passageway off the track. Just as he was about to leave the stadium, Viren stopped and turned. He looked back across the infield, putting his hands on his hips and lingering, as if not wanting the moment to end. Taking a last look, Viren then turned and walked off the track.

Viren entered his second Olympic Marathon at the Moscow games, but pulled out with nine miles to go. It was his last Olympic race, and the end of what Cordner Nelson of _Track & Field News_ called the "most spectacular Olympic distance career in history." Summing up Viren's career, Eino says, "In Finland, we have a saying, 'Big words don't fell the trees.' That's what Lasse did in his running. His races speak louder than his words."

Viren's club, Myrskylän Myrsky, continued holding a race in Lasse's honor, called the Lassen Hölkkä. After the Moscow Olympics, several of Viren's rivals, including Yifter and Emiel Puttemans, came to the race to show their respect.

Viren would often travel from Myrskylä to road races during the following years. Viren also attempted some marathons, but mostly he showed up to lend his name—one of the biggest names in the sport. "I'm happy to see a new generation take its place in the running world," said Viren. When Grandma's Marathon in Duluth, Minnesota, wanted to put on a first-class event, Viren was the runner they brought in. Says Bjorklund,

> Race director Scott Keenan used to say, "Foot races are like horse races; you can either assemble a exciting field, or bring in the Secretariat." That's what Lasse Viren was: a Secretariat. Minnesota just loves him. Lasse is a guy like Zatopek. If you've never

met them, you'd think they were 20-feet tall. They are not big men; they're both soft-spoken and polite. But when Lasse or Emil put shoes on to race, a different look came into their eyes. Some people are transformed into a different kind of person when they race. That's the way Viren is.

Viren kept training at a low level and gave some thought to making a comeback for the 1984 Olympics, but he was unable to find a sponsor willing to support his training. He retired in 1985 and remains "the king" in Finland, giving lectures, attending youth camps, and appearing at events such as the "Finland Run," a relay run across the length of Finland. "He is always out there giving back to the people," says Eino. "That's one of the things Lasse learned as an athlete, and he takes that responsibility very seriously."

Training

From the time of Hannes Kolehmainen, Finnish runners have known how to peak, and getting ready for championship races was the theme of Viren's training program. Shorter compares Viren to miler Noureddine Morceli, in that Viren could win when he wanted to. Many of Viren's competitors were also talented, but they were not able to perform when it counted. To be a champion, an athlete has to be able to relax in front of 100,000 spectators, says Eino. "Lasse always had the inner strength to be with himself, to stay relaxed."

Viren's year was divided into sections: Winter was for basework, speed training started in the spring, and the racing season was May through September, after which he took a break. Unlike runners like Shorter and de Castella, Viren did not have a regular, weekly schedule. But like them, he was very wise about his training, and he monitored his training carefully. Haikkola geared Viren's training to increasing his heart rate during intervals. A typical week leading up to the Olympics included:

He had several standard workouts, such as 5,000 meters of alternating 50- or 100-meter sprints, which he once ran in 13:43. Viren also ran loops on a beautiful "special" hill outside Myrskylä. He knew when he was in shape by his times on this loop and when he could run an interval session of 10 × 400 meters in 59-60 seconds with a 200 recovery. Altitude training was very important for Viren, and he spent much of his winter months at altitude, often in Brazil at a town called Penedo populated mainly by people of Finnish descent.

Sunday: A.M., 25 kilometers keeping pulse at 96 beats per minute (1:46:00);

P.M., 12-kilometer fartlek run (52:00).

Monday: A.M., 12 kilometers including 8 × 600 meters uphill keeping pulse at 180 beats per minute (1:02:00);

Noon, 15-kilometer fartlek run with surges every 2-4 minutes keeping pulse at 122 beats per minute (56:00);

P.M., 12-kilometer fartlek run (52:00).

Tuesday: A.M., 12 kilometers keeping pulse at 84 beats per minute (50:00);

Noon, 12-kilometers of intervals; 2 sets of 10 × 200 meters with 200 meter floats in between and 5 minutes rest between each set (50:00);

P.M., 17-kilometer fartlek run keeping pulse at 90 (1:08:00).

Wednesday: A.M., 15-kilometer fartlek run keeping pulse at 84 beats per minute (60:00)

P.M., 20 kilometers (1:25:00).

Thursday: A.M., rest (rain);

P.M., 22 kilometers keeping pulse at 122 beats per minute (1:30:00).

Friday: A.M., 12-kilometer fartlek run including 1 × 1 kilometer at 172 beats per minute (1:00:00);

Noon, 15-kilometer fartlek run with 2-4 minute surges keeping pulse up to 134 beats per minute (58:00);

P.M., 12-kilometer fartlek run (52:00).

Saturday: A.M., 12-kilometer fartlek (50:00);

Noon, 16-kilometer fartlek (1:05:00);

P.M., 10-kilometers (42 minutes).

© Photo Run/Victah Sailer

Lasse Viren continued racing after his retirement.
Here, in 1989, he made an appearance at the New York Games.

Mostly what Viren had was what other great runners had: the determination to train hard and consistently, with no expectations of instant
success. Once, Viren was driving through Lapland in northern Finland.
Passing a pleasant-looking lake, he decided to run around it. He stopped
the car and did the run. The next day he came back and measured it
with his car, and it turned out to be 50 kilometers around the lake. Viren
had run that far, by himself, simply because he had made up his mind
he was going to do so. That is the attitude that fueled his training.

Living in Finland was a big plus for Viren, Bjorklund believes.

Finland is so isolated that kids there grow up fearless. He was able to run all those miles on a soft, dirt surface in the woods. That's what made him tick. Then there were the 200-mile weeks back-to-back, up to eight in a row [during his base-building period]. Can you imagine coming back down to sea level after all those miles at 7,500 feet? Lasse was naturally gifted anyway, with what seemed like a 38-inch inseam.

Every athlete starts his career thinking he or she can be a champion, says Bjorklund, but most learn along the way that will never happen. Viren knew he was going to be one, and Haikkola "structured his career so that he would hit his peak on a certain day. There may have been runners as good as Viren, but no one prepared as well as he did." Tuominen agrees with Bjorklund, saying, "Lasse's greatest talent was that he was fearless. His 'secret' was that he prepared well and he trained hard."

Winding Down

For much of Viren's career, and even after he retired, Viren was asked in every interview about his "reindeer milk." Once, when in New York City as a guest of the marathon, he was spreading lotion on his legs.

"What is that, Lasse?" an anxious reporter asked, looking over his shoulder to make sure no one else would get in on his scoop. The reporter thought he had uncovered one of the great Viren's secrets.

"Reindeer s—," Viren replied, showing he hadn't lost his sense of humor.

Says Eino,

A good sense of humor is one of his trademarks. He teases everyone. What made him a champion was not only his athletics, but that he was able to relax by never taking things that seriously.

In 1994, Viren put his gold medals up for sale. He asked $200,000, and this price was not negotiable. Viren did not give an explanation to journalists for why he was selling his medals, but friends say it was because he wanted to put his three children through school. The four gold medals sat in a box at his house, and Viren wanted someone to buy them and donate them to a museum. The plan was blasted in newspapers and magazines, but Viren, as usual, kept quiet. "They weren't interested in what Lasse had to say about it," says Eino.

His children are growing up and he wants them to have an education. The point is that Lasse never went into athletics for money, but in the spirit of being the best he could be. If he were running now, he'd be wealthy, but he was too early.

Viren, 46, was still poking fun at journalists in 1995, when it was reported he was going to make a comeback for the marathon at the World Championships.

Taking some visitors around Helsinki several years after he had retired, Lasse Viren gestures through the window of his late-model Peugeot, pointing out the sights of downtown Helsinki to his visitors. There, he says, is the national theater. And over there, the harbor. Here is the Olympic Stadium, with the bronze statue of the naked Nurmi, in mid-stride on the corner. (In 1994, a statue of Viren was added to the spot, confirming his position as one of the two greatest Flying Finns.) "Helsinki is very nice," Viren says. "But I prefer the countryside."

More than three-fourths of Finland is still forests, mostly pine, spruce, and the tough birch, which can grow where no other trees are able to grow. Ten percent of the country is lakes and rivers. Finland was the last country on Earth to be uncovered when the glaciers retreated during the last Ice Age, 10,000 years ago. Much of the soil was scraped away then, and it is said that in Finland, the ground is dug "with dynamite instead of a spade." What's left is some of the hardest rock in the world and some of the hardiest people and runners. This is the land that forged the Flying Finns.

Distance running suits Viren's—and the Finnish—soul. The long winters make for independent men and women, accustomed to hardships, who take discomfort unflinchingly. Finns are closer to nature than the rest of us. They watch the sky through the winter, waiting for the darkness to retreat. The summer is so short in Finland that Finns greet the return of the sun with exuberance, as they know that winter is not far behind. This gives an existential bent to life in Finland, a sensitivity usually found only in great artists and those who understand the words of the poet Nikos Kazantzakis: "Life's a brief lightning flash; great joy to him who grasps it in time." The Finns are a people who understand this, having had to battle invaders and the elements all their history, and they rewrite the couplet in the following way: "Summer's a brief lightning flash; let's do all we can before the darkness returns."

During a career at the highest level of competition that did justice to his country and his Finnish running heritage, Viren rewrote it a step further: "An athlete's career is a brief lightning flash; let me do as much as I can with it before it ends."

7

El Caballo

Born November 12, 1950, Cuba

World record: 800 meters

Olympic gold, 400 and 800, 1976

Two-time Athlete of the Year, *Track and Field News*

In 1971, there was a forward on the Cuban junior national basketball team who had a decent jump shot but was prone to running with the ball instead of dribbling it. It is a good thing for the sports world that the young Alberto Juantorena wasn't a great basketball player. One year before he would make his first appearance on the track in the 1972 Olympic Games, he gave no thought to running, spending all of his time playing basketball.

Juantorena was energetic, tall, and fast and played good defense. Sometimes, however, his feet did not keep up with his mind, and he was prone to getting traveling calls and making other rule violations while sprinting up the court. One day during a practice early in 1971, the national team basketball coach called him over to the sidelines.

"Alberto," the coach said, "We think it's time you thought about switching to athletics."

"Thanks for the offer, but no, I'd rather not," Juantorena replied. "I've told you before that I cannot switch. You know basketball is my life."

"We're sorry, but it's already been decided that you will change sports. Starting tomorrow, you are a runner, not a basketball player."

"Why?" Juantorena asked.

"Really, Alberto, it's because you have no chance in basketball."

Juantorena was crushed, because he had a passion for his favorite sport. "Basketball is very emotional," he explains. "Much of running is done alone; it's boring, with so much sacrifice." But he quickly recovered from his disappointment and reported for track practice, vowing to become a success in his new sport.

Cuban officials knew Juantorena had talent—during his basketball years, he had beaten all the members of the national track team in some 600- and 1,200-meter races in his hometown of Santiago de Cuba on the south side of the island. The clincher came when Juantorena clocked 50.8 for 400 meters—wearing his high-top basketball shoes. "All the time, they were trying to convince me to switch to track," Juantorena recalled. "I always said no,'because I really loved basketball."

The officials were adamant, however, and so started the track career of *El Caballo* (the Horse), as Juantorena was nicknamed, for he ran with a stallion-like power. He would go on to bring glory to Cuba and its revolution by becoming, in 1976, the only athlete to win Olympic gold medals in the 400- and 800-meter races. Success in sports was the main way the revolution showcased itself to the world, and Juantorena won in such a way that all the world—even those opposing the revolution—marveled at his boundless power and strength and the way he galloped over the track when he ran, towering over his opponents. And if Alberto had only been able to hit a baseline jumper with more consistency, he might never have started running.

Early Career

Juantorena is a child of the Cuban revolution, born November 12, 1950, in the old colonial city of Santiago, where the revolution against Fulgencia Batista first gathered strength. His father owned a small grocery store, and his mother stayed at home raising Alberto and his brother and sister. He came from a close-knit family; his father and brother, who look just like him, though not as tall, are best of friends with Alberto. Life was pleasant in Santiago, with Juantorena spending most of his time outside playing in the warm, tropical weather. "I had a normal childhood," he says. Juantorena harbored three loves when he was growing up: for his family, for sports, and for his dog named Campeoán (champion).

Juantorena attended the Ernest Bacardi school, named for the rum manufacturer who is still very famous in Santiago. Juantorena had a fiery temper that was usually kept in check, but sometimes he would fight with the other school kids and get into minor trouble. Yet he was also very sensitive of others, even as a youngster. One day he came home without any shoes. When his mother asked him where they were, Alberto replied he had given them to a classmate who didn't have any shoes. At first his mother was upset, but then she told her son, "You did a very good thing today."

In 1956 a young lawyer named Fidel Castro Ruz led an attack on the Macando military garrison. The raid did not come off as planned; Batista's soldiers killed most of the young rebels, and Castro was captured and sent to prison. Alberto was not old enough to understand those first shots of the revolution, but 20 years later he would become one of its greatest sports heroes.

The exiled Castro returned from Mexico in 1958 with a boatload of followers on the ship *Granma*. It was a dangerous time in Santiago, and when the bullets started flying, Juantorena's mother said, "Go inside and stay there." Alberto waited out the fighting in the house, watching and hearing the bullets going back and forth. When the Castro-led revolution toppled Batista on January 1, 1959, there were many changes, including redistribution of land and the nationalization of some industries. Sports, especially sports for the young, became one of the three major areas of emphasis for the revolution, along with islandwide medical care and literacy. Under the new government, nearly everyone in society did some kind of physical activity.

Like all Cuban school children, Juantorena and his classmates spent two hours a day, three days a week, playing different sports. Juantorena was a superb athlete, blessed with fine reflexes and eye-to-hand coordination, and he was good at whatever he tried. He took part in gymnastics, volleyball, soccer, track, and basketball. Baseball was one of his favorite sports. He was also an excellent swimmer, and for a time considered joining the navy.

"We participated in every sport when I was young. Maybe you are better in this sport or that one, so you begin to specialize," Juantorena explains. He was more athletic and taller than most of his classmates, so in the 9th grade, he began specializing in basketball. He still ran in school track races, becoming a regional high-school champion in the 800 and 1,500 meters. When he was 16, one friend was always telling Juantorena, "You will be a big man one day. I don't know in what, but I know you will be."

The Cuban sports system is set up as a pyramid, with seven levels. It starts with grade-school sports on the base and ends with the national team at the top. There are two aspects to the sports setup: the social system (such as factory teams), and the school system. Juantorena, like more than 85 percent of the athletes on the Cuban Olympic team, came up through the school system. All students are required to take part in athletics and in school sports, with the best being selected for further development. From those competitions at the Bacardi school, Juantorena was selected to continue playing basketball at the next level. He continued playing until officials finally told him, "Alberto, there are other basketball players taller than you, but there aren't many runners faster than you. You are losing time playing basketball." "I was very disappointed," he says.

Once reconciled to being a runner and not a basketball player, Juantorena quickly channeled his overflowing energy into athletics. On March 8, 1971, Juantorena was given his first test as a track team member. His friends laughed at him when Juantorena showed up dressed in his basketball uniform. "We just want to look at your form," the coaches told him. Without any experience or proper shoes, Juantorena went through 500 meters in 1:07, a good indication of his potential.

One evening not long after making the switch to track, he told his father, "I have a dream and a goal in my mind. That one day I will be an Olympic champion."

Juantorena's golden journey began when he was sent to ESPA, Cuba's school for top athletes, for six months of training. In a time trial—wearing spikes this time—he ran 46.7 for 400 meters, good enough to earn him a place on the national track team, where his coach was Eneas Muñoz. Soon after, Juantorena hooked up with Sigmunt Zabierzowski, a Polish coach who had been sent to Cuba to train athletes. They immediately hit it off and developed a special relationship.

Zabierzowski took the young, restless bundle of energy that was Alberto Juantorena under his wing and carefully planned out his career. At 6'-3", 180-pounds of lean muscle, Juantorena had the talent and mental concentration, Zabierzowski believed from the start, to be one of the best ever.

After finishing at ESPA Juantorena enrolled at the University of Havana. He lived with his aunt not far from the famous Tropicana nightclub and began training and studying.

Because he was on the national team, Juantorena's schooling was paid for by the government, and he also received a small stipend to live on. After he joined the national track team, he went every day to the national stadium on the east edge of Havana. The outgoing Juantorena had fun with his new teammates, all the while getting stronger and faster under the watchful eye of Zabierzowski. Juantorena soon had a reputation for being able to push himself harder than anyone on the team. The overflowing energy and exuberance he had shown on the basketball court was successfully transferred to the track. He would run interval sessions so hard that he would collapse, sometimes having to be packed in ice to bring his body temperature down.

Realizing His Potential

Juantorena had been training only a year prior to the Munich Olympics. Early in 1972, he went with the Cuban national team on his first trip to Europe, where in April he ran 46.2 in the 400 to place second behind South African-born Marcello Fiasconaro. The trip helped motivate Juantorena to train even harder, because he enjoyed traveling and seeing some of the world.

In Munich, Juantorena clocked 45.94 in his first preliminary qualifying round and 45.96 in the quarterfinals to advance to the semifinals. But then in the semis, he missed qualifying for the finals by less than an inch. Even more than 20 years later, Juantorena's eyes flash when he talks about that Munich semifinal. "I ran 46.07; he ran 46.05. I'll never forget that guy," Juantorena says. "Munich was too early for us," Zabierzowski said. "We still had too much to learn, too much to refine."

What they learned was that Juantorena needed to get stronger to be able to handle fast racing in several qualifying heats. Despite not making the finals, Juantorena's performance at Munich was significant in that he was voted "Rookie of the Year" in Cuban sports, kudos which gave him more encouragement and support from track officials. The close call at the Olympics fueled the emotional Juantorena, giving him motivation to train through the tough interval workouts Zabierzowski knew were essential for an Olympic champion. They had four years to wait and train for Juantorena's next shot at Olympic glory, and they planned them carefully. And though he never told Juantorena, Zabierzowski had the 800 in mind for his star pupil as early as 1972.

Great things were forecast for Juantorena after Munich, and they began coming true in 1973, when he won the Budapest World University Games in a personal best of 45.36, beating David Jenkins of Britain. His wife was expecting their first child when he left for Budapest, and Juantorena says he won the race for his newborn son. He missed a lot of schoolwork traveling to races, but Juantorena took extra classes to make up the requirements, eventually getting his degree in economics.

Juantorena's success continued in 1974, when he became a force on the European track circuit, going undefeated over 400 meters and running a personal best of 44.7. (He ran one 800 meters in 1973, clocking 1:49.8, then ran another in 1974; they were to be his only attempts over the two-lap distance until 1976). Juantorena capped the year by winning the Santo Domingo Games 400 meters in 45.56 seconds.

After a solid season of training in Havana, Juantorena ran 44.80 early in the summer of 1975, followed by 44.45. However he injured his foot and missed most of the remainder of the 1975 season, though he still came back to grab the silver medal (in 44.8) in the Pan American Games behind American Ron Ray.

Because of his injury, Juantorena was ranked just fourth for the year in the 400 meters and was not considered the favorite for the following year's Olympic Games in Montreal. That was to change, however, when a healthy Juantorena was able to do the interval training Zabierzowski devised for him in the spring of 1976.

Training: "You Must Sacrifice for It"

Juantorena used the periodization method of training, brought to Cuba by Zabierzowski and other foreign coaches after the revolution. What Juantorena calls his "General Training," from October through February, was designed to build up his overall stamina. He says that that training was tough. "We used to run on sand in hills, two times day, up to 25 kilometers a day; 15K in morning, 10K in evening."

After several months of this stamina work, Juantorena began speed-specific training. The core of this training was repeat 200s, 150s, 350s, 300s, and 500s. Then came middle-distance workouts—600s, 1,000s, and 1,200s.

Mondays and Wednesdays were interval sessions on the track. Standard interval workouts were 20 × 200 meters or 15 × 300 meters. The speed of the 200s varied depending on the season; in the spring, they would start at 30 seconds and progress through the workout down to

28, 26, and 25 seconds. "When I was peaking, they would be in 21, 20.5, and 20.8," Juantorena says. "Very free, very smooth."

Thursday was reserved for long weight-lifting sessions, with no running. In the weight room, Juantorena would bench-press 80 percent of his body weight 30 or 40 times.

Friday, depending on the season, was an overdistance day. Tuesday and Thursday were recovery days, and Sunday was taken completely off. "Sunday was always our rest day. I liked Sundays, after the hard week of training."

"The secret to being a good runner," Juantorena says, "is that you must sacrifice your life for it. You must train hard, eat well, with not too many parties and not too much sex. You must have a lot of discipline, and, over everything else, you have to really want to do something. And you must get a lot of help from your family."

Juantorena ran some fine early-season times in 1976 off this training. Then came a key moment in his career. In April, while at the track in Havana training just before the Cuban National Championships, Zabierzowski called him over.

"Alberto, I have a favor to ask you. The runners in the 800 (at the championships) need a pacemaker, so I want you to enter the race and run the first lap hard," he said. "You don't even have to finish if you don't feel good; just try to reach the end if you want, to pull the others along."

Juantorena not only reached the finish, but it took him just 1:46.1 to do so, after a first lap of 50 seconds. "Hey, that wasn't as bad as I thought it would be," he told Zabierzowski after catching his breath. "You know, coach, maybe I *can* run some good 800s."

Zabierzowski simply smiled and did not say anything. He knew his star had a sprinter's mentality— anything over a lap was anathema to him, something he viewed as a distance race. He was aware that it was rare for a 400-meter runner to move up to the 800; but he also knew Juantorena had the physique and talent to be a great two-lapper. If Zabierzowski had told Juantorena straightaway he was going to be running the 800, Juantorena might not have accepted it as easily as he did. The pacemaking chore was the coach's way of getting Alberto to try the 800 without putting any pressure on him.

With confidence from his 1:46.1 800-meter/45.4 400-meter double at the Cuban nationals, Juantorena went to test himself on the European circuit. An 800 meters in Formia, Italy, gave him a good lesson in tactics. Because of his inexperience, he was boxed in during the first lap. After freeing himself on the second lap, he swung wide to pass the entire field, winning in 1:45.2. Despite the fast time, he said, "The 800 will have to wait until next year. I wish to be Olympic 400 champion first."

Juantorena ran one more two-lapper before Montreal, July 10, in Havana, clocking 1:44.9. With his injury from 1975 obviously healed, he was by now one of the favorites in the 400, but was not given serious consideration in the 800, because of his inexperience. Zabierzowski, however, knew he had a good chance, and when Juantorena came to Montreal after his undefeated European season, his coach took him aside and pronounced him fit and ready to spring a surprise on the world.

If Juantorena had his choice, though, he would have gone to Angola to fight instead of to Montreal to run. Juantorena had in fact made up his mind to join Cuban forces backing rebels fighting the South African-backed Angolan government. But Fidel Castro told him, "No, for Cuba, it is more important if you go to the Olympics and win a gold medal."

A Cuban Comet Descends on Montreal

Juantorena's reputation as one of the all-time greats was formed at Montreal. According to *Track & Field News,*

> If he had been better known before Montreal, maybe he wouldn't have made such an incredible impact on the sporting world. On the other hand, considering the performance of the 24-year-old Cuban Comet in Canada, it's hard to believe that his achievements still wouldn't have been simply astounding.

At the prerace press conference in Montreal's Olympic Village, Juantorena was his easygoing, charismatic self. He had about him the confident air of someone who is strong, fast, and smart—and knows it. He jokingly said that the "Danger" in Alberto Juantorena Danger (Danger is his maternal name) was a warning for the Americans in the 400. He was hardly asked about the 800 meters.

But Zabierzowski had been thinking about the 800 for four years. Once settled in Montreal, Zabierzowski came up with a plan for the 800, which would be run first. They knew Juantorena had better speed than anyone else in the race, having run 44.4 seconds for 400 meters just before going to Montreal. They tried to outsmart the other 800-meter runners, deciding to keep as low a profile as possible in the heats, in order to take the others by surprise. Before each heat, Zabierzowski and Juantorena sat down and reviewed the list of competitors. They looked at the "pedigree of the runners" and selected the two best in each heat.

"Let them go," Zabierzowski told Juantorena. "You run with the group. Run as easily as you can, just so you can qualify."

"Don't you want me to finish first in the heat?" Juantorena asked.

"No. Never qualify in first or second place," Zabierzowski replied. "Look over the races, and qualify easily—it doesn't matter if you are in third or fourth place—without risk of not qualifying."

Juantorena tried to hold back and not win his heats, but he felt so good that he won his first heat on July 23 in 1:47.2. Still running well within himself, he was first in his semifinal as well, in 1:45.9. He said it helped that he was not one of the favorites, because it kept the pressure off him. "That's why you saw me all the time looking over my shoulder [in the heats]," he said. "I didn't want to use too much energy." Journalists misinterpreted Juantorena's looking over his shoulder, writing he was arrogant.

Juantorena was also helped by politics rearing its ugly head in sports. "Kenya boycotted [to protest the presence of New Zealand, which had sent a rugby team to South Africa, which had a policy of apartheid] and [Mike] Boit was not there," Juantorena said. Boit was the Munich 800-meter bronze medalist and fourth-place finisher in the 1972 Olympic 1,500. He was the one 800-meter runner with the speed and strength to match Juantorena. Boit had never faced Juantorena, but had beaten Montreal favorite Rick Wohlhuter of the United States, the 800-meter world-record holder, four of the six times they met in 1975. The other prerace favorite in the 800 was Ivo Van Damme of Belgium. Of the world's top 800 runners, Juantorena said, "All are dangerous, but Boit is the one I respect the most."

Wohlhuter had the fastest time of the year among the Montreal finalists (1:44.78 in winning the U.S. trials in June) and was facing a tough 800/1,500-meter double of his own. Van Damme, the European indoor champion with 46.4 400-meter speed to his credit, was said to be peaking at the right time.

Juantorena's other rivals in the 800-meter finals included Carlo Grippo of Italy, Steve Ovett of Great Britain, Yugoslavia's Luciano Susanj, Sri Ram Singh of India, and Willi Wulbeck of East Germany. All were fast and capable of winning if the pace was slow enough through the first 600 meters. That was not going to be the case, however, as Zabierzowski's plan for Juantorena was simple: "Don't let the other runners take a big lead during the race. Make sure you are ahead with 200 meters left."

As he got ready to step to the line, Zabierzowski told Juantorena, "You can win. Try to burn off the energy of others. You are ready to run the 400 and 800; they are aiming for the 800 and 1,500. Try to get the others to follow your pace."

Many observers, said *Track & Field News*, "placed their odds on Wohlhuter or on Ivo Van Damme." Says Juantorena, "You know how many times I ran the 800 before Montreal? Only a few times. But I had run 1:44.9, so you see, my coach said, 'You have a good chance.'"

The 800 final started at 5:15 in the evening, and Juantorena executed Zabierzowski's strategy to perfection. He followed Wohlhuter through the first 200 meters in 25.5, passing the first lap in 50.85 seconds. Singh took the lead, but Juantorena grabbed it on the backstretch, shadowed by Wohlhuter, who looked to be in perfect position to add a gold to his world record and follow Munich champ Dave Wottle in keeping the 800-meter gold in the United States.

Juantorena, however, dug down deep as he and his much smaller rival entered the final 100 meters, and with his "ground-eating, nine-foot stride" Alberto powered away from Wohlhuter, who was then caught at the tape by Van Damme. Juantorena's 1:43.5 gave him both the gold and the world record. Van Damme's 1:43.86 was good for the silver, while Wohlhuter clocked 1:44.12 for the bronze. Germany's Wulbeck was fourth (1:45.26), followed by Ovett (1:45.44), Susanj (1:45.75), Singh (1:45.77), and Carlo Grippo (1:48.39).

It was a glorious victory for Juantorena and for Cuba. Watching him sprinting down the straightaway, towering over Wohlhuter, the Cuban did look like the new style of runner. Juantorena "made the impossible achievable, the miraculous human," gushed *Track & Field News*. Juantorena "didn't just run the distance and defeat all comers, he over-powered them with sheer, brute strength." The crushing win gave him the aura of a superman. In *Wizards of the Middle Distance*, Roberto Quercetani quotes excerpts from Van Damme's diary in which he writes of being told by Roger Moens, the 1960 Olympic silver medalist and an ex-world-record holder, that he could win the 800. Writes Van Damme, "Neither of us had taken Alberto Juantorena into account, an excep-tional athlete who, after the race, I looked upon like a God."

Sebastian Coe, in *The Olympians*, says Juantorena's performance "be-gan to impress on me what the Olympics signified." Coe was "in awe of Juantorena."

> Here I was, a thin, eight-and-a-half-stone 19-year-old who hadn't yet run under 1 minute 50 seconds but who was supposed to be a prospect at 800 meters. And there was this huge Cuban, over six-feet tall with a nine-foot stride and the build of a rugby player who was looking to run close to 44 seconds for the 400 meters and 1 minute 43 seconds for the 800 meters.

British coach Harry Wilson told Coe not to get depressed over Juantorena's size and strength. "He said that Juantorena was a one-off phenomenon, and he turned out to be right. But what an amazing runner the Cuban was!"

Juantorena was jubilant at his postrace press conference, saying he "had succeeded in hoodwinking the world. I was not laughing at my opponents. I was just happy that my coup had succeeded." His coup brought the 800 to a new level and gave the world a new star. "Today, July 25, is the anniversary of our revolution which gave me the chance to become Cuba's first gold-medal winner in athletics," he said. In perhaps no country more than Cuba does sport play such a major role in a nation's psyche. It is the one area where the extremely poor country can compete on the level of the First World nations. "I still can't describe the feeling I had when I won," Juantorena says years later.

Juantorena remained humble, giving credit to his coach, his training partners and the Cuban people. "The medal is not for yourself. It couldn't be done without the support and help of my people, runners, and coaches," Juantorena said, not mentioning his talent or hard work. "We are educated in the principles of modesty, not individual honors."

Cuban president Fidel Castro was delivering a speech at Pinar del Rio when news of Juantorena's victory came, and "it was Fidel himself who told us of Alberto's win," remembers coach Lucas Lara. "It was a very happy moment, shining with emotion. All the people received him as a hero and we started . . . partying immediately." *Cantare Victoria*— victory songs—were written for Juantorena in Cuba, and the news of his victory was sent to soldiers fighting in Angola.

The 800-meter win meant Juantorena could be relaxed for the 400—he had his gold, for himself, "for the revolution and for all of Cuban people." Juantorena also celebrated that night and slept well; he needed to, because the heats of the 400 meters began the next day, and he had two to run. After making it through those heats, finally there came a rest day. The next day, Juantorena cruised through his semifinal with a 45.10 win.

The 400 final was run on July 29, and there was a pack of fast, fresh runners waiting for a piece of Juantorena, anxious to knock off the gold medalist. The top contenders were the American duo of Fred Newhouse and Herman Frazier. It was Newhouse who took the lead at the gun. Juantorena moved closer down the backstretch, then took the lead just 20 meters from the finish, winning with a low-altitude all-time best of 44.26. He needed it to beat the two Americans, who ran well. Newhouse took the silver in 44.40 while Frazier's 44.95 gave him the bronze.

Some claimed Juantorena's time was superior to Lee Evans' world record of 43.8, run at Mexico City's 7,200-foot altitude. The quality of Juantorena's time is reflected in the fact that no one ran faster at sea level until Harry "Butch" Reynolds turned in a 44.10 in 1987.

How did Juantorena feel after winning his historic double? "Tired. I had to come from behind, and it seemed harder to me than my win in the 800. I am especially proud of my 400 victory." When Juantorena talked about his wins, he never mentioned his sacrifice; it was always "Cuba's sacrifice."

Juantorena had run seven races in six days to get his two gold medals, and he was not finished yet. In another display of his great strength, he ran a 44.1 anchor leg to get the undermanned Cuban 4 × 400-meter relay team into the finals. In the final, Juantorena received the baton far back in seventh place, with no chance of getting into the top three. But the indefatigable Cuban went after the runners in front of him as if he were going to break 40 seconds and get his country another medal, passing the 200 in *20.2* seconds. Finally running out of gas, Juantorena slowed to 44.7 and Cuba finished in seventh.

On the eighth day, Juantorena rested and reaped the laurels that were justly his. His Montreal performance was called "the greatest exhibition of speed and durability in Olympic history," and his competitors did not disagree. Silver medalist Newhouse had perhaps the best observation about Juantorena, saying, "He ain't God, but he sure is one good 400 man." Coach Zabierzowski called Juantorena "an ungodly talent."

Added Frazier, "I doubt anyone will fall down and worship him. But he sure is good. It's really the test of a great athlete to run the 800 and then the 400. If anyone else had done that, they wouldn't be standing up today."

Staying on Top

Juantorena stood tallest in his homeland. He and his teammates flew from Montreal to Kingston, Jamaica, then on to Havana, where Castro, an ex-minor league baseball player who remains close to sports, greeted the team at its arrival at Jose Marti airport. Juantorena was an immediate national hero in Cuba, but he did not get wealthy off of his medals. He says he did not get special treatment and that he remained one of the guys at the track in Havana. "I was not privileged and didn't have any advantages. Nothing; I was still among the ordinary people." It was not until three years later, in 1979, that Juantorena received a car, a house, and a telephone in recognition of his status as "Cuba's No. 1 athlete." He was also voted 1976's Athlete of the Year by *Track & Field News*.

"Alberto's Olympic victories were really important. His first places gave us the courage to follow him," said coach Lara. "For the younger generation of Cuba, Alberto is an example to follow and somebody who inspired us."

Juantorena's victories were front-page news in newspapers throughout Latin America, with some papers devoting five pages to his exploits.

He was the handsome, gregarious model of the Latin Man, charming enough to make women swoon. He was also the sensitive, intelligent paradigm of the "New Man" championed by the Cuban revolution, a speaker of words and a doer of deeds. This giant of a runner was one of the outstanding figures in Cuban sports, his athletic success complemented by an unselfish attitude and fierce loyalty to his beleaguered island nation.

His gold medals inspired him to train even harder in 1977, and he started the next track season like he would never be beaten. The difference was that in 1977, Juantorena was the best-known track athlete in the world. In 1976 he had sneaked up on people in the 800, but this year he was the favorite in all his races, which suited him just fine, as he rose to the challenge with another spectacular year. To further his mystique, Juantorena rarely talked about his training. When asked why not, he would reply, "*Porque son secretos.*"

During the year, Zabierzowski, who had returned to Poland when his contract with Cuba expired, died of a heart attack. The coach was "my second father," says Juantorena, who went to Poland for the funeral.

The highlight of 1977 was to be his eagerly awaited matchup with Mike Boit. In Juantorena's first European races, in June in East Berlin, he clocked 44.98 for 400 meters—he was the only man under 45 all season—and 1:43.7 for 800 meters, just 0.2 seconds off his world record.

Continuing his tough 400/800 doubles, Juantorena dominated races in Europe, then lost to Seymour Newman at the Central American Games. Angered by the loss, Juantorena vowed to show what he could do at the World University Games, held August 21, 1977, in Sofia, Bulgaria's Vasil Levski Stadium. The race turned into a time trial for Juantorena. After an opening 400 of 51.4, no one in the field could stay near him. He came back with a second lap of 52.0 seconds to finish in 1:43.4, breaking his world record. Second place was more than two seconds behind.

With another world record under his belt, the stage was set for his showdown with Boit, who had run several tune-up races in the 1:44 range. The matchup came three days after the World University Games at the Weltklasse meet in Zurich. A standing room-only crowd saw a race that lived up to its billing. After a first lap of 49.6, led first by Kenyan Sammy Kipkurgat and then by Juantorena at the bell, Boit accelerated on the backstraight in an attempt to take the lead. But Juantorena refused to let the Kenyan pass. He fended off several of Boit's attempts, then powered away to win in 1:43.6, one second up on his rival.

Then, on September 2, came the year's biggest race, the World Cup in Dusseldorf with another Juantorena-Boit clash. This superb race was called by *Track & Field News* "the classic's classic," while Quercetani terms the race "one of rare excellence."

Surprisingly, it was Sri Ram Singh who led the field through a first lap of 52.3, followed by Juantorena and Boit. Mal Watman of *Athletics Weekly* described the race:

> With 200 remaining, Juantorena was three meters in front; into the straight the margin was down to two meters. The Cuban glanced round, to see the Kenyan on the point of drawing level. Faster and faster they raced along the finishing stretch, with Juantorena always just fractionally ahead but with Boit never easing the pressure on him. This was racing at its highest level, and at its most basic—two evenly matched rivals, slugging it out every inch of the way. Only in the last five meters, said Juantorena, was he confident of winning.

Juantorena's winning time was 1:44.0, and his second lap of 51.5 "was probably the swiftest ever recorded by the winner of a fast race," Watman writes. "But even in defeat Boit (1:44.1) was never greater." With the year's four fastest times, Juantorena had now proven without a doubt that Boit's presence in Montreal would not have changed the awarding of the gold.

The fiery, emotional side of Juantorena was seen at the World Cup the following day, when he attempted his by-now characteristic double. When the gun went off to start the 400 meters, Juantorena stepped out of the blocks, thinking that someone had jumped the gun and that a false start had been called. Looking behind him, Juantorena saw to his dismay that the other runners were flying down the track past him. Juantorena started running hard, but ended up just short, finishing third.

A very mad Juantorena kicked a lane marker and stomped about, yelling at whoever he could find. Cuban officials successfully appealed the result, and in a rerun of the race the next day, Juantorena won in 45.36. He ended 1977 with a 44.65 win in Havana and was again named track's Athlete of the Year, being top ranked in both the 400 and 800 meters. Juantorena and U.S. great Mal Whitfield are the only two men to be ranked number one in both 400 and 800 meters in the same year, and Juantorena had now done it two years in a row.

Whitfield praises Juantorena as "one of the best runners ever. Alberto in 1976 and '77 was just terrific. I have great admiration for him. He was a great performer and one of the most powerful runners ever."

Despite his large size, says Whitfield, Juantorena "was very light on his feet, with a good, fast stride. To win two golds, you need, first, good, strong competition, and second, a man with the ability to do it. Alberto was that man."

Juantorena's "secret," says Whitfield, was that "he had speed he could pick up anywhere in the race. His accelerated leg lift made it hard for anyone to pick it up on him." Whitfield goes on to say that once he saw Juantorena in the preliminaries in Montreal, his 800 win

> didn't surprise me. He had good endurance to go with his speed. It just wasn't publicized. In those days the socialist countries kept a lot of secrets. The moment I saw him run, I knew he could do both. He was the greatest; what he did in the Olympics separated the man from the boys.

What was left for Juantorena? He had defeated every top 400- and 800-meter runner in the world, won championships and gold medals, and grabbed scores of victories. Most 400-meter runners, if they double, run 200 meters, and most 800-meter runners, if they double, go up to the 1,500 meters. Juantorena had showed himself exceptional by making the difficult 400/800-meter double seem commonplace, and fans now wondered when he would take up the 1,500, with '76 Olympic gold medalist John Walker going so far as to say Juantorena was the prototype of the future in the metric mile. With his muscular legs and long quads, and rare combination of strength, speed, and ineffable determination, Juantorena seemed destined for success in the 1,500. But he never had a chance to try it.

Superman Gets Injuries

Juantorena was born with flat feet, which led to pains in his back and neck when he ran. He had surgery to correct the problem, and in 1978, he continued his Superman act by going undefeated over 400 meters once again. Juantorena ran an early season 1:44.4 in the 800 meters, but during a race in August, he lost his first 800 race ever, finishing a dispirited sixth to Boit. So much world-class 400- and 800-meter running was taking its toll, and even Juantorena was weary. But he continued training and racing.

After Juantorena lost a 400-meter race in Jalapa, Mexico, the Jamaican runner who won came up to Juantorena and offered congratulations, saying "I know I am not the best, Alberto. Somehow something happened today and I won, but you are the best."

Juantorena took a long break in the winter and had a lackluster 1979, running 45.24 and 1:46.4. Injuries continued to creep up; this time, it was his hamstring that bothered him.

The upcoming 1980 Moscow Olympics were important to Cuba, because the Soviet Union was the country's main benefactor. Before the Games, when asked what athletes he admires most in history, Juantorena said distance runners Paavo Nurmi and Emil Zatopek, and sprinter/ long jumper Jesse Owens. Juantorena made a valiant effort worthy of those greats at Moscow, despite not having raced at all that season. He made the finals, and placed fourth in the 400 in 45.09. Then Juantorena had an operation on his hamstring and was inactive throughout 1981.

Juantorena made a successful comeback in 1982, ranking No. 2 in the world off his 1:45.1 800 meters, a full decade after his first Olympic appearance. Training went well enough in the spring of 1983 for Juantorena to believe he had a chance to win the gold in the inaugural World Championships, set for August in Helsinki.

He clocked 1:44.6 coming into the meet, which brought together an Olympic-caliber field. In his heat, Juantorena looked to be qualifying easily, coming down the stretch in second place. Then disaster struck; bumped by another runner, Juantorena stepped on the curb lining the track and twisted his ankle. He fell to the infield in agony with a broken metatarsal bone and four torn ligaments. In an image frozen forever in track annals, he was carried off on a stretcher, his face framed in a desperate scream as he clutched his foot. Like a great racehorse at the end of his career, Juantorena looked to be finished.

Juantorena's body may have been broken, but his spirit was not. After missing half a year to recover from the injuries, he made another comeback, starting his background training early in 1984 for the Los Angeles Olympics. With his training going well, Juantorena was looking to make another bid in the 800 meters. After clocking 1:44.8, Juantorena pronounced his comeback nearly complete, saying he was ready to make a run for a medal. But he never got the chance to compete in his fourth Olympics, as Cuba followed the Soviet Union's lead and boycotted the Games. Thus ended the illustrious running career of *El Caballo*.

A New Career

Juantorena, however, was not put out to pasture like an old warhorse. He immediately put all his energy into his new position as head of the Cuban Track Federation. It was a good choice, says coach Lara, because "Who can better represent Cuba than Alberto?"

Who indeed? He's the father figure of sports Cubans know best. Photos of revolutionary Che Guevera look down on Juantorena in his modest office in the National Institute of Sports. His desk is piled with papers and a fax machine. The walls behind his secretary's desk are filled with life-sized, black-and-white photographs of Che and Fidel

Ana Quirot

Ana Fidelia Quirot is another example of the success of the Cuban sports system in identifying top athletes. One of the world's best women's 800-meter runners, her career almost ended in agony.

Quirot began competing at 12, and by the time she was 13, she was winning races. In 1985, Quirot realized she could be a champion when she won a Grand Prix meet in Czechoslovakia. Ana climbed level by level up the pyramid of Cuban sports, getting selected for EIDE and ESPA, the initiation school for the top junior athletes.

She was the best female 800-meter runner in the world for several years, taking the bronze at the 1992 Barcelona Olympic Games. But early in 1993, she was severely burned from her face to her waist when a pot of oil exploded in her kitchen. She continued running, with difficulty, and later in 1993 placed second in the Central American Games.

However, the third-degree burns were slow to heal, and Quirot took 1994 off, concentrating on coaching. It seemed her career had ended; she had several skin grafts and was continuously in and out of the hospital.

But in a stirring story, Quirot came back to qualify for the 1995 World Championships in Göteborg, Sweden. She made it to the finals, where Mozambique's Maria Mutola, the defending World Champ, was the favorite. Mutola, winner of 42 straight races, had narrowly defeated Quirot early in the summer. In a shocking development, Mutola was disqualified after her semifinal for stepping on the line, leaving the door open for Quirot.

And Quirot took advantage of it, winning the gold medal in 1:56.11, faster than she had run in the 1992 Olympics. Statuesque and powerful, she raised her fist as she crossed the line, and on her victory lap, Juantorena gave her a hug and a Cuban flag which she wrapped around herself. "I never thought that I could come back so strongly," she said. "This is the most beautiful victory of my life."

Castro playing baseball. Like Che, Juantorena is a man of the people, and he takes pride in helping his country.

Retiring from competition was not difficult for Juantorena, because he looked at his new post as another way of doing his duty for the revolution.

> It's just a very different way of thinking. We are a team here. We work to produce many things, to improve the social life and the standard of living in Cuba. We really are one family. My workers don't look at me as a boss, but as a friend, someone they can deal with in confidence.

When undertaking a new project, Juantorena's approach is the same as when he was training—he jumps right in and gives it his all. He has had great success since taking over as head of Cuban sports: Javier Sotomayor, world-record holder in the high jump, was first recognized when he was 16 as a talent by Juantorena.

Juantorena is a hard taskmaster as coach of the national team. National athletes, who get a stipend and attend classes, "have to have good grades. There were several top athletes who missed trips because they didn't keep their grades up," Juantorena says. "We're interested in their life outside of athletics, and helped them become coaches or teachers. We protect the athlete this way."

The system works: Cuba grabbed 31 medals, including 14 golds, at the Barcelona Olympics, fifth-highest of any nation. One reason for the success centers on Juantorena, whose charisma and hard work keep sports going during the hardships of the "special period" of the U.S.-led embargo. Life in Cuba has become much more difficult since the disintegration of the Soviet Union, Cuba's main trading partner and oil provider. In 1994 Juantorena had already set Cuba's goal "to do better in Atlanta. But it's going to be hard, with so many countries sending good athletes now."

Juantorena remains a gentle man, still one of the most famous personalities in Cuba. He is a hero not just for his athletic success—that could have faded long ago—but because he remains sympathetic to the plight of the poor and less fortunate in Cuba. He still lives the ideals of Castro's revolution, eschewing the riches he could have gained by defecting to the West; he drives a small car and lives a modest lifestyle.

Juantorena has an existentialist philosopher's view of the human condition that gives him empathy with those who suffer. He did not get a "big head" from winning the golds or going so often to Europe. Indeed, his travels made him humble, something reinforced, Juantorena says, by his understanding that "Everybody has a home at the end of his life. A tomb."

Human beings, Juantorena says, "are not all different. I look at you, and I see one head and two eyes—maybe they are green, maybe they are blue or black—but there are not four eyes. We all have two, and that's what makes us in common. That's my philosophy."

That philosophy "came from life," Juantorena explains. "From life, living, traveling, and the experience of talking to many people."

That gives him an awareness of life's brevity and the need to help out those who struggle. His competitive side drives him to make his national team as good as possible, but he also takes an interest in the nonelite of Cuba. His special concerns are programs to help out children and what he calls the "grandmothers of the revolution." Juantorena-inspired programs encourage the elderly to stay active, and every day in parks all over Cuba, older people and schoolchildren can be seen exercising.

The outgoing Juantorena remains extremely popular with Cubans. During the running of a road race through Old Havana, children yell out "Correr Juantorena!" at the lead runners. In the Ramon Foust sports hall, built for the 1991 Pan American Games, Cuba houses its Sports Hall of Fame. The country's most important mementos are there, such as a baseball medal from 1878, given later to Martin Dihigo, "*el Maestro*," the only man elected to four baseball halls of fame: Negro, Venezuelan, Mexican, and Cuban.

The chess table Jose Capablanca used to win the world championship is also in the hall of fame. The proudest possessions of the sports hall, however, are the Adidas shoes and uniform Juantorena wore while winning his double gold medals in 1976. They are housed in a glass case, beneath a life-sized photo of the lean, muscular Juantorena raising his arms in victory.

"Alberto is the most outstanding athlete of Cuba," says the hall of fame director. "Historically, Cuban people have liked sports, and with Alberto's help they are now still moving upwards." This is difficult in the "special period," because of a lack of shoes and equipment. "But we have not stopped sports."

Under Juantorena's leadership, Cuba had an outstanding performance in the 1991 Pan American Games, winning nearly as many medals as the United States. The highlight came when Alberto Cuba won the marathon gold medal for Cuba. "It was something spectacular," says Emperatiriz Wilson, Cuban record holder in the 10,000 meters and one of Juantorena's star athletes. Thousands of Cubans volunteered to build the Pan Am sports facilities, commuting one day per week to the *villa Pan Americano*—the "sports city"—between Old Havana and the fishing village of Cojimar, where Ernest Hemingway's "old man" in

The Old Man and the Sea trudged each day after failing to catch a fish. Its 34 rooms house 71 of the top Cuban athletes overseen by Juantorena. Coaches also live at the sports village, and the facility includes a hospital, gym, sauna, and nursery. There are also similar training centers in the provinces, from which young athletes are selected for the junior teams.

Juantorena often praises the "anonymous heroes of the revolution." That includes teachers, doctors, and sugar cane cutters (something Juantorena is proud of having been when he was competing.) "Sports are always important in any society," he says. "We are not working for the top, but for the health of Cuban people. And that's how we came to have good athletes. It is much more important that men and women are healthy and strong."

The driving force behind the fitness movement keeping the Cuban people healthy and strong remains Juantorena, says Osvaldo Ryuez Rasoririz, director of Estadio Panamericano.

Alberto represents for the Cuban people the revolution's model of a new man. He's a symbol of what the revolution has made since 1959 up to now, and for us, he is an example to follow. All our kids and young people would like to be like him.

But we know that there will never be another Juantorena.

8

Queen of the Marathon

Born October 1, 1953, Norway

World records: 3,000 meters, 10K, and marathon

Nine-time winner of New York City Marathon

Five-time World Cross-Country Champion

Early one morning in Oslo during the fall of 1978, Jack Waitz had a conversation with his wife, Grete, that caused her to cover her ears with her hands and exclaim, "No! No, *absolutely*, no!" She definitely would not try a marathon. Grete Waitz was one of Europe's best track runners, a former 3,000-meter world-record holder, the reigning World Cross-Country champion, and the World Cup 3,000-meter gold medalist, but she had never run more than 12 miles at a time. Now her husband was suggesting that she run *26.2 miles* through the streets of New York City. The idea was anathema to her, and she wondered if Jack had lost his senses.

Waitz, 25, told her husband that she had a good career, and that perhaps it was time to start winding it down. She did not see any reason to try the marathon, a race she thought was reserved for those unable to run fast on the track. Fortunately for Grete and for all women runners, Jack persisted, and, after some more urging, Grete agreed to enter the demanding, quixotic world of marathoning. Her record in the years to come speaks for itself: four world records; nine-time winner of the New York City Marathon; 13 marathons under 2:30.

Waitz has no rival in terms of depth and breadth of career. Her place as the pioneer of women's marathoning is secure, and it is not farfetched to say that women's marathoning entered the modern era when Waitz entered New York in 1978. There were good runners before then, but they were recreational runners compared to Waitz, a first-rate athlete and the first female track runner to bring her skills to the marathon.

There have been few runners, female or male, who have had an effect on running comparable to that of Waitz's. When she started running in 1966, there were no women's 3,000-meter, 10,000-meter, or marathon races in the Olympics; no women-only races; no prize money; and scarcely a modicum of respect for women's running. By the time her career ended in 1990 with her tenth New York City Marathon, women's running had nearly equal status to men's. It was not all her doing, of course, but the 24 years of Waitz's career tell the story of one of the greatest champions in running, or any sport.

Starting Out

Waitz grew up in the long Norwegian tradition of outdoor activity and exercise, where hiking during the summer and cross-country skiing in the winter came as naturally as breathing. The Norwegian culture encourages physical activity, and Waitz, who looked at exercise as something everybody did, enjoyed all kinds of sports as a child. She calls Norway a "sports heaven." Her two brothers, Jan and Arild, by including her in games with other boys, helped her develop the toughness that would come in handy once she started racing. Waitz had the reflexes and coordination of a natural athlete, and she says, "Ever since I was a young girl, I have always been strong." She played team handball, skied, and did gymnastics.

Grete "always loved competition," she writes in her book, *World Class*. She would race against cars and buses, and she would time herself to see how fast she could get to the grocery store and back. "As children, we used to play cops and robbers, and it was from this game that I sensed for the first time that I had some running ability. When I was a robber, no one wanted to be the cop to chase me, as I simply wore them down by continuing to run for such a long time." She had a natural liking for running, and her first "training" came when she put on an old pair of World War II-era track spikes that were lying around her house. Grete wore them while running on a grass strip behind her house.

Waitz, then Grete Andersen, joined Oslo's Vidar Sports Club when she was 12, inspired by one of her neighbors, Terje Pedersen, the javelin world-record holder. She did a variety of events, including the high jump, long jump, and shot put. Her first prize, a silver spoon, came in a ball-throwing contest. She did not have success in her first running races, over 60 and 80 meters; she often came in last. She did better when the distance was 300 meters, and so she started training for the 400 and 800 meters. Her training included "long runs" of six miles with some of the older boys in the club. Though they were stronger and faster, Waitz doggedly hung with the boys. It was on those runs, Grete says, that she first realized she was a distance runner. Her parents, however, were not so sure they wanted her to be a runner; they asked Grete to stay home and do chores or practice the piano instead of going to the club. Despite a lack of support at home, Grete kept running.

In 1969, when she was 16, Grete won the Norwegian junior 400- and 800-meter titles and began serious training for the 1,500 meters. In 1971, she won the Norwegian open 800- and 1,500-meter titles, and she set the European junior record by clocking 4:17.0 in the 1,500. Grete was selected for the 1971 Helsinki European Championships, but she ran poorly. After failing to qualify in her heat of the 1,500, she cried for two hours in the stadium bathroom. It did not help that team officials and coaches "kept their distance," writes Waitz. "I was disappointed, perplexed, angry, and only 17 years old . . . . My bitterness fed my desire to excel. Just as with my parents, this denial of support strengthened my determination."

In 1972, the year following Grete's entry into international running, she suffered a blow in her personal life. Then 18, her boyfriend and coach was an older runner in the sports club. He became ill and passed away in the hospital. Grete sat in his hospital room every day for several weeks and sadly watched her boyfriend die, something that made a lasting impression on her life. She stopped eating and running for awhile. Her Vidar teammates helped her get through the pain and encouraged her to keep running. She writes, "I used that running to help me forget, to help me begin to do other things, to try to live normally again."

It was not easy for women runners in the early 1970s, even in a progressive country like Norway. When Grete entered a 3,000-meter event in an Oslo track meet, one journalist wrote, "Oh, save us from these women running seven laps around the track." That was the attitude nearly everywhere. Some people overtly discriminated against women by not letting them run; others were just insensitive. Grete's brothers provided encouragement by doing their hard workouts with her, and it was to be Waitz who once and for all put to rest the idea that women could not run as far or as hard as men. But Waitz never imagined she would be the one breaking new ground for women by one day running 26.2 miles with a grace that would attract many to the sport. Her concern during the early years of her career was figuring out how to develop a finishing kick that would enable her to compete with the Soviet and Eastern European athletes in championship races. Waitz had developed into a good 1,500-meter runner, but she would invariably get outsprinted at the end of races. During those early years, she was training more miles than most 1,500-meter runners, miles that would later help her make a smooth transition to the marathon.

From Munich to Montreal

When she was still 18, Grete made the Norwegian 1,500-meter team for the 1972 Munich Olympics. She calls it "a turning point" in her life, saying she was awed by the Olympic Stadium. Her dorm room was just 200 yards from the room where terrorists took Israeli athletes hostage. Waitz writes that the death of the Israelis left her "perplexed, sad and frightened."

Living in the Olympic village for three weeks solidified Grete's belief that she, too, could become a top runner. The 1,500-meter final was loaded with talent, as several women broke the Olympic record. But though she ran a personal best of 4:16, Grete did not make it out of the preliminary heats.

Later in 1972, Waitz began attending a teacher's college in Oslo, getting up at 5:30 A.M. to train before school. Her progress continued, when, in 1974, she took the 1,500-meter bronze medal at the competitive European

Championships, helping her to be named Norway's Athlete of the Year. The following year was also a good one for Grete. Building her confidence by running a 2,000-meter workout at world record pace, Grete set the 3,000-meter world record of 8:46.6 in only her second 3,000-meter race. Time trials were to remain a key part of her training throughout her career. Waitz ended 1975 ranked as the top runner in the world in both the 1,500 and 3,000 meters (the only other runner to do that was the United States's Mary Decker). That year, she also married Jack, a former clubmate at Vidar. The two were nearly late for their wedding after getting lost on a long run, and their "honeymoon" the next day was an interval session on the track.

Waitz had been running roughly 100 miles a week, and, leading up to the 1976 Montreal Olympic Games, she had not missed a day of training for two years. She seemed a lock to medal at the Olympics. There was only one problem; there was no 3,000-meter race in which she could compete. Instead, she entered the 1,500 meters, still the longest race women were allowed to run in the Olympics. This time, Waitz advanced out of the quarterfinals, but her semifinal heat was heavily loaded with race favorites and she placed only eighth. That was not good enough to qualify Waitz for the finals, even though she ran a personal best and set the Scandinavian 1,500-meter record in the semifinal.

The Norwegian press blasted Waitz for not making the final, souring Waitz's relationship with the media. She had trained for the Olympics twice a day while teaching full-time and also spending two hours a day commuting. Norwegian newspapers, she writes, "added to this already enormous pressure, creating a weight that threatened to crush me. Despite my warnings, the Norwegian people were led to simply assume I would win. I became a victim of the Norwegian expression 'a silver medal is a defeat'—if you don't win, you lose." Waitz cried, "first from disappointment, then from anger" at the high expectations others were putting on her.

Later in 1976, Waitz showed she would have been hard to beat had there been an Olympic 3,000 meters, lowering her personal best to 8:45.4. She did not get a gold medal for it, but it was another world record.

Track and Cross-Country Triumphs

Waitz reduced her running during the winter of 1976-1977, while continuing to work full-time as an elementary schoolteacher. "I was tired from training and leading such a busy life, tired of having to bear the pressure and come through for others," Waitz writes. "I decided to run

Women's Olympic Running

It is reported that a woman named Melpomene took part in the first Olympic Marathon in 1896 in Athens, running some-where around 4-1/2 hours. This would be the only running women would do in the Olympics for 32 years. Pierre de Coubertin, the French baron who founded the modern Olym-pic Games in 1896 in Athens, was quoted in *Running* magazine as saying in 1928 that "As to the admission of women to the Games, I remain strongly against it. It was against my will that they were admitted to a growing number of competitions."

The one group that supported women's running during those dark years was the Federation Sportive Feminine Internationale [FSFI], founded in Paris on October 31, 1921, by five countries: England, France, Italy, Czechoslovakia, and the United States. The group grew to include 30 countries, and until being disbanded and absorbed into the International Amateur Athletic Federation (IAAF) in 1936, it kept records in the few track and field events in which women could compete. These events included the two-handed shot put and discus throw, the standing high jump, and the 50- and 80-meter dashes. The longest race for which the FSFI kept records was 500 meters.

Despite the Baron's objections, women were allowed to compete in events, the longest being 800 meters, in the 1928 Olympics. Unfortunately, some women collapsed after the two laps, and the 800 meters was taken off the Olympic schedule and not reinstated until 1960. The 1,500 meters was added in 1972. The 3,000 and the marathon were added in 1984, and the 10,000 meters in 1988. For the 1996 Atlanta Olympics, the 3,000 was replaced by the 5,000 meters.

on my own, without the support of the Norwegian Federation scholar-ship, responsible only to myself." She increased her cross-country ski-ing during the winter, the break from running rejuvenating her. When she resumed full training, later in 1977, her motivation had returned.

Waitz would head out the door for her first run of the day at 5:30 each morning, when Oslo was still dark. Sticking to that routine devel-oped the determination she needed to race well, Waitz believed. When the snow was deep, she would put on boots and run. One day, she could only find a quarter-mile strip of plowed road to run on, and, rather than not train, she ran back and forth on it for eight miles. Even after she became a star and stopped teaching in 1979 to have time to travel to races, Waitz still got up at 5:15 every morning. One reason was to avoid traffic, especially when visiting a big city. "The only drawback is that by the time 9 P.M. comes along, I'm so tired I have to go to bed," she said in an interview with Stefan Bakke.

That discipline paid off in the summer of 1977, when Waitz finally ran to championship gold, taking the 3,000 meters at the inaugural World Cup meet, defeating Lyudmila Bragina, who had broken Grete's world record earlier that year. It was one of those "once-in-a-lifetime-type" races, she writes. "I felt great the entire way, with everything under control. Whatever moves the other runners made, I knew I could respond. If I had to, I could run faster. I felt if I had to, I could fly!"

With that win, it looked as if Waitz had done just about all she could on the track. Then came 1978. After another winter of solid training, she went to Glasgow, Scotland, for the World Cross-Country Championships. Despite a muddy course in Bellahouston Park, Waitz went to the front early, with only two Romanian runners, Natalie Marasescu and Maricica Puica, going with her. Romania won the team title, but Waitz won the 5K race in 16:19, thirty seconds in front of Marasescu. That was the start of her domination of cross-country over the next seven years.

The biggest meet of 1978 was the European Championships in Prague, an event of great importance for Norwegians. The Norwegian newspapers were "at it again," Waitz writes, penciling her in for the gold. Waitz took the bronze in the 3,000 and was fifth in the 1,500 meters with a personal record of 4:00.5. She was strong and fast, but, once again, she could not match the kicks of the Eastern Europeans. The next day one paper ran a photo of Waitz beneath a headline that read "SORRY NORWAY." Waitz "strongly considered" retiring. She had a good track career, but felt that she would never be able to outkick the Eastern European runners no matter how hard she trained. (She may have been right; some of those runners tested positive for anabolic steroids in 1979.)

Giving the Marathon a Try

In the fall of 1978, Waitz received an invitation from Fred Lebow, director of the New York City Marathon, to come to his race. Grete was hesitant, but Jack felt that with her good form and strength from years of training, she would do well in New York. Grete told Jack he had been reading too many running magazines, but, after much cajoling, he convinced Grete to run, "just to see how it would go," and to see what the road racing scene in America "was all about." Lebow came up with another ticket for Jack to come with her, and the Waitzes finally flew to New York two days before the race, figuring that they would at least enjoy a long weekend in America

Coming off her best track season ever, Grete was in excellent shape. Fast track times, however, were no guarantee that she would be able to run 26.2 miles. Waitz had never run a road race, had never run in the United States, and had never run more than 12 miles at one time.

New York is a good place to shatter barriers. It was in the 1971 New York City Marathon, then run entirely in Central Park, that Elisabeth Bonner of the U.S. became the first woman to break 3 hours for the marathon, running 2:55.22. By the time Waitz lined up for her first marathon, the record had dropped to 2:34:47.5, set by West Germany's Christa Vahlensieck in the 1977 German championships.

Waitz, her blond hair tied in a ponytail, lined up with 13,000 others on the Verezano Bridge in Manhattan. The gun fired. Waitz ran with the other women until 16 miles, then she took off on her own. She felt well within herself for another two miles. Then the race began dragging on and her legs started cramping. Feeling mounting fatigue and "pain all over," Waitz kept waiting for Central Park to appear. She ran in to finish in a world record 2:32:30, far in front of Martha Cooksey in second. Her only prize was $20—for a cab ride to the airport.

Grete was inundated by reporters after the race, because it was a story the media loved—the lean, blond Norwegian running her first marathon and beating the competition by more than nine minutes and breaking the world record. She and Jack flew back to Norway the next day, telling reporters, "I had to get back to work. And I was really glad to get back. In New York, the phone in the hotel was ringing constantly. Everyone wanted to talk to me."

What everyone wanted to find out was how she had done it. Waitz said, however, that "There is no secret to my training," just lots of speed work on the track and consistent training weeks of between 60 and 100 miles. When Waitz returned to Oslo and her teaching job, she tried to explain to her students how far a marathon was. "I told them it was 26 miles," Grete said in a magazine interview,

> but they didn't understand what that meant. So, I said, "It's 42 kilometers." They still didn't quite comprehend. Finally, I said, "It's the distance from Oslo to this town over here." Then they said, "You ran that far without walking or stopping?"

It is ironic that Waitz became the winner of the most visible race in the world in the most visible city in the world, because she is a private person who eschews publicity. Grete never liked the attention running brought her. She would rather spend the day with her husband, hiking, reading, or relaxing. But from that fall day in New York until well beyond the end of her career, she has been one of the best-known figures in running. Said Waitz of the 1978 New York City Marathon, "I lost my anonymity forever"—and so did women's running. Like Frank Shorter, Waitz brought an aura of class and professionalism to running, and suddenly thousands of people wanted to know her thoughts on nearly every subject. What Waitz really wanted was to be left alone, running back in her beloved Romsas woods outside Oslo. Waitz's 1978 New York City Marathon win marks the beginning of modern women's marathoning, with Grete leading the way in the first wave of elite women's marathoners—soon to be joined by Ingrid Kristiansen, Joan Benoit, and Rosa Mota, the "Big Four" of women's marathoning during the next decade.

Staying on Track

Waitz continued training for track and cross-country. In 1979, she repeated as World Cross-Country champion in Limerick, Ireland, by beating Raisa Smekhnova of the Soviet Union, 16:48 to 17:14, over a rough 5K course. That summer, she set a world road best of 53:05 for 10 miles, and, in the fall, she broke her world record and the 2:30 barrier in New York, running 2:27:33.

Waitz found that cross-country racing in the spring was a good base for a marathon later in the season, and she followed that pattern for the next several years. In March, 1980, Waitz won her third consecutive World Cross-Country Championship. On a horse race course in Lonchamp, France, Soviet runners tried to gang up on Waitz, taking second, third, and fourth, but no one was close to her at the front. Far behind in 26th place was a U.S. runner named Joan Benoit.

That summer, Waitz ran a world record 30:59.8 for a road 10K at the L'eggs Mini Marathon in New York's Central Park. Waitz was back at the New York City Marathon in the fall, setting another world record of 2:25:42. Waitz was far ahead of anyone in the world, and would have likely won a women's Olympic Marathon, if there had been one and if Norway had not boycotted the 1980 Games. She continued to show her strength by racing 20 miles in 1:51:23, a new world best. However, she would have to wait four more years for her shot at Olympic gold.

Despite three world records in her three marathon attempts, Waitz still looked at herself as a track runner, not a marathoner. The only change in her training was that she did several 1-1/2 hour runs in the month leading up to the New York Marathon, at the end of her track season. Everything else was the same as when she was racing 3,000 meters. When asked if she was a marathoner, Waitz would emphatically disagree. "She really did run those first marathons on her track schedule," Jack told journalist Bakke, "although you might say that she's always done more distance work than most women track runners."

It was more than her world bests that made those early New York wins some of the most significant in the sport; it was also the world-wide exposure they received. The races were televised, and audiences saw the seemingly calm, cool, nonplused Waitz run through "the wall" to set the world records, showing that women could do more than finish a marathon; they could race it.

Men's modern running had many stars; all were names the public knew. But there had not been any long-distance stars for women. Waitz's New York wins and her running and winning road races around the world made her a personality known to the general public and one of the biggest stars on the road-racing circuit. She was a regular at race clinics, patiently answering the questions of a generation of women who now saw possibilities for health and fitness where none had existed before. Her 15 minutes of fame have lasted over 17 years.

In March 1981, Waitz returned to the World Cross-Country Championships at the Hippodromo de la Zarzuela in Madrid, Spain. Romania's Puica, tired of losing to Waitz, shot off into the lead. But Waitz caught her and went on to yet another win, her fourth in a row. Puica dropped out. It was not until after her 1981 summer track season that Waitz finally admitted that she might indeed be a marathoner. The women's marathon had been added to the 1982 European Championships in Athens, and the first World Championships were scheduled for 1983 in Helsinki. Waitz made those two races her goals, cutting down on her track running and adding more long runs. "I started training more specifically for the marathon, which meant I included one long run of about 25 kilometers (15 miles) once very 10 days, and I was a lot less on the track than before," she said. "I also ran longer intervals."

Unfortunately, the following year an injury kept Waitz out of the Europeans, and she watched Rosa Mota win the gold. Before the World Championships, the Waitzes hooked up with Norwegian national coach Johan Kaggestad, who also coached fellow Norwegian star Ingrid Kristiansen. They took on Kaggestad "because we felt we knew very little about marathon training. He was coaching Oyvind Dahl, among others, and we reckoned he could supply us with the professional help we needed," Waitz said in a magazine interview. As with Dick Quax and Lorraine Moller, and Bob Sevene and Joan Benoit, Kaggestad was more of an advisor to Waitz than an actual coach. Waitz knew what worked for her, and she kept to her schedule like clockwork, allowing few distractions in her life.

Training: "Hurry Slowly"

Waitz writes that while she "reached the top somewhat haphazardly," she did not stay there that way. "In the world of running and fitness, there is an art to consistency and longevity . . . . The bottom line, as far as I'm concerned, is simply hard work and enjoyment." She says the theme of her training program is best summed up by the Norwegian expression "'Hurry slowly.' Be dedicated and disciplined and work hard, but take your time. Move ahead, but be patient."

"Grete was one of the first women to train like a man," says Frank Shorter. Before Waitz, coaches would take men's workouts and modify them, because they did not think that women could handle the stress, Shorter says.

> She's the one who opened it up. More than any marathoner, Grete was the first not to fear the distance. She was a ferocious, well-prepared competitor. She was always thinking of ways to beat you. She made the transition from middle-distance track runner to the marathon, and kept it going. She translated her middle-distance running into marathoning.

Waitz did not do the extremely high mileage of Joan Benoit Samuelson, Uta Pippig, Lisa Martin, or other top women marathoners who were to come after her. Waitz preferred, like Mota, to do quality. She called her training "a mixture of marathon training and track training." Twenty miles a week was a lot for Waitz when she first started training for the 1,500 meters. During her peak track years she averaged about 100 kilometers (60 miles) a week, and when she became a marathoner, she averaged 160 kilometers (100 miles) a week.

Like Benoit and Mota, Waitz ran quickly during training. On her easy days, Waitz would start out slowly but, after a few miles, would be clicking off a 6-minute mile pace. When she and Rob de Castella trained together in the days leading up to the 1983 World Championships, Deek recalls having to slow Grete down, because she ran faster on many of her runs than he did.

The danger in running quickly all the time, says Jack, is that the speed sessions can suffer if a runner is tired from running too fast on recovery days. Sometimes when Jack would run with Grete to slow her down, he would be told by Grete that he was in poor shape.

Long runs are key to marathon training, Jack told *Athletics Weekly*.

> Those runs should be the easy ones. If they're fast, they become tough and thus come on top of all the other hard sessions you do. The result is that your long runs wear you down instead of building you up.

In racing and in training, Waitz was as tough as the Norwegian winters. "I am stubborn," she explains, saying she had such a long, successful career because she enjoyed her training. Coaching was a team effort, between Kaggestad, Jack, Grete, and her brother, Jan. Jan was crucial to Grete's training as he did the actual running with her, including interval sessions that were too fast for Jack. Waitz's training program was based on quality, even after she became a marathoner. When preparing for a marathon, Waitz would do three hard days a week: one short- and one long-interval session (rarely wearing spikes) on the Bislett track in Oslo, and one fartlek session. A typical week building up to a marathon included:

Sunday:	2 hour run.
Monday:	A.M., 45 minutes, 4 minutes per kilometer pace; P.M., 55 minutes.
Tuesday:	A.M., 45 minutes; P.M., 6 × 1,000 meters in 2:55 with 1-minute rest, in the track. Or 5 × 1 mile with lap recovery, or 5 × 2,000 meters.
Wednesday:	A.M., 45 minutes; P.M., 55 minutes.
Thursday:	A.M., 45 minutes; P.M., fartlek on dirt trails in the woods or on the road, 6-4-3-2-1 minutes with 2 minute recovery, or 1-2-3-4-3-2-1 minutes. Or, a 20-minute tempo run.
Friday:	A.M., 45 minutes; P.M., 55 minutes.

Saturday:	A.M., 50 minutes;
	P.M., two sets of 10 × 300 meters with 100-meter jog recovery, and a 5-minute jog in between sets.

When getting ready for a shorter race, Grete would do 10 × 300 meters at a faster pace, or a "ladder" on the track of 1,000, 800, 600, 400, and 200 meters, and she would cut her long run to 1 hour, 30 minutes. Waitz would vary the days she ran the hard workouts, depending on how she felt. The key for her was getting in three quality sessions a week, along with the long run. Like Mota, she would rather run 1 hour, 30 minutes quickly than 2 hours, 30 minutes slowly. The track runner in her never left, she says. "My training is, and always has been, very intensive. That's how I like it." That was the main difference between her training and that of countrywoman Ingrid Kristiansen, Waitz told Bakke.

> Ingrid will happily go out alone for a slow three-hour run—and enjoy it. I can't do that. I think Ingrid got used to long, slow sessions in her days of cross-country skiing. And she really does like them! I have to train on the track and do intensive intervals. All my training has to be intensive.

Waitz did not lose her track speed when she moved up to the marathon. In 1982, she ran 15:08.8 for 5,000 meters at the Bislett Games, a European record and less than a second off Mary Decker Slaney's world record. In July, 1982, she also ran 1:07:50 for a half-marathon in Oslo.

In March 1983, Waitz won her record fifth World Cross-Country Championship at Riverside Park in Gateshead, England. She ran 13:29 for the 4.41 kilometers, while Joan Benoit placed fourth. A month later, Waitz matched her world record by winning the London Marathon in 2:25:29. She was well prepared for the World Championships.

She came to Helsinki the favorite in the marathon and ran like it, crushing the field by over three minutes. She got stronger as the race went on, running her last 10 kilometers in less than 33 minutes. Afterwards, Waitz said she felt so good she could "easily have run another 10 kilometers. No trouble!" It was the only marathon Waitz did not feel like dropping out of, she said. It is appropriate that Waitz, the First Lady of marathoning, won the first event in those first-ever World Championships.

1984 Los Angeles Olympics

Waitz ran in her last World Cross-Country Championships in March, 1984, at the Meadowlands near New York City. She was not planning on competing, but she did so as a favor for New York City Marathon director Fred Lebow. This time, Puica beat Waitz, outkicking her down the last straight of the 5K course for a two-second victory, 15:56 to 15:58. (Puica went on to win the 3,000-meter gold and 1,500-meter bronze at the Los Angeles Olympics.)

Waitz was the co-favorite for the 1984 Olympic Marathon, along with Joan Benoit, who had broken Waitz's world record at Boston with a time of 2:22:43. There was tremendous pressure on Waitz and Kristiansen in Norway, with the media penciling them in for first and second. It did not matter what order they finished in; it was just assumed that the first two would be Waitz and Kristiansen.

The Olympics brought together the best women's field ever. Waitz "went to the line in Los Angeles as not only the handicappers' favorite but also, in a way, the sympathetic favorite," wrote journalist Hal Higdon. "I'm going to cheer for Joan, or maybe Julie Brown, because I'm an American," added another observer of the world marathon scene. "But let's put it this way; I won't be disappointed if Grete wins. In fact, I'll be delighted."

If the Olympic Marathon had been run a few days earlier, it may have unfolded differently. Grete was in the best shape of her life heading into Los Angeles. On an accurate 5K course on an Oslo road, she ran 15:09 in a time trial, 14 seconds faster than before the World Championships the year before. And she had "a superb" track workout the Wednesday before the marathon. Waitz was ready for Benoit's expected fast pace, but a back injury hampered her mental preparations. The problem arose two days before the marathon, when she and her brother Jan changed rooms so that Grete could get as much rest as possible. "Now, his bed was softer than ours, and I occasionally have problems because of slipped discs, so Saturday morning my back hurt a little when we went for our jog."

Jack wanted Grete to go to the doctor right way, but she declined, saying it "will get better soon." But it got worse, until by lunch on Saturday, Grete was "hobbling about like an 80-year-old. I couldn't run at all. I couldn't even straighten my back! I was given lots of treatment, none of which seemed to help." Waitz thought she might not be able to start the marathon "Everything collapsed like a house of cards," she told Bakke. "I usually have trouble sleeping the night before a big race, but I was so exhausted mentally by night time that I went out like a light the minute my head touched the pillow."

Her back was better on race morning, but Waitz had lost her focus. She was not concentrating on the marathon as she normally would; her focus instead was on whether her back would allow her to compete. Waitz says she had "no aggression—my head wasn't tuned in." Waitz was the center of attention, with everyone in the race keying off her. Everyone, that is, except Benoit. The American, who had reached a mental and physical peak, did not know of Grete's back problems. Waitz, known for her ability to finish strongly over the last part of the marathon, let Benoit go when Joanie took off at the three-mile mark. We will never know what would have happened if Grete had gone with Benoit when she made her historic break. We do know it would have been fun to watch the two best marathoners in the world battling it out. But it was Benoit who was alone in front after taking the gamble and making her early surge away from the field.

Benoit's gap quickly grew, reaching 1:30 by 10 miles, and 2 minutes by 13 miles. Waitz, feeling "sluggish," ran with Kristiansen, Mota, Moller, and Welch in the trailing pack. Benoit's early break was, as it turned out, the best possible tactic she could have thrown at Waitz that day. "Then, suddenly, halfway, things started functioning and I felt the brakes were off," Waitz says. "There was nothing holding me back." Waitz slowly cut into Benoit's big lead, and

> When I caught sight of her back with about 5K to go, I just for a moment thought I might yet win. But I soon realized it was asking a bit much to haul back a minute over 5K when somebody's traveling at 2:25-marathon pace! So then I just ran for the silver, and I was really delighted when I got it.

Waitz's time was 2:26:18, 1:26 behind Benoit. "I ran the way I felt I was able to and had to. I would have let the rest of the field go as well if they had run any faster. I just ran the way my body dictated."

Waitz did not make excuses afterwards, taking pride in her silver medal and giving credit to Benoit. The heat did not bother her, Waitz said.

> It turned out to be just about the coolest day of the Games. We started early in the morning with no sun whatsoever. The heat was not a problem at all, apart from the last 10 kilometers being a little unpleasant. There had been far too much focus on how dreadfully hot it was going to be.

Waitz cried when she finished, relieved that the pressure was off and happy to finally have an Olympic medal. "My crying was due to a combination of happiness over winning the silver, pain in my legs and back, and—more than anything—relief that it was over."

The Norwegian media once again were not satisfied, painting her silver medal as less than a complete success. That has happened often in her career, Waitz writes.

> I often experience that people around me expect much more than I do; they're more disappointed than me. It almost makes me laugh. I think, "Why are you disappointed? You haven't run. I'm the one who has run, and I'm satisfied, so why can't you be satisfied as well?"

One reason she was satisfied was that Benoit ran "a superb race," Jack said. Added Grete, "I'm sure that had I gone with her . . . I don't know . . . I think she had even more in reserve; it looked like it. That's the way it is when you run a good race. Like me in Helsinki [at the World Championships]."

Post-Olympic Success

Waitz kept rolling after the Olympics with a theme song of "New York, New York." In 1985, she won New York for the seventh time. Waitz, improving as she got older, recorded her personal best in 1986 at the London Marathon, with a 2:24:54 win, nearly six minutes ahead of second-place finisher Mary O'Connor. In the fall, Waitz returned to New York and won for the eighth time, and she won it for the ninth time in 1987. Waitz was hoping to run in the 1988 Olympic Marathon, but an injury kept her out of it. In 1989, she had a stress fracture that kept her from running for several months. She came back in 1990 to run 2:34:34 at New York, good for fourth place. It was her last competitive race, and appropriate that her competitive career ended in New York, where her marathon career had started.

Waitz continued running after retiring, dividing her time between Oslo and Gainesville, Florida, where she and Jack bought a house. In 1992, she returned to the New York City Marathon after a one-year absence. Her goal was to cut 3 seconds off the combined time of her first two world records at New York: 2:32:30 and 2:27:30; in other words, she wanted to break five hours, running with race founder Fred Lebow. Lebow, 60, was the president of the New York Road Runners Club, and he was running his five-borough course instead of directing the race from the lead vehicle. "For the first time in all these years I'll get to see what the marathon is like from a runner's perspective, back in the pack," Waitz said in *Runner's World*. "When you are there in the front line, there's a lot of pressure. You are so running within yourself that you

Grete Waitz runs the Asbury Park 10K in 1985 as preparation
for her seventh New York City Marathon win.

can't pay attention to the spectators. Now I can relax a little more and enjoy the atmosphere." She had plenty of time to do that, as she and Lebow took 5:32:34 to finish the course. Waitz, saddened that her friend was dying of cancer, cried as she and Lebow finished, because she knew it would be the last time they ran together. Two years later, he passed away.

Waitz still shows up at the New York City Marathon every year, but she says, "I have no more interest in competing."

A Norse Treasure

Waitz, hollow-cheeked, running tall, her long, blond hair pulled in a ponytail behind her head, has carried women's running into the 20th century. Women's opportunities and abilities in running have come a long way in this century. Waitz was a pioneer in all aspects of running: cross-country, track, and road racing, and her appeal has extended beyond just runners.

Just as statues of Paavo Nurmi and Lasse Viren stand guard outside Helsinki's Olympic Stadium, so was a statue of Grete erected outside of Oslo's Bislett Stadium. Grete is called a "Norse national treasure," and with her wins came a new enthusiasm for staying in shape, not just in Norway but around the world. The largest women's race in the world is the Grete Waitz 5K run in Oslo. In typical, low-key, Waitz fashion, she does not much publicize the race outside of Norway. "Are you sure there were 42,000 runners? And all women?" Lisa Martin asked journalist Katy Williams. "I didn't even know Grete had a race named after her."

Williams puts Waitz's place in Norway like this: "The runners will remember Ingrid; the women will remember Grete. I think Grete is eternal. She does so much for the people of Norway and represents Norway so well." In addition to the race, she is involved in the Norwegian Olympic movement and with a program to get the inactive people of Norway out exercising. Williams adds,

> Grete is the one people adore. She is just a warm person. She went out of her way and spent hours showing me around town. I was so enchanted with her. There was so much written about her and she is so much in the public eye, yet she's so charming and so genuine. I had read about her for years, and thought it was just a gimmick. But it isn't.

That opinion is echoed by many who know Waitz. "Grete is one of the truly genteel women in running," says Boulder Road Runners' president Rich Castro. "She's always polite and remembers names."

Rosa Mota, one of Waitz's rivals in the 1980s, is also one of Waitz's many fans, saying,

> I always admired Grete; the way she runs, the way she talks. She was the one I looked up to. I think she is just very friendly. Grete was always popular with the people, always nice, never stuck-up. And she won a lot of races. She is one of the best ever.

9

The Runner's Runner

Born August 4, 1955, Wales

World record: marathon (2:08:05)

Winner, Chicago, London, and New York City Marathons

Nine-time Welsh Cross-Country Champion

Royal Air Force (RAF) Corporal Steve Jones did not expect to make running history when he awoke in a Chicago hotel room on the morning of October 21, 1984. All he knew was that he was going to run as hard as he could for as long as he could, wherever that would take him.

Where it took the square-jawed Welshman was to a marathon world record and a new way of running the distance. Few runners in few races have smashed boundaries, opening the way for others to follow: Paavo Nurmi, Emil Zatopek, in distance races, Roger Bannister, Filbert Bayi, and Kip Keino in the mile and middle distances. Jones did it in the marathon, boldly going where no runner had gone before. He raced the 26.2-mile distance like it was 10,000 meters, taking Frank Shorter's tactic of a hard, midrace surge a step farther. In a 26-year career, Jones was continually asked to prove himself—by federation officials, race directors, and shoe companies. In succeeding, he earned the respect of runners throughout the world; he became known as the "runner's runner," a man who trained hard, and raced with integrity, a man admired for his "blue-collar" approach to training and living.

Jones's running roots go deep into the muck and mire of Welsh cross-country. There was nothing fancy about his training or his racing—no gimmicks— just fast, tough running. Come with me if you can, he said, and not many runners could. All the while, he remained humble in the face of the precariousness of the long-distance runner, realizing, he said after his world record, that "you're only a hamstring injury away from oblivion."

Steve's Life as a Punk

The Vale of Glamorgan, a beautiful green valley in south Wales, is a land of steelworkers, miners, and farmers. Steve Jones was born near there in Tredegar on August 4, 1955. The Welsh are notorious for being tough, and Jones's upbringing in the nearby Ebbw Vale lends credence to that belief. The son of a steelworker, Jones was something of a roughneck as a kid. He smoked cigarettes for seven years, beginning at age 12, and spent much of his childhood hanging out with local punks. Jones left school when he was only 13 years old in order to learn a trade at an industrial school. His main exercise was running away from the Ebbw Vale police force, which, fortunately for Steve, could never catch up with him. His troublemaking, mostly minor incidents such as grabbing vegetables from the local greenhouse, was "nothing to be proud of." The communities of south Wales had a type of "us-versus-them" class structure that permeated Jones's upbringing, encouraging him to always try and prove he was better than others.

Jones was a hard worker during his childhood, even when he was an amateur hoodlum. He was a paper boy, milk boy, and butcher boy at various times, sometimes doing all three at once. "Even though I may have been a bit of layabout and smoked and drank or whatever, I always worked for my money," he recounted to Mel Watman in *Athletics Weekly*. "It's because of that sort of upbringing that I appreciate just what working means."

The only place tougher than his neighborhood was the Royal Air Force, and the 15-year-old Jones fit in when he signed up for its Air Training Corps.

Fifteen is also the age at which Jones was coerced by a friend to run his first cross-country race. It was 5 kilometers over grass, and he finished 5th, a high enough finish to qualify Jones for a regional race. Placing 6th there qualified Jones for nationals, representing the cadet team. At nationals, Jones was 23rd, and his team finished seventh, earning Jones his first medal. It might as well have been gold. "It all went from there," he says.

It was the start of a career that went from cadet runner to club runner, then to national champion, international track runner, and, finally, world-record holder. Some runners love the track, others the roads, others still the mountains. Cross-country running is where Jones earned his stripes, and cross-country perfectly fits his personality as a sport that requires guts and toughness above all else.

Rugby is the Welsh national sport, and one of Jones's ambitions as a youth was to play rugby for Wales. Running also is popular, and Jones knew the story about a famous runner named Guto Nyttn Bran who lived at the turn of the century. The story goes that Guto had an important message to deliver to town, and he had to get back home before a kettle of water boiled. He ran and delivered the message, and he returned home, just in time, in a state of complete exhaustion. "Well done, Guto," his wife said, slapping him on the back, after which he collapsed and died. Guto was from the area where Jones grew up, and his grave rests atop a nearby mountain.

The cadet championship was the big race for Jones each year, and, until he was 18, the only running he did was in cadet races three times a year. Jones placed near the front and was the top runner in his cadet group, despite the "fags," or cigarettes, he was still smoking, sometimes in the back of the bus on the way to a race. During his second year of running, Jones was second in the local cadet race, won regionals, and finished ninth at the national race. He also won the cadet's "Duke of Edinburgh Award" for all-around fitness. Along with doing well in races, Jones was also motivated during his first years of running by the attention it brought him. He was encouraged when he received notes after races, such as one from the Wing Commander congratulating him on a race: "This has brought much credit on yourself, your squadron, the Wing and the Region. Well done!" Jones still has these notes.

When he turned 18, Jones joined the Royal Air Force. "Somebody told me I should run for the Air Force," he recalls. "I said, 'I could never do that, because there are too many good runners. You have to be really, really good to run in the Air Force.' And I was right." Jones set himself a goal of becoming one of those really, really good runners. There was nothing easy about it, simply a lot of running through the wind and the rain. He was assigned to St. Athans RAF base near Cardiff in South Wales as a fighter-plane mechanic. What separated Jones from the others he ran with was his determination to train twice a day, sometimes even three times a day, while working full-time. He ran hard during training, speeding down the road as if he had an important message he was in a hurry to deliver. "Where I got that drive from I don't know. I'm single-minded," says Jones. "Running wasn't something I wanted to do when I started out, but I quickly realized it was the only thing I was good at. I was trying to be good at something, and running was it."

The motivation Jones showed throughout his career illustrates what the Welsh call *hwye*, a word usually associated with rugby. It means a passion to succeed, to prove others wrong, to show that the underdog can win. Like *sisu* for the Finns, *hwye* is an inner drive that some are born with and that cannot be learned or taught. "Steve was constantly proving something," says Welsh runner Clive Thomas. "He was always showing that he was better than the other runners. The thing about Steve is that he was able to drive himself past his physical limits. Obviously he was talented, but he also had great strength of determination."

Jones's heroes during his early years of running were tough British runners like Tony Simmons, silver medalist in the 1974 Europeans, and Dave Bedford, who set the 10,000-meter world record (27:30.8) in 1973. "I admired Bedford because he was a trier," explains Jones.

> For all Dave's faults, he was a real gutsy runner. I remember watching the 1972 Munich 10,000, and I just admired him, the way he took on the 10,000. He said before the race, "Nobody can touch me." And he wasn't dragged around. He took them on and just ran himself into the ground. He had a go at the race.
>
> Then, in the 5,000, he tried again. He told me that whenever he tried to slow it down, Pre would pick up the pace. I remember watching those races, and seeing Lasse win both of them.

Jones watched those Olympics with a girlfriend. "I remember saying to her that I would beat Lasse Viren one day. It was a lot of bravado, since I had a cigarette in my hand when I said it." Jones finally did beat Viren in a 3,000 at the Coca-Cola meet in Crystal Palace in 1980. "I thought about that when I beat him. I was pretty pleased."

There was plenty of competition for Jones. He started running in inter-county races for St. Athans and for his club, the Newport Harriers. "It kept going from there. There were no scholarships then. Nobody gave you shoes. You just went out and ran. That's what I did." Jones found a role model in those early years in Tony Bednarksi, a clubmate who was one of the first runners from Great Britain to get a college athletic scholarship to the United States. When Jones was starting out, he was clocking 17 minutes for 5K, and Bednarksi helped him.

> Tony was the best runner, and just running with him or being in the same van was a help. I keyed off him. I wasn't thinking of going to the Olympics or anything like that. I was just competing for the team. It's like you are on the C team, then the next season try to make it to the B team, and maybe if you work hard, you can go from there. It was a progression for me. Running's difficult. You just have to work very hard, really. If you want to be the best, you have to work very hard.

Jones did work very hard, pushing himself during his runs to and from the airbase. His first coaching advice came from Bob Wallis, an officer at RAF Lyneham who later became his coach. Jones's focus was cross-country, and his breakthrough came in 1976 when he placed seventh in the Welsh Cross-Country Championships at Cardiff. Most people were shocked, but Jones was not too surprised, as he had been running 70 miles a week for several years. "I don't think I have too much talent particularly. I just work hard." Others disagree with that modest assessment, and those who know Jones echo Clive Thomas and say his greatest talent is his ability to push himself in training and racing. Running to his limit, to the extent that he would vomit during workouts, was Jones's trademark. Talking about cross-country racing, he says, "If I'm still standing at the end of the race, hit me with a board and knock me down. Because that means I didn't run hard enough."

That national cross-country race was the most important in Jones's development into a world-class runner. He was just establishing himself as a top runner, and, despite his high finish, he was not selected for the Welsh team competing in the 1977 International Cross-Country Championships, to be held in Chepstow, Wales. There were nine people on the team, plus four reserves, and Jones was not picked. He was not yet well-known in Wales, and "Not getting picked really upset me," Jones said. But he did not let it get him down; he, instead, used it for motivation. He vowed that he would run so well that next time there was no way the selectors could leave him off the team. "That was really the kick up the backside I needed. I said, 'Next year, I'll make sure you'll *have* to pick me.'"

1977—Getting Even

The following year a determined Jones followed up on his vow by winning the first of his nine Welsh national cross-country titles. This victory earned him a trip to the first of his 11 International Cross-Country Championships, at Dusseldorf, West Germany, where Jones finished 103rd. In January, 1978, his drive to succeed intensified when his father passed away. "Dad's dying was the real source of motivation for me," Jones said. The elder Jones spent his life in the British Steel mills in Ebbw Vale, and, when he died of a heart attack at only 47, there was found in his pocket a clipping from the local paper. "Steve Jones second to Ovett," read the headline on the article, which described how Jones was just 11 seconds behind star Steve Ovett in the inter-county cross-country championships in Derby, the best finish in the history of the event by a Welsh runner.

That race was on Saturday, and his father had clipped the article from the paper on Sunday, the day he died. "He had it in his pocket to show the boys at work on Monday. He never got to work to show them." Jones's father died without ever seeing his son run. "Dad was a provider," Jones said, meaning he put a roof over his children's heads and supplied food, but he never took Steve to a soccer game or to the park. His father, however, had always encouraged him, telling him he could be a good runner. "He'd tell me to give up the cigarettes," said Jones, and, after a cross-country race, he might say, "No wonder you're good in the mud, Steve, there's not much of you there," because Jones was lean and strong even as a kid. "When he'd go to work, his coworkers would ask my Dad, 'How'd the boy get on in his race?' When Dad died, running was a release for me. I tend to store things inside me, and it's only when I go out for a run that I get it all out."

The improvement in Jones's running was remarkable. Two months later, running for his father, Jones returned to the World Cross-Country Championships and pulled a shocker, placing 11th. He had improved 92 places in a year, and he was just behind established stars like John Treacy, Alexander Antipov, and Karel Lismont. Afterwards, Jones said that he could not have run another step. It was, wrote a paper at the time, "a rapid rise to the top. In just over three years, Steve Jones has risen from virtual obscurity to become one of Wales' most promising athletes."

For the next six years, Jones concentrated on cross-country and track, building a background that gave him the strength he would need for the marathon. It is hard to know what cross-country in Europe is like if you have not experienced it. "It's very popular, with crowds lining the course and whole families coming out to watch," says Jones. He placed in the top 11 in the World Cross-Country Championships four times, and in the top 30 six times. "Cross-country was me. It's where I'm from, a working class sport, going through mud up to your eyeballs, through ditches, over haybales. I just enjoyed cross-country." Off his cross-country racing, in 1978 Jones dropped his 5,000-meter personal best from 14:27 to 13:47 in a track race in Greece. That earned him a spot on the Commonwealth Games team. He placed 11th in the Commonwealth 5,000 in Edmonton, won by Kenyan star Henry Rono. Competing against Rono and top British runners Mike McLeod (who would win the silver in the 1984 Olympics 10,000 meters) and Brendan Foster, the 1976 Olympics 10,000-meter bronze medalist, gave Jones the confidence that he would beat them one day.

During the next four years, running and wrenches (or "spanners," as the English call them) were Jones's entire life. Steve and wife, Annette, a nurse in the RAF, had two children and little money. Jones did nothing but run and work. He would run seven miles to the air base in the morning, spend several hours tuning fighter planes, then do a workout during his lunch break. He would often run another seven miles home in the evening. He was buying his own shoes, and just running, running, and running. There was not even enough money for a drink, except after his 15-mile Sunday run. "With that background I became real strong," Jones says.

The Proof Is in the Running

In aiming for the 1980 Olympic team, Jones did not try to run 200 miles a week, like Bedford; Jones preferred, instead, fewer miles and higher quality. In a pattern he was to keep all of his career, he ran about 100 miles a week during the winter and 80-85 miles a week the rest of the year. Jones was injured the winter of 1979-1980, and he switched to the steeplechase in an attempt to make the British team. He ran 8:32.0 in the steeple and was fourth in the British trials for the Moscow Olympics, not making the team. In hindsight, he says he should have gone for the 10,000 meters, which he skipped because he did not think that he was fit enough for the race. He probably was, however; later that summer he ran 28:13 to finish second in the British Championships to Nick Rose.

Despite his fast times, Jones was not getting respect from the British track authorities, partly because of where he was from. "It's a Welsh thing," Jones explains.

> When you're from the other side of the bridge you're always having to prove yourself. Although I was the best in Wales, it was looked at like I wasn't quite up to the level of British runners, because the standards in Wales are lower. But it's when you're starting out that you need the help, to get into races and such, not when you're already at the top.

In 1981, Jones's season was geared to running a very fast 10,000 meters at the Bislett Games. Early in the summer, he ran the 1,500 and 5,000 meters in the Air Force vs. the U.S. military meet, followed by a 10,000 and 3,000 meters in Finland. When he got back to the base, British promoter Andy Norman was waiting for Jones, and he asked Jones to run a 5,000 meters in the Britain vs. West Germany meet. Jones did that, followed by another 10,000 meters. When Jones returned home, British officials called and asked him to run in the upcoming Europa Cup. "I'm really tired and need a break," Jones said in turning down the invite. The British Athletic Board did not like that, and they refused to give Jones permission to run at the Bislett Games in Oslo. "Mick McLeod had gotten out of running the Europa Cup by getting a doctor's note saying he was sick. I could have done that, but being 'Honest Steve,' I told them the truth, and they wouldn't let me run [at Oslo]."

A frustrated Jones said some things in the papers, and he vented his bitterness by running a fine 10,000 meters the next week at the British-Soviet Union meet at Gateshead. Jones ran at world-record pace for 10 laps, passing 3,000 meters in 8:03, before slowing to 28:13, a stadium record. He lapped both Russians in the race and finished with his fists in the air. He then made his point by giving the two-finger salute (the English version of an obscene gesture) to the section of the stands where the British officials were sitting. It was a race he calls

> my most satisfying win ever, along with the '77 Welsh cross-country title. It was just so frustrating. I wasn't getting that many doors open for me, to get to Brussels or to Oslo, and then they slammed the door in my face. I wasn't a Steve Ovett or a Steve Cram, who could just show up and get in a race.... All my wins are satisfying, but that's why Gateshead was an especially satisfying result.

Jones said in an interview afterwards that if he had "been able to hold myself back a bit I would have come out with a really fast time. It was a matter of controlling my effort, which I didn't do very well." That race showed the fast, front-running style for which Jones became famous in the marathon. He always felt more comfortable running from the front because that way he could push the pace and make sure everyone was working as hard as he was. "I'm not afraid of anybody; if they want a race, I'll race them," Jones told Watman. "I think that's why I get on quite well in Europe."

Race directors began wanting him in their track 10,000 meters, because they knew Jones would ensure a fast, exciting race. On the circuit, he was known as "Madman Jones," and even if Jones did not always win, anyone beating him would know afterwards that they had been put through a wringer.

Another big victory for Jones came when he won the 1981 United Kingdom Inter-County Cross-Country title, the first Welshman to do so in 50 years. His continued to progress from "just the bloody hard work he did," said Clive Thomas, who raced against Jones. "He had a lot of determination and was the underdog. He wasn't expected to do well, and always ran like he had something to prove. What made Steve great was hard work and guts."

In 1982, Jones improved his 5,000 meters to 13:18.6 on the track. He placed seventh in the 1982 European Championships and eleventh at the Brisbane Commonwealth Games, both in the 10,000 meters. He was scheduled to run his first marathon there, where he would be matched up against Rob de Castella and Juma Ikangaa, but a bout with food poisoning kept him on the sidelines. "I wish I was in there. I would have run with the leaders like I did in Chicago the next year."

Hitting the Roads

Jones was looking for a championship medal the following year, and he dropped his 10,000 personal best to 27:39.14 heading into the World Championships in Helsinki. Jones ran four sub-28 minute track 10,000s in 1983, more than anyone in the world, but he finished just 12th in the 10,000 at the World Championships. That fall he went to Chicago to run the marathon at the invitation of agent Bob Wood, who had been trying for more than a year to entice Jones into trying some road races.

Jones was very fit when he went to Chicago. The night before the race, he went for a jog. Nearly back in the hotel, he bumped into fellow Brit Hugh Jones, who asked Steve to jog another 20 minutes with him.

That extra bit of running put Steve over the edge, and he pulled a tendon in his foot. "I thought it was just sore, and didn't think it would affect me." In the morning, Jones laced his shoe up as tight as he could and started the race. With his typical toughness, he ran through the pain. But by 16 miles Jones was hobbling, trying to run on one leg, and he pulled out of the race, for the first time in his career. He had gone through halfway in 65 minutes, and 16 miles in 79 minutes, still with the group of seven that was leading the marathon.

> I covered every break in the race until then and I wasn't even breathing heavily. But then the pain came back and I was reduced to hopping and had to pull out. I felt disappointed about having to stop because I felt really good and was confident about staying with the leaders. It was the easiest 16 miles I've ever run. It was just five-minute miling and I felt quite comfortable.

Jones limped back to his hotel room and watched Joseph Nzau outkick Hugh Jones by one second in a course-record 2:09:44. That night, Jones approached race director Bob Bright to give back his $2,500 appearance fee. "That's not the way we work," Bright said. "You get to keep it."

Jones's tendon healed during the winter, but, early in 1984, he missed two months of training with an ankle injury. Jones came back and showed he was ready for the Olympic year by beating de Castella at the Combined Services (all branches of the British military) cross-country race in March. Jones also won the Welsh cross-country title for the seventh time in a close race at Swansea. Then he took the bronze medal in the World Cross-Country Championships in New York, behind Carlos Lopes, who won for the second time. Jones passed American Pat Porter 30 meters from the finish to get his medal. "It was fantastic," said Jones, who was only looking to break into the top 10.

Jones next finished second in the 10,000-meter United Kingdom championships at Cwmbran. He ran 28:12.5, faster than the Olympic qualifying time, but he was told by federation officials that only winner Nick Rose was on the team. If Jones wanted to be on the British Olympic squad going to Los Angeles, he would have to run another 10,000 meters in the AAA championships. "Pick me now, says furious Jones boy"; "Jones blasts unfair trial"; and "Jones fury at Olympic selectors" read the banner headlines. Jones won the AAA race and was selected for the team, but he said afterwards, "I should never have had to run today." He was still having to prove himself.

That second, high-quality 10,000-meter race in a short time might have taken too much out of Jones; he placed eighth at the Los Angeles

Olympics. His mental outlook was also shaken when his coach, Bob Wallis, retired soon before the Olympics, not giving Jones any inkling that it might happen. Mike McLeod, whom Jones had beaten handily in both trial races, finished third, and he was awarded the silver medal when Finland's Martti Vaaino was disqualified after testing positive for a banned substance. Jones shook off his Olympic disappointment and returned to Wales, vowing to redeem himself at Chicago in two months. He wanted to make sure race director Bright got his money's worth this time.

1984 Chicago Marathon

Steve Jones came to the United States to run road races for five weeks before Chicago, mainly "as a holiday" for his family. Jones's agent, Bob Wood, had the race pay for tickets for Annette and the boys to come over. Wood also talked with New York City Marathon officials, who declined to match the fee Chicago was offering. "I wasn't trying to prove myself at Chicago," says Steve. "I was trying to justify the race's faith in me, and was treating it as a chance to come to the States and train hard and race on the roads."

Based in Park City, Utah, he trained with Hugh Jones of England, and ran 80-95 miles a week, with a long run of 18 miles. Jones's goal at Chicago was to break the Welsh national record of 2:12, and he said, "I would have been happy with 2:10 and 10th place." He saw an indication of his fitness a month before Chicago when he lost to Carlos Lopes by six seconds over 15K in the Run against Crime in El Paso, Texas. Then he won a half-marathon in Dayton, Ohio, in just over 62 minutes, despite stopping to help up a wheelchair competitor who had fallen. "I had been chatting with Mark Curp along the way during the race, so I knew I was fairly fit," Jones said.

When the runners lined up in the Daley Plaza for the start of America's Marathon (as the race was called then), it was cold, windy, and raining—typical late-fall, Chicago weather, perhaps better suited for a Chicago Bears football game than a marathon. But Jones was not thinking about the weather; his only concern was the other top runners, a group called the "most glittering array of distance talent outside the Olympics." Race director Bob Bright had gone head-to-head against the New York City Marathon and had put together a stellar field. Bright said in an interview, perhaps only partly tongue-in-cheek, that New York should consider moving to the spring, so that it did not conflict with Chicago.

Strong words, but Bright backed them up, thanks to the deep pockets of Beatrice Foods, the marathon's sponsor. Rob De Castella (Deek), the 1982 Commonwealth Games and 1983 World Championships gold medalist, was there. So was Olympic champion Lopes; Kenyans Simeon Kigen, Gabriel Kamau, and Joseph Nzau; Mexican Martin Pitayo; and Englishman Geoff Smith. Deek received a reported $35,000 appearance fee and Lopes $50,000 as part of Beatrice's $1 million commitment to America's Marathon.

Jones did not get any publicity before the race. The media talked about Deek and Lopes, two of the best marathoners ever, and the rest of the experienced marathoners in the field. Jones had been racing against Lopes since 1976, and he had been beaten by Deek at the World Cross-Country in 1983. "We'd nod to each other and then duke it out. Carlos and Rob were the stars, and the whole race was built up around them." Jones, on the other hand, had started one marathon and finished none. Keen observers would have recognized Jones's pedigree. But to most, Jones was a track and cross-country runner, viewed as someone who would run with the leaders until 20 miles, then drop back.

The runners started off through the rain and cold, going through the first mile in five minutes. Moving together were de Castella, Lopes, Pitayo, Nzau, Smith, Jones, and Kigen, who had soundly thrashed Lopes at a 10K in Denver, running 28:03 at mile-high altitude. Jones looked over and spoke to Deek, who was pushing the early pace. De Castella was running like the world's best marathoner he had been leading up to the Olympics, easily going through five miles in 24:24, a 4:53 per mile pace. "I was following Rob," said Jones.

Lopes looked loose as usual, running in the back of the pack. His gold medal in Los Angeles two months earlier capped a distinguished career that included a silver in the Montreal 10,000 meters and two World Cross-Country titles. The pack stayed at 10 men through the early going, with a 4:51 mile bringing the runners through six miles in 29:15. The runners were spread out five and six across the road, looking like racehorses waiting for the stretch run. Lopes dropped off the pack when someone stepped on the back of his shoe and pulled it off. He quickly put the shoe back on and rejoined the pack.

Annette watched her husband pass by at 4 miles, then went to the family's hotel room, where she battled with sons Dafyd and Matthew to keep the race on TV. "The kids wanted to watch cartoons, and we kept flicking the television back and forth," Annette says. Jones was like Wile E. Coyote, sitting in the pack and covering the surges. When the leaders went through nine miles in 43:40, Alberto Salazar, who was doing the TV commentary, said, "They have to start slowing down."

But they did not slow down, and, among all those top runners, Jones looked the best. He ran relaxed, glancing around at his competitors.

After hearing the 10-mile split of 48:40, Jones, who was feeling very good, turned to Deek and asked, "Is that right?"

"What's the matter? Too slow for you?" Deek replied.

Well, it *did* feel slow to Jones, which is why he was surprised to hear those splits. The others, however, were beginning to feel the pace. Kigen, the willowy Kenyan, was the first to drop back. Jones, Deek, Lopes, Smith, and Nzau stayed together. At the next aid station, Deek picked up his water bottle and shared it with Lopes. Jones skipped the water stop. De Castella, the cool Aussie, had felt the pressure before Los Angeles, going into it as the favorite. With the Olympics over, he was running relaxed. "It's much more difficult staying on top than getting there," Deek said before the race.

Jones ran smoothly behind de Castella, occasionally coming to the front of the pack. He ran with his head cocked to the side, as if he were listening to the others' footsteps, trying to determine if they were feeling as good as he was. "Just before 16 miles, de Castella looked across at me and surged. Every time he surged, I surged with him, and covered. That's when I knew Rob was thinking about me." Jones was not as worried about Lopes, "who was up and down. I knew on a given day, Carlos was the best in the world, but he was not always at his best. He wasn't always consistent."

At 18 miles, the pack of eight passed a water station, where Kamau tried to cut across the road to the water table. He tripped and fell, knocking Geoff Smith off balance. Smith began falling to the ground and Jones, without breaking stride, reached down, grabbed his arm, and held Smith up until he regained his balance. "That showed I was aware of what was going on," Jones says.

At this point, he was aware that he was entering a no-man's land. Jones had run farther than 20 miles only once in his life, and he remembered the advice that 1984 Olympic bronze medalist Charlie Spedding had given him: "When you feel like going, wait for a couple of miles. And when you want to go again, wait for another couple of miles. Then, when you're ready again, wait for a couple more minutes."

At 19 miles, they were still on a 4:56 per mile pace, looking to be heading for a 2:09 marathon. Then, all at once, the break came. Kamau, with adrenaline flowing from his fall, surged to the front. Jones quickly was with him and then past the Kenyan. Deek hung back and, when he realized Jones was going to run hard to the tape, went after him. That move broke up the pack and brought Lopes up with Deek, and together they chased Jones. Could a runner who had never finished a marathon before drop the two best marathoners in the world? "I didn't feel strong enough" to go with Jones, said Lopes, while de Castella figured Jones was running too fast and would come back to the pack.

Jones kept getting farther away from the other runners, concentrating on keeping his form. "My legs were sore more than heavy, mostly at the top of my quads," Jones says. "I wasn't in a panic, and I never looked behind me." Soon, he was no longer running easy. Gritting his teeth, his brow furrowed in concentration, he focused on forcing the pace, the wind at his back now. "I felt good up to 20 miles," Jones said. "It was tough after that. I did have an edge. Everyone was telling me I'd collapse and hit the wall, but I didn't experience any of that." He ran miles 20 and 21 in 4:47 and 4:42, and he passed 24 miles in 1:57:24. Now, with two miles to go, someone in the press truck yelled out Jones's 24-mile split, which did not mean anything to him.

"Two more five-minute miles and you can get the record!" he heard. Jones did not know what record was being referred to.

> I thought he meant the course record. In the last two miles my legs were a bit sore, but in those weather conditions, cold and windy, you're bound to get some tightening up. Anything could still have happened. I was first aware of the exact time only right near the end, when I saw the finish clock reading 2:07:32, and I had to watch it ticking away over the last 200 meters. I thought, "the clock's going too fast," not that I was running too slow.

Jones drove hard down the finishing straight as the clock reached 2:08. "I was tired, but I put my head down and sprinted. I didn't know what the record was." A final 10 kilometers of 29:38 had brought Jones home in 2:08:05, a new world record—only Jones still did not know it. "Some reporter came up and stuck a big microphone in my face, and said, 'Do you realize you broke the record?' It didn't sink in right away. It was all new to me."

While Jones was answering questions, there was a race for second between the Olympic Champion and the World Champion. De Castella made the first move and took the lead, but Lopes passed him near the end, finishing in 2:09:06, three seconds up on Deek. Those were fine times coming off the Olympics, but still a minute behind Jones, who was showered with attention. "I'd never done interviews like that. It hasn't been the same since then. The phone kept ringing [that night] and I couldn't sleep."

It was only an inkling of the attention Jones was to get, as newspapers around the world picked up on the theme of the "World-beater from Nowhere." De Castella called it a "sensational run. What will Steve do if he runs a marathon when it's fine? On any other day that run was worth under 2 hours, 7 minutes."

Charlie Spedding wrote in *Athletics Weekly* that Jones had come to Chicago "physically and mentally primed."

> His opponents were the best in the world. The course was fast, the weather was cool. He let the pack take him to 19 miles at perfect pace and he then found himself in the right place at the right time to move into the history books with an eyeballs-out, lung-busting, gut-wrenching six-mile surge to the finish. But there is nothing sensational about that for Steve Jones . . . that is the way he always runs.

The record increased the rivalry between Chicago and New York to be the premier marathon in the United States. "There's a lot of needle between the two," said Jones. "And this has added fuel to the fire. It's helped their [Chicago's] cause a bit." Jones was asked to go to Boston and New York for promotional work after the race, but he turned down the offer, instead returning to his wrenches at St. Athans.

Jones and his family arrived back in Wales to a roaring welcome. Jones's RAF mates gave him a reception and presented him with a medal. In the background, on a fighter plane, hung "Harry the Spider," a big wire and paper spider brought out by the RAF squadron on special occasions. Steve and Annette were pulled around the base in a homemade chariot. "They are a great company," Jones told Cliff Temple. "They are the people I work with and get my hands dirty with. They could relate to me because I'm just Steve to them, not someone like Sebastian Coe or Steve Cram, whom they just see on TV." On the Saturday after returning, Jones ran in the annual cross-country race between the Air Force, Army, and Navy. "This is what really matters: running. This is where I know where I am," he said after winning the race. The next day he ran in the Swindon Halloween Half-Marathon with teammates from his former club, the Swindon AC. Then Jones took a little break and did "a bit of celebrating. I was running on empty for a bit after that. I've never known a week like it. I didn't know there were that many reporters in the whole world."

Jones's win added to the depth of British marathoning, as he, Charlie Spedding, and Boston winner Geoff Smith were a formidable trio of marathoners. But the new world-record holder caused quite a bit of consternation when he said he was still a 10,000-meter runner, not a marathoner. "I still think the marathon is easy if you are mentally and physically prepared for it." A good 10K runner, Jones says, has at least one good marathon in him.

Back to Work

Corporal Jones spent the winter of 1984-1985 repairing fighter planes at St. Athans RAF Base and rebuilding his base, putting in 100-mile weeks in difficult conditions along the Welsh coast. He was committed to the RAF for another 11 years. He would by then be a chief technician or flight sergeant. Jones liked his job and his coworkers, but he said after his record that the "frustrating aspect is that I still have to get permission to go to a race at which I might win 10,000 or 15,000 dollars, far more than I earn in a whole year with the RAF." He had the option of buying out his contract, but he decided to stay with the Air Force for another year.

As usual, Jones began cutting down his mileage in the spring of 1985 and adding speed sessions. He got an indication of his fitness level in March in Birmingham, when he set a world record for the half-marathon (1:01:14), running by himself. He broke Paul Cumming's record by 18 seconds, a feat that surprised friends, because Jones had been at a wedding the night before, draining several pints of strong cider.

Jones next finished 35th in the World Cross-Country Championships, but he was only 45 seconds down on Lopes, the winner. After a month more of training, he was off to London for a showdown with Spedding. "I'm going into London exactly the same way as I went into Chicago," he said. "Not really sure of what is going to happen other than I know I am prepared for it."

London remains Annette's favorite of Steve's marathons, because "It was on our home ground." London is one of the biggest and most prestigious marathons in the world. The race was cast as a showdown of the purist Spedding against the athlete Jones. "Charlie had foregone running for the money," said Jones. "I had won money, but it just happened. That's not what I had gone to Chicago for," but it is what the journalists focused on—something that bothered Jones. He said Spedding was a "specialist" in the marathon, "while I am just an athlete who can get fit for the right race at the right time." If you are going to be in an alley brawl, "Jonesy" is the one runner you would want on your side. One Welsh writer said Jones had "an unquenchable thirst for competition and never-say-die spirit. When the chips are down, no one is tougher than Jones."

At London, in 1985, Jones showed that spirit. A pack of five ran together behind the rabbit through the early miles: Jones, Spedding, Christoph Herle of West Germany, Denmark's Henrik Jorgensen, and Pat Petersen of the U.S. The leaders stayed together until a 4:50 mile by Jones at 20 miles left him with only Spedding for company. Jones, running strongly, threw in a 4:43 mile but failed to shake Spedding. Jones was then hit by stomach cramps. "The farther I went the worse it got, and when Charlie started making his move I felt in a bit of discomfort." At 22 miles, Jones had to stop and relieve himself. "I had to do something about it. I thought at one stage I might have to pull out, but that would have been too embarrassing."

Jones quickly caught up to Spedding, the defending champ, and the duo ran together until 23 miles. Passing through a tunnel beneath Blackfriars Bridge, it suddenly became very quiet. Only one spectator was in there, and he happened to be a Jones fan. The man's cry of "Come on, Steve!" gave Jones a jolt, and he immediately surged and broke Spedding. When they came out of the tunnel, Jones had a 10-meter lead, and he went on to win by 17 seconds in 2:08:16, the fastest marathon run in the United Kingdom. The underrated Welshman had finally arrived. Ingrid Kristiansen set the women's world record that day, running 2:21:06, and another record was set when more than 16,000 runners finished, the most ever in a marathon.

Spedding said he knew when Jones was going to make his move: "The trouble was I couldn't hold onto it. He was that little bit stronger and sharper than me. He is one of the best runners in the world and is as hard as they come."

"I never felt I was better than the other runners, except London and Chicago in '85. That's when I felt I really was the best in the world. There was a time, too, when I felt I was one of the best cross-country runners." Jones said he was able to run relaxed at London because the day before, Lopes had broken his record by running 2:07:12 at Rotterdam. Jones now had finished two marathons, and he had two of the fastest five marathons ever run.

> My one objective was to win, and win well to put myself firmly on the map as far as British athletics is concerned. I've been struggling for about 10 years to be recognized among the top men in the sport here, and knew I needed a win like this to achieve that.

Jones followed London with a good summer season, running 15 track races, ranging from 1,500 through 10,000 meters, topped by a 27:53 for 10,000 clocking at Stockholm. A look through his training log shows that he did some good workouts that summer when getting ready for the 1985 Chicago Marathon, including a 7:58 3,000 meters by himself. Another entry reads, "Six miles in 27 minutes. Bloody hard. Struggled a bit at the end." No wonder. That is 4:30 a mile for six miles, on a *training* run. Other favorite workouts for Jones before Chicago were 16 by one-minute hills, 12 × 300 meters in 43 seconds, three sets of 4 × 200 meters in 27-28 seconds, and 10 × 90 seconds hard. Jones ran most of his quality sessions on the grass, wearing spikes. "You don't get worn down that way," he said.

He ran three quality sessions a week; two of them were 1 hour and 30 minute runs, during which he did his fartlek sessions.

Nobody Keeps Up With Jonesy

Jones kept to the same plan that had worked so well the year before, going to Park City, Utah, in September for five weeks of high altitude training, and coming down to sea level on the weekends for road races. He won the Freedom Trail road race in Boston, and, on the Monday before the 1985 Chicago Marathon, did a workout of 6 × 5 minutes hard, with a 2-1/2 minute float in between. "It was the best set I had ever done, and I was confident of being able to race Deek," said Jones, who knew there would be no sneaking up on people this year.

> I realized Deek came back to Chicago specifically to beat me. De Castella had run 2:08:18, and must have thought, "Heh, this unknown came and got the record. I'm going to see what I can do."
>
> I took it personally that he was coming back to have a go at me. No matter how friendly race directors are, whether it's Chris Brasher [London Marathon race director], Fred Lebow [New York City Marathon race director], or Bob Bright, they all bring guys in to go after you, trying to set you up. Bob matched me up against Deek and the Djiboutians at Chicago, and I took that personally as well. I said all right, if Deek or the guys from Djibouti were going to beat me they had to earn it. I decided I was going to take off at the gun and was going to run as fast as I could for 26 miles.

Sprinting off the line at the start, only the rabbit, Carl Thackery, and Kenyan Simeon Kigen were with him. Bright had hired Englishman Thackery to tow the field through the half-marathon in 63 minutes. But the rabbit's pace was too slow, and Jones flew by him at two miles, passed in 9:28. After a third mile of 4:43, Thackery dropped out, while Jones and Kigen went through four miles in 18:55.

It was a race that changed the way marathons were run. Never had anyone gone so fast so early and tried to keep it up so long, not even Juma Ikangaa in the '82 Commonwealth Games. Just as Kip Keino and Filbert Bayi changed tactics with their front-running in the middle-distances, so did Jones in the marathon. He showed that marathons could be raced hard the whole way. Jones, concentrating solely on winning the race, had no indication of the time as the miles flew by. Kigen, barely hanging on to Jones's pace, bothered Jones by stepping on his heels.

"Simeon, quit stepping on my shoe," Jones said. "Come on up and take the lead."

"No, thank you," replied the polite Kenyan. "I'm fine where I am."

That did not sit too well with Jones, who put his head down and ran a 4:34 mile. That was too much for Kigen, who dropped out after seven miles. "I kept wondering where Deek was," Jones recalled. "I felt quite comfortable, and didn't see any reason to slow up." De Castella was leading the chase pack and wondering how long Jones could keep it up, as he passed 10 kilometers in under 30 minutes, 10 miles in 47:01, and an incredible 61:42 at the half-marathon mark. "I knew we were running fast," Jones said. His splits for the first 13.1 miles were 4:46, 4:42, 4:48, 4:39, 4:59, 4:34, 4:39, 4:37, 4:39, 4:38, 4:44, 4:42, and 4:44. Jones passed 25 kilometers in 1:13:30, two minutes ahead of Lopes's world-record pace. "I wasn't noticing the times," said Jones. "I felt comfortable out there. I knew it would hit me. It was just a question of when."

Jones kept his sense of humor even while running faster than anyone had in a marathon. At 18 miles, he turned a corner and passed Bright and Wood, giving them a big wink. "I began struggling a bit the last six miles. I wasn't running for the record. I didn't care how fast I ran, as long as I beat Deek and the Djiboutians."

A 4:54 mile brought Jones past 20 miles in 1:35:22. "After that, it was just survival," Jones said. He kept telling himself that the bigger the gap he opened, the harder it would be for anyone to reel him in. At 22 miles the car carrying the clock sped off, and Jones was on his own, except for the press truck, which he said was

> getting on my nerves. I found it hard to concentrate, and I couldn't do anything about it. The police were shouting at people to stay on the pavement and it was breaking my concentration. If there is such a thing as a wall, I almost hit it.

Jones ran 5:07, 5:06, 5:05, and 5:13 for his last four miles. Coming down the straight to the finish, he pumped his arms in a furious sprint, finishing in 2:07:13 and missing the world record and a $50,000 bonus by one tick of the clock. It was one of the most amazing running performances ever, and Jones did not know how close to the record he was, because there was no clock to watch. "When the crowd started going wild on the final straight I thought they were trying to tell me someone was catching me, and by the time I could see the clock it was too late," he told the Daily Express. "If I had a pair of binoculars I would have smashed the record, because I would have started my sprint sooner."

> I wasn't even disappointed that I didn't get the record. I did set a personal record. I came to win. The wind was strong, not all the way around,

but right in your face in the open places. It was very tough, particularly in the last six miles. I was so tired. The last five miles hurt, really hurt. I just lost my concentration. But there will be other races.

Joan Benoit won the women's race, and she also just missed the world record, running 2:21:21, 15 seconds outside of Kristiansen's record.

Jones was in a state of fitness at Chicago seldom reached by anyone.

I was just so strong, and I was never tired in training. I didn't need much recovery. From 1980 to 1985 I never got tired. Whatever I did in the morning I was always able to recover by the afternoon. It helped that physically, I'm a strong person. That whole year [1985] I felt I could do anything I wanted to do in every race. Every race I entered I felt I could win.

De Castella was stunned afterwards. He walked into the media tent, came up, and shook hands with Jones. "Steve surprised me a great deal, first of all because he was able to go out so fast, but mainly because he was able to continue on and only slow down a little bit." That praise meant a lot to Jones, who said, "I was in awe of de Castella, and have tremendous respect for him. I hadn't talked to him much before that. I was just happy to be around him at races."

De Castella said in a newspaper interview that with his win, Jones had taken marathon running into "a new era." Said Deek,

The way he ran showed a total disregard for the marathon as an endurance event. Before the weekend I didn't believe it was possible to see a race run in a faster time. Now I know it is possible and after witnessing the aggressiveness with which Steve ran, I am sure he can take the marathon record into new realms.

What made Jones's run the most impressive marathon ever was that it was done on his own. The greatest amount of stress in a marathon is mental, says de Castella. "It is much harder to run on your own than in a pack. I think he can run around 2 hours, 5 minutes, certainly somewhere in the low 2:06s. He went out at a suicidal pace in Chicago, but with a better strategy he can certainly go faster."

Some observers feel Jones's mark is superior to that of Lopes and record holder Belayneh Densimo (2:06:50), both of which were run at Rotterdam, where a pace car blocks the wind for the runners, moving at a constant speed of 3 minutes per kilometer, and pacemakers lead much of the way. Jones's 2:07:13 was done by himself, off the front.

One reason for Jones's marathon front-running was his track background, believes Froude. "Steve had some of that attitude track runners have, where he chased times on the track, and looked down his nose a bit on road times. So when he did run on the roads, he went for the wins, not the times."

The Ebbw Vale in Jones kept him from getting a big head after his wins. He never considered himself a better person than his clubmates. "As far as I'm concerned all I've done is run fast marathons. It doesn't make me a superstar or a hero or anything. I'm just plain me, and I run because I like running and not because I have to," he told Watman. "Athletics doesn't rule my life. I don't watch what I eat, watch what I drink, or the amount of sleep I get in. It's only a sport."

Jones explained his drive to keep training and racing at a top level by saying,

> I'm not a hard person, but mentally, I feel I can achieve most things and I pride myself on my training. I get myself into good condition and just run the race. I can get stuffed by the next man in a set of efforts in a track session, but it's not all in the legs, is it? I run with my head, my heart and my guts, because physically, I don't think I've got a great deal of talent or ability. I started at the very bottom and worked up.

When asked what was different about marathon running, Jones said, "To me, it was just running. I'm just as happy with a five-miler." After Chicago, Jones kept his $60-a-day RAF job and continued with his routine: running to the base early in the morning, training for 45 minutes at lunch, then running home when he finished work. "My job is the Air Force," he said. "Running is my sport, my hobby. I'm not a professional runner. I run because I enjoy it, not because someone wants to pay me. I make my decision to run a race, and if they want to pay me that's all well and good." The money Jones earned went into a trust fund set up by the British Athletics Association and managed by three trustees. Jones got a training stipend every month, but he had to make a written request to the trustees anytime he wanted to spend any of his winnings.

Trapped in the Marathon

Even after his second Chicago Marathon win, Jones still considered himself a 10,000-meter runner. But he discovered that when you are successful at the marathon,

You are always preparing for a marathon, and having to run well in the marathon. To do that, you have to run fast track times, but you can't do that if preparing for the marathon, because you are tired. So you get caught in a vicious cycle. Once you've had success, the marathon becomes the most important thing. It just happened.

Jones had a down year in 1986. An injury kept him out of Boston, and he focused on winning the 1986 European Championships in Stuttgart, for which he had been preselected 18 months in advance. But first, staying true to his roots, he competed for the Newport Harriers in the European Clubs Cross-Country Championship, and he went into the European Championships as the overwhelming favorite. That was the race that really made Jones a marathoner. He had raced the marathon harder then anyone ever had, and, when he hit the wall for the first time at Stuttgart, he hit it harder than anyone ever had. He started out just as he had in his three great victories, grabbing an early lead. This time, however, it did not work, as Jones himself presaged before the race when he said, "I am under no illusions as to the task that lies ahead of me. On paper, the rest of the field may be much slower than me, but the gold medal is not decided on previous times." He was inspired after watching friend Rosa Mota win her second of three European Marathon gold medals.

Jones appeared to have his gold medal well in hand, racing to a big lead at halfway. He looked to be cruising along to the win when all at once, at 20 miles, he hit the wall. Jones was slowed to a shuffle and could have dropped out. In fact, he should have dropped out. There was no chance for a medal, no chance for a fast time—but Jones would not stop. He refused to give up in races. Jones struggled home to finish in 20th place with a time of 2:22:12. He realized afterwards that the problem was that he had not taken enough water in the weeks leading up to the race, and he was dehydrated even before he stepped to the line. Newspapers called his loss a "failure" in big headlines, and what bothered Jones the most was the feeling that he had let his countrymen down. "It was his most foolhardy race. Steve was always trying to drive himself beyond what he was physically capable of doing," said Clive Thomas.

Jones bounced back into his training. His "secret," Annette says, "is his commitment and dedication to the sport. Most of them back down, but Steve goes out training all the time, in 80-85 mile per hour winds along the cliffs with pouring down rain." Later in 1986, Jones got his championship medal in the Commonwealth Games, taking the bronze in the 10,000 meters with a time of 28:03.

1988 New York City Marathon

After an easy year in 1987, Jones finished ninth at the 1988 Boston Marathon in 2:14:07 and was left off the British Olympic team heading to Seoul. Then, his contract with Reebok expired two days before the New York City Marathon. Reebok did not renew it, and Jones, now 33, ran the race wearing a plain white singlet. "I knew I was fit before New York, but I didn't argue with them," Jones said. "I just decided that I'd show them. I'm a person of principle. I didn't think they were being fair with some of the things they were asking me to do." As whenever he was written off, he came back with a vengeance. Jones did not say much; he just got a glint in his eye and ran the second-fastest New York ever, 2:08:20, crushing the field and beating second-place finisher Salvatore Bettiol of Italy by over three minutes. "To run 2:08 on that course is incredible," said John Treacy, who placed third, nearly five minutes behind Jones. "It's comparable to running 2:06 at Rotterdam."

Jones won New York with a new strategy, hanging off the front in the early going. He did not take the lead until near halfway, after the Pulaski Bridge, saying it was "a measure of my restraint that I held back. That was the plan." After taking the lead, Jones kept hammering, saying afterwards that "You try to keep the pressure on yourself, try to keep the feeling that somebody is chasing you down." Once again Jones had shown that he does not get mad; he gets even. Two days after his win, Reebok re-signed him.

The only sour note of Jones's race was that Lebow refused to recognize his time as a New York course record. Salazar's course record of 2:08:13 had been adjusted to 2:08:40 after the route was found to be 43 yards short of the full marathon distance. Lebow, however, refused to recognize the adjusted time and did not give Jones the $15,000 bonus promised to anyone breaking Salazar's record.

Throughout his mid-30s, Jones remained a fixture on the road-race circuit. He divided his time between Wales and the U.S. He kept a simple lifestyle. The only trapping of success he had was the Harley-Davidson motorcycle he liked to ride. In October, 1992, Jones, by now 37, showed he still had the right stuff by winning the Toronto Marathon in 2:10:06, once again out front by himself. "I always seem to run my best races alone," he said afterwards. Jones was more than three minutes up on second place finisher Don Janicki. There was a $50,000 bonus for a sub-2:10, and Jones ran the race as he did his Chicago runs, going through the halfway point in 1:04:04 and pushing himself the rest of the way. Toronto made him the fastest marathoner of all time, based on a runner's

Men's Marathon World Best Performances

2:55:18	John Hayes (USA)	London	July 24, 1908
2:52:45	Robert Fowler (USA)	Yonkers	January 1, 1909
2:46:52	James Clark (USA)	New York	February 12, 1909
2:46:04	Albert Raines (USA)	New York	May 8, 1909
2:42:31	Henry Barrett (GBR)	London	May 26, 1909
2:40:34	Thure Johansson (SWE)	Stockholm	August 31, 1909
2:38:16	Harry Green (GBR)	London	May 12, 1913
2:36:06	Alexis Ahlgren (SWE)	London	May 31, 1913
2:32:35	Hannes Kolehmainen (FIN)	Antwerp	August 22, 1920
2:29:01	Albert Michelsen (USA)	Port Chester	October 12, 1925
2:27:49	Fusashige Suzuki (JPN)	Tokyo	March 31, 1935
2:26:44	Yasuo Ikenaka (JPN)	Tokyo	April 3, 1935
2:26:42	Kitei Son (JPN)	Tokyo	November 3, 1935
2:25:39	Yun Bok Suh (KOR)	Boston	April 19, 1947
2:20:42	James Peters (GBR)	Chiswick	June 14, 1952
2:18:40	James Peters (GBR)	Chiswick	June 13, 1953
2:18:34	James Peters (GBR)	Turku	October 4, 1953
2:17:39	James Peters (GBR)	Chiswick	June 26, 1954
2:15:17	Sergey Popov (URS)	Stockholm	August 24, 1958
2:15:16	Abebe Bikila (ETH)	Rome	September 24, 1960
2:15:15	Toru Terasawa (JPN)	Beppu	February 17, 1963
2:14:28	Leonard Edelen (USA)	Chiswick	June 15, 1963
2:13:55	Basil Heatley (GBR)	Chiswick	June 14, 1964
2:12:11	Abebe Bikila (ETH)	Tokyo	October 12, 1964
2:12:00	Morio Shigematsu (JPN)	Chiswick	June 12, 1965
2:09:36	Derek Clayton (AUS)	Fukuoka	December 3, 1967
2:08:33	Derek Clayton (AUS)	Antwerp	May 30, 1969
2:08:18	Robert de Castella (AUS)	Fukuoka	December 6, 1981
2:08:05	Steve Jones (GBR)	Chicago	October 21, 1984
2:07:12	Carlos Lopes (POR)	Rotterdam	April 20, 1985
2:06:50	Belayneh Densimo (ETH)	Rotterdam	April 17, 1988

five fastest marathons. Jones's average is 2:08:24.0, ahead of Juma Ikangaa's 2:08:27.2 and de Castella's 2:08:28.6.

After Toronto Jones's training was erratic, but he remained competitive in races, running near 29 minutes for a 10K. "Running went back to being a sport again," he said. "I keep doing it because I enjoy running." While his contemporaries such as Lopes and de Castella retired, Jones kept going, as dedicated as ever to his training, and he was looking forward to making his mark in the masters division. At the New York City Marathon in 1994, Jones, 39, ran 2:29. He was so upset with that time that he broke down in tears afterwards. "At 18 miles, I was a minute down on the leaders; by 26, I was 18 minutes behind. Emotionally, physically, and mentally, I was completely drained."

Training

When Jones set the world record, many runners wondered how he could do it on 80 to 90 miles a week. Like most of the runners who reach the top, Jones kept to a simple schedule during his 25-year career, explaining that "I've done the same kind of training through it all." He focused on quality sessions, and the key was that he trained the way he raced, pushing himself as hard as possible.

"Steve is intense," says Derek Froude.

Intense in work and intense when he has fun. He's very focused on one thing at a time. When he was getting ready for a big marathon, he would not drink a drop of alcohol for three months, not even a beer with dinner. But afterwards, he'd have three months' worth in 24 hours. Steve trains very, very hard. I'm not sure he knows how to run slow. He had to be at the front. In 1988 . . . Steve wasn't all that fit when he started training with us, and wasn't racing that well. He'd be in the back of the pack in hill sessions. But by the middle of October, he was running 8 × 1,000 meters in 2:50 with less than 60 seconds float in between. I remember we went to the track to do that session, and after five, most everybody stopped. But Jones was right back on the track doing one more. Shortly after that he was hammering us into the ground [in workouts]. He went from last in the group to first in only a few weeks. It was like night and day. We said, "Whoa, Jonesy is in shape."

Marc Plaatjes, the 1993 World Championships marathon gold medalist, calls Jones "an animal" in workouts. "Nobody gets more out of themselves than Jonesy," says Plaatjes.

Steve Jones remained a strong competitor through his late 30s.

I remember the first time I did a workout with Steve and Rob [de Castella]. I knew who Steve was, of course, and we did a hill workout. After the first one there was Steve, hunched over at the top of the hill, vomiting. I looked over at Rob and said, "Is he all right?" "Oh yeah, that's just Jonesy," Deek said. And after each hill, Steve was there vomiting. He just runs so hard.

Unlike most marathoners, Jones did his long run on Thursday. His three hard days were divided into one hard session at his race pace for 5 kilometers, another workout at his 10-kilometer race pace, and the third at his marathon race pace. Jones ran those days very hard, and he had three days a week where he ran just one 40-minute run. A typical weekly schedule before he set his world record in Chicago was:

Sunday:	90 minutes. 5:45 per mile pace.
Monday:	40 minutes easy.
Tuesday:	A.M., 5K at race pace, such as 12 × 90 seconds on dirt trails, as hard as possible; P.M., 6 miles.
Wednesday:	40 minutes easy.
Thursday:	A.M., 5 × 5 minutes at marathon race pace during 90-minute run; P.M., 40 minutes "easy, easy."
Friday:	40 minutes easy.
Saturday:	A.M., track session of 200-, 400-, or 1,000-meter repeats or 10 × 2 minutes at 10K race pace; P.M., 6 miles.

Says Jones, "It's the effort that matters on the hard days." That philosophy got him personal bests of 1:53 (800 meters), 3:42.3 (1,500 meters), 4:00.6 (mile), 7:49 (3,000 meters), 8:26 (2 miles), 13:18.6 (5K), 27:39.2 (10K), and 8:32 (steeplechase). Jones did not favor a depletion/carbohydrate-loading diet before his marathons, because it made him weak and tired. He might eat some extra pasta before a marathon, but he did nothing special.

Jones remains a big fan of running and says,

High school athletes, and to a lesser extent, college athletes, are still the bread and butter of our sport. Once you leave school, you just have to enjoy yourself. Set little goals for yourself. If you are a 38-minute 10K runner, don't say you're going to make the Olympics, but seek your own source of motivation, and don't rely on any monetary motivation. . . . Just keep working hard and don't rush it. You'll have time to get there. You just need to stay in running and enjoy yourself.

That is a philosophy Jones kept when he turned 40 on August 4, 1995.

There's still a light at the end of the tunnel. I'm looking forward to it. It's a challenge to see if I can get back under 29 minutes for 10K. I'm an old bastard now, and this is a completely new career for me isn't it? It opens up new doors and new career potential, although I have to say that I don't want to be a masters runner. . . . I just want to get fit again.

For Jones, running was becoming more than a hobby again. What he noticed as he got older was that he needed a couple of recovery runs between his hard days. "I do feel a bit worse for the wear," he said. Jones also started lifting weights three times a week.

Jones had his eye on Martin Mondragon, the Mexican who in 1993 become the first master to run sub-29 minutes for 10K on the road. (Martti Vaino had done it on the track). Jones was picking up some paychecks as a master, but that was not his focus. "For me, earning money goes hand in hand with performance. And I still want to perform my best. That's been my undoing, because I don't compromise."

That was evident when Jones returned to the Chicago Marathon in October 1995 for his first race as a master. He ran just behind the leaders, passing 10 miles in 49:26 before pulling out at 21 miles. "I didn't run that smart, but I'd rather not talk about it. I'll be back at it," said Jones.

Despite nearly 90,000 miles of training in a quarter-century of running, much of it at under a 6-minute-mile pace, Jones is just as motivated to train today as he was when he took his first run in October, 1970, in Wales. Now, when asked if he is a marathoner or a 10K runner, a road racer, cross-country, or track runner, he says, simply, "I'm just a runner. I will always be a runner because I just love the sport." Things have changed over the years, adds Jones, but in the end, running remains pretty basic.

The enjoyment is still there. It's pretty much like it was 25 years ago, when I was running in the cold and snow, and didn't have a pair of shoes. It's still cold and snowy when I go out and train; the only difference now is that I have a proper pair of shoes on my feet.

There is one other difference. Jones also has the respect of runners around the world, along with a legacy as one of the greatest marathoners ever.

10

The BodyMind Connection

Born June 1, 1955, New Zealand

Masters World records: 5K and 4-mile

Olympic bronze, marathon, 1992

Sixteen major marathon wins

In the Olympic village dining hall the night after the women's marathon at the 1992 Barcelona Olympics, an Italian official got down on his knees, bowed his head to the floor, and kissed Lorraine Moller's feet. He was doing penance for having doubted that the 37-year-old New Zealander would win a medal.

The Italian was not alone. Moller surprised—in fact, shocked—the athletic world with a brilliant bronze-medal run in the heat and humidity of Barcelona that capped a 20-year international career that spans the length and breadth of women's running. Some of those shocked individuals worked in promotions at the shoe company which had dropped its sponsorship of Moller just before the Olympics, telling her she was too old to continue as a world-class runner. But Moller showed at Barcelona that 37 is not too old to keep racing well and improving— as long as you believe you can do it.

This is why the one person not surprised at her medal run was Moller herself. She had run in both the 1984 and 1988 Olympic Marathons and had been aiming for the Barcelona Olympics since August of 1990, when she underwent an operation for a bone spur in her foot.

> I wouldn't have had the operation if I didn't want to run another Olympics. I didn't want any attention before I went. . . . I deliberately kept a low profile, because then I could quietly go about my business and do what I knew how to do best.

What Moller does best is use consistent, smart training to fuel one of the longest careers in women's running. Her training is guided by the principle that "what the mind can believe, you can achieve."

"When I go into a race, I go in with the intention of winning it," Moller says. "My goal was to figure out how I could win the Olympics. I had a plan and I trained with that goal in mind."

Her plan had everything in Moller's life geared to winning a medal: nutrition, training, sleep, even who she spent time with and what she did outside of running. Moller had visualized the Olympic Marathon over and over during her training, and that total devotion paid off.

Moller is one of only two women to have run all three Olympic Marathons (she was fifth at Los Angeles in 1984 and 33rd at Seoul in 1988), and she plans on competing in Atlanta in 1996. She is one of the most prolific marathoners ever, and calls the bronze medal the highlight of a long career which includes 16 major marathon wins, two world-bests on the roads, and two masters world records.

"The Olympics are held in an esteem that the other races can't match," Moller says. "It has such an historical significance, and it's such a big event that, really, to win an Olympic medal for me is moving up into a new league. I'm in an exclusive club, something I have aspired to since I was a teenager."

Some might argue that Moller has been in an exclusive club from the beginning of her career in 1969—that club whose members are the pioneers of women's running. "Women's distance running just didn't exist," Moller says of her early racing years. "My career coincided with the evolution of women's distance running. I was able to get on at the beginning of it and ride it right through. Things have changed a lot, for the better."

Starting Out in Putaruru

Lorraine Moller had a recurring kidney problem as a child, and when she was eight years old, she was placed in the Princess Anne Hospital in Auckland. Her room overlooked the Domain, the large park where many of the great New Zealand runners have trained. "I remember looking out the window and wondering what was out there and, now and then, I'd see a runner go by."

She vividly recalls one day overhearing the doctor tell her mother, "I'm sorry, but there is nothing more we can do for Lorraine," and that she was eventually going to die.

"I thought, well, I just won't let that happen," recalls Moller. "In my mind I had things I wanted to do. I wanted to be famous, I wanted to be an actress."

And five years later Lorraine Moller did cause quite a stir as a 13-year-old when she began running through the pine forests near Putaruru, her hometown of "5,000 people and several hundred thousand sheep" on New Zealand's north island.

"It's not good for a girl to be running. Lorraine will be ruined for later life," neighbors warned her father, Gordon. They said she would become masculine, and even some doctors at the time told girls they shouldn't run. There were other obstacles for girls wishing to become athletes, Gordon recalls. "For example, in primary school, girls were discouraged from running by limiting them to the 60-meter dash, silly little things like that." Says Lorraine, "That was the attitude that existed back then. There were so few women runners."

The neighbors soon changed their tune when young Lorraine started winning races and getting a bit of fame. First it was 60-meter dashes in grade school; then she really blossomed in the "longer" high-school 400-meter contests, sweeping through school and district competitions. Running on a grass track in bare feet, Moller, at age 14, won the New

Zealand national 400-meter title in 58.6 seconds, and was eighth in the 800 meters (2:13.7)—with no serious training. "The environment in Putaruru was conducive to outdoor living and sports," Moller says of her early success. "And there was a Golden Era of New Zealand athletics, with Peter Snell and John Davies, that I was certainly aware of as a child."

Moller's father is a World War II navy veteran and businessman. He remembers the first race his daughter ran in Putaruru, a cross-country

New Zealand's Running Tradition

New Zealand is a small country of roughly 3.4 million people. There's nearly a score of cities in the world with more people than inhabit all of New Zealand. But despite its small size, this island nation has a running tradition that rivals that of Finland's greatest years.

It began with Jack Lovelock, who set the mile world record of 4:07.6 in 1933. He followed that with a gold medal win in the 1936 Berlin Olympic 1,500 meters (3:47.8), also a world record. New Zealand produced a plethora of stars in the years to come. The greatest was Peter Snell, winner of the 1960 Olympic 800 meters in a thrilling race over world-record holder Roger Moens of Belgium. Less than an hour after Snell's victory, Murray Halberg won the 5,000-meter gold for New Zealand.

Snell and Halberg were both disciples of Arthur Lydiard, one of the best-known coaches in the world. Lydiard's difficult training, that included 22-mile runs even for milers, continued bearing fruit the following year, when Snell broke Herb Elliott's mile world record. A week later, he broke the 880 record by a whopping 1.7 seconds.

Snell trained for the 1964 Tokyo Olympics by running up to 100 miles a week and won both the 800 and 1,500 meters, establishing himself as one of the best middle-distance runners ever. John Davies, another Kiwi (New Zealanders are nicknamed "Kiwis," after the rare wingless bird that is their national symbol), was another international star. Snell went on to break the mile record again, running 3:54.1, before retiring in 1965. "Kiwis," says Moller, "outrun predators, since they can't fly."

Snell was followed by a trio of stars in the 1970s: John Walker, the first man to break 3:50 for the mile and the 1976 Olympic

1,500-meter gold medalist; Rod Dixon, third in the 1972 Olympic 1,500 and winner of the New York Marathon in 1983 in 2:08:59; and Dick Quax, silver medalist in the 1976 Olympic 5,000 and a world-record holder in the 5,000 meters. Walker, Dixon, and Quax were known as the "Big Three." On the women's side there was what was chauvinistically called the "Little Three" of Moller, Anne Audain, and Allison Roe, a marathon world-record holder.

In the early 1990s, John Campbell added another chapter to the legacy of New Zealand running, clocking 2:11:04 in the Boston Marathon to set the masters world record. He broke the record set by yet another Kiwi, Jack Foster, a bicyclist who turned to running in his 30s and competed with the best in the world in open races. Campbell set masters world bests at six distances, including a 1:02:28 half-marathon in Philadelphia.

race against Val Robinson, then New Zealand's best female runner. Halfway through the race, 13-year-old Moller was running side by side with international runner Pam Kenny. Lorraine was breathing so hard and was such a pale skinny girl that Kenny looked over and said, "Slow down, Lorraine," fearing that she was going to hurt herself.

> I thought she was telling me that so that she could beat me, so I stuck to her like glue. In the last few hundred meters, she told me to slow down again. Everything was going black and I couldn't see what was in front of me, and I thought, "What's the difference, I might as well sprint."

Lorraine finished second to Robinson and then collapsed. Gordon Moller immediately took his daughter home, put her in a hot bath, and told her to go to bed.

But Lorraine would not stay away. She was soon back at the starting line, watching the other races. "You could tell even then that running was something in her blood," says her father. "She was just a little mite, and she beat everyone except Val, which was not expected. She was a natural right from the start. That race was the beginning."

Moller did a lot of easy mileage in her formative years, something Gordon, who has run 40 marathons, says was critical to her later success.

"It was not training back then. It was enjoyment, but she was getting the mileage in, too. But while Lorraine was enjoying it, I was suffering!"

Lorraine and her father would go running together through some of the thousands of acres of bush surrounding Putaruru, and they were known to get lost now and then.

No matter how late Lorraine came in from her bush runs, her mother, Maisie, would have the table set for her. "She was very supportive and always had meals ready. That support was very important in her athletic development," says Gordon. Sometimes Lorraine and her father would not return from their runs, and Maisie would get a call in the middle of the night from a farmhouse as far as 20 miles away. It would be Gordon and Lorraine, lost again, needing a ride home.

Lorraine always had a "lovely personality as a child, and was never cheeky," recalls Gordon.

> She'd poke me in the stomach and say, "Come on, fatso. Let's go run." Once I was on a trip and came home rather late. There was Lorraine, curled up on the kitchen chair, waiting for me to get home to go on a run. That was Lorraine; she had a routine and she stuck to it, even then. She was always serious about her running, and she did her best in everything.

Moller's development was furthered by the Putaruru Athletic Club. Most towns in New Zealand, even ones as small as Putaruru, have running clubs and grass tracks. Competitions are held once a week, and that's where Moller had some of her first races, in the summer after school was out.

Unlike some talented children, Moller was not pushed into competition too quickly. Her parents, along with a brother who ran, helped her build her strength slowly, keeping her from overdoing it. Says Gordon,

> Early easy mileage, without pressure, is the most important thing with young people. Whether it's rugby, boxing, ice hockey, or athletics, parents and coaches have to know to let them develop.

"We were just muddling along," says Moller.

Despite the family support, Moller is a self-made athlete, her father emphasizes.

> Lorraine knew she had the ability and she sacrificed a lot of what teenagers do, parties and things like that. Lorraine always stood out. She would have done well at whatever she chose. She could have been a brain surgeon. Lorraine has been a person on her own. She's had help along the way, but she's done it herself.

Moller did it on her own because there was not a path for her follow. There were few role models for young women runners when she was starting out, no prize money, no sponsorships, no women's races. Moller, along with Anne Audain and Allison Roe, blazed the trail for women's running in New Zealand, and from there, to the rest of the world. They joined Grete Waitz, Katherine Switzer, and Joan Benoit, among others, in bringing name recognition to women's running. And when it was time, Moller and Audain put their careers on the line to help break the charade of amateurism that runners competed under.

Early coaching help came from former New Zealand star John Davies, who coached Moller as a teenager. She then enrolled at the University of Dunedin, where "there was tremendous training and encouragement, running with the young fellows," says Gordon. "Not many girls were running at the time, but there was a good group of young athletes who had some strenuous training. Lorraine built herself a name by keeping up with the guys."

Moller recalls how she hooked up with the group.

I was standing on some steps at the university and when the group ran by, one of the guys said, "Going to come run with us, chick?" I took up the challenge and kept up with them. It became a regular thing, and they adopted me as "one of the boys." It was a great honor, and soon I was going on 20-mile runs with them on the weekends. I remember someone saying to me, "Lorraine, you're running more mileage than even the Russian women are doing!" I was the only woman to run with the men, and I became the team mascot. It was great support and not competitive at all.

Women's Running Evolves

Moller took part in her first international competition at age 17. In 1974, when she was 19, Moller ran a personal best 800 meters of 2:03.6, good for fifth place at the 1974 Christchurch Commonwealth Games. In 1975, she placed fifth in the World Cross-Country Championships in Morocco. Three other New Zealand stalwarts who were progressing at the same time helped pave the way for the acceptance of women's running: Anne Audain, Allison Roe, and Diane "the blonde bombshell" Zorn. "They all stuck to their guns when women were not treated as equals," Gordon said, adding, "Women are still not there yet, are they?"

Maybe not, but they are getting closer. As the sport began to change in the 1970s, so did the distance of Moller's races. Moller got better, too. She raced primarily on the track and in cross-country through her early 20s, mostly because there were not many road races for her to compete in. When she was 23, Moller tried her first marathon, on a whim, in 1979 at the Grandma's Marathon in Duluth, Minnesota. Not expecting much more than a long training run, she won in 2:37:36, then the sixth-fastest time ever. "I couldn't see what the big deal was," she said. "I wondered what I'd do with proper training."

She raced all over the world. In 1980, she won the Avon Women's World Championship Marathon in London, the first time the streets of London were closed for a sporting event. Moller stopped at each aid station to drink water, saying she ran the race like doing intervals, running a few miles, stopping, then starting up again. Moller also went to Rio de Janeiro, Brazil, where she won the Maratona Atlantica Boavista. She also won the Nike OTC Marathon in Eugene, Oregon, and again at Grandma's.

As she began running marathons, Moller saw the inequities in the way the sport was run, and she was outspoken about the need for open prize money for athletes. And in 1981, she put her (lack of) money where her mouth was.

The Cascade 11

The boycott of the 1980 Olympic Games brought to a head the resentment felt by runners over their lack of say in racing matters. But while many elite athletes bemoaned the fact that there was only limited, secretive, under-the-table prize money available, Moller and several others decided to do something about it. She, Allison Roe, and Anne Audain, along with Colombian Domingo Tibaduiza and several U.S. runners, went out on a limb by accepting prize money at the 1981 Cascade Run-Off 15K in Portland.

There had been a couple of marathon prize-money races, but they were not taken seriously by top runners. In 1980, the Association of Road Race Athletes (ARRA) was formed, with Frank Shorter as its head. Road racer Benji Durden named the organization, getting inspiration in part from the rock group, Abba, which was popular at the time.

ARRA's legal counsel was Chuck Galford, race director for Cascade, and the group decided to make the Run-Off the test case to openly take prize money. They wanted to make a circuit of events that would help runners make a living and not be left "swinging in the air by ourselves," Durden says. "This was when the fabric of amateurism began to tear."

Even on the morning of the Cascade Run-Off, there was much discussion over who would actually defy the archaic amateur rules and accept prize money, risking being banned. Frank Shorter ran on the side of the course to show support. Bill Rodgers raced and finished second, but did not take the prize money. Eleven runners did take the prize money. The Americans, such as Durden, Greg Meyer, and Peter Pfitzinger, were threatened with a ban by The Athletics Congress (TAC), the governing board of track and field in the United States. After the race, they were still "legal," pending the outcome of TAC hearings that dragged on.

New Zealand, however, had no due process procedure, and Moller and Audain were immediately banned from all competition. If the ban was upheld, neither would be able to race internationally again. "Lorraine and Anne took a big risk," said Durden. "They were hassled every time they tried to run." (Roe had returned to New Zealand and gotten reinstated.)

Six weeks after the Cascade Run-Off, matters came to a head at the Bobby Crim 10-Miler in Michigan. British runners Nick Rose and Dave Murphy refused to run if Moller was allowed in the race. They didn't want to risk being "contaminated" and face possible sanctions from their own federation. "The race was going to dump Lorraine and Anne," says Durden. "They called our bluff."

With runners lining up against the banned New Zealanders, it looked as if Moller's career might be at an end. But it was none other than road-race star Bill Rodgers who rescued Moller, saying he would not run unless Moller and Audain were permitted to race. Rather than risk losing Rodgers, the biggest draw on the roads, Bobby Crim officials caved in. "Billy turned the corner," says Durden. "He also gave ARRA $5,000 in seed money."

Moller has always had "a strong opinion on these issues," says Durden. "From early in her career, she's felt athletes, especially women, don't generally have the voice. One of the things she pushed for was equality of prize money."

ARRA eventually agreed to a modified version of a trust fund idea proposed by Frank Shorter. With public sentiment going against the New Zealand federation, the ban on Moller and Audain was lifted. "With the compromise Frank came up with, Anne and Lorraine were not hounded, and we got back to the business of running," says Durden.

"It was one of the few times we had solidarity among the athletes," Moller says. "It became a political issue."

Audain and Lorraine "stuck to their guns, and went for what they deserved," says Gordon. Moller and Audain were responsible, in large part, for altering the framework of women's running, not just in New

Zealand, but around the world as two of the first women to make their living from running road races. "I'm quite proud of it," Gordon adds. "That, in my opinion, is her biggest victory."

Back to Running

Moller had plenty of victories on the road and track, as well. After getting reinstated, she was selected for the 1982 Commonwealth Games in Brisbane. She showed she had not lost much leg speed by winning 1,500- and 3,000-meter bronze medals.

Moller split her time between New Zealand and the U.S., and was married to 1968 U.S. Olympic marathoner Ron Dawes for a year. She had a stellar 1984, winning in Boston (2:29:28) and at the Avon Women's World Championship in London and placing fifth in the inaugural women's Olympic Marathon (2:28:34).

Durden, who has followed Moller's progress through the years, says what sets her apart is that "Lorraine has learned what she can and can't do in training. She can focus and really believe in herself when it counts."

Moller had a good 1985, running on the track. She qualified for *four* events in the 1986 Commonwealth Games: 1,500 meters (4:10), a New Zealand record; 3,000 meters (8:53); 10,000 meters (32:40); and the marathon (2:34:55). She also ran 15:35 for 5,000 meters on the track.

Early in April 1985, Moller ran 53:48 at the Cherry Blossom 10-Miler in Washington, D.C., second behind Rosa Mota's new world best of 53:09. But after placing fourth at the New York City Marathon, Moller was dropped by her sponsoring shoe company. Like Steve Jones, Moller used that as motivation to come back even better.

She did so early in 1986, winning Japan's Osaka Marathon. In June, she set a new world best of 20:23 for four miles at the Steamboat Classic in Peoria, Illinois, despite heavy training preparing for the Commonwealth Games. A week later, Moller returned to Portland for the Cascade Run-Off for a race against Grete Waitz, whom she had never beaten.

"I was thinking that if I had any chance at all of beating Grete, I'd race her on the downhill," Moller told *Running Stats*. "I know my strength is as a downhill runner, and I know Grete doesn't like the downhills."

Waitz looked like she might run away with the race early, hitting the first mile in a fast 4:55, with Moller already 10 seconds behind. Moller passed 5K in 17:08, but was losing ground. Then, not long after 10K, she caught a glimpse of Waitz. "I got excited seeing Grete," Moller said, and she got even more excited when she passed Waitz at seven miles.

Moller expected the Great Grete to come back on her, but she never did, as Lorraine ran the last downhill 5K in 15:25 to finish in 49:09, nearly 30 seconds up on Waitz. That time placed Moller fourth on the all-time 15K list, behind Ingrid Kristiansen, Waitz, and England's Wendy Sly.

Next up was the Commonwealth Games Marathon, where Moller had a battle with a big rival, Lisa Martin of Australia. Moller was as fit as she had ever been, and passed halfway in 1:14:48, saying she was waiting for Martin to "make a mistake." But Martin never did, winning the gold (2:26:08) with Moller getting the silver. Despite having to walk twice because of cramps, Moller finished in a personal best 2:28:17.

She ended 1986 with two good road-race wins. The first was at Falmouth, where she hooked up with Joan Benoit Samuelson. As typical, Moller started out running within herself, then passed Samuelson at two miles on her way to the win. Afterwards, second placer Marty Cooksey told *Running Stats* that Moller "runs like a race horse, and I mean that as a compliment. She has those loping strides." Samuelson, who was fifth on a bad day, said, "I was totally outclassed. I can't take anything away from what Lorraine did." Moller then won a 10K in Texas in 33:36, beating her other big rival, Anne Audain, by seven seconds.

Moller continued racing at the top in 1987. In January, she returned to the Osaka Marathon, where she had another duel with Lisa Martin. When the two raced, it was not just Moller versus Martin, but also New Zealand versus Australia.

It was cold at the start in Osaka, and Martin showed up wearing long, white gloves that covered her arms up to her elbows. Moller and Martin watched each other through the early going, content to sit in a huge group of roughly 250 women that went through the first 5K in a very slow 19:06.

The pace gradually picked up, but so did the snow, and after passing halfway in 1:17:08, the lead pack was down to eight. The runners had the wind at their backs after the turnaround, and Moller's smooth stride lengthened. She went to the lead at 25K and upped the pace. One by one the others dropped back, until three were left: Moller, Martin, and Misako Miyahara of Japan. "All I was aware of was that Lisa was on my shoulder because I could hear her feet."

Moller stood out against the snow in her pink running shorts and top. The crowds lining the course were cheering for Miyahara, who dropped back at 35K. Moller was feeling good, but behind her back she could always hear Martin's soft footsteps staying near. With the temperature dipping into the 30s, Moller cranked it up another notch, running the next 5K in 17:10, but still Martin hung directly behind her.

Then, with two miles to go, Martin moved up alongside Moller. The live TV audience saw Martin pull off first one long glove, then the other, and toss them to the side of the road. Martin had thrown down the gauntlet, and Moller thought, "Looks like Lisa is ready for action."

Moller, however, was ready as well. She dipped into her bag of tricks to use one of her favorite tactics. Whenever she gets tired and is passed, Moller will try to go back in front of the runner passing her. When Martin began to make her move, Moller responded with a surge of her own, and sure enough, Martin dropped back. Moller went on to the 2:30:40 win, with a second 13.1 miles of 1:13:22.

That was a good start to 1987. In June, Moller went back to Peoria for the Steamboat Classic 4-Miler. She was aiming to run 5-minute mile pace, and went out in 4:56. She slowed in the second and third miles, but finished with another 4:56 to break her own world best with a time of 20:16. "I got the first mile right and the last mile right," she told Paul Christman. "Now all I have to do is work on the middle."

A week later, Moller tried to defend her title at the Cascade Run-Off, but placed second, running the 15K in 49:30.

In the winter of 1987-88, Moller began aiming for the 1988 Olympics. In January, she placed second to Ingrid Kristiansen in a 15K in Australia. Afterwards Moller said it's "impossible to beat Kristiansen over this distance." Moller was feeling tired in her training and racing and had to pull out of Osaka. She was diagnosed as having anemia, and did not run for a month.

After resuming training, she ran 15:40 on the roads at the Carlsbad 5K. She followed that with a road 10K of 32:06. Though she was running well over the shorter distances, her low-iron blood count prevented her from putting in the mileage she needed to train for the marathon. That showed at the Seoul Olympics, when Moller had to drop back from the second pack at 20 miles. Running in, she passed Carla Beurskens of Holland standing on the side of the road. The two jogged in together, finishing in 2:37, in 33rd and 34th place.

Moller's anemia persisted through the fall, and after her disappointing showing at the Seoul Olympics, some speculated that her career might be over. "Everybody was saying that would be my last race," Moller remembers.

In January 1989, Moller returned to Osaka for a race against Olympic champ Rosa Mota. Moller led early in the race before Mota took over, pushing the pace after halfway. Typically when she did that, Mota would have the race to herself. Moller, however, stayed right with the Olympic champion, and a little over 5K later, Mota was forced to drop out with a pain in her calf. Moller ran in for her third win at Osaka.

Training: The BodyMind Connection

In 1990, Moller's foot was bothering her, and she decided to have the operation to remove bone spurs. She was already thinking about the 1992 Olympics. Once again, some wrote her off after the operation, but Moller knew she was not finished. She had the utmost confidence in the coaching of Dick Quax. When training for the Olympics, she ran 80-mile weeks planned by Quax, ate a low-fat diet, and used sessions at The BodyMind Connection, the "wholebrain" technology shop she owned. While some said Moller was "too old" to beat the best, she did not consider her age a disadvantage.

© Photo Run/Takashi Ito

Lorraine Moller runs in for her third win at Osaka.

I never thought of age as an issue until people brought it up afterwards. Because age is just a number. I never thought there were any sort of barriers or anything like that. And I think when I'm 41 and go to the Olympics, I'll probably speak to a lot more people than I did at 37.

With the wisdom gleaned from her long career, Moller speaks to all those who want to continue getting better as they get older. "The neat thing is that I know how the program works," she says. "I know how to do it. I figure I can do it again and do it better."

Moller almost didn't get a chance to do it at Barcelona; New Zealand picks its Olympians via a committee, and politics within the federation kept her from being named to the team until early in the summer.

Earlier, in May, she was diagnosed with having low-iron blood again. Moller was "weak all the time" until she made a radical change in her diet, cutting out sugar, tea, and—despite "a mild addiction"—coffee. "I just decided that everything I put in my mouth had to count and be supportive of my goal."

Each morning her "support crew"—future husband, Harlan Smith—squeezed her fresh pineapple, apple, orange, or banana juice. In the evening, it was fresh-squeezed vegetable juices; carrots, celery, and, especially, beets. "It has concentrated minerals and vitamins," Moller said. "It made a huge difference."

Doctors had told Moller it would be three months before her iron would be back to normal. However, the juices helped her iron count double within two weeks, and she was ready to continue with her training, which emphasized both the physical and the mental. "You can't separate them," she says. "One is a function of the other. People ask me [to give] a percentage, and I say, 'It's 100 percent physical and 100 percent mental.'"

Moller has never been a high-mileage runner. Leading up to Barcelona, she put in 100-mile weeks only twice. She rested when she thought her body needed it, saying, "I'm very conscious of balancing work periods with adequate recovery periods. I'm kinder to my body than a lot of other professional athletes."

"I didn't do the high miles or really hard training before the Olympics. But it was very good training and very balanced training," Moller recalls.

If you look at my training schedule and my races and the way it worked out, it looked like I was cutting it pretty fine, because my races weren't spectacular. I absolutely peaked at the right time. Just three weeks before the Olympics, everything clicked and every run was feeling great.

Moller's weekly training schedule leading up to the Olympics was:

Sunday:	A.M., long run of up to 2 hours, 45 minutes, as fast as 6:30 per mile, usually on trails.
Monday:	Recovery day: A.M., 10K; P.M., 10K. "I rarely run slower than a 7-minute pace. And if I'm not feeling that strong, I might cut out the second workout or swim for 40 minutes."
Tuesday:	5K steady-state run. "When I can break 16 minutes for 5K (during this training run), I know I'm all right." (Moller's fastest before Barcelona was 15:40.)
Wednesday:	15 miles at a 6:30- to 7-minute pace.
Thursday:	Recovery (same as Monday).
Friday:	Recovery (same as Monday and Thursday).
Saturday:	A high-quality interval session or a race. This session might be 20 × 400 meters in 74 seconds, or 10 × 1 kilometer, each with 400-meter recoveries.

What was Moller's secret to doing that? "There is no secret," she says. "There is no one ingredient anyone could point to."

The one thing central to Moller's training not used by other elite runners was The BodyMind Connection, a quiet refuge just off the rambunctious downtown Pearl Street Mall in Boulder, a short jog from Moller's home. It is here that Moller and several other athletes did their mental training. Moller says that in a sense, the shop is a metaphor for her own personal BodyMind Connection, and that it's not a coincidence that she started racing well again when she began investigating how the mind works.

Moller is a student of comparative mythology (she brings to races a pendant of Hermes, the Greek messenger god), and the key to better running and better living, she believes, is to be found in the ancient Greek axiom, "Know Thyself." The BodyMind Connection is a "Know

Thyself" shop, offering a variety of high-tech, new-age "tools" all aimed at helping people develop physically, emotionally, and mentally. Moller says this is just as important as long runs for anyone wanting to reach his or her potential.

"Our thoughts and beliefs are the blueprints from which we create our physical reality," she explains. "Your body follows the directives of the mind. Racing is such a direct feedback system that whatever thoughts you are holding are immediately represented in your body."

The cutting-edge mental training Moller uses will one day be a regular part of an athlete's training, she says; it is what separates the champions from the ranks of the merely talented. Her philosophy is that people can "create their own reality" by selecting what to pay attention to from the myriad messages bombarding us. "I've been written off so many times in my career, and I never believed any of it," she says. Moller adds that we can "paint a picture" of our lives, choosing what to "put down on the canvas." For her, that means painting images of wins and achievements.

However, thinking about winning is not enough, Moller warns. "We can't just settle down and visualize and not do anything. Everything has to be backed up with action." Moller believes that

> We put the idea out there, and then we go to meet it. It's as if you set your destination, where you want to go, so you have a direction, and then you figure out how you're getting there from where you are. So you plan your training and your diet, and figure out what else you need to do to get you from this point to that point.

Moller explains the mental part of her training like this:

> Believe in your program, do what you can, be prepared for life's surprises, expect the unexpected. I think the difference is that I treat everything as a learning experience; then you become divested of the result and more invested in the experience itself.

Moller credits her "support crew" with building her confidence leading into Barcelona. "I didn't want anyone around me telling me I was wasting my time, or couldn't do it, or was doing it the wrong way. The people I had around me were like, 'We believe in you, we know what you want to do. How can we help you?'" The BodyMind Connection helped by letting Moller concentrate on her goals and maintain a high self-image. "My initial motivation for getting into these gadgets was that I wanted to improve my athletic performance. To me, the key is having very clear ideas about what you want to do."

Moller does this partly with dual-induction hypnosis tapes, called hypno-peripheral processing, which send different stories into each ear, thereby "overloading" the conscious mind and letting the desired message in. Moller often listened to the tapes (a favorite is titled "Achieving Excellence") while on the Graham Potentializer—a rotating bed with an electromagnetic field whose motion simulates that of ocean waves. "It's very effective. The tapes provide a positive dialogue with your subconscious mind."

The "sound and light" machines at the shop also let Moller get into relaxed, meditative states very quickly. That is when she visualizes winning a race or having a good workout.

> We also get all sorts of neurotransmitters and endorphins released in response to the deep relaxation; that is just excellent for recovery. If you can't relax, then you can't train hard. It's a total thing. I'm not one of these people who is just going to muscle through and win. It doesn't work for me. Everything in my life has to be going well and in agreement for me to do well.

To help her do well, Moller traveled to Spain in August 1992 to review the marathon course.

> I wanted to see what it was going to be like. It's very hard to train for something you have no idea about. I think it was invaluable to see the stadium and what it would be like running through Barcelona. And also to feel the atmosphere of the country, the sights, the sounds, and the smells.

Moller planned on running a conservative race in Barcelona and letting high-profile runners like Lisa Ondieki (the former Lisa Martin, who had married Kenyan star Yobes Ondieki) and Wanda Panfil break up the field. Moller was not afraid of anyone in the race. "I had beaten Lisa in head-to-head battle, and had run in races with [fields] just as tough."

Coach Arthur Lydiard told Moller beforehand that 80 percent of Olympians perform below their potential. "That was great," Moller said, "because it meant I only had 20 percent to worry about. I just had to perform at my best."

Moller was surprised at the slow early pace, which played right into her plan. She stayed in the large pack that gradually thinned out. Just past halfway, Valentina Yegorova, of the Commonwealth of Independent States team, took off for the front.

Moller was feeling great, and says the Olympic Marathon overall "felt like such a jog. I told myself, 'I'm going to win this thing.'" Whenever she did begin to tire, Moller used her favorite tactic, and went directly to the head of the pack that was chasing Yegorova.

Dick Quax's Coaching Advice

Dick Quax had a lot of thrills during a running career that spanned three decades, most notably grabbing the silver medal behind Lasse Viren in the 1976 Montreal Olympic 5,000. The next year, he set a 5,000-meter world record of 13:12.8 and, in 1980, ran a 2:10:47 marathon in his first attempt over the distance. Quax, a three-time Olympian, then retired and turned his talents to coaching, including Moller, whom he's known since she was a teenager.

Of all his experiences in track and field, Quax says Moller's bronze at Barcelona "is one of the highlights of my career. And I believe Lorraine still has a lot of improvement to come. She knows how to train. What she really needs is not so much coaching, but advice." The five keys to long-distance training Quax identifies, applicable to any level runner are:

• **Consistency:** As a coach, he expects his runners to train in a regular and consistent manner. "Training must be planned well in advance and the athlete should maintain an accurate record of all training," he says.

• **Caution:** After Quax prepares a training program for Moller, he puts it aside for a while before reviewing it. "Overtraining is much more of a problem than undertraining." Quax's coaching motto is, "If in doubt, be conservative."

• **Rest:** The body adapts to the stress of training not during the training itself, but during the following periods of rest, explains Quax. "Without rest, there is no training effect—just stress."

• **Volume:** "In all races over 1,500 meters, the volume of training is of primary importance." But, Quax warns:

> This does not imply mile after mile of slow jogging, but running at varying intensities and terrain. This is the basis of all distance-running success. No anaerobic or lactic tolerance training should begin until there is a foundation on which to build.

• **Individuality:** Every runner is unique, says Quax. "I have never coached two runners who have reacted in the same way to training. There is no recipe for success—only sound physiological principles, which must be adhered to."

That works really well for me. Because you can start having negative thoughts, and begin looking at the other runners and thinking that it's going to be hard. So I thought, nothing makes you
feel better than going to the front. I'd stay there a little while and
start feeling great. You feel like you are winning.

Actually, as far as marathons go, it was one of the easier ones
I've run. It didn't really beat up my body; my legs weren't stiff. I
didn't feel like I wasted myself or pushed myself to the limit.

It would have been interesting if Moller had pushed herself to the
limit. She says her only mistake in Barcelona was not going with eventual silver medalist Yuko Arimori with about 10 miles left in the race,
when the Japanese runner bridged the gap to Yegorova. "I wanted to
make sure I finished strongly, so I held back."

Moller went into third at about 18 miles and looked lean and strong
coming up the final hill at Montejuc. She finished with a surfeit of energy
and the satisfaction of knowing she was now an Olympic medalist.

After winning her bronze medal, Moller was invited to Japan to
give a talk. The Japanese runners were very interested in her training schedule which she passed out. They couldn't believe that was
all there was; they lifted up the paper, looking on the other side,
asking where the other pages were. "They thought there must be
more," Moller said.

For me, running is a lifestyle and an art. I'm far more interested
in the magic of it than the mechanics. It's that interest and explo-
ration that make running fun for me. It's easy to become out-
come-focused; for me the unfoldment of self is what is meaningful in running and outlasts any medals.

Believe in Yourself

Moller's future includes more races and more wins. Her advice to people
wanting to follow in her footsteps is,

You have to be focused on your dreams and tune in to what sup-
ports that. If people are around who are telling you that "Oh,
you're too old," get away from them. The only problem people
have is their own concept about age. People who think 37 is too
old to be doing something are probably old in attitude themselves. I suggest they do some revising. Because age is an attitude. In fact, in endurance sports, you get better as you get older.

Moller took a year off after Barcelona and, on June 1, 1995, became a masters runner. She says,

> The biggest plus to turning 40 is that sponsors were seeing me at the end of my career. Now, they're seeing me at the beginning. For me, age is like time in a marathon; far too much emphasis is put on it. I just want to win—in the open competition. I don't see any reason why I can't keep improving. There are so many mistakes people make; two are not believing in yourself and arrogance. And arrogance is usually followed by a good lesson in humility.

Moller's first race as a master was an excellent 16:56 for 5K at altitude in Denver. Her goal in the winter of 1995 was to reach the New Zealand Olympic Marathon qualifying standard of 2:33:30. Moller showed she wasn't missing a step, setting masters world records of 16:03 for 5K and 21:05 for 4 miles in the fall.

Despite 23 years of top-level competition, Moller says

> I still feel like I'm better than I've ever been. As you get older, you have more experience to draw from. I still really enjoy racing. It's the most fun way I know to earn a living, and it's still a challenge for me. I really think I can do better. I thought my day would come, because I hadn't done what I wanted to do yet. And I still feel that way. I'd like to have another go at it in '96. I'd
>
> I never expected to have this long of a career when I started running. When I was growing up the longest race for women was 800 meters. I wasn't inspired to be a marathoner then. It wasn't even in a little girl's vocabulary.

Thanks in part to Lorraine Moller, it is now, and her career is an example not just to those of her age and sex, but to all of us seeking the most out of life. Training partner Kim Hartman says that for Moller, running and racing was "never just a job. Few exude such joy in the act, the process of running. The exemplary liver and lover of life in the classical Greek sense is Lorraine."

11

Sebastian Coe

Father and Son

Born September 29, 1956, England

World records: 1-mile, 800, 1,000, and 1,500 meters

Olympic gold, 1,500, 1980 and 1984

Olympic silver, 800, 1980 and 1984

As Sebastian Coe sprinted around the final turn in the 1980 Moscow Olympic 800 meters, he looked up and got a sick feeling in his stomach. Steve Ovett had five steps on him, and Coe knew he was not going to catch his archrival and might not even get a medal. Coe drove his arms and accelerated from fifth into second place in the last 100 meters down the homestretch, earning "only" the silver medal.

Silver medalist in the Olympics would not be a bad effort for any other runner, but to the millions watching on TV, to the 100,000 packed into Moscow's Lenin Stadium, to Peter Coe, Seb's father and coach, and to Coe himself, it was an utter, complete failure.

A stunned Coe walked off the track with the sinking feeling of not having run the race he could have run or should have run. He was the clear favorite and had been knocked about like a novice. Simply put, Sebastian Coe, the 800-meter world-record holder, had choked.

A distraught Coe sought refuge in the Olympic Village, but could not find any. Wherever he turned, people reminded him that he had blown it. There was perhaps more pressure on him and Ovett than any pair of runners before, pressure that grew to monstrous proportions in the following five days leading up to the 1,500-meter final. Crowds of reporters and cameramen followed Coe around, even driving beside him on a training run, hanging out of car windows and snapping pictures to send back to athletics-crazed England. "Trail of Shame" read the headline on one British paper, emblazoned above a photo of Coe.

Redeeming himself in the 1,500 meters was the only way out of the pit of despair in which Coe found himself. Nothing but a gold medal would do, and it would not be easy. The 1,500-meter final was being billed as the "Race of the Century" and the roles were reversed from the 800-meter event. This time it was Ovett who was the favorite. He had not lost a 1,500 or mile in three years, an amazing streak of 45 races in a row. If Coe lost to Ovett again, as many expected, he would forever be labeled a loser, despite his world records, and Ovett would earn unanimous acclaim as the best middle-distance runner in the world.

A Love of Running

Yorkshire County in northern England is a place of rolling hills and dales. Sheffield, a steel town of more than a half-million people, is its biggest city, and it was here that Peter Coe, an engineer, and his actress wife, Angela, raised their family of four children. The oldest was Sebastian, born September 29, 1956, in Chiswick, West London. Peter Coe was a decent cyclist and Seb's grandfather had been a sprinter in the early 1900s. Seb was an athletic youth and had a well-rounded child-hood that included both sports and art. He went to the theater and museums with his parents and played soccer with his friends.

Coe always liked to run as a kid. In fact, he preferred running around town rather than riding a bicycle. Coe recalls that his first jog came when he was three. "I never walked anywhere, it seems. I had a genuine, instinctive love of running," he writes in *Running Free*, coauthored by David Miller. His first "official" run came when he was 12, and even in those first years of running during his early teens, self-motivation was never a problem for Coe. "I think he was the only one of the four children who would let father stand behind him and shove," Angela Coe told David Miller. "He always had an ability to get the maximum out of what he's got." Angela says that if her son had not become a successful runner, he would have found a sport at which he would have excelled.

Peter knew nothing about running when his son began training, but he could see that Sebastian had potential. Peter's first day as a coach was the day Sebastian took his first run. While Peter did not have a background in athletics, he did have intelligence and that ineffable British attitude that he could do whatever he set his mind to. "I was seeking a coherent training rationale and found I had to create it," said Peter.

Moreover, Peter knew many people who did know a lot about athletics, and he talked with them and read all he could about running. He had a high enough opinion of himself to say, "Hey, I can coach as well as any of these guys." He took what he thought would work for "his athlete" —Seb—and discarded the rest. Peter's skill was in being able to separate the gold from the dross in the training material floating about. "There is nothing revolutionary in what I have done with Seb, but it has been tailor-made for his physique," Peter told Miller. "An athlete to a great extent determines his own training by his response to the tasks you set for him and by his racing results. The coach must adjust to his athlete."

Peter set out a very difficult task for his son. When Sebastian was 14, he won the Yorkshire County 1,500 meters in 4:31. Afterwards, Peter sat down and laid out a plan that would have Seb running sub-3:30 for 1,500 meters (five seconds under the world record) and getting the gold medal at the 1980 Olympics, still 10 years away. Peter had an uncanny ability to predict performance, as shown that day in 1970 when he guessed what the world records would be in 1980 or 1981, the years he thought Seb would be ready for a go at them. Peter correctly predicted the records then would be 1:43 for 800 meters and 3:48 for the mile.

"When Seb was 14 I knew he was good; at 16 I had a strange kind of certainty that if I was patient I had a world beater," said Peter. Bold plans, but Peter used his engineering skills to develop a training program for his son. It worked because Coe was devoted to his father and had complete faith in him, along with a great deal of talent and the capacity to endure extremely hard work. Sebastian Coe the runner is inseparable from Peter Coe the coach. They had a symbiotic relationship, unique in track annals, that allowed them to put in the meticulous work that would prove Peter's predictions correct.

"Seb respected his father, because his father worked very hard to get it right. And Peter respected Seb very much, because his son worked very hard to get it right," says Dr. David Martin, a family friend and physiologist from Georgia State University. They were not sure what distance Sebastian would be a world beater in, at first thinking it might be 5,000 meters, before deciding to concentrate on increasing his speed and tackling the 800 and 1,500 meters. Peter took a different approach from the emphasis on long-distance work favored by many. He wanted Seb to run fast, so he devised a training program that would build up his strength and stamina enough so that he would be able to handle the speedwork needed to run world records.

Everything was thought out; nothing the pair did was casual. Peter succeeded precisely because he did not know anything about the sport when Sebastian started running, and so was not limited by preconceived notions about what a young runner could and could not do, or should and should not do. There were no barriers for Peter. Coe said his father "had no idea what a hard workout of, say, repeat quarters in 60 seconds or repeat halves in 1:55 felt like."

Peter and Sebastian Coe had a special relationship, says David Martin. What made it work was that in addition to the admiration they had for each other, "both developed the capacity to completely shut off the coach/athlete relationship when they were finished training." The moment they left the track, Peter and Sebastian became father and son again.

The only athlete Peter coached was his son, meaning he could give him his full attention and modify the training to suit Seb's needs. "Most coaches in the United States don't work with athletes," says Martin.

> They are out recruiting, buying plane tickets, talking to booster clubs, teaching, and counseling the anorexics and bulimics. And none of this has anything do with coaching individuals. Peter didn't have to worry about that. He was *coaching* and not running a program.

Running no more than 30 miles a week under his father's watchful eye, Coe kept improving. In 1970, in addition to winning the Yorkshire County 1,500 meters, Coe also won the Yorkshire School Cross-Country Championship. He then finished 10th in the English Schools Cross-Country Championships in which a runner a year older than Coe, by the name of Steve Ovett, placed second. The two runners were not acquainted with each other at the time, although they would certainly get to know each other *very* well in the years to come.

Through his midteens, Coe competed in British Amateur Athletic Association (BAAA) competitions, as "these were the logical stepping stones for progression up the ranks of sport in the world." From school races in Sheffield, he went to county meets, then area races, and finally to the English Championships. By now he was winning nearly all his races, and Angela says she sometimes wished her son would lose, because other mothers would say, "Oh, it's only going to be Coe again. I don't know why we bother to race."

Angela Coe found Sebastian's self-discipline early in his life astonishing. For years she heard stories about training and how Peter thought their son would be "world class" one day, but she was not as confident as her husband. "I didn't want either of them to be disappointed," she says. "Because I saw less of what was happening up there on the hills, I suppose I probably had less faith in the ultimate success."

What was happening in the Yorkshire hills were repeat hill sprints that built up Coe's strength and form. Seb ran the uphills very hard, but Peter would not let him run downhill as a youth; instead he drove him down in the car to avoid stressing Seb's growing bones. When an injury did show up, Coe never ran through it like many runners. Instead, he stopped training completely until it was healed, even if it meant missing races.

In July 1973, when he was 16, Coe won the English Schools Championship 3,000 meters in 8:40.2 and ran a 3:55.0 (a Championship record) for 1,500 meters in winning the BAAA youth title. He also ran 51.8 seconds for 400 meters that year and 1:56 for 800 meters. Coe's development slowed when he suffered a stress fracture in 1974 and was not able to run from April through November. But his training was given a boost when he enrolled at Loughborough University in Leicester. There Peter Coe asked George Gandy, head of the university track program, "to provide Seb with coaching assistance on circuits and weight training and to get him to join the 400-meter squad." Gandy's advice proved invaluable to Coe's program. "George produced a much strengthened athlete," says Peter.

When Coe was 18, he won the 1975 Northern Counties under-20 3,000-meter title in Blackburn, where he showed his racing guts. Coe was having a "pits of a race," falling behind by 200 meters with three laps to go. But he "dug in" and caught the leaders to set a personal best of

British Running Tradition

Britain's deep middle-distance tradition stretches all the way back to the middle of the 19th century. Beginning in 1853, sixteen different British runners, both professional and amateur, set 23 different mile world records in the years before the International Amateur Athletic Federation (IAAF) began keeping its records in 1913. The most prolific of these was the charismatic Walter George, who brought the mile record down from 4:24.50 seconds in 1880 to 4:12.75 in an 1886 one-on-one match race against Walter Cummings, another of the era's great runners. It was to be *37 years* before anyone ran faster than 4:12 for the mile, when Paavo Nurmi clocked 4:10.

Before Coe and Ovett, England had three one-mile world-record holders in the IAAF era: Sydney Wooderson (4:06.4 in 1937); Roger Bannister, the Oxford grad who shattered the four-minute barrier with his 3:59.4; and Derek Ibbotson (3:57.2 in 1957). Bannister finished a disappointed fourth in the 1952 Helsinki Olympic 1,500 meters. Bannister, training only four days a week, no more than thirty minutes at a time, had trained exactly to run two races, and stronger runners beat him in the final. Bannister, however, won enduring fame on May 6, 1954, by breaking four minutes on Oxford's Iffley Road track, perhaps the most famous race ever. The "four-minute mile" has since entered our vocabulary as meaning something difficult to achieve. Scores have run faster than four minutes since Bannister, but he will always be remembered for doing it first.

8:14.2, telling Miller, "I was pretty chuffed about that." He also ran 3:49.1 for 1,500 meters in winning the United Kingdom junior 1,500-meter title, a victory that led to his selection to the European junior championships that year in Athens.

Coe had a breakthrough in Athens, taking the bronze medal and lowering his personal best to 3:45.2. That race boosted his confidence and showed Peter he was on the right track. But it also showed him that Seb had to develop a finishing kick, which they worked on through winter weight training and very fast interval sessions.

There was a great group of junior milers in 1975. Besides Coe, there was Ray Flynn of Ireland, Jose Abascal of Spain, and Ari Paunonen of

Finland, who won the world junior 1,500-meter title. "Seb was very skinny, and his father was always with him," recalls Flynn, who competed against Coe for years, beginning with the UK school championships. "He really wasn't a prodigy when he was young." But what was most noticeable about Coe, even as a youngster, was that he had "a drive to be successful. He had the type of personality and the drive where he was going to be a successful guy. He had an agenda."

Flynn, a 3:49.7 miler who ran against Coe more times than he can count, remembers

> He had great acceleration. But he worked on it. I wouldn't say it came naturally. To run at the level he got to is still 80 percent hard work, 20 percent talent. There is just so much work involved that you have to be self-driven.

In 1976, Coe reached the elite level when he broke four minutes for the mile for the first time. His 3:58.3, run after leading most of the race, was good for seventh at the Emsley Carr Mile in London's Crystal Palace at the end of August. Coe ran one more mile, in just outside four minutes, before ending his 1976 season. After a month break, he resumed weight training, doing three days a week of hard lifting. "Seb was fully committed to weight training as a building block and foundation for his track expertise," says David Martin. Coe started off with 35 miles a week of steady running, increasing that through the winter up to 70 miles.

Searching for Speed

Peter was very smart when it came to making decisions about Seb's career. In 1977, Coe was at the point where it might seem logical to start running longer distances. That is the way most runners' careers went. Peter, however, decided to reverse the normal trend and have Sebastian move *down* in distance, all the way back to 400 meters. If the Coes had not gone back to speed, Seb might have ended up running marathons.

"There's only a limited possibility of improvement in distance work, going up and up, but coming back down again, we could see the benefits were very much better," Seb writes. "I needed the leg speed. My stride length had never been a problem, but on occasion, maintaining a fast cadence was." Added Peter, "You can no longer go up distance to hide from speed. It's speed, speed, speed."

Part of the speed training was designed to develop what Frank Shorter calls Coe's "elegant style," and others have called "poetry in motion." This had to be worked on, because Coe had "a cramped high-arm action and excessive shoulder movement" when he first started running, writes Peter.

Despite Peter's wishes for his son to become a world-class runner, he insisted that school was more important than running. Peter believed academics and athletics went hand in hand, that success in running bred success in the classroom. During his years at Loughborough University, Coe was what he terms a "part-time runner."

When Coe began making a name for himself in running, his family served as a balancing influence. They helped keep him humble, chanting "boring, boring," if Sebastian talked too much about running at dinner. When the Coes left the Sheffield track after training, "neither one was particularly interested in track-groupie conversation, where every minute of the day is numbers, splits, and races," says David Martin.

> Seb and Peter were far more cultured than that. They had a very cultured, close-knit family. When they came together, they couldn't care less what Seb had done at the track. None of them had any identification with how hard or how easy it was to do a 22-second 200 meters.

Coe's family helped imbue him with that special British sense of becoming a well-rounded citizen of the world, combining the artistic background of his mother with his father's scientific bent. He developed an interest in jazz (his favorite style being Dixieland), literature, and the theater.

Early in 1977, Coe twice set the United Kingdom indoor 800-meter record, and then won his first major championship, the European indoor 800-meter gold medal in 1:46.5, just outside the world record. That summer, he outkicked 1,500-meter world-record holder Filbert Bayi of Tanzania to win the Emsley Carr mile. That was followed by the 1977 World Cup 800 meters. Coe learned about tactics in that race, when Willie Wulbeck of East Germany knocked him about on the last lap. Coe ended up fourth in a race he says he should have won.

Chasing Ovett

No matter how careful a runner is, obstacles can spring up when least expected. Coe's progress was interrupted in 1978 when, during a training run on the Loughborough campus, he stepped in a hole and badly strained the ligaments and tendons in his leg. It was a serious injury, which could have ended his career. Several top runners have had their careers ended by stepping in a hole; among them are former half-marathon world-record holder Stan Mavis and U.S. 1,500-meter national champ Jeff Atkinson, who was tenth in the Seoul Olympic 1,500. Neither was able to come back after an injury similar to Coe's.

Coe missed a month of winter basework while his tendons healed. He went with his family to train on the Adriatic coast before the 1978 European Championships in Prague, the biggest race of his life so far. Ovett was the star of the British team in Prague, and he played mind games with Coe by not declaring whether he would double and run the 800 along with the 1,500. Wrote Coe, "Many athletes can't help feeling that Steve has had kid-glove treatment from the Board," because he did not have to declare what races he would be entering until the last minute.

Peter decided Sebastian should run from the front in the 800 meters, saying, "I want to see what the bastards are made of." Coe did lead from the start in the 800, going through the first lap in an extremely fast 49.3 seconds. But it was not enough to shake off Ovett, who passed him off the final turn. But in the shocker of the championships, Ovett was in turn passed by 21-year-old Olaf Beyer of East Germany for the gold, with Coe getting the bronze.

Ovett and Coe ended their 1978 seasons with fine wins at the Coca-Cola Invitational in London's Crystal Palace. They did not have a rematch of the European Championships, as Coe won the 800, breaking 1:44 for the first time, while Ovett set a world record for two miles in a duel with Kenyan star Henry Rono. Ovett had taken two weeks off after Prague, and was not expecting much at the Coca-Cola race. "It's a meet at the end of the season, making it difficult to be at top form," Ovett told *Running* magazine. "They always expected us to come back from championships and almost perform better than we did at the championships. It's very hard if you've just come back after a tough competition to motivate yourself to do it."

It was Rono's great season, when he set four world records, in the 3,000, 5,000, 10,000, and steeplechase. But Ovett outkicked Rono down the homestretch, breaking Brendan Foster's world record with a time of 8:13.5. Coe wrote that Ovett "treated (Rono) shoddily" by

> coming level with him in the finishing straight, giving him a stare, and then waving as if to say good-bye as he sprinted for the tape. I really cannot condone so much of Steve's behavior on and off the track. He is without question a wonderful athlete and my admiration of him as such is sincere and unbounded, but he does conduct himself in a way which regularly leaves so much to be

desired. He should not belittle inferior opponents in lesser races the way he sometimes does. That is sheer bad manners.

Training: Patience and Quality

The 1978 season over, Coe went back to classes at Loughborough. Many of Coe's teachers looked at his running as no more than a hobby, a diversion that interfered with his university studies. Coe was caught between running and schoolwork, unable to devote his full attention to either. "Grafting into world-class athletics and picking up a decent degree is tough, and you can't mess about," said Peter. "Life is too short; everything you do has got to be meaningful."

That is the philosophy father and son took into training. Everything mattered, nothing was wasted. The focus was not on counting miles but on counting quality sessions. None of that long, slow jogging stuff for Sebastian. Even winter basework was done at a good pace, "much at 5:15 to 5:30 per mile," says Peter. "Of course, you need the base, but what you need is *quality* base," adds Martin. "And the quality has to be good quality over distance. Seb and Peter were not particularly megamileage."

"If you are noticing the scenery, you probably aren't working hard," Coe says. Rather than running 100 to 120 miles a week like many runners—even some milers like John Walker—Coe would run 60 to 75 miles a week of basework. Says Martin, "The purpose of the base phase is to build up your aerobic system." He did try to have fun when possible in the winter. Sometimes Coe would do "Sunday slogs," in which he and other Haringey club runners ran. They would often leapfrog back and forth, carrying a training partner on their backs while running up and down a steep slope.

Martin says Coe "would occasionally test himself in stage relays which are very popular in Britain." The races include short and long legs between 3 and 6 miles. Those stage races were "a good way to run real hard, and he couldn't care less where he placed. In this way he never lost his racing skills, to surge, bump elbows, run hard off a hard pace up hills. That never left him."

Coe's running followed the seasons in Yorkshire. The Coes took the periodization approach to training. First, there was a recovery period for himself, when Coe would hang up his shoes. Then, November through March or April was the base-building period, what Martin calls "the purgatory of training." What Coe was doing during this time, as

Steve Ovett

Steve Ovett and Sebastian Coe's rivalry, heightened by the media, was real, but the pair did respect each other. Coe says he had "tremendous respect for (Ovett's) athletic ability. He is one of the most talented runners there's ever been, and his range, from 400 meters to a half-marathon, is unsurpassed." (Ovett's range was illustrated in the summer of 1977, when he jumped into a half-marathon and won, beating a British Olympic marathoner in the process.) Coe also praised Ovett's "enormous athletic talent and unparalleled record of racing achievement."

Those achievements started with the 800-meter gold medal in the 1973 World Junior Championships, followed by an unexpected silver medal in the senior race in 1974. Those wins foretold great things, and unlike most talented youngsters, Ovett delivered on his promise. It was in a victory in the 1,500 meters against Swedish junior runners, won in 3:54.9, that Ovett was first seen waving down the final straight, something that was to become his trademark as he developed into the top 1,500-meter man in the world.

In 1976, Ovett was fifth in the Montreal Olympic 800 meters, won by Alberto Juantorena, and was eliminated in the semifinals of the 1,500 meters. "It was disastrous," Ovett said, vowing "never to run as badly again in a major championship." He rebounded the following year at the 1977 Dusseldorf World Cup, where he won the 1,500 meters in 3:34.5, setting the British record. He beat a top field that included John Walker, Thomas Wessinghage, and Eamonn Coghlan.

That Dusseldorf race was, Coe told *Running* years later,

the best 1,500 meters I have ever seen. You wouldn't get a better field. . . . You had a guy like John Walker, who had won the [Olympic] 1,500 meters the year before, stepping off the track with 200 meters to go, just shaking his head, disbelieving what was going on at the front. [Ovett] took 10 paces out of the best mile field assembled within the space of about 20 yards. It always sticks in my mind.

It brought it home that middle-distance running was really our game now. It was our race and it was the first time anyone in the UK had truly won a world championship. We had had good medals and good positions, but this was the first time a guy had won it.

1977 was the year, agreed Ovett, that Britain really broke through.

Up until then I don't think we were considered seriously as a world nation in terms of middle distance. That race actually started Britain on a decade of dominating middle-distance racing. I am still proud that we are a part of that era.

But, Ovett added, "The race didn't really stick in my mind as being as good as that."

de Castella, Barrios, and others have said about their own training, was "going to work." Says Martin, "His job was his training. It was hard, hard work."

After doing strength work in the fall and winter, mixed in with a few road races, Coe moved more and more to speed, until by the summer he'd be doing only 30 miles a week. But he would be running tremendous interval sessions. "It's a matter of just being a little bit better at what you're doing than everyone else is. He wasn't interested in making excuses. If there was ever a choice to substitute quality for quantity, Seb chose quality. Endurance will get you to the finish line, but speed will get you there first."

In May, there was a "subtle change in the mix," and a gradual change over to anaerobic work. Three weight sessions a week went down to two; one or two tempo runs a week went up to two tempo runs plus track workouts.

Training before the big summer races was essentially maintenance. "At this point, he always took plenty of time to rest." It was low mileage, but with "incredible quality," says Martin. One of the best sessions Coe did in the late 1970s was 6 × 800 meters on the Rivelin Valley Road outside of Sheffield. In one session Coe averaged 1:52 for the repeats; the last was clocked at 1:49.

His approach was difficult to beat. And when it worked once, the Coes did not make major alterations in their program. "If it works, don't fix it," was the attitude. "So you didn't find Coe doing things like going up to altitude," says Martin.

Coe would begin running in smaller races in the spring, but he "preferred time trials on the track to let himself know what kind of shape he was in."

Repeat 200s were the workout for him. Seb found the ability to run repeat 200s at a given speed and given recovery gave him a sense of rounding into form. He would run the repeats quicker and quicker with less and less recovery, getting more and more anaerobically fit. And what wins 800 [meter races] is anaerobic power, not just a high aerobic base.

After each 200-meter interval session, Peter would tinker with the training. "It was just a matter of sitting and adjusting the mix to the situation," says Martin.

Kenny Moore recalls once doing a 200 workout with Coe on a track in London.

We were running the 200s in 29 seconds. I was struggling, but keeping up, thinking "this is great." Then he starts running faster, and he did not look any different running 25 seconds instead of 29s. He just looked effortless. Others weren't like that. With Eamonn Coghlan, you could see it in his arms, but not with Coe.

Martin, having worked with the Coes for many years, knows Seb perhaps better than anyone except his family. Martin met Seb in 1978 at the European Championships. He was having lunch in a restaurant where Coe was being interviewed by some East German journalists. "They just assumed Seb spoke German." He did not, and Martin served as translator for the interview, while Coe wondered what the heck an American was doing behind the Iron Curtain.

Peter Coe approached racing and training as an engineering project, and asked Martin to dissect the 800, saying, "Let's take the 800 and divide it into two 400-meter laps. Tell me what percentage is aerobic and what percentage is anaerobic in each of the two laps."

Says Martin,

It turns out you run the first 400 more aerobically and the second more anaerobically. If you look at that notion . . . then the secret to racing is to get the biggest aerobic capacity possible, so you do not have to put as much anaerobic into it. Just run as aerobically as possible, then you are not in oxygen debt. This *anaerobic tenacity* is the secret to winning the 800.

Martin says that the English club system helped form Peter's philosophy—that sooner or later, runners will meet at the club championships and see who is best. Martin describes Coe's training as "a

long trip through the tunnel of training and work, with the only interest being a supreme effort months later in June, July, August, or September. Seb always channeled everything toward peaking, from the time
he ran in the European junior championships all the way to the time he
retired. Peaking was his sole reason for being." According to Martin, in
a personal interview,

> Europeans are basically that way, and Seb was willing to do more
> work, with very little play. He's very intellectual. You wouldn't
> find him partying in the bars playing snooker after training. He's
> much more sophisticated than that. He had been so patient for
> so long a time and worked so hard for so long a time, that he
> would just be so hungry when June and July came around.
>
> Seb obviously has the genes. You don't get anywhere without
> genes. But to get the job done you have to have patience, and he
> was perfectly content to have one supreme peak each year.

While many runners today often race every other weekend for the
entire year, Seb didn't.

> He and his father developed a pact together; Seb wanted to be
> the best he could be, and his father wanted him to be the best he
> could be. Seb understood the reality very quickly that to be able
> to be the best on the track, you have to do one of two things; be
> the best at major championships, or be the best you could be at
> other big races.

Coe was not a trainer, but a competitor, Martin says, and two things
would happen in the summer: Physically, Coe was incredibly fit and
mentally he was ready to race.

> Then, all you have to do is back off with the training and get the
> load off, and you'll feel fresh off that. Cutting back to 60 miles a
> week and then to 30 miles a week, Seb would get so fresh he
> didn't know what to do with himself when he got on the track to
> run. You run like a feather, and that's fun. You get a thrill, and
> think, this is nice. Run and win, and get the rush. Nothing ever
> beats the rush of victory.

Coe did win against some great runners. And his training, besides
being geared to produce the proper mix of anaerobic and aerobic work,
was also designed to beat certain athletes, such as Ovett or Steve Cram.
Peter Coe knew Ovett's racing tactics very well and spent hours pouring over splits of his races. In fact, he studied the races of all of Sebastian's

rivals, to see what strategies they favored. The question Peter and Seb were always asking was, "How can we train to make us more able to cope with their strategy?"

After determining what an opponent's likely tactic would be, Coe trained to counter that move. For example, if Cram was known to make his move with 600 meters to go, Coe "would either make his move with 601 meters left or be exactly right behind him to get dragged along. If you get caught short, even three steps, it can make all the difference," says Martin. Writes Coe, "You must be committed willingly, without any doubt, to endure at least one moment longer than your adversary." Coe endured because he knew he had prepared properly. Each of his workouts had a specific purpose. For example, 400-meter intervals were done to allow Coe to put in a "submaximum short sprint" in a race to stay on the shoulder of the lead runner.

When seeing Coe run, what you first notice is his legs. Powerful, lean, muscular legs, the kind Michelangelo would have sculpted if Coe had grown up in Renaissance Florence. Weight lifting and hill repeats developed the strength in Sebastian's legs. He used both Nautilus machines and free weights. Six keys to weight training identified by Coe and Martin are:

- Train regularly.
- Train the muscle groups most in need of conditioning and that will be of greatest benefit to running.
- Ensure muscle balance by training opposite muscle groups (antagonists as well as agonists, that is, quadriceps as well as hamstrings).
- Provide a progressive overload stimulus.
- Work the muscles through their full range of movement.
- Allow adequate time between training sessions for recovery and physiological adaptation to occur.

Peter, ever the engineer, drove around Sheffield until he found a suitable hill to run repeats on, one with the proper grade. The hill could not be so steep that Coe could not sprint up it, but it had to be steep enough so that it was a tough climb. On some very long hills, Peter would sit in the car, start the stopwatch, and drive behind Sebastian as he ran up the hill. Hill workouts let Coe build up his speed without pounding his legs, as he would run the downhills very easy. (After Peter allowed him to start running downhill, that is.)

"My advice, if anybody wants it," Peter Coe writes,

> is not to get too far away from the basis of what you are doing, because modern 800 meters and 1,500 meters demand a considerable

amount of leg speed, and you're not going to get it from running slowly in training. You have to develop this and train the mind, as well as the body, to run fast. A lot of it is coordination.

Much of that coordination came naturally to Coe—Peter joked to Kenny Moore that Seb got his athleticism from him and his susceptibility to colds from Angela—but Seb's coordination was worked on through circuit training. The idea was to use gym work in the winter to develop overall stamina and fitness.

As set up by coach Gandy at Loughborough, this training involved a circuit of exercises that Seb did in rotation, such as repeatedly stepping up on boxes, chairs, or low tables. There were also half-squats, bent-knee sit-ups, push-ups, and back extensions. Coe could do the circuit training when traveling, and he also incorporated stretching into his weekly regime. Everything was designed to let him have a full range of motion in his joints. "I wish I had known when I was a young runner what Coe knew about training," says Kenny Moore.

There is a theory in economics called the marginal rate of return; it studies the benefit derived from the next incremental increase in a given input. Such was the approach the Coes used to training. What could they do to maximize the return on their training? They tried to get the most benefit from training with the least amount of mileage, because excess mileage can lead to staleness and injury.

"Peter Coe back in those days had some very revolutionary ideas and approaches, based on the quality rather than the quantity," says Coe's agent, Brad Hunt. "He is very opinionated, very proud of the fact that he was Seb's coach. To Peter, coaching is a matter of management. Find your goals and figure out the steps you need to use to get there."

In response to critics who said he was dominating his son, Peter said through the years that Seb was not dependent on him—he was "*coach-oriented* but not *coach-dependent*. His strength is his discipline, and you have to be brave to be disciplined, not just an automaton."

Like de Castella, Kristiansen, Barrios, Seko, and others, Seb had complete confidence in his coach, saying, "I can rely on the guy 100 percent. I'd like him even if he wasn't my father." Coaching for Peter was an intellectual pursuit, but also an art in that it changed depending on how "his athlete" changed. It was scientific training, not in a cold, hard sense, but rather science softened by British humanism. Peter was not interested in coaching many people; just his son, although later he took on a few athletes, such as British runner, Wendy Sly.

In the summer of 1979, Coe was still a relatively obscure Loughborough economics student, overshadowed by Ovett, who had already won the Europa Cup, World Cup, and European

Championships 1,500-meter titles. That would all change, however, in the space of 41 magical days beginning July 3 in Oslo, when Coe showed that his father's predictions nine years earlier on when his son would be ready to break the world records had in fact been a tad too conservative.

Forty-One Days

Coe's goal for 1979 was not to break records, but rather to finish final exams and earn his degree in economics. It was Scottish historian Thomas Carlyle who dubbed economics "the dismal science," and the winter of 1978-1979 was indeed dismal in Sheffield. It was, David Miller writes, "endlessly depressing, an expanse of fog and ice and little daylight, the evenings seeming to begin soon after lunch."

Through December, January, and February, Coe would "often be running by the light of the moon on snow-covered pavements, foot-paths, and lanes, every stride a potential hazard," Miller writes in *Running Free*.

Despite the poor winter of training and being over his head in studies, Coe kept his focus. Running for Loughborough at the end of April, Coe clocked 48.3 for 400 meters. He dropped his 400 personal best down to 47.6 seconds, then 47.4 on May 23. Studies were at long last finished in June, and for the first time ever, Coe was able to train like he and Peter wanted. He ran only two races in June: 1:46.3 for 800 meters at the Northern Counties Championship on June 16, and 1:46.6 at the Europa Cup in Malmo on June 30.

Four days later Coe stood on the starting line of the 800 meters at the Bislett Games. With the stress of exams and school gone, Coe ran like a freed man and surprised everyone, even his father, although they had an inkling Sebastian was ready to pop a good one when he ran a set of 200-meter intervals in under 23 seconds the week before Bislett.

In the Bislett 800 meters, Leonard Smith of Jamaica led through 400 meters in 50.5 seconds, followed by Coe in 50.6. Kenyan great Mike Boit was already trailing by 15 meters. Coe took the lead and ran his next 200 meters in 24.8, then came home in 27.0 seconds (a second 400 meters of 51.8) to finish in 1:42.33, breaking Alberto Juantorena's world record. Juantorena, the great Cuban runner, had made a big impression on Coe. Coe might not have been as large as Juantorena, but on this July night in Oslo he ran a second faster than *El Caballo* ever did. And afterwards, Coe said he could have run even faster, that he was not tired at the end of his race.

Peter did not go to Bislett, and he said, "Possibly what pleased me the most was that he did it on his own. My real joy was not only the record, but that it was one in the eye for all those who suggested he couldn't do anything without his Dad."

Coe returned to London and broke 47 seconds for 400 meters for the first time, clocking 46.85 at the BAAA championships on July 14. Three days later, he went back to the Bislett track for the Golden Mile. Despite his recent 800-meter record, Coe was not listed among the favorites. He was a babe among veteran milers like world-record holder John Walker, Eamonn Coghlan, and Steve Scott. Ovett, who had won the inaugural Golden Mile in Tokyo the year before in a tactical 3:55, did not show up, saying any mile race without him in it would be "hollow."

Coe, who had run only four 1,500-meter or 1-mile races in the previous four years, came into the Golden Mile the slowest in the field. He was a world-record holding 800-meter runner trying to move up in distance. It sounds like it would be easy to do, but it is not. Track history is littered with half-milers who could not make the transition to the mile. Talking over race strategy with his father, as they always did, Coe realized it was on the third lap where problems might arise. Coe knew he would feel good for the first 800 meters; the third lap against a great field would take him into unknown territory.

Coe need not have worried. American Steve Lacy led through two laps in 1:53. When Lacy stepped off the track, Steve Scott took over and pushed the pace on the third lap. Coe tucked in behind Scott and waited for the pain to come—but it never did. Coe ran easily, up on his toes, and never tied up. Once Scott and Coe separated themselves from the field, Coe tried to relax behind the American. Up the straightaway nearing the bell lap, he smoothly went by Scott.

Coe ran alone on the last lap, pushing as hard as he could. He glanced over his shoulder several times down the homestretch, unable to believe he was so far ahead and worried someone might be coming up on him. He thought Walker or Coghlan might make a move, but they were far behind. "I was afraid someone would come surging up. I had a nagging doubt that I had done something wrong or unorthodox against a world-class field, and that a big kicker would come through," Coe told Miller. "When I looked back twice in the final straight, it was fear, not pain." Coe finished in 3:48.95. He had demolished the fastest mile field ever assembled, with 10 runners coming home inside of 3:55, and he had made the others look like a bunch of school kids. Coe knew Walker had the world record, but was not sure what it was (3:49.4). Upon learning he had broken it, Coe felt good about bringing the mile world record back to England, 22 years after Derek Ibbotson held it. Coe became a national hero overnight. TV crews camped out in his front yard and laid siege to his house. Letters from around the world piled up on his doorstep.

Next up was an assault on the 1,500 record a month later. In early August, Coe ran two 800-meter races. The first was an easy 1:50.0 at a race in Italy, followed by a 1:47.3 win at the Europa Cup in Turin. Before the start of that race, Coe refused to shake hands with East German Willi Wulbeck, the man who had pushed him around in the World Cup back in 1977. Coe, by now experienced in the ways of international track running, had not forgotten. This time he hung at the back of the pack, just to prove wrong those who said he could only run from the front. Coe sprinted with 200 to go and won easily. Afterwards, his revenge on Wulbeck finished, Coe shook the East German's hand.

Coe then went to Zurich and the Weltklasse meet to make his bid on the 1,500-meter record. With the 800 and mile records in hand, Coe was recognized as one of the top runners in the world, and Zurich promoter Andreas Brügger hyped his attempt at a third world record. Miller writes that Ovett was kept out of the 1,500 meters in Zurich for fear that a tactical race would result if the dynamic duo hooked up. Fast times sell at the big European track invitationals, and Brügger wanted a record in the 1,500 meters, one of track's glamour events.

A record had not been on Coe's mind when he committed to race in Zurich in the spring of 1979, but the pressure for another record bid by now had momentum of its own. After breaking two world records already that summer, Coe had no choice but to go for another.

The race started at 7:45 in the evening, and the weather was cool as Coe followed Kenyan Mike Koskei through a very fast first lap of 54.2 seconds, a 3:37 mile pace. The crowd roared and jumped to its feet when Coe passed Koskei and took the lead coming up the homestretch for the second time. He passed 800 meters in 1:53.2, thinking "the record is there if I want it badly enough." He did want it, maintaining his form and holding on for a 56.9 last lap to finish in 3:32.1, breaking Filbert Bayi's 1974 record by one-tenth of a second. Craig Masback of the United States was second (3:37.0).

This time the pain and "hollow feeling" were there. Coe was completely spent, physically and mentally. "It was the only time I've ever gone for a record," he told Miller. "As a piece of even paced running, it was pretty diabolic. Everybody was supposed to chip in and help set the pace, but the first lap was wrong. It was a long run for home."

With that win in Zurich, Coe joined Jim Ryun as the only person to hold the 1,500-meter, 1-mile, and two-lap world records (Ryun's was for 880 yards) at the same time. Coe says he was most proud of that 1,500 meters "in terms of endurance," having been able to get the record running alone the last lap. "I would never want to go through that particular race again," he wrote. The hard effort left Coe with an "emptiness" when he returned home. Once again he could barely open his front door because of all the mail piled there. It had been a fulfilling 41 days.

The Rivalry Builds

Steve Ovett had always said he ran for wins, not records. But spurred by Coe's three new records, Ovett had gone for his own in the summer of 1979. Coe writes that Ovett "said dismissively that if that was what gave me pleasure, it was up to me. Yet by August he had a carefully orchestrated, record-breaking circus on the road with the help of (promoter) Andy Norman. It seemed that my records forced him to break cover. He'd never previously exposed himself, running tactical races from the back to win in 3:35/3:37 (for 1,500 meters)."

And win Ovett did. He used a simple strategy in running to 45 victories in a row. Ovett would hang just behind the leaders until sprinting into the lead with a little less than 200 meters to go.

The greatest athletes need the greatest rivals to push them, and Coe had that in Steve Ovett. Not only were the pair running faster than anyone in history, but they were from the same small, island nation—even casual observers could see that there was something unique about these two exciting athletes.

What made the Coe and Ovett rivalry all the more intense was Britain's insular media, which puts public figures in a fishbowl in a frantic, never-ending attempt at one-upmanship. Ovett quickly tired of the scrutiny and stopped talking to the press in 1977. He rarely granted interviews or even showed up at press conferences after a major win. The media helped fuel the rivalry by portraying Ovett as "Mr. Nasty" and Coe as "Mr. Nice."

They did not race against each other in 1979, which only whetted the public's appetite for the Moscow Olympics. Ducking opponents was common, Miller writes, " the most bizarre" occurrence being at a 1977 meet at Crystal Palace "when Juantorena would not run against Ovett and Ovett would not run against Boit, so Boit finished up running an almost meaningless 800-meter race without serious opposition."

Both Coe and Ovett had fine support systems from their families as they geared up for the Olympics. Coe had the world records, but he was not sure he was the best in England. That praise was still reserved for Ovett, who had reached the top level before Coe. Coe recounts that Ovett said after 1977 that Seb "would never be fast enough to run a really world-class 800 meters." Two weeks after that, Coe ran 1:44.95 to set the United Kingdom record. Ovett also ignored him after his 1979 records, said Coe.

"Ovett was a strength runner, Seb has sustained acceleration," says Coe's agent, Brad Hunt.

> They were not friends, though there was a great deal of mutual respect. Seb had a very pragmatic approach to his athletics. He planned out his goals and knew what steps were required. Sebastian had a very, very professional approach to his craft. He was very deliberate with what he wanted to do.

Leading up to the Moscow Olympics, fans around the world were intrigued that one of these two greats was going to lose. The strengths and weaknesses of both were endlessly discussed in pubs across Great Britain, with everyone knowing that the arguments could be settled in only one way—on the track in Lenin Stadium.

1980 Moscow Olympics

However much he tried to ignore it, Coe felt pressured by the public in the year before the Moscow Olympics. Like a thick fog coming down from Hampstead Heath, the pressure wrapped itself around Coe wherever he went: to the grocery store, for a walk, on a run. He was constantly being greeted by well-wishers, who slapped him on the back and told him to bring home the gold. "There wasn't an ant in an anthill who didn't know who Seb Coe was," Martin says.

To find some privacy, Coe spent part of the winter of 1979-80 at a friend's home on a private country club outside of Rome. This was the first winter he was a full-time runner, and Peter wanted Seb to do more stamina work to prepare for his 800 / 1,500 double in Moscow, where he would run six races in eight days. Ovett, meanwhile, made a point of training in Brighton, as if to say he stayed in England while Coe had fled.

Coe spent three months training in the mild Italian winter, running on the grass and weight training at the local school outside the compound. What Coe found in Italy, he says, was the "intensity, regularity, and quality of training" he needed.

A problem arose, however, when politics entered the sporting scene. Late in 1979, troops from the Soviet Union invaded Afghanistan, to support the Afghanistan military government's fight against Islamic rebels.

British Prime Minister Margaret Thatcher, following the lead of the United States, advocated a boycott of the Moscow Olympic Games to punish the Soviet Union. But the British Amateur Athletic Association said its athletes should be able to compete if they chose.

Coe hesitated, but in the end decided he would go to Moscow. The "should-we-go or should-we-stay-away" controversy drained him, as it did many of the athletes preparing for an Olympics in which they might not compete.

Despite the distraction, Coe had the best training of his life, doing "soaring, scorching runs of 6 or 10 miles which would carry him across the golf course almost as fast as a seven iron could drive a ball," writes Miller. After his sojourn in Rome, tests showed Coe had the physiology of a top marathon runner, and that he also had "three gears," that allowed him to accelerate while already sprinting. Coe would need all his gears when he faced Ovett.

Coe was ready for Moscow and confident he could win both races, saying that "In the 800 meters I don't think there is really a serious challenge. Not one." That assessment, Miller writes, "took my breath away when stated so baldly. To be that certain in your own mind was to carry around a responsibility to yourself which could be unnerving."

Wrote Coe, "It's a far worse situation to be in, knowing that you have to do something stupid *not* to win a race, than thinking that you will have to do something startling if you *are* to win it. There was nothing, including Steve, that I'd seen at either distance that worried me."

Coe did have a sciatic nerve problem that led to a sore hamstring. It got so bad that he could barely reach down to hit a ball when playing tennis. Coe was still able to race well before Moscow, testing his strength out in local races in May and June. On July 1, he went to the Bislett Games and broke American Rick Wohlhuter's 1,000-meter world record, running 2:13.4. This world record was for his mother, he said. "I'd given her a little something back for all those months and years of patience and attention she had given me."

Coe now had four world records—but not for long. An hour after Coe's 1,000-meter record, Ovett snatched his mile mark, clocking 3:48.8, raising expectations for their Moscow matchup even higher.

Ovett was not done. A week before the Olympics, he tied Coe's 1,500-meter world record. As the Games got underway, Coe and Ovett could not have been more evenly matched: Each had two world records and were co-owners of a third. (Though Peter Coe comments that the tied record was "Not strictly true. Ovett's time only equals Coe's after 'rounding up.' Coe's was the faster time.") "Things were brewing up for a good series of races in Moscow," said Peter.

On the flight to Moscow from England, the airline lost Coe's luggage. Fortunately, Coe had learned from his travels to keep his spikes with him in a carry-on bag at all times. Ovett said in a rare interview before the Games started that he felt 50 percent sure of winning in the 800 and 90 percent sure in the 1,500. Coe, of course, did not agree. He says that on the track "Speed hurts, sustained speed kills," and he felt certain he could maintain his speed longer than anyone.

A Silver Medal Failure

Coe looked at his races as chess matches, says Martin. "Who were the competitors? What are the scenarios? What are the others likely to do? And he kept an open mind." The Coes always did their homework, "like TV announcers getting ready for a football game." The 800 meters was up before the 1,500, and both Coe and Ovett breezed through their heats. Before the 800-meter finals, Peter and Sebastian debated how to run the race. They were not sure what tactic to use, and in the elevator in the athletes' village, observers heard Peter going back and forth, saying, "You can go from the front. Or you can go from the back."

The Coes eventually decided Seb should not lead from the start, because of the danger of doing all the work and "then getting stuffed on the run-in" by an inspired runner. They chose instead what they thought was the safest strategy, with Coe positioning himself "in the right place at the right time."

"I've never known pressure like it," Coe wrote. "I thought people had exaggerated, but they hadn't. There was no comparison." Coe had his worst night's sleep ever before the 800-meter final, just lying in bed listening to his heartbeat. At breakfast the morning of the race, he knocked over his orange juice and dropped his cream into his coffee, wasting nervous energy. "I suddenly felt ungainly, conscious of my own awkwardness."

Coe needed his father to snap him out of it, but Peter kept quiet, not wanting to undermine his son. "The point was that at 800 meters he had to be so bad to lose," Peter told Miller. "I knew he was, at his best, immeasurably better than anyone else in the race."

Finally, the 800 was underway. The first 400 meters was run in a slow 54.5, and Coe hung at the very back of the field, running wide, almost out into lane three at times. Ovett, meanwhile, looked to have gotten himself boxed in on the inside. But he shoved Germany's Wagenacht aside to free himself. Dave Warren, Britain's third 800 entrant, briefly took the lead down the backstraight of the second lap, but it was Kirov of the Soviet Union who started his sprint first. Around the final turn,

Ovett was just behind Kirov, with Coe still stuck behind the pack of runners. Ovett then sprinted into the lead and Coe, despite passing four runners, was too far out of position to catch him down the homestretch. The fastest 800-meter runner in the world had waited too long, and Ovett had the gold. Coe received the silver in what he called a bumbling and inept performance.

There is no overstating how badly Coe felt. It was a "crushing loss," says Martin.

> When you work so hard, you don't lose. There's no explanation except that it was just a bad day. Seb still can't explain how he got in such a predicament. Things didn't come together; it was as if his mind was blank. It was that inability to cope that frustrated him the most. He wasn't sick or injured; he didn't have pneumonia; he wasn't afraid of the other guys, and they weren't more fit. Some days you just don't get it right.

Kenny Moore says that if Coe had just run as if he were going for a world record, he would have been out in front and gotten the gold. But he had lost to his archrival, and Coe said when he awoke the next morning it was "worse than any hangover."

Friends tried to cheer him up by saying, "You got the silver."

"There is only one medal that counts," snapped Coe. "There's one more race, and I have to make sure it doesn't happen again."

Fans wondered after the 800, and rightly so, whether Coe was a runner who could break records but who could not handle the pressure and pushing of championship races. Peter made things worse by telling reporters the next day, in his inimitable, blunt way, that his son had "run like an idiot."

A Lane of One's Own

Coe was at a crossroads. If Ovett won the 1,500, he would be acknowledged as the world's top middle-distance runner, with Coe relegated to the realm of Ron Clarke—a great runner who could break records when running by himself, but unable to grasp the Olympic gold.

"It is when things go wrong that a good coach is priceless," says Seb. Something had gone terribly wrong in the Moscow 800 meters, and he says he was fortunate to have the chance to show what the "real Coe" was made of in the 1,500. Seb was getting advice from all sides on how to run, and he and Peter formulated a different plan for this race. This time he was going to simply run as he knew best—aggressively from near the lead.

When the starting gun went off, Coe broke to the front and settled into second place behind East German Jurgen Straub. The first lap was a slow 61.6 seconds. The pace then slowed even more on the second lap, to a pedestrian 63.3 seconds, for an 800-meter split of 2:04.9. Suddenly, Straub accelerated in a long bid for home. It was now Coe's kind of race, one of fast, sustained running, which he knew he could hold longer than anyone in the world. "I found a rhythm, a lane of my own," he told Kenny Moore in *Best Efforts*.

Straub led, running with his head down, his eyes fixed on the track in front of him, followed by Coe and Ovett. Both looked magnificent, strong and fluid, two of the best runners ever battling stride for stride in a bid for the gold medal. They dueled through the last lap. Coe took the lead around the final bend, followed closely by Ovett, both giving everything they had. "We were into an area where we were no longer middle-distance runners, where the hours of conditioning in training were needed: 'sprint, drive, work the arms.' I put in a semi-kick at 180 meters and that carried me past Jurgen," Coe wrote. "There was daylight and I could hear his feet receding."

"Over the last 300 meters, each successive 100 meters got faster, culminating in a devastating 12.1 seconds for the last 100," remembers Peter.

Coming off the final bend, Coe kicked again, looking over his shoulder.

> I was now running for the tape, the mental agony of knowing I had hit my limit, of not knowing what was happening back there behind me. I was not to know they were fading too. I tried to drive again at 40 meters out, and in the next few strides I knew I had nothing left if anyone came back at me. The anxiety over the last 20 meters was unbearable, and it showed in my face as I crossed the line.

Indeed, when he finished, Coe's face was twisted half in agony, half in disbelief at having won the gold. It is one of the most famous photographs in running, Seb Coe crossing the 1,500-meter finish line ahead of Straub in second and then Ovett, who said he just could not get "up" for another race. Coe's arms are outstretched, his head thrown back, mouth agape, and face lighted as if to say "I can't believe I won the whole thing." In Coe's expression is summed up all the pressure of Olympic running. Coe knelt down and bowed his head on the track, looking like a weary English explorer who had reached land after a stormy ocean crossing. Still kneeling on the track, Coe put his hands on his head, then got up for an elated victory lap.

The agony was over, and Coe says he felt so good that he flipped. Wrote Coe, "They were dreadful days. I'd bottled it all up, and now the emotion was coming out like champagne that had been shaken." As he ran his victory lap, Coe's felt he was finally free. "I knew I could now retire at any point and feel a satisfied man." On the backstretch of his victory lap, Coe spread his arms wide, in imitation of an airplane gliding along.

A relieved Peter Coe did not even stay to watch the closing ceremonies. He told Moore that "the last thing I want to remember about these Games is that picture of elation as Seb crossed the line, a man who had borne up and gone out and done exactly what he had set himself. You can hang the rest."

The question of who was the best was not yet settled. Coe and Ovett had each won a gold medal in the event the other was favored in. They joined the ranks of other top 800-/1,500-meter doublers in the Olympics. Albert Hill, who went on to coach Sydney Wooderson, had doubled in 1896, along with Australian Edwin Flack. Americans James Lightbody and Mel Sheppard did it in the early 1900s, along with New Zealand's Peter Snell in 1964.

After the Olympics, Coe went back to England to prepare for an attempt on the 1,500-meter record, which he held jointly with Ovett, falling just short in 3:32.19. It was Ovett who got the record at the end of August, running 3:31.36, with Wessinghage also dipping under the old mark.

Between Olympics

Fans eager to see Coe and Ovett race after Moscow were disappointed. The pair did not face each other the year after the Olympics; in fact, they would not race again for another four years. Frank Shorter says it is a shame because of what might have been if the two had been in a record race together.

"Coe and Ovett were the first of the modern runners to practice active avoidance," says Shorter.

> And because of tactics and running for the medal, the Moscow Olympics weren't the flat-out races they could have been. If Seb and Steve had met at Zurich, Brussels, or any of the other big track meets, there could have been the mano-a-mano, classic battle of the titans. But they just never had those races against each other.

However, Peter Coe says it is "not totally correct" that Seb and Ovett practiced active avoidance. "Examples would only raise old rivalries as to who kept whom out."

Shorter thinks Coe and Ovett both would have run below 3:30 for 1,500 meters if they had raced each other more often. What the two raced against were the records, and Coe's record breaking continued in the winter of 1981. On February 11, he set the indoor 800-meter world mark of 1:46.0 in the United Kingdom vs. West Germany indoor meet, breaking Italian Carlo Grippo's record by .37 seconds.

Then, in Florence in June of 1981, Coe smashed his 800-meter record with a time that 15 years later still stands. Peter Coe calls the 800 "probably the most unforgiving of all track events. It requires a combination of strength, raw speed, anaerobic endurance, and split-second judgment." Running in the *Citta di Firenze* meet at Florence's Comunale Stadium, Coe showed he had all those qualities. The race started at 11 P.M., and Coe, wearing a white singlet and white shorts, ran like a ghost whipping through the night.

Kenyan Billy Konchellah led through 400 meters in 49.6. Coe then took over the lead and, running far out in front, sped his next 200 meters in 25.3, followed by another in 26.7 (for a second lap of 52.0) to finish in a phenomenal 1:41.73. The finish-line equipment failed, and Coe's final time was arrived at by analyzing the three photocells at the finish. Coe's 800-meter record is one of the longest-lasting in track, testimony to the remarkable peak of fitness he had reached.

Coe was on top of the track world, and Peter Coe said that when you are at the top, you do not necessarily have to go down—you can go sideways. Coe continued at the top in August 1981, during a nine-day stretch in which he and Ovett passed the mile record back and forth like it was a game of pin the tail on the world record. Coe always said his records were only borrowed, and he and Ovett certainly proved it that summer.

Coe struck first, reclaiming his mile record from Ovett by running 3:48.53 on August 19. A week later, Ovett took it back by running 3:48.40. Two days after that, it was Coe's turn again when he ran 3:47.33 in Brussels, a mark that would stand until July 1985, when Steve Cram ran his 3:46.32. (Cram's record stood for another eight years until Algeria's Nourredine Morceli broke it in 1993.)

Coe was a special runner in 1981, says Frank Shorter, who was at the Brussels race doing TV commentary.

Seb created an aura that he was the best ever, better even than Peter Snell. He made people think that they couldn't beat him. Scott, Abascal, and all the best runners in the world were there, and when the rabbit went into the lead, everyone just looked at Coe and fell in behind him. That was a real indication of his mental control; none of those other guys in the race thought they had

800 Meters/880 Yards (804.68 Meters) World Record Progression

1:52.5y	James "Ted" Meredith (USA)	Stockholm	July 8, 1912
1:52.2y	James "Ted" Meredith (USA)	Philadelphia	May 13, 1916
1:51.6y	Otto Peltzer (GER)	London	July 3, 1926
1:50.6	Sèraphin Martin (FRA)	Colombes	July 14, 1928
1:50.9y	Benjamin Eastman (USA)	San Francisco	June 4, 1932
1:49.8	Thomas Hampson (GBR)	Los Angeles	August 2, 1932
1:49.8y	Benjamin Eastman (USA)	Princeton	June 16, 1934
1:49.7	Glenn Cunningham (USA)	Stockholm	August 20, 1936
1:49.6y	Elroy Robinson (USA)	New York	July 11, 1937
1:49.2y	Sydney Wooderson (GBR)	London	August 20, 1938
1:46.6	Rudolf Harbig (GER)	Milan	July 15, 1939
1:49.2y	Malvin Whitfield (USA)	Berwa	August 19, 1950
1:48.6y	Malvin Whitfield (USA)	Turku	July 17, 1953
1:48.6y	N. Gunnar Nieson (DEN)	Copenhagen	September 30, 1954
1:47.5y	Lonnie Spurrier (USA)	Berkeley	March 26, 1955
1:45.7	Roger Moens (BEL)	Oslo	August 3, 1955
1:46.8y	Thomas Courtney (USA)	Los Angeles	May 24, 1957
1:45.1y	Peter Snell (NZL)	Christchurch	February 3, 1962
1:44.9y	James Ryun (USA)	Terre Haute	June 10, 1966
1:44.3	Ralph Doubell (AUS)	Mexico City	October 15, 1968
1:44.3	Dave Wottle (USA)	Eugene	July 1, 1972
1:44.6y	Richard Wohlhuter (USA)	Los Angeles	May 27, 1973
1:43.7	Marcello Fiasconaro (ITA)	Milan	June 27, 1973
1:44.1y	Richard Wohlhuter (USA)	Eugene	June 8, 1974
1:43.5	Alberto Juantorena (CUB)	Montreal	July 25, 1976
1:43.4	Alberto Juantorena (CUB)	Sofia	August 21, 1977
1:42.33	Sebastian Coe (GBR)	Oslo	July 5, 1979
1:41.73	Sebastian Coe (GBR)	Florence	June 10, 1981

Note. Times followed by y denote times for 880 yards.

a chance. He was very smooth, with good acceleration, and he had real good top-end speed once he was sprinting. Seb was a very light, powerful runner, and had the strength of Snell.

Seb was one of the first to pick his races to create a persona. Many of his opponents felt there was a mystique around his training and racing. John Walker also had that kind of mystique in 1976 when he won the Olympic 1,500 without having a great race.

Yet Peter Coe says, "Neither Seb nor I cared or worried about what others were doing; we just stuck to our plan."

"What makes any great champion great?" Ray Flynn asks. Whatever it is, Coe showed he had it by producing when it counted. Zurich and the other big track races are "like the major leagues, with packed houses. There's a lot of pressure there."

Track is a major attraction in Europe, says Flynn,

> with a lot of media attention, like the NFL and NBA seasons in the United States. Coe and Ovett were the stars of the sport, the marquee attraction. They brought track and field in Great Britain into the Golden Era. Their rivalry was on the one hand the best thing to happen in the sport and on the other the most disappointing, because the rivalry was based on chasing records.

That looked to change in 1982, when extensive plans were made for three meetings between Coe and Ovett, in Nice, London, and Eugene. Three distances were to be run: 800 and 1,000 meters, and the mile. But injuries kept them from racing, with Coe suffering through a stress fracture for most of the summer and Ovett nursing his thigh.

In the end Coe believed it was for the best that he and Ovett did not meet often. "In hindsight, I think thank goodness it did work out like that. People remember the Moscow race in a way they wouldn't remember, say, Gateshead (England) on a Tuesday night," he said years later. Seb also said that he was glad they met at the Olympics; no one could say that they only raced each other for money.

Ovett says fans expected he and Coe to break records and win medals, and that is what they did.

> We had to aim at a target for the season and that target quite often was the most important championships. A lot of the time to do that we sacrificed and missed out on quite lucrative race schedules, both of us. To do that, we decided we wouldn't race as much as other people.

That paid off, Coe says, not financially, but by the fact he and Ovett dominated the mile. "But the public and the media always wanted more.

I think the amount of pressure we had at championships was more than most athletes had ever encountered before."

Despite the pressure, Coe remained a nice guy, as Austrian journalist Knut Okresek recounts,

> When I was starting out as a reporter, I called Seb Coe up at his hotel at a meet in Lausanne. I got through to his room, and he asked me how I got his number, then hung up. I desperately needed a story to clinch a newspaper job I was going for, so I rang him again. He was about to hang up, and I said, "Wait, Seb! I used to be a 1,500-meter runner, and you were my idol."
>
> "Well, how fast did you run?" Coe warily asked.
>
> "4:03."
>
> "4:03. Well, that's pretty good. OK, I'll give you the interview."

After his stress fracture healed, Coe got ready for the 1982 European Championships in Athens. There he was upset by Hans-Peter Ferner of West Germany, and once again the 800 silver was seen as a failure, as it had been in Moscow.

In 1983, Coe set two indoor world records. First, he returned to Cosford and broke his own 800-meter record with a 1:44.91, a mark that stood until Kenyan Paul Ereng broke it by .07 seconds at the 1989 Budapest Indoor World Championships. Coe also set the 1,000-meter indoor mark. That summer, however, he was diagnosed with severe toxoplasmosis, a blood infection, that forced him to pull out of the 1983 Helsinki World Championships, where the 1,500 meters was won by Steve Cram. The infection was serious enough to threaten to end Coe's career, and it appeared unlikely he could recover in time to defend his title at Los Angeles.

Los Angeles Olympics

Coe was sick with toxoplasmosis during the winter of 1983-84, and some in the media believed he was finished. And even Coe himself wondered. A year and a half of setbacks had left him uncertain of his ability to defend his Olympic 1,500-meter title in Los Angeles in 1984. He did not start running until after Christmas, saying it was a long shot to make the team. He recalls Sunday runs during the winter with his Haringey clubmates, running with 12- and 13-year-olds, then reading in the paper the next day that Ovett had run 3:34 in Australia, where the Southern Hemisphere's summer track season was taking place. Cram and Peter Elliott, the last of the "Big Four" of British miling, were also running well. "It was at that point," says Coe, "that making the Olympic team seemed as far away as anything I'd ever done."

But Coe was selected for the team, and decided to avoid distractions by going to Oakbrook, Illinois, a suburb of Chicago, to start his Olympic countdown. There he stayed with Coach Joe Newton, the most successful Illinois prep coach ever. He would not see Peter again until he was in the Olympic Village. In marked contrast to Moscow, there was little pressure on Coe in Los Angeles, because "most people had written him off," says Brad Hunt.

> Cram was the world champion, and Coe had seemingly been usurped. And Seb basically took that as a challenge. He is very serious, sets his goals, and tries to understand all the components that come into play. He lets very little come in his way. Seb had goals related to medals and goals related to wins.

For the five weeks leading up to the Los Angeles Olympics, Coe's weekly mileage totaled 38, 36, 31, 24, and 17 miles. And he ran progressively better intervals. "The principle is simple: First establish the speed; then begin decreasing the recovery time to bring speed endurance into focus. This is done by eliminating the added rest time between sets," Martin and Peter Coe write in *Training Distance Runners*.

In the book, Coe's schedule before Los Angeles is described, including a tearing-down phase, done on the track, and a recovery building-back phase, which included tapering speed sessions. It was a multitiered training philosophy divided into volume, intensity, density, and frequency. Coe's shorter intervals were 200-, 300-, and 400-meter repeats, while pace work was mile repeats and pyramid workouts. The following is the week of July 16-22, 1984, leading up to the Los Angeles Olympics:

Sunday:	6-mile recovery run.
Monday:	The first of the harder tempo runs. A.M., after warm-up, 6 ×800 meters in 2:00 with 3-minute recovery, 2-lap cool-down at 90 seconds a lap, followed by easy jogging; P.M., 4 miles easy.
Tuesday:	The first cadence session. A.M., 5 miles easy; P.M., warm-up, 10 ×100 meters steady acceleration to 60 meters, maximum speed to 80 meters, then float to 100 meters, walk back to start, and repeat.

Wednesday:	Progressing from the previous Saturday's workout of 2 sets of 3 × 300 meters at 39 seconds with a 3-minute recovery. Same session, but 2 seconds slower and as a single set. A.M., 6 × 300 meters at 41 seconds; P.M., 4 miles easy.
Thursday:	Short intervals to sharpen speed and still maintain a good heart/lung stimulus but keeping mileage low. A.M., 20 × 200 meters in 27-28 seconds; P.M., 5 miles easy.
Friday:	Adjusting to increasing speed with increasing distance—11 sprints, progressing in distance from 100 meters to 200 meters in 10-meter increments, increasing from 14 to 25 seconds, with jog-back recovery to start position.
Saturday:	Maintained endurance run, but without locking into a set pace—6 to 7 miles including mixed accelerations (mini-fartlek).

The Coes had learned from the 1980 Olympics to approach a championship double, the 800 followed by 1,500, like a bicycling stage race, says Hunt. "With Sebastian's physiology, as fit as he was for championships, he'd almost get better day by day. The ultimate goal was to win the 1,500 gold, and the 800 was built up to that. Peter tried to adapt that cycling stage-race approach, seven races in nine days, so that each race was building his strength up one notch."

Coe and Ovett finally met again in the Los Angeles 800 meters, but there were other, new, fast runners by now. Coe was relaxed in the heats, which Hunt says "were a breeze for him." In the 800 final Coe made a strong bid for the gold. He ran wide on the first lap, tucked in right behind Ovett in the early going. At the bell Coe was running relaxed in fifth place. Joaquim Cruz, the young Brazilian, moved up on the leader's shoulder, with Coe running outside of American Earl Jones just behind. Coming through the final turn, Coe started past Jones in an attempt to take the lead, but at that very moment Jones was also moving wide. Jones's right elbow hit Coe's left arm, knocking him slightly off stride. Cruz accelerated to the front and gained a two-meter lead. Coe sprinted but failed to catch Cruz, though he did hold off Jones for the silver medal. Ovett, stricken with asthma, faded off the last turn and jogged home last.

Coe was indeed getting stronger as the Olympics continued, and he was "happy and confident" he could defend his 1,500-meter title. Peter predicted his son was going to win, and Coe went to the line with a "This medal is mine attitude."

At the start of the 1,500 meters, Coe briefly took the lead before settling into second place. It was a tactical race, and the field remained bunched together. Heading into the bell lap, Abascal of Spain led, followed in a row by Coe, Cram, and Ovett, Britain's three great milers. But Ovett stepped off the track on the turn, leaving it a three-man race. Abascal led into the backstraight. Just past 300 meters to go, the tall, lanky Cram gathered himself and came alongside Coe, who was running in second directly off Abascal's right shoulder. For an instant, Cram inched ahead of Coe. But Coe was prepared for Cram's move and accelerated, squeezing between Abascal and Cram into the lead.

Into the final turn it was Olympic Champion Coe and World Champion Cram racing for the gold medal. Cram tried to pass Coe on the curve, but Coe held him off. And once they turned into the final straightaway, Coe simply blew Cram away, finding his "third gear" and easily sprinting home to win his second 1,500-meter gold medal. Cram, looking like he was running through mud at the end, held on for the silver.

"That must go down in history as one of the greatest achievements in our sport," Ovett told *Running*.

> It was bloody impressive. People expect you to do it and it's hard when it's expected. To do it on top of that a second time around was great. I wish I hadn't been carried out on a stretcher to watch it, but it looked pretty impressive from what I saw of the race.

When he finished, Coe's joy at winning all at once turned to anger at the media, which had criticized him during the previous year. He turned and made a gesture to the press box, his retort to all those who had written him off. Hunt explains,

> Seb's motivation was the spirit of the competition. Ultimately, any athlete who is going through the pain and rigor isn't driven by finances. Seb wanted the accomplishment, and he knew there was more left in him than people expected, and he wanted to show that in Los Angeles.

Coe took a break after the Olympics, then resumed his purgatory of training. He was not ready to hang up his spikes just yet, because he still had more to accomplish.

David Martin recalls a vignette that he says is "vintage Seb" and which illustrates his competitiveness. After running an indoor 3,000 meters in 1985, the only indoor meet Coe ever ran in the United States, New York City Marathon race director Fred Lebow came up to him.

"Good job at the Olympics," Lebow said.

"Thanks, Fred, but I only won one race," Coe replied.

1986 European Championships

Coe says his most satisfying race is not either of his two Olympic 1,500 crowns, but rather the 800 meters in the 1986 European Championships in Stuttgart. Despite his two Olympic gold medals and two silver medals, Coe did not have a European outdoor title. Ovett had won Olympic *and* European golds, and Coe wanted to match his rival win for win. "In terms of what I was doing, it was a gap in my career," Coe said.

Coe had the 800 world record, but he had not gotten the gold medal in the 800 at Prague in 1978, Moscow in 1980, Athens in 1982, or Los Angeles in 1984. "He didn't like getting beat, especially in the 800 meters," said Martin.

> We spent the better part of 1985 going over Seb's training log and reached the conclusion that what he needed to do was continue his weight training longer in the summer. The 800 is more of a strength event than the 1,500.

There was good news and bad news to doing more weight training. The good news was that Coe became stronger. The bad news was that with the extra stress from the weight training, Coe came down with a cold. "Seb very seldom got injured. What stopped him was sickness," Martin explains.

Illness kept Coe from running in the 1986 Commonwealth Games, which turned out to be a "blessing in disguise," says Martin. First, it made Coe hungry for competition, and second, it kept him fresh. "Seb was so strong in the summer of 1986 that there was not a soul in the world who could beat him. Then it was a matter of very subtly changing his routine to arrange for a peak." At the beginning of August, Coe ran his personal best in the 1,500 meters. He then faced a rematch with Steve Cram at the August 28 European Championships, in both the 800 and the 1,500 meters.

Coe, the experienced veteran, was content to stay in the back of the pack as the field went through the first lap of the 800 in a moderate 52 seconds. Around the bend on the second lap, Coe followed Cram and

Tom McKean, the third British 800-meter runner at Stuttgart. McKean led through the final turn, and once in the straightaway, Coe passed Cram and went after McKean, nailing him just 50 meters from the finish to earn his long-awaited 800-meter gold medal. Britain got a medal sweep, as McKean took the silver and Cram the bronze.

"I was very calm, and that feeling was reinforced after the first lap," Coe told *Track & Field News*. "The split suited me well and I was ideally placed in Steve's wake. This victory was more important to me than any other." Coe also ran to the silver medal in the 1,500 meters. After a slow first 800 of 2:07.8, Cram ran the last 400 meters in 50.9 to hold off Coe, 3:41.09 to 3:41.67.

Racing into Politics

In 1988, the British Amateur Athletic Board changed its Olympic selection policy, giving two spots to the first and second placers in the British Olympic trials, with the final spot held in reserve. With the way he trained, aiming for a peak later in the summer, Coe was not ready early in the season and, suffering from a bad cold, he did not make it through his qualifying heat in the British trials. There was still a spot open on the team, but Coe was not selected, and neither was Ovett. Many say, however, that Coe would have had a great shot at a 1,500-meter Olympic three-peat in 1988. One of those is Brad Hunt. "That race in Seoul was made for him. It's only speculation, but in a sit-and-kick race he would have won. He had 1:43 (800 meter) speed at the time and 46-second (400 meter) speed." Little-known Kenyan Peter Rono won the 1988 Olympic 1,500 meters.

An indication of Coe's long career was that he ran his 1,500-meter personal best in 1988, nine years after his first world record. But Coe, 33, was fighting illness, and he eventually retired after the 1990 Commonwealth Games in Auckland, as did foe John Walker. Coe wanted to end his career with a medal, but finished sixth in the 800 in 1:47.24. Walker fell in the 1,500, then got up to place twelfth. Notes Peter Coe,

> Seb lasted 13 years at the top and got out at the top. A few days before his 33rd birthday he ran 1:43.33 [800 meters] to beat the best of the Kenyans before he quit. How many would stop at that level?

After Coe and Ovett retired, and then Cram and Elliott finished their careers, the Golden Age of British miling was over. Fans quickly realized that when, at the 1992 Barcelona Olympics, Britain failed to advance a runner to the 1,500-meter final for the first time since 1960.

Coe, meanwhile, was on to other tasks. In 1992, he became an honorable member of Parliament from Falmouth and Camborne. Coe, a member of the Tory, or conservative, party, had narrowly won, helped in part by going around the district shaking as many hands as possible.

"I'd known since I was 12 that I wanted to get into politics," Coe said after getting elected. He found political life a little tougher than he had anticipated. "It's been very different. You don't go in there with any system at all," he told *Sports Illustrated*. "There's nobody to greet you officially at the House [of Commons]. You literally just turn up and that's it." Coe said he was fortunate to latch on to a couple of older members of Parliament who helped him out.

There is a connection between Coe's running and political careers, as both are manifestations of his drive to excel that Angela Coe had noticed so many years before. He often works 18-hour days. Coe still runs to keep in shape, and has run a marathon in under three hours.

Steve Ovett, however, is unable to run anymore. He was seriously injured in 1993 when hit by a car while bicycling near his castle home in Dumfriesshire, Scotland. While that accident ruined his shot at becoming the first master to run a sub-four-minute mile, Ovett's place in track history is secure, and is inextricably bound up with that of Coe. Ovett first, followed by Coe, brought the forefront of miling back to England. Ovett remarks:

> We both came through the era when not a lot was expected from our middle-distance runners internationally. We were always a nation which hoped they [its runners] would do better than they did. . . . People would say that we didn't have the facilities, or we weren't born at altitude, or we don't have the summers that the Australians or the New Zealanders have. I remember thinking that they were all excuses rather than reasons that we were not performing all that well. It's pleasing to me to be part of proving them wrong. Seb and Steve (Cram) and everyone else who came along just accentuated the point that it's not necessary to have any of those factors to dominate. You just have to go out and run bloody hard.

Running bloody hard is what Coe and Ovett will always be remembered for. And as time goes on, the pair become more and more the stuff of track lore. They met only five times in their careers, but those races "stand out as perhaps the most gripping races ever in athletics," because of the hype, the tension, and the unpredictability, writes *Running*. All English running fans, and indeed track fans around the world, still have their favorite Coe and Ovett races, and while most of their "borrowed" records have been broken, "the memories of their glittering achievements will remain in athletics fans' minds forever."

12

Family Comes First

Born March 21, 1956, Norway

World records: 5,000, 10,000, 15K, half- and full marathon

World Championship gold, 10,000, 1987

Winner of 14 major marathons

When Ingrid Kristiansen walked down the street carrying her son Gaute and holding husband Arve's hand, she looked like any other mother, wife, and homemaker out for an evening stroll. With her wire-rimmed glasses and ready smile, she did not seem like an athlete who had done something no other runner, male or female, had ever done. Ingrid looked so . . . normal. But that is Ingrid Kristiansen—an ordinary woman who did extraordinary things in running.

Kristiansen is the only runner, woman or man, to simultaneously hold world records for 5,000 meters (14:37.3), 10,000 meters (30:13.7), and the marathon (2:21:06). She is also the only athlete to win World Championship titles on the track, on the road, and in cross-country. During her long career, Kristiansen also set world road bests over 10K, 10 miles, 15K, and the half-marathon, and she ran 15 marathons faster than 2:35, the most ever by a woman. Kristiansen also has to her credit five of the fastest marathon times run by a woman—quite a record for a woman who would rather spend time with her family than go to a race.

Kristiansen not only was faster than any other woman during her career, she was also years ahead of her contemporaries in training ideas, making regular use of treadmills and heartrate monitors. She was "cross training" years before it became popular, using winter skiing to supplement her running. She was able to get the most out of her training by analyzing what would give her the biggest physiological benefit and taking the hard/easy system of training to the extreme.

A cancer researcher by trade and an elite cross-country skier before she was a top runner, Kristiansen monitored her body carefully. She would ask herself, "What am I supposed to be doing today? Running easy? Then I'll run easy." Recovery runs and long runs were well over eight minutes a mile. But when it was time to run hard, she ran very hard.

That approach worked. The times the women were starting to run in the 1990s, and their training techniques, are just beginning to catch up with Kristiansen, whose goal was to be the first woman to break 2:20 in the marathon and 30 minutes for 10,000 meters.

Running In Grete's Long Shadow

Kristiansen set the groundwork for the world records and victories during family hikes she took with her parents and older brother around their home of Trondheim, on the northwest coast of Norway. Outdoor activity is a way of life for nearly all Norwegian families, says Kristiansen, whose maiden name is Christiansen. She was an athlete from the time she was born.

"Every weekend we were skiing or hiking, from the time I was one year old. In the summer we went hiking for one or two weeks at a time." It was those walks and ski excursions that first piqued Ingrid's interest in exercise and fitness. She had a natural inclination to working out, saying, "It made me feel good."

What made her feel the best was skiing, and she joined a sports club in Trondheim along with other kids her age. "Like all Norwegians, Ingrid had skis on her feet before she could walk," says British coach Dave Welch. In 1971, the Trondheim sports club won Norway's cross-country skiing championship, and as it turned out, skiing was the best conditioning possible for the running Ingrid would do in the summer. It gave her "big cardiovascular development from the time she was 4 and 5 years old, into her teens," explains Welch, adding that Grete Waitz, also an excellent skier, achieved the same sort of fitness from skiing. (German marathoner Uta Pippig is another top runner who makes extensive use of cross-country skiing to build her winter base.)

Later in 1971, Kristiansen, then 15, ran the 10,000 meters in the European Junior Championships in Finland. She was knocked off the track during the race by another runner and did not finish, an incident that reinforced her preference for skiing.

Kristiansen remained primarily a skier during the 1970s, competing in national skiing events well enough to earn gold, silver, and bronze team medals at the European Junior Championships from 1973 through 1975. In 1976, she made the Norwegian Olympic team: "I learned a lot [in the Winter Olympics]; it was a good experience for me."

Kristiansen's best skiing finish came at the 1978 World Championships, where she placed 21st in the 20K cross-country race. Even though she was skiing in the winter and racing only in the summer, Kristiansen became Norway's number two runner behind the great Grete Waitz. After doing several months of skiing in the winter, followed by eight weeks of running in the spring, Kristiansen brought a high level of fitness to the summer track season, along with fresh legs that had not grown weary from too much mileage.

Kristiansen had tried her first marathon in the summer of 1977, clocking 2:45:15. In the summer of 1978, she broke nine minutes for 3,000 meters on the track for the first time. Dave Welch, who watched that race, says Kristiansen was "a big, strong girl," with a developed upper body from all the skiing she had done. "I couldn't believe the difference the next time I saw her, after she'd been running for a long time," recalls Welch. "She'd lost at least 10 pounds." Later in 1978, Kristiansen placed tenth in the European Championship 3,000 meters.

Kristiansen says, "[In 1979] my coach told me if I switched over to running, I would become one of the top in the world. But I liked skiing better, so I skied for one more year." One reason Kristiansen finally made the switch to running was that competitive skiing "takes a lot more travel. There is not always snow where you live. It's easier to be a runner, because you can run anywhere."

When she did turn all her attention to running in 1980, Kristiansen had immediate success, winning the Stockholm Marathon in 2:34:25 and making the 1980 Norwegian Olympic team. She did not get to run in Moscow, however, because Norway joined the U.S.-led boycott of the Olympic Games.

With all the strength she had built up from the years of cross-country skiing, Kristiansen kept getting faster, but remained Norway's "other" runner, behind Waitz, who beat Ingrid scores of times. It was to be five long years before she stepped out of Grete's shadow. They were both at the New York City Marathon in 1979. Waitz set her second world record there while Kristiansen was forced out by an injury.

In 1980, Grete Waitz won New York for the third straight time, with Kristiansen third. In 1981, Ingrid married Arve, an oil engineer, and set her first world record, clocking 15:28.4 for 5,000 meters at the Dulux Games in Oslo's Bislett Stadium on July 7. Kristiansen went through 3,000 meters in 9:02 on her way to breaking American Jan Merrill's record by 2.2 seconds. That fall, Kristiansen improved to second place at New York behind New Zealand's Allison Roe. In 1982, she dropped her 5,000-meter time to 15:21.8.

While she was moving into the ranks of the top runners, Kristiansen continued working, showing it was possible to be an elite runner while holding down a rigorous job. She worked full-time as a medical engineer in the town of Stavanger until 1983. Kristiansen ran for 45 minutes early in the morning before starting her job studying cancer cells at 8 a.m., then did her second session in the afternoon after work. "The only place I was tired was in the head, in the concentration," Kristiansen says. "I think too many runners today are too serious about their running. Of course you have to be serious, but you can do other things, too."

Kristiansen really started making her name on the international scene in 1983, after giving birth to her son Gaute, an experience about which she said, "I'd rather run two marathons back-to-back than give birth again." She started running a week after leaving the hospital, and just five months after Gaute was born, Ingrid won the Houston Marathon in 2:27:51, a little more than 2 minutes off Waitz's world record.

Kristiansen credits Arve and her baby-sitter, Hannah, with providing the environment that allowed her to train and race well while raising a child. "I am the runner, and do the work, but they also support me. We are a good team. They help me and don't push me. And that is really important if you want to be at the top and have children."

In the spring of 1984, Kristiansen won the London Marathon in 2:24:26, the fastest time of the year, giving her a good shot at a medal at the Los Angeles Olympics.

An Olympic medal did not pan out, however. Kristiansen finished fourth in 2:27:34, behind Joan Benoit, Waitz, and Rosa Mota, saying afterwards, "I was very disappointed." Writes Michael Janofsky in the *New York Times*, "By that point she realized she could never reach her full potential as a marathoner, which meant defeating Waitz, without psychological help." Eventually, Ingrid found a doctor in Oslo who needed no more than an hour to recognize her mental block. "He told me, 'You have one problem: You don't think you can beat Grete.' I started to think, 'Maybe that's right.' It was still in my mind that she is better than me." Recognizing that she had a mental block was the first step to removing it, and Kristiansen renewed her training in the winter of 1984-85 with the attitude that, yes, she was just as good as Grete.

Ingrid knew she was better than anyone but Grete after the June 28, 1984, Bislett Games where she proceeded to break the 15-minute mark in the 5,000, setting the world record. Kristiansen took the lead at 3,000 meters, passed in 8:59.8, then pulled away from Aurora Cunha of Portugal to finish in 14:58.89. Cunha was second in 15:09.07, with Rosa Mota sixth in 15:30.63. Kristiansen's amazing 400-meter splits were 70.3, 74.5, 74, 70.5, 70.3, 72, 72.2, 72, 72.8, 72.2, 73, and 71.8, with a last 200 of 33.3 seconds.

Making Her Own Name

With the psychological block gone, in 1985 Kristiansen began beating everybody, including, at long last, Waitz. Not once, but twice in the same week, at the Norwegian Cross-Country Championships and in a road race. In March 1985, she placed third in the World Cross-Country Championships.

It was the 1985 London Marathon where Kristiansen finally ran out from under Grete's shadow. She and coach Johan Kaggestad started thinking about the race six months earlier. Ingrid could never take Joan Benoit's gold medal away, but she could get Joanie's world record, and she trained for it all through the winter of 1984-85.

Women's Marathon World Best Performances

3:40:22	Violet Piercy (GBR)	Chiswick	October 3, 1926
3:37:07	Merry Leper (USA)	Culver City	December 16, 1963*
3:27:45	Dale Greig (GBR)	Ryde	May 23, 1964
3:19:33	Mildred Sampson (NZL)	Auckland	July 21, 1964
3:15:22	Maureen Wilton (CAN)	Toronto	May 6, 1967
3:07:26	Anni Pede-Erdkamp (FRG)	Waldniel	September 16, 1967
3:02:53	Caroline Walker (USA)	Seaside	February 28, 1970
3:01:42	Elizabeth Bonner (USA)	Philadelphia	May 9, 1971
3:00:35	Sara Mae Berman (USA)	Brockton	May 30, 1971**
2:46:30	Adrienne Beames (AUS)	Werribee	August 31, 1971
2:46:24	Chantal Langlace (FRA)	Neuf Brisach	October 27, 1974
2:43:54	Jacqueline Hansen (USA)	Culver City	December 1, 1974
2:42:24	Liane Winter (FRG)	Boston	April 21, 1975
2:40:15	Christa Vahlensieck (FRG)	Dülmen	May 3, 1975
2:38:19	Jacqueline Hansen (USA)	Eugene	October 12, 1975
2:35:15	Chantal Langlace (FRA)	Oyarzun	May 1, 1977
2:34:47	Christa Vahlensieck (FRG)	Berlin	September 10, 1977
2:32:29	Grete Waitz (NOR)	New York	October 22, 1978
2:27:32	Grete Waitz (NOR)	New York	October 12, 1979
2:25:41	Grete Waitz (NOR)	New York	October 26, 1980
2:25:28	Grete Waitz (NOR)	London	April 17, 1983
2:22:43	Joan Benoit (USA)	Boston	April 18, 1983
2:21:06	Ingrid Kristiansen (NOR)	London	April 21, 1985

*uncertified course
**probably a short course

Organizers of the London Marathon let the women start with the men, unlike the previous year when there was a separate start. This gave Kristiansen people to run hard with in the early going. Despite experiencing stomach pains, Kristiansen went through 10 miles in 53:29 and halfway in 1:10:10. She reeled off several faster miles to stay under record pace at nearly 5:20 per mile, then came in to finish in 2:21:06, breaking Benoit's mark of 2:22:43 set at Boston in 1983.

"I planned to run the same speed the whole way," Kristiansen told *Runner's World*. "I saw the time 2:22:43 in front of me and I told myself I must carry under this 2:22:43."

With the world record came many invitations from race directors. But Kristiansen was careful not to over-race, saying, "If you run too many races, you can run well, but not so many great races. And I like to do some real good races."

After London, Kristiansen knew she was in excellent shape. She went to the Bislett Games on July 27 for the 10,000 meters. Ria Van Landeghem of Belgium set the pace for the early going, leading the field through 1,000 meters in 3:13.2, 2,000 meters in 6:18.3, and 3,000 meters in 9:22.3. Kristiansen then took over, passing 5,000 meters in 15:34.54. She ran negative splits, hitting her second 5,000 in 15:24.48 for a time of 30:59.42 to become the first woman to run faster than 31 minutes for 10,000 meters on the track. Her time broke the world record of Olga Bondarenko of the Soviet Union by 14 seconds. Once again, Cunha finished second (31:35.45) and in sixth place, in 32:33.5, was Rosa Mota.

Kristiansen ended her great 1985 season by battling Joan Benoit Samuelson in the Chicago Marathon. After an epic duel, with the two runners throwing everything they had at each other, Kristiansen fell off the torrid pace, and Samuelson went on to the 2:21:21 win.

A satisfied Kristiansen went home and rested. She did not mind doing more skiing and backing off on her running during the winter, and showed that her program worked in the winter of 1986. At the end of January she traveled from Oslo to Miami for the Orange Bowl 10K. Despite having done limited running, she ran 31:31, beating second place finisher Wendy Sly by over a minute. "I came from Norway and lots of snow six days ago, and it's not easy to run in this heat," Kristiansen told Paul Christman afterwards. "But I feel I'm in good shape with my training in skiing and on the treadmill."

Kristiansen ran the Boston Marathon for the first time on April 21, 1986. Benoit Samuelson was not there, and there was little competition for Ingrid. She started the race very fast, running 5:10 miles, and passed halfway in 1:09:44. She slowed over the hills in the second part of the race to win with a time of 2:24:55. Boston showed Kristiansen was ready for another record-breaking summer.

On July 5, 1986, she returned to Bislett Stadium to try for a new 10,000 mark. Lesley Welch of the United States led through seven laps. When she dropped out, Kristiansen took over and passed the first 5,000 in 15:11.33. Far out in front, Kristiansen ran 15:02.41 for her second 5,000, to finish in 30:13.74, another world record. In second place, over a minute behind, was, once more, Aurora Cunha.

In 1985, Zola Budd, then of Great Britain, had broken Kristiansen's 5,000 record by running 14:48.07 at an invitational in London's Crystal Palace. Ingrid had been second in that race in 14:57.4, with Lorraine Moller third.

Kristiansen got her 5,000 record back on August 5, 1986, in Stockholm. There were few women close to her level on the track, and once again running by herself, Kristiansen clocked 14:37.33, more than a minute and a half up on the second finisher, Dorthe Rasmussen of Denmark. After running a 30:20 10K road split for the Norwegian team at a Japanese ekiden, Kristiansen was ready for the European Championships in Stuttgart. It was an important race in women's running history, as it was the first time women were allowed to run 10,000 meters in a major track championship.

Kristiansen showed she was far above anyone else then competing by soloing to the second-fastest 10,000 meters ever. "I had to run alone because no one followed me," Kristiansen told *Track & Field News*. No wonder, as she ran her first 5,000 meters in 15:07.9. With the race and the gold medal well in hand, Kristiansen still came back with a second 5,000 of 15:15.4 to finish in 30:23.3. It was the fastest women's 10,000-meter race ever, as Olga Bondarenko became the second person to break 31 minutes (30:57.2), and seven other women ran faster than 32 minutes.

Said Kristiansen, "My motivation is that I always like to train, and like to have great competition, so I feel it's easy." Priscilla Welch adds, "Ingrid worked jolly hard at it. She was very ambitious, with a lot of objectives. You couldn't sway her from her goals."

Going for the World Championships

Kristiansen had another great year in 1987. Coming off her typical winter of cross-country skiing and treadmill training in her Oslo home, Kristiansen knew she was in shape early in the year. Competing in the Norwegian championships on April 5, Kristiansen ran a world half-marathon best of 1:06:40—comparable to sub-50 minutes for 10 miles. The course, however, was not certified, and Joan Benoit Samuelson's world best of 1:08:34, set in Philadelphia in 1984, remained the record.

Kristiansen was at the peak of her career, and she focused on breaking her marathon world record, picking London on May 10 as the place to do it. The 2:20 barrier was in sight as she passed half-way in 1:09:27. Kristiansen gave it her best shot, but slowed in the last miles to win in

Women's 5,000 Meters World Record Progression

16:17.4	Paola Pigni (ITA)	Formia	May 11, 1969
15:53.5	Paola Pigni (ITA)	Milan	September 2, 1969
15:41.4	Natalia Marasescu (ROM)	Oradea	March 16, 1977
15:37.0	Janice Merrill (USA)	Mainz	July 11, 1977
15:35.5	Kathy Mills (USA)	Knoxville	May 26, 1978
15:33.8	Janice Merrill (USA)	Durham	May 19, 1979
15:30.6	Janice Merrill (USA)	Stanford	March 22, 1980
15:28.4	Ingrid Kristiansen (NOR)	Oslo	July 11, 1981
15:24.6	Yelena Sipatova (URS)	Podosk	September 6, 1981
IAAF Era (After event recognized for record purposes)			
15:14.51	Paula Fudge (GBR)	Knarvik	September 13, 1981
15:13.22	Anne Audain (NZL)	Auckland	March 17, 1982
15:08.26	Mary Decker-Tabb (USA)	Eugene	June 5, 1982
15:01.83	Zola Budd (RSA)	Stellenbosch	January 5, 1984
14:58.89	Ingrid Kristiansen (NOR)	Oslo	June 28, 1984
14:48.07	Zola Budd (GBR)	London	August 26, 1985
14:37.33	Ingrid Kristiansen (NOR)	Stockholm	August 5, 1986
14:36:45	Fernanda Ribiero (POR)	Hechtel	July 22, 1995

2:22:48, more than four minutes up on Priscilla Welch in her masters world record run. Even though Kristiansen's time was the fastest of the year and the fourth best in history, she was again disappointed, saying afterwards she "was fit enough" to break 2:20.

After her victory at London, Kristiansen took a short break and set her sights on breaking 30 minutes for 10,000 meters on the track. In July at Bislett Stadium, she ran 30:48.5 for 10,000 meters, giving her the three fastest 10,000-meter times ever. But she sustained a calf injury from the race that forced her to miss three weeks of training. Kristiansen typically trained at altitude for two or three weeks before a marathon or big race, and in August, she went to St. Moritz for some high-altitude workouts before the September 4 World Championships. But, because of her injury, the only running Kristiansen could do in St. Moritz was in a swimming pool.

By the time Kristiansen got healthy, there were only two weeks left before the Rome World Championships. The other women in the

Women's 10,000 Meters World Record Progression			
38.06.4	Ann O'Brien (IRL)	Gormanstown	March 26, 1967
35:30.5	Paola Pigni (ITA)	Milan	May 9, 1970
35:00.4	Julie Brown (USA)	Los Angeles	March 29, 1975
34:01.4	Christa Vahlensieck (FRG)	Wolfsburg	August 20, 1975
33:34.2	Loa Olafsson (DEN)	Hvidovre	March 19, 1977
33:15.09	Peg Neppel (USA)	Los Angeles	June 9, 1977
32:52.5	Mary Shea (USA)	Walnut	June 15, 1979
32:30.80	Olga Bondarenko (URS)	Moscow	August 7, 1981
IAAF Era			
32:17.20	Yelena Sipatova (URS)	Moscow	September 19, 1981
31:35.3	Mary Decker-Tabb (USA)	Eugene	July 16, 1982
31:35.01	Lyudmila Baranova (URS)	Krasnodar	May 29, 1983
31:27.58	Raisa Sadreydinova (URS)	Odessa	September 7, 1983
31:13.74	Olga Bondarenko (URS)	Kiev	June 24, 1984
30:59.42	Ingrid Kristiansen (NOR)	Oslo	July 27, 1985
30:13.74	Ingrid Kristiansen (NOR)	Oslo	July 5, 1986
29:31.78	Wang Junxia (CHI)	Beijing	September 8, 1993

10,000-meter race thought she would wait and sit in the pack. Kristiansen, however, surprised the field by blasting away on the second of the 25 laps on her way to burying the field. Ingrid's World Championship gold medal solidified her claim as the world's best women's runner.

"It's just a great relief to have this race over," Kristiansen told *Runner's World*.

> My advantage was that I had raced 10,000 meters on the track several times, while many of the others had not run it often. I believe some are still learning how to race it. It was a frustrating season for me, because I was battling the leg injury all the time. If I had been healthier, I could have produced much better results.

Those better results continued to come after Rome, as Kristiansen took advantage of her fitness to set the 10-mile road world record, clocking 50:31 at Amsterdam in mid-October. She followed that by winning the IAAF 15-kilometer road championships in another world record, running 47:15.

Kristiansen, 31, was racing better as she got older, and said, "If you still have your spirit and want to go for it, it's good to be in your 30s." And having children does not have to hinder a runner, Kristiansen believes, as long as she has a good support system.

"More and more runners are coming back after having babies," Kristiansen said.

> I tell them to keep on going some years after their mid-20s. Some runners are good at 18 and then don't improve for some years. But if they stop running, they'll never reach the top. You can be a serious runner and mother, but you have to have a husband or someone you live with who will help you. I am doing the running, but behind my good races there's a lot of work.

Looking Forward

In 1988, Kristiansen went back to London for yet another shot at the 2:20 barrier. Once again she passed halfway in under 1:10 (1:09:45), but ended up running 2:25:41, her fourth victory at London and still nearly five minutes up on second place Ann Ford of Great Britain.

Heading into the 1988 Seoul Olympics, Kristiansen was the overwhelming favorite to win the gold medal in the 10,000 meters. Running easily, she won her semifinal heat in 31:44.7. In the final, Kristiansen was content to stay in the pack for the first two kilometers before surging into the lead.

Kristiansen quickly got a gap on the field, looking to be well on her way to adding an Olympic crown to her European and World titles. But after seven laps, Ingrid was forced to drop out due to a fractured bone on the arch of her right foot suffered while training in spikes before the Games. After stopping, she fell to the infield and had to be carried off on a stretcher, crying as she was brought off the track. It was a crushing blow for Kristiansen, "really sad," she said. "I could have won, but you never know about the sport. It's really hard when you get injured and can't make it." But she was glad Bondarenko of the Soviet Union won.

Kristiansen quickly put the Olympics behind her, finding solace in her family. "When I came back to the hotel and saw Gaute, he didn't care I didn't have a medal," she told Dick Patrick of *USA Today*. "Life must go on. I came back to the hotel and told Arve, 'Maybe I would have won the race.' He said, 'Forget it. It's history. Look forward.'"

Jacqueline Gareau, winner of the 1980 Boston Marathon, says Kristiansen remained relaxed and confident even when she lost or was injured. "Part of her mental preparation was laughter. Ingrid liked to laugh a lot, and thought it was good for us." Once the injury healed, Ingrid continued looking forward to the elusive 30-minute and 2:20 barriers, because the DNF at the Olympics left her feeling she had something to prove in 1989.

"I came back this year to let people know I am still one of the best runners," she said in the spring of 1989. Instead of taking an easy year, as she would have if she'd won the gold medal at Seoul, Kristiansen focused on running fast at the Boston Marathon in April and the Bislett Games in July.

She tuned up in March by placing second to Great Britain's Liz McColgan in the Red Lobster 10K in 31:39. The following week, she went to the snowy New Bedford Half-Marathon. "I think it's important to run some races before a marathon," Kristiansen said. "Of course, you get beaten, but it's good to do some shorter stuff."

At New Bedford, Aurora Cunha hung with Kristiansen through three miles in 15:40, but a mile later Ingrid was running as she usually did in races—up front and alone. She went through 10K in 31:40, then put in 4:53 and 4:50 miles on her way to finishing in 1:08:31, a new world best by 3 seconds.

On April 9, in her last race before Boston, Kristiansen broke Lorraine Moller's course record in winning the Freedom Trail 10K in 30:59. Then it was back for another try at her marathon world record.

Kristiansen was as ready as she was ever going to be, and it looked as if she might get her sub-2:20 in the early going of the April 17 Boston Marathon. She passed 5 miles in 26:00 and halfway in 1:09:31, with Joan Benoit Samuelson roughly a minute behind. But as the temperatures climbed during the second half of the race, Kristiansen, and most everyone else in the race, slowed. "When I got to 25 kilometers, I thought it was a little too hot, so I concentrated on winning," she told Paul Christman after winning in 2:24:33. "It was nice hearing the crowds cheer for me." Samuelson, fighting a hip injury, finished ninth.

Johan Kaggestad, Kristiansen's coach, said that Ingrid would have been close to 2:20 had she run the London Marathon six days later, where the weather was much better. The difference in the days is seen in that London had roughly *100* men running under 2:20, while at Boston only *11* men ran that fast.

"But I was pleased with the Boston results when I came to the finish and saw my time," Kristiansen said. "I never felt so great after a marathon. I had no problems going down steps. Normally, after a marathon I have to take the lift."

In the fall of 1989, Kristiansen went to the New York City Marathon, which had been Grete Waitz's race. Once Kristiansen became a star in 1985, she and Waitz stopped competing against each other. Some said Grete was ducking her rival, but Waitz said no, it was that their schedules did not match. They both ran the 1,500 meters in the Sweden-Norway dual meet in 1985, but did not race each other the rest of the decade.

"We are almost never in the same place. It is strange that we never meet," Kristiansen told the *New York Times*'s Janofsky before the New York City Marathon, which Waitz had to miss because of a stress fracture in her right pelvis. Earlier in the year, after her win in Boston, Kristiansen had conjectured that perhaps she was not as welcome in New York as Waitz was. "Maybe he [race director Fred Lebow] makes invitations to me. But invitations never get to my mailbox." Lebow said there was no truth to that. "Let me think. I don't recall inviting her. I don't recall not inviting her," Lebow told Janofsky.

By this stage in her career, Kristiansen was driven by the desire for records, not just wins. At New York in November 1989, she once more went out in world-record pace, passing halfway in just over 1:10:20. Running in warm conditions, Kristiansen says it "was feeling so easy until 17 miles, and then I had some stomach problems. I had to slow down and it's difficult to get going again after you've slowed." No one threatened her, and Kristiansen ran the second half in 1:15:10 to finish in 2:25:30, good for $31,000.

That victory made Kristiansen the only person to win both the Boston and New York marathons until Uta Pippig did it in 1993. It is Pippig who has taken up the challenge of breaking Kristiansen's marathon world record, which Ingrid is surprised still stands. Despite the great improvements in time women have made, Kristiansen is not one of those who think women will one day run as fast as men. "Women will never beat the fastest man in a marathon, because men have more strength," she told *Athletics Weekly* in 1992. "My world record stands at 2:21, and I believe in the next five years it will come down to 2:17. The men's is 2:06 and that will come down to 2:05. So, you can see there's a big difference."

Kristiansen had said after her marathon world record that it was the mental barrier that was keeping women from running sub-2:20. "Perhaps more mental training is what it will take," she told *Runner's World*. "There are so many boys running under 2:20, and many of them don't train any more than we do. So why do these boys run under 2:20? Because there are so many other men running under 2:20."

Training: A Balance

When Kristiansen won the New York City Marathon in 1989, a group of runners was watching the race on TV. When Rich Castro's 7-year-old son saw Kristiansen crossing the finish line, he excitedly turned to his dad, exclaiming, "Look! There's Gaute's mommy."

"Gaute's mommy" is a title Kristiansen cherishes more than her records or wins. Running was only a part of her life, as she also spent her time studying cancer cells at work, taking care of her children, and being a wife and homemaker. "I do my best races with them [my family] around me instead of lying around the hotel worrying. A lot of athletes think it would be tiring to have a six-year-old boy around. For me, it's important to feel their atmosphere," Kristiansen told Dick Patrick. Added Arve, "It's not good to get accustomed to limos or hotel suites. You must do something to keep your feet on the ground."

That was Ingrid's "secret": pursuing disciplined, scientific training while always keeping in mind a sense of what really was important to her. She was too busy with her life to get fanatical about her running, and she kept a good balance between her workouts and her recovery days. She *always* knew the reasoning behind her workouts. "Many people go too hard on their easy days, and too easy on their hard days," she explains.

As with Frank Shorter, Rob de Castella, and others, it is surprising how easy Kristiansen ran on her recovery days. Starting out on a run with her, the pace would be close to eight minutes per mile. One might think it would get faster, but it never did. "I think it is better to run a little bit too slowly, so you don't break down. It may be nice to train in a group," Kristiansen said,

> but there is always one person who wants to go faster, and the rest go with him, even when they are tired. When I run with other people, they try to run too fast, maybe to try to impress me. So I do the training by myself.

Training too fast on easy days often means runners leave their best efforts in the workout, Kristiansen says. "Then you go to a race in shape, but you are too tired to run well."

Jacqueline Gareau says she hesitated the first time Kristiansen asked her to go for a run, thinking it would be too quick.

> But Ingrid said, "No, no, I don't run crazy fast." And when we ran I saw she was right. It was very relaxed and very fun. It was very easy to get friendly with Ingrid. She's very generous and kind, and

Ingrid Kristiansen runs in to win New York City in 1989.

was always giving me advice. She'd tell me, "Come over and use the treadmill if you want." And if I was by myself, she'd say, "Come and join us for dinner." It's fun to have known her other side.

After a long run, most elite runners rest and nap. Not Kristiansen. She could be found out riding her bike with Gaute or Arve. "Ingrid has very good family values," says Gareau. "She wouldn't be able to live without her family."

When Arve was looking for a business graduate school to attend, the Kristiansens moved to Boulder, Colorado, after the 1988 Olympics. "It's easier to go to a place where you know somebody," she said. When Ingrid and Arve were shown around their house in the Wonderland Hills section of town, where most of the elite runners lived, she said, "Ohh, Dynasty," upon seeing the vaulted ceiling in the master bedroom, referring to a popular TV show of the time.

But she and Arve refused to sleep in that master suite, eschewing ostentation for a simpler bedroom downstairs. So it was with Ingrid's life and her running, domestic simplicity and a focus on the basics. She had no interest in keeping up with the gossip of who was doing what, who's in or who's out in the running world. "I am a person who, when I am training and competing, I really concentrate, but during the rest of the day, I don't want to think about running. I feel if you read too much what others are doing, you will have doubts."

While some world-class runners lead ascetic lives, with diets and sleep carefully measured out, Kristiansen never took a nap and ate what she wanted to. "I feel I rest better if I am sewing or cooking, and not lying in bed."

Says Rich Castro, "It's interesting to see the other side of her, when she is with Arve and the kids. The intensity is gone, and she is just a wonderful lady." Adds Paul Christman, "Ingrid has a good sense of discipline without obsession, a sense of humor, the ability to lose, and she has a full life outside of running."

Kristiansen's philosophy of running is simple. She says, "I always train a lot, because I like to train." Like Waitz, Ingrid received coaching advice from Johan Kaggestad, but she and Arve shared the daily coaching. Her training was geared to producing good results in a few major races a year, and she had no problem taking breaks from running. After a marathon, Kristiansen took one week completely off, followed by a week of easy running. "After a marathon, I feel my body needs a rest." And if Kristiansen was tired after coming back from the track circuit in Europe, she again took several days completely off from training.

When she was training at her peak, Kristiansen ran 110 to 120 miles a week during the summer, including three workouts. Her intervals were usually run at faster than her 10,000-meter race pace. Kristiansen followed the hard/easy idea of training to the extreme. She used a heart rate monitor to make sure she was recovering, and was one of the first to make heavy use of a treadmill. "It was critical to her training," said Katy Williams. So critical that when she moved to the United States, Kristiansen had her $25,000 treadmill shipped over.

"Ingrid did some *horrid* sessions on her treadmill, just some great speedwork," remembers Priscilla Welch. Kristiansen started using the treadmill as a way to train through the Norwegian winters once she made the switch to being a full-time runner. The treadmill "helps you keep an even speed and keeps you going when you feel you're tired," says Kristiansen, who would sometimes run on the treadmill five times a week in the winter. She would do two-hour runs on it, along with intense speed sessions such as 1,000-meter repeats with a three-minute

Ingrid's Racing Advice

You do not have to be a multi-world-record holder to get the most out of racing, as long as you compete at your own level, says Kristiansen. Her advice: It is more beneficial to undertrain, by going for 45-minute training runs, instead of overdoing it by trying to do too many long runs. "I think it is better to go for more short runs. [They] take less time, are easy to do, and fit into your schedule. And your legs won't get stiff."

Anyone taking a race seriously, however, needs to get in a hard workout at least once a week. People training a minimum of four times a week should do intervals—fast sprints followed by a short recovery that increase a runner's ability to hold a quicker race pace—at least once a week.

Vary the hard workouts, one day doing hill repeats, and perhaps going to the track for the next workout, Kristiansen advises. "Do something different, so it is not the same every time. I think it is really important to have a variation in your training. That's the way my coach trains me."

recovery, or 10×60 second intervals hard, with a minute recovery.

"The main reason I train on the treadmill is to try to feel comfortable when running great races," she says. "It's important to feel the speed is not too bad. It's important to go into races relaxed." Kristiansen still ran on the treadmill two or three times a week in the summer. "I feel I can relax on the 'mill,' and find a good rhythm that translates into races. It helps my form and makes me more efficient."

Priscilla Welch calls Kristiansen

a very special lady. She is a dedicated mother and athlete with a certain toughness so typical in Norwegians. She is a good friend and good training partner on our long runs. She just went out there and enjoyed it.

Kristiansen's long runs were very easy, at a pace between 7:30 and 8:30 per mile. "That's the Norwegian method of training," Kristiansen says.

"I was impressed with Ingrid's long runs," said University of Colorado coach Toby Jacober. "I made the assumption that her long runs were going to be fast. They weren't, but she really hammered her hard workouts. That stuck with me, and is what I still often tell my athletes."

Like Frank Shorter and Said Aouita, Kristiansen sometimes appeared aloof as a competitor. "People get confused when Ingrid sounds confident," Welch told journalist Theresa Smith.

They think she's arrogant, but she's not. She's just more advanced in her training, and she knows what she can do. Ingrid's just a very ordinary person when you get to know her. She likes to cook and sew, and she has a wonderful sense of humor. To us, she's just another runner who happens to be the best.

Jacober agrees, saying she found Kristiansen

very personable. There is a complete lack of arrogance given her level of great running. She likes to go out and run easy. She's good company and there is no competition in the training when you run with her. Ingrid liked to just run and talk. And if she ran faster than me, she'd come back and pick me up.

When training for a big race, Kristiansen had a unique way of stoking her motivation. She would tape photos of top opponents on the inside of the garage door in front of the treadmill. Before a marathon it might be Joan Benoit Samuelson, Grete Waitz, or Rosa Mota. Before a track race, Scotland's Liz McColgan or another top 10K runner. Later, posters of the London or the New York City Marathon would go up, to spur her training for those races. Running on the treadmill, Kristiansen could check her form by watching herself in a mirror, and dream that she was at last breaking 2:20.

Kristiansen's schedule during the winter, as told to journalist Kim Wrinkle in *Runner's World*, included:

Sunday:	A.M., 10K on the treadmill in 40 minutes, or 6:30 per mile;
	P.M., 10 miles on the treadmill in 1 hour, or 6 minutes per mile.
Monday:	A.M., 50 minutes on the treadmill at about 6 minutes per mile; 15 minutes of jumping exercise to strengthen the calf muscles;
	P.M., 2 hours of cross-country skiing.
Tuesday:	A.M., 1 hour on the treadmill at 6 minutes per mile or faster;

P.M., outdoor training session including 2 × 15 minutes at 5:00 to 5:15 per mile, with 4 minutes of easy running between efforts—total of 12.5 to 15 miles.

Wednesday:	A.M., 50 minutes on the treadmill at about 6 minutes per mile; P.M., 1-1/2 hours of cross-country skiing.
Thursday:	A.M., 1 hour on the treadmill first 30 minutes at 6:10-6:30 per mile, second 30 minutes at 5:20 per mile; P.M., 1-1/2 hours of cross-country skiing, 15 minutes of jumping exercises.
Friday:	A.M., 55 minutes on the treadmill at about 6 minutes per mile, with 5 × 100-meter strides closing the session; P.M., 1-1/2 hours of cross-country skiing, 15 minutes of jumping exercises.
Saturday:	2-1/2 hours of easy cross-country skiing.

Kristiansen's treadmill has a top speed of 2:30 per kilometer, a pace of 25 minutes for 10K, or 4:12 per mile. That's very fast, and what happens if a person cannot keep up with the pace the machine sets? "You fall off," Kristiansen said, shrugging her shoulders.

And has Ingrid ever fallen off? With her ever-present laugh, she answers, "No, never. And I don't plan to."

Slowing Down

Kristiansen had a quiet year in 1990, going through a difficult pregnancy. "It was a trying time," Welch says. Kristiansen kept in shape by using a Stairmaster and a stationary bicycle. Her second child, daughter Marte, was born on August 1.

Kristiansen returned to the racing scene in March 1991, showing she was still fast at age 35 by running 1:09:05 for a half-marathon in Holland, beating the up-and-coming Uta Pippig, who was third in 1:10:35.

Kristiansen did not go to the 1992 Olympic Games, because of injuries, and gradually raced less and less. She went back to her roots and started cross-country ski racing again. She is also involved with the Norwegian Track Federation, going to international races with national teams. And she gets to spend more time at home with her family now that she is not running track and road races.

Kristiansen lives in the outskirts of Oslo, Norway, above windy streets that rise up to a hill with the ski jump used in the Winter Olympics. Her home is near a lake, and there are trails nearby on which to train. Joy Rochester and Arturo Barrios visited Kristiansen there, saying it's a "warm" house, and not ornate. "Ingrid and Arve have things accumulated from trips, but there aren't trophies all over the place. The house is not a shrine to Ingrid."

The Grete Waitz Lopet 5K run in Oslo draws 42,000 people, making it one of the biggest races in the world. Ingrid, too, has a race in her honor, a smaller one in the town of Stavanger, where she lived before she became famous. In 1994, Kristiansen, Waitz, and many other past champions of the New York City Marathon gathered at the marathon. It turns out that even past stars go unrecognized, as a man came up to Kristiansen, asking, "Are you a jogger?"

No, Kristiansen will never be "a jogger." This Norwegian will forever be one of the stalwarts of running, because no one else has come close to her combination of wins over 5,000, 10,000, and the marathon. She won 14 of 23 marathons, nearly all of her track 5,000s and 10,000s, and was a World Champion in three venues. She is, U.S. coach Catrina Campbell said in 1995, "probably the greatest women's distance runner ever."

> Even though her (track) records have been broken, Ingrid will always be unique for what she did. And what makes her even more amazing is that she did it while leading a balanced life. She wasn't a one-dimensional person.

Adds Jacqueline Gareau, "Ingrid excelled at all those distances for a long, long time. It's hard to imagine anyone will ever match her records or her career."

That career might not be over yet. Ski racing has kept her fit, and Priscilla Welch says, "Ingrid, like Joanie (Benoit), is one of the toughest ladies out there, and I think we'll see her racing again. She still doesn't fill out her tights. I was talking with some Norwegian friends, and they said Ingrid's training was going well—and that we should watch out for her in [the year] 2000 in Australia."

13

The Zen of Running

Born July 15, 1956, Japan

World record, 30,000 meters (track)

Winner, Boston, London, Chicago, and Tokyo Marathons

Four-time winner, Fukuoka Marathon

The Olympics were held in Tokyo in September 1964, just 19 years after the end of World War II. Since the war, the Japanese had quickly rebuilt their country, and hosting the Olympics was the signal that Japan had reentered the first family of nations. The Olympics were highlighted by the inauguration of the Shinkansen bullet train, which sped Japan into the modern world.

It was a stellar Olympic Games, with Peter Snell winning the 800 and 1,500 meters, Abebe Bikila repeating his gold-medal performance in the marathon (this time wearing shoes) just a few weeks after having his appendix removed, and Native American Billy Mills shocking Ron Clarke and the rest of the 10,000-meter field with a fantastic last-lap kick.

One of the highlights for the Japanese was Kokichi Tsuburaya's 2:16:23 bronze-medal performance in the marathon, after getting passed for second on the homestretch of the track in the stadium. It was the best finish ever by a Japanese runner in an Olympic distance event, though Japan had had two marathon world-record holders in the 1930s, and two Koreans running for Japan, Kitei Son and Shoryu Nan, took the 1936 Berlin Olympic gold and bronze medals. The best marathon finishes by Japanese had been wins at the Boston Marathon, in 1951 by Shigeki Tanaka, by Keizo Yamada in 1953, and Hideo Hamamura in 1955; no Japanese had ever won a medal in an Olympic distance event. Tsuburaya, only 22, was highly honored in Japan for his bronze medal in Tokyo. And he was expected by most Japanese to win another medal, hopefully a gold, at the next Olympics in Mexico City.

It would be nice if this story had a happy ending, but, Tsuburaya's tale doesn't have a golden conclusion. Instead Tsuburaya, unable to train after being felled by an injury to his Achilles tendon, committed suicide, *jissatsu*, about three years after winning his bronze medal. A note to his father was found beside his body, reading, "Sorry; can't run anymore." The suicide has been attributed to post-race depression.

While Kokichi Tsuburaya was running in the Olympics, Toshihiko Seko was running around his elementary school yard, having no inkling that 15 years later he would be the one to bring Japanese marathoning to renewed prominence. Seko's victories, fast times, stoic appearance, and, especially, his ascetic, Zen approach to running made him one of the biggest names in marathoning in the 1980s. He is an enduring figure who exemplifies the Japanese approach to running, which is far different than that of any other country.

A Child Born With *Makenki*

Seko was born July 15, 1956, in the Mie prefecture on the island of Kyushu, weighing in at 4 kilograms. He was the youngest of three children, all boys, born to the owner of a small shop that sold straw goods to farmers. After a typhoon caused severe damage in the area, Seko's father switched his profession to ironworks.

Baseball was Seko's first love as a child, as it was for nearly every other Japanese child (that is, until a soccer craze hit in the 1970s). In fact, Seko did not take part in any of the races his elementary school put on when he was growing up, preferring to play baseball instead. In middle school, he was a pitcher on the local baseball club. However, Seko slowly discovered that, like many others, he was drawn to running. Whenever he had to run, he simply enjoyed it. During his second year of middle school, Seko entered his first track meet sponsored by the Mie prefecture (there are 47 prefectures, or "provinces" in Japan).

Though he did not win his first race, Seko had found his sport, and he started running more. The following year, he qualified for the national middle-school regionals. After that, he put away his baseball glove and bat for good and rechanneled his energy from baseball to running. Even as a child, Seko had what Japanese call *makenki*, or the "spirit of not losing." Seko apparently never grew out of this "hating to lose" and brought it to his running

Whatever the exact translation, *makenki* is what runners such as Aouita, Coe, Shorter, Barrios, Benoit, Waitz, and Keino all displayed. It's called by different names in different languages, but is something universal that all champions have in common—that something extra that separates them from the other talented runners of their times. Says Seko's father about his son, "He wasn't very big, but his will not to lose was strong. Even when he fought, he wouldn't cry."

Meeting Mr. Nakamura

Seko continued running when he enrolled at Kuwana Technical High School near Nagoya. He trained with the school track team, competing in ekidens—relay races with legs of varying distances that are a very popular cultural tradition in Japan. The New Year and many major calendar events are celebrated by the running of ekidens. (The New Year ekiden is the equivalent of America's Super Bowl. Friends and families gather to eat and watch five hours of live coverage of the race.) Seko also competed in the Japanese inter-high school championships and the prestigious *Kokutai*, the national championships.

His second year at Kuwana, Seko won the inter-high school championships in both the 800 and the 1,500 meters. In the fall of 1972, his third year of high school, Seko won the 1,500 and 5,000 at the Kokutai championships in Chiba. That double victory earned him the nickname *Kaibutsu*, which can be roughly translated as "Monster." Later that year, Seko also set the Japanese high-school 1,500-meter record of 3:53.3.

While he was winning on the track, Seko was not as doing as well in school. He did not pass the competitive entrance exams to get into Tokyo's Waseda University his last year of high school, but he's not entirely to blame, according to Brian Sheriff (who works and competes for a Japanese firm), because high-school athletes have rigorous, year-round training, sometimes to the extent that they live away from home, holidays included, so that they can train. For a champion high-school runner like Seko, there was already total immersion in running.

Still, failing the university entrance exams is a social stigma in Japan, so Seko spent some time near Boston, in the United States, during high school. His disappointed parents then sent him to the University of Southern California (USC). Seko did not make it through his freshman year of college, however, and when he returned home, in the summer of 1976, he had grown chubby, looking nothing like a good runner. Friends teased him, calling him by the names of Sumo wrestlers—not the famous ones, but those wrestlers who were extra huge. It seems Seko had fallen in with two other Japanese athletes at USC who, like him, did not really want to be there. "None of us really practiced," Seko told journalist Hans Maler. "We just sat around all day and ate." For a time when he returned to Japan, Seko stopped running completely, and his promising career as a runner was at a crossroads.

When Seko's parents saw their son come home so overweight, they were aghast. Worried about his future, they decided to take drastic action. They sent Toshihiko to the small, historic, wooden house in Tokyo where lived Kiyoshi Nakamura, coach of Waseda University and of the corporate team for S & B, a major food processor. Nakamura was one of the most interesting coaches in running. He was a very wealthy man, most likely a millionaire, whose humbleness was reflected by the small house he lived in.

All told, Nakamura had a stable of roughly 100 runners. Impressed with Seko's running form, Nakamura told Seko's parents that "within five years he will be a world-class marathoner." Nakamura did not just say Seko "might" become a world-class runner. He "promised" that he would and when a Japanese of Nakamura's stature makes a promise, he delivers on it.

Seko's parents, however, had their doubts. "I'm sorry," Mr. Seko said to Nakamura, "But my son doesn't have the disposition or the mental attitude to be a marathoner," adding that he wouldn't be able to handle the "terrible, cruel lifestyle. There's no way, he can't do it."

Even Seko himself at first did not think he could do it, saying, "I had no confidence in this plan. My parents and I thought he was crazy, especially since I held high-school records in the 800 and 1,500 meters."

But Nakamura persisted, telling the Sekos that if Toshihiko "does the work, he will become a marathoner." How could Nakamura be so sure? Because, he said, repeating the idea that formed the basis of his training philosophy: *Tensai wa yugen da go, doryoku wa mugen da.* "Talent is limited, but effort is unlimited."

Seko says, "By these means, he managed to drag me into the world of marathoning."

The World of Marathoning

That world was one of total commitment to Nakamura and the ascetic, almost religious lifestyle he required his athletes to follow. Seko moved in with the coach so that Nakamura could watch over every detail of his life. In a way, Nakamura was like Sebastian Coe's father, who when asked to coach other people said he would have to move in with them first. Nakamura had the same concept of what is required for a coach, only he did it on a grand scale. Nakamura told Seko that "People are fearful, because they don't know what thing they possess. You can't really know what your potential or possibilities are until they are shown to you. Someone needs to draw them out of you."

That someone, of course, was Nakamura, who devoted his life to making sure his runners devoted theirs to running. Says Seko, "On this point, I can't really find words to thank him." If Seko had not fallen under Nakamura's spell, he likely would not have continued running, or if he did continue running without Nakamura, he would not have become the runner he did.

Most of the officials in the Japanese Track and Field Federation came from Waseda University, and they did not want to see Seko go to another school, where he might come back and beat Waseda. However, once you fail an entrance exam in Japan, it is difficult to get into the school. Entrance exams to Japanese universities are so competitive that parents sometimes start prepping their children for them as soon as they start elementary school. After finishing high school, students will often spend a full year studying for the entrance exams. Seko took his

Waseda entrance exam once again and passed this time, causing some cynics to wonder if he had taken the exam himself or if someone had taken it for him. How much pressure is there to get into a good school in Japan? So much that Seko was to later call passing the exam "the greatest thrill of my life, even greater than winning Fukuoka." Seko majored in physical education at Waseda and was coached by Nakamura.

In pursuits of Japanese life there is "the way," called "-do." Examples of this include taekwon-do, karate-do, and bushi-do. And for the Japanese, there is also "the way" to train for a marathon, explains runner Brendan Reilly, an American who lived in Japan for six years and who is translating Seko's autobiography into English. That is what Seko was searching for and that is what he found under the enigmatic Nakamura, whose "-do" of coaching is so unique as to be hard to believe.

Nakamura, a former Japanese 1,500-meter record holder, believed in heavy mileage—lots of it. According to Nakamura, because they are not as big or as strong as some of the foreign athletes, Japanese runners have to work much harder and need to be capable of "unlimited effort." That belief formed the basis for the extraordinarily hard work Seko and the other Japanese runners put in. Long runs of 50 kilometers and even 50 miles were a regular part of training, along with fast, long, tempo runs and 200-mile weeks (with three runs a day), during intense training camps called *gasshuku*.

Not surprisingly, it took Seko a while to understand Nakamura, and giving himself entirely to his coach was difficult at first. He was confused for a year by the strict discipline required to be in Nakamura's training group. He chafed under the strict rules and one day left the Nakamura household and tried to return home. But when he got there, Seko's parents closed the door on their son. They called Nakamura and told him, "Do whatever you must with him; he's yours."

With no where else to go, Seko returned to Nakamura's house. One story has it that the coach put him on a diet of a piece of lettuce and a piece of toast a day to make him lose the weight he had gained at USC and gave him literally 24-hour-a-day attention. Seko eventually accepted the discipline required by Nakamura and gradually worked up to a routine of 120 miles a week. Nakamura set up a five-year plan for Seko, who trained at first for 5,000 and 10,000 meters, with an eye toward excelling in the marathon down the line. His first marathon was a 2:26:00 tenth-place effort in Kyoto in February 1977. Seko improved on that in December at Fukuoka, finishing fifth in 2:15:01 behind Bill Rodgers at 2:10:55.

Nakamura's athletes had 100-percent faith in him, to such an extent that they even prayed to him during races. "We call out his name and ask him to guide us," one runner told Maler. "If Mr. Nakamura pointed to a piece of white paper and said, 'This is black,' then his runners would say, 'Yes, that is black.' The athlete doesn't have his own mind," says Hideshi Okamoto, another Japanese coach.

"We thought of and tried everything humanly possible to enable Seko to become the world's best runner," Nakamura told Hans Maler. "God gave Seko to me, and I want to thank God by making Seko the best."

Seko admitted that Nakamura ran his life. "Everything in me, down to the smallest detail, has changed since I met Nakamura *sensei* (teacher). I am what I am and who I am because of him. I believe in everything he says." He gave himself completely to Nakamura, who was his coach, mentor, manager, supervisor, and in loco parentis. In this way, Seko represents everything the Japanese value; he epitomizes the Japanese respect for their elders. He and Nakamura had what Japanese consider the perfect coach-athlete relationship, "the super-subordination," says Brendan Reilly. "He listened to his elder, respected his elder, and did what his elder told him to do."

Nakamura had this kind of relationship with each of the more than 1,000 runners he coached since he started in 1965. It was *sunao*, or "total obedience." The team was very private, like a close-knit family. They had to wear the same haircut, and they couldn't have girlfriends, go out at night, or drink beer. Seko gave Nakamura a 100-percent, total commitment, and their relationship was very much like that of a priest/disciple. "They were even closer than father and son," says Reilly. The dark side of that total commitment and the hard, near fanatical training he did was that Seko was battling injuries throughout his career. "He was like a machine. I used to think they were just stories, but he was really like that," says Reilly. Adds Hideshi Okamoto, "He is not human. His training with Mr. Nakamura was like being in the army."

"There will never be a second Nakamura," Nakamura told Maler. "When I read to my runners the stories of Jesus, the disciples, and the other great religious leaders they believe the stories because they see me and the kind of life I am leading, and they know people like that can really exist."

After living with the Nakamuras for six months, Seko moved to an apartment nearby, though he continued spending most of his time at his coach's house. There Nakamura's wife fed steak dinners to her husband's runners; usually four or five were selected a night. Nakamura paid for all the food.

Maler said Nakamura spent roughly $15,000 a year of his own money feeding his runners. When he started coaching, he used to beat his runners, who nicknamed him "Satan, because of his brutal, Spartan-style practices," Maler reports. "I gave up hitting my runners when I discovered that words were more effective," Nakamura said. His brand of coaching was called by some in Japan "Nakamuraism."

"The relationship between American coaches and their athletes is generally confined to practice, and all they talk about is strategy," Nakamura told Maler. "It's more important for the runner to be with the coach day in, day out so he can learn how to live and think."

Nakamura said, "Most Americans don't practice as hard. They take breaks and cut down on distances. Seko and most Japanese runners run every day, even after a marathon. Just imagine what the bigger, stronger foreigners could do if they trained like Seko, or if they had me as a coach."

Running With Zen

The 1978 Japanese Track and Field Championships were the turning point in Seko's career as he ran an excellent 27:51 for 10,000 meters. After that, Nakamura had him marathon training full-time. He ran Fukuoka in 1978, and was a surprise winner in 2:10:21, beating Bill Rodgers, the 1976 Olympic gold medalist Waldemar Cierpinski, Leonid Moseyev, Garry Bjorklund, and Shigeru Soh, who in February had run 2:09:06 at the Beppu Oita Marathon, the second-fastest ever. This gave the world its first inkling that a new Japanese running star was rising in the east.

As was to become his marathoning style, Seko sat in the pack. Soh led through splits of 30:26 at 10K and 1:04:12 at the half-marathon. Seko and Australian Olympian Chris Wardlaw then passed Rodgers, who was slowed by the flu and a cramp. Soh led through 35K in 1:47:30 before Seko and countryman Hideki Kita passed him. Seko pulled away for the win, with Kita second and Soh third. Recalling the race, Rodgers wrote in *Marathoning*, "All I could think of was 'The Japanese have returned.'" In April 1979, Seko finished second to Rodgers at Boston, running 2:10:12.

Seko's life was running, totally and completely. After graduating from Waseda, he worked for S & B from 8 a.m. to noon Monday through Saturday. He ran in the morning before work, then again in the afternoon. Nakamura liked to have his runners train over a measured loop outside Tokyo's Olympic Stadium so that he could control their pace and watch them run.

The asphalt loop around Meiji Jingu National Garden next to the Olympic Stadium is a perfect oval and is exactly 1,325 meters long.

Every 100 meters is measured and marked off to within 10 centimeters of accuracy. Here Seko ran lap after lap after lap, sometimes as many as 50 in a row. He did not look to the left or the right, but ran lightly over the ground with his eyes fixed in front of him. Once each lap he passed Nakamura, who carefully timed each lap in an attempt to mold Seko's raw talent and develop it until Seko was renowned throughout the world for his marathoning prowess.

"Seko finds meaning and happiness in life through running," Nakamura said. "There's never been a harder worker or a more serious athlete. He doesn't go out at night to clubs and he's never received even one call from a woman. He doesn't have time for that."

Seko added, "The marathon is my only girlfriend. I give her everything I have."

"Look how smooth he runs," Nakamura told Hans Maler while watching Seko run one day in 1980. "Did you see his relaxed expression? That's the key to his strength. It's Zen. In the old days we had samurai. Their most lethal weapons were their swords. But even more important than their swords was their understanding of Zen. With Zen in their hearts and minds, they could control every emotion and thought. That's what Seko does. Next time he comes by, watch his face. He's in total peace; his heart is pure."

Zen is a form of Buddhism, originally from China, that concentrates on the enlightenment of the student. Nakamura called his philosophy of training "Zensoho," or "running with Zen," Maler reports. "The idea is to clear your mind of everything and to let your body function naturally, undisturbed by thought," Nakamura said. "That's something most Americans and foreigners can't understand."

Just as important as the hard, high mileage in Nakamura's training was developing a positive mental attitude in his athletes. He saw that his role as a coach was bringing that out and fostering it. "Physical training is only 10 percent of the total preparation; the other 90 percent is mental. We have to do things like this so we can overcome the larger, stronger foreign competitors."

Nakamura's mental training involved studying the great teachers of history. Each night he would read to his runners selections from different wise men. Buddha means "the enlightened one," and Nakamura used his teachings and those of others, ranging from Jesus to Japanese poets, to enlighten his charges on how they should face the marathon. A favorite aphorism, Maler tells us, was from Daruma-taishi, a Buddhist monk:

"Welcome the hardships when they come. Be patient and work through the burdens. Only then can you overcome them and grow stronger."

Others from Nakamura's treasury of inspirational sayings he repeated to his runners included:

- "If you think you are going to win, you'll lose. Moreover, if you think you are going to lose, you'll lose."
- "The marathon is an art; the marathoner is an artist."
- "One sketches the spirit and impression of youth on a 42.195 kilometer canvas."

There is something to learn from all religions, "just like everything in life," Nakamura told Maler. "We must study the Bible, Scriptures, and all famous works. We must study nature; mountains, rivers, stars, sun, and moon. All of them are our teachers."

Nakamura also said he and Seko must study

the other top runners like the Soh brothers, Rodgers, Cierpinski, and Ito and take their best qualities and mold them into Seko. That way he's still Seko, but he has a part of all his competitors in him, which will enable him to beat them.

It is often hard for people in the West, raised in the tradition of individualism dating back to the classical Greeks, to understand the Japanese culture that produced Seko. Even people who have lived in Japan for years find it hard to understand. In Japan, the individual is subordinate to the community and the country. This gives people a sense of belonging, yet it can lead to great pressures, as Tsuburaya found out in the 1964 Olympics. It's the Japanese culture which allows for the "unlimited effort" Seko and others put in. Japanese runners are not just running for themselves, but for their 120 million countrymen; and even beyond that, for the millions of ancestors who live on in the memories of their descendants.

The Japanese approach to running is unlike that in the United States, Britain, New Zealand, Australia, Kenya, or any of the other countries with a deep running tradition. "The one thing in common is the competition. Other than that, everything else is different," says Brian Sheriff,

As I've come to realize by living and training in Japan, competition is not what we athletes aim for. It's more the Spartan commitment to living the almost secular life of the *dojo*. Our existence is an extension of our supporter's own inner life. We realize for them through our commitment to our lifestyle that almost spiritual superiority of their individual group (or company) over their rivals.

The difference is that for Rodgers, Shorter, and Viren, the race itself was the goal of training. Not so for Seko and Japanese running today, believes Brian Sheriff. He says that Seko was

> the epitome of Nakamura-san's dedication to the Zen way of life. Through Seko, others could find solace, encouragement, pride, and honor. Competition is in itself a mere extension of the *dojo* athlete's life, not the ultimate reason he is training.

The basis of Nakamura's relationship with Seko was the great respect Japanese people hold for their elders and their ancestors. In shrines all over Japan, along roads, in fields, on street corners, you see shrines set up with candles lighted in memory of ancestors. The tradition goes back centuries and is still alive in everyday life. Elders are always referred to as Mr. or Mrs. and are seen as being teachers to the younger generation.

That teacher/pupil relationship Nakamura and Seko shared, called *shitei*, was not unique: It is found all over Japan, in areas such as music, pottery, or the famous tea ceremony. In such a relationship, the leader of a corporate running team is more than a coach, though he is not a "buddy"; the athlete does not go out with the coach after training, explains Brendan Reilly. "But at the same time, there is not a distance between them, either. Not a friend, but not distant." In the morning, runners get in a circle around the coach, who gives words of wisdom for the day. The runners bow, then go to their workout. When they return, they again gather in a circle around the coach and bow again, thanking the coach for his guidance and for coaching them.

All this is often mysterious to foreigners and after his win at Fukuoka in 1978 and second at Boston the following year, Seko embodied for the rest of the world all the mystery and discipline that is Japan. He had an otherworldly aura around him. The stories of his training came out of Japan along with his victories, and since Seko rarely revealed his emotions, the mystique grew.

Nakamura helped Seko make the transition from university runner to elite runner. Universities are farm systems for the corporate teams, which are the major leagues of running in Japan. The rivalries come to a head every New Year's Day, at the national ekiden. The team competition of the ekiden illustrates the team approach that underlies Japanese running. No one runs alone. The Japanese often go single file or in pairs on long runs while the coach drives at the head of the line, playing music and giving out splits. Workouts can involve 15-20 runners on the track, and they will all do the same workout, in single file. Seko, however, had more of an individualistic streak in him than most Japanese runners. In training, he kept to himself and his privacy was extreme. Even many in Japan did not know much about him or what he was thinking.

That was part of his game plan in racing as well. Foreign runners never knew how fit Seko was or how he was feeling, says ex-marathon world-record holder Steve Jones.

> He was a tough cookie to run against. With some people you know what they are thinking, but with Seko you never did. He was very private, and you never heard how his training and racing were going beforehand. It was hard to go into a race with a game plan against him.

"It's fine for runners of other countries to come right out and say what they think. But we Japanese won't say exactly what is on our mind," Seko told journalist Dan Schlesinger in 1984.

Seko was short and powerful, built like a sparkplug, and very efficient when he ran. Rodgers was one of the runners he had beaten at Fukuoka, and Seko came to Boston in April 1979 to try and win another major marathon. This time, they were on Rodgers's home turf, and he vowed to win. In the early going, it looked as if neither would, as Tom Fleming, and then Gary Bjorklund, ran in the lead. Rodgers ran in the chase pack, followed by Seko.

Near 18 miles, Seko passed Rodgers and went after Bjorklund. But Rodgers was as tough as they come, and he followed behind Seko. Rodgers then repassed Seko, and they both went by Bjorklund. Fearing a repeat of the 1978 Boston , where he had to outkick Jeff Wells, Rodgers ran harder, and got a safe lead over Seko, finishing in 2:09:27, with Seko second in 2:10:12. There was no shame for Seko in finishing second to Rodgers, who was impressed by Seko. "I can't believe this guy is only 21," Rodgers said afterwards.

In December 1979, Seko returned to Fukuoka and won in 2:10:35. That second Fukuoka win made Seko one of the favorites for the Olympics. One running magazine wrote that

> Seko seemed to be the one man who had everything in its proper place to beat everyone in Moscow. He was strong, he was fast, he was smart, and he knew how to peak. On August 1, 1980, with the honor of his country at stake, Toshihiko Seko could most likely have become the first Japanese to win the Olympic Marathon.

Seko, however, never got the chance. Japan joined the U.S.-led boycott which kept the Japanese star at home. Many Japanese believe that 1980 was his year, and that by 1984 he was already past his peak. The heavy mileage and total devotion inherent in Japanese running leads to burnout, and careers often last only a few years. One day on a summer run, José Pedrosa, coach of Rosa Mota, explained, "You see, today's the anniversary of Hiroshima (the atomic bombing), and look at Japan today—it has the world's most powerful economy. Incredible. It's the same effort they put into their running." When one runner is gone, another steps in to take his place. Elite Japanese marathoners don't bemoan the end of their career or try to hang on. They just continue working for their corporation, where they often have lifetime employment. Seko's career was long by Japanese standards.

"Without the (1980) boycott, I believe the marathon would have been won by Toshihiko Seko," said Yoichi Furukawa, who founded the prestigious Ohme 30K race in 1967 to honor the memory of Kokichi Tsuburaya. "We all believed there was absolutely no way anybody could have beaten him."

"I was disappointed" in not being able to run in the Olympics, Seko said. "My country put faith in me, and I was not going to let them down. I trained especially hard because I was representing all of Japan."

Nakamura helped Seko get over his disappointment by telling him more stories of people who have overcome adversity. "I like it when he reads to me," Seko said. "It calms me and makes my thoughts pure. This is especially important before a race. After the race, I like to be alone. I usually go to a temple and meditate."

Instead of the Olympics, Seko went back to Fukuoka at the end of the year. He was extremely anxious to race Waldemar Cierpinski, who repeated as gold medalist at Moscow. Cierpinski was quoted in Japanese papers before Fukuoka as saying he would have won at Moscow even if there hadn't been a boycott and runners such as Seko and Rodgers had been there.

Maler was at Fukuoka in 1980 and gave a report in *Runner's World* that gives some insight into Seko's relationship with Nakamura. An hour before the race, Nakamura summons his runners, saying, "'Seko, come. It's time.'

"'Yes, master,' Seko replies." Nakamura then leafs through his "time-worn and frayed Japanese Bible," with his favorite passages underlined. "'Here we are: Jeremiah 1:19.' He read in a soft, steady tone. 'And they shall fight against thee: but they shall not prevail against thee; for I am with thee, said the Lord, to deliver thee.'" Seko listened intently with his hands folded behind his back.

Seko "prevailed" at Fukuoka for the third time. "Cierpinski is a great runner and I respect him," Seko told Maler. "Winning Fukuoka obvi-

Japan's Marathoning Tradition

With his incredible dedication and patience, it seemed likely that Seko would break the world record one day and add to Japan's marathoning tradition. It began with Fusashige Suzuki, who broke Albert Michelson's world record, which had stood for over nine years, by running 2:27:49.0 in a race from Tokyo's Jingu-Stadium to Rokuyo and back on March 31, 1935.

Three days later, on the same course, Yasuo Ikenaka knocked more than a minute off that time with a 2:26:44.0. Suzuki also ran this race and was second in 2:33:05. Third was someone listed as Kitei Son of Japan—but his real name was Sohn Kee-Chung, and he was from Korea, not Japan. In November 1935 Kitei Son broke Ikenaka's world record by two seconds, running 2:26:42 in a marathon in Tokyo. The next year, Kitei Son would win the gold medal at the Berlin Olympics, running for Japan. In the 1960s, Toru Terasawa broke Abebe Bikila's world record at the Beppu Oita Marathon in 2:15:15.8. After Bikila reclaimed the record at the Tokyo Olympic Games, Morio Shigematsu (now a corporate team coach) broke it in 1965, with his 2:12:00. Furthermore, Seiichiro Sasaki took second when Derek Clayton broke Shigematsu's mark. Japan's Kenji Kimihara continued the tradition, taking the silver medal in the marathon at the Mexico City Olympics in 1968.

"The marathon is recognized and appreciated by the public at large in Japan," says Frank Shorter, who never lost a marathon there. "It's not so much the social situation, but more the psychological support runners get. Performances are appreciated and marathoners have different status. It's part of their heritage." Everyone knows running in Japan, Shorter adds, even elderly people. "It's always been fascinating to me. "

ously doesn't mean I would have beaten him in Moscow, but it did help ease the pain of not running in the Olympics." But even Seko's 2:09:45 was not good enough for Nakamura, who told Maler, "I scolded him for two weeks following that race. He didn't run that well."

Seko did, however, run well the following spring. Each March, Nakamura took Seko and some of his other runners for a month's training in New Zealand. There, Seko would put in huge mileage, while the coach would go hunting. Seko's capacity for hard work really did seem "limitless," according to some of the stories that surfaced. During one of Seko's sojourns in New Zealand, the story goes, he ran 1,200 kilometers in eight days, or *150 kilometers a day* (nearly 90 miles), saying afterwards, "My body was a little confused after that, but I did it."

On March 22, 1981, Seko went for the 30K track world record in Christchurch, breaking Jim Alder's 11-year mark by more than 2 minutes. Pushed by a S & B teammate, Seko passed 5,000 meters in 14:48.7; the first 10,000 meters in 29:34.1; 15K in 44:17.4; and 20K in 59:11.1. Seko passed 25K in 1:13.55.8, breaking Bill Rodgers's world record, and finished in 1:29:19. His three 10K splits were 29:34.1, 29:37, and 30:07.7.

That record showed Seko was ready to pop a good marathon when he returned to Boston a month later. He was facing Rodgers, Craig Virgin, Greg Meyer, and Kirk Pfeffer. Virgin and Seko battled. Virgin was faster over 10,000 meters, and also was the 1980 World Cross-Country Championship winner. But Seko was too strong and too experienced, and he powered away to win in 2:09:26, breaking Rodgers's course record by one second. Virgin was exactly a minute behind, with Rodgers third in 2:10:34.

Seko was forced to take off the rest of 1981 with a knee injury. But he never did anything in half-measure, not even rest. "We're gearing up for L.A.," Nakamura said in a 1982 interview. "Toward that end, I plan to have Seko rest for one whole year." With the help of acupuncture treatment, Seko got better, and in February 1983 he entered the Tokyo Marathon, his first marathon in nearly two years. Many wondered if would be able to come back after a lay-off, but some, like Shorter, knew he would be back.

"Nakamura was an excellent coach, a masterly, super coach, and Seko was a good talent," he said. Nakamura, says Shorter, "Made marathon training a sacrament. . .," meaning injuries didn't lessen his commitment.

Seko faced a top field at Tokyo, including Juma Ikangaa, Mexican Rodolfo Gomez, and Cierpinski. He held back in the early going. Gomez took the lead, but slowed at a hill at 19 miles. Seko passed him, followed by Takeshi Soh. Seko ran strongly over the final miles to show in stunning fashion that he was indeed back by winning in 2:08:38, 20 seconds off Rob de Castella's best. It was the fourth-fastest marathon ever run. Soh also broke 2:09, in 2:08:55, showing that Japanese runners were back on top.

In March, Nakamura took Seko and his teammates to New Zealand for their traditional spring training. But after his stay in New Zealand, Seko suffered a bout of hepatitis, "reportedly aggravated," Dan Schlesinger wrote, "by drinking too much beer after long training sessions." Too much, once again, in the extreme. Seko had to stop training; instead, he walked every day. "Outsiders said he could be seen walking everywhere with feverish intensity, his face and neck swollen by either the effect of hepatitis or medications." Bingeing on beer might seem contradictory for someone with Seko's incredible self-control, but perhaps it is an illustration of what such extreme self-control can do to a runner.

It appeared Seko might be down for the count this time. But this great Japanese warrior rose up again to do battle. Reports began filtering out of Japan that he was running as much as *six hours at a time* because his rivals, Takeshi and Shigeru Soh, had been doing very long runs. It's said that on a training run, Seko set the world record for 50K. Says de Castella, "Seko's main strength is his upbringing and philosophy. He has incredible mental strength. He can do incredible training sessions like 50- or 60-mile runs. It's mind-boggling."

"I always have the passion to get better," Seko told *Runner's World* after Tokyo. "Salazar has the best time, but I haven't run against him yet, so I'm not afraid." For Seko, "getting better" meant running more miles. One report had him running a workout before Fukuoka of two 20K time trials—both in sub-58-minutes.

After setting a Japanese record over 20K, Seko got his chance to face Salazar at Fukuoka in December 1983, along with Ikangaa and his great Japanese rivals, the Soh brothers, Shigeru and Takeshi. He won Fukuoka for the fourth time, once again breaking 2:09, this time outsprinting Ikangaa on the track to finish in 2:08:52. It was Seko's fifth major marathon win in a row, and when he finished, he bowed to Nakamura. He was now, along with de Castella, acknowledged as one of the two best marathoners in the world.

One of Seko's legacies, says Shorter, is that he turned the marathon into a 1,500 meters. "Nobody thought they could beat him in a sprint, and that was his tactic." Shorter says Kenyan Ibrahim Hussein (winner of the Boston and New York City Marathons) was the only one who had the same ability. "You didn't want to take the risk of being on the track with either of them. Seko never did lose a sprint."

Training

Seko never had a fixed weekly routine. He trained from race to race, trying to stay one step ahead of injury. Nakamura gave him the daily workout, varying each day's session depending on how he looked and how he felt from the previous day's training.

Seko ran twice a day—10 to 15 kilometers in the morning, speed sessions or up to 30 kilometers in the evening—except when at a *gasshuku*, when he'd train three times a day. When gearing up for a marathon, Seko would run 10 miles in the morning and up to 20 miles in the evening. High mileage was the foundation of Seko's training.

Once a week, he ran a tempo run of up to 20 kilometers at race pace (faster than five minutes a mile), and there would usually be one track session a week. In general, Seko aimed for intense sessions in two out of every three of his workouts. His long runs would be as much as 80 kilometers, sometimes 70 or 80 laps of the oval in front of the Olympic Stadium. The system worked for one reason—Seko did whatever Nakamura told him to do.

Says Steve Jones about Seko's training, "There was absolutely no distraction. Absolutely none. He kept his pain to himself. Sometimes that works, and sometimes it doesn't. It's just like with all kinds of training."

In his autobiography, Seko gives the following daily schedule for a training camp before the Seoul Olympics:

6:30 A.M.	Wake-up. Morning run.
8 A.M.	Breakfast, followed by morning nap.
11 A.M.	2nd workout; a time trial, if feeling good.
Noon:	Leisurely lunch of udon noodles or sushi (raw fish), followed by afternoon nap.
Evening:	Hardest training. 20-30 kilometers. Sometimes Seko ran so hard he could not eat, and had to skip dinner. If his stomach was not upset, he would have dinner with one or two beers. If his stomach was upset and he couldn't eat, he might have as many as 10 (!) beers.
9 P.M.	Lights out.

Seko often went to Hokkaido for his *gasshuku*. There's a little bit of altitude there, and it was his favorite place to train.

Very long runs are part of the running tradition of the Japanese, who place the utmost importance on overdistance training. Some Japanese runners have been known to run *eight hours* on their long run, says Reilly. "They try to overcompensate by doing incredible workouts."

And when he was injured, Seko would do very long walks, of up to 25 miles. That tradition continues; Japanese runners with the corporate teams that train in Boulder can often be seen walking single-file up the mountain roads, going on regular 20- to 25-mile walks.

Seko was able to endure all that heavy training because of his mental approach to it. "To me, Zen and running are the same. Most people must consciously try to be patient. To me, this comes naturally. Zen is sitting. People sit for a long time relaxing. To me, running is the same." Indeed, you would have to be very patient to follow Seko's training.

The spiritual training is as important as physical training, Seko said. "Track and field isn't a mere footrace. You run with your whole body and whole soul, making the competition a sacred or divine matter. By no means can you neglect the spiritual side and run at all."

One of the themes running through the lives of the great runners is how they had the luck or the sense to know what approach would work for them. The coach and the athlete have to be just right for each other, like Nakamura and Seko, or the relationship will not click. Frank Shorter gives the example of coach Bob Timmons and miler Jim Ryun; the two were perfect for each other. Says Shorter:

> There's an element that has to be there to be successful. It's not just hard training—it's the human relation and the way you go about training and the way you go about dealing with the competition and the coach.
>
> There are variations on the theme, and there is no one way to do that. I think that in the end a good athlete gravitates instinctively to what works. And you are lucky if you have the support system that works. Some of it is serendipity. In Ryun's case, he lived in Wichita (where Timmons was coaching). And Seko was able to find Nakamura.

Los Angeles Olympic Games

Heading into 1984 and the meeting of Seko, Salazar, and de Castella at the Los Angeles Olympics, Seko was rated a four-to-one favorite (Deek was listed at two-to-one) by *The Runner*, which wrote of Seko's chances: "With his spotless record, fanatical training and deadly kick, victory could well be his, though he's not raced in the heat or competed much outside his country."

De Castella is among Seko's many admirers, citing his speed, strength, and "the best self-control of probably any marathoner. That may come from his very disciplined lifestyle, or just the Japanese lifestyle in general," he told *Track & Field News*. "You have to be able to hold yourself back in a race, to utilize your fitness and your strengths as best you can. His approach to running is superb. I respect him a great deal."

Deek said Seko's only flaw, maybe, was "that he hadn't run a summer marathon. Nor has he run a marathon in a championship event. Japan boycotted the 1980 Olympics. They didn't run the World Championships." And he's also had some injuries. "He's got a couple of things to think about."

The Japanese public also gave Seko something to think about, as he was being counted on to win the gold medal for his country. The pressure on Seko "was enormous," says Brendan Reilly. "You can't imagine the pressure there was on him." For many Japanese who lived through the exploits of Seko, their nation's honor was at stake.

If Seko was feeling pressure, he did not show it when the Olympic Marathon started. Seko sat in the lead pack in the early going, running next to de Castella through ten kilometers in 31:15. Wearing a white baseball cap turned backwards, he ran comfortably with the leaders—de Castella, Carlos Lopes, Juma Ikangaa, Alberto Salazar, Joseph Nzau of Kenya, Great Britain's Charlie Spedding, John Treacy of Ireland, Mexico's Rodolfo Gomez, and Rod Dixon of New Zealand—until 21 miles, looking in complete control. But just when he seemed poised to make his move and take the lead, Seko fell back off the pace. Lopes won the gold medal, while Seko finally struggled into the Coliseum in 17th place, a finish viewed as a national disaster in Japan. The heat had gotten to Seko, and he became very dehydrated. Other runners understood that, but not many back home did. "In Japan, all these people think that if you have a strong mind, you should be able to control a heat wave," says Hideshi Okamoto.

Afterwards, Seko and Nakamura tried to explain to the hordes of Japanese media what had happened. Wrote Eric Olsen in *The Runner*,

> Japanese newsmen surrounded them [Seko and Nakamura] protectively, all stunned by his impossible defeat, all as silent and still as if they'd just learned someone dear to them had died and perhaps in a sense, someone had, such is the intensity with which Seko strives for victory and the intensity with which the Japanese demanded he succeed. . . . The Japanese operate in an entirely different milieu than we do, an intense ascetic modern samurai tradition in which death is always preferred over failure, or at least a failure to fight to the end.

When he failed to win a medal, it was not just Toshihiko Seko's failure—it was the country's failure, as well. He received another blow when Nakamura died. The coach was found floating face down in a stream where he had gone trout fishing. The death was officially ruled an accidental drowning, but rumors persisted that he had committed *jissatsu*.

Seko said after the 1984 Olympic Marathon, "I tried my best. I feel sorry I couldn't do my best. Now I need rest, I'll try again in four years."

It was not until London in 1986 that Seko ran another marathon. He went there for redemption, saying, "I want to make up for my disappointment in the Olympics," adding that he wanted to get as close to 2:07 as possible. Seko led from the start at a 2:07 pace, but stiff winds and a lack of competition forced him to settle for a 2:10:02 victory, his seventh win in 11 marathons.

Seko put in heavy training over the summer, pursuing a world record. Tired from his training, he ran 29:31.9 to take the 10,000-meter bronze medal at the Asian Games in Seoul at the end of September. A month later, he went to Chicago. Steve Jones had won the race the previous two years, setting the world record in 1984 and running 2:07:13 in 1985.

Seko, too, wanted a fast time, and he thought Chicago was the place he could get it. He said beforehand that he wanted to go through 20 kilometers in an hour, and he was just about on pace when he passed 20 kilometers in 1:00:20. Trailing the lead pack of Charlie Spedding, Martti Vainio, and Michael Musyoki, Seko hit halfway in 1:03:42.

Seko patiently waited, occasionally glancing at his watch. Just at 25 kilometers, he looked at his watch, then threw in a 4:50 mile. Only Ahmed Saleh could stay with Seko, and the two took turns surging on each other. At 23 miles, Seko ran a 4:46 mile, and Saleh was broken. "When I was in the lead I watched his face and he was tired," Seko told Paul Christman. "So I made the move." Seko ran in to finish in a new personal best of 2:08:27.

Back to Boston

The following year, Seko showed up in Boston with his race face on, along with a big entourage. "It seemed like there was a lot of secrecy involved, and the language was a barrier," said Rich Castro. "He was always very polite, but there seemed to be a line drawn that he didn't want to cross over. There was a real air of mystery about him, and also invincibility, that he had come there on a special mission."

Seko was the mystery runner to his opponents, unsmiling when he ran, seemingly unbeatable, with great strength, deep patience, and endless fortitude. He was feared because he combined the discipline of a Buddhist monk with the kick of a 1,500-meter runner.

Seko's "special mission" at Boston was for his family, as he explained before the race. "I will do this for my son," he told *Running Stats*. "Having a family and a baby gives relaxation and encouragement." For Seko, it was not a question of doing his best; that was a given. He was there for one reason only—to win. Before the race, Seko and the other Japanese went into the Bill Rodgers Running Center. After he left, Charlie Rodgers said, "That is the fittest human being I've ever seen. Just sitting there, you could see that this guy was really ready to rock."

And he did, but not until Heartbreak Hill. Despite a deep field brought together by John Hancock, it was a tactical race, with a large pack of runners staying together through 16 miles. The early pace was pushed, as usual, by Juma Ikangaa, who towed the field into a headwind. De Castella, who had won Boston the year before in 2:07:51, was in the field, but a mishap with the starting rope had tripped him up at the start.

Geoff Smith and Steve Jones pushed the pace up the hills, dropping Ikangaa, Eddy Hellebuyck of Belgium, and Japan's Tomoyuki Taniguchi. Seko followed easily behind Jones and Smith, then just ran away from them over the hills. Once clear, he put in a 4:52 mile to seal the victory. "We kept an eye on each other in the early going. Seko was the guy to beat, and when he took off, he just left us for dead," said Jones. "He had so much power that it was all over once he left us. Seko was metronomic when he ran, with no knee lift. He had perfected that style. He was awesome."

Seko came across the finish line in 2:11:50, good for $40,000 and a new Mercedes, 47 seconds up on Jones, who outkicked Smith in the last 200 meters. Seko "kind of surprised you," says Castro. "He wasn't the most fluid runner; he was just tenacious."

Seko was well-recognized in the United States, said Pat Lynch, invited athlete coordinator for John Hancock. "Seko was one of the people in the sport with real charisma. Along with Deek, Juma (Ikangaa), (Gelindo) Bordin, and Steve Jones, he had that charisma. Seko was a known person here; he had run here twice, and because of the mystique surrounding him, it was a big deal when he won."

A Last Shot at Olympic Glory

Later in 1987, Seko was once again felled by injuries, and his prospects for making the Japanese team going to the Seoul Olympics were dim. Japan does not have a separate trials race, but selects its Olympians based on their performances at important Japanese marathons. For the 1988 Olympics, the two races designated for Olympic hopefuls were

Toshihiko Seko celebrates his 2:11:50 win at Boston in 1987.

Fukuoka and Tokyo. Because of injuries, Seko could not run either of them, but Japanese officials bent over backwards to aid his comeback attempt, extending the qualifying period to include the Lake Biwa Marathon. Two spots had been taken, by Taniguchi and Nakayama, and Seko trained to make that last place on the team.

Seko prepared by going to a *gasshuku* in Okinawa early in January 1988. He ran 30 to 50 kilometers a day, with speedwork mixed in. At the end of the month-long training camp, Seko said he felt ready for a sub-14-minute 5K. After the *gasshuku*, he put in another period of intense training, capped by a 40-kilometer time trial in 2:03. On a very hot day, Seko ran 2:12:41 at Lake Biwa. Two other Japanese runners also trying for the last spot on the Olympic marathon team had run faster at Tokyo and Fukuoka, but Seko was chosen, partly because of the weather at Lake Biwa.

In the Seoul Olympic Marathon, Seko ran in the pack in the early going, eventually finishing eleventh, as Italy's Gelindo Bordin won the race. But he wasn't disappointed, and he crossed the line with an ecstatic look on his face, his fists clenched, in what Japanese call a "guts pose." It's not just raising your arms at the finish, but raising them and clenching your fists, as if to say, "Yeah, I did it," explains Reilly. That caused some consternation in Japan, where critics wondered what Seko was celebrating, since he hadn't won.

Seko was ecstatic that he had come back from injury and had placed higher than at the Los Angeles Olympics four years earlier. He finally had his redemption for Moscow and Los Angeles. Seko says Seoul was his best race, because the previous year had been such a struggle. Soon afterwards, Seko announced that he was going to retire on December 18, 1988, after the International Chiba Ekiden.

Seko's last race was moving, an event of national importance. "Who won the race was incidental," explains Reilly, who compares it to baseball player Lou Gehrig's retirement ceremony at Yankee Stadium in 1939. More than 10,000 people showed up to watch Seko, not to see him at the top of his racing; that was past. Rather, they came to pay their respects to this man who for almost exactly a decade (from his first Fukuoka win on December 3, 1978) had come to symbolize Japanese running. "Just to see that race was really something special," recalls Reilly.

Following Mr. Nakamura

With the pressures of training for the marathon gone, Seko became a different person after he retired. He was much more open, much more outgoing in public, much more a "regular" person. He opened up to people and they liked him. "Toshihiko is very down to earth, and a great guy," says Brian Sheriff. "He's a family man, the complete opposite of his image. He came up to me at a race, introduced himself and asked where I was from. Then he advised me on my prerace meal." Seko took over as coach of S & B, and now the circle has been completed for him: He is the one standing along the loop outside the Jingu Garden near the National Stadium, in the same spot where Nakamura once stood. He is there watching his runners, coaching the same teams Nakamura did. But he is not the same as Nakamura; he is lighter, more relaxed, trying to let his runners have some fun, to expose them to the things he missed. For example, he takes a group of runners to Europe to run in some of the summer track races.

Seko is there in Tokyo, carrying on the strong Japanese marathoning tradition, waiting and watching for the next Toshihiko Seko to emerge. Japan has had several world class marathoners, both men and women, since Seko retired. Hiromi Taniguchi won the 1991 World Championships Marathon held in Tokyo. Taniguchi, in marked contrast to Seko, was garrulous at races and always telling stories. Near disaster struck in the 1988 Olympics when someone stepped on his foot, pulling off his shoe. Instead of getting angry, Taniguchi shrugged his shoulders afterwards, saying *Sho ga nai*, or "Well, it couldn't be helped." That response endeared him to his countrymen. Brendan Reilly puts it this way: "Seko is more respected in Japan, Taniguchi is more loved."

Then, at the 1992 Barcelona Olympic Games, Koichi Morishita and Yuko Arimori won silver medals in the men's and women's marathon, and Japanese runners also took fourth in both races. And at the 1993 Stuttgart World Championships, Japanese women won the gold and bronze in the marathon. Still, says Reilly, Seko will never be replaced. "Seko is still the guy in Japan. He made his mark and is a god for life in Japan."

14

Train Smarter, Not Harder

Born February 27, 1957, Australia

World record: marathon, 2:08:18

World Championship gold, marathon, 1983

Commonwealth Games gold, marathon, 1982 and 1986

Rob de Castella came to the United States in the summer of 1981, still unknown to most of the world, to compete in a series of road races. After finishing third to Americans Herb Lindsay and Jon Sinclair at the Maple Leaf Half-Marathon in Vermont (where Lindsay set the American record), he attended a running camp in Winter Park, Colorado. One evening after dinner, the day's workouts done, the campers sat relaxing over a beer, telling stories and chatting about training with the amiable Australian. The inevitable question came up, as it always does with elite runners: "What's your secret?"

All at once de Castella's smile vanished and his face hardened. Setting his beer down, he leaned across the table and answered in a low voice tinged with steel: "Nothing gets in the way of my workout." Then, after a moment's pause, he added emphatically, *"Nothing!"*

There were several seconds of silence as the campers were taken aback by the seriousness of his response. Then, just as quickly, de Castella leaned back and took another sip of beer. A quick smile broke the serious mood, and the relaxed, friendly Aussie was back, open to talking about what it takes to be a world-class runner.

"Running well is a matter of having the patience to persevere when you are tired, and not expecting instant results," he said. "The only secret is that it is consistent, often monotonous, boring, hard work. And it is tiring."

"Then what keeps you going?" he was asked.

De Castella, or Deek as he's known to runners around the world, leaned forward again, this time eagerly, and his eyes flashed as he said, "To run well you have to run with a passion. If that is quenched, you can't do it."

Draining his beer, he got up from the table, saying, "And I have a passion for running."

In that brief exchange were seen the two, seemingly irreconcilable, sides of Rob de Castella—an unruffled, friendly, outgoing demeanor that takes things in stride, coupled with a drive and commitment to running as solid as the Australian continent; a drive, he said that day, to become the best marathoner in the world.

In the following years, de Castella did just that in running to a stellar record: A world record of 2:08:18 in the Fukuoka Marathon, two Commonwealth Games gold medals, the first-ever World Championships gold medal, and wins at New York and Boston (2:07:51), along with scores of road victories over shorter distances and several world bests, and he's the only man to finish in the top ten in three Olympic Marathons.

De Castella was born in Kew, a suburb of Melbourne, on February 27, 1957, the eldest son of Rolet and Anne de Castella. Rolet, an executive with the Nestle Corp., and Anne, a part-time nurse, were able to provide their five sons and two daughters with an upper-middle-class life, including education at Jesuit schools. Rolet also gave Rob something else that was to be the foundation of his athletic career—an approach to running that saw the sport as something to be enjoyed, not a chore to be endured.

When Rob was 11, he started accompanying Rolet on his early-morning jogs, often making a game out of finding shortcuts to beat his father home. Rolet, says Deek, was one of the three major influences on Rob's athletic life, someone with whom he could always discuss training and racing. Rolet, a bit of a character, puts his whole effort into whatever he is doing. If Rolet was going to paint the family house when Rob was growing up, he wouldn't just buy a can of paint and a brush. That'd be too easy. Rather, "He'd put on three layers of filler, four layers of undercoat, and another three layers of paint," says Rob. "His attitude is that if something is worth doing, it's worth doing well." That attitude was ingrained in Deek as well.

Armed with his father's determination, commitment, and even fanaticism, tempered by a running-as-enjoyment attitude, Rob joined the cross-country team at Burke Hall, where he was the fourth or fifth best runner on the squad. He played other sports, mainly Australian rules football and cricket, but did not excel at them. He was strong, but a bit awkward. De Castella knew he had chosen the right sport at Burke after he won his first race, a 400-meter dash.

"I went out really hard and ended up dying like a shot duck. It's just one of those special things you remember when you're little." The race was motivating, Deek says, because winning "makes you feel a little different and helps you enjoy the running."

Because he liked the improvement he was seeing in himself and the satisfaction running was already giving him, Deek, 14, decided to join the cross-country team in the fall of 1971 when he entered Melbourne's Xavier College, a preparatory school comparable to a U.S. high school. In one of those serendipitous twists of fate that make you think the gods must be runners, de Castella's history teacher and cross-country coach at Xavier was Pat Clohessy, a former top Australian middle-distance runner. Clohessy was a two-time NCAA three-mile champ (1961-62) at the University of Houston who had seen his promising career cut short by injuries. He knew how to coach; Deek had the motivation to run; and beginning in 1971, they formed one of the most productive, rewarding coach/athlete relationships ever.

At first, Deek was just one of the pack in the large group of Xavier runners, finishing in the middle of the field in cross-country races. But under Clohessy's creed of gradual adaptation to higher levels of fitness through relaxed, consistent training, Deek became stronger and fitter until he was the best in the school. Talent had a lot to do with it, but, "I got better as the races got longer," Deek says. "I was able to master the training, stick to it consistently, and gradually I started to improve. That was more motivation. And the farther I went, the stronger I got, and I just kept it going."

There was an incident in an early race at Xavier that made a career-long impression on Deek. Running on a muddy cross-country course, one of his shoes came off his foot after getting stuck in the mud. Deek, mad at himself for not lacing up his shoe tighter, sprinted off , running faster. He ended up improving 20 places after losing his shoe, something that made him realize that "by being aggressive with myself, I could draw out a much improved performance."

This kind of aggressive running, what he calls "running over the top of people," became one of de Castella's trademarks and helped him start winning regional races. His last year at Xavier, when he was 17, Deek broke several Australian junior records that had been held by Aussie greats Ron Clarke and Herb Elliott. The highlight came in the summer of 1974, when he broke 1960 Olympic 1,500-meter gold medalist Elliott's junior two-mile record by clocking 8:46.

The Tree Begins to Grow

From their first season together in 1971, Clohessy believed Deek had the potential to be a world-class marathoner, because he had strength, dedication and, most importantly, a personality that was able to accept the need for long-term planning. It would be eight years before de Castella would run a marathon, but Clohessy knew from the start his protégé had the ability to be the best in the world.

By the time de Castella arrived at Xavier, Clohessy had refined his coaching ideas into a system he calls "complex training," which, despite its name, is quite simple; it has a certain workout for each day of the week, with the same pattern repeated 52 weeks a year. The emphasis varies depending on the phase of training.

It's called complex training because it incorporates many varied aspects of running into a weekly schedule. Under this system, there is not a specific build-up phase, followed by a peaking phase; the base work is done over years of injury-free training, with the peaking done through what de Castella calls "freshening up."

Deek took to Clohessy's training like a koala bear to a eucalyptus tree. He raced well over a wide range of distances after finishing school at Xavier in 1974 and enrolling at Melbourne's Swinburne College. There, he began training with older runners on their long runs on dirt trails in the forests, starting out at 12 miles for the Sunday runs and eventually being able to keep up as the distances got longer.

After one Sunday run when Deek was 17, one of the senior runners came up to talk with Clohessy, recounts Brian Lenton in his *Through the Tape*, complaining that Deek was starting to push the pace of the long runs. Clohessy didn't say anything; he just smiled at this sign that de Castella was moving up to the next level.

Training partner Chris Wardlaw, a 1976 and 1980 Australian Olympic marathoner, nicknamed Deek "Tree" because of his strong legs, which have often been compared to Australian gum trees. That strength meant Deek never missed a workout, even when he was up late, which was apt to happen at times. Lenton tells the story of how Deek was once blindfolded as a prank by his fellow Boy Scouts, brought out to the countryside, and dropped off. He had to run home at 3 A.M., then get up a few hours later for a cross-country race. He raced wearily with bags under his eyes. When Clohessy found out, he told Deek, "If you ever do that again, you're off the team." Deek never did it again.

"Train smarter, not harder," was Deek's training program motto. This refers not just to the actual workouts, but to everything in a runner's life. "Being an athlete means living a certain kind of lifestyle," Deek said. "You don't recover from a late night out in one day—sometimes it can take up to a week. To be a top runner, you have to make choices."

Deek learned that the hard way during the transition period after graduating from Xavier and starting to run with Clohessy's more experienced runners. (Swinburne College did not have a team, and Deek stayed with Clohessy after finishing at Xavier.) He did not always run as well as he and Clohessy thought he should, though Deek was winning senior races now and becoming one of Australia's top runners.

Deek was going out and having fun at night, while at the same time increasing his mileage. But because he was not getting enough rest, he wasn't "absorbing the training," Deek says. "If you are training but resting little, your performances will often fluctuate dramatically."

When he was 18, de Castella clocked 29:11.8 for 10,000 meters on the track, then improved to 28:50.4 the following year. In 1977, he had a taste of international racing, finishing 137th in the World Cross-Country Championships in Dusseldorf, Germany.

The turning point in his career came at the 1979 World Cross-Country Championships in Limerick, Ireland. Deek ran poorly and finished devastated in 62nd place. Deek had been steadily improving and thought he would run better. But he wasn't even the top Australian at the race, as he had expected to be. Deek was at a crossroads; two paths diverged into the future following that race, and de Castella took the more difficult one. That night Deek took inventory of his life, realizing that his poor showing came about because he wasn't focused. He decided he was going to dedicate himself to becoming a world-class runner.

De Castella got his first chance to show his new attitude a week later at the Cinque Mulini cross-country race in Milan, Italy. It's one of the unique races of the world, with a course, crowded with spectators, that winds through five barns. It attracts many of the top competitors from the World Cross-Country Championships, and Deek redeemed himself with an eighth-place finish, just behind British miler Steve Ovett. After the race, Clohessy took de Castella for a walk to get some *gelati*, telling him, "This is what you can do if you discipline yourself, if you want it badly enough. If you really want to succeed, you have the ability. The rest is up to you."

That 1979 trip to Europe was important for two other reasons: Deek read British star Brendan Foster's biography and was struck by one sentence in particular that seemed to encompass what it means to be a long-distance runner: "All top international athletes wake up in the morning feeling tired and go to bed feeling very tired." It was a line Deek would remember often through the years of training that lay ahead.

Also, it was on this European trip that Deek became friendly with the third great influence (after his father and Clohessy) in his life, Gayelene Clews, a dynamic, talented Australian runner. They had met three years earlier when Gayelene, then 13, asked the 17-year-old de Castella for an autograph after he won the Australian cross-country title in her hometown of Perth. In Europe, Gayelene, now 18, and Rob, 22, hit it off, spending most of the trip together.

"Basically, Robert's a good listener," Gayelene said, "and we fell in love."

They did not become a couple for another year, since Gayelene lived in Perth, 800 miles from Melbourne. After a courtship through the mail, they married in 1980, when Rob moved to Perth to prepare for the Moscow Olympics.

"There has to be a lifestyle that provides support for anybody wanting to be a top athlete," Gayelene says. "Rob had that all along, with the school system, with Pat (Clohessy), with his parents, who really encouraged him, and with his relationship with me."

It was after the 1979 European trip that Deek started to think he could be a world-class runner, telling Brian Lenton,

The incredible contrast in those two racing performances (in Limerick and Milan) was very motivating and showed I had the potential to be a good runner. Once I realized that, it was just a matter of making a commitment to train hard and become more professional and serious in my approach.

"But you never know," he recalled years later. "I was hoping I could make it (as a world-class runner). You always have to believe you can be the best, even if you don't know whether you'll get there."

Becoming a Marathoner

Clohessy knew Deek would get there when he won the 1979 Victoria Marathon Championship in 2:14:44, six months after Cinque Mulini. That was his first marathon, and the win qualified Deek for the Australian national championships, where he took another win, in 2:13:23.

Next up was the 1980 Australian Olympic Marathon Trials. Deek took a year off from his studies at Swinburne College so that he could train full-time. He and Gayelene moved to Ferny Creek, a town in the mountains where Australian great Ron Clarke had trained. De Castella was fit and motivated, and his mileage reached 145 to 150 per week. But even with careful coaching and preparation, Deek fell victim to overtraining. With plenty of time to train, he dug himself into a hole.

Deek found out just how deep the hole was one day when he came to the track for his regular session of 8 × 400 meters with a 200-meter float. Usually, the 400s were run in 63 to 64 seconds. This time, with the same effort, he hit the first one in 75, the slowest since he was a teenager. Clohessy did not let Deek finish the workout, instead sending him straight home to rest.

In hindsight, Deek realized he was not giving his body time enough to recover from the hard workouts. Instead of a hard/easy schedule, he was running hard/hard. Hard workouts make a runner stronger only if she or he can recover from them, de Castella says, and he was not recovering. Clohessy told Deek to have confidence in his fitness level and just jog, with no quality sessions or long runs. "It was recovery, recovery, recovery," Deek says. "Fortunately, I came right just before the trials."

De Castella climbed out of the hole to take second in the Olympic trials in 2:12:24. Each of the three marathons he had run so far had been faster than the last.

Deek was now an Olympian, but the joy of making the team was tempered by the realization that he might not get to compete in Moscow. U.S. President Jimmy Carter was pressuring allies to boycott the Olympics, to protest the Soviet Union's involvement in Afghanistan. After months of acrimonious public debate, with marathoner Chris

Wardlaw taking the role as athletes' spokesman, the Australian Olympic Committee voted to send a team to Moscow, despite the wishes of Prime Minister Malcom Fraser.

In Moscow, Deek trained in the forests outside the city with Wardlaw. The 1980 Olympic Marathon was a race of surges, and Deek was impressed by repeat winner Waldemar Cierpinski of East Germany, who let the leaders go on their surges, content to run a steady pace that eventually brought him to the front at 35 kilometers. It was a lesson in patience that Deek was to keep in mind in the years to come. "You can either go with all the surges and hope to be there at the end, or you can run like Cierpinski: run at a pace that maintains contact with the leaders but which does not dramatically change your tempo." Deek learned that Cierpinski's method was "the best way to do it."

Deek ran with Cierpinski and a large pack until 30 kilometers before losing contact and eventually finishing a satisfying tenth in 2:14:31.

Returning to Australia, de Castella took a job as a bio-lab technician at the Australian Institute of Sport, and had three months of good training before Japan's Fukuoka Marathon. There he ran eighth in 2:10:44, a nearly two-minute personal record that was the 14th fastest in the world in 1980. Toshihiko Seko of Japan won the race in this first meeting between the two. Seko was at a level higher than de Castella at that time, he says. "I wasn't racing Seko at Fukuoka; I was only running against him at that point in my career."

Back in Australia, de Castella ran shorter races through 1981, gearing his training toward a return to Fukuoka. He declined appearance money and an invitation to run the New York City Marathon in order to concentrate on his training. He had consistent 120-mile weeks of training throughout 1981, without any time off. Those close to him knew he was going to run well, as he had clocked 13:34 for 5,000 meters on the track before Fukuoka. So when he first came to the world's attention in December 1981 with his 2:08:18 win at Fukuoka, it was not a surprise to Clohessy, Gayelene, or his training partners.

Garry Bjorklund, the U.S. 10,000-meter Olympian from Minnesota, led the field at Fukuoka through a blistering pace. Deek and the rest of the runners, including Japan's Shigeru Soh and Ito, were hanging on to "BJ" even from the start.

Bjorklund, cut from the same tough mold as de Castella, had spent two months before Fukuoka isolated in upstate New York at a cabin owned by Bob Bright, race director for the Chicago Marathon. There he spent his time running, chopping wood, and working with the sled dogs Bright was training. "I was training to crack that 20- to 21-mile 'meltdown,' and Fukuoka is the ideal place for that, because it is flat as a pancake," Bjorklund said. "I wanted to run 15-minute 5Ks for as long as I could. My theory was that if I could run through 30K at that pace, there wouldn't be anyone around. And I was wrong."

De Castella and the Japanese hung on to Bjorklund, passing him at 30 kilometers with a surge that left BJ in awe. "When you're in the company of a de Castella and he has a flyer going, and he puts the hammer down and runs away from you when you're running as fast as we were, you can only shake your head."

Ito was the only one able to go with Deek, but he, too, soon fell back, and de Castella ran in alone to break Derek Clayton's course record by 1:18. "And Deek didn't look any worse for the wear afterwards," said Bjorklund. "I always tried to give an honest effort in a race, and Rob was strong enough to keep it going."

Deek, too, was known for giving an "honest effort." "I always like to run hard in my races. I have always believed that after a race you should know honestly within yourself that you couldn't have run any harder," he said in an interview with *Track & Field News*.

> If you go into a race to run as hard as you can, you won't be able to look back and think or say what you "might" have done. Likewise with my career, I don't want to get five or so years in the future and look back and say, "I wish I had done this or that." I want to do *now* everything that I feel I should be doing. I believe that fulfilling your potential and running the very best you can is more important than making as much money as possible by racing often.

De Castella's Fukuoka performance was the fastest marathon ever run on a loop course, five seconds off of Alberto Salazar's 2:08:13 at New York five weeks earlier. "To run so close to 2:08 was surprising, but it wasn't totally unbelievable," Deek said.

Deek's time, it turns out, was the world record until Steve Jones's 2:08:05 at Chicago in 1984, as New York was found to be short. (Salazar's time was eventually listed in the record books at 2:08:40).

As it was with Frank Shorter, Fukuoka is a favorite with de Castella, because it was the race that confirmed his entry into the ranks of the elite. According to Deek, Fukuoka was where he went from being "just" an international competitor to being "a real international force."

1982 Brisbane Commonwealth Games

After Fukuoka, de Castella was the overwhelming favorite at the October 1982 Brisbane Commonwealth Games, in which all the former colonies of the British empire compete. It was a major event for Australia, and the entire country was counting on Deek for a gold medal.

However, de Castella had a slight muscle strain in his back and was worried that he might have overtrained a bit and not given himself enough time to "freshen up." As was their habit, Deek and Clohessy got together and formulated a race strategy. Based on his Fukuoka performance, Clohessy figured the field would just sit on de Castella and let him set the pace. So the night before the marathon, Deek and veteran Kevin Ryan of New Zealand agreed to share the lead if the pace were to dawdle. As thousands of spectators and a shocked national television audience soon saw, that wouldn't be necessary.

Even before the predawn start, the staging area in Brisbane was filled with fans. Most knew that Deek had a time three minutes faster than any other entrant, and they were looking forward to a gold medal to celebrate the last day of the Commonwealth Games. But two Tanzanians were ready to crash Australia's party.

Gidamis Shahanga, 10,000-meter gold medalist a week earlier on the opening day of the Games, and his unknown teammate, tiny Juma Ikangaa, took off and left the field behind after the first 5 kilometers. Deek was not worried—at first. Clohessy had taught him that relaxation is key in racing as well as in training. Deek's theory of racing marathons, what he tells runners seeking advice, is:

> Run with the group the first half of the race, and don't worry about the time. Just be comfortable. In the marathon it is important to feel good the last five miles, to run up, run strongly and get carried along passing people, as opposed to tying up. During the first half of a marathon, look around, have fun, and watch the crowd and the surroundings. If you are hurting by 13 miles, you're in trouble. Then press and run aggressively over the last part of the race.

That theory was severely tested at Brisbane as the Tanzanians upped their tempo to close to 4:50 per mile, getting a big lead.

Deek was feeling great as he passed halfway, running well within himself with a pack that included Ryan and Scotland's John Graham. But Ikangaa and Shahanga were also feeling great and were well out of de Castella's sight, running below world-record pace on a very hot and humid day, on a very difficult course. Still following Clohessy's plan of holding back with the pack, Deek ran 5:05-mile pace through 15 miles, all the while falling farther behind Ikangaa and Shahanga. Sharing the lead, the Tanzanians had a two-minute lead by 15 miles. It looked like Deek, the fastest marathoner in the world, was destined to finish third.

"I watched the race from various points on the course, and didn't think Rob could win from so far behind," recalled Gayelene. Finally, Deek left the pack at 18 miles and took off alone after the Tanzanians, who were still a minute up. "Rob was just a dot way behind Juma and Gidemas that finally started getting larger and larger," says Dave Welch. Deek began running "aggressively" and at 23 miles a struggling Shahanga was finally within sight; he offered no resistance as Deek swept by.

Ikangaa was caught at 24 miles, but Juma was not going to relinquish the gold without a fight. After giving de Castella a look described as being "full of terror," the Tanzanian army colonel responded with a surge of his own. Deek caught back up and passed Ikangaa, but Juma retook the lead. Deek then repassed Ikangaa, who in turn repassed Deek again. Finally, Deek surged up a hill at 25 miles, and the tough Ikangaa was broken. Deek broke the tape in 2:09:18, in one of the greatest come-from-behind wins ever at a championship marathon. Those who have seen both courses say the Commonwealth win was as good or better than Deek's 2:08:18 at Fukuoka.

Deek said it was the confidence he had in Clohessy's training that kept his spirits up when he was chasing the Tanzanians. De Castella told Brian Lenton,

> I knew I had done the work. I kept believing I could win. I didn't know if I would, but I had to believe it was possible, or else I couldn't have kept pushing myself. I could have run a faster time; but I wasn't out to run a fast time, I was out to win the gold medal. It was an incredibly emotional experience to feel as though you were out of it at one stage, and then catching the leaders, passing them, and finally running away from them.

It also thrilled Australia, making Deek a national hero. The response from the public was overwhelming, as he was featured in several television commercials and feted by the Prime Minister. The Commonwealth win illustrated to the world who de Castella the marathoner was. He is able to relax when necessary, but can summon great concentration when racing. "What amazes me is the way Rob can block everything out," says long-time training partner Derek Froude. "He'll run so hard in races he'll come in with bloody feet and missing toenails. It's something unique."

Reaching the Top

After his Commonwealth win, Deek was acknowledged as one of the two best marathoners in the world, along with the undefeated Alberto

Salazar. Deek, like Salazar, always wanted to race the best. Both were having their business affairs handled at the time by International Management Group (IMG), and they agreed to hook up in the spring of 1983.

It appeared at first that a new race would be set up for them on Australia's Gold Coast, but the $100,000 proposal was nixed by the IAAF. So, the showdown came instead at Rotterdam; the course was fast, the weather promised to be good, and a top field, including Mexican Rodolfo Gomez and Carlos Lopes of Portugal, was already lined up.

"Rob and Alberto were the two fastest marathoners ever, both seemingly unbeatable. Throw in Gomez and Lopes, and it was a classic, one of the watershed races in running, because it brought worldwide attention to the marathon," says Dave Welch.

Indeed, the media loved it, hyping the race as if it were a world championship boxing match. Deek versus Alberto. The fastest ever on a loop course versus the fastest ever on a point-to-point course.

Deek told journalist Brian Caulfield before the race.

We decided that we wanted to race against each other. There's been a lot of talk about whose marathon was the faster, who had the world record, and who was the better runner. There is no way you can compare performances on different courses. You have to be in the same race on the same day. This was something both of us felt.

De Castella knew he was ready when he ran a world record of 42:47 in winning the Gasparilla 15K in February. Deek spent time training isolated in a forest in the weeks leading up to Rotterdam. As always, he remained calm. (On the bus to race starting lines, he could often be seen reading a book while others frittered away energy. "No sense using up excess energy," he explains. "The race will be here soon enough.")

Despite what papers might have tried to stir up, there was no animosity between Deek and Alberto. De Castella admired Salazar and still considers him a good friend. They had dinner together the week before the race, warmed up for a track workout together, and Salazar even lent Deek his Finnish masseur, Ilpo. Deek told Jon Hendershott before the race,

Salazar is without a doubt one of the most competitive and determined of all athletes. He has incredible drive. We approach the marathon from different angles, Salazar concentrating on his speed and me on my strength. I've got a lot of respect for him— but I think I can beat him. When we meet, it should be a very close and exciting race.

And it was. Rotterdam was beamed live around the world and lived up to its billing. After the 8 A.M. start, John Graham tried to set the record pace he had been hired to do, but the top guns were content to watch each other and not go rabbit hunting. The first 13.1 miles were run in over 1:06, making a world record unlikely.

This was a race, though, not a time trial—these top marathoners were going for the win. The pack stayed together for 35 kilometers, when Salazar finally dropped back. Gomez then surged, with Lopes and de Castella taking off after him. The Mexican dropped off at 38 kilometers when Deek increased his speed and took the lead, with Lopes a step behind. Lopes followed directly behind Deek past 40 kilometers, with the pace getting faster and faster, until, 800 meters from the finish, Lopes began to pass the Australian. The race seemed to be Lopes's for the taking, as he had 27:30 10K speed to his credit.

But Deek would not give it away; he dug down, pumped his arms, lifted his knees, and pulled away from Lopes to win by two seconds. Deek's last mile was 4:32; the last 400 meters an astounding 61 seconds, and he finished in 2:08:37.

The race was a huge event in Australia and de Castella's influence in his country was tremendous. When he used a sponge to wipe off the back of his legs, after having to relieve himself during the race, many watching thought he was doing so to cool down his legs. So in races in Australia, you would see runners sponging off the back of their legs, just as they had seen Deek do on TV. That year, de Castella was voted more popular than the prime minister.

"I consider Rotterdam one of Rob's best races," says Gayelene, "because of the competition and the way he won it."

> It's a lot tougher to run that way than to run 2:07:51 on your own. On paper, it looked as if Carlos would be able to beat Rob in a sprint. But Rob didn't care what was on paper or that Carlos was faster. He outsprinted him, after he just kept winding it up and winding it up.

The rest of the world thought it one of Deek's best races as well, as he was now seen as the best marathoner in the world. De Castella looked to make that title official in August at the inaugural World Track & Field Championships Marathon in Helsinki.

Deek ran with the pack for the early part of the race. At 15 miles, there were still 18 runners in contention, including two-time Olympic champ Cierpinski. Deek did not take the lead until 34 kilometers, when a surge took him away from the field. Only Kebede Balcha of Ethiopia could follow him, and he stuck directly behind Deek for the next 4 kilometers. At

38 kilometers, the course turned onto a narrow path winding through a forest and up a hill. Deek surged here again, and at the top of the hill broke Balcha, and ran in waving to the crowds, wearing a big grin on his face when he entered Helsinki's historic Olympic Stadium to take the gold medal in 2:10:03. Balcha took the silver and Cierpinski outsprinted Sweden's Kahl Eric Stahl for the bronze.

Frank Shorter was among the many observers awed by Deek's power over the last six miles, which he ran in close to 4:50-per-mile pace. "De Castella is stronger over the last stages of a marathon than any marathoner ever before," said Shorter.

> He didn't take the lead until he was ready to make his move, and just ran hard when he needed to. He showed in this race that if anyone is going to beat him, he'll have to be ahead of him with six miles to go. To run the last six miles as fast as Rob did would be impossible for almost anyone else to do.

A large wreath was put on his head, and Deek jogged a victory lap inside the stadium, satisfied that he had proven he was indeed the best in the world.

1984 Los Angeles Olympics

Deek went into the Los Angeles Olympics as the clear favorite. There did not seem to be any tactic that could beat him. He had run 2:08:18 from the front at Fukuoka, won the Commonwealth gold from behind in the heat and humidity of Brisbane, beaten Salazar and outkicked Lopes at Rotterdam, and won the competitive World Championships over a hilly course.

The only thing missing from his resume, to perhaps complete his goal of being ranked the best marathoner ever, was to win the Olympic gold and defeat his one remaining rival, Toshihiko Seko of Japan. They would meet in Los Angeles in what Brendan Foster called "the greatest field of marathon runners ever assembled."

Foster, ex-Olympic record holder at 5,000 meters and world-record holder over 3,000 meters and two miles, was one of many picking Deek to win the race. Before Los Angeles, he wrote in *Olympic Heroes,*

> Rob de Castella is a warm, likable character, but ice runs through his veins when he is competing, and I expect to see him take command in the last third of what promises to be one of the greatest marathon races ever staged. He has proved himself able to

handle any pace and any situation. Deek never looked anything but a winner in the world championships in Helsinki, and has since been pouring all his considerable concentration and intelligence into preparing for the race of a lifetime.

Lining up against Deek were Salazar, Lopes, Seko, two-time defending champ Waldemar Cierpinski of East Germany, European champ Gerad Nijboer, Ikangaa, and several other fast Africans.

Deek trained in Canberra, then came to the United States and won again at Gasparilla. After that, he brought Gayelene and daughter Krista to Boulder, Colorado to get used to the time change and to train in isolation. In March, Deek ran a personal best 27:48 10K in the Continental Homes 10K, five seconds behind Tanzanian Zach Barie. Running a sub-28-minute 10K for the first time was motivating for Deek, despite getting outkicked: "It tells me my preparation for Los Angeles is right on schedule."

Faith in his training further boosted Deek's confidence; he said that with his complex training, he was continually getting stronger and fitter, as long as he was able to absorb his training. Deek could control his training, but not the television networks. A major difference between Helsinki in August 1983 and Los Angeles in August 1984 was the evening starting time in Los Angeles; it was great for American prime-time television viewers, but dangerous for the marathoners. Not only the hot weather and smog, but also the intangibles were against Deek, as he told journalist Marc Bloom.

> There are a lot of disadvantages—the pressure and the expectations, a lot of media attention. It's hard to concentrate and prepare without becoming distracted by the carrying ons. And I don't believe a favorite has ever won the Olympic Marathon, at least the last few.

Unfortunately, Deek was right—he finished fifth, in 2:11:12, while Lopes took the gold, followed by Charlie Spedding of England and first-time marathoner, Irishman John Treacy. Deek lost contact with the leaders between 30 and 35 kilometers, but never stopped running hard. "After I dropped back, I was in eighth place. At the end, I ran over a few people," to move back up to fifth.

It was Deek's single-minded focus that might have cost him the medal most thought he was going to get. After the World Championships, he had a year with no marathons before the Olympics. He cut down on his races to concentrate entirely on training, saying, "I might have overdone it, taking a year off, trying to give everything to L.A. In giving everything, I overtrained a bit . . . . That's the way I approached things."

As the Olympic favorite, de Castella was in great demand, which also hurt his preparations, as he had predicted. "There was too much happening, and I made the mistake before Los Angeles of doing too much traveling. You can't train hard and travel a lot."

Deek, however, does not offer any excuses. "The Olympics come only once every four years. You just have to prepare as well as you can and hope you are in great shape. It just didn't work out. It would have taken a spectacular run to beat Carlos that day. Chances are that no one could have beaten him." Deek shrugged off his Olympic disappointment and, after a short break, which included some skiing on his return to the Australian winter, he was right back into his old routine. He went back to his roots with Clohessy to recharge and plan for the future.

Coaching: Patience and Understanding

You cannot understand Rob de Castella without understanding Pat Clohessy, a man who has unselfishly given himself to coaching all levels of runners. He has become head coach at the Australian Institute of Sport since beginning to oversee Deek's training in 1971.

Clohessy is a "low-key" coach, the complete opposite of Percy Cerutty, the other famous Australian coach, who was known for his dogmatic approach to coaching. Cerutty's style was to tell his athletes what they should be doing; Clohessy, on the other hand, "will almost never tell you what to do," says Derek Froude.

> If Rob says he wants to run Rotterdam, Pat will say, "Great idea." Then he'll say, "Maybe your legs are tired, and maybe you want to give yourself more of a rest." He'll suggest more than tell an athlete what to do. Rob learned to read between the lines; when he'd say yes, more often than not that would mean no.

"Pat's greatest gift is his patience and his ability to spot talent," says Deek. "Pat has been essential not only as regards my training, but especially my mental and psychological approach to the sport," he said in Brian Lenton's *Through the Tape*.

> I have incredible respect for Pat's views on training and competition. Since I was 14, he has molded the way I have grown as an athlete. I believe that is the ideal role for a distance running coach.

Pat tries to mold an athlete into the type of person who knows himself, what he should be doing, and why he should be doing it. That is the approach Pat has taken with me. I still rely on him very strongly for a little more confidence prior to a race and also working with me in determining the best program of competition.

Another of Clohessy's coaching gifts is his ability to build up the self-esteem of runners. Deek learned that from the beginning with Clohessy, who always gave positive reinforcement to his athletes. "Pat *never* says anything negative. No matter how you run, he always finds something good to say that you can take away with you."

I remember one race where I didn't run well. I came off track, Pat came up, patting me on the back, saying, "You really looked great that last 100 meters!" That's the kind of guy he is.

Clohessy, Deek says, looks at the effort, not necessarily the result.

Clohessy won two NCAA titles at the University of Houston. He overtrained, however, before the 1964 Olympic Trials, and his bid for medals was cut down by foot and hip injuries. The injuries that kept Clohessy from the Olympics ended up helping Deek, because Clohessy learned that workouts such as 40 × 400 meters left him flat as a pancake.

Clohessy's ideas on training are rooted in a 1961 European track tour he took with the Arthur Lydiard-led New Zealand team that included Rome Olympic 5,000-meter champ Murray Halberg. From Lydiard, the celebrated New Zealand coach, Clohessy learned the importance of long runs, and from his injuries he embraced the concept of undertraining.

For over ten years, Deek averaged 120 miles a week, missing only about 15 days during that time. "I had to lay off for several days in 1981 or 1982, when I hurt my ankle," he recalled. "It takes so much training to build to a high level. You can lose fitness pretty quickly, and I figure it took me a long time to get in shape, so I never wanted to take too much time off."

The groundwork was laid in the Dandenong Hills outside of Melbourne. Clohessy brought his older athletes there, and Deek began doing Sunday runs with the group. Herb Elliott sprinted up the same hills, Ron Clarke ran his famous two-mile repeats up there (he'd run fast repeats up a steep hill, then get driven down to start his next repeat), and Clayton ran his 20-mile runs at a five-minute pace there. Clohessy modified Deek's training to prevent injury.

Said de Castella, "I have as much confidence in Pat as you can possibly have in another person. I think you can do it without a coach, but it's

Australian Running Tradition

Deek is the culmination of a deep and rich Autralian running tradition. The lineage stretches from miler John Landy, who waged the epic duel with Roger Bannister to be the first to break the 4-minute-mile barrier. Bannister did it first, running 3:59.4 on May 6, 1954, but Landy dropped the world record to 3:58.0 six weeks later in Turku, Finland. Bannister then beat Landy in the classic "Mile of the Century" at the Vancouver Empire Games (the predecessor to the Commonwealth Games).

Though he lost to Bannister, Landy sparked interest in Australian running, an interest that was increased by the 1956 Olympic Games in Melbourne. Landy begat a slew of top athletes: Pat Clohessy, Randy Thomas, and Herb Elliott, who set the mile world record, won the 1960 Rome Olympic 1,500-meter title, and retired undefeated. In the 1960s, Ron Clarke and Derek Clayton became two of the best runners in the world.

Clayton set two marathon world records. The second, 2:08:33.6 in Antwerp in 1969, was one of the greatest single runs ever. Clayton pushed himself so hard he was vomiting bile at the end, and he never fully recovered from that race, which stood as the record until 1981.

Clayton's ability to push himself past the limits of endurance is part of the Australian legacy that was passed on to Deek, but with a difference: Deek tempered his training, undertraining over years, while keeping Clayton's same ability to push himself in races.

Clayton suffered groin and spinal injuries that ended his career, because he trained harder, but not smarter. Deek succeeded because he took Clayton's iron will and softened it with Clohessy's hard-earned wisdom.

a lot harder to succeed. You have to be a very strong individual to do it." Starting with Clohessy's groups at Melbourne, he got used to group runs, and Deek trained with others his entire career. Some were elite, others high-schoolers.

Deek ran his off days at whatever pace he needed to recover. The regular 10-mile recovery was run in a quick 62 to 63 minutes, but at times he would slow down to a 7-minute-mile pace, if needed. You have to recover in order to absorb the training, he says, and that means running slowly at times.

"If you are running with someone who is running faster than you want or need to, just turn off, and go another way," Deek said. "That way they'll be out of sight so that you won't be tempted to pick up the pace."

De Castella was always willing to share his training with anyone who, like him, had a passion for running. And most were surprised at the simplicity of his "complex training."

The program is basic, yet powerful when followed for years, as Deek was able to do. There are long runs Sunday (22 miles) and Wednesday (18 miles), hill repeats on Tuesday, track intervals Thursday, and a race or tempo run Saturday. Deek's heaviest training loads included weeks of up to 145 miles, but surprisingly, one of the keys to de Castella's training was that he often left workouts "feeling like I could have done more, if I had to."

"You need variety in your training, and you have to be able to train at a high level for years," de Castella explains. "You have to have a long-term approach." Under Clohessy's tutelage, Deek repeated the same simple workouts week after week, year after year, until he was the strongest marathoner in the world.

Deek was also blessed with good genes, says training partner Barbara Moore, the 10,000-meter bronze medalist (32:42) at the 1990 Commonwealth Games in Auckland. "Rob has ability; great ability. He has unbelievable talent, plus he put in all that hard work." De Castella, friends and family agree, has incredible mental discipline; not the discipline to do each workout as hard as possible, though he was capable of running tremendous sessions (for example, once doing three miles of sprinting the straights and floating the turns in 13:42, at altitude). Rather, it was the discipline to be consistent and stick to Clohessy's training schedule, no matter where he was or what he was doing. As his strength built up, he was able to handle more and more mileage, which in turn made him even stronger. The cycle then kept on repeating, like clockwork. "Consistency is the secret to improvement and success," Deek says. "You have to keep training when others lose interest."

Few know de Castella better than Derek Froude. The marathoner from New Zealand trained with Deek for many years. Froude says

His [Deek's] strength is his consistency. He rarely missed a day because of injury. He has a lot of natural strength. None of his workouts, relative to other runners of his stature, are so difficult. But he was just so consistent. Rob is a great believer in not overtraining any one day or any one week.

Says de Castella, "Injury and illness are the two great enemies of runners. Once you make up your mind that you are an athlete, you do the things necessary to succeed." That includes going to sleep early even when you'd rather stay up and have fun. Deek is a night person who loves to socialize or read at night; but he forced himself to go to bed early. "One hour of sleep before midnight is worth two afterwards," he'd say, leaving a party as it was getting into full swing.

"There's no sense doing the workouts if you aren't going to get enough rest. You can keep it going for a while, but eventually it catches up with you," Deek said. Once he made the commitment to be a world-class runner, he was very careful to get nine hours of sleep a night.

Deek took the same pragmatic approach to all parts of his training; for instance, he liked to drink coffee in the mornings, but when he thought it might be affecting his adrenal glands, he gave it up, cold turkey.

Clohessy's creed of gradual adaptation to training and racing within the body's present level of tolerance is geared toward getting his runners stronger and fitter over years. "It's like putting money in the bank," Deek would say, heading out on a run. "You clock in and clock out." Deek built up to his 20-mile-a-day training gradually, starting with 50 miles a week when he first entered Xavier. The sessions gradually got faster, but the basic weekly schedule never changed; the emphasis just varied depending on the season.

When Deek woke up each morning, he never had to think about what he was going to do: every Tuesday for 15 years was a hill session, every Thursday, 8 × 400 meters on the track, every Sunday a 22-mile run. "If I had to think about what I was going to run each day, I'd have trouble getting out the door."

When asked once if he thought U.S. distance runners didn't train hard enough, Deek responded, "No, not at all. There are plenty of runners in the United States who work hard. But *training hard* means *training consistently*, and doing it with *patience and confidence*."

He added, "I think the only solution for U.S. running is to develop a club system. And there needs to be an accreditation system for coaches."

Hill Workouts

One of the foundations of Deek's training program was his weekly hill session. In Canberra, he'd incorporate the hills into a 10-mile fartlek run; his favorite loop had 12 hills of varying lengths which would be run nearly all-out. In Boulder, where de Castella spent half the year after the '84 Olympics, he favored a workout that started, after a 20-minute warm-up, with a two-mile sustained run in about 9:40. After a

Sunday:	Long; hilly, 22-mile run.
Monday:	Recovery. A.M., 10 miles; P.M., 6 miles.
Tuesday:	Hills. 2-3 mile tempo run, followed by 8 hill re-peats; or hilly, 30-minute fartlek run.
Wednesday:	Long. A.M., 18 miles; P.M., 6 miles.
Thursday:	Track session, such as 8 × 400 meters or 16 × 200 meters.
Friday:	Recovery, same as Monday.
Saturday:	A.M., race or tempo run; P.M., 6 miles.

short jog to one of two hills, either on Dellwood or Gillaspie Avenues, he'd run the hill eight times at a very strong effort. Each was never more than a minute of hard running.

"Hill running is maybe the best overall training you can do," Deek said. "It makes you strong, helps you get faster, and improves your running form." It is more important to run strongly and aggressively for a short hill then to go longer and lose form, he says. "Hills are a great way to simulate sprinting when you're tired at the end of a race."

De Castella was not concerned with timing the hill repeats; it was the effort that mattered. There are different ways to run hills, and Deek says the greatest benefit comes from sprinting all-out at the start of a short, fairly steep hill, rather than running steadily and trying to sprint at the end.

"That way you get the lactic acid built up immediately, and you must concentrate on maintaining your form all the way to the top." During one hill session with the group, one runner stopped before the end of the hill. When the runner was told he should run to the end, Deek disagreed, saying, "The top of the hill is wherever you make it."

Track Workouts

Deek was sometimes accused of being "slow," but there were several races in his career in which he outkicked runners with faster track times. The reason Deek never broke 28 minutes for 10,000 meters on the track was that he was always training for the marathon. His speed, which was enough to run a 58-second 400 meters at the end of a 10,000, came from three standard track workouts, plus the hill session. On the track he rarely ran more than three miles total, including the rest intervals. His basic track workouts were:

- 8 × 400 meters in 63-68 seconds, with a 200-meter "float" for recovery.
- 12 laps of sprinting the straights and floating the turns.
- 16 × 200 meters, in 30-32 seconds, with a 100-meter recovery.

The 400-meter intervals were tough because of the 200-meter float, often run in 45 seconds. If he had wanted, Deek could have taken a full recovery in between each 400 and run them faster. These intervals Deek called an "anaerobic threshold" session. (He defines anaerobic threshold as "your fastest maintainable speed.") He'd go over his threshold on the 400s, then drop down just below the threshold on the recovery, before starting another 400.

"We had a few classic workouts," Froude explains, "but nothing really of great difficulty. But for the 400 intervals, the range was enormous, depending if Rob was recovering in the winter versus when he was in peak shape and flying."

The entire three miles might be run in 15:30 on a "bad day," with the 400s run in 68 seconds, down to 14 minutes on a day when Deek was "flying." "Some people could do the 400 workout once, but it's the consistency over years that counts," says Froude.

The track sessions were much less in quantity than those of Arturo Barrios, Priscilla Welch, Lisa Martin, Lorraine Moller, or the local university runners. Barrios and de Castella had many discussions about training over the years, finally "agreeing to disagree on training ideas," says Froude. "Rob did less specific quality than Arturo. They are two totally different athletes, and neither is right or wrong."

In track workouts, Deek emphasized "aggressive" running "up over the ground," keeping up on his toes. "I like to wear spikes for track workouts year-round, so my legs are always used to the spikes." Track workouts started with a 25-minute warm-up, at a relaxed pace, around 6:30 per mile. The warm-up loops, as with all Deek's runs, were standard and never varied. Like Joan Benoit, he felt running the same loops made it easier to be consistent.

Even after his medals and wins, it was the physical act of running that remained its own reward for Deek, just as it had been for the 11-year-old trying to keep up with his Dad. After one interval session on a cold, dark evening on an empty track, with only a flapping flagpole for company, he said, "I got as much satisfaction out of that run as any I've ever done."

Recovery Runs

Recovery is an integral part of complex training. The purpose of recovery runs, Deek said, was "to absorb the harder sessions. So the distance and pace should be whatever it takes you to recover." For Deek, the runs were sometimes between a 6:00 and 6:20 pace, but other days, when Deek was feeling a bit "stuffed," they were easy enough that high-school runners could keep up.

"I first met Rob at Stramilono, in Italy, in 1979," recalls Barbara Moore. "We went out on some training runs, and he used to tell me how fast I trained." The ability to run easy is just as important as the ability to run hard workouts, Deek says.

One runner in the group who never ran easy was top American marathoner Kirk Pfeffer. Sometimes on a 15-kilometer recovery run, Pfeffer would be 50 meters ahead of the group after the first mile. Deek could only shake his head, telling Kirk, "There's a difference between running slow and running easy." But the talented Pfeffer (with a 2:10 marathon PR) could not grasp that concept, and his promising career was cut short by injury. Pfeffer set the world junior record for the marathon by running 2:17 when he was 17 years old. "If Kirk could have trained like Deek did, he might also have run 2:07," said Catrina Campbell, a coach at Oklahoma State University. "But not too many people could train like Deek. That's why there's only one of him."

Long Runs

The key to Deek's strength and success were his regular long runs of two to two-and-a-half hours. "Long runs are the hardest part of training to do, and the Sunday long run is the most important part of my training," he said, something even the most casual observer would be able to tell from the all-star group that showed up for the weekly 22-miler that started from Deek's house on Poplar Avenue in Boulder. You could look around the training group and count the gold medalists and world-record holders. Neighbors within a stone's throw included Arturo

Barrios, Rosa Mota, Steve Jones, Ingrid Kristiansen, and Priscilla Welch. Deek was a gracious host, and runners in town knew he'd be leaving his house at 9 every Sunday morning. Sunday runs were a great social event; Deek worked hard when it was time to train, but would relax afterwards, serving tea and bagels.

The pace on Sunday long runs, as on all his runs, started out very slowly, but gradually picked up to close to six-minute miles. When a visitor, such as American distance ace Pat Porter, would visit Boulder from his home in Alamosa, a high and isolated town five hours to the southeast, the tempo would dip down to near 5:40 pace.

The long run wound through a residential section of town, then past the 5-mile mark at the Boulder Reservoir, where dirt roads and rolling hills began. Deek would run the hills hard, leaving the slower runners behind, then regroup and run the downhills with the others. "Running the uphills strongly is a way a faster runner can run with slower runners," he said. At the base of Old Stage Road, the 18-mile mark of the 22-mile loop, was a very steep, mile-long hill. Once a cyclist came by at the base, passing the group, saying as he sped by, "I'll see you guys at the top." Deek kept running steadily, and by halfway up the hill had passed the startled cyclist. At the top Deek was standing there, waiting for the cyclist. "Reckon so," was all he said, a grin on his face.

While some in the group would struggle to finish the long run, Deek was always running well within himself. Invariably, he would pick up the pace the last mile, to simulate running hard at the end of a marathon; "I do that to get used to sprinting after two hours of running," he said. The 22 miles would take anywhere from 2:10 to 2:18; Deek thought it best to run for the time he'd be on his feet in a race, not the full marathon distance, during training.

De Castella always liked training with other people, elite or not. Running with a group gives stability to a training program, he says, because it makes you accountable to do a workout on a specific day at a specific time. This helps you train consistently, which is more important than doing any individual workout as hard as possible.

Absorbing the workouts is harder a mile above sea level, and as a concession to Boulder's thin air, de Castella switched his track intervals to Fridays, giving himself an extra day of rest to ensure, once again, that he was getting the full benefit from his hard days. Another adjustment to living at 5,400 feet included more recovery between intervals.

"Training at altitude is harder than training at sea level. With the group we had, the quality sessions were really tough. Everyday, someone in the group would be feeling good," Deek said. "There are still a

Robert de Castella's strength and success were due largely
to his regular two-hour runs.

lot of unanswered questions about altitude, and we might have overdone it while in Boulder [from 1984-92]."

There are two aspects to running well, de Castella believes: skeletal
strength and cardiovascular fitness. By putting a wide range of variety
into the weekly workouts, complex training was always increasing both.
Long runs are the key workout because that's where you get skeletal
strength; that built-up-over-years strength in turn allows you to avoid
injuries and do the intervals, tempo runs, and hill sessions that increase
cardiovascular fitness. Deek had such a long career because his strength
came before his fitness.

"Injuries come when your fitness level exceeds your strength level,"
he explains. Find your own optimum level of training and stick with it
consistently, Deek advises.

"You have to understand the theory behind the training, so that you have faith in the workouts and don't go jumping about from one system to another. That's how you get hurt." Being a top runner means facing the ups and downs of training, racing, and life with equanimity. When he had a bad training session, Deek would shrug it off with "No worries; I'll be out banging away again tomorrow."

De Castella's philosophy is summed up in the axioms he would refer to on training runs over the years; one is the simple idea that: "There are no shortcuts."

Be patient and look long-term, Deek advises runners, both elite and beginning, who ask him for advice: "If you go on a crash course of training, you'll end up crashing and burning."

From 1979, when he won his first marathon, to 1992, when he began the "process of retiring" after the Barcelona Olympic Games, Deek averaged 105 miles a week. During that period, his times dropped from 2:14 in his first marathon to 2:07:51, from 30 minutes for 10K to 27:43, and he won scores of major races. All thanks to an unchanging series of workouts repeated in all seasons.

It's not the people with the most talent who succeed, Gayelene says. "It's the ones who keep putting in the training, putting in the training, putting in the training."

When the group would be off in a cold snowstorm or rainstorm, and conditions were at their worst, someone might complain about the weather. Deek would then yell out, his voicing rising against the wind, "What's the first rule?" The wet, soggy runners would respond with a drawn-out "Nooo whinjing"; the ensuing laughter invariably made the rest of the run easier. "Whinjing" is Australian slang for "whining or complaining." That's Deek: solid, rolling through his training with no complaints.

Motivation

De Castella was motivated by the recognition, wins, and medals, but also from seemingly minor things such as running a good hill or track session. Deek and training partner Steve Jones both said financial success had not dimmed their motivation to train, even after they had reached the top. Through the years, there were major races with big appearance fees that both passed up because they were not ready to run their best. "It's a matter of wanting to achieve something and enjoying it," Deek explained not long after being voted the top marathoner of the 1980s. "There are not many areas where people have a chance to be number one in their chosen fields." Being the best in the world is what drove Deek for years; it was the primary motivation for the races he picked, how he trained, and where he traveled.

Barbara Moore saw another motivating factor: "I think the reason Rob has been on top as long as he has is that he doesn't overrace, and he really enjoys his running. He's a serious, dedicated athlete, but he enjoys his training." A big part of that enjoyment came from his training partners. In Melbourne, he ran with "The Pack," a group headed up by two-time Australian Olympian Chris Wardlaw. In Canberra in the early 1980s, the training group included Deek's brother-in-law, Graham Clews, Derek Froude, elite female runner Lynne Williams, and physiologist Dick Telford. Lisa and Ken Martin also joined in for two years.

"The group in Canberra could match Rob stride for stride," recalled Froude. "Rob dominated the training, not in a physical sense, but by the force of his personality." Much of the training there was done on the soft trails of the Stromlo Forest, where a street is named "Deek Drive."

Once, an American 2:12 marathoner showed up for some training runs in Canberra. He was very competitive during the group runs (the antithesis of Deek's approach to training), picking up the pace in training and dropping people.

"It's the foolish idea that if you do a little more, faster, then you'll get better than the rest," de Castella says, "and it ignores the fact that you must train at your *optimal level*, not your *maximum level*." That went on for a while, until one day Deek showed up for the Wednesday morning long run with race numbers, which were handed out to his fellow runners as if to say, "So you want to race during training, then, by gosh, we'll race."

The group started off at a quick pace, and by the third of the scheduled 18 miles, the pace had dropped down to 5:05 per mile. The American was barely hanging on, and he was soon dropped by the leaders, who then hid in the trees—when he went struggling by, Deek and the others jumped out and jogged easily back home. Training never got competitive after that.

Deek didn't mind stopping for water or to wait for slower runners during training. He took interruptions in stride. "Rob always trained with a lot of people," said Gayelene.

> Some runners don't want to share what they know or don't want others to benefit from their experience. Rob's not like that at all. Because he knows he doesn't have some magic formula, he is really happy to see people improving, even people he is competing against. The point is that he has his own personal level of accomplishment, to be as good as he can be. And as a consequence of trying to be as good as he could be, he did become better than anyone else.

Race Preparation

De Castella prepared for a marathon through what he calls "freshening up." Five weeks before all his major marathons, he'd do a 30-miler, "which gives me confidence in going past the marathon distance." His father sometimes also did the 30-mile runs, carefully driving over the course beforehand and setting water bottles out along the route he and his son would follow. The only difference was Rob's 30-miler would take a little over three hours, while his father's would last five hours or more.

"On the 30-miler, you want to run to the point of depletion," Deek explained. "Your body will overcompensate, so that the next time you will move to a higher level. By going slower on the long runs, you burn more fat; if you run faster, you burn glycogen more quickly. The idea of all the long runs is that your body becomes more efficient." But, Deek warns, "there is a fine line between depleting and going too far and hurting yourself." After these very long runs, Deek would walk for 15 minutes, then "take it quietly" for a couple of days,

The last long run, a 15-miler, was always "rolled through" 10 days before a marathon. That run was Deek's "depletion run" for the modified carbohydrate loading/depletion diet he followed before marathons. He'd cut out carbohydrates for two days before the depletion run, then gradually eat increasing amounts of carbohydrates such as potatoes, rice, and pasta.

The race countdown then began the week before the marathon: three miles at race pace five days before, two miles at race pace the next day, then one fast mile three days before the race. "You want to freshen up before a race; take it seriously if you are racing, and don't say you are using a race as a 'training run.'"

Deek always tried to go into races rested and at his peak. Those who do not, who say they are going into races as "training runs," face the risk of injury at worst, or staleness at best. What many runners forget is that the purpose of their training is to reach new levels in racing, Deek said. Before any competition, Deek would reduce both his mileage and the intensity of his workouts: To "sharpen up," he'd run a few short, fast track sessions, the most typical being 8 × 200 meters in 30 to 32 seconds, with a quick 100-meter float between. If a slower runner was with him, Deek would run in lane two so they could run side by side.

When you're racing a marathon, "you're really running off of your last four years of training," Deek says. No one workout is going to make the difference; success comes from the accumulated benefits of years of training. After one training run, Deek said, "When I struggle through a

10-mile run, I sometimes wonder how I can run 26 miles in 4:50 per mile. It always amazes me." Such is the mystery of the marathon.

A noticeable change came over the gregarious and laid-back de Castella when he raced. Says Froude, "There is more of a difference between how Rob trained and how he raced than anyone else. He's an intense competitor in a race. He's really quite capable of doing himself damage, because he just shuts out everything. He's often finished marathons physically quite ill."

Froude got an up-close example of that when he saw part of Deek's attempt to set a world record at 25K. De Castella ran 75 minutes, seconds off the world record, with Froude more than three minutes back in second. "Rob was nauseous, his feet were bloody; and he had just done himself in, when he didn't have to. It was quite awesome to watch; he just has a fierce determination in a race."

Deek had that determination even in minor races. Once he came out to support a five-mile race in Boulder with about 500 people, which was raising money for charity. He decided to push daughter Krista in a jogger stroller. But de Castella was not satisfied with just jogging through the race; he wanted Krista to be the first woman in, ahead of stars such as Rosa Mota, Lorraine Moller, and Barbara Moore.

Pushing the stroller, Deek went through the first mile in 5:09, and Krista had the lead. Things went fine for another half-mile, until the course took a sharp turn. Deek took the turn, but the stroller didn't, recalls local runner Conrad Truedson: "I looked behind me and the stroller was up on one wheel. The wheel fell off, and Rob had to stop. I thought he was out of the race, but at about four miles, he came flying by me, pushing Krista, with this . . . this look on his face." Krista ended up third, in 28 minutes.

"Rob's mental attitude is just amazing," says Gayelene.

It's his belief in his own ability. He's motivated to achieve his personal best. He measures performance in relation to how good he could be, rather than who he beats. When you race to be as good as you can be, you are consistently setting goals and working to achieve a level of constant improvement. In everything Rob does, he is constantly moving out of the comfort zone and setting new goals.

Another Run in the Windy City

In the fall of 1985, de Castella returned to Chicago to have a go at Steve Jones, who had set the world record there the year before, with Lopes second and Deek third. This year Jones took off from the start to finish in 2:07:13, with de Castella third in 2:08:48.

De Castella could have gone to any race in the world, running marathons he would be guaranteed of winning. But it's not surprising that Deek would go to Chicago to race against Jones, says Dave Welch.

> De Castella was running for pride. Deek was running to win races. Racing was what he was about, not about maximizing his income. He came out of the British/New Zealand/Australian tradition where you were going out to do the very best you can do.

In 1986, de Castella had a good year training in Canberra, getting ready for his first appearance at the Boston Marathon. John Hancock had signed on as sponsor; for the first time appearance money was paid, and a good field was signed up, including two-time New York winner Orlando Pizzolato of Italy, 1983 Boston winner Greg Meyer, and young Mexican Arturo Barrios, who would go on to dominate the roads that year.

Five weeks before the Boston Marathon, Deek did a 30-mile run, as before all his marathons; this time he ran at 9,000 feet above sea level.

After the 30-miler, Deek walked for a mile for two, and he kept it "quiet" for the next couple days of training; his quads were sore for several days, because of the 3,600-foot drop on the 30-mile loop.

But the downhill run paid off, because he flew down Boston's hills. De Castella crushed the field, passing 10 kilometers in 30:08 and 10 miles in 48:42, and passing halfway in 1:03:38 on his way to a course record 2:07:51, more than three minutes up on second-place finisher, Art Boileau. It was the third fastest marathon ever run at the time. Deek still rates it among his best races.

The training group in Boulder got larger and faster that summer when Steve Jones bought a house two blocks away from the de Castellas. The runners training with Deek knew each other better, meaning they could have fun and enjoy each others' company more, he said. He had three months of solid training leading up to the August Commonwealth Games Marathon.

In August, Deek repeated as Commonwealth Games gold medalist with a "comfortable" 2:10:15 win over Canada's David Edge. He wanted to set a Commonwealth record in the low 2:09s, "but the way the race went, it just wasn't on. Because I thought I would be running New York later in the year, I tried to conserve as much as I could so I could recover quickly and get back into training."

Running a marathon three months before New York was putting his performance at the Big Apple at risk, but de Castella always placed the utmost importance on championship races. "I would have been disappointed with myself if I had just jogged through it [the Commonwealth marathon]. I felt that because it was a major championship, I had a responsibility to myself and to my country and to the spectators."

The New York City Marathon was a race Deek had wanted to run ever since Salazar's 2:08:13 there in 1981. "I want to get one of my best races in New York, and then rank that up against Alberto's best," Deek said. "It's just an extra challenge to see who's the best." Deek finished third there in 2:11:43.

The summer before the 1988 Seoul Olympics, Deek had some of his best training ever. Several runners in his training group ran personal bests and won major races. But Deek's back began hurting in 1988, perhaps from the accumulated stress of training, and after returning to Canberra in late August, he missed eight weeks of training. Letting the leaders go in the Olympic Marathon, he finished eighth, a performance Gaylene rates as one of his most courageous.

"It's one of the races he ran as well as he could. He couldn't run at all beforehand, because of the back injury. He used to have to get driven down the downhills during training; he was struggling." The seriousness of the back injury forced Deek to take three months off after the Olympics to get healthy.

His second injury, to his leg, came before the 1990 Commonwealth Games, where Deek, the two-time defending gold medalist, finished 13th. Says Gayelene, "Before the 1990 Commonwealth marathon, Rob 'lost the plot.' He came home to Canberra, and for several months wasn't training well at all."

If it had been any other race, Deek would have skipped it. The leg injury, which wasn't serious enough to make him quit training, slowed him down in the race. After halfway, he lost contact with the leaders and ran in with longtime rival Ikangaa. Deek was disappointed in his failure to win a third Commonwealth gold, but afterwards reiterated his fundamental tenet that athletes, especially at his level, have to maintain a nonplused attitude about their races: "It's important not to be too emotional. You need a stable commitment. You don't get too excited about the good times, and not too upset about the bad. You just go and roll with the punches."

The "Process of Retiring"

Following the Commonwealth Games, de Castella accepted the job of director of the Australian Institute of Sport. For the next two years, he tried to combine running and working and found it extremely tiring. He was picked for the 1992 Barcelona Olympics, which was to be his fourth Olympic Marathon (he is the only runner in history to compete in four Olympic Marathons).

Deek was in a hole before Barcelona, brought on by trying to work full-time at the Institute while continuing to train. Nevertheless, after three weeks racing on the track circuit in Europe, he was getting "right" just in time for the Olympic Marathon, which once again would be run in hot weather. The heat in Barcelona slowed everyone down, and most of the prerace favorites dropped off the pace by halfway. Deek ran with Froude, finishing just under 2:20. "It was very tough conditions," he said, "and there were so many new guys from Asia. They ran well"

"I think Rob ran as well in Barcelona as he could," said Gayelene.

> He had been only tenth in a national half-marathon in Australia not long before. He couldn't do the training he needed to do to run at the Olympic level. He'd work 60 hours a week and still try to run as well as everyone else in the world.

Despite the difficulties, Deek kept training after the 1992 Olympics while working in his new job. He still traveled to road races as head of the Diadora racing team, which sponsored several Australian athletes. And to the very end of his running career, he remained committed to his training.

One morning on a visit to Boulder, he woke up to discover that someone had taken his shoes from the porch of Derek Froude's house, where he and his family were staying. But no whinjing was heard from Deek. He simply laced up his Diadora dress shoes and went on a 10-mile run over the three steep hills of the "hogbacks" that form the western edge of north Boulder. "Even with those shoes on, Rob was pushing it up the hills," said Froude.

In 1993, de Castella was working more and training less, saying, "It's not just physically being at work, but also the mental energy you use up. I'm not retired. I'm in the process of retiring. Before, I was living running. Now, it's not my whole life."

When de Castella emerged as a world-class runner in 1981, his full-time job did not have the same responsibilities as the directorship position holds. "It depends upon the work you are doing. Then, I had a relatively flexible job, and it wasn't emotionally draining."

Now, he was in charge of 22 programs and managed 70 people—including Clohessy—and the same drive that guided Deek's training went into making sure Australian athletes are among the best in the world.

From Deek, the Australian torch has been passed to younger runners, such as Steve Moneghetti (coached by Deek's ex-training partner, Chris Wardlaw), Sean Quilty, and Pat Caroll, who took first, second, and fifth respectively in the 1994 Commonwealth Games Marathon. But despite the good coaching and facilities at the Institute, there may never be another Deek. The runners coming from Down Under in the years to come could be like the Finnish runners after Lasse Viren, mere mortals chasing the shadow of a once-in-a-lifetime runner.

At a party held in his honor at Priscilla and Dave Welch's house, Deek explained to his many friends about his new career saying that he wanted to spend more time with his family and look for new challenges.

Gayelene puts it this way: "Rob didn't make the transition; the transition was made for him. It was harder for me." Gayelene was ranked the number one triathlete in the United States in 1985. Injuries finally forced her to the sidelines in 1987. Gayelene was always interested in the psychological dimension of running, and she is now a specialist in sports psychology at the Australian Academy of Sport.

Early in 1995, de Castella resigned as director of the Institute, saying the rigors of the job left him "pining for the simple pleasures of the marathon." Deek has begun working in private business for the first time, as one of two directors of a Melbourne-based firm, Focus on You. The company designs health and fitness programs. "This is a new challenge for him. Rob felt if he didn't leave the Institute now, he might become a bureaucrat forever," says Gayelene. "There's always a lot of risk when you make a change. But so what? You have to give it a try. That's what Rob has always done."

Rob de Castella will always be remembered as part of a special era in marathoning. His battles with Alberto Salazar, Carlos Lopes, Toshihiko Seko, Juma Ikangaa, and Steve Jones are classics.

"Rob is one of the all-time greats," says Froude. What Bill Rodgers and Frank Shorter were to the '70s, Deek and Alberto are to the '80s. They are the names people really associate with the marathon."

Adds U.S. Olympic marathoner Benji Durden,

Deek had something we need a lot more of in the sport right now. He didn't compromise. Deek *never* compromised. He was the last of the personalities. We'll have more personalities, but we're in a dry spell now.

Reviewing his career, Deek says, "All the races were special, because they were all run under different conditions. The World Championships is special, because it is prestigious; so is Boston, where I ran my fastest time."

However, despite the wins, medals, kudos, and records, Deek still says, "I always wanted to do more than I did. I wanted to win an Olympic gold medal."

When told that some observers say that if circumstances had been different, and the Los Angeles Olympic Marathon had started early in the morning instead of in the afternoon heat, he would have been battling Lopes for the gold, de Castella scoffs. He doesn't take any solace in such second-guessing:

"Circumstances? Life is circumstances," he says. "You do the workouts the best you can and hope you get there in great shape."

Then, speaking of his last major competition, he says, "It felt a bit sad finishing at Barcelona, because I knew it would be my last time running in the Olympics. But that's the way it goes. If you don't have any regrets, it means you weren't challenged in life.

"I don't have any regrets about the way I did things; just that I didn't win an Olympic medal," he adds. "But nothing goes exactly the way you want it to. There is never a perfect life, and there is never a perfect career."

But there are some, as Rob de Castella showed, that come close.

15

The Will to Win Is Nothing Without the Will to Prepare

Born July 19, 1957, Tanzania

Six times under 2:09 in marathon

Winner, New York City Marathon, 1989

The clock tower in the center of the town square of Arusha, Tanzania, marks the exact north-south midpoint of Africa, sitting halfway between Capetown, South Africa, and Cairo, Egypt. Juma Ikangaa passed by the tower every day on his way to the dirt roads outside Arusha, where he put in the huge training weeks that made him one of the world's best and most beloved marathoners and the greatest sports hero in Tanzania, a country that finds itself poised between the modern world and the old. As Ikangaa trains, he passes people walking along the roads carrying loads on their heads, who still work the fields by hand, while new Toyota pickup trucks zip by.

Ikangaa took his cue from the beauty of his country. "You feel inspired to run here, don't you?'" he asks. Indeed, a visitor is struck by Tanzania's beauty, not just of Mt. Kilimanjaro, but the beauty of its people, exemplified by Ikangaa, a gentle man with an unyielding drive. He did not run for money or for awards. All he did, he did for his country. Juma was totally immersed in training; it was for him a national duty, in which he was representing his country on the world stage. He was known for the serious look he wore while running, as if carrying a great burden. In fact, the way he trained was serious, and he got serious results: six sub-2:09 marathons and nine marathons faster than 2:10, the most ever.

The tiny Ikangaa (5'-3", 117 pounds) is a quiet, graceful man who was one of the best-known marathoners of the 1980s. Along with Steve Jones, he pushed back the limits of marathoning, giving a supreme effort in every race. No marathon was complete without Ikangaa in its field. Ikangaa won New York in 2:08:01, the fastest time ever run in the Big Apple, as well major marathons around the world including Fukuoka, Tokyo, Melbourne, and Beijing.

But he is perhaps best-known for his three consecutive second-place finishes at the Boston Marathon, each time setting a scorching pace that dropped all his competitors except one. And though he finished second more often than he won, Ikangaa was first in the hearts of runners around the world, winning fans with his warm personality and gutsy front-running—when he entered a race, the promise of a world record was always there. Ikangaa was praised for the dignity he showed, a dignity that made him not just one of the foremost men of Tanzania, but, as U.S. coach Joe Vigil puts it, "the most complete human being I've ever met."

A Love of Running

Juma Ikangaa was born near Dodoma in the middle of Tanzania on July 19, 1957, the youngest of six children. His father was a farmer who told his children that nothing in life comes without hard work. Ikangaa is of the Rangi ethnic group, one of the more than 100 in Tanzania. Like most of the children he grew up with, Juma ran to school every day; in his case, it was 10 miles each way.

"It's different from a developed country like the United States, or Europe, where children can take a bus or a car home. There were no cars or buses for us," Ikangaa told journalist and runner Don Kardong. "We had to wake up early in the morning and run quickly, and get to school early to avoid punishment from teachers."

While soccer was the most popular sport with his schoolmates, Ikangaa always preferred running over soccer. In his first race ever, he won a bicycle, which inspired Ikangaa to try running on a regular basis.

Ikangaa went to high school near Lake Victoria, on the western border of Tanzania, where he continued winning local competitions. After finishing school in 1975, he entered the Tanzanian army, which sent him to Cairo, Egypt for artillery training. He drew attention there when he won the Army Games 5,000- and 10,000-meter championships. In the army, he was given equipment and supported in his running. "Juma loved running and was successful at it from the beginning," says Vigil, a U.S. national coach who was to become a friend and confidant of Ikangaa's. "He didn't become a success internationally until after the [1982] Commonwealth Games."

The world first noticed Ikangaa in his epic duel with Rob de Castella (Deek) at those Brisbane Commonwealth Games. He had run his first marathon a little over a month earlier, winning the African Championships, but had not been noticed by those getting ready for the Games. All the attention was on the Australian de Castella, who had emerged as one of the best in the world with his 2:08:18 at the Fukuoka Marathon the previous December.

Ikangaa ran the Brisbane marathon in the manner that made him one of the most feared racers in the following decade—setting a blistering pace from the start that forced his competitors to run hard the entire distance. Ikangaa and teammate Gidamis Shahanga took off at below world-record pace, getting so far ahead of the field that Deek could not even see them until near 20 miles. Deek was the second fastest marathoner in history, but much to the dismay of his countrymen and women lining the course, he did not even look like he was in the same race as the Tanzanians. Deek finally reeled in and passed Shahanga at 23 miles, then caught up to Ikangaa a mile later. In the denouement of a classic battle, the two took turns surging on each other over the hills. A spent Shahanga had not offered any resistance, but Ikangaa showed his character by staying with de Castella when the Australian took the lead, then passing him in turn. Back and forth they went in the heat and humidity, until Deek finally pulled away to win the gold by 21 seconds. Ikangaa ran 2:09:30 for the silver medal, a new African record that made him a hero in Tanzania. Said one Tanzanian, "Everyone wanted to be like Juma after that."

What Ikangaa showed in that first major marathon was what a joy of running, coupled with a military-like discipline, could do. In the following years, he became one of the major players in international marathoning. "I don't train to beat another runner," he said. "We are out there together, competing with the marathon, and I train to run the marathon as fast as I can." To do that, he trained very fast, with many of his runs near a five-minute-mile pace. "To run fast in the marathon you have to run fast in training."

Ikangaa chose the races with the deepest fields, eschewing easy victories for the chance to run with the best in the world, to see how fast they could push each other. It was always Juma out in front in the major marathons, pushing the pace, and pushing back the limits of marathoning, each time trying to go faster than the race before. And if he did not get the victory or the world record he was chasing, he simply dusted himself off and said, "I'll prepare better next time."

Running Fast out Front

"It seems out of all the runners, Juma was the one who maximized his potential," says journalist Paul Christman. "For his small size, he was better than anyone I've ever seen. Juma is a remarkably engaging character with a sly sense of humor."

Ikangaa, though he wore a serious expression when racing, sometimes let that sense of humor show through. In the 1983 World Championship Marathon in Helsinki, he and de Castella, who had become good friends, were running along in the pack. Rob Tabb of the United States was up front leading, and, de Castella recalls, "Juma looked at me and winked. Then he went all the way around the pack to the front, just in front of Tabb, then slowed down. Then he drifted over to the side of the pack and came back next to me. I looked over and he had a big smile on his face." De Castella went on to win the World Championships, while Ikangaa dropped back to 15th.

At the end of 1983, Ikangaa dropped his personal best to 2:08:55 at Fukuoka. He pushed the pace, then was outkicked by three seconds by Toshihiko Seko of Japan. Ikangaa, though usually the smallest runner in a race, nearly always did the majority of pulling the pack along.

Heading into the 1984 Olympics, Ikangaa was one of the favorites, along with de Castella and Seko, but Juma finished sixth after leading the early part of the race. In 1985, Ikangaa had an off year, with his best marathon being "only" 2:11:06.

He rebounded in 1986, running personal bests on the track that summer: 13:41.0 for 5,000 meters and 28:15:13 for 10,000 meters. In October, he went to the Beijing Marathon, where he led through 19 miles. Though Japanese runners Kunimitsu Ito and Taisuke Kodama passed him, Ikangaa ran a personal best of 2:08:39, with Kodama finishing in 2:07:35 and Ito in 2:07:57.

Ikangaa followed that with a 2:08:10 win at the Tokyo Marathon, and in December he won the Fukuoka Marathon. This time, he stayed in the pack before pulling away at the end for a 2:10:06 win. Ikangaa was ranked the number one marathoner in the world for 1986 by *Track & Field News*.

Juma showed that to get a fast marathon you need more than a flat course and pacemakers, says Steve Jones. "You need competition and Juma was a competitor."

In April 1987, Ikangaa went to his first Boston Marathon. After leading into the wind early on, he ended up finishing only 11th. After the race, he went shopping for three hours. *Running Stats* reported that Ikangaa spent roughly 40 percent of his five-figure appearance fee on clothes, but not for himself. Ikangaa, by now a major and artillery instructor in the Tanzanian army, bought them to bring back to children in Tanzania. When asked how he knew something he was buying was the correct size, Ikangaa replied, "Oh, that does not matter. It will fit someone."

It was also windy when Ikangaa returned to Beijing in the fall of 1987. After the previous year's third-place finish, Ikangaa was looking for a win. He ran with the pack through a first half of 1:06. Five runners remained through 35K, and with two miles to go, Ikangaa took off to win in 2:12:11.

In February 1988, Ikangaa was part of a deep field at the Tokyo Marathon, joining Rob de Castella, Ethiopia's Abebe Mekonnen, and Douglas Wakiihuri. It was an Olympic-caliber field, with the bonus of cool temperatures and no wind. A large pack stuck together through a fast first 13.1 miles of 1:03:56. Soon after, Ikangaa went to the front and pressed the pace, splitting up the pack. Soon it was down to six runners: Ikangaa, de Castella, East German Jorg Peter, Mekonnen, Ralf Salzmann of West Germany, and Japan's Isamu Sennai.

With about two miles to go, it was down to Ikangaa, Deek, Mekonnen, and Peter. Then, at 40 kilometers, Mekonnen went to the front and pushed in for the 2:08:33 win. Ikangaa, once again, was second, in 2:08:42. Peter set a new East German record of 2:08:47, and Deek was fourth in 2:08:49.

Filbert Bayi

The Tanzanian front-running tradition was started by Filbert Bayi. Born on June 23, 1953, Bayi grew up on a farm within sight of Mt. Kilimanjaro. Like many other African runners, Bayi spent his early years running around the fields, herding cattle. He was inspired to start running by Kip Keino and John Stephens, the first Tanzanian runner to race internationally.

After finishing school at 17, Bayi moved to the Tanzanian capital of Dar es Salaam, on the Indian Ocean. It's a hot, humid place, and Bayi raced city buses down the crowded streets in a kind of crude interval training. He would sprint alongside the bus for as long as it was moving, then rest while the bus loaded and unloaded its passengers. That kind of rudimentary training got him in shape to run 3:52 for 1,500 meters in 1971, when he was 18.

In 1972, Bayi clocked 3:45 and 8:55 in winning the 1,500 and steeplechase at the Tanzanian championships and was selected for the Tanzanian Olympic team. At the Munich Olympics, he failed to qualify for the finals though his times showed promise: 8:41.4 in the steeple and 3:45.4 in the 1,500.

Bayi gained his first international notice three months later in Lagos, Nigeria, when he beat four-time Olympic medalist Keino at the 1973 African Games in 3:37.2. Despite suffering from a bout with malaria just before the race, Bayi led from start to finish. Afterwards, Keino told Bayi that he could break the world record with proper training.

In mile races in Europe during the summer of 1973, Bayi went through the first half of the race faster than anyone in history, startling opponents and fans alike. In June at the Helsinki World Games, he started out in 53.4 and 1:51.9 for his first 800 meters, finishing in 3:34.6 for 1,500 meters, the fourth fastest all time. In his next race, Bayi started even faster, passing the half in 1:51.0 on his way to a 3:52.6 mile, finishing second to Ben Jipcho's 3:52.0. Those were the second and third fastest all time.

He changed his tactic during a race in the summer of 1974. Responding to criticism from journalists complaining about his fast early pace, Bayi dropped back in the pack in the early going. The new tactic did not work, however. Bayi ended up getting spiked and was forced to take the rest of the year off.

Certain races are defining moments in sport, times when you know you are watching history being made and are seeing a new era dawning. Such a race was the 1974 Commonwealth Games 1,500 meters in Christchurch, New Zealand. The race brought together the best milers in the world. Kenya's Ben Jipcho and Mike Boit, Rod Dixon and John Walker of New Zealand, Graham Couch of Australia, and England's tough Brendan Foster. Rounding out the field were Tanzanians Suleiman Nyambui and Bayi. Bayi was fit and rested after placing fourth in the 800 meters.

Bayi went out in 54.9 seconds for the first 400 meters, with Boit right behind him, followed by Jipcho and Dixon. After passing the 800 in 1:52.2, Bayi had a gap over the field. The boyish-looking Tanzanian slowed only a bit in running his next lap in 58.6, passing the bell at 2:50.8. He continued to hold his form around the bend while the pack gained on him. Walker, Dixon, and Jipcho all continued getting closer to Bayi as the crowd, sensing a record, stood and rocked the stadium with excitement and noise.

The tall Walker, his long blond hair flying behind him, was spurred on by his home country fans and gained on Bayi, putting in a tremendous effort by running his last lap in 54.4. Down the last straightaway, Bayi glanced over his shoulder at the onrushing Walker, then stretched out to break the tape in a new world record of 3:32.1, 0.4 seconds ahead of Walker. Jipcho was third in 3:33.1, followed by Dixon (3:33.8), Crouch (3:34.2), Boit (3:36.8), Foster (3:37.6), and Nyambui (3:39.6). That race was immediately recognized as a race for the ages. Bayi "was now the front runner to end all front runners," wrote *Track & Field News'* Cordner Nelson.

On May 17, 1975, he took aim at Jim Ryun's mile world record at the International Freedom Games in Kingston, Jamaica. After opening laps of 56.9 and 59.7 (1:56.6), Bayi was two seconds up on Eamonn Coghlan and Marty Liquori. A third lap in 58.7 brought him to 2:55.3 at the bell. Bayi kept the lead on the last lap and sprinted home in 55.7 seconds to finish in 3:51.0, breaking Ryun's eight-year-old record by a tenth of a second. Liquori was second in 3:52.2.

"Bayi did what Keino had done earlier," not waiting until the last lap to start his kick, says Liquori. "When I knew I'd be running against Bayi, I'd do different workouts, gearing them for getting into oxygen debt and hanging on. Against Filbert there was no sense in working on your kick. He changed the whole way of training."

One of Liquori's workouts was 600-meter intervals. If, for example, Liquori was training to race Jim Ryun, the first 400 might be in 60 seconds and the last 200 in 26 seconds.

"But if I was trying to beat Keino or Bayi, I would do 32 seconds [for the first 200 meters of his 600-meter repeat], 28 for the second 200, and 30 seconds for the third. You had to learn to run that way."

Ikangaa then came to Boston vowing to redeem himself for his subpar performance the year before. To prepare, he went to 7,500-foot Alamosa, Colorado, for six weeks of high-altitude training. He told friends in Alamosa he was going for the world record in Boston. Three days before the race, he did a workout of 15 × 400 meters in 64 seconds, followed by some strides.

Ikangaa looked like he might get the world record early on, leading a large pack through 14:32 at 5 kilometers, 10 miles in 47:57, and halfway in 1:03:12. One by one the other runners, including Steve Jones, Italians Gelindo Bordin and Gianni Poli, and John Treacy dropped off until it was down to Ikangaa and Kenyan Ibrahim Hussein. No African had ever won Boston. It was clear one would this year, and anxious onlookers wondered which one.

"With one mile to go, I looked at Ikangaa and he looked at me, and I knew it was going to be a 100-meter kick," said Hussein. Ikangaa was in front, with Hussein right behind. With 600 meters to go, Ikangaa still had the lead. But in a sprint finish, it was Hussein getting the one-second win over Ikangaa, 2:08:43 to 2:08:44. It was one of Boston's best races, wrote Joe Concannon of the *Boston Globe*. "To some, it was Boston's greatest" race.

"It's the most memorable race to me," Ikangaa told Concannon. "I made a slight mistake. You don't break, though. I was prepared. I was ready. I wasn't lucky enough to win." Ikangaa had been second, but once more he had ensured a fast, exciting race.

Stung by the close loss, Ikangaa went back to Arusha and trained even harder, running up to 220 miles a week and increasing the speed and distance of his tempo runs and track sessions. All year long he told the runners he was training with the idea that he was going to win the 1988 Olympics and then Boston.

Ikangaa, going for a medal, ran a conservative early pace at the Seoul Olympic Marathon, leading a large pack of runners through 15 miles. Italian Gelindo Bordin began pushing the pace, and within three miles de Castella and Seko had fallen back.

Ikangaa ran with Bordin, Douglas Wakiihuri of Kenya, Ahmed Saleh, and Japan's Takeyuki Nakayama near the lead. But with about four miles to go, Ikangaa dropped back, eventually finishing seventh in 2:13:06. Bordin won the gold (2:10:32), followed by Wakiihuri (2:10:47) and Saleh (2:10:59).

When he returned to Boston the following year, he told people who questioned his kick that he had run a 3:56 mile and that he would go as fast as necessary to win. In an attempt to keep the 1989 Boston Marathon from coming down to another sprint finish, Ikangaa went even faster, passing halfway in a Steve Jones-like 1:02:23. And once again, Ikangaa shook off all his competitors except one; this time it was Ethiopian Abebe Mekonnen who pulled away from Juma over the last miles to win. Mekonnen clocked 2:09:06 to Ikangaa's 2:09:56.

It's Up to You, New York

Ikangaa was looking for a major win in the United States, and that fall he went to New York. Under near-perfect conditions, Ikangaa once again set a blistering fast pace in an attempt to drop what was called "one of the best marathon fields ever assembled." He was going up against Olympic champ Bordin of Italy, along with Belayneh Densimo of Ethiopia, the world-record holder (2:06:50), and Steve Jones, the defending New York champ.

Despite running near 4:50 miles, a dozen runners were still in the lead at halfway. "I don't like the little surging," Ikangaa later told Merrell Noden of *Sports Illustrated*. "Surge and stop, surge and stop. That can cause muscle cramps. It is better for someone to surge completely." It was Jones—who had defined marathon front-running with his solo 2:07:13 in Chicago in 1985—who surged, but he could not shake Ikangaa. And when Juma threw in a 4:34 mile soon after, Jones couldn't respond, and the Tanzanian was clear.

Recalls Jones, "I surged just before the bridge at halfway, and Juma just kicked away after that. He did exactly what I had done the year before." Jones was running with American Ken Martin about 150 meters behind Ikangaa after he had taken his lead.

"Do you think Juma will come back to us?" asked Martin.

"No way," said Jones.

Martin, who went on to finish second, chased Ikangaa, but there was no way of catching the Tanzanian.

"It was Juma's strength and flexibility that allowed him to run that fast," said Joe Vigil. "It was such a dramatic surge, and he was gone so quick," Martin told Noden. "I thought, 'He's not going to keep it up. He can't.'" But Ikangaa did, running by himself the rest of the race to get the 2:08:01 win. "It was the greatest race I've run," he told Noden. "It was a personal record, a course record, and I am the second African to win this race (Hussein was the first)." Jones agrees, "To run 2:08:01 on that course against that competition was incredible." Ikangaa's time is still the New York City Marathon course record. The quality of the mark is seen in that German Silva of Mexico won the 1994 and 1995 New York City Marathon with times three minutes slower than Juma ran.

Ikangaa won over $36,000 in prize money, but was especially pleased with the Mercedes Benz he took home. "I want this car to be used by my mother, because she was a bit angry the last two years when I did not succeed in winning one."

After finishing, Ikangaa evoked memories of Abebe Bikila, Ethiopia's great two-time Olympic champion, by doing exercises to show that he wasn't tired. (Bikila did something similar after winning the 1960 Rome Olympic Marathon.) "I could have run another five miles," Ikangaa told reporters, some of whom said he was showboating. Not so, explains Vigil. "Juma did those calisthenics when he finished just to get his blood flowing. He wasn't showing off, like some criticized him for."

Indeed, Ikangaa was anything but a showoff. He dressed in plain cotton sweats and lived simply. He went to bed early, woke up early, and read the Koran every day. "Juma had great emotional control in his life and in his racing, something that is often lacking in distance runners," said Vigil. "Too many runners get in there and run somebody's else's race, not their own. He always knew what he wanted and had confidence that he could do it."

Ikangaa, says Jones, "was the key person in any race."

Juma ran like clockwork. When he was in a groove, he could just pick it up any time he wanted. He also liked being in the front; he was never a pack runner. No matter what kind of shape he was in, he always ran hard. Juma was very, very consistent. People respected him more for his consistency, which is what makes any good distance runner and gives a runner his reputation.

Ikangaa's confidence sprang from his training, because he knew when he stepped on a starting line that no one could be running as fast as he was in training. Something in Ikangaa—perhaps it's a genetic trait, perhaps because he was running for his country—allowed him to push himself relentlessly, in training and racing.

Training: It Must Be Fast

Arusha is a town of about 100,000 near Mt. Meru in the northern part of Tanzania, not far from the border with Kenya. Countless miles of dirt trails run along the base of 14,979-foot Mt. Meru, the fifth-highest peak in Africa. The Tanzanian national teams are headquartered in Arusha, which is the gateway to the game parks: the Serengeti and the famous Ngorongoro Crater. The green hills of Arusha are lush, the land very fertile.

The first *Homo sapiens* are thought to have emerged in the Olduvai Gorge, 60 miles from Arusha, and were probably running through these plains millennia ago. Ikangaa lives the primal rhythm of our first ancestors, with his day corresponding to the movement of the sun. He goes to bed about 9:30 P.M. and awakens each morning at 5:30. After drinking some tea, he begins the very serious business of training.

"Juma is successful because he trains very hard," says Filbert Bayi. "His morning run is up to 50 kilometers once a week. At a pace of perhaps 5:20 to 5:45 per mile."

Ikangaa says, "If you want to run 2:08 marathons, you must train fast." Once or twice a week, he also runs 30 to 35 kilometers at close to five minutes per mile. He does his hard workouts with the national team, and as a national coach, he tries to be a good role model. "They can become world-class runners by using simple food, a simple life. You have to go step-by-step," Ikangaa said. "One way is to encourage them. I run with them and pretend I'm not in shape . . . . I could go faster, but I want to encourage the young runners."

Ikangaa takes his meals at the Pic-Nic restaurant, near the track, and the Safari Inn Guest House, where he stays in Arusha. Next door is the Fortune Boutique and Hair Stylist and the Bora Stationery Shop, typical of the family businesses that dot the city. When Ikangaa was a struggling runner, the owner of Pic-Nic recognized his potential. "He told his sons and daughters to give me free meals," Ikangaa relates. "Now, when I have some money, I still eat here." His typical meal is rice with some liver, chicken, or fish.

Ikangaa is like the mayor of Arusha. When he walks into the Pic-Nic cafe, he is greeted by several players on the women's national basketball team, who come up and hug him. Other customers stop by his table to ask how his training is going.

Ikangaa does his first run of the day very early in the morning. "You see, before 10 o'clock it is very cool here. From noon to 3:30 it is very hot. It is cold later, not like in Dar es Salaam [the coastal capital], so it is easy for us to train here. I can run in any direction I want. There is a lot of food. There are no distractions here, and the climate is good. Yes, this is a good place to train."

Ikangaa looks you directly in the eyes when he talks about his training, fixing you with a gaze that has in it all the struggle and hardships of his young country. He takes his role as a spokesman for Tanzania very seriously. He is very polite, very considerate. "Are you comfortable?" he asks. "Do you need anything else?"

Ikangaa is solicitous to his guests. When a Japanese film crew comes to film Ikangaa, he arranges for a rented four-wheel drive truck so they can follow his run. When an American journalist interviews him on the run, Ikangaa slows down, looking over his shoulder now and then and asking, "Is this pace OK for you?"

The other runner nods, because he is too deep in oxygen debt to answer. Ikangaa's favorite run goes through coffee, wheat, and maize fields, past Masai tribespeople, easily distinguished by their colorful capes. Invariably, the people passed on the roads, going to work or school, say hello to Juma. Running on one of the dirt roads outside Arusha, he says, "To break the world record, you must put in mile after mile, week after week, month after month. That way you hit the wall in practice, not in the race."

The visiting runner, very tired by now, asks, "How far does this road go?" hoping it leads back to town.

"All the way to Nairobi," Ikangaa said. "I can run here as fast and as far as I want," he adds, picking up the pace. "Don't forget; the tougher the training, the easier the competition," he says, disappearing into the distance.

Back in town, just a javelin throw from the stadium, Ikangaa points out the house where former Tanzanian president Julius Nyerere gave his famous "Arusha Declaration" speech in 1967. Nyerere is their revered *Malimu*, or teacher, the George Washington of Tanzania. Nyerere is called the father of African Socialism, famous for his focus on "self-reliance." The Arusha Declaration formulated Nyerere's brand of African socialism, or *Ujamaa*. There, on the trails and green hills of Arusha and on its track, Ikangaa formulated an Arusha Declaration of his own: to become the best marathoner in the world; not to win money, but to bring fame and progress to Tanzania.

President Nyerere gave two conditions of development in his Declaration: "hard work and intelligence." Ikangaa is a mirror of his country and of that philosophy, training as hard as anyone in the world.

His training philosophy is simple: "The will to win is nothing without the will to prepare," he often said. And Ikangaa prepared very well, running up to 220 miles a week before marathons. He believed in isolation in getting ready for a major race, so that he could focus solely on his training.

Says Steve Jones, "Juma was an enigma, because he was very secretive in his training and very Spartan in his lifestyle."

When he stood on the line at a race he was more serious than anyone. If Juma was in the race, you knew he would always be right up there, always in the front and that it was going to be a hard race.

Ikangaa divided his training into two parts: his "conditioning" program, which he followed until four to eight weeks before a major marathon; and his "specific training," which was geared to whatever marathon he was preparing for. "It's important to know a course to know how to train for it," he said. For example, when getting ready for Boston, Ikangaa increased the amount of training he did on rolling hills.

Ikangaa's workouts are legendary among other Tanzanians. The "will to prepare" meant the will to do extraordinary workouts: his weekly 50-kilometer long run, 30-kilometer tempo runs at close to a five-minute-mile pace, and 50 × 200 meters. Even in the midst of his workouts, however, he would stop and advise the younger runners, urging them to run with him.

"What impressed me," Tanzanian coach Claver Kamanya told journalist Cheryl Bentsen, "was how hard he worked and how he seemed to know what he was doing. He's very intelligent, very cool, and well-mannered. I've never seen him try to do anything the easy way; mentally he is very strong-willed. Physically, he has better form than most marathoners and a lot of flexibility."

That flexibility was worked on every day, by doing bounding drills on the grass, stretching, and isometrics. His rooms at the Safari Inn Guest House are spotless; after training, he changes clothes, showers, and brews a cup of tea. He carries himself like someone in the army. Ikangaa kept a medicine ball in his room, to build his strength after workouts. That was critical to Ikangaa's success, says Vigil, because "distance runners on average are weak and inflexible."

The three aspects runners need to develop are flexibility, cardiovascular fitness, and strength, says Vigil. Ikangaa had all three. "He used body isometrics. They don't have fancy health clubs in Tanzania, so he used resistance, bounding on grass, to build up his muscle elasticity."

If he was fatigued, Juma would hold off on his workout a day. He often didn't time his runs, saying, "I usually run how I feel." Juma's weekly schedule in his "specific training" program a month before a marathon would include:

Sunday:	Long run, 30-35 miles.
Monday:	A.M., 12 miles; P.M., 13 miles.
Tuesday:	A.M., 5 miles; P.M., 25 × 400 meters on track, 50 ×200 meters, or fartlek on grass field.
Wednesday:	A.M., 5 miles; P.M., 20 miles.
Thursday:	A.M., 3-mile warm-up, 30K at 5-minute-mile pace; P.M., 10 miles.
Friday:	A.M., 12 miles; P.M., 13 miles.
Saturday:	A.M., tempo run, or repeat miles or halves; P.M., 10 miles.

After doing his basework or conditioning work in Arusha, or wherever his military duties took him, Ikangaa often went to the high altitude of Alamosa, Colorado. Just as in Arusha, he lived a simple life when training in the United States. The runners at Adams State College in Alamosa never knew when to expect Ikangaa—he would just show up one day. He always took a room at the Best Western Motel, off of Highway 60 on the edge of town.

"Juma was friends with everybody," says U.S. cross-country star Pat Porter. "He knew all the busboys at the hotel and took time to learn the names of the maids. Everybody loves him."

"He is somebody you would like. He has basic, sincere values that you don't find in everyone. He was very sincere about everything he did," says Joe Vigil's wife. Adds Vigil,

Juma is just a great person, and of course, he had a passion for running. His secret was that passion. He's a great runner because he's a great guy. I've never met a person more compassionate than Juma. He had a lot of natural talent and wasn't like a typical American runner; he didn't run for money. He trained hard, and the money came. He put in the volume necessary it took to be the best.

One difference in Ikangaa's training was that instead of saying he was going to run 10 or 12 miles at a five-minute pace, he'd instead run that fast for as long as could, trying to push himself farther and farther. The farthest he ever got at five-minute-mile pace in Alamosa was 17 miles, rolling through the Fort Garland foothills outside of town. As in Arusha, nearly all of his running was done on dirt.

"Training was very serious business for Juma. He wasn't a jokester. When he was tired or fatigued, he would just call it quits for the day. Otherwise, he was running hard every day, unless there was a long run," says Vigil.

Even the long runs, up to 35 miles, were at six minutes per mile. When not doing his long run, Ikangaa tried to average 25 miles a day, divided into two sessions, depending how he felt. In the morning, he might run 5 miles, followed by 20 in the afternoon. Or, he'd break his training up into a 12-mile run in the morning and 13 miles in the afternoon. That mileage did not include the warm-up or warm-down. He'd jog three miles before starting the run, then jog afterwards. Ikangaa's hard days were on the track, tempo runs, or fartlek on grass. One standard workout when getting ready for a marathon was six repeat miles at 4:30 per mile.

Ikangaa was not a partying person; he read a lot at night. He also ate a healthful diet, with no processed food, Vigil says. He would eat meat, but followed a low-fat diet. "Juma espoused megamileage. He was able to work harder than anyone else and recover quickly. He was small, so he wouldn't burn as many calories."

Another Run at Boston

In 1990, Ikangaa vowed not to get beaten at Boston again. He decided to set so fast a pace that no one could possibly be able to stay with him. He told Vigil he was going beat Belayneh Densimo's marathon world record of 2:06:50, set in Rotterdam in 1988.

Juma Ikangaa's ability to push himself, in training and racing, set him apart.

Ikangaa and fellow Tanzanian Simon Naali flew through the opening splits, with the lead pack passing the mile in 4:26, five miles in 23:05, and 10 kilometers in 28:44. Juma led through halfway in 1:02:01 and 20 miles in 1:36:53.

That dropped everyone except 1988 Olympic champ Gelindo Bordin, who ran off the back of the pack and passed Ikangaa to get the runaway win. For the third year in a row, Juma was second. He did not have enough to hang on at the end that day, and when asked by reporters, "Juma, why did you run so fast?" Ikangaa replied, "How fast do you have to run to run a world record?" Says Vigil, "He was right on pace. He was doing what he said he'd do."

If Ikangaa was fated to be second at Boston, he was number one with the people of Beantown. Fans loved him, and he became one of the most popular runners at the race. Before the 1990 Boston Marathon, he and Steve Jones attended a Boston Celtics basketball game at the Boston Garden. When Ikangaa and Jones were introduced, they received a standing ovation.

There was adulation in his own country as well. Popular with people from all walks of life, he is well-respected as one of the leaders of the young country, a role he sees being as important as his racing.

Always, Ikangaa was thinking about others' and Tanzania's future. It's a poor country—in fact, the third poorest nation in the world, according to the World Bank. Like Nyerere, Ikangaa felt a responsibility to help bring Tanzania into the future. And like Kenyan Kip Keino before him, Ikangaa saw running as a way to do that.

"Juma has a great spirit of nationalism. He goes out into the countryside to encourage young people to run and to get an education," says Vigil. "He's very concerned and was always talking about his country's future and making progress."

When he would leave the United States, Japan, or Europe after a race, he would take back with him suitcases full of underwear and clothing for the people in Arusha. A visitor getting ready to leave Arusha after a visit was pulled aside by Juma, saying, "If you have any shoes you can leave the runners here, it would be very much appreciated. They are too proud to ask."

Sometimes Ikangaa pushed himself too relentlessly. In 1991, he suffered a leg injury that caused him to miss a spring marathon. In 1992, he came back to place fourth at Boston. He returned to Arusha afterwards to train for the Barcelona Olympics. In the heat of Barcelona, though, he faltered, like many other of the top runners, finishing 34th in 2:19:34, not far from his friend de Castella, 10 years after their first race together. Ikangaa said his mistake was training in the coolness of Arusha rather than somewhere hot and humid. "It was very hot," he told Joe Concannon. "I should have trained in a place that resembled the climatic conditions of Barcelona. It was just the heat. I dehydrated and was feeling bad after 21 kilometers."

Later that fall, Ikangaa placed fourth at the New York City Marathon in 2:11:44. He is still racing around the world, adding to his resume of more than 40 major marathons run at the world-class level. He won eight of those marathons and finished second in some of the best marathons run, after leading most of the way.

Ikangaa's ability to push himself, in training and racing, is what set Juma apart. Vigil doesn't know where it came from, but says,

> Any mental trait is learned, and it was just that Juma knew what he needed to do to win and to set the world record. It was never an ego thing. I never saw him say anything about himself. It was always for his family, his military, or the good of the country. He never focused on himself; the focus was always on a higher order. He had a good word for everybody, like the barbers in town. Everyone just loved him. He may not have gotten the world records he wanted, but Juma is one of great marathoners of all time.

16

Running Into History

Born May 16, 1957, United States

World records: 25K, 30K, and marathon

Olympic gold, marathon, 1984

Winner, Boston and Chicago Marathons

The sharp, searing pain in Joan Benoit's right knee came all at once at the 17-mile mark of her regular 20-mile run on the quiet roads along the outskirts of Freeport, Maine. Benoit had suffered many injuries in the 10 years since she started running as a high school student in Maine; most pain she simply put out of her mind and ran through, but this was different. This was the kind of pain that told her immediately something was seriously wrong. She hobbled through two more miles before the knee locked up completely, forcing her to walk home. It was March 17, 1984, eight weeks before the U.S. Olympic Trials race that would select the three runners to represent the United States in the inaugural women's Olympic Marathon, and as Benoit finished the run by trudging home, it appeared that her Olympic dreams were finished as well.

For three years Benoit, the fastest women's marathoner, had been aiming for the 1984 Los Angeles Olympics, in which women would be allowed to run a marathon for the first time. It had been a long struggle for equality since the modern Olympic Games were established in 1896. In the original Olympic Games in ancient Greece, women were forbidden, under the penalty of death, of even entering the stadium and watching the men compete.

Finally, in 1928, women were allowed to run the 800 meters. In 1972, the women's 1,500 was added, and now, after much lobbying, women were to be featured in an Olympic Marathon. Benoit was one of the favorites for the race, based on her world record of 2:22:43 set the year before at the Boston Marathon. But now, her leg packed in ice, it looked like she would be watching the historic race from the sidelines.

Benoit struggled with the injury the next several weeks, resting for several days, then running on it until the pain again became too great. In desperation, she went under the knife just 17 days before the trials. The arthroscopic surgery was successful, but when she was allowed to start training again, only 10 days remained. Though she could now run pain free, it looked as if Benoit's chances of winning the gold had come crashing down when her knee collapsed. There did not seem any way for a runner to come back so soon after major knee surgery and run a quality marathon, observers said.

Or was there?

A Natural Athlete

Maine is a unique region of the United States, populated with independent, laconic people. Closer to Canada than the rest of the United States, in both spirit and geography, Maine's people have a hardiness that helps them through the long winters. That Maine toughness was ingrained in Benoit, and it fueled her drive to become the best marathon runner in the world.

After Benoit made it to the top, folks in her hometown of Cape Elizabeth erected a sign on the lawn of her parents' home reading, "It all started here"—in the woods and on the streets of Cape Elizabeth, a small town where Benoit grew up as a sports-crazy kid. She was a tomboy, almost by necessity, growing up with three athletic, and not very sympathetic, brothers. She spent her early years playing all kinds of sports. No matter what the Maine weather—snow, rain, cold, heat and humidity—Joanie was outside, following her brothers around.

Benoit is one of those people who know they want to be an athlete from the time they're kids and who had to win in whatever she was doing. She played a variety of sports and had a plenty of excess energy as a child, which she channeled primarily into skiing. Skiing was her first youthful love, and like Frank Shorter, her dream was to become a world-class skier. During the winter she would ski nearly every weekend with her parents on the slopes of New England ski areas. Her father, owner of Benoit's Clothing Store in Cape Elizabeth, had served in World War II in the Tenth Mountain Division of the U.S. Army—the troops that were trained to fight on skis. He became an expert skier and passed along a passion for skiing to his four children.

Benoit's "competitive drive and a sense of adventure" drew her to the "speed and freedom" of skiing, she writes in her autobiography, *Running Tide*. Skiing was, she said, "my best early teacher. It was a wonderful introduction," because it "taught me about sacrifice, about picking myself up and going on in spite of adversity, and about striving." The bad conditions sometimes found on the New England slopes—very icy and cold—did not stop Joanie from skiing, just as bad conditions did not later stop her from running. No matter how cold it was, Joanie would keep going up and down the mountainside; she may even have done permanent damage to her fingers and toes by staying out in the cold so long.

In addition to the "pure exhilaration" of flying down the slopes, what Benoit learned from skiing was "tenacity," she writes. "If it appears that running in pain doesn't bother me, it's because I learned to manage it when I was a young skier. I found a part of myself which could go on in spite of it, and I developed that part."

Benoit's interest in sports increased as she got older. While most girls her age wore white ice skates, Benoit had black hockey skates just like the guys. She played tennis and every summer, the Benoit family went to "The Island," a special place off the coast where she'd row, swim, and dig for clams.

Benoit also liked the island people with their "quiet, self-effacing ways. What is mistaken for reticence is the Island watchfulness, the attitude that it is better to listen than to talk," she writes. What she learned from the islanders helped her later on as an athlete. She writes,

> I learned to put something besides myself at the center of my universe. That came in handy whenever I tried to feel sorry for myself. I was taught to be tough, to meet challenges without flinching. I was also taught to love myself but strive to be a better person. I learned to value silence and contemplation. I learned how to earn respect. I came away knowing when to laugh.

Benoit's running talent surfaced early; when she was eight, she won five first-place blue ribbons at a field day at a local country club. She continued to excel during elementary school at field event days.

Benoit's sporting activity increased when she went to Cape Elizabeth High School, where she played field hockey. She was a forward, which involves constant sprinting up and down the field. Even more important than the physical benefit Benoit received from field hockey, however, was the mental boost she got from her coach, who told Benoit and the other players that they "were terrific kids who could do whatever we set our minds to. Her confidence gave me confidence." Benoit developed the self-image that she was a good athlete, an image she lived up to in the years to come.

High-School Running

Benoit went out for track as a freshman in the spring of 1971 and was a successful runner from the start. Receiving a pair of real running shoes for Christmas that winter, she put them to good use in track. She ran a variety of events, from the 100-yard dash on up, as well as competing in the long jump and high jump.

Even as a high-school freshman, Benoit showed a champion's drive to train. As in most high schools, coaches used running laps as punishment for players who messed up. Most dreaded "running laps." For Benoit, however, it was a great pleasure, and she looked forward to those occasions when she made a mistake and was forced to run. After field hockey practice was over, Joanie would run more laps on her own. On weekends she would go on five-mile runs by herself. Benoit showed even then what Frank Shorter calls a "runner's personality," meaning she had to exercise every day or she would feel guilty.

Joanie was the only girl in her high school—in fact, in the entire town—running. Then, in 1972, the Cape Elizabeth boys' cross-country team held a meet against a school that had one girl runner who ran in races with the boys. Midway through field hockey practice, Joan changed from her cleats into her running shoes and ran her first cross-country race, beating the other girl and feeling "loose and terrific." After finishing, she went back to field hockey practice. That was the race that gave Benoit the "first real inkling of my potential," she writes. "I'd been training hard in hockey and running the roads, but I wasn't under anything like a tough runner's regime, and yet I had beaten someone who was."

Flushed with that success, Benoit trained harder, aiming for the following spring's state meet. In February 1973, though, she suffered a serious skiing accident. Most skiing accidents come at the end of the day, when skiers are tired and perhaps not concentrating as well as they should be. Perhaps it was inevitable that someone like Benoit, who pushed herself relentlessly even as a child on the slopes, would sooner or later end up injured. She had been doing slalom runs on Pleasant Mountain, a ski area in Maine. Benoit knew she should call it a day, but she "wanted one last try at a perfect run." Instead, what she got was a perfect leg break when she ran into a slalom gate. It was a serious break, and kept her out of track that season. "The leg was not my first injury and it would not be my last," she writes. Indeed, Benoit's life has been full of scrapes and injuries brought on by pushing herself beyond all reasonableness, whether it be in school, or sports.

That fall, Joanie was back to her athletic self, running, playing field hockey, and skiing on the weekends. Then came the day when she knew she was truly a runner, not a skier. Throughout her youth, Saturdays had always been reserved for all-day skiing trips, but one Saturday she cut short her day of skiing on Pleasant Mountain to go to a road race. That spring, she ran 2:24 for 880 yards, but in the state meet was disqualified for passing on the inside lane.

Benoit joined the Boston-based Liberty Athletic Club and began competing in more road races around the region. Her junior year of high school, she went to the Junior Olympic Cross-Country Championship and finished far back from the leaders, which motivated her to keep on training. By now, Benoit was getting attention for her running; a feature article in a Portland, Maine, newspaper made her out to be "a cross between Jesse Owens and Abraham Lincoln," she writes.

Benoit was a dedicated runner, even sneaking off campus to run during the day, in violation of her high school's policy requiring students to stay on the grounds. That drive helped her to a state record of

5:15 in the mile. She ran in all kinds of weather, something she says New England runners have in common with Norwegians and is one reason why both produce so many good runners. "We learn to cope with physical hardship."

College "Muddle"

Benoit enrolled at Bowdoin College in Maine, where she continued adding to her busy schedule. There was no women's cross-country team yet, but she played on the very competitive varsity field hockey squad and continued running on her own. Benoit compares her athletic career to a pyramid, with a wide variety of sports at the base, narrowing to running at the top. Training about 50 miles a week, she placed second in a half-marathon in 1:19:24. She beat her brother Andy for the first time that day and got Bill Rodgers's autograph.

Life at Bowdoin was "a muddle," with Benoit's full schedule of classes, field hockey practices and games, a social life, and running beginning to be too much, even for a workaholic like Joanie. After the half-marathon, she was tired and did not play well in her field hockey match, and was demoted to the junior varsity squad. But she would not lighten her load and quit—"the word gives me hives." In her next match, she played like a madwoman to show the coach she had made a mistake, sprinting all over the field until stepping in a hole and hurting her knee.

It was the Bowdoin doctor who told Benoit that people who had seen her run thought she had potential and that she should give up field hockey. That was just the message she needed. Benoit never would have stopped on her own, but once ordered to, she finally stopped playing field hockey. From that point on, she would no longer be a part-time runner. However, she remained in a kind of lethargy, worn out because of her hectic schedule. Not long afterwards, she was beaten by Lynn Jennings, then a prep star. That snapped her out of her slump. Benoit wrote later that Jennings reminds her of herself; Jennings has gone on to win three world cross-country titles, nine U.S. National Cross-Country Championships, and the bronze medal at the 1992 Olympic 10,000 meters.

Freed from field hockey practice, Benoit began training with Bowdoin's men's team, averaging 50 miles a week, and finally broke five minutes for the mile at the New England AAU Championships. She won the Falmouth road race the summer of her sophomore year. She then transferred to North Carolina State for her junior year, because she thought the big Atlantic Coast Conference school would be better for her running.

As usual, Benoit overdid it and came down with mononucleosis that spring. She felt lost in the large university. At N.C. State, practices with collegiate stars Julie and Mary Shea often turned into races. Too much hard running put her in a hole.

Back home in Cape Elizabeth after the semester ended, Benoit spent the summer running with Bruce Bickford, another top runner from Maine. Benoit was happy in Maine and did not want to go back to North Carolina, but the coach told her they had a good cross-country team coming back and convinced her to return. She did, with a better attitude and a refreshed body. That fall, Benoit broke through with a world record for a road 10K in the Bonne Bell 10K. It was her entry into world-class running. Her commitment to N.C. State finished, Benoit reenrolled at Bowdoin for the spring semester.

Benoit was traveling to road races now, and in January she won a 10K in Bermuda. She writes that she knew she was going to win before she started. She says her confidence in certain races such as this one "isn't euphoria, exactly, and it isn't overconfidence. It's as if I'm an inventor; I created this body and now I'm watching it work." Benoit passed another "psychological milestone" in her Bermuda win, beating Julie Shea for the first time.

Benoit's single-mindedness is reflected in her actions the following morning. She woke up and took a run; then, out of the blue, she decided to enter the Bermuda Marathon. Benoit had never run 26 miles before, but "Adrenaline took over from reason. I never got tired," writes Benoit, who won in 2:50:54, a good time over a windy course that follows rolling hills in a loop around the edge of the island.

Once again, Benoit had pushed her body beyond its limits, and the next day, the beating she gave her body took its toll. She couldn't run at all that morning, and her heel hurt. She flew back to the mainland and went straight from the airport to a track meet at Bowdoin she was supposed to run. Despite being in pain, she raced for the third straight day, and now her body really hurt. Benoit was used to little aches and pains—she just ran through them—but this was serious. She was taken to Dr. Robert Leach in Boston. He brought her to a room where Dutch star Jos Hermans, world-record holder for the hour run, was lying on a table with casts on both feet. The doctor pointed at Hermans, telling Benoit that this is how she'd end up if she didn't take it easy. Benoit listened, but nothing was ever going to slow down her training, and her heel would hurt her on and off for the remainder of her career.

1979 Boston Marathon

After recovering from heel surgery, Benoit decided to aim for the Boston Marathon. She sometimes made the drive to Boston to train with the Liberty Athletic Club. She liked the city, and she was ready to see what she could do in a marathon if she really trained for it. The consistent, 100-mile weeks Benoit had put in prepared her better than she could have imagined.

Benoit was still new to the marathon and was calm coming into the race. She had no reason to worry, she writes. "It was a private test, Joan running for Joan's sake, so I could afford to be peaceful." Still a college student, wearing a Bowdoin singlet, she beat Patti Lyons, the top U.S. marathoner, and set a new American and Boston record of 2:35:15. Benoit ran behind Lyons in the early going, then took the lead at 18 miles and ran into history. She asked one of the men running near her when they were going to hit the famous Heartbreak Hill. "You've already passed it," she was told. At 23 miles, a student from a Bowdoin fraternity jumped out of the crowd holding a bottle of beer and a Red Sox hat, telling Joanie, "Either drink the beer or wear the hat." She chose the hat.

The win took its toll, beating up her legs so much that it felt "like walking on blazing hot tar." When she reached the Portland airport the next day, she was hobbling so much that someone asked her if she needed a wheelchair. Back at Bowdoin, Benoit received a standing ovation when she walked into the school's dining room, something she describes as "a great moment in my life," because she realized that "the college community would always support me if I pursued my running with devotion and sincerity."

That's what she did, but before she could go on to new goals, there were other duties to take care of. Boston is the most visible marathon in the world, and Benoit's win made her a star, giving her what she calls "sudden, unwelcome fame." Some of the trappings of fame were fun, such as when she and men's winner Bill Rodgers had dinner at the White House with President Carter and the prime minister of Japan. In December, Benoit graduated from Bowdoin, ready to try a career different from any of her classmates—that of a professional runner.

Benoit's myriad interests, while making her tired, actually helped her career, says Rodgers.

Joanie is a terrific person, with the same kind of focus as Grete [Waitz]. She's funny. She had room in her life for a lot of things, which I admire because I'm not like that. She was really focused, but she made space for the rest of her life. A lot of time it's observed that runners don't make room for other things in their lives, but Joanie did. It's hard to do, but it's a part of her that makes her a better runner.

Fighting Fatigue

Like other female distance runners, Benoit was limited in her options when it came to thinking about the Moscow Olympic Games; the longest race for women was 3,000 meters, which was too short for her. With no 10,000 meters, "Joanie was pushed into the marathon a lot sooner than she wanted to be," says Bob Sevene, a Boston Athletic Association coach who advised Benoit for many years.

In 1980, Benoit placed a fatigued fourth in the first Avon Women's "World Championship" Marathon in London, won by Lorraine Moller. Despite her loss, she impressed Frank Shorter. The 1972 Olympic Marathon champ, always an astute judge of talent, knew Benoit was going to be great. "I was just so impressed with the way Joan ran in that race," says Shorter. So impressed that he went up and talked with Benoit and her mother.

> I congratulated her and told her she was only going to keep on getting better, once her training caught up with her mind. It was only a matter of time. I had the feeling in 1976, after seeing Carlos Lopes run, that he would be a good marathoner, and I had that same kind of feeling about Joan. She ran and competed like a marathon runner. So, it didn't surprise me when she did well later on.

Nike, which sponsored Benoit her entire career, sent her to New Zealand for some track races and warm-weather training that winter, but she was not happy being there. A recurrent motif throughout her career was how her training faltered when she was away from her beloved Maine. She was like the giant, Antaeus, in Greek mythology: every time he was slain by Hercules, he returned to life and regained his strength when he came in contact with the ground, and so it was with Joanie; her strength and confidence were replenished each time she came back to Maine and was able to run on her favorite training loops. "I've never left Maine without wishing I didn't have to," she writes. "I'm not at peace anywhere else, and, consequently, I don't train as well."

Despite being homesick, she ran well in New Zealand, clocking 4:45 for the mile in the race where Mary Decker set a world record of 4:21.7. Revved up by Decker's performance, Benoit set a new mark of her own, running 2:31:23 to break her American record in a marathon in Auckland. Suddenly, Benoit was the second fastest female marathoner, behind Grete Waitz.

Benoit was not able to build on that success right away. Another of the recurring themes of her career is her perpetual tiredness. She became very tired during her New Zealand tour and returned home early to get ready for her next big race, the World Cross-Country Championships in Paris. She was still tired when she got there, so tired that she could not even climb the stairs at the Louvre to see a Picasso exhibit. Benoit's great powers of concentration were both a blessing and a curse. It allowed her to train harder than any other woman, but it also allowed her to push her body far past its limits, until something broke.

Benoit discovered the source of her fatigue while in Florida for a road race—appendicitis. She had run through the pain and didn't bother seeing a doctor until it felt like "broadswords" were piercing her stomach.

After recovering from an appendectomy, she was back training full-time while teaching full-time at Cape Elizabeth High School. She calls the next two years "building years for my career"—building for the 1984 Olympic Games, where there were hints that the IOC would finally enter the 20th century and allow women to run the marathon.

Benoit took a job with Nike's research lab in Exeter, New Hampshire. She continued racing, but still felt sluggish, reaching the nadir of her career when she hit the wall at the Columbus Marathon, where she ran 2:39:07. Her heels hurt her and, it turns out, she was anemic. Benoit gained new respect for the marathon at Columbus, saying she learned you can't go into a marathon unprepared and that anything can happen in a long race. Benoit compares the marathon to the ocean: beautiful but dangerous. She had yet another operation, on her heels and Achilles tendon, and spent the winter rebuilding her strength, wondering if her career was at an end.

Blistering the Records

Benoit made a quick recovery from surgery, breaking her own American 25K record in May 1982. She ran several more road races throughout the summer, then raced in Europe on the track before setting a course record at Falmouth.

A year after hitting the wall at Columbus, Benoit looked around for a marathon to run, to prove to herself that she had not lost her skills. She chose the September 1982 Nike/Oregon Track Club Marathon in Eugene, redeeming herself in a spectacular way with a new American record of 2:26:11. She felt good and strong the whole race, and her heels had held up well. It was a fine way to end a long two years and was a sign of great things to come.

Benoit kicked off 1983 with a bang, lowering her mile best to 4:36.4 and placing fourth at the World Cross-Country Championships in Gateshead, England. As with Rodgers's third-place in the same race in 1975, Benoit's high placing in the competitive cross-country race showed she was ready for the Boston Marathon, which she approached with "a detached grimness."

Benoit quickly detached herself from the rest of the field at Boston, running her first mile in 4:47. As was to be her strategy in many big races, she wanted to get a big cushion early on. Passing 10K in 31:53, she already had a lead over Roe. She went through halfway in a fantastic 1:08.22. "Joanie was running into unknown territory," said Sevene. Roe dropped out on Heartbreak Hill, but it did not matter. Benoit was on a mission, and nobody was going to catch her this day, as she shattered the world record with a 2:22:43 clocking. As always, Joanie ran how she felt, and this time she felt great.

The only blot on the performance came when some said that Kevin Ryan, a New Zealand marathoner who covered the women's race for New Zealand radio, paced Benoit, a claim she calls "patently ridiculous." (Pacing is not allowed in U.S. marathons, though it is in Europe.) Ryan ran in the same general area as Benoit from 10K on, giving reports. She said his presence was "a nuisance."

That Boston race gave a good illustration of the Benoit toughness. Benji Durden recounts,

> I finished limping, with a bad case of blisters, and Joanie finished looking good. But afterwards, we sat in a hallway in our hotel and pulled off our shoes. We compared feet, and hers looked worse than mine, just a mess. The difference is that she refused to acknowledge it. She set the world record and would not let on that her feet hurt. But they did hurt, because officials had to carry her away. And I was annoyed she went out dancing that night.

Durden had been on world-record pace himself that day, before slowing and placing fifth. "The difference," he says, "is that Joanie had a tenacity about her and the willingness to suffer more than you can possibly suffer to win the race." Durden is among the many runners who agree with Sevene's observation that Benoit is the toughest athlete he's ever met. "That's accurate. Lasse Viren's the only runner I've known with the level of toughness that Joanie had. And Viren was tough at the Olympics only; Joanie was tough all the time."

Boston was followed by a great year. Benoit took the 3,000-meter gold medal at the Pan American Games in Venezuela and won several major road races, including the Philadelphia Distance Classic in 1:09:16 in September. Then it was back home to Freeport, Maine, where Benoit had bought an old farmhouse, to begin her buildup toward Los Angeles. Training went smoothly through the winter and spring until March 17, 1984, the day of the ill-fated 20-mile run. She "felt glorious" until the pain came, a pain that felt "as if a spring were unraveling at the joint."

Olympic Trials

Benoit immediately went to Dr. Leach, who injected the knee with cortisone and told her to rest. That seemed to work, as she was able to get back to her 120 miles a week, thinking, "the problem was solved." It was not, however, as she found out on April 10, when the pain returned with a vengeance after a track workout of three sub-five-minute miles. The morning after that workout, Benoit had to walk home when she tried to run. After a day off, she went out for 12 miles, but could barely lift her leg over a twig. There was nothing to do but take more time off.

When the knee did not get any better, Benoit flew to Eugene, where she was examined by Dr. Stan James, who had operated on Frank Shorter's ankle in 1977. She tried running with Sevene and could not even keep up for two easy miles. It didn't look good, and Benoit writes that "I thought my heart would break." On April 10, James did the arthroscopy, finding and removing a "fibrous mass called a plica, which had become inflamed and was interfering with the joint."

After the surgery, Benoit took another week off, and on May 2 began running again. There were 10 days left before the Olympic Trials, on each of which Benoit put in 15 hours of training, getting up early to swim, run, go to physiotherapy, lift weights, and take a whirlpool. She naturally favored her right knee, which had been operated on, causing stress on her left leg, and she pulled a hamstring. To treat the hamstring, Benoit underwent 6 to 10 hours of electrical stimulation with a Myopulse for five days in a row.

"Joanie is a very intense, driven woman, no question about it. She has a drive few of us can equal," says Sevene. Benoit still did not know if she would be able to run the trials, so, on May 9, she did a 16-mile run. After that, she knew she would be able to start the race but didn't know if she would be able to finish it.

Benoit drove with fiancé Scott Samuelson, her college sweetheart, to Olympia, Washington, knowing she needed a miracle to make the team. She got one, breaking away from Betty Jo Springs at 14 miles and running in alone, though still with the pain in her knee, for a 37-second victory over Julie Brown. Her time was 2:31:04. It was, she says, "the race of my life." Sevene calls it one of the greatest runs by an American athlete ever, saying, "She worked her butt off on an exercise machine, and she wins the whole damn thing."

Adds Durden, "Here is a woman who refused to accept defeat. She just powered through it. I don't know how many of us, even good runners, would be able to do that. Most of us would say, 'It's not meant to be today.'" Benoit, however, refused to give up.

Los Angeles Olympic Marathon

There was no time to bask in the trials glory. Beating the other American marathoners was one thing; beating Grete Waitz, Ingrid Kristiansen, and the best women in the world would be quite another. Benoit returned to Maine to strengthen her knee and hamstring. She knew her comeback from surgery was complete when she won the "exhibition" 10,000 meters at the U.S. Olympic track trials in the Los Angeles Coliseum in 32:07. She went back to Freeport for her last month of training.

Benoit needed an isolated place to train for the Olympics, and she found it on Cliff Island, off the coast of Maine, where she took a cottage. There she'd go out for 20- to 22-mile runs at 6:10 per mile, by herself. "That taught her to be totally into herself and to run faster and faster," says Sevene. "It was something she did on her own."

The media were hyping the showdown between Benoit, the world-record holder, and Grete Waitz, the 1983 World Champion and five-time New York City Marathon winner. That motivated Benoit even more, said Sevene, because she liked to key off the other competitors. Facing fast runners inspired her, made her hungry, even made her mad. There was no prerace socializing for Benoit; she didn't want to share any energy and wanted to save the aggressive feelings that were building up.

Joanie was full of energy before the Olympics. You run a marathon off of what you've done the past four years, Rob de Castella says, and Benoit had averaged 100 miles a week for those years. She was strong and rested, saying, "I was feeling so good and so fast that it was all I could do to hold myself back in my training. When I'm in that condition, I want to run until I drop."

Benoit flew to Los Angeles, where her presence was already felt—Nike had painted a huge mural of Benoit winning Boston on a brick wall near the Coliseum. One morning, while running with Lorraine

Moller, Benoit ran past the mural. A tourist was getting ready to take a photo of the mural of Benoit as Joanie and Moller ran by. "Hey, get out of the way!" the tourist yelled. "She didn't realize that it was Joanie herself running past," says Moller.

Almost everyone else in the city recognized Benoit, though. She found that she was so well-known that she could not go for a run without having people running alongside her, trying to show her they could keep up with her. Benoit said she felt like a gunslinger in the Old West, having to continually prove herself.

Benoit decided to attend the opening ceremonies and then stay with Sevene in Oregon to get away from the hype until the marathon. She says she got "tingles walking into the Coliseum, thinking, 'I wonder what it would be like to come into the stadium alone and leading the marathon.'"

Benoit then flew to Eugene, where Sevene picked her up at the airport. She told Sevene, "I've been talking about getting a medal for three years. And you know something? There's only one medal: the gold medal. The rest is just a cop-out."

Benoit and Sevene flew back to Los Angeles two days before the marathon.

Three years of planning, training, and plotting was coming to a head. Some falter and fade under challenges, choking under the pressure. Benoit thrived on it. This would be the biggest race in women's long-distance history, and she was ready to meet the challenge head-on.

Benoit's plan was to stay with the leaders—to try to keep the pace honest—until 18 miles and then make a move. She and Sevene decided on a 2:27 pace because of the projected weather conditions in Los Angeles. "I really felt she was two minutes better than the rest of the field, and that is what we thought she could run in the heat," said Sevene. With such a good field, there didn't seem to be any way a runner would be able to get away early. But when the early pace of the marathon was too slow for Benoit, she took off after three miles. "Joanie said, 'Damn, let me out,' and dropped it to 5:11 for a couple of miles, and it was the gold medal," explains Sevene. "No one responded, and she got away totally on her own."

Once out in front, Benoit skipped the water stop and pulled farther ahead. The shocking thing about her break was not that she had made a move that early in the race—the pace was not that fast—but rather that none of the others went with her.

"It was like a dream," she wrote later. "Here I was, running comfortably and in control of the Olympic Marathon with no visible opposition." The gap widened as each mile ticked off. The other runners were all keying off Waitz, and because she did not go with Benoit, no one else attempted to. Grete expected Benoit to come back to the field.

But there was no coming back. Once off the front, Joanie was gone for good; all those miles and careful training were paying off. Benoit concentrated on staying relaxed, and smiled when she ran past a Bowdoin banner. She had visualized winning the race so many times during the previous three years. She believed right along that she was going to win.

Says Frank Shorter,

> In essence, it was one of the best tactical races ever tried in an Olympic race. When you do that, you deserve to win. Sometimes, you reach a point as an athlete where you have to say, "Look, let's go out and see who is the best runner." Joanie did that. She took a risk and no one went with her. It was amazing that Grete, Ingrid, and the others let her go. She was able to keep focused on her goal, and that's what made Joanie so tough. She reminds me of Karel Lismont (a Belgian marathoner who placed second to Shorter in the 1972 Olympic Marathon). If you are a woman, the last person you wanted to see was Joanie, just as for the men the one guy you didn't want to see was Lismont. They were both so tough, able to put down their heads and just run.

Benoit felt good running by herself, and the hot weather never materialized. When Benoit reached 18 miles, "she was so programmed to go that she put the pedal down, and by 21 miles it was over. She was almost on world-record pace, and said, 'Wait a minute, I'd better slow down and get the win,'" says Sevene.

"If Grete had been the one who had made the move, Joanie would have covered it." Little known at the time was that Waitz was not ready physically or mentally. She had hurt her back and until two days before the race was uncertain whether she'd be able run. Waitz said even if she had gone on the break, Benoit would probably still have won.

Benoit ran far in front of the field, and as she reached 22 miles with a minute-and-a-half lead, it was clear she was not going to be caught. When she entered the tunnel beneath the Coliseum, she thought, "Once you leave this tunnel your life will be changed forever." On the last lap, Benoit allowed herself a smile of victory, and began waving to the full house that had packed the stadium. Benoit felt so good when she finished that she could have run another marathon; she wrote, "Real success comes when a person is able to say of one of her accomplishments, 'That is a good job well done,' and then leave that accomplishment behind."

So it was that after the 1984 Olympic Marathon, Joan Benoit could finally take a deep breath and say, "Yes, that was a job well done." That was the sentiment of many who watched her stirring performance. The impact of her win is hard to overestimate. She became a role model for many who had never had a woman athlete to admire before. "Joanie's race in the Olympics is the greatest marathon ever run," says Kristy Johnston, a top U.S. marathoner. "It was inspiring for so many of us."

Mary Crawford, a professor at West Chester University, called it an illustration of "female strength and courage," and wrote in *The Runner* that "There's no question that Benoit's victory has energized other women runners." She quotes one young runner as saying, "After 17 miles I knew the race was hers, not from the splits, but from the look on her face—total absorption, concentration, and focus. I want to train as intelligently as she does. But most of all I want to be as *mentally* tough."

Crawford writes,

> When I grew up in the 1950s, girls and women weren't allowed to test themselves in sports . . . . The absence of images of physically competent women had real effects that women of my generation are still working to overcome. Perhaps this was the reason I watched the first women's Olympic Marathon with tears of joy at the accomplishments of the runners. The image of Joan Benoit's face, full of determination as she pulled ahead of the pack and stayed there, compelled my attention and empathy. . . . As the miles rolled by I began to understand how very much she controlled that race, and my heart was with her.

Crawford mentions a 27-year-old mother who said of Benoit's win, "I was glued to the set. At 10 miles I started to cry, and the tears poured down all the way to the end. I felt that every fiber of my body was with Joan Benoit in her effort. She *had* to do it."

Post-Olympic Success

Benoit took advantage of her Olympic fitness by setting the half-marathon world record of 1:08:34 in Philadelphia that fall. (She ran faster through halfway at Boston; that's not a record because the course drops more than one meter/kilometer.) In December, she married Scott. The music at her wedding included the theme to "Chariots of Fire," the same song she had listened to the night before the Olympic Marathon.

After a break picking berries in Maine, Benoit (now known as Benoit Samuelson) was back on the road and back following a hectic schedule.

It felt like it was harder being the Olympic champion than it was getting there, as Benoit was inundated with hundreds of requests for her time. And her heel began hurting again.

In April 1985, Ingrid Kristiansen had broken her world record with a 2:21:06 clocking at London. That motivated Benoit, but she still was feeling a post-Olympic flatness.

In May, she set a course record in the Bay-to-Breakers race in San Francisco, the second largest race in the world, after the Tower Round the Bays in Auckland, New Zealand.

Benoit was set to run New York in the fall of 1985. Her agent had clinched a deal with New York race director Fred Lebow. Then she found out that Kristiansen was going to run Chicago, along with 1984 Olympic bronze medalist Rosa Mota. That afternoon, Benoit went for a run with Sevene.

"What kind of shape do you think Ingrid is in?" she asked. Benoit often used Sevene as a kind of sounding board. "Joanie knew all the time what kind of shape Ingrid was in, but she had to hear somebody else say it," says Sevene.

"Oh, Sev, Ingrid's in great shape."

"But she's not doing 23-milers like you."

"What do you think about me running Chicago?"

"If you want to be number one in the world you need to run against Ingrid. It's the only way to be ranked number one."

Benoit mulled this over for a minute, then turned to Sevene. "Let's go to Chicago."

Thus was the stage set for a classic battle, the Olympic champion versus the world-record holder. For good measure, Rosa Mota, the European champion who got faster every time out, was in the race. Before Samuelson could commit to Chicago, however, she had to first talk to Lebow. The Chicago and New York marathons were each competing in the fall to draw the best field possible. But Lebow didn't try to change Samuelson's mind, saying, "I'm never going to deprive an athlete of the chance to race against the best competition."

Kristiansen spent the fall running road races in the United States, running as fast as 30:50 for 10K. She was coming to Chicago in an attempt to break 2:20. Benoit ran 30:51 for 10K and read how Ingrid trained on her treadmill with Benoit's picture taped up on the wall in front of her. "That gave Joanie something to focus on," says Sevene.

When the gun went off in Chicago, Benoit pushed it much faster than a 2:20 pace. She opened with 5:09 and 5:07 miles, ran 5:08 for mile 3, followed by 5:34 for mile 4, then a 5:04. She passed 10 miles in 52:42 and continued mixing up her splits. But she could not shake Kristiansen, who hung on her shoulder for 18 miles. No matter how fast Samuelson went, Kristiansen hung right with her after each surge. There was a point when Benoit nearly had to let go of the pace, says Sevene. "Ingrid almost broke Joanie, and she had decided at 20 miles 'If she stays with me, I'm out of here.' But Joanie looked behind her and Ingrid was gone."

Benoit was on world-record pace, running alone now. "I had no idea she was going that fast," says Sevene. Scott Samuelson was watching the race with Sevene, and when Benoit passed them, Scott screamed at her, and she "just took off," finishing in 2:21:21, just 15 seconds off Kristiansen's record. Many observers think that without the sometimes strong winds that prevailed, Benoit would likely have gotten the record.

That race showed her side as a "nasty competitor, like Rodgers," says Sevene. "She had health problems and a bad year," but she ran what remains the second fastest marathon ever. "She was convinced she could beat Ingrid; you almost had to die to beat her. She did things that at the time appeared to be crazy, but weren't crazy. She ran with just reckless abandon."

Chicago topped off a great streak for Benoit. She did not lose a marathon from 1982-85, and her *slowest* time was 2:31. She was planning to make Chicago her last marathon, but it wasn't. Her career after that race was slowed by injuries, but she has continued competing.

Training: When in Doubt, Train Harder

Benoit ran very high mileage in her career, often up to 120 miles a week, saying, "Mileage is my safety blanket." Before the Olympic Games, she did one long run, one semi-long run, and an interval session a week. Getting in two long runs a week was important for her training. Her marathon preparations began about four months before the race with a 20-mile run. As the marathon drew near, she increased the frequency of her 20-miler to once every five days. In between, she averaged 10 miles in the morning and "six" in the evening.

"Joanie's ability lies in her training. Joanie was very tough and able to train very hard and focus on the goal," says Shorter. "Her training was very regimented; she could just focus and cut everything out. That was her unique talent as much as her physical talent."

Benoit never liked training with women. She raced as fast as many men and liked training with elite men such as Greg Meyer. "Joanie liked to bury people," is how Sevene explains it. "She would play with me when we ran together. She'd test herself against the men, and she'd run hard." Not surprisingly, Benoit ended up training frequently by herself. Benji Durden would run with Benoit when they saw each other at races. "I remember going with Joanie to do a training run the Friday after Boston, and she just hammered me, really hammered me, chattering away the whole time."

Benoit was comfortable in Maine and was not tempted to try high-altitude training. She had a home in Freeport that she had restored, and her family is there. "Joanie is very family-oriented. She came from a rural background and had a whole support system. By leaving, she found she was giving up more than she was gaining," Sevene said.

Benoit had five or six runs that she ran repeatedly, following her footsteps from run to run, and it was the times on her regular training loops that let Benoit judge her fitness. She gained her strength—both mental and physical—from this repetition. She'd make big, wide turns around the corners, staying in the same grooves. That way, she would know when she was really flying, and the times on the course would mean something.

Benoit's thoroughness in training was seen in how she'd run when she reached an intersection. Approaching a left-hand turn, she wouldn't just turn left, but instead would go right and all the way around the perimeter of the intersection, making sure she took the longest possible route. And when the run was over, she'd touch the mailbox in front of her house, then run another half-mile down the road and back.

"Joanie is a very compulsive trainer," says Durden. "If you would go on a workout with her, if it was a workout she had done before, there would be a standard loop, and you *did not* cut the loop. If there was a tree on the loop, you don't go inside the tree, but go outside it."

Benoit's racing strategy was to force the pace as early as she could and drop the other runners. To be able to do that, her training philosophy was "When in doubt, run harder." She ran hard in the morning, then got through the afternoon run as best she could, saying, "It's the second run of the day that makes me the competitor I am."

While most runners will pad their mileage to make it seem like they're running more—so that a 6.5-mile run becomes 7 miles—Benoit was on the opposite extreme. No matter how far she ran in the afternoon, she still called it six miles. She *undercounted* her mileage. When Joanie went for a training run, she *never* did less than what she'd planned for. If a 10-miler was scheduled, she not only did the 10 miles, but often would make it more like 11 miles.

One training partner, Englishman Giles Norton, recalls, "When we'd go skiing on the weekend, she had a loop from the ski area. It was 10 miles in 65 minutes on the way down, then back up in 60 minutes. Then she'd ski the rest of the day."

After a run, Benoit would come back in the house and cook brownies, talk on the phone, or do chores, while her training partners collapsed on the couch. Benoit had the will-power to push her body far beyond the point where most people, even most elite runners, would have stopped and rested.

Every once in a while, her body would rebel and her overachieving, frantic life would catch up to her. She'd finally be forced to stop running because of injury, or forced to rest because of illness. "Joanie's stubborn," Sevene explains.

Perhaps the best example of Benoit's career is that of Sisyphus, the Greek whose punishment for angering the gods was to endlessly roll a rock up a mountain, only to see it roll back down when he reached the top. So it was to be for Benoit: endlessly training, reaching the pinnacle at a race, then getting injured and having to start the climb all over again. The only failure, Benoit said, is the failure to try.

Benoit rarely talked about her training to outsiders. Racing for her was as much a mental as a physical challenge, "which is why," Sevene says, "she didn't want to give her opponents any reason to key on her."

Benoit is one of those people who just loves to run, and better yet, to run hard. Over and over again through the years she pushed herself to the edge, seeing how far she could go and still come back. There were no easy days scheduled in Benoit's training program. "She wasn't out there on the roads to goof off," says Sevene. "She was there to do her best every time she lined up."

That's why Benoit wouldn't compete if she was not 100 percent ready to race. That was sometimes frustrating for race directors, who wanted to pin down a commitment from her, but Benoit, like de Castella and Jones, would pass up large paydays if she knew she was not fit enough or healthy enough to give her best effort.

Because of injuries, Benoit became an expert in cross-training long before it was popular. First came long swimming sessions after her heel surgery, then biking on an exercycle after her knee surgery in 1984.

Benoit's training was a constant race to get in world-record shape and run a race before injuries slowed her down. The "secret" to her training was that, like Shorter and Zatopek before her, "Joanie honestly believed that she was working harder than anyone in the world," said Sevene. "Whether she was or not, she was always mentally ready. She was that tough."

Joan did work extraordinarily hard. "I kept to the same basic schedule during those [peak] years," Benoit Samuelson recalled late in 1995. "I'd do two long runs a week, one speed session, with the rest being filler." A typical week leading up to a major marathon included:

Sunday:	A.M., 6-13 miles; P.M., 6 miles.
Monday:	Same as Sunday.
Tuesday:	A.M., 15-16 miles (no P.M. run).
Wednesday:	Same as Sunday.
Thursday:	A.M., 6-13 miles; P.M., track workout or fartlek run.
Friday:	Same as Wednesday.
Saturday:	A.M., 20 miles (no P.M. run).

Benoit would sometimes do her two long runs on Sunday and Wednesday, and move her speedwork to Friday. She was able to run most of her runs at a quick pace, because, she says, "I guess it is just the nature of the beast."

Benoit's runs weren't comfortable, fun runs. "Slow to her was a six-minute-mile pace," says Durden. "Joanie was respected and admired by everyone. You'd hate to get beat, but if you got beat by Joanie, you knew she was able to do it because she had put in the work. And who could begrudge that?"

Indeed, Benoit is acknowledged as one of the classiest of runners, someone who won the gold medal through relentless hard work. "If I feel good nine straight days, I run hard for nine straight days." She took easy days only when her body couldn't be pushed any further.

The purpose of her training was to build up her endurance far beyond that of any other runner, to "neutralize" the speed she thought her opponents had. Not that Benoit was slow: She cracked 60 seconds for the quarter-mile in college and had a 4:36 mile to her credit. Her 10K and marathon training was similar; the main difference was that she ran more track workouts while building up for a 10K.

She'd get a "feeling of emptiness" after a marathon, a letdown that took her a long time to overcome. What worked best was setting a new goal that she could devote her enormous energy to.

© Photo Run / Victah Sailer

Joan Benoit Samuelson returns to Chicago in 1994 where she qualified
for the 1996 U.S. Olympic Trials by running 2:37.

Going and Going

In 1986, Benoit set records over 10 miles and 25K, but didn't run a marathon. Even when she couldn't run Boston in 1987 because of her bad knee, she still went to the marathon to sell her special blueberry jam. She was raising money for the Samantha Smith Foundation, set up in memory of Samantha Smith, a young girl from Maine who went to the Soviet Union in 1983 and was killed in a plane crash in 1985.

In 1988, Benoit took a break to have her first child, Abigail, and it was her daughter who forced Benoit to do what friends, family, husband, and coaches couldn't—get her to back off on her training. She cut out one of her two daily training sessions after Abigail was born, adding swimming to her schedule. The baby's needs came first, and Benoit's focus was now her daughter, not the marathon.

Pregnancy was no problem for Samuelson; she jogged and swam straight through it. Giving birth, however, was as difficult as running a marathon, she told Marlene Cimons. "I said running a sub-2:20 would be a cakewalk after this. When it was over, I told Scott, 'Never again.' But then again, I said the same thing after my first marathon. The pain of being an athlete is nowhere near this kind of pain."

Samuelson's running form was thrown off after childbirth. She planned a comeback for the 1988 Olympic Trials, but problems with her leg kept her from full training. Plus, the motivation wasn't as great, she told Cimons. "For me, nothing could match what I did in Los Angeles. That win was something special. Even if I could win another medal, it wouldn't be the same as that first win in L.A.... I hit the Olympics at just the right time in '84.

Shorter says that in Benoit's case, "if the biomechanics are not there, then what is basically a minor injury can become serious." As Shorter found out with his own training, when he had trouble regaining top form after surgery, sometimes "it's just enough of a change that it just never gets right again."

That got to be a problem for Benoit, who wouldn't go into a race unless she had full confidence in her training. "This is what I am going to run, and anybody who beats me, beats me," Shorter puts it.

> Joanie would have the feeling before the race that she wasn't afraid of anyone. Her way was to prepare so well. The problem comes when you can't duplicate past training. At the highest level, it's interesting to think of what, out of all the training, makes the difference. In Joanie's case, it was running those certain loops very fast.

In the fall of 1994, Benoit Samuelson returned to the scene of her great win over Kristiansen and ran the Chicago Marathon in 2:37, qualifying for the 1996 U.S. Olympic Trials. Joanie was 39 in 1996, and it was 12 years since she hobbled home on the bum knee before her first Olympic Trials. Samuelson told *Runner's World* in 1994, the 10th anniversary of her Olympic win, "I'm just trying to maintain right now. You can't go back to the well too many times. But the spark is still there. The Atlanta Olympics are appealing, especially because they'll be back on home soil. That's one of the reasons I was so pumped out in 1984." She finished 13th at the 1996 Trials, however, a strong performance, but not one that would put her on the Olympic team.

What defined Benoit during a long career that stretched from the late 1970s through the 1990s was that no matter how fast she ran, how many world or American records she set, how many races or medals she won, she was never, ever satisfied. Each time she reached a goal, she set a newer, more difficult one, with the ultimate being breaking the 2:20 barrier in the marathon. And although she never did, in getting close, Benoit, like her rival Ingrid Kristiansen, brought women's running to a new level with a mental toughness that allowed her to run through pain, fatigue, and injury.

The legacy Samuelson has left for young runners, says Sevene, is that their dreams can indeed come true, and that hard work can overcome many obstacles. "I tell the kids, 'Don't be afraid.' She and Billy (Rodgers) are two classic cases of individuals who had a dream, and did not give up on the dream. Finally, they reached the point where it came true. They were both nasty competitors, feisty, who liked getting down and dirty in races. They both knew exactly where they were going and developed all facets of their running to do it.

"Joanie was always in control and knew where she was going and how she was going to get there. You knew Joanie was going to get there. She did it the right way."

"All athletes who strive for excellence share the same story," writes Samuelson. What Benoit learned from her story, she wrote, was the importance of perseverance, humor, friendship, and hard work. Her advice to young runners:

> Love yourself, for who and what you are; protect your dream and develop your talent to the fullest extent. Don't lose sight of your goals. No matter what the obstacles are, don't let anything deter you from your best effort. Don't allow anyone to tell you what you can and cannot do. Be tough, be stubborn, love yourself, and find friends who believe in you.

And above all, Samuelson adds, "Recognize your victories."

17

Said Aouita

"It Must Remain a Secret"

Born November 2, 1960, Morocco
World records: 1,500, 2,000, 3,000, and 5,000 meters
Olympic gold, 5,000, 1984
Olympic bronze, 800, 1988

Said Aouita's face is a picture of concentration as he bends over the far side of the pool table. He frowns and narrows his eyes, and his forehead furrows as he carefully sights down the cue and takes a bead on the balls. His 5'7", 125-pound body tenses as he attempts a difficult bank shot.

A little body English urges the cue ball on. It lightly taps the eight ball, which, after a moment's hesitation, drops into a side pocket. Aouita straightens up and gives a quick victory yell, pleased at having won another game from Faouzi Lahbi, his training and playing partner. Lahbi, a 1:46 800-meter runner who paces Aouita through workouts, throws his hands up in dismay and stalks away.

Dezza Abderrahim, Aouita's physiotherapist turns. "Said is good for just learning the game, no? In a few years, he will be a *very* good player."

Aouita was already a very good runner by this time, the spring of 1991, acknowledged by most as the world's top middle-distance runner. The Moroccan 1984 Olympic 5,000-meter gold medalist held five world track records: 1,500 meters (3:29.46); 2,000 meters (4:50.81); two miles (8:13.45); 3,000 meters (7:29.45); and 5,000 meters (12:58.3). Aouita also set the 3,000-meter indoor world record, and his 3:46.7 mile was the fourth fastest ever run.

Aouita was the preeminent track athlete of the 1980s, running not just to win—it was assumed that he would win any race he entered—but to set records. Aouita brought a fire and cockiness to the track world. "Aouita is scary for the number of times he went to the line and raced exceptionally well. He missed the world record in a number of events by just fractions of a second, and that was in addition to the ones he got," U.S. runner Doug Padilla told *Track & Field News*. "It's scary when a guy is so strong and can go out and do that so often."

The majority of Aouita's records and wins came in a stellar four-year stretch, beginning in 1984, during which he lost just two races (one of those a steeplechase, a race that was not his event). Those races were against the best in the world—Steve Cram, Sebastian Coe, Steve Ovett, Steve Scott, Sydney Maree, Arturo Barrios, Yobes Ondieki, and Abdi Bile, among others.

Aouita's talents were so overwhelming and wide-ranging that some of his countrymen in sports-crazed Morocco believed their charismatic national hero could do anything on the track, in any event that he entered—even win the 100 meters against the top sprinters in the world. "It's true," Aouita says, taking a break from the pool table. "There are many people in Morocco who think it is easy for me to beat Carl Lewis in the 100. But not everybody, just some people who don't know very much about athletics."

Those who do know athletics rank Aouita among the most versatile runners ever. That includes Steve Cram, ex-world-record holder in the mile (3:46.32) and one of Aouita's chief rivals through years of international track racing at the highest level. "Said's range was unbelievable," says Cram. "He could win any race he set his mind to."

Sebastian Coe agrees. "Said broke all the rules," Coe told journalist Pat Butcher, who made a film about Aouita entitled "The Arabian Knight." "Besides winning 800s, he could run a brilliant 1,500 meters and an unbelievable 5,000 meters. In terms of range of distance he's unsurpassed. The biggest gap is between 1,500 and 5,000, and he made the jump with sublime indifference."

U.S. miler Steve Scott, who waged many battles with Aouita, said in an interview that Said "isn't afraid to race the best competition. He didn't dodge anyone. Aouita is exciting because every time he goes out, you know the race will be a barn burner. He can run either way, from the front or coming from behind." U.S. 10,000-meter runner Bruce Bickford told *Track & Field News*,

> You can't really say you race against Aouita. He runs his own race; *he* dictates the race. When you race him, the main thing you notice is that *he* controls everything. His strength definitely is his head. We all know he has tremendous talent, but without the head to go with it, a talented athlete won't go nearly as far. Aouita is just very confident of what he can do, and goes out and does it.

Aouita does not take much interest in such discussions. Of his racing, he said simply, "I run for Morocco and for that I am very proud. I want to run fast. I want to win. I want to break records."

From Last to First

Like one of the unstoppable desert *siroccos* that sweep down from the Atlas mountains along the north coast of Africa, Aouita had an inexorable determination to be the best since he was a child selling roasted watermelon seeds in Fez, Morocco. Born in the Mediterranean Sea town of Kenitra, Morocco, on November 2, 1960, Said was the oldest of six children of a paper-mill worker. When Aouita was nine, his family moved to Fez, one of the old imperial cities of Morocco, after his father lost his job in the paper mill. As a youth, Aouita spent his time roaming the narrow streets of Fez before turning to athletics.

In photos of Aouita as a youth, he is invariably smiling, and his aunt, Khadija, told Pat Butcher in an interview that "Said was always a happy boy. He did not sit still for a moment and was always running in the streets." Aouita was also always fast. Like nearly every young Moroccan, he played soccer from the time he could walk, and one story has it that his running talent was discovered when his soccer team was running laps after practice—and he set a new national junior record during the practice laps.

Aouita's youth soccer coach, Aziz Debbagh, says that Aouita was "no different than the other children" when he started playing. But Aouita "was keen to improve," Debbagh remembers. One day when the coach was late, most of the children left. Not Said. He had changed into his practice gear and went out running.

One day, Aouita's best friend was running in a cross-country race. Aouita came and watched. His friend won, and afterwards Aouita came up to him, saying, "I could beat you."

"That's not possible, Said," his friend said. "You've never trained, or run a race."

"Next week, I will run a race."

Aouita showed up and won. "I was very sick after the race, but I did beat him," Aouita told Butcher.

While still playing soccer, Aouita began training with a sports club and winning local races. He would stay out in the streets, playing running games, and his friends would make fun of him. This did not bother Aouita; rather, it gave him the "ambition to win."

Aouita ran his first international competition in 1978, at the junior division of the World Cross-Country Championships in Glasgow, Scotland. He had won the Moroccan junior championships and expected to do well in Glasgow. It was cold and the course was thick with mud. The 17-year-old led for the first four kilometers, before fading to 34th. "I was very unhappy with that, because I wanted to win," Aouita told Butcher. "I said, 'I will never run that badly again.'"

When he was 18, Aouita ran in the World University Games in Mexico City. "I don't like to speak about this," he says in a soft voice. When asked why not, he replies, "Because I was the last." Aouita shakes his head as if still shocked by such an inconceivable occurrence. "Yes, I was last. . . . It was terrible for me."

But Aouita's running potential had caught the attention of the Moroccan Track Federation, which sent him to school in France, where there were better facilities for training. He showed his potential by running 8:40.2 for the steeplechase later in 1979. In 1980, he clocked 3:37.3 for the 1,500, making him one of the top young middle-distance prospects in the world.

French doctors tested Aouita's maximum $\dot{V}O_2$ uptake on the treadmill. He tested out at 96. "I didn't know what it meant," Aouita told

Butcher. "It was the highest number they had ever heard of. They said, 'He must be a great athlete.'"

In 1981, Aouita started what he called "intensive training." He returned to the World University Games, this time in Bucharest, and got redemption. "I won the 1,500 (in 3:38.43), and from that time many people said that maybe I can become a good athlete in the future. In 1982, I decided to make just athletics [my career], and from there, I started to run hard. Things have gone good since then," Aouita recalled.

Giving up soccer for track was indeed a good choice, as Aouita quickly became a force on the international circuit in 1983. He left Morocco and moved to the historic Italian hilltop town of Sienna, so he could be near Enrico Dionisi, an Italian banker and manager of a Sienna-based track club. Dionisi has managed Aouita's financial affairs ever since. But Aouita devised his own workouts, saying, "I decided to be my own coach."

When he first met Aouita, Dionisi had the impression that Said "was older than he was. He reminded me of Sebastian Coe at the same age, so nervous to arrive, so wanting to be someone," the Italian told Kenny Moore. Aouita was not yet well-versed in track and field. When he ran his first 5,000-meter race, Aouita did not know how many laps it was. "I just ran hard."

In 1983, he blasted 3:32.54 for 1,500 meters in a meet in Florence, fast enough to get him his first corporate sponsorship. Aouita went on to run the 800 in 1:44.38 that summer, and he geared his training to peak for the first-ever World Championships in Helsinki. Despite his fast times, Aouita was still an unknown when he came to Helsinki, says Cram, who was focusing on rivals Steve Scott and Steve Ovett. "I'd heard a little about Said, but I really didn't know much about him."

Aouita's plan was to surprise Cram by starting a hard kick from 500 meters out, far earlier than most 1,500-meter runners begin sprinting. But a slow early pace meant that the rest of the field was able to go right with Aouita when he moved into the lead and began accelerating. Aouita led at the bell and down the backstretch, until Cram passed him going around the final turn. Aouita told Butcher that getting passed "upset me so much that I lost interest." Scott also passed Aouita. And Aouita clocked 3:42.02 with his characteristic head-rolling sprint, holding off Ovett for the bronze medal.

That loss was a turning point in Aouita's career, because he realized, Moroccan official Aziz Daouda says, that "training is not enough to be a world champion." There was a change in Aouita, from a focus on the physical to the physical plus intelligence. From now on, he tried to outthink his opponents as well as outrun them.

Choosing a Gold Medal

Aouita missed some training in the spring of 1984 because of an injury, but still ran well in the summer. Returning to Florence in June, he ran a 13:04.78 5,000 meters, placing him second on the all-time list. In July, he added to his list the third fastest 1,500 ever, 3:31.54.

With his broad talent, Aouita never had an easy time making up his mind what event, or events, to run at championship meets. He assumed he could win every event he entered, and hated missing out on any race. Two weeks before Los Angeles, Aouita announced he was going to run the 1,500, setting up what would be a spectacular showdown against Steve Cram, defending gold medalist Sebastian Coe, Steve Ovett, and Steve Scott.

But on race day, there was Aouita on the starting line of the 5,000. An injury had kept Aouita from doing the speedwork he needed for the 1,500. While he looked to be the favorite for those who followed the sport, he was virtually unknown to the casual fans among the full house in the Los Angeles Coliseum. The 5,000 field featured world-record holder David Moorcroft (13:00.42), ex-mile world-record holder John Walker, Ray Flynn of Ireland, Doug Padilla of the United States, and Kenyans Wilson Waigwa, Paul Kipkoech, and Charles Cheruiyot. Coming into Los Angeles, Aouita, just 23, had the year's fastest times in both the 5,000 and the 1,500.

It was a scintillating 5,000, which, unlike most dawdle-and-kick championship 5,000 meters, was fast from the start. Antonio Leitao of Portugal, knowing he could not match Aouita's last-lap speed, teamed up with countryman Ezequiel Canario to string out the field by opening with a 62-second first lap. After two and a half laps, Leitao took over the lead, pushing the pace to well below that of Brendan Foster's 13:20.3 Olympic record. It did not bother Aouita. He tucked in right on Leitao's shoulder, where he would remain until it was time to start his kick. The field ran in single file behind Leitao and Aouita, and the challengers dropped off one by one, until with three laps to go the pair had just four runners for company—Cheruiyot and Kipkoech, Markus Ryffel of Switzerland, and Tim Hutchings of Great Britain.

Entering the bell lap, Aouita was still sitting on Leitao's shoulder. Then, down the backstretch, Said accelerated and easily moved past Leitao, with only Ryffel able to go with him. Ryffel tried to pass Aouita on the curve, but Said had plenty of speed left. He sprinted down the homestretch as if out for an evening stroll, waving to the crowd, to win in 13:05.5, the third-fastest 5,000 ever and a new Olympic record by nearly 15 seconds. Ryffel (13:07.5) took the silver with Leitao (13:09.2) hanging on for the bronze.

Afterwards, the world had its first glimpse of the Aouita cockiness that was to characterize his career. "Usually, I like more of a challenge," he told the press. "It was a very easy run." The Olympic win made him a national hero not just in Morocco, but in all Arab countries. The train from Rabat to Casablanca was named "The Aouita," and King Hassan II telephoned Aouita after the race and rewarded him with a villa outside of Casablanca.

Aouita had a huge theater installed in his villa, stocked with over 2,000 movies and videos of his races. He added a weight room to the basement, to work on improving his strength and settled in the villa to train with an eye for setting world records in 1985, especially in the 1,500.

A Record Year

The first attempt at a world record came against a stacked field on July 16 at the Nikia Grand Prix meet in Nice.

"Said was still relatively new then," Cram recalled. "We all had our eyes on Joaquim Cruz, who had won the [800-meter] gold medal in the Olympics the year before." To get away from the Brazilian, Cram took off with over 400 meters to go, earlier than normal in a 1,500, and built a big gap down the backstretch. Aouita had been sitting in fifth when Cram made his jump and was caught by surprise.

The tall, lanky Cram was always difficult to pass once he had the lead on the last lap of a race. The crowd was making so much noise that Cram could not tell how close Cruz and Aouita were. Aouita gave it his all, running his last 300 meters in 39.0, faster than Cram's 39.8. In the last 200 meters, Aouita gained nearly a second on Cram, 25.0 to 25.9, and his last 100 meters took just 11.8 seconds, to Cram's 12.2.

Cram heard the crowd cheering louder in the final meters, and out of the corner of his eye, just before the tape, saw the charging Aouita. Cram had just enough to hold off the fast-finishing Aouita down the stretch, as both broke the record. Aouita clocked 3:29.71. Cram set a new world record of 3:29.67, beating Aouita by a meter. "We were both happy," said Cram, "but I was slightly happier."

The indefatigable Aouita was stunned by the loss and vowed to come back. His next race was over 5,000 meters on July 27, 1985 at the Bislett Games in Oslo, Norway. There was no better place to take aim at Moorcroft's 5,000 world mark than venerable Bislett Stadium, the site of 54 world records through the years. Aouita faced a good field which included Sydney Maree, Alberto Cova and Francesco Panetta of Italy, Ireland's John Treacy, and Peter Koech of Kenya.

After following rabbits through 3,000 meters in 7:51, Aouita took the lead, running the next kilometer in 2:41.1 and his last 1,000 meters in 2:28.24. He needed a very fast finish to get the record, and Said responded with a final 400 meters of 54.4 and a last 200 meters of 26.7. Down the final straightaway, Aouita ran with his eyes closed, his head rolling from side to side, finishing in a new world record of 13:00.40, one-hundredth of a second inside Moorcroft's three-year-old record. When Moorcroft set his record, breaking Henry Rono's standard, he was so far ahead of the field that the second-place runner thought Moorcroft had been a pacemaker and had dropped out. That wasn't the case in this race, as Aouita beat Maree by less than a second, not passing the American until the final turn. Aouita had not expected to run a world record, as he had missed 10 days of training. A niece had died, and the saddened Aouita just had not felt like training. He told Butcher that "it was as if the record had just dropped out of the sky."

On August 21, he just missed Cram's mile record (3:46.32) in running 3:46.92. Two days later, at a Grand Prix meet in Berlin's Olympic Stadium, Aouita took aim at Cram's 1,500-meter record. Rabbit Volker Blumenthal towed the field through splits of 56.8 and 1:53.5 before Frank O'Mara of Ireland took over, with Aouita tucked in right behind. They ran the next 400 in 55 seconds to pass three laps in 2:48.5. Running the last lap by himself, Aouita used a 41.0 last 300 to grab the record in 3:29.46, a time that nearly left him in tears.

Former world-record holder Sydney Maree of the United States was second, 3.5 seconds behind. Aouita's last 800 was 1:50.0; his last 400 meters took just 54.5 seconds. When he finished, Aouita jumped up in the air, then lay face down on the track. He got back up and ran a victory lap, pumping his fists in the air and blowing kisses to the crowd. The high standard of the record is seen in that it was to stand for eight years, until Algerian Nourredine Morceli broke it in 1993.

Aouita was characterized by a tremendous desire to win, and was known for his all-out efforts in the last laps of races. Here's how Kenny Moore of *Sports Illustrated* described Aouita's ferocious running style in his 1985 world record 1,500 race: "Aouita came flailing into the stretch of the 1,500 meters looking as if his teeth were going to crack. His head seemed in danger of rolling right off. His arms were pumping so high, his fists were above his ears." When asked about such descriptions of his form, Aouita says, simply, "I do everything I can to win."

Maybe that is why such an aura of invincibility developed around him, and why so many, Emil Zatopek among them, admired him. The Czech said the three modern track runners he had seen who impressed him most were Aouita, Barrios, and Coe. Perhaps it was Aouita's same grimace of almost superhuman effort on the last straightaway of his races that impressed Zatopek. Both sprinted at the end of races as if their lives depended on winning; and maybe they did.

Aouita's competitors also had high respect for him. Cram said Aouita and Coe were the most difficult to race against because he could never be sure what tactic they would choose. Sometimes they would go from the front, other times they would sit back and kick. "You never quite knew," said Cram, who had a great year himself in 1985. After Aouita broke his 1,500 record, Cram set the mile world record with a 3:46.32 (which stood until 1993) and the 2,000-meter world record. Cram's mile record was set at the Bislett Games.

Aouita said that if he hadn't been injured part of 1985, he would have set four world records, instead of two. "If someone breaks my records, it won't bother me," he said. "It gives me a reason to train even harder."

Hollywood Material

Aouita was now one of the top stars of track and field. Along with a few others, such as Cram, sprinter Carl Lewis, and hurdler Edwin Moses, Aouita commanded large appearance fees (up to $40,000 per race) and first-rate treatment wherever he went. That lifestyle seemed suited to Aouita's personality, and after more success in 1986, he bought homes in Fez, Morocco and Malagra, Spain. He showcased his talent in 1986 by running the only 10,000 meters of his career. He finished in 27:26, then one of the fastest times ever. He said the 10,000 meters on the track was an easy race.

Aouita began training in Davos, Switzerland, Mexico City, Italy, and the United States, flying across the globe to find the best setting for his training. He was the first elite runner to have a jet-setter's lifestyle, living in plush surroundings where he could do his workouts in secret. Even among the elite track athletes at the Grand Prix track invitationals, Aouita stood out. He would show up at meets in a stretch limousine, stepping out with a large entourage in true Hollywood style. He took over meets by the sheer force of his personality, brashly predicting that no one would be able to stay close to him, then proving himself right.

In 1987, Aouita had what he calls his best year. He got the record in the two-mile run, clocking 8:13.45 in Turin, Italy, in May during an Italy-Soviet Union dual meet.

In the two-mile record race, Moroccan Brahim Boutaib, who would go on to win the 10,000 meters at Seoul (and who was coached by Aouita), took Aouita through splits of 55.3, 1:56.3 (800 meters), 2:59.4, and 4:02.5 for the mile. Aouita took the lead on the sixth lap and ended up beating Salvatore Antibo by more than seven seconds.

Aouita next broke Cram's 2,000-meter record in Paris, clocking 4:50.81 on July 16, 1987. The race was specifically set up as a record run. At 800 meters, which rabbit James May of the United States led in 1:55.5, Aouita was a second behind. He moved up onto the shoulder of Dave Reid at 1,200 meters (2:56.3), then passed 1,600 meters in 3:56.02 before finishing strongly to break Cram's record by .58 seconds.

Aouita then took aim at his own 5,000-meter record six days later in the Golden Gala Grand Prix meet at Rome's Olympic Stadium. Most of the Romans had fled to the seashore to escape the heat and humidity, and Maree was back to challenge Aouita, along with Portuguese Olympian Ezequiel Canario. After following through a 7:46.3 3,000 meters, Aouita took the lead and left the other runners far behind. A next 1,000 meters of 2:39.68 put him at 10:26.05 at 4,000 meters.

Running alone, Aouita increased his pace, running his last 800 meters in 2:00.7 and his last 400 in 57.4 to become the first runner to break the 13-minute barrier, with a time of 12:58.39. Second-place finisher Maree was 26.6 seconds behind. "People said it wasn't possible to break 13 minutes, but I did it," Aouita said.

"Of all the runners I have raced, Aouita may be the gutsiest, because when he is ready, he just goes," Maree told *Track & Field News*.

> It doesn't matter who is in the race, or if his race plan has been jeopardized somewhere in the middle of the race. Aouita sticks to his guns. He is one racer who lays out a plan for a race and then sticks to it.
>
> He lets nothing come between him and his plan, regardless of the distance. A runner with that frame of mind will think only positively toward the future. I'm sure a lot of runners would love to hold both the 1,500 and 5,000 records, but they didn't *believe* they could do it. Aouita *knew* he could and did it.

Aouita often came off as self-centered and cocky. His reputation for being a bit arrogant was solidified by his comments at the 1987 World Championship 5,000. Then 26 and with an Olympic gold and four world records already under his belt, Aouita showed up at the prerace press conference with several chain-smoking underlings. Ben Johnson had just beaten Carl Lewis in a world-record 9.83 in the World Championship 100-meter final, and Aouita vowed to make fans at Rome forget about the sprinters.

Said Aouita, "My 5,000 record has days to live. I will run in the front of the field and *basta*! I want to run 12:56 on Sunday and show the whole world that Ben Johnson is not the king of the World Championships."

This time, however, Aouita was blowing as much smoke as his cronies. He did not run from the front, but was content to let the pace dawdle at 68 seconds per lap before easily running away from his overmatched competitors with a 52.5-second final 400 meters. His winning time was 13:26.44.

Then, at the postrace press conference, Aouita spoke of how he had not really been challenged at all, and chided several runners, including Belgian Vincent Rousseau, for spiking him. "I am the top runner in the world," Aouita said in *Runner's World*. "There is not a race tactic that can beat me. If I choose, I can run world records. It was easy for me to win the gold medal here. My time was of no importance to me."

Still, the 1987 World Championships gold medal solidified Aouita's nearly universal reputation as the best runner in the world. Indeed, he was nearly invincible, winning over 50 races from the time of his gold medal in the Los Angeles Olympics through the Seoul Olympics. Amazingly enough, after the 1987 track season ended Aouita said, "I was not pleased that I didn't break more world records." Three world records in a year weren't enough.

"Said's quest was to push back standards," Cram told Butcher. "He was always trying to improve, which is what the good athletes have to do. His positive attitude endeared him to me. He enjoyed racing and never showed up and went through the motions." Cram says what separates winners like Aouita from the also-rans is their mental approach. "He had the energy to put his head on the chopping block," at the big track meets, performing like an actor. But that approach meant that by the end of the summer, says Cram, Aouita was always "very tired, trying to break world record after world record."

Seoul Searching

With his record-breaking year behind him, Aouita took aim at the 1988 Olympics. Heading into Seoul, he was the favorite in whatever race or races he decided to run. Rumors flying across the track circuit were that he would try an unheard of triple, going for wins in the 800, 1,500, and 5,000 meters. Everyone was waiting to see what Said would do—but even he did not know. Part of his decision was made for him when the Olympic schedule was released, showing that the 5,000 final would start just 20 minutes before the 1,500 final. "I am not Superman," Aouita said, in explaining why he didn't defend his Olympic title in the 5,000, a distance in which he had not lost a race in five years.

Instead, he entered the 800- and 1,500-meter races, saying of the 1,500, "I must win that race." He believed it would take 1:42.50 to win the 800, and said he was capable of that. But for the first time in four years, things didn't turn out as planned.

> In Seoul, I was the defending gold medalist. Everybody wants to know why I ran the 800. I think it is easy to run 800, because I know I am fast in that race. I know I have enough power to run a good 800. In 1988, I beat Johnny Gray, who had run 1:42. I beat Joaquim Cruz. I beat everybody in the 800. If I wasn't injured, I would have won the race. I am not lucky.

The injury came when Aouita strained his hamstring training in Tokyo, three weeks before the Olympics. "I was alone; my physiotherapist was not with me. When I was injured, I didn't have anybody to help me."

By the time Aouita was able to resume training, there was just one week left before the track prelims started. To top it off, he pulled another muscle two days before the racing began. "It was too late. When I went to run fast in training, I was injured for a second time in Seoul. And maybe I made a big mistake. I was told not to run the 800 because I can't run good, because I am injured."

Telling Aouita he can not do something is like waving a red cape in front of a bull—it makes him charge. In this case, he stubbornly went ahead and ran the 800. "I had the 800 in my head, and I couldn't make a change," Aouita said. Pat Butcher called Aouita's attempted double the "bravest, and foolhardiest, in Olympic history."

According to Abderrahim, it was a matter of pride for Aouita, who he says was only 90 percent healthy for Seoul. "We said, 'Wait, Said. Run the 1,500.' But he told us, 'I said I will run the 800 meters, and so I will run the 800 meters. I have to try.'" He tried, but this time it was Kenyan Paul Ereng with the fastest finish, while Aouita took the bronze. "My mistake was running the 800 with my bad leg," Aouita said. A team doctor had told him, incorrectly it turned out, that his leg would be OK by the time the 800 final came around. Instead, it did not get any better, and three days after the 800 Aouita took himself out of the 1,500 semifinals after making it through the first round. If he had skipped the 800, his leg would have had more time to heal before the 1,500.

But Aouita would not be Aouita without boundless confidence, so coming away from Seoul with "only" a bronze medal did not affect his self-confidence. When asked if he would have won the gold if he had not been injured, or if he would have entered the 5,000 if it had not been scheduled on the same day as the 1,500, Aouita responded: "In the 800, I would have won, no problem. In the 1,500, you know I'm the best. In the 5,000, I had broken the world record two times." So there you have it; three gold medals that should have been his.

Unlike 1984, when he returned home from the Olympics a conquering hero, Aouita this time was endlessly questioned in Morocco for not winning the gold. "When I won, everyone was my friend," he recalled. "When I didn't win, people spoke bad of me." Two days after coming home, a fed-up Aouita had heard enough criticism. He and his wife packed up their daughter and went to Orlando, Florida, for a long vacation. "I have the medals and the records," Aouita said. "I don't have to prove anything." These words rang hollow, as it was plain to see that Aouita did still have something to prove, that he was not satisfied. The bronze medal was an albatross around his neck that gnawed at him. He vowed that he would be back in 1989, saying he had more ground to break, more records to set.

"I *have* to get the mile record," he said. And, when talking about the 1988 Olympics, his expression turns to a scowl when he says, "I *must* get another gold medal." Second place means nothing to Aouita. If he did not win, it was a failure. He said in *Sports Illustrated*, "If I weren't flat-footed and didn't have my two annual bouts with Achilles tendinitis, which force me to stop for a time, I would already have achieved incredible times." When asked about that quote, Aouita shrugs and says, "It's true."

Training Must Remain a Secret

An athlete of Aouita's range and abilities must have a bevy of coaches watching over him, giving him advice, and monitoring his workouts, right?

Wrong.

"I have no coach. I prefer always to be alone," Aouita said when I interviewed him in 1991, as he watched Lahbi rack up the balls for another game of pool.

It's surprising to learn that Aouita is a novice at pool. He plays the game well, and he tries to win every game. This drive to master pool right away, says Abderrahim, is a reflection of Aouita's personality, which helps illustrate why he is so fast on the track. "Other athletes would not be able to learn pool in two weeks. It's the first quality of Said, I think," the portly physiotherapist adds, racking up the balls for yet another of their seemingly endless games of pool.

"When he says he will do something, he does it. That's something I think not every athlete has. Said is one in a thousand that way."

Abderrahim gestures toward Aouita and Lahbi battling over the table. "Here are two athletes who both want to win," he says. "Said wants to be the first in every competition. For that he works very hard. And when he thinks he cannot win, he prefers not to participate."

It is this overwhelming desire to be the best at whatever he does that is the key to Aouita's track success. "People say, 'Said does it for the money.'" Abderrahim pauses, and, moving closer, drops his voice, as if revealing a great secret. "If everybody knew his training, and followed his training for one year, they would know the money is nothing. Can you understand this? Nothing."

Holding his hands out in front of him in imitation of a scale, Abderrahim indicates that the money does not balance out the training by holding one hand far below the other. "The training is much harder." But, he adds with a sigh, "everybody does not know that. Many people think it is easy."

Aouita's training is not easy, and only an athlete with tremendous concentration could do the intense workouts year after year. Abderrahim has been with Aouita since the mid-1980s, and is the closest person to a coach he has. Abderrahim provides massages and is Aouita's sounding board. "I can't tell you the specifics of the training," he says. "For that, you'll have to ask Said."

When asked once by a reporter what his training involves, Aouita replied, "It would take me a week to tell you, and I know you don't have the time." In other words, it is none of anyone's business. He told Butcher that "my God has given me the intelligence to prepare a program, and the willpower to follow it."

Despite a reputation for aloofness, Aouita is pleasant and patient in person. His Islamic religion prohibits alcohol, but when Said learns that some visitors like a beer now and then, his refrigerator quickly becomes stocked with several six-packs. He is willing to talk about anything: religion, diet, drugs in sports, and the general principles of his training program—but not any of the specifics.

"I train mostly with friends," Aouita says.

> Steve Cram lives just 10 meters away, not far from me [in the same condominium complex in Boulder]. But I never see him in training, and he never sees me in training. I respect other athletes' training, and they respect mine. It's important to have the right style, your own style of training. I make the training [fit] my physique.

Aouita, says one American friend, "would make a fantastic camel trader. He keeps his training very close to the vest."

"Let's go out for a jog," the friend recalls asking Aouita.

"No," Aouita replied. "We have special techniques. We always train alone. And we always run alone."

Aouita's "special methods," as he calls them, vary depending on what race he will be running. These methods are, he lets on, what allows him to prepare for yearly assaults on whatever world record he feels like tackling. He just did not like others watching his preparations. Before the 1988 Seoul Olympics, Aouita was doing his high-altitude training in a rented villa in Davos, Switzerland. When reporters began photographing him and timing some of his track workouts, Aouita called the police to clear the stands before he would resume the session.

He takes a scientific approach to training. Soon after arriving in town, he hands a local runner a couple of $100 bills. "I must have an altimeter," he says. "Get me the best one you can find." When told that topographic maps produced by the county give very accurate altitudes of all the roads, trails, and peaks in the area, Aouita shakes his head in exasperation. "No, no. Listen to me. I must know *exactly* what the altitude is." Aouita had to personally gauge the altitude, reading it before he would believe it.

Abderrahim just smiles when he hears this, and explains it by saying that Aouita trusts only his own senses. His training is based on careful preparation that leaves nothing to chance. Hard track sessions were the foundation of his program. The first thing you notice when watching Aouita do a workout is the very long time he spends stretching, then the long warm-up he takes before starting his intervals. Those intervals are extremely hard, and he runs them with a wide-eyed ferocity. "When I train, I'm serious," he says.

This day while training in Boulder in 1991, he is running repeat 400 meters in 57 seconds, with a minute rest. Aouita has a small chest and long legs. His stride is huge, and he runs so smoothly that it appears he is running 77-second instead of 57-second 400s. He runs four sets of three 400s with a three-minute rest between each set. But this April day, winter's chill still creeps down from the deep snow of the Rocky Mountains, and Aouita, despite all his experience, slightly pulls a hamstring muscle. "I was stupid. I must change with the weather. It was cold, and I must not try to run fast." Fortunately, it is not a serious injury.

"I train between 50 and 70 miles a week," Aouita says. His training is specific for the track. "I have no experience on the roads. There are many weeks of 50 miles, 50 miles, 50 miles," he says, moving his hands back and forth, as if swinging a pendulum. When making an assault on a world record, Aouita first breaks the race down into smaller increments, then trains at a pace faster than that of his target times. He has three kinds of training: for 800 meters to 1,500 meters; 1,500 meters to 5,000 meters; and 5,000 meters to 10,000 meters. Each kind of training has its own sets of intervals.

When pressed for more specifics about individual workouts, Aouita politely says, "I'm sorry. I hope you understand, but that must remain a secret." When pressed more, the wily camel trader grins, then relents enough to explain that the principles of his training "have been the same since I started. Speed; speed endurance; and volume resistance." He was often asked if would ever run a marathon. Aouita says that's not likely. "I have never run over 15 or 16 kilometers. I don't know if I can run over 40 kilometers. I think a marathon would be very hard for me."

What was important to Aouita was not the number of miles he ran weekly, but rather the quality of his hard workouts. "I train with hard and easy days," he says, adding that he is not tied to a set schedule. He took off as much time in between workouts as he thought he needed. "*Always* I am following my feelings," he adds.

On his easy days, Aouita ran for time, not distance. When asked how many kilometers he ran in the morning, he said, "I don't know, but it was 50 minutes. You see," Aouita finally says, his patience growing thin. "There isn't any secret to being a great runner. You must just train very hard. Very, very hard. That's the secret."

But another, more subtle key to Aouita's dominance, Abderrahim says, is that Said has what he terms, in French, *psychometricite*.

> It's the liaison between the brain and the body. All the time, Said knows his body very well and he always listens to his body. It is another of his best qualities, I think. Many athletes turn in a good performance, but can't keep it going all the time. When they turn in a good performance, they take a rest. Said never takes a rest.

Training partner Lahbi agrees, saying, "Said works very hard, and runs very fast in his training. He can recuperate very fast."

Aouita is, says Rich Castro, "a perfectionist. He likes to be in control of his training and wants things done his way." That is seen by the training partners he handpicked to train with him in different locales around the world. All were very fast in their own right. "Said basically supported them," says Castro, "and they were there so he could do a workout when he wanted to do it and how he wanted to do it. Said wanted things done his way. Period."

Aouita's agent, Vicente Modahl, was an elite runner and sometime training partner of Aouita's who became a sports agent. Modahl recalled for Paul Larkins of *Athletics Weekly* some of Aouita's workouts.

At Mexico City, where Aouita would go for his yearly stint of high-altitude training, Aouita once ran 10 × 400 meters with 90 seconds rest, averaging 54.5 seconds per 400. "He was very proud that he could actually make that because he had read that Sebastian Coe had done 10 in just under 56," Modahl said. Another time, Aouita ran a 7:33 3,000 meters in training, Modahl recalled. "He measured a lot of what he did in the beginning [against] Seb Coe. He was a great fan of his."

"I am an athlete, and I respect all athletes," says Aouita. "I admire Sebastian Coe and I respect Miruts Yifter. I like him very much."

Aouita says training is "sometimes hard to do during Ramadan." Islam is the Arabic word for "submission," and Aouita submits to the duties of his religion, including observing the fast of the holy month of Ramadan, the ninth month of the Islamic calendar. During this month, Muslims do not eat or drink from dawn to dusk. "Religion is first for me, and for every Muslim," says Aouita. "It is the first thing our family teaches us when we are young," adds Abderrahim. "We think we are safe when the religion is good."

During Ramadan Aouita does not eat during the daylight hours. "No, I can't eat. I am Muslim and I want to respect my religion. It is very important to me. It is very hard for us. You know, athletes need water, and during Ramadan we can't drink water. I think as for eating food, it's no problem."

Aouita prefers Moroccan food, but admits, "I haven't a diet. I eat everything." Boxes of American cereals piled on the kitchen counter testify to that.

Chasing More Records

His Olympic gold medal remains more important to Aouita than his world records. "It was very nice to win the Olympics," he says.

> It is very hard to speak about my feelings at that time. I was very happy. I am most proud of winning the Olympics. The gold medal is better. The world records are for the sponsors and the money. The Olympics and World Championships are for Morocco.

After the disappointment of not getting another Olympic gold in Seoul, Aouita vowed to show he was still the top runner in the world. To his way of thinking, and because the next Olympic opportunity was four years away, there was only one way to do that—by setting more world records.

After returning to Morocco for base training, Aouita came to the United States in February 1989 to run some indoor races. "After my third place in Seoul," he told the *New York Times*, "I want to prove I am the best. I will start indoors and then go outdoors." Aouita had raced indoors only once in his career, two years earlier in Spain. "If everything is OK, I'll like indoors," he said. "The first race might be hard for me, but I will try to break the world record."

He didn't get the indoor record, but in the summer of 1989 Aouita was after, as he had been for several years, Henry Rono's 11-year-old 3,000-meter record of 7:32.1. The field for his record attempt at the August 20 "Weltklasse in Koln" Grand Prix meet in Mungersdorfer Stadium was deep, with Dieter Baumann (1992 Olympic 5,000-meters gold medalist), Maree, Kenyan Yobes Ondieki, Americans Mark Nenow and Doug Padilla, and Khalid Skah of Morocco (1992 Olympic 10,000 meters gold medalist) all in the race. Aouita left the others running for second place, as he recorded 400-meter splits of 59.3, 61.6, 60.9, 59.7, 61.8, 60.7, 56.8, and a final 200 meters of 28.65 to get the record in 7:29.45. Such was Aouita's dominance over this world-class field that he beat second-place finisher Baumann by nearly 11 seconds. Afterwards, Aouita said that Rono's record had been the most difficult of all his records to break.

Things were looking promising that winter, but in January 1990 Aouita had to have surgery on his calf muscles. He then was forced to skip most of the indoor season with a cold. After recovering in Morocco, he returned to the United States in April. "What really interests me is the (1991) World Championships in Tokyo and the Olympic Games in Barcelona. I will prepare for them without overdoing things," he promised

Aouita resumed training that spring, and in May won the New York Games mile in the last few strides. In the fall of 1990, he ran the Mercedes Mile on Fifth Avenue in New York, challenged by Abdi Bile of Somalia, the gold medalist in the 1,500 meters at the 1987 World Championships and the 1989 World Cup. It was the first time in two years the pair had met. Aouita won.

Aouita found that he liked the United States and came to Boulder in the spring of 1991, scouting out possible training sites. It wasn't the rarefied air that attracted Aouita. "For me, it's the same, altitude or not. I'm here just because many athletes are here for training." Frank Shorter, the 1972 Olympic Marathon gold medalist who was the first of the elite runners to move to Boulder, said Aouita likes the city for the same reason he, Cram, Arturo Barrios, Rosa Mota, Lorraine Moller, Ingrid Kristiansen, Rob de Castella, and other Olympians do—athletes are respected for their abilities, but at the same time are left alone.

Said Aouita ran for Olympic redemption at the
1991 World Championship 1,500 meters.

"There is an empathy for athletes here," Shorter says.

I don't know if it is paradise, but I think for someone like Said, it
is very nice to go where he is respected, but where he can also
live a reasonably normal life. What he is getting in Boulder is the
environment he needs to train the best he can.

That's true, agreed Aouita, explaining that he is well-known in Morocco, perhaps too well-known. Track champions are treated with the same hype and hoopla given to baseball, football, and basketball stars in the United States. Aouita felt trapped by the attention.

> Everybody comes to ask me for autographs, and it is very hard for me to stay in Morocco without being asked questions. I feel I just want to change the place. I don't like to run every day in the same place, and for that reason I like to make a change sometimes. That's why I am coming to the United States, because I don't like my concentration to be interrupted for the Olympic Games, for the World Championships.

The summer of 1991 was an off season for Aouita. He said he wanted to set "only" two or three track records in Europe. He wanted to lower his 5,000 meter record—"I think my record is not so strong. I must lower it before someone comes and beats it"—as well as the mile record then held by Cram. "This year, I don't have anything, but will try for two or three world records later (in the summer)," he said at the start of the track season. "I want to reserve my power for next year. It's very important for me, the World Championships and 1992 [Olympics]."

Aouita's big race in the summer of 1991 was a 1,500 meters in August against Noureddine Morceli, who had emerged as the world's top middle-distance runner. It looked as if Aouita would beat his young rival, hitting splits of 55.9, 1:54.3, and 2:51.8. The pair entered the last lap together before Morceli edged away. The Algerian won in 3:32.04 with Aouita a satisfied second in 3:33.28. Cram was fourth (3:34.9), 1988 Olympic champion Peter Rono of Kenya was fifth, and Bile was eighth. That was Aouita's best race of the summer; later he overdid his speed training and reinjured his hamstring.

Morceli says that Aouita is a role model for youngsters in the Arab countries of North Africa. "There have been many good athletes from North Africa over the years, but it was only noticed when Said appeared," Morceli told *Athletics Weekly*. "As a young man, Said Aouita was my idol, and what he has done is amazing."

Despite his injuries, Aouita ran in the 1991 Tokyo World Championships, which was to be his redemption of Seoul. It was the new star, Morceli, however, who shined in Tokyo. The Algerian won in 3:32.84, with his hero Aouita a distant, injury-slowed 12th. Aouita finished his season in October, with an eighth-place, 4:04.9 mile in Monaco. Both Aouita's shins were then operated on for compartment syndrome.

Though he traveled around the world to train, Aouita never abandoned his native land. "Morocco is my country, it is my home," Aouita said. He continued living in Casablanca and also trained near his home in Spain before the 1992 Olympics. "It's not far from Morocco, just 20 minutes from the frontier, and I have a sponsor in Spain," he said.

Having the Barcelona Summer Olympics so close to his home did not give Aouita any extra motivation. The driving force remained his desire "to beat everybody," to be the best in the world and win back his gold medal. "Every athlete thinks about 1992, and I am like other athletes. For me, Barcelona is special because I lost my gold medal in Seoul," Aouita said before the 1992 Olympics, his dark eyes flashing and his voice lowering.

As the Barcelona Games neared however, Aouita decided against the 10,000, saying he was going to run the 1,500, because the 5,000 "was too easy. I want to show that I am not at the end. I want to show that I am just starting."

But his injuries would not go away, and he did not get a medal at Barcelona. In desperation, he turned to Dr. David Caborn, a Scottish sports medicine specialist Aouita met through the doctor working with Roger Kingdom, the U.S. Olympic 110-meter hurdle champion. "I had lost everything," Aouita told the *New York Times*. "I needed someone to orient me."

Aouita was told the cause of his injuries was the seven-day-a-week weight training program he followed for much of his career. "This was the biggest thing," Caborn said. "Any time an athlete with such a natural talent wants to meet so many goals, one who had relatively little down time experiencing any injuries, suddenly finds himself injured, he has no ability to understand or comprehend what's going on."

According to Caborn, Aouita's injuries caused him to lose races, which in turn lessened his enjoyment of the sport and thus his motivation to train. After decreasing his weight lifting and adding some flexibility exercises to his workouts, Aouita returned to his record setting ways in 1993, setting his first indoor world record, running 3,000 meters in 7: 33.66.

Can He Come Back?

But with the rise of Morceli and other new athletes, Aouita knew it was time to move on. He retired in 1993 and began managing Moroccan athletes. Early in 1994, he took the job of technical director of the Moroccan national track team. "I don't think there is any secret to my system, just hard work," Aouita told *Running Times*. "I plan the training very well and try to do the best thing for the athletes. I know which day we can be great and which day we are not. This comes from my experience."

Moroccan athletes had good success under Aoutia in 1994, winning major races and having six 5,000-meter runners faster than 13:13. The Moroccans also won the World Road Relay Championships over the Kenyans and Ethiopians. However, the fiery Aouita clashed with federation authorities, and he was fired later that year.

In 1995 Aouita, age 35, moved to San Diego and was back training, saying, "I love track, and I miss it." Aouita's first race back after just six weeks of training was an indoor 3,000 meters at the Hamilton Games in Ontario, where he placed third in 8:10.45. He quipped to Dick Patrick of *USA Today* that "I can make a comeback if (boxer) George Foreman can. He's 11 years older than I am, and none of my rivals is trying to punch me."

Aouita's comeback was the talk of the track world, with Sebastian Coe telling Pat Butcher, "How he goes will really depend on how he's taken care of himself. But it's often not so much the physical nature of decline as the mental thing. It simply ceases to be the most important thing in your life."

Coe says he "admires [Aouita] immensely. I suppose, like myself over the 800 meters, he rescripted the way the 5,000 meters is run. And if that's what he's coming back to [running world-class 5,000 meters], it's a long way to hurt. Comebacks, like political careers, very rarely end happily." Coe continued, "The psychology of retirement is interesting. Is it because he's got nothing else to do? Because when you get past 30, distance lends enchantment. You forget how hard it was. You've really got to be brutal with yourself. The saddest retirements are those that end in disaster."

And the most exciting careers, as Said Aouita showed, are those that end in wins, medals, and world records. During his peak years, when asked about his next challenge, Aouita said, "I say, 'Why not?' I always say, 'Why not?' Because in this sport, anything is possible."

18

Friendships and Fast Running

Born June 29, 1958, Portugal

Olympic gold, marathon, 1988; bronze, 1984

World Championships gold, marathon, 1987

European Championships gold, marathon, 1982, 1986, 1990

At the 38-kilometer mark of the 1988 women's Olympic Marathon, Rosa Mota was running stride-for-stride with Lisa Martin and Katrin Dörre. She was beginning to worry that the race might end up coming down to a sprint finish, when, going down a slight hill on the course through the streets of Seoul, she saw her coach, José Pedrosa, who nodded his head and yelled out, "Now! Go now, Rosa! Go!"

Rosa surged, pulling away from her two rivals in the final miles to run to a special place in track and field's archives. Her 2:25:40 gold medal run made her the only runner, male or female, to win Olympic, World-Championship, and European-Championship gold medals and capped a 10-year, gradual fitness buildup that made Mota one of the best women's marathoners ever. Her sensible approach to training stressed longevity, enjoyment, and above all, friendships. Mota is one of the most beloved of runners, with her outgoing personality endearing her to runners and fans around the globe. From her first marathon at the 1982 European Championships through the World Marathon Cup in 1991, she was the most consistent women's marathoner in the world, training and racing with an exuberance and dedication that makes her one of the stalwarts of women's running.

Promise in Porto

When Rosa was a little girl in the coastal city of Porto, Portugal, she had no idea she would be one of the best women's marathoners. Instead, she dreamed of being a kindergarten teacher when she grew up. She did not grow up to be very big, standing just 5 feet and 1 inch, and weighing only 95 pounds with her shoes on. But she stands tall in the annals of women's marathoning, having won 15 major marathons and over 50 international races during a career that started in 1975. Scores of other talented women appeared and disappeared from the racing scene, but Mota's long-term approach to training and racing allowed her to reach the top of the sport and stay there for nearly a decade.

Porto is a rough and tumble city on the Atlantic coast of Portugal, and Rosa resembles her city: tough, determined, and never letting up. Until Mota came along, the city was known mainly for the port wine that is aged there. Sports in Porto, as in all of Portugal, started and finished with soccer. Mota grew up in a modest household in the old fishing-village area of Porto called Foz, where the city meets the sea.

When she was in high school, there were no races for women, and Rosa never thought about running until a competition was set up against a neighboring school in the fall of 1974. "We didn't have sport at that time in my school, but they asked, 'If you want to run, bike or do swimming, write your names in.'" Mota, then 16, was eager to have the chance to compete in any kind of athletic event, and she did not want to miss this opportunity. "So I wrote in cycling, running, *and* swimming."

The running race was two kilometers on a cross-country course. Rosa won, receiving a small trophy as her prize. Her school team also won, receiving a larger trophy. "This is good," she thought. Three weeks later, she went to a regional race, which she also won. A few weeks after that, she lined up for the Portuguese national meet and scored another victory in the schoolgirl division. Three races; three wins. "After I won the nationals, my teacher said, 'Rosa, you look like a runner; you can be very good. It's better that you go to a club.'" Mota's younger sister Paula started running at the same cross-country meet. Paula says she and Rosa did well in those first races because they were so active while growing up.

After their wins, the two sisters were invited to join the local club near their home, the Futebol Clube da Foz. It did not have a track, so all of Rosa's and Paula's early racing came in cross-country races through the mud and the woods. They did no training except for a little jogging a few days a week. "I would play different games with friends, and we'd race our bicycles around the block and run around the block," Rosa says. She continued doing well, winning nearly all her races over the next several years and developing into one of Portugal's top runners. "Rosa was always the best from the time she started running," says Paula, who would end up being a good middle-distance runner herself. "She always liked to run." Rosa recalls that "It wasn't so tough then, because there were so few girls running. If I had started running a few years later, I would not [have been] able to win right away like I did."

There were not any women runners in Portugal for Mota to use as role models when she started out, but she was inspired after seeing Grete Waitz win a race on television. Rosa also received steady encouragement from her very close-knit, Catholic family, especially her father, José, a mechanic, and her mother, Helena.

> My parents always said to me that it was good to be in sports. To do my best. They never thought I was going to be a world-class runner. But they said, "Go and do your best. And be honest with yourself and with your friends."

"My father likes all sports," adds Paula. "He always told me and Rosa that 'sports is good for you.' He encouraged us a lot." This was important, because Rosa and Paula were sometimes jeered at by locals, who had never seen girls running before. "Women at that time were not going out. They stayed at home. When we ran through the streets, they would say, 'Go home! Go home and help your mother wash the dishes.' Things like that," recalls Paula.

There are no athletic teams in Portuguese schools. As in most European countries, athletes compete for their towns's clubs. Mota stayed with her local club in Foz for five years before joining Porto's largest sports club, the Futebol Clube do Porto. But, she says, "I don't like big clubs, so I changed to the club I'm in now. That's where my friends are. We don't have a track, nothing. We meet together once a week in one place and we talk and train." Mota's attitude toward running illustrates the value she places on friendship. Her outgoing, friendly nature, however, masked a deep determination to succeed, one reason she kept up her running.

She continued winning, competing after 1975 in races sponsored by the Portuguese Track Federation. Because Portugal does not have high-school and college running programs, as the United States does, students compete in races sponsored by the federation. Rosa typically ran 800 and 1,500-meter races. "Sometimes I'd lose, but always it was fun." She increased her training in 1978 so she could start running 3,000-meter races, which she usually won.

Getting Over the Hump

The turning point in Mota's career came in 1980, when she met José Pedrosa, nicknamed "Zé," a medical doctor who was to become her coach and advisor the rest of her career. Pedrosa worked in a hospital in Sabrosa, a town about two hours from Porto. Mota asked him for a ride home from the track one afternoon, and they have been inseparable ever since. Like nearly everyone who meets her, Pedrosa liked Mota from the start. "When I first met Rosa, I thought she was a nice person, and had a nice personality," says Pedrosa. Mota and Pedrosa made a good pair. She was motivated to become a world-class runner like Grete Waitz, but health problems had slowed her development. Pedrosa had medical training and an interest in running, and he was the one who helped Mota recover and showed her the way to the top. "I think Zé was very, very important for Rosa," says Paula. "Maybe there are others like her, but they never got the chance" to train and race. With Pedrosa to lean on, Mota made the most of her chance to become a runner.

Pedrosa is an energetic, intelligent man, with an understanding of physiology and psychology that, through the years, helped Mota avoid the overtraining trap into which so many runners fall. When he met Mota in 1980, however, there was another problem. Mota had begun racing poorly, finishing far back from the leaders. Doctors told Rosa her problem was all in her head, but Pedrosa thought otherwise, that perhaps she was suffering from some kind of respiratory problem. "The doctors told me to forget it, and meanwhile she was getting worse and worse. She was so depressed," Pedrosa told journalist Marlene Cimons. "She couldn't tell it was her breathing. She just felt tired in her legs. . . . All she knew was her legs just didn't run fast."

For a while, Mota thought maybe she had gone as far as she could in running, and she never would reach the international level. The other runners in Porto's big sports club did not help her, and she considered quitting running. "They weren't very supportive," Mota told Cimons. "They said I was not strong enough to keep up. It was a very competitive club with a lot of pressure to perform well. When I wasn't going so well, they said I was not sporting enough."

Pedrosa, however, kept his faith in Rosa and finally diagnosed her as having exercise-induced asthma.

> I just decided to help her as a patient, to get her proper care like any other patient. In the beginning, I just tried to help her so she could enjoy life and running again. That's what mostly concerned Rosa.

It was a long road to recovery. After several months taking different medications, along with "physical and psychological rehabilitation," she was back in full training. Pedrosa said after Mota was able to run pain-free again,

> It took so long for Rosa to get to that bad spot, and so long for her to recover from it. The first part of the recovery was psychological, helping her believe that it was possible to recover. What I noticed about Rosa is that definitely, she enjoys running very much.

That enjoyment fueled Mota's drive, as it does for many other elite runners, and it kept her motivation up when she was running poorly.

Mota's first international race came at the end of 1981, when she won the New Year's Eve São Silvestre race in São Paulo, Brazil, the first of her six victories there. In the spring of 1982, Portuguese authorities picked Rosa for the team going to Athens for the European Championships. She wanted to try the marathon for the first time, but federation officials wanted her in the shorter race. They did not think she had any chance to place in the marathon, and she was given permission to run the marathon only after agreeing to compete in the 3,000. Mota finished near the back of the pack in the 3,000, but wasn't bothered by this placing because she was focusing on the longer race, even though she had never run farther than a half-marathon before.

European Championships Marathon 1982

That 1982 European Championships Marathon in Athens was history's first all-women's championship marathon. In view of its significance, organizers filled the race with symbolism. It started in Marathon, Greece, near the battlefield where in 490 BC a small band of Athenians and soldiers from some of the other Greek city-states defeated a much larger Persian army that had sailed over from Asia. The marathon followed the route of Pheidippides, who is said to have run from Marathon to Athens after the battle. Upon telling his fellow citizens in Athens, "Rejoice, we have conquered," Pheidippides fell dead.

The 1982 race also followed the course of the first Olympic Marathon, held in 1896. Aware of this marathon's significance, Pedrosa talked with Mota, and they decided, "Yes, this is the right day for Rosa to start her marathon career. There were a lot of important things going on."

Mota was not among the favorites when the marathoners lined up in Athens. She was just one of the pack expected to fill in the ranks behind Norwegian Ingrid Kristiansen. But Pedrosa believed Rosa had potential in the longer event and had devised a plan for her: run very conservatively in the early going and hope the leaders burn out and come back to her. Pedrosa says, "I knew she *could* do well."

Mota was not as sure as Pedrosa; driving the course two days before the marathon, Mota was shocked at how long the race was, and she worried she would be unable to finish. "Forget it, Zé. It's too far and too hilly," she relates to Cimons. "Then I think: the important thing for me is to finish. That's all. If I don't save myself as much as possible, I might get into big trouble and die like Lazaro or Pheidippides."

Lazaro was a runner from Portugal who died the day after competing in the 1912 Stockholm Olympic Marathon. "At that time, running was a poor people's sport, and there was very little knowledge about physiology," says Pedrosa. Lazaro tried to give himself every edge possible, such as wearing a light racing singlet. Lazaro knew he typically lost a lot of fluid during races. Realizing that the more he sweated, the weaker he became in his races, Lazaro came up with a novel solution— he spread a thick lotion on his skin to keep him from sweating. Explains Pedrosa,

It was some kind of cream water-proofing material. . . . What happened was that he burned himself up and died from over-heating. That's a story about Portuguese running many people know, and they thought marathoning was dangerous, because Pheidippides died and Lazaro died. So, you should be careful. It was really unfortunate, because the guy was so dedicated and took it so, so seriously. He tried. It was just that the knowledge and experience then was not so great.

Rosa knew the story of Lazaro, of course, and says, "Often when we talk about a poor guy in Portugal, we say 'just like Lazaro.'" She held back during the first part of the race, running in last place and trailing the leaders by over a minute in the early going. It was a very hard course, with lots of uphills, and it was a hot, humid afternoon. Temperatures were close to 90 degrees, and the humidity was over 90 percent. Despite the conditions, Mota was feeling strong, and she gradually moved up, picking off runners until she joined Kristiansen and Italian Laura Fogli in second place at 30 kilometers. "I was running, but not to win," Mota says. "Then [at 30 kilometers], I said, 'Let's try to go,' and it felt easy." Kristiansen, Fogli, and Mota trailed Carla Beurskens of Holland by 30 seconds, but by 35 kilometers, the trio had taken the lead. For the first time, Mota began to try to win. "I knew how fast Ingrid was and wanted to avoid a fast finish," she said. Running into the gathering darkness, "I saw the stadium lights and I could see the motorcycles start to go faster to open up the crowds," Mota told Cimons.

I decided to take the lead. I look behind me and Ingrid and Laura stay. I am still afraid of sprinting from the other girls, but nothing happens. When I crossed the finish line, I smiled, and I see José taking pictures and crying.

He had good reason to cry. Mota's victory over the extremely challenging course was vindication for Pedrosa, who had gone out on a limb with the Portuguese Federation by advising Mota to run the marathon. "I kept thinking that if something happens to Rosa, the whole country will kill me," he told Cimons. "I will have to ask for political asylum someplace else. . . . We never thought of winning. Rosa just wanted to participate." Pedrosa had no need to worry. Not only did Mota win but she felt good doing it, showing she was a natural for the marathon.

It was a big surprise for me, to beat Ingrid. I was very surprised. I finished and I wasn't even tired. I think: This is so good for my country and for my friends. Afterwards, I went running with my friends from Portugal.

It was the first European Championship gold medal for Portugal and the race was televised live there. "We were all so surprised, because Portugal is so small and had never won anything so big as the Europeans. After this, everybody knows Rosa," said Paula, who had driven from Porto to Athens to watch Rosa run.

> We were waiting in the stadium, and no one knew who was winning. Then when we saw Rosa, we said, "No, it's not possible. It's not her." We were so happy. And she didn't look tired at the end. Only happy.

After that win, "My life changed," Rosa says. She immediately became a heroine in Portugal, a poor country going through difficult times in the early 1980s.

"We were suffering from a long dictatorship, a regime that was really anti-development, anti-cultural, anti-human rights, and anti-everything," says Pedrosa. A revolution in 1974 brought a new government, but it would take a long time before the country began to recover. The people of Portugal had needed a boost, and Mota gave it to them. The small country on the edge of the Iberian peninsula, somewhat cut off from the rest of Europe, had beaten all the other countries of the continent; it was a win for all Portuguese, something that made the fishermen, the farmers, and the grape pickers proud. The phone never stopped ringing at Mota's home, and she was feted and honored with champagne and parties.

Says Mota, "It was my first marathon; my first European Championships, and then after that I started training for the marathon." She upped her mileage to a consistent 100 miles a week. "I said, well, let's train seriously, to see if I can be a good marathoner."

Mota rented an apartment around the corner from her parents' home, as did her brother and sister. "Family is very important to Rosa; she's always stayed within spitting distance of them," said Steven Campbell, a Boulder chiropractor who treats Mota. She was recognized wherever she went after her European win, and she began spending time each year overseas to get some privacy.

> In Porto, people always want me to visit schools and houses for old people. I like doing it, but it takes away from my training, and I don't like to say no. And in Porto, people always want to talk to me, and newspaper reporters are always coming to my house. In the U.S., I have more time for training and resting. Sometimes I spend several weeks or several days in Japan, because I have a race and I need to go some days before because of the travel and the differences in time.

Hitting the Roads

Using a principle of gradual adaptation to higher levels of training and racing, Mota's trademark became running faster in each of her successive marathons. She showed she was ready to stake her claim among the world's best in 1983. Rosa ran her second marathon at Rotterdam in April, where she PR'd (set a personal record) with a 2:32:27. On May 14, she set the 20,000-meter world record on the track in Lisbon, clocking 1:06:55.5. Then she ran 2:31:50 in the marathon to place fourth at the first World Championships in Helsinki. The race was won by Grete Waitz, with Marianne Dickerson (USA) second and Raisa Smeknowa (USSR) third.

Following the World Championships, Mota's shoe sponsor gave her a ticket to the United States to compete in some road races, starting with the Danbury Connecticut Classic 10K, followed by the Maple Leaf Half-Marathon in Vermont, and the Coliseum 10K in Los Angeles, held to drum up interest in the upcoming Olympic Games. "Rosa was extremely quiet when she first came to the U.S., because she didn't speak much English yet," said Dr. Robert Rinaldi, who hosted Mota and Pedrosa in Danbury. Mota won the Connecticut race and Rinaldi helped her get her check for placing second in the Maple Leaf Half-Marathon behind Anne Audain of New Zealand. "What's this?" Mota asked when Rinaldi handed her the check. Notes Rinaldi, "It became immediately impressed upon me that money was secondary to Rosa and José. In fact, they didn't know what to do with it. What she came here for was to run the race and win the race."

On the way back from the west coast in October 1983, she stopped in Chicago for its America's Marathon. She won it in a course record 2:31:12, picking up a large paycheck. "They [Rosa and José] were flabbergasted that she won that much money," says Rinaldi. "Our first impression of Rosa and Zé is that they were interested in the sport, in reaching the highest elevation of the sport. They were very altruistic, and Rosa never lost that very pure concept of wanting to run as fast as she could."

That win in Chicago was the only time in her career Mota ran against the clock, says Pedrosa. Even though she had won the European championships the year before, she was not yet well known, so she wanted a fast performance to rank her among the top marathoners in the world. "That was the only race where we were concerned about the time," says Pedrosa. "After that, Rosa was only concerned about winning."

Three marathons in 1983, three personal bests with steady improvement. But Mota was not considered to be much of a factor heading into the first-ever women's Olympic Marathon at the 1984 Los Angeles

Olympics. Grete Waitz and Ingrid Kristiansen, the marathoning greats from Norway, along with Joan Benoit of the U.S., were the favorites. On paper, the best Mota could hope for was fourth, but that did not stop her from giving an all-out effort to prepare for the Olympics. Pedrosa even quit his hospital job and Mota stopped going to school in order to devote all their time and energy to the Olympics.

That dedication was something some in Portugal had trouble understanding, partly because Portugal was still a "man's country." One indication of the status of women was that it was not too long ago that schoolteachers could not get married without the government's approval. Under the dictatorship, "Women were put in a lesser position," says Pedrosa. "Legally men had more rights than women. It takes a while to change that mentality." Mota and Pedrosa took a "100-percent professional approach to her training, which was hard for some to accept," says Pedrosa. "It was only after the [1987] World Championships and the [1988] Olympics that they finally realized that it was logical. This serious approach took a while to be accepted."

The "serious approach" began to pay off. After a winter spent training twice a day in Porto, Mota ran her fastest track times ever, running 8:53 for 3,000 meters in the spring of 1984. Regular racing was part of her buildup for Los Angeles. Mota ran against good competition on the weekends whenever it fit into her schedule for the year and a half before the Olympics, and she came to Los Angeles in great shape. When Joan Benoit clinched the gold medal with her early breakaway, Mota stayed with the pack, as did Waitz and Kristiansen. She gradually moved up and took the bronze medal by passing Kristiansen in the last three kilometers. Her time shocked even Pedrosa— 2:26:57, a 4-minute and 15-second PR.

The Olympic bronze medal, however, was not enough. "After the Olympics, when I get third, Zé said, 'Let's do everything for Seoul; let's train hard for the next Olympics.' Because we think that if everything is OK, we can get first place."

Getting Better and Better

After Los Angeles, Mota returned to Chicago in the fall of 1984 for another duel with Kristiansen. The duo ran side by side for nine miles, until Mota put in a surge that left a struggling Kristiansen behind. Mota ran another personal record and broke her course record by more than five minutes with a 2:26:01 win. "The men are running fast. I think the women should be able to also," she said. At the awards ceremony, Mota got up, saying she "dedicated the race to Deek [Rob de Castella], the person who helped me the most in training for Chicago."

In 1985, Rosa came back to Chicago for a rematch with Kristiansen. Joan Benoit Samuelson also was scheduled to compete there. It was one of the most important women's marathons to date, because of the attention it drew in the months leading up to the race. In the spring of 1985, Kristiansen had smashed Samuelson's world record with a 2:21:06 clocking in London, and media speculated that the record could fall at Chicago. Even non-running fans in Chicago got excited about the showdown.

Samuelson was worried about Mota. Samuelson's coach, Bob Sevene, told Cimons that Samuelson had seen Mota running along the Olympic course before Los Angeles and that "she looked great." "She was more concerned with Rosa than with Ingrid. Joan worries about people who are young and hungry. And Rosa's the hottest thing out there right now. She just gets better and better." Mota's strategy remained the same—hope the duo would go out too fast and blow up, allowing her to pick up the pieces in the later stages of the race. But, Kristiansen and Samuelson went out fast and held on. Samuelson won, and Mota came on strong in the second half of the race to finish third in 2:23:29, 20 seconds behind Kristiansen. It was Mota's seventh marathon and her seventh PR in a row; it also made her the third-fastest women's marathoner ever.

Mota continued getting stronger, biding her time until she would be able to beat Samuelson. In 1986, Mota concentrated on shorter races, running several 10Ks near 32 minutes. She ran the fastest-ever road 20K, clocking 1:05:38, and also set a world best for 10 miles, 53:09, at the Cherry Blossom race in Washington, D.C. With her light stride and low body weight, Mota looked like she was floating through races.

> I'm a marathon runner. I'm not fast enough to do 10Ks, but I run them. My favorite distance is the half-marathon. Because you can do it almost every week. It's not like a marathon. I like to compete a lot, because it's fun to compete. And it's easier to do a half-marathon and easier to recover. And in 1:10, 1:15 it's over.

Late in the summer of 1986 in Stuttgart, West Germany, Mota defended her European-Championship Marathon gold medal, reinforcing her status as one of the best in the world. The key was her consistent training. She had put in years of 100 miles a week, with many of the runs very quick. That resulted in some minor aches and pains in 1986, and, for the first time, she had to stop running and take a three-week break. "Some people keep running when they get hurt. It wasn't hard for me to take time off, because I did not want to get hurt again," said Mota.

Chiropractor Steve Campbell, who treated her "minor injuries" and gave her treatment for the rest of her career, describes her as "mischievous. When Rosa and her sister, Paula, stayed with me, it was like the Ringling Bros. Circus between the two of them. If something wasn't mischievous, Rosa wanted no part of it." She was, however, very dedicated to her training. "Rosa's life was eat, sleep, and run when she was in the United States; that's it," Campbell recalled. "She tried to avoid distractions, and training always came first for her. Rosa got so many invitations to do things, and she would turn them down if they interfered with her training. Rosa was very serious about it." The one invitation Mota always accepted was when she was asked to talk to students.

During the next several years, Mota competed all over Europe, Japan, and the United States. For several months each summer in the United States she would train with Rob de Castella. She became one of the most popular runners on the roads. Mota was "absolutely a great natural talent," Campbell said.

> She was petite, but real strong and real tough, mentally and physically. She had that championship attitude that is the difference between the top people and those just below them. And Rosa did it fighting minor injuries. Usually when someone gets a "5-percent" injury, that's it. But Rosa was able to fight through it.

Mota says she went for longevity in her career, taking Grete Waitz as her model. She also admired countryman Carlos Lopes (1984 Olympic gold medalist at age 37). "I think he's a tough guy."

In April, 1987, Mota won the Boston Marathon in 2:25:21, good for 40th overall. It was the tenth-fastest women's time ever. There was speculation by some in Boston that she would try for Samuelson's 2:22:43 course record, but that was not something Mota herself ever worried about (except at Chicago in 1983). "Winning is most important to me," she said. Added Pedrosa, "Rosa never ran for time, because they don't mean as much in a marathon as a track race. You can't compare times on different courses."

She won Boston easily, and in a fast time, despite being slowed by a steady headwind. "I felt good the whole way," she said. "I was motivated to win not only for myself, but for the Portuguese people of Boston. They were with me all the way and made winning this race the nicest moment of my life."

In the summer of 1987, Mota won another championship, grabbing the gold medal at the World Championships in Rome, once again saying the win was not just for her, but for her country. Rosa knew she was in great shape, having earlier in the year run 31:35 on a 10K looped course and 31:18 on a point-to-point course. She changed her strategy for this race, going hard from the start, expecting a battle from Australian Lisa Martin. But Martin dropped back early, and by the three-mile mark near the Vatican, Mota had the race won. Her lead kept building and building until when she finished in 2:25:17, Mota was an incredible 7 minutes and 21 seconds ahead of the silver medalist. It was the biggest winning margin in any championship marathon ever run. "That, I think, was the most remarkable of Rosa's performances," says Pedrosa. "It was the best shape she was ever in. At that time she was the best in the world, but we weren't expecting such a big difference in the race."

Most importantly, Mota felt good winning Worlds, showing that the injuries had cleared up and leaving the road clear for her to train for the Seoul Olympics. The World Championships win gave her the confidence that she could indeed win the Olympics, says Campbell. "Even top runners need to win a big race like that to believe they are the best. That was the race that did it for Rosa."

Training

Paula Mota, who ran 2:05.2 for 800 meters and 4:24 for 1,500 meters, has often been asked why she was not a champion like her sister.

> That's the question people always ask me, for many years. What I say is that Rosa has something in her that is more than talent. She is able to do a lot of work. She has lots of resistance, to run and run and run and not get tired. Really, that's it. Rosa is good because she is able to do a lot of work.

Most of that work was done in Porto, the second-largest city in Portugal. With its crowded streets and lack of open space, the city would not seem to be a good place to train, and it really is not, Mota admits. "Porto is a town with lots of houses and lots of traffic. We don't have forests in Porto; we have only streets for training, and we have only a small park."

But Mota stays there to be near her family. "For me, training in Porto is good. Because it's the place where I was born, and I've always been there. Porto, that's my city, the place I love the most." It was in Porto where Mota got accustomed to doing most of her training on the roads, a habit she kept up her whole career. Mota was rarely seen on the track, going there only to do strides or visit with friends. "I don't like to run on the track, because I just never got used to it." That is because there was no track for her to train on in Porto until one was built in 1987.

During her peak years, Mota ran 100-110 miles a week on two runs a day. When told that is a lot of miles, Mota shrugs, saying, "Sure, but some people do more." She was very regimented and rarely missed a run. Mota always ran one hour in the morning, often with a group, because she enjoyed the company. She said "relaxation" was the key for her training and the camaraderie of the group kept her loose.

Her hard days were fartlek sessions on the roads. Mota had two hard days, and one or two long runs of 13-15 miles, per week. The length of her long runs was another habit from her early days in Porto, where it was hard to find longer loops to run. Nearly all marathoners do runs longer than Mota's regular one hour, 30 minutes, but she sums up her attitude about long runs by saying, "For me, that worked. There's no reason to kill myself. If I have to do two hours, I need to go slow. And I think it's better to go faster. Two hours or more is too slow. And the races are not slow."

When she was training with de Castella and his group, Mota would start out with the runners who were doing 22 miles, then stop at *precisely* one hour, 30 minutes. She would then climb into the car Pedrosa drove alongside her. She ran on dirt loops whenever she could, but she did not mind running on the asphalt. The longest run she ever did was one hour, 45 minutes, as a compromise with de Castella, whose long runs were over two hours. He ran shorter and she ran longer that day. Mota had no trouble keeping up with de Castella. In fact, it was often the men who had trouble keeping up with Rosa. "I know that the men are very good, and I think, why not the women? I feel good. I like to train well, and I like to run the way I feel. It's my job."

The rest of Mota's runs were done "how she felt," but typically at 6-minutes-per-mile pace, or faster. Many of her runs were at 5:45 pace. She was quick from the start of her runs, speeding down the street looking as if she were late for an appointment. She was so quick that de Castella remarked, only half jokingly, "Rosa is a great trainer. We're going to have to bump her off because she is pushing the pace too hard." Adds Rinaldi, "I've known Rosa for 11 years, and for 11 years, Rosa has always said, 'I run too fast on my training runs.'"

Mota did not keep to a strict weekly schedule; she varied the workouts after consultation with Pedrosa. Hard days might be 10 × 1 minute fast with a 1 minute slow jog in between, or 10 × 2 minutes fast with a 2-minute recovery. Mota's shortest workout was 10 times 30 seconds fast and 30 seconds slow. She also did longer fartlek runs on the road, such as three-, four-, or five-minute repeats. She wore a watch that beeped every 30 seconds, so she would know when to start the next repeat.

Mota loved to race, in big or small competitions, and she tried to jump in a race on the weekends whenever she could as a way to get in a tempo run. "Sometimes in Porto we have a lot of small races, 10Ks and 15Ks. I would go and run the race for a workout. It's my job, yes, but I like to run the way I feel."

Pedrosa and Mota do not like to talk about the specifics of their training, because they had what he calls a "bad experience" in Portugal. Once, Pedrosa explained about the details of Mota's training, which turned out "to be the opposite of what everyone else was doing. It created so many problems that we decided not to speak publicly again about what Rosa does until she retires." Mota, however, never declined to give young runners advice when they asked. The three main points of her training were: (1) she ran quickly much of the time, (2) she did not do the long, long runs like many marathoners, and (3) she was able to train consistently for long stretches.

Mota ran twice a day, but she always took one afternoon a week off. "And if I was tired, I'd take more than one off." Like many runners who reach the top, Mota paid attention to her body, and, if she was overly tired, she would cancel her workout and run just five easy miles for the day, followed by a nap. In fact, napping was a regular part of Mota's training; "rest is essential," she says. She slept about seven hours a night, but she *always* got a nap in. When it was time to nap, "everything stopped," Rinaldi said.

Pedrosa enjoyed talking until "the wee hours of the morning" about training, said Rinaldi.

> He's a very exacting coach. They approached running as a team. Zé was the technical part of the team and Rosa did the work. Even in races, Zé would be so involved, telling her to run the first 10K at such and such a pace.

The pair usually discussed training and tactics by themselves, in advance of workouts or races, and, between them, they would come up with the workout or race strategy. The philosophy underlying all her training is not complicated, Mota says. "My secret? Never do too much. That way you won't get hurt."

"José was like (pool player) Minnesota Fats when it came to discussing strategy. I look at it like they were going into the race with a plan, and Rosa would hustle people. I think she was really sharp," says Rinaldi. In competition, Mota would "shark them," running behind her competitors, up until a certain point. The race Rinaldi remembers best took place in 1985 in a little town in Portugal.

> It was about 10K. They never really measured the courses there; whoever came across first won. José and I were going to follow the race in a car, and watch Rosa run. So the gun goes off, boom.

We were supposed to follow, but José got himself in front of the race, driving right alongside Rosa, to protect her from traffic.

The course went across some train tracks, and, as the leaders neared the tracks, a train appeared. "We could all see the train coming. Rosa looked at Zé; Zé looked at Rosa, then back at the pack, and said 'Run faster, Rosa! Run faster!'" Rosa sprinted across the tracks just in front of the train, leaving the rest of the pack on the other side of the tracks. Mota went on to an easy win, and signed autographs for three hours afterwards. "On the way home, we ran out of gas. And Zé joked, 'Rosa, get out and push.' That was a most memorable race."

The adulation accorded Mota was tremendous, not just in Porto, where the city's sports pavilion is named after her, but all over Portugal

In the early days, even before she won the Olympics, we'd go for a ride and Rosa would show us the sights. Wherever we'd get out, there would be crowds of people, saying "Rosa, Rosa, Rosa." Everyone wanted her autograph.

Mota never failed to oblige her fans, waving, kissing people, and signing her name until the last person had an autograph, even if it took several hours. "Once we stopped in a poor section of town, a ghetto," Rinaldi said. "There was a little boy there, who took Rosa by the hand and led her to his house. It was a shack, literally made out of cardboard. And on the door of the shack were two pictures: one of Queen Elizabeth, the other of Rosa."

1988 Seoul Olympics

Mota built on her World Championship win with another good winter of training. She was the clear favorite for the Olympic Marathon, and Mota prepared like it, averaging 110 miles a week for the entire year before the Olympics, despite conflicts with the Portuguese federation. Officials didn't like her and Pedrosa's independence. Rosa was supremely confident in her training, but she did not say that she was going to win. All she ever said before a race was, "I promise to try my best."

Others were trying their best as well in the Seoul Olympic Marathon, and, in the first part of the race, the patient Mota bided her time in the warm conditions, waiting and watching the others. A large pack passed 5K in 17:10 and 10K in 34:13. She thought about what she always does in the early part of a race:

First off, I think about myself, and the pace I'm running. I don't want to run too fast during the first part and then [drawing a finger across her throat] hit the wall. And I try to look at the runners, to see what they are doing. This one might be running too fast, and not be good enough to keep up at that pace. And I try to enjoy it, and wait for the finish.

After a pack of 13 passed halfway together in 1:12:45, runners began, one-by-one, dropping off the pace. One of those was Grete Waitz; still recovering from knee surgery, she dropped out of the race. Mota stayed in control, until

We were only four: me, Lisa [Martin], Katrin [Dörre], and the girl from Russia, Tatyana Polovinskaya. And then, she [Polovinskaya] stayed behind at 30K, and we three stayed together. And I said to myself, "Well, I'm going to get a medal. I don't know what kind, but one medal is for sure."

When Mota passed by Pedrosa on the side of the course and heard him shout with 4 kilometers to go, Mota said to herself, "'Let's go.' And I did." After taking the lead, she was still worried about one of the other two coming back on her.

I knew I had the gold medal only when I crossed the finish line. Because anything can happen in the marathon. We were so close until 38K. When I finished, it was almost a dream, because I had wanted to win three titles in a row: European, World Championships, and the Olympics. I'll always remember the race; I always remember the stadium, going into the tunnel, then showing up in front of all those people. And you think . . . All the people in my country, they are watching and they are happy. And I think people I know in other countries are happy also. I think all my friends live my races.

Mota finished in 2:25:40, with Martin (2:25:53) getting the silver and Dörre (2:26:21), the bronze. It was Mota's tenth win in 13 major marathons, and made her the first woman from Portugal to earn an Olympic track and field medal.

Upon returning to Portugal, Mota went straight from the airport to a giant party. A huge crowd welcomed her back, and there were lines of people, side-by-side, along the entire 10-mile route back to town. The president of Portugal, Mario Soares, was waiting to congratulate her, and Mota showed him the gold medal. Now, she keeps it in her room at home.

When I go to schools to talk to children, I bring the medal so they can touch it. Sometimes they look at me, and I tell them, "I'm the same as you, like this [pinching her skin]. I'm not different. I'm not a superwoman. I work hard, and I did this." And they say OK.

© Photo Run / Victah Sailer

Rosa Mota runs to her third consecutive European Championships Marathon win in 1990.

"Rosa always said that the most important people in the world are children, and she was always going to visit schools," says Rinaldi. "She's a sage, and takes a genuine interest in the children. Rosa found her talent in running, and wanted to use it to better help other people." Her greatest talent, he adds, is that "Rosa is a very strong person mentally, the strongest person I ever met. She would put a plan down and follow the plan. She was always mentally prepared, and physically, she treated her body like a racing machine."

Portugal's leaders continually invited Mota to state parties and affairs; one was a state dinner with U.S. President Ronald Reagan—this time, even Zé had to wait outside. Mota was "probably the most highly visible person in Portugal," said Rinaldi, but she favored a quiet lifestyle.

> Rosa does a lot of things with her family. She loves parties with families and friends, and loves being with people. She doesn't drink, but she eats sweet things. She's a very sincere person; it's not put on. Family, friends and children are important to her. She tries to teach children that they have to work for good things. That way, they will appreciate them more.

Post-Olympic Injury

In January of 1989, Mota was forced to drop out of a race for the first time because of sciatic pain in her left leg. She came back in March to place second in the Los Angeles Marathon, despite having the sciatic problem continue to act up. After leading the race early on, she dropped back and ran in for second in 2:35:27, behind Zoya Ivanova, who had been second to Mota in the 1987 Rome World Championships.

Mota looked to be recovered in 1990, when she won the Osaka Marathon and then got her *third* consecutive European Championships gold medal, this time in Split, Yugoslavia. "That's enough," she said afterwards. "I've won it three times, and I think that is good." Mota's run-conservative-early strategy helped her avoid "hitting the wall" in marathons. The closest she came was at Split, when she started too fast.

> It was a hilly course, and hot. And then the Russian, Valentina Yegorava comes, at 25K, and starts to run a little bit faster till the end. That was my most difficult marathon. The difficulty of marathons depends on the course. But I always try to run relaxed.

Mota's relaxed attitude changed in May 1991, when she had an operation to remove an ovarian cyst the size of a grapefruit. She also had stomach problems that forced her to drop out of the World Cup Marathon in London.

> After 14 miles, I wasn't able to run fast. I was in reasonable shape. But at times the pain comes in the races. Sometimes it goes away, and other times it comes back. It never really goes away completely. But the stomach problems had nothing to do with my surgery.

The pain and surgery made Mota reflect on her life. "I think only about my health. That's what is important. Some people think we runners are machines. But we are people, and we have problems." After the surgery, Mota decided to defend her World Championship title in Tokyo in 1991. "We decided to train for it only because it was in Japan," said Pedrosa. "Even though it's a short time [after the operation] and even though she is not in top shape, we believed she was in shape enough to fight for a medal."

Mota raced often in Japan through the years. She was very popular there, and there is a park named after her. The Japanese even put out a book called *The Life of Rosa Mota*, complete with pictures of her first communion. "The Japanese love Rosa as much as the Portuguese do," explains Rinaldi.

Mota had to drop out of the World Championships Marathon. She recuperated over the winter, and, by the time she turned 34 on June 29, 1992, Mota was back in full training, looking to defend her Olympic title at Barcelona.

Gearing up for an event like the Olympics or the World Championships puts a lot of pressure on a runner, Mota says.

> This will be my last one [Olympics]. I will train hard for big marathons, like Boston, New York, Chicago, Berlin; all the big ones. But the Olympics . . . I don't like to think about the Olympics, because it is four years to wait. If, in four years, I feel like going, I'll run. But I don't want to be pressured with thinking about four more years of training, and concentrating so much. I want to be relaxed with my training.

Mota's approach was to go "For one year, then another year. In 1996, if I feel good, yes, I'll go. . . . I don't want to feel the pressure about one more Olympics. But I'm not going to retire."

Being the defending Olympic champion did not add to the pressure, Mota said.

> Every race is different, and the real pressure was in Seoul, because I wanted to get a medal. And because in Portugal, people

say, "She needs to get a medal." Now, I can say I won first place. So I'll do my race, and will try to get a medal. The race will be very tough, with the hill at 40 kilometers, and it will be very hot and humid.

Mota's battle against injuries continued before the 1992 Olympics, as she had "several small problems that did not allow her to train normally," says Pedrosa. But they believed Rosa was in good enough shape to win a medal, because of the difficulty of the course and the fact that it would be hot when the women's marathon would be run; Mota was a good heat-runner.

Ten days before the race, however, Mota went on a training run. She felt fine when she started, but, by the end of the run, her hip was hurting her. It was an injury that forced her to withdraw from the Olympics and that would keep her from training for nearly the next two years. "If the injury hadn't happened, I still think Rosa would have made a run for a medal at Barcelona," says Pedrosa. "From what I know about Rosa and from looking at the course, I think she would have had a chance. That's why it was a huge disappointment for us." New Zealander Lorraine Moller, Rosa's friend who went on to win the bronze medal, agrees that it would have been a totally different race with Mota, the defending champ, in it.

But she was not in it, and telling her countrymen and women that she would not be able to defend her Olympic title was one of the most difficult things Mota had to do during her career. Mota was so crushed she declined to even attend the nearby Barcelona Olympics. "It broke her heart," said Rinaldi. "She wanted so badly to be there, and felt she had let her country down. It was very upsetting because Rosa is so patriotic. Her country and her people are so very important to her."

And so ended the "first part" of Rosa's career with the injury just before the 1992 Olympics. What she calls the "second part" of her career would not begin until 1994, when she was healthy and finally able to train again.

Staying in Porto

With her success, Mota could live anywhere in the world, but she never considered leaving her native city. "I think if I moved to another place I wouldn't feel good. I have my people, my city, my family. They get very happy when I win some races. And when I have a bad race, they always give me encouragement, and say, 'Next time, we hope you will be strong.'" She also has a second home in San Pedro de Moel, a country resort town two hours south of Porto, with beautiful forests and roads that run between high pine trees. Mota bought the house in San Pedro to be able to train better, away from the traffic of Porto. "Conditions there are a little bit better," she says.

The question invariably arises when talking about top runners: Is success in running due mostly to hard work, or is it genetics? Rosa falls on the side of hard work, saying there is something about the Portuguese culture that made her a good runner.

> I think what we have in Portugal is perhaps what the Mexicans and Africans have. We don't have a lot of facilities. . . . We need to work very hard to get things. And almost all the long-distance runners in Portugal come from big families and are not rich, perhaps so-so, at most. . . . They learned how to suffer.

The good things Rosa got from her running include her apartment and her vacation home in San Pedro. But she did not buy a lot. She had simple tastes before she was a success, and she kept those simple tastes afterwards. Mota has advice to young runners wanting to emulate her success:

> First, enjoy the things you are doing. You need to choose a sport you like, not a sport your parents like. Mothers and fathers sometimes say, "Do this, or do that." The girls themselves need to choose a sport. Then, you need to start slowly. The only thing I can say is that it was only after 10 years of running that I got my first Olympic medal. They have plenty of time. The first year, take it easy. Sometimes people start running, and after one or two years of running a lot they are doing well and win everything—then they disappear. So I'll say it again; I think it's better to wait. Enjoy yourself. Start slowly. When you mature, then OK, you can train very hard and win some races.
>
> I think it's the pleasure I have doing my training and my racing that has helped me. I like to run with the people, with friends. I really enjoy the training; I never feel I'm killing myself doing it. I always think that I can do more than I do.

Adds Pedrosa, "It's really that Rosa runs for no other reason except that she likes to run."

Young runners, girls especially, should not become fanatics about their diets, Mota says. She did not watch what she ate, preferring Portuguese fish and meat dishes.

> I eat everything. Except I don't like lobster, or crab, but not because I'm a runner. I just don't like it. I eat everything, and I like

almost everything. When I eat meat, or cookies and ice cream, I'm just as strong as before.

Mota did not eat much when out at restaurants, sometimes taking just four or five bites a dish. But at home she would eat a lot of small meals. Says Campbell, "Rosa's head was always in the refrigerator."

Mota is most proud that she made a difference with the women in her country, where it is acceptable for women to be out on the streets running now.

It was after my first medal that they start running more. And more important, even those who are not running are jogging. *A lot* of women started jogging. Those with small kids, or with their mothers, they walk. Before, they would have stayed at home.

It has given her pleasure to be seen as a role model for young girls in Portugal. "There are a lot of people who started running after Rosa," says Paula, "and no one says 'go home' now" like they used to say to women running on the street. Good runners followed Mota, including Albertia Diaz, Aurora Cunha, Manuela Machado (the 1995 World Champion and 1993 silver medalist in the marathon), as well as Fernanda Ribiero (who broke Ingrid Kristiansen's 5,000-meter world record). Rosa continues to be a heroine in Portugal, staying busy, giving talks, and making appearances. In the middle of her runs, the fishermen still yell out, "Go, Rosa, go!" and Rosa still stops to give little kids kisses.

Mota says her most memorable races are

the Olympics, the Worlds, the Europeans, where I got my first medal, and Boston. Those are my favorites, and the people I met, everything about them. I did what I wanted to and had fun. It's a good life; it is. If I was not a world-class runner, there are so many friends I wouldn't have been able to meet. Besides the medals I have in sports, it's my friends who are most important to me. When I finish being a competitive runner, I can come and visit them, because they will always be my friends.

Despite her problems with injuries, Mota remained upbeat, saying in 1994, "As long as I can run every day, that's what is important."

She began getting back into competitive shape, running small races in Portugal. Rosa was happy one day in July of 1994 to take second in a mile race in Portugal. "It's a little short for me, but I beat Paula!" she exclaimed proudly. In September, she won a half-marathon in Europe in 1:11:10. Mota started the Tokyo Marathon in November 1994, her first marathon since

1991, but she was forced to pull out. Mota remained optimistic and vowed to continue running and to try another marathon.

Many people thought her career was over, but now, in the "second part," she is healthy and training fast again, says Pedrosa. "Starting after the operation [in 1991], Rosa just had so many small problems," such as a lung infection, and knee and respiratory problems that did not allow her to train at a high level. But he believes the potential is there for Rosa to be competitive again, "which," he says, "is not something many people wanted to believe."

> We're hoping to prove those people wrong, those who didn't think Rosa could come back. We fully understand the feelings of those who thought her career was over, but it's something that particularly annoys us. Rosa has always been extremely fair and honest in everything she's said during her career. I don't know if we can prove those people wrong, but we are going to try.

In the fall of 1995, Mota was elected to the Portuguese Parliament, and will now divide her time between Porto and Lisbon. She also plans to compete in the 1996 Atlanta Olympic Games. "I'm healthy now and have more time to train since the election is over. We'll see what happens."

Mota had, by the spring of 1996, been running for 22 years. She had won the races she had wanted to win, and she and Pedrosa were financially secure. What then keeps her going, to continue training for the Olympic Marathon? Simple, she says. "I love to run. It's the same as when I started running, only now, I enjoy it even more." Running was its own reward for Mota at the beginning and remains that way today.

> Yes, it's true. I enjoy running more now than when I started, because of all the people I've met. If not for running, things wouldn't be so good, and I wouldn't have friends to visit. I get satisfaction from winning a race, and traveling and training in different places. Like yesterday, I was out training, and a man came running by, saying, "Rosa, hi!" Then I saw a deer, and I was so happy, and I thought to myself, "You know, Rosa, it is good to be a runner. Yes, it is very good."

19

"I Train for Good Luck"

Born December 12, 1963, Mexico

World records: 10,000, 20,000 meters, and hour run

First person to run half-marathon under one hour

Pan American Games golds, 5000, 1987 and 1991

One afternoon not long after Arturo Barrios moved to Boulder, Colorado, from his native Mexico City in 1986—the same year of his startling emergence onto the world road racing scene—a large pack of elite runners, including Rob de Castella, Rosa Mota, and about a dozen others, were on an easy, 10-mile training run along Boulder Creek. There is a path there that winds down the mountains along the creek through the center of town. Near downtown, it passes through a small sculpture park, and as the runners went past the statue of Chief Niwot, several touched the statue as they passed by, as was their wont.

"What did you do that for?" asked Arturo.

"For good luck," one runner replied. "We always touch the statue for good luck. It's a tradition."

Barrios looked puzzled but did not say anything as the group continued east down the path past the statue, beneath Broadway Avenue, through Central Park, and past the high school. About a mile later, just below the University of Colorado, he spoke up. "You know," he said, a serious look on his face, "I *train* for good luck."

At the time, some of the runners thought Barrios was exaggerating. Surely, the newly crowned 10K loop-course world-record holder (27:41) did it with superior genetic talent. But as the years have gone by, and Arturo's wins and records have piled up, the running world has seen that he was right—his good fortune has come from extremely hard training and meticulous preparation that leaves nothing to chance; a great talent, of course, but talent stoked and fueled by an ineffable fire that has made him into what Frank Shorter calls "one of the best runners in history."

Engineering an Escape

Barrios was born with a ferocious drive to succeed, to explode out of a background of poverty in Mexico City and become somebody. Thousands of people never escape the crowded Mexico City valley. But even as a little boy, Barrios knew that he would make it out beyond the mountains that ring the valley and do something important. When he was four years old, Arturo was asked, as all children are at one time or another, what he wanted to be when he grew up. Whereas most youngsters will say a fireman, policeman, sports hero, or doctor, the young Barrios had a different dream—he wanted to be a petroleum engineer. A petroleum engineer, you might say, is not your typical childhood career choice; but then, Barrios is not your typical person—or runner.

Years after that first dream, Barrios smiles when he tells the story. "Mexico was one of the top oil-producing countries then, and they were always talking about oil production and engineers. And I told somebody, 'This is it. This is the dream, the thing to be.' And so when people asked what I wanted to be when I grew up, I said a petroleum engineer."

Barrios became an engineer when he grew up; not a petroleum engineer, but a mechanical engineer, earning his degree from Texas A & M in 1985, and he is as proud of his education as he is of his four world records.

> I chose to major in mechanical engineering because of the many labs and field trips on the weekends in petroleum [engineering]. I was running for the school and didn't have the time to do both [petroleum engineering and running]. But I did have a choice, and so my dream was coming true.

It was his swift legs that paid for Barrios's education. He was born December 12, 1962, and raised by his mother, along with two brothers and five sisters, in the Agricola Oriental section of Mexico City. As a skinny, 99-pound 15-year-old, he began running in high school, not at all because he liked running, but rather to be with his best friend, Luis Zavala.

> In Mexico, when I was a kid, I never got exposed to different sports, like basketball, baseball, or tennis. In Mexico, it's not like it is in the United States, where you have the chance to play different sports. I'm happy with my choice, of course. But I never played sports like soccer.

Good thing he did not, because Barrios's running talent was soon evident. In high school he clocked 3:49 in the 1,500, 4:04 in the mile (when he was only 17), 14:26 for 5,000 meters, and 30:20 for 10,000 meters. He did not train much in high school, hitting highs of only 50 miles a week, which helped him avoid the burnout common with many young runners today. "I don't think somebody in high school should be training twice a day," Barrios says. "When you're young and training two or three times a day, you can beat everybody your age, but you'll only last a few years."

Barrios has lasted more than a few years—he has been a world-class runner for 10 years, and his times in some road races in 1994 were faster than those in the same races when he set his first world record in 1986. Barrios is one of the longest lasting of the elite runners for two reasons: he took a gradual approach to being the best, and he trains with more intelligence than most runners.

Arturo first drew notice when he was selected to represent Mexico in the 1980 Central American Junior Championships in the Bahamas. A coach from Rice University was there scouting. Seeing the 17-year-old Barrios win three races in three days, the coach told Barrios he was good enough to get a scholarship to Rice. There was a problem, however. Arturo did not speak any English. So he enrolled at Wharton Junior College in Wharton, Texas, where his priority was learning English and getting a start on his college degree.

During his first year at Wharton, Barrios studied math, physics, and English. Being a stranger in a strange land was a shock for the 18-year-old Barrios, and he had a difficult time adjusting. He ran slower his first year at junior college than he had in high school.

"My goal there was to improve myself and improve my running," he said. Barrios did the latter his second year at Wharton, winning junior college national titles in the steeplechase and 5,000 meters in 1983. The times were not spectacular, but that was OK, Barrios thought; the fast times would come when he got his scholarship to Rice. Barrios realized early and throughout his running career that it is best to take the long-term approach to running; there is no quick path to the top.

But things did not go as planned; after turning down recruiters from several big colleges, Barrios was not offered the scholarship he was promised by the Rice coach. Barrios still has not forgotten, and his black eyes flash when he recalls the snub. Instead, he accepted a scholarship to Texas A & M, and had a very good, though not spectacular, collegiate career. (He is proud that he never lost to a runner from Rice.)

Training still came second to getting an education for Barrios, but he never stopped believing he would make his name in running after finishing school. He had the self-motivation to steadily plug away at both, getting up at 5:30 to train in the cool of the morning, then studying and attending class all day. Arturo was a diligent student, receiving good grades and never missing a class. During semester breaks, he would return home to visit his mother and train in Mexico City. And he always kept his long-range goals in mind, careful not to overdo his running.

"I didn't start training twice a day until I was a junior," he says. "As a freshman and sophomore, I was training once a day. When you're 18, I don't think you can take the mileage." Barrios averaged about 60 miles a week while at Texas A & M, not much more than many high school runners do.

> Really, what you should do in college is to relax and enjoy your time there. Just maintain and keep your scholarship. That's what I did. . . . I was just running enough to score points and keep my scholarship so that I could get my degree, just making sure I was always on the team.

You're going to see that people who are beating you aren't going to last. That's why I say that I don't think you should be training twice a day when you're young.

Barrios was fortunate to have a coach at Texas A & M who recognized his potential, not pushing him to overrace or overtrain as is so often the case with college coaches anxious to squeeze all they can out of their athletes. Training at his own pace, often by himself, Barrios did do well on the track. In 1985, his senior year, he won the 5,000- and 10,000-meter races at the Southwest Conference outdoor championships, then placed second to Ed Eyestone of Brigham Young University in the NCAA 10,000-meter championships. Good, but not good enough for Arturo, who was getting ready to really start training and see where he could go with his running. "Arturo was a different runner back then," recalls Eyestone. "'Oh, Barrios; he's that guy from Texas A & M,' we might say. We didn't have big battles back then. Education always came first to Arturo, but after finishing his schooling, Arturo went and did tremendous quality training."

Unknown No More

Barrios graduated in December 1985 and, engineering diploma proudly in hand, returned home to Mexico City. He was ready to make running his priority and to start improving his times. Tadeusza Kepka, little known in English-speaking countries but considered a coaching genius in Latin America, became his coach. Arturo's family supported his decision to pursue running. In order to have time to train twice a day, Barrios turned down a lucrative job with Nissan and borrowed subsistence money from his sister. His brother chipped in by loaning him a car, so that Arturo could make the 15-mile drive each day to the *Desierto de Los Leones*, the high-altitude forest outside of Mexico City where some of the best runners in the world train. Barrios, a careful planner in all areas, gave himself exactly one year—not one day more, not one day less—to make it as a runner. If he had not made it within a year, he would take an engineering job and give up running.

It did not take Barrios that long. Six weeks after returning home, he won a local 10K and used his first prize money ever to fix his brother's car and buy new tires for it. His next race was a personal best 28:59 10K at altitude, good for $400. Then came a conversation that was to change his life. During a training run in the *Desierto* in March 1986, Martin Pitayo, a 2:10 marathoner, casually mentioned to Barrios that he had been invited to the Continental Homes 10K in Phoenix, Arizona, the following weekend.

"Why don't you come with us?" Pitayo suggested.

"How deep does the prize money go?" Arturo asked. Being unknown to the race director, he knew he would have to pay his own way to Phoenix. He scraped together $375 and bought a plane ticket—one way, because he did not have enough money for the return trip home. He was hoping to pay for his way home by finishing in eighth place, worth $800.

Pitayo and Barrios arrived in Phoenix the night before the race not knowing the race director's name or at what hotel they would be staying. Boulder Road Runners President Rich Castro, an agent for some Mexican runners, finally showed up and gave them a lift to the hotel, where Barrios spent an uneasy night sharing a bed with Pitayo. Barrios became more uneasy when he learned of the field he would be facing the next day. Looking at the list of entries, Barrios thought, "This guy's going to beat me, this guy's going to beat me. . . . There were maybe 20 guys, and I said 'I guess I'm not going to make any money, but I'm going to try.'"

Barrios had three months of good training going for him. He had averaged 110 to 120 miles a week on trails 9,000 feet above sea level. "When you train that hard at that altitude," he says, "you are ready for anything. My goal was just to finish eighth and be in the money." Wearing bib No. 69 out of 69, Barrios, unknown to everyone in the elite field except his fellow Mexicans and college foe Eyestone, ran at the back of the 20-runner lead pack that included Steve Jones of Wales, American Bill Rodgers, John Treacy of Ireland, Tanzanian Zak Barie, and Kenyans Peter Koech and Ibrahim Hussein. At two miles, passed in 8:54, he was still in the back of the front pack, which was led by defending champ Koech.

Despite running against some of the best road racers in the world, Barrios's confidence increased the longer he stayed with the lead group. "I was feeling good, and just kept telling myself to hang in there. I knew if I could stay close to the leaders for five miles, maybe I could kick it in and see what happens."

People in the press truck did not know Barrios, and some wondered whether the newcomer with the high number had actually started the race, or had just jumped in somewhere along the course, Marc Bloom reported. Barrios was with a group of 10 that broke away from the rest of the field after halfway, and, watching the others' form as they ran, he began counting down the runners, seeing which he had to beat to earn his plane ticket home. Eyestone dropped back between miles four and five, and when Barrios ran the sixth mile in 4:16, he was all alone with Koech. The Kenyan surged but could not shake Barrios. Barrios waited until the final 400 meters to start his sprint, and he ran away from Koech to win by five seconds in 27:41, a new road 10K world record. Treacy was third in 28:02.

"That was the first time we had seen Arturo, and all I knew was that some skinny newcomer from Mexico had paid his way to the race and blown everyone away," said Steve Jones, then at the peak of his marathon career. "The field was particularly good that year. What I remember most about Arturo is how young he looked, and how compact a runner he was. Arturo was efficient and never wasted any energy when he ran."

It was not a bad U.S. road debut for Barrios. His win and world record were good for $5,000—more than enough for the plane ride home and some gifts for his family. Now everybody knew Barrios and wanted him in their races. He obliged, following Continental Homes with one of the best road racing seasons ever, grabbing wins in an amazing 13 out of 14 races against the best runners on the circuit.

First came the Jacksonville River Run 15K, a 43:18 win. Then Crescent City in New Orleans on April 5 (28:16). Then the Boston Marathon, done "on a whim"; it was his only loss that season, a 2:14:09 fifth-place finish. Barrios bounced back with victories at the Bolder Boulder 10K (28:46), the Steamboat Classic 4-mile (17:33), a world best for four miles that stood for nine years, the Cascade Run-Off 15K (42:36), and the Falmouth 7.1-mile road race (32:17). A star had been born. *Running Times* featured Barrios on its cover with the headline, "Move over, Carlos! Suddenly, Arturo Barrios is the best male distance runner in the world."

Chief Niwot's "Blessing"

Something else happened in 1986. Arturo found a home in the United States and a girlfriend, helped along by Chief Niwot. Niwot was the Arapaho Native American who helped the first European gold prospectors, back in 1859, survive their first winter in the Colorado mountains. Niwot, who with other Native Americans wintered at the natural springs in nearby Eldorado Canyon, helped them even though he knew the arrival of the prospectors foretold the end of his people's way of life. Legend has it that Niwot laid a curse on Boulder to the effect that anyone coming to the area will fall in love with the mountains and the beautiful valley it sits in, and will always return. And so many will come that they will eventually ruin the valley's beauty.

So it is that visitors to Boulder always come back, including Arturo. Except for him it has turned out to be a blessing. He met his wife, Joy Rochester, in Boulder, and they are raising their twins, Monica Rosa (named after Rosa Mota) and Alex there. And it is in Boulder where he trained for his world records, mostly on the dirt roads that spread north from the Boulder Reservoir to the plains east of town. Barrios some-times jokes that "I own the reservoir," because he is there so much.

Barrios first visited Boulder in May 1986, two months after his world record at Continental Homes, to train at altitude along with three other Mexican runners. He had been living at 7,200 feet in Mexico City, but he needed a base in the United States from which to travel to road races. He liked the anonymity of living in Boulder, where he was just another lean and hungry-looking young man, no different from the hundreds of other runners, rock climbers, skiers, bicyclists, triathletes, in-line skat-ers, and other thrill-seekers who fill its streets and trails. "This is the perfect place to train," Barrios thought after his first visit.

Joy was a Bolder Boulder race official who was asked to house Bar-rios in her townhome in the Wonderland Hills section of North Boul-der when he first arrived. Joy said he could stay for a few weeks until close friend Rosa Mota came in April. Mota arrived, but Barrios did not leave. Within a year, he and Joy were married.

Barrios won the first of his four Bolder Boulders that year with a three-minute surge up a hill at the four-mile mark to break away from Koech and another strong field. That late-race surge became Barrios's trademark. "You have to be able to change the pace, because you never know how the race will go. You have to be ready to make a move."

Joy had been around many elite athletes, and she knew right from the start that her husband-to-be was somebody special.

> He has a fire inside him that is different. It . . . drives him on in a way very few people have. He thinks it's normal. . . . He doesn't understand that ability to focus; he thinks that everybody has that same sort of determination in them. But not everybody has what he has.

Breaking the Track World Record

There is no hesitation in Arturo's voice when asked which is his favor-ite race. "The most important race has to be August 18, 1989," the day he set the 10,000-meter world record.

Barrios took a patient approach to breaking the record. He had two more stellar years in 1987 and 1988, winning 18 major road races, but was beginning to focus on the track instead of the roads. All the great runners have a race when they are developing, when they say, "Yes, I can run with the best in the world," and Barrios's race came when he dropped his personal best on the track down to 27:25 in the summer of 1988, and then finished fifth in the Seoul Olympics. That was the race he says that gave him the confidence to run with anyone in the world. As soon as the 1988 Olympics ended, he and coach Kepka began planning his assault on the 10,000-meter world record.

First, Barrios cut down even more on his non-track racing. In 1989, he ran just two road races; the Bay-to-Breakers 12K (which he won for the third straight year) and the Crescent City 10K, a 27:50 win. The 10,000-meter record he had his eye on was 27:13.81, set by Portugal's Fernando Mamede in 1984. In going for the record, Barrios followed the formula he and Kepka developed during the previous two years: race in Europe starting in June, return to Boulder to train, then back to Europe for a series of fast races and then the record attempt.

Barrios ran well in some shorter track races early in the summer of 1989, and after placing third behind Said Aouita and Yobes Ondieki in a 3,000 meters in Sweden, was ready for a run at the record. He chose July 3 in Stockholm. Following a rabbit, Barrios passed halfway in 13:41, then took the lead with 11 laps to go. He ran negative splits, hitting 13:37 for his second 5,000 meters to finish in 27:18.45, 4.6 seconds off the record. It was the fifth-fastest 10K ever run. Kepka had told his star pupil before the race that he was fit enough to run 27 minutes, and now Barrios believed him. "I knew then I could get the record," he said. He had to wait a little longer, however. A week later in Nice, Barrios finished behind Ondieki again, running a new Mexican record of 7:35.71 for 3,000 meters. Four days later, it was London and another Mexican record, 13:07.79 for 5,000 meters.

Barrios then returned to Boulder for three weeks of training, returning at the end of July for his second record attempt, at the Mobil Grand Prix meeting at Berlin's historic Olympic Stadium, where Jesse Owens had won his gold medals in 1936. Barrios had a light meal the night before and slept well; he was rested and ready. Italy's Salvatore Antibo, who had the year's fastest time of 27:16.5, was scheduled to race Barrios, but ducked out, leaving the crowd of 33,000 to watch Barrios follow rabbits Doug Padilla and Steve Plasencia through 3,000 meters in 8:08.1. A lap and a half later, Padilla dropped out and Plasencia took over, leading until close to 5,000 meters, passed in 13:32.39, well below Mamede's record pace.

"I was feeling good. Up to halfway, I was just trying to stay with Plasencia. When I'm racing, I just try to stay with somebody and go with him," Barrios said. There soon was nobody to go with, as Plasencia, his pacing work done, stepped off the track. Barrios needed a 13:45 last 5,000 meters to get the record, and he would have to run the last 12 laps by himself. He was up to the task. "After that point, I was thinking, let's just try to keep it up. Just keep it up." Barrios, known in Europe as

Le Metronome for his even, rhythmic running style, hit each of the next seven laps between 66.1 and 66.6 seconds.

"Then, with five laps to go, you realize you really have a good chance at breaking the record. That's when I really tried to go faster and faster." The only question was whether he could hold his pace to the tape. He could, hitting the last kilometer in 2:35.6 and the last lap in 59 flat to finish in 27:08.23, a new world record and an average of close to 4:21 per mile.

In the postrace interview, Barrios told reporters, "My coach said I could run under 27 minutes, but let's stop this. I've got to phone my wife." That was the end of the interview. Joy remembers the call, in which he told her he was "happy with the record, but especially with the way he felt that day, so strong and so totally in control."

"I wasn't really sure I had the record until the last straightaway," Barrios says.

> You know in a 1,500 whether you are on record pace; three and a half minutes, and you are done with it. Here, you can lose the record with two laps to go. So I just tried to keep it up with five laps to go. That was the difference between breaking the record and not breaking the record.

"It's hard to describe how I felt that day," he says, picking his words carefully.

> But it's like this: When you cross the tape, you feel like you were always training for something, and now I was there. Like when you go to school. You go to school because you want to get a degree. Then you get the degree, and you say, "Hey, I did it!" You train and train and train, and sometimes you ask yourself, "What am I training for?" Then you get in the race and you say, "This is it."

Rob de Castella praised Barrios, saying, "He has the ability to make a plan and the drive to stick with it to make it happen." Barrios took a complete month off and then began his buildup for his assault on the one-hour run record, one of the longest-standing in track.

It took another year of training, but once again Barrios's careful preparation paid off. In March 1991, in La Fleche, France, he turned in another great performance, setting the world record for the one-hour run by averaging 68 seconds a lap for an incredible 52-3/4 laps in a row. He ran 21.101 kilometers in an hour, passing the half-marathon (13.1 miles) in 59:59.6, becoming the first man to run that distance in under 60 minutes. (The hour record still stands, and Barrios's 10,000-meter record stood until Kenyan Richard Chelimo broke it 1993, followed in quick succession by countrymen Yobes Ondieki and then William Sigei. Haile Gebrselassie of Ethiopia now has the record, 26:43.53.)

Training: Patiently Fishing for Peak Fitness

Most weekends when he is not racing, Barrios and good friends Steve Jones and chiropractor Steve Campbell can be found in the mountains west of Boulder taking in an afternoon of fishing. It is his only hobby, a way to relax from the rigors of training.

The first time Campbell took Arturo fishing, they went to an isolated mountain lake where there was a "ton" of fish. Campbell found a likely spot, where fish could be seen from the bank, and told Arturo to sit there until he caught one. When he came back two hours later, Barrios was still sitting in the same spot. "He hadn't moved," Campbell says. "He was determined to stay there until he caught a fish. He would have stayed all night if I hadn't dragged him away."

That's the kind of patience and determination that fuels Arturo's training, too. Most of it is done on the soft dirt roads around the Boulder Reservoir or on dirt roads in the mountains at 8,000 to 9,000-feet altitudes. Barrios prefers the reservoir for another reason; it is isolated, and he likes to train alone. He will occasionally train with other runners, but not too many can keep up with him.

Barrios is blunt when explaining why he favors training by himself.

I don't mind training with somebody, once a week or twice a week. But if they want to run with me they have to run my pace and they have to do my training. I'm not going to do somebody else's pace, and I'm not going to do somebody's training. . . . I don't want to be arrogant, but I have my training.

The training goes on no matter what the weather. In December 1991, while Barrios was doing basework for the Barcelona Olympics, Boulder was hit with a two-week, sub-zero cold snap that dropped the temperature to minus 25 degrees. But, it did not stop Barrios.

"Even if it's snowing, I go out. Just being out there when it was minus 25 degrees helps me. I think simply by training in bad conditions, it is going to make you tough, physically and mentally."

He bundled up beneath several layers of clothes, only his face visible under a hat, hood, and scarf. He came back from his run with serious frostbite on his nose and ears.

10K World Record Progression

30:58.8	Jean Bouin (FRA)	Paris	November 16, 1911
30:40.2	Paavo Nurmi (FIN)	Stockholm	June 22, 1921
30:35.4	Ville Ritola (FIN)	Helsinki	May 25, 1924
30:23.2	Ville Ritola (FIN)	Paris	July 6, 1924
30:06.2	Paavo Nurmi (FIN)	Kuopio	August 31, 1924
30:05.6	Ilmari Salminen (FIN)	Kouvola	July 18, 1937
30:02.0	Taisto Maki (FIN)	Tampere	September 29, 1938
29:52.6	Taisto Maki (FIN)	Helsinki	September 17, 1939
29:35.6	Viljo Heino (FIN)	Helsinki	August 25, 1944
29:28.2	Emil Zatopek (TCH)	Ostrava	June 11, 1949
29:27.2	Viljo Heino (FIN)	Kouvola	September 1, 1949
29:21.2	Emil Zatopek (TCH)	Ostrava	October 22, 1949
29:02.6	Emil Zatopek (TCH)	Turku	August 4, 1950
29:01.6	Emil Zatopek (TCH)	Stara	November 1, 1953
28:54.2	Emil Zatopek (TCH)	Brussels	June 1, 1954
28:42.8	Sandor Iharos (HUN)	Budapest	July 15, 1956
28:30.4	Vladimir Kuts (URS)	Moscow	August 11, 1962
28:18.8	Pyotr Bolotnikov (URS)	Kiev	October 15, 1960
28:18.2	Pyotr Bolotnikov (URS)	Moscow	August 11, 1962
28:15.6	Ron Clarke (AUS)	Melbourne	December 18, 1963
27:39.4	Ron Clarke (AUS)	Oslo	July 14, 1965
27:38.4	Lasse Viren (FIN)	Munich	September 3, 1972
27:30.8	Dave Bedford (GBR)	London	July 13, 1973
27:30.5	Samson Kimobwa (KEN)	Helsinki	June 30, 1977
27:22.4	Henry Rono (KEN)	Vienna	June 11, 1978
27:13.81	Fernando Mamede (POR)	Stockholm	July 2, 1984
27:08.23	Arturo Barrios (MEX)	Berlin	August 18, 1989
27:07.91	Richard Chelimo (KEN)	Stockholm	July 5, 1993
26:58.38	Yobes Ondieki (KEN)	Oslo	July 10, 1993
26:52.23	William Sigei (KEN)	Oslo	July 22, 1994
26:43.53	Haile Gebrselassie (ETH)	Hengelo	June 5, 1995

Barrios has missed only one workout since 1981. It was late in December 1992, when he was in the middle of his basework. A Pacific front came quickly over the Rockies, dumping more than two feet of snow on Boulder. Even then, Arturo drove his four-wheel drive truck to the reservoir and tried to run through waist-high snow drifts. Making little headway, he was forced to turn back.

> I started running, and I ran 15 minutes, and I said, "Forget it, there's no way I can run," so I went back. It's just like running when it's windy. It can be very windy in Boulder, up to 100 miles an hour. But I think by [training through] that, when you are racing someplace else, it's going to be easier.

But still he admits that the powerful Chinook (a Native American word meaning "snow-eater") winds that come sweeping off the Continental Divide are what bother him the most. "I can run when it's 110 degrees, when it's minus 25. But the one thing I hate is the wind. Especially when I go to the track, because when I go to the track, I have to run specific times."

Persevering in bad conditions is important, Arturo emphasizes.

> I think that is why I'm lucky to live in a place where we can get snow, we can get heat, cold, and rain. Basically, we have everything. It's not like, say, California, where it is always sunny. When it's 45 degrees here, we think its great; and you can ask a California guy, and he'll say, "Oh, man, it's too cold."

Barrios calls driving early each morning to the reservoir "going to work." He parks near the entrance gate, and runs a counterclockwise loop around the reservoir. The first 200 meters are fairly easy, but he quickly falls into his rhythm, and within a few minutes he is running between 6 and 6:20 per mile. His standard 10.7-mile loop is run in 62 minutes. It has a beautiful view of the Front Range of the Rocky Mountains and the 13,000-foot, white-capped peaks of the Indian Peaks Wilderness Area and the Continental Divide. The ranchers and farmers in the area know Barrios, giving him a friendly honk and a wave when they pass by. Nevertheless, even training in nice surroundings can get tiring, so Barrios has a couple of mental tricks to help him get through the run.

> When I start running every morning, I know I'm going to do 10 miles. In the beginning, it's always tough. "Here I go, one more time," I think. After a few miles, I'm OK, because I have loops, and I know how far I have to go. So by that time, after a half-hour, it's just another five miles. And I want to run as fast as I can in training, so that it's over.

One of the "secrets" of Barrios's training regime is the complete break from running he takes each October. It's tough for even ordinary runners to take time off, and many of the elite runners train year-round. But the same focus that allows Barrios to do great track sessions and never miss a workout also gives him the discipline to take a month *completely* off from training. "If you train 365 days every year, and you don't take a break, you might do it for two or three years, but then it's going to get you. It's going to catch up with you."

Runners are surprised by this, and those who don't know Barrios think he's disingenuous. "People say, 'Oh, you are still running once a day.' I say, no I'm not. I think that's a problem, that people just keep training. It's boring if you do not take a break."

It must be difficult for a full-time, professional runner to take time off, knowing the competition is out training for those 30 days, right? "No, no, not at all. Resting is easy," Arturo says. "It's the training that is hard."

On Tuesdays and Fridays, instead of driving to the reservoir, he heads to the University of Colorado's Potts Field track for his track workouts. He is all business at his "office," warming up by running for 20 minutes on the grass that rings the track, or going out on the bike path for 10 minutes, then returning.

After 10×100-meter strides, he starts the workout, often with Joy timing him. She knows him well enough to tell him when he is on or off. Although Barrios will joke or make small talk while warming up, he is all concentration while running the intervals. He stares intently at the track in front of him as he runs smoothly and rhythmically, hitting the splits right on. People can yell out his name and he won't acknowledge them.

Track workouts have been basically the same since Barrios began training with Kepka in 1986: $10 \times 1,000$ meters between 2:45 and 2:50, with a 60-second recovery; 20 by 400 in 63 seconds; or five 2,000s. When training for the marathon, his times are "maybe a little bit slower, but not that much, because the secret is for me not to lose my speed for the 10,000 so I can move up to the marathon."

Mark Coogan, top U.S. runner and an occasional training partner of Barrios, says,

> [Arturo] has great talent, but he also works harder than anyone. He does killer track workouts, then will go to the pool and swim for a mile, stretch, and get a massage. In the afternoon, he might run some hills the same day, or after his second run, do 10 3 100 meter strides. Stuff like that makes him so tough.

Barrios pays close attention to his form, like a Formula 1 racer monitoring his engine. One day on the track, recovering from a slight muscle pull, he yells out, "Am I leaning at all?" as he sprints by, a worried look on his face. Efficient form is key, he believes. One way he maintains his form is with bounding drills. Sometimes after the morning 10-mile run, he drives to the base of a 200-meter, fairly steep hill. He bounds up the hill, extending his legs like a long jumper taking off, as if jumping over a puddle of water. He lifts his forward knee high while extending his back leg.

"It's a mistake to do only distance, distance, distance," Barrios believes. "If you don't do bounding, or stretching, after you've been running for a long time your style is going to change." Barrios does his bounding five months a year, three times a week, on a soft surface; either on the hill or on the track, for 50 to 100 meters. Sometimes he does it before his workouts, sometimes after. "There are so many kinds of bounding," he says.

> No matter what people say, age does make a difference. You get heavier and your form can change. For me, it's important not to change my style; that's why I do the bounding. It only takes 10 to 15 minutes, three times a week. And it really helps.

Bounding is incorporated into one track workout Barrios has been doing for a long time, 30 × 200 meters in 30 seconds. He wears a watch that beeps every 30 seconds, keeping him on pace. The workout is divided into 3 sets of 10 × 200s; in between each set, he does 6 × 50-meter bounds on the grass inside the track. Watching her husband run lap after lap, Joy talks about his mental edge. "Obviously, he's physically gifted. . . . But he's also born with a mental gift. He is incredibly determined and focused."

That's why he never has trouble training. Even after he achieved financial security, there was no decrease in his motivation. Barrios still has the same attitude toward running as he had as a poor 23-year-old looking to escape Mexico City. There's never a question of getting burnt out or missing a workout. Says Joy,

> There are some people who mentally can't get out the door unless there is someone waiting for them. Arturo doesn't need somebody to get him out. When he wants something, he wants it badly, he wants it for a lifetime, and he's willing to wait for it and work for it.

Barrios has never set foot on a treadmill and never uses a heartrate monitor when he does his track work, which begins only after months of laying a base. Base training commences November 1, unless he is running the New York City Marathon; then, he takes a month off after the race and starts his basework in early December. His mileage was 90 miles a week when training for the 10,000 meters and 100 miles a week when doing marathon training. His winter training is all distance work.

The major change in his training when Barrios switched to the marathon was increasing his long run to 24 miles. That would be followed by a nap. The 24-miler takes about 2 hours, 30 minutes.

Barrios is not fanatic about hitting an exact pace on his easy or long runs, unlike his carefully planned track workouts. After a distance run in the mountains one Saturday, he was asked what his splits were. "I don't know," he shrugged. "I didn't time them." It was the first time he had run this particular loop in the mountains; when he was finishing, he was told the loop was exactly 17.4 miles, knowing he had wanted to run 18 miles. "That's close enough," he said.

After eight weeks of basework in the winter, Barrios runs a couple of road races in warm climates: the São Silvestre in Brazil, a race in Uruguay, then the Bob Hansen 10K in Indonesia, at the end of January. The latter race offered a $500,000 prize for anyone breaking Barrios' road 10K record, and he tried for three years to get it. In 1993, Ethiopian Adiss Adebbe broke his road loop world record by one second, running 27:40. Barrios was second in 28:01.

After those early-season races, Arturo returns to Boulder for two more months of base training, and then begins incorporating bounding drills into his regime. The scientist in Barrios is evident in the way he approaches his training; everything, from diet to sleep to track workouts to easy days is planned out. Especially rest days. Barrios follows his rest days as strictly as his workouts.

His smarts were also evident during the hot, dry Colorado summer. When a large group would be leaving Rob de Castella's home to start training at 9 every Sunday morning, there would be Arturo, standing in front of his house, already showered and dressed from his run, which he had done early in the day to escape the heat. He would wave as the runners went by, smiling, happy to have his run done early.

A typical week in Barrios's schedule is:

Sunday:	18-24 miles, flat, 6:15 to 6:30 pace.
Monday:	A.M., 10 miles on dirt; P.M., 6 miles, 6:10 to 6:30 pace.

Tuesday:	A.M., 20 × 400 meters in 63 seconds;
	P.M., 6 miles.
Wednesday:	A.M., 15 miles at 8,000-feet altitude.
Thursday:	Same as Monday.
Friday:	A.M., 6-10 × 1,000 meters in 2:50;
	P.M., 6 miles.
Saturday:	10 miles on dirt.

It Is How Long You Last

1991 was a year of changes in Arturo. It was not a great year for him on the track, though he won his second Pan American Games gold medal, in the 5,000 meters in Havana. His twins, Alex and Monica, were born in August, and fatherhood becomes Barrios, who spends hours playing with the kids.

Becoming a parent, says Barrios, has helped his training, as well.

How can you describe being a father? I can sum it up in three words: It's just great. Even when we didn't get a lot of sleep the first three months, it didn't matter. We'd be getting up at 2 or 3 A.M., but it didn't affect my training. In fact, it was just the opposite; it gave me strength to train hard and to keep on training. If you are really happy with what you are doing, no matter what happens, you get used to it, even if you sleep only 5, 6 hours. If you are not happy, forget it, because even if you are getting 20 hours of sleep, it won't help.

After his usual month-long rest in October, Barrios looked toward the 1992 Barcelona Olympics. This time, he would be one of the favorites. In an attempt to win a medal, he changed his training in 1992. After São Silvestre and Bali, he did not run a race from February 16 until the middle of May, concentrating instead entirely on his training in an attempt to get stronger. "This is the first time I've done this," he said. "We'll see if it pays off. Basically, what I'm doing is a lot of miles and quality track workouts. I'm doing all the training without racing."

Kepka and Barrios used his experience at the 1988 Seoul Olympics to formulate a new strategy that they hoped would bring him a medal. The Seoul 10,000, however, "was a surprise for everybody," Barrios said.

We were expecting a slow, tactical race [in Seoul]. It wasn't. I know now, and everyone knows, that to win a medal in the Olympic final you have to go out from the beginning even if it's 58 (seconds for the 400 meters). The leaders will slow down, but they will not break down. We saw that in Tokyo (at the 1991 World Championships), where they were on world-record pace for eight laps. They did slow down, but they didn't break down. If you start out in the second pack, you might get closer, but you won't catch the leaders. I have to be with the pack. I have to be right there in contention, so when a move is made, I can go. If you're 20 or 30 meters behind, there's nothing you can do.

Barrios ran near the front in the early part of the race. He was with the leaders for five laps, but when Richard Chelimo, a 21-year-old Kenyan, made his move, Barrios could not go with him, and he ended up battling with Italian Alberto Cova for fifth. "I did all I could do; obviously, I wanted to place higher," Barrios said.

But he wants to be judged over his whole career, not by one race.

The way I see it is that it's not what you do for one race, but what you do for 10 years, or however long. It's how long can you last. For me, it's better to be able to perform at a world-class level for 12, 14 years, instead of being at the top for 3 years. You see people who are still young and have to retire. If somebody gives me a choice, to get the gold medal and retire at 22 or not get the gold medal and retire at 36, I go for the 36.

When pressed, Barrios explains his motivation to keep training: "I always wanted to do something in life. I used to see these people getting married and having kids. They used to be here," he says, raising his hand to chest level, "and now they are here," he adds, lowering his hand down to waist level.

"So I used to say, look, I have to do something, otherwise I will never get married. Because if I'm going to suffer, it's just going to be me. Why bring somebody else into the world? Why bring one more or two more or three more?"

Like Alberto Juantorena, Rosa Mota, Steve Jones, and others, Barrios has empathy for the less privileged of the world. After setting his world records, he founded the Arturo Barrios Invitational to provide scholarships for underprivileged youth in Chula Vista, California, outside of

San Diego. Several of Barrios's world-class friends run the race for free, to support the scholarship fund, which has raised more than $70,000.

Once, after a friend returned from a visit to Mexico City, Arturo asked what he thought. "A beautiful city," the friend said, praising the National Archeological museum, the art galleries, the Aztec excavations, and the broad Avenue de la Reforma.

"Ah, then you stayed in the Zona Rosa," Barrios said softly. "Did you get to the northwest side of the city? It's not the same. You'll see the poor people there. Life is very difficult for them." Even after he was making a good living from racing, Barrios never forgot his humble upbringing.

Moving to the Marathon

After Barcelona, Barrios made one of the biggest moves of his career—to the marathon. Meticulous preparation is his trademark, and that is why his most disappointing race is not the 1992 Olympics, but the 1986 Boston Marathon. He did it "on a whim," thinking it was going to be "a piece of cake."

And up to 25 kilometers, on a 2:09 pace, it was easy for him. "It was like, 'So, when are we going to start running?' And then I started getting tired. It was really disappointing." De Castella went on to win in 2:07:51, while Barrios, despite walking several times, finished fifth in 2:14:09. "It was one of those crazy things you do in life," he explains. It was to be seven years before he would enter another marathon.

He points to longtime rival Ed Eyestone as a 10K runner who has been able to run good marathons. "It's one more step, then, from being good to being one of the best." And being the best is what continues to drive Barrios, whether it's in his choice of professions, in school, fishing, or even in making friendly sports wagers with friends. A group of runners has a 10-mile "beer relay" every year, in which runners alternate running a mile with drinking a beer. When Barrios found out marathoners Steve Jones and Don Janicki were a team, he quickly formed his own team.

"But Arturo," someone reminded him. "It's the week before the Bolder Boulder."

"Never mind," he said. "We'll kick everyone's butt."

Says Jones,

The main thing about Arturo is that he's a competitor. He's competitive in everything he does. He always says he catches five more fish than everyone else, they're always a pound heavier than anyone else's, and he always says he drinks 10 more beers than everyone else. That's Arturo.

Barrios showed in road races in 1993 that marathon training wasn't affecting his speed. He won the 1993 Bolder Boulder in a gutsy performance that illustrated what he's made of. Barrios came down with a fever the week before the race, but declined to tell anyone about it. "I said I was going to run, and I will run," he said. The fever broke two days before the race, and Barrios dragged himself to the starting line. He hung with the pack before surging at five miles. Countryman Martin Pitayo and Kenyan Thomas Osano were the only ones able to go with him. Osano was dropped, but Pitayo took a 10-meter lead with a quarter-mile to go. He looked to have the race won, but a grimacing, hurting Barrios dug deep down and sprinted past Pitayo just before the finish. Barrios summed up the drive he has to be the best by saying afterwards, "I was either going to win the race or die."

The well-known Barrios brought new publicity to the marathon, with many observers waiting eagerly for his appearance in the New York City Marathon in the fall of 1993. He made the change to the marathon to give himself a new challenge, a way to direct competitive urges. When asked if he thought he could get faster at 30, he replied, "30! I'm not 30. I'm 29 years, 345 days." But hitting 30 was one reason he made the switch. "I think it's time for me to move up. I see it as a new challenge. I'm excited to see what I can do in the marathon. And I hope I do OK, otherwise I'll have to go back to the 10K."

Barrios brought his engineering background to his marathon training. He's analyzed the race and disagrees with those who say the 26.2 miles will eventually catch up with whoever runs it.

> People say it's because they are racing every week. That may have a part in it, but I think it's the training . . . that kills you. The marathon is not going to kill you. Almost anybody who runs even 40 miles a week can run a marathon. Obviously, they aren't going to run 2:07, but they can run and finish it."

Barrios finished third at the 1993 New York City Marathon, behind Andres Espinosa of Mexico and Bob Kempanien of the United States. He was in good position to challenge for the lead, but bad blisters forced him to slow down. He wore racing shoes that he uses for shorter road races and developed hot spots that turned into blisters. Barrios did not make a big deal of it after the race, but the blisters were the size of small pancakes on the bottom of his feet.

After his customary month break, Barrios trained through the winter and lined up in the 1994 Boston Marathon. Facing a deep field, he placed fifth in 2:08:23. "Now, I'm a marathoner," he said.

Barrios became a U.S. citizen on September 16, 1994—ironically enough, Mexican Independence Day. The reason for the switch was a continuing conflict with the Mexican track federation. Less than 24 hours after receiving his citizenship certificate, on just three hours sleep, Barrios won his first U.S. title at the national 10K road championships in Kingsport, Tennessee, clocking 28:43. Support there was great, as runners shook his hand and wished him well, said Barrios, adding, "I have peace of mind now."

The switch was hot news in the running community, with comments roughly 80 percent in favor of Barrios on the Internet computer bulletin boards. While some said Barrios became a U.S. citizen because it would be easier to win prize money, more typical was the response of Catrina Campbell, women's cross-country coach at Oklahoma State University and a friend of Barrios's. "I'm surprised, because Arturo has always been so loyal and dedicated to Mexico. But now he will be just as dedicated to his new country."

Julian Nuños is president of the Mexican track federation, who, Barrios says, heads up a corrupt organization. Women's marathon star Olga Appell is another Mexican runner who became a U.S. citizen, after being asked to give the federation $10,000 of her winnings from the 1993 New York City Marathon. Changing his citizenship was a difficult decision for Barrios, but he says he felt shackled by Mexican track officials, who reneged on promises and never paid for tickets to international meets, even the Olympics.

As usual, Barrios was remaining true to himself, no matter what the consequences. There was a bit of sadness at leaving the country for which he had toiled so long, but he quickly regained his focus and continued training for the 1994 New York City Marathon and beyond.

The 1994 New York City Marathon offered a good field, and Barrios was ready for his first marathon win. After running with the pack, he took the lead at 22 miles and pushed the pace, dropping everyone except Mexicans German Silva and Benjamin Paredes. But Barrios fell back, running in to place third, while Silva, despite taking a wrong turn just before the finish, won.

Barrios's next marathon was Los Angeles in March 1995, and again he fell back after leading the race. This time it was Rolando Vera of Ecuador who won, while Barrios was fifth. His leg was hurting during the race. Barrios found out afterwards that he had pulled a hip muscle. It was his first major injury, after 17 years running, and he had to take

Arturo Barrios runs the 1994 Bobby Crim 10-miler in Flint, Michigan.

six weeks off. He resumed training in the summer of 1995, slowly at first, and doing more stretching exercises. In late July, he did a track workout of 15 × 400 meters in 62 seconds, exclaiming, "I'm back!"

Training Is One Thing, Racing Is Another

At a track party not long after Barrios set the 10,000-meter world record, an ex-runner, slightly drunk and with a nascent potbelly bulging over his belt, began boasting of bygone glories. There is nothing sadder than listening to a runner gone to seed, bragging about past exploits, and this was no exception. The longer it has been since a runner has been out of running, the greater those exploits become.

"Barrios? You're talking about Arturo Barrios? I used to beat him," he boasted.

"You did?"

"Yes. The steeplechase at junior college nationals," he said.

Arturo has no trouble admitting that the drunk ex-runner beat him, along with many others while he was in college. "Sure. A lot of people beat me," he says. "I didn't make it to the NCAAs in track until my senior year. I made it to nationals twice in cross-country; I was 86th and 39th." Then his eyes narrow, his brow furrows, and he asks, "The guys who used to beat me in college—where are they now? They cannot beat me now."

They're certainly not running fast 10Ks and marathons. Eyestone and Kenyan Yobes Ondieki, who ran for Iowa State, are two of his few college rivals still competing at the international level. The difference is that Barrios was able to keep putting in hard training year after year, without injury or major illnesses. Careful training is the reason for that, says chiropractor Steve Campbell, who gives Barrios electrical and ultrasound treatment for minor aches.

"When you look at Arturo's career, you see he has had one major injury and only a couple of little injuries. All of these guys have talent, but the guys who stay healthy and train smart are the ones who succeed."

Barrios likes to pass those smarts on to young runners. He always has time for them, even providing workouts for and training with some of them. He is a popular speaker with the local running club, and after a talk college runners will corner Barrios, anxious to pry out his secrets. Arturo is gracious with them, patiently giving advice.

One tip he gives is to be extra careful when living and training at altitude, to avoid overdoing it. Many runners come to altitude to live, but train so hard that they are either not fresh when they go to races or are injured. Barrios avoids this by running at a much slower pace on his easy days than he is capable of (though it is still faster than many people's race pace).

> When I'm doing my distance runs at altitude, or I'm on an easy run—this is my belief—I cannot train under six minutes. To repeat, somebody like myself can't run under six minutes, because

it will take a lot out of you. You can do it for maybe two weeks and then, when you're racing, you're going to find out that's not the right training for you.

Most runners, from the ordinary to the elite, train too fast, Barrios says, explaining it like this:

There are people who are great trainers but they are not great racers. So whatever your pace is when you are racing, you have to run about a minute or a minute and a half over that in training. That's what is going to be right for you. When I'm racing, I'm running about 4:30 per mile pace. So when I 'm training, I'm going about 6:10, about 1:40 slower.

Someone running a 45-minute 10K, 7-minute pace should be running about an 8-1/2- or 9-minute mile pace in training. Because when you are running faster than that, basically you are racing every day. You might be able to do it in training—but don't forget, training is one thing, racing is another.

Barrios typically trains at a pace between 6:10 and 6:30, "but in the last mile I might run a little bit faster, maybe about a 6-minute mile. But I think that whatever your pace, you have to find a formula that's going to be best for you."

Un Hombe Entre Hombres

One reason Barrios and the other elite runners like Boulder is that they can go about in public and not be bothered, or even noticed. Being a professional athlete is a legitimate profession in Boulder. In Europe, Barrios, like most of the big track stars, is besieged by fans, and in Mexico he was a national hero on the order of a football star in the United States. I had a glimpse of this on a trip to Mexico City. At the airport, I was delayed while two customs officials went through my bags, asking for a receipt for the fax machine I was carrying. Thirty minutes passed, and I was beginning to get worried. When a supervisor finally came, I opened my briefcase to get out my passport. There was a stack of signed, color postcards of Barrios from his 10K record race, which Joy had provided to pass out to young runners.

"Conoce a Arturo Barrios?" the supervisor asked.

"Yes. Here. These are for you," I said, handing him a stack of cards. They proved popular, and soon half a dozen workers appeared, asking for photos. I passed them out and pointed to my watch. *"Adelante,"* the supervisor said, waving me through to where Mexican 2:14 marathoner Gerrardo Miranda, one of Arturo's best friends, was waiting.

"You should have just mentioned Arturo's name in the first place," Miranda said. "It would have saved a lot of trouble."

Miranda says, "Now, we'll go to the forest." The forest is *El Desierto de Los Leones*, the place where Barrios laid the base for his future success with countless miles over the years. The city soon gives way to smaller buildings, and all at once the forest appears up on a hill, green, thick, and quiet. "It's a national resource," says Miranda. The tall pine trees and dirt trails of *El Desierto* stretch for miles on a high ridge along the outskirts of the city. Sitting at 9,000 feet above sea level, just 15 miles from downtown Mexico City and its 20 million people, it's the most popular training spot in Mexico.

It is hard to say what Barrios's becoming a U.S. citizen will do to his popularity in Mexico, but he is happy with his decision and with the support he has received from Mexican friends and runners, who are still trying to follow in his footsteps, training in his old stomping grounds. Even at 7 A.M. on a Saturday morning, the forest is full of activity. The side road leading up from the main tollway out of town is lined with cars; groups of brightly clad runners pass by a grassy opening in the trees, some in full stride, others in an easy jog. Vendors sell shoes, squeeze fresh fruit, and cook food for the runners. The smell of *pinos* trees fills the air. Suddenly, a wide-eyed Salvador Garcia, winner of the 1991 New York City Marathon, sweeps out of the trees a step ahead of a pack of runners. He passes by several times during the next hour, and when he finishes, barely out of breath, he indicates the forest behind him with a sweep of his hand: "This is where we train. It's a special place."

"All the elite runners in Mexico go here," adds Miranda. "This is the place. This is where Arturo got started." Barrios was one of the first of the scores of world-class runners in Mexico to find fertile training ground in *El Desierto*, which translates as the "The Desert of Lions." It's hardly a desert, but it is full of "lions," the training athletes.

The King of the Forest is Kepka, Mexico's national coach, whose patient training methods have brought Barrios and other Mexican runners into the world's spotlight. He is called *Profe*—the professor—and he fits the part. The erudite Polish native has taught at the University of Mexico since 1966, when he came to Mexico City to prepare athletes for the 1968 Olympic Games. Kepka liked the city; the Mexicans liked him, and he has been here ever since, weaving his magic. The 65-year-old father of two is paid by the university and the government.

Even though Barrios has raced and trained all over the world, the forest remains a special place for him. "Even runners who have never been here have heard of it," he says. "Everybody trains there. Everybody."

"Everybody" is not much of an exaggeration. It is not only Barrios and the best Mexicans who train in the forest, but the very best in the world. On this summer day, besides the elite Mexicans running in *El Desierto*, several Algerians, former multi-world-record holder Said Aouita, world 1,500-meter champ Tatyana Samolenko, and others from the Soviet middle-distance team were passing each other on the forest's many loop trails. Members of the German, Cuban, Polish, and Japanese national teams also train there.

Barrios says the forest was critical to his success. The training is solid and good there. It's isolated from Mexico City's cars and crowds, but close enough to get to easily; the many trees give it a pleasant, oxygen-filled atmosphere; the surface is soft dirt and ground-down pine needles, and the mild climate allows for year-round, high-altitude training. The forest has several measured loops, where Barrios and the others can do long runs, easy runs, tempo runs, and fartlek workouts. And, most importantly, "It's much clearer there, with low pollution," says Barrios.

When he would go to Mexico City to visit Kepka, Barrios's day started at the Mexican Olympic Training Center, a large complex where young athletes get coaching in basketball, gymnastics, soccer, swimming, weight lifting, and other sports. Noureddine Morceli and other visitors stay at dormitories at the center.

Once a year, the Mexican Olympic Committee gave physical exams to Barrios and the other Olympic runners. Barrios's resting heart rate was 25 beats per minute during his last exam, in 1994. The Mexican athletes also get psychological testing at the Olympic Training Center, and Barrios's response to one question gives perhaps the best insight into his character.

"Have you ever failed?" the psychologist asked.

"No. I have never failed," Barrios replied. "And I never will."

The next question was, "What do you do when you fail?"

Barrios replied, "One more time; I have *never* failed, and I *will never* fail. Bad experiences, yes. But never failure."

Now, the forest blooms with the fruits of Mexico's running boom, as women, children, and club runners crowd the paths. But they defer to the stars, moving aside to let the world-class runners pass by. Kepka and former star Rodolfo Gomez each supervises an elite group that trains in the forest. "All the guys winning in races around the world run here all the time," says Barrios. The groups pass each other on the trails, like running matadors, though they save their duels for races.

The "friendly rivalry" is healthy, Kepka says. "It's good for the sport. It increases the competition and gets more people training."

There are many small running clubs in Mexico City, sponsored by businesses. For a monthly fee, club members get membership in a health club and entry into races. These club runners spend as much time socializing in the forest as they do training, mingling with the who's who of international running. Barrios is their hero; "*Arturo es un hombre entre hombres*," Miranda says.

Will the *desierto's* popularity and this influx of runners spoil the forest? No chance, says Barrios, in his sensitive and intelligent manner, befitting someone who may be a *Profe* himself one day. "This will always be a special place."

It appears he is right. A sign at its entrance reads: "If you run in the forest, plant a tree." Despite the hundreds of athletes who use it every day, the forest is spotless, with no trash visible.

Barrios, still proud of his native country, wishes Mexican runners well, especially those coming from poor upbringings. Heading off on a training run in the forest one day, Barrios (who still visits Mexico City) reflected on how far he—and Mexico—have come.

> It makes me very happy to have helped popularized running in Mexico. It is the one thing I'll take credit for—I want to be remembered not as the guy who set the world record, but as someone who opened up new doors. That's what I want to be remembered for.

Barrios, though, competitive to the very end, cannot resist one last, parting shot before running up over a hill and disappearing into the distance. "Just one more thing," he yells out over his shoulder. "Make sure you say that I am the best fisherman, and that I can beat anyone in the world."

20

Free to Run

Born September 7, 1965, (East) Germany

Winner, Boston, New York City, and Berlin Marathons

Third-fastest Women's Marathon, 2:21:45

The most difficult run Uta Pippig ever took was not the Olympic or World Championships 10,000 meters or the New York City or Boston Marathons, or any of the scores of races she has won. It was the one that began in East Berlin early on a January morning in 1990 and ended in West Berlin and freedom. Most runners have to worry about the wall that comes stealthily and furtively at the 20-mile mark in a marathon; the wall Pippig faced was 15-feet high, made of steel-reinforced concrete, and topped by barbed wire, watch towers, guard dogs, and machine guns.

The Berlin Wall, erected in 1961, symbolized a divided Germany and a divided world. While West Germany followed the path toward democracy after World War II, East Germany turned toward socialism and the east. One of its greatest achievements was the establishment of a sports system that rivaled that of any in the world. Pippig was one of the stars of that system, which helped her develop into one of the best marathon runners in the world. But whenever she wanted to test herself against the best from the west, Uta ran into a bureaucratic wall. She was kept in a "kind of prison," not allowed to travel, race, or pursue the training she and her coach wanted. Pippig, the top women's runner in East Germany and a member of the East German army through her army sports club in Potsdam, was taking a great risk when she left East Berlin. If caught, she would be considered a deserter. After the dismantling of the Berlin Wall two months earlier, she and Dieter Hogen, her coach and boyfriend, decided to run for freedom. Uta and Dieter put three suitcases in the back of their small car and drove off into the morning rain. It was raining on the other side of the wall, too, but somehow, this was a kinder, gentler rain. When she arrived in West Berlin, Uta stepped out of the car, letting the rain flow down her face. She was free for the first time in her 24-year-old life.

Free at last from the shackles of the East German sports federation, Pippig blossomed into the biggest star in women's running, clocking fast times and winning races with an élan that brought new life into women's running. "I've had three dreams in my life," Uta said. "Coming to the West was one of them."

Pippig's running took off with her new-found freedom, as she trained and raced with an uncommon focus, intent on becoming one of the best ever. At a time when road running was waiting for new runners to emerge and take the place of the Big Four who had dominated women's marathoning—Rosa Mota, Ingrid Kristiansen, Joan Benoit Samuelson, and Grete Waitz—Pippig burst onto the scene like a fresh wind, a forerunner of a new kind of woman runner. Pippig is the fastest marathoner for her age, clocking 2:26 when she was 26 years old in 1992. She ran 2:21:45 at the 1994 Boston Marathon, the third-fastest marathon ever, and, with her best years still ahead of her, many think she will be the first woman to finally break the 2:20 barrier.

Making Sport

Pippig was born in Leipzig, Germany on September 7, 1965, when Leipzig was part of East Germany, and she lived there until she was four. Her parents, both medical doctors, then changed their practice and moved with Uta and her younger brother to the countryside outside of Berlin. "It was a nice place to grow up," says Uta. "There are lots of forests and many lakes." Pippig had a quiet upbringing, spending her time reading and playing with other children. The biggest influence on her life were her parents, who installed in her a Faustian love of learning and a tremendous capacity for doing difficult work. Through the centuries Germans have had the reputation of being hard workers, and Pippig has continued that strain on her way to becoming the top women's distance runner of the 1990s and the model of the new kind of female runner of the future.

Pippig got into athletics as most young East Germans did, through her town's sports club. She began doing gymnastics when she was 10. When she was 13, Uta joined the local sports club in Petershagen, where she lived, and she stopped gymnastics and started running (though she was not seriously training). "It was fun. We also played a lot of games, like soccer. That's the sort of thing I like. It was a nice time, because I grew up not too serious in track and field. It was for fun."

Those small, local clubs were the backbone of the East German sports system. It was a good system, says Hogen, a top German coach, "because in the former East Germany, every kid made sport."

> Sport was a very exciting thing, and everybody was interested in it. You see, someone who was good in sport had some possibilities to make their life better, to go to other countries. You could get a lot of nice things and travel. That's why many kids are going in not just for track and field, but all Olympic sports.

The system worked; East Germany was a sports power from its first appearance in the 1956 Olympics to its last showing in the 1988 Olympic Games, grabbing the third-highest number of medals behind the Soviet Union and the United States.

Children were judged on body type, build, or athletic skills. For some sports, such as gymnastics or ice dancing, the selection came very early, Hogen explains:

> They would say, "OK, this guy is fast, he'll go into sprints; this guy is very tall, he goes into rowing," or whatever. And so most of the kids are attached with sport; that's why East Germany had so many champions. That's the biggest reason. A lot of hard

and serious training, many, many full-time coaches, and also a very good system to select kids for sport.

Surprisingly, Uta was not selected for running right away. Her first athletic endeavors came in gymnastics. She might have had a future on the rings, "but then I became too tall, and the second thing was that I was too afraid." Instead, she turned to running. Her running remained low-key, however, because Uta's parents, in addition to providing tight family bonds, encouraged her to be a success in academics, not athletics. Pippig was a good student, earning top grades. Instead of watching TV in the evenings after school, Uta read books, and she has remained curious her whole life. She was, and is, always reading. "When I was a little girl, my parents said studying was the most important thing. 'You need your job in the future, not sport,'" they told her. "You have to do your job. They couldn't believe running would be such a big thing for me." Pippig did not, either, as she was still running for fun with her clubmates, expecting to be a doctor when she grew up, not an Olympic runner.

The question often arises as to why some athletes have the discipline to continue difficult training while others just as talented stop. Pippig believes it was her upbringing. "It's how you grow up, your friends, your education, your total character." Pippig learned from her strict upbringing that hard work "is one of the best things in life," says Hogen. "It gives you satisfaction. Look around and you can see how many people really are not happy with their life. They don't know what real life is, what is worthwhile."

What motivated Pippig when she started running and what continues to motivate her is the satisfaction she gets from the effort she puts in. "Many great athletes came from poor families, or big families, where life was not easy," says Hogen. "And hard work makes tough people."

Pippig was pushed to work very hard by her parents, to give not just 100 percent but 110 percent in order to get good results in everything she did, whether it be school, athletics, helping around the house, or playing the piano. Even when Uta excelled, it sometimes was not enough to please her parents.

One incident illustrates the drive that characterizes Pippig. She was extremely talented as a child, and, at a sports day in her town, Uta competed in a variety of events, winning 11 medals—10 gold and one silver. She was very proud of her haul, of course, and ran home to show her parents. Her father's reaction? Instead of praising the 10 wins, he angrily asked his daughter, "What about this silver?" Pippig has never forgotten this, and she has spent her life trying to answer her father's question.

Too Early a Marathoner

At age 16, Pippig began training more seriously, and her running potential continued to show. When she was 17, Pippig was told by officials, as many athletes were told, to take the steroid Turinabol every other day. Steroids are a problem in many sports, and Pippig, a leading proponent of healthful living, isn't reticent to talk about it. "I was too young to understand," she says. "The federation told me to take this, like they told all young athletes," saying it was just what others did and that there was absolutely no risk. Fortunately for Uta, her mother disagreed. She sat down with Uta one evening, telling her daughter that "The pills are not good for your body," and so Uta did not take them. But she could not tell the sports officials. If she had, "I would have had to leave the club. I wanted to keep running, so I said nothing. But I knew my family was with me and that was the important thing." Indeed, her family remains the central support in her life, and she became a good enough runner that the officials never suspected she was not taking the pills.

Pippig, driven to be a success in running, knew she had to move on, because she most likely would never realize her potential at the small Petershagen club. So, early in 1983, still 17 years old, she approached some bigger clubs, saying, "Look, I can run very good." They saw her talent, and she was invited to join the Army Sports Club in Potsdam, known as ASK. It was one of the top clubs in East Germany, and here she would meet Hogen, who was coaching 800- and 1,500-meter runners.

Hogen had turned to coaching after seeing his career cut short by injury. In just his second year of training, Hogen had run 3:45 for 1,500 meters and placed second in the East German nationals. But his coaches "had no patience; they wanted results in a year," sometimes entering him in three races a week. After increasing his mileage from 2,000 kilometers a year to 8,000, he suffered an abductor injury, and, at 22, his promising career was finished. That injury formed his philosophy of training. "If you make a big mistake, then it's over, and it never comes back," he says. "You have just this one body, and you can't change parts."

But Hogen was not her coach yet, and Pippig, who finished high school in 1985, started running longer distances, though not by her own choice. After showing her talent by winning short races, Pippig was told by coaches that she should try the marathon, so her "official" marathon training started when she was 19. That, Pippig says with hindsight, "was too early. For me, it would have been much better to train first for middle distance, and then to grow up with the miles." What happened was that her first coach in the ASK club made it easy for himself by sending Uta out with some of the other girls he was already training. There was not as big an interest in women runners as in the men, and "He said, 'Oh, it's easier if she goes with the marathoners, so she would not be training alone.' It was easier for him, too, so I started too early this long-distance." Her first marathon came that year when she ran 2:47, fast enough for her to be pegged as a marathoner for good.

Pippig had a fine support system at ASK, which has a long tradition going back to the 1950s. It is one of the most famous running clubs in Europe. In 1960, it won its first medals in the Olympic Games when Hans Grodotzki took silver medals in the Rome 5,000 and 10,000 meters. "Then in the '60s, '70s, and '80s we had *so* many medals in the running," says Hogen. Two of the top runners were Olaf Beyer and Jurgen Straub.

"So, in the end, we have a tradition from 30 or 40 years, and a lot of kids running in the club. And Uta was one of them," Hogen said. Pippig was a dedicated trainer and continued improving until she was the best young runner in Germany. "I won a lot, but I was very often second, too," she says. When she was just 20, Pippig won the German Marathon Championship.

In 1986, Hogen, the top coach in the club, was asked to coach Uta, its most promising runner. It turned out to be a perfect match. The handsome, rugged-looking Hogen was smart and dedicated. He had not coached long-distance runners before, but he learned everything he could about marathon training by watching and talking with two-time Olympic champion Waldemar Cierpinski and other German stars, spending as much time with them as he could.

Marathon Ideas

"I made my own ideas about the marathon," says Hogen.

> That was the good thing about East Germany. There were many, many, very good athletes, world-class athletes, like Cierpinski. Every year, we spent many weeks together in training camps. You could see all day how they trained. You could speak with their coaches. Sometimes I was in one room with his coach, and we spoke about long-distance training all day.

Hogen was always reflecting, always listening, always absorbing training techniques through those long hours together with top runners and coaches. Like Peter Coe, he was able to cull out what was important and discard the rest. "It was a very good experience. I saw how they trained, and what worked for the marathon, and what didn't work. And I said, 'OK, if Uta is a marathoner, and she is in my group now, we have to go for it.'" And go for it they did, with a passion and precision that brought Pippig along slowly until she was strong enough to race the best in the world.

The enjoyment she got out of running, along with her success at regional championships, motivated Pippig, who was nearing elite status. The only problem was that she could only read about the best women runners; she could not test herself against them, because the DVfL, the East German Running Federation, refused to let her leave the country. Her applications to run in international road races were "consistently rejected."

Hogen's coaching was working; at her next marathon that year at Leipzig, Pippig ran a personal best by seven minutes, winning in 2:30:50. When she won the Leipzig Marathon again the following year, Pippig began receiving a stipend from the East German government and support in her training. That support included medical tests, equipment, free housing in a dorm with other female athletes, and coaching from Hogen.

Hogen felt there were benefits to coaching within the club system. "Everything was very close; that was the system. And the parents were proud that the kids are in the sports club. That's important for your work, so you have no problems. I could try different things, and make my own ideas," says Hogen.

This was the part of the East German system that was "really good." The bad part was the close-minded officials, who looked askance at some of Hogen's innovative ideas. Even though Pippig was one of the best runners in the country, she and Hogen felt stifled in their training. "It was not easy, because we couldn't go for our own ideas; we had to do the government's ideas," he says. Hogen wanted his athletes to do more speed work, but the higher-ups did not agree. He was acknowledged as a top coach, but his outspokenness caused officials to distrust him. They did not think he would come back to East Germany if he and Uta left the country to go to a race. So Uta was always training and training without getting a chance to race. When Dieter questioned this, officials became even more wary of him. "They thought if we went to a race together, we wouldn't come back." Which was true.

Uta and Dieter continued to dream of making their great escape. After the 1987 Rome World Championships, where Uta ran the marathon but did not medal, Hogen and Pippig decided to defect to the West. But after talking it over with her parents, Uta changed her mind. Her mother told Uta that if she left, the ubiquitous Stassi secret police would "make trouble" for Pippig's family, and her parents would lose their jobs. Instead, Pippig stayed in Potsdam, running up to 150 miles a week but racing infrequently, and Hogen continued butting heads with sports officials. It did not help that Pippig turned down officials' requests that she join the Communist Party. All Uta and Dieter could do was read about races in other countries, wondering how Pippig would have fared against Rosa Mota, Grete Waitz, and the other world-class runners.

Pippig would have done very well, according to tests conducted by East German officials. Once a year, complete exams were given to all their top athletes. During the tests, Pippig would run 15 kilometers on the treadmill. After 5 kilometers, she would stop for one minute while blood was withdrawn. Then, she would run 2 kilometers wearing a mask that collected gases to be analyzed. "These tests showed she could run 2:25 back in 1986," Hogen says.

Invitations for Pippig from around the world continued to pour in, and Hogen continued to ask for permission to go to international road races. But officials continued to say no. "I was very sad about it," Pippig says, "because if you train very hard and do big workouts, you want to race." Instead, Pippig's "races" were in the vast woods behind the club, where she ran workouts. "It wasn't so much fun," she says.

Pippig and Hogen were even forbidden to read western running magazines. "You could ask for permission, but it was never granted," Hogen explains. Hogen was fed up, and he said "No more. We had many of these situations, and finally they said, 'OK, you can't go. You will never leave the country.'"

"That's one thing," says Hogen. Another was the bonuses he did not get. In the East German system, coaches received a base salary, which was "good money," Hogen says.

He was supposed to get all the bonuses, because his runners were among the best in the country. "They had all the points, all these medals and all these championships in East Germany. But I never got the bonuses. They always cut the bonuses because I spoke my mind. . . .That was the system. That's all," he says without bitterness.

East German athletes were told that "people in the West were not our friends." West Germany was the biggest enemy. "In these countries there are very bad people," they were told. "There were just very different ideas for everything. So we had a lot of problems."

So did the country. People were tiring of Communist rule, and, after changes in the Soviet Union, changes came to East Germany as well, culminating in the dismantling of the Berlin Wall on November 10, 1989. "We were very, very happy when the wall came down," Uta says. They spent the night celebrating with friends, and, the next day, they went to

West Berlin to talk with different people to see what the future held for them, their country, and Uta's athletic career. "I made a picture of what's possible and what's not." What was possible was the chance that Uta would at long last be able to travel and test herself against the best women in the world. She had missed so many races and now it seemed certain she would get to race in the west. "Then, we waited a little bit, to see if things are changing. But they didn't." Pippig was still denied permission to travel. The same bureaucrats were still in charge, with the same hardened attitudes. Adds Hogen, "Yes, after the wall came down, it was still the same, and then we said OK, now we go."

Go West, Young Woman

Dieter did not tell Uta that they were leaving East Germany until the January day before they were to flee, so that she would not have too much time to think about what was happening. It was a decision fraught with danger. By leaving, she was deserting the East German army, a serious offense. She telephoned her parents that night and cried. Because of the desertion problem, Pippig could not tell anyone except her parents that she was leaving. "I was calling just my parents and they were sad. 'Are you crazy? No you can't do it.' It was a big risk more for me than Dieter because I was directly in the army. But sometimes you just have to try."

Pippig packed up two suitcases, while Dieter had just one. "You see, we couldn't take anything that would arouse suspicions." They were worried their car might be stopped at the border. They loaded the car in the rain and drove across the border leaving their old life behind. Even though she was fulfilling a dream, it was a difficult move for Pippig.

Says Dieter, "We wanted to leave before they build up the wall again. We thought it was possible at this time." For several months after the wall came down, East Germany was in limbo, teetering between the east and the west. But the fuzzy political situation eventually cleared up in March 1990, when the East German people voted to work with a party from West Germany.

What they found was a new world, one in which the old support systems were gone. On their own for the first time, Pippig and Hogen got by with a little help from their friends. "We knew somehow we can find a way. We can go to a club in West Germany and ask them if they will help, since at this time I was not so bad as a runner." Some runners in a West Berlin club did agree to help them. Uta and Dieter went to Stuttgart, where they "had a little room, in the highest level under the roof. It was not an easy time," Pippig says. They stayed in Stuttgart for a year, before receiving a "very good" offer from SC Charlottenburg [SCC], a well-established West Berlin sports club and the organizers of the Berlin Marathon. "We said, OK, let's go back to Berlin."

Hogen was offered a full-time coaching job and the couple was given "a very nice apartment." That was important, because, says Dieter, "It was not easy to get an apartment, because *so* many people came from East to West! Everything in town was closed." But their running friends in Stuttgart knew some people who had connections, who found them the apartment in Berlin. "You know how these things go," Hogen says. "It's the same all over the world."

Finally, they had a home, and then, says Uta, "We were really happy." Pippig and Hogen have been with SCC ever since, where Dieter trains club members, both elite and "fun" runners. SCC includes many sports besides running. There are 200 marathoners of all abilities, and 1,500 total club members. Funding comes from organizing races such as the Berlin Marathon as well as Germany's largest cross-country race and largest all-women's race. The money from these races goes to putting on more races and paying the coaches. The club prospers, says Dieter, because, "People like sport so much."

Pippig likes SCC in part because of its location. The clubhouse (really a large health club, behind which is the stadium with an all-weather track, and facilities for table tennis, weight lifting and other sports) is on the rim of a big forest, full of soft, dirt trails. "It means you can go out the door into the forest and run for hours. We have everything we need, and conditions are really good for running." It was also good for her studying, as Pippig, now in medical school, could get from the classroom to the clubhouse very quickly.

Free at Last

At long last, Uta was free to race in the west, and she made the most of it. Uta's racing and training were fueled by a new enthusiasm and euphoria, the kind only someone who is set free after have been shut up her entire life can feel. After a good winter of training, averaging 120-130 miles a week, she won the 3,000 meters at the German Championships. The elite 5,000-meter runners in East Germany trained over 100 miles a week, so it was natural for Hogen to have Pippig doing high-mileage training. In February Uta set the world record for the indoor 5,000 meters, clocking 15:13.71 to break Sonia O'Sullivan's record. This and other races showed that Pippig would have had success in shorter distances if she had not been moved to the marathon so early in her career. "I had it in me to make fast times earlier. But I'm not angry, only sad."

Her first competition in the west came at the 1990 Boston Marathon, three months after leaving East Germany. "We had heard so much about the Boston Marathon that we said, 'Let's go to Boston . . . . We have to try it; you can run fast there, for sure. Let's go.'" Not everyone thought that was a good idea, however. Friends and other coaches in Stuttgart urged them to run the Frankfurt Marathon instead. "I said no—we go to Boston." It was a good decision, as Uta ran 2:28:03 for second place behind Rosa Mota. That earned Uta $24,000. It seemed to many western observers that Uta had appeared out of nowhere. But she had been running for a decade already, and she had taken the best from the efficient East German system to develop into a strong, solid marathoner.

Pippig spent the summer of 1990 getting ready for September's Berlin Marathon, which for the first time would go through East and West Berlin. The race, first run in 1974, is the largest in Germany. From 1981 through 1989, the marathon started in front of Berlin's most famous landmark, the Brandenburg Gate, at the border between East and West Berlin. In 1990, with the fall of the Berlin Wall, runners could pass for the first time through the gate into East Berlin.

The prospect of reunification had left all of Germany on an emotional high, and, for Pippig, the race was the fulfillment of a dream. The marathon was run just three days before the reunification of Germany, and 25,000 people streamed through the streets of Berlin. Pippig went to the front of the women's race soon after the start and led to the tape, buoyed by the cheers of the crowds lining the course. Polish national record holder Renate Kokowska made a late bid, but Pippig won by 33 seconds in a course-record 2:28:37.

"When I passed through the Brandenburg Gate, I realized that it was time to look forward and not back," Pippig told *Running Stats* afterwards. "For me it was a new beginning." Steve Moneghetti of Australia took the men's crown in 2:08:16.

In 1991, Pippig came back to Boston and lined up against one of the best women's marathon fields: Joan Benoit Samuelson and Kim Jones of the United States, Norway's world-record holder Ingrid Kristiansen, Wanda Panfil of Poland, and Kamillah Gradus of Poland. Pippig let the leaders go during the early downhill portion of the course, but she ran strongly over the second half of the race. Panfil won in 2:24:18, and in the closest finish of a women's marathon ever, Pippig finished 12 seconds behind Kim Jones in third. It was a symbolic changing of the guard, as Pippig outkicked Samuelson to finish third in 2:26:52. Samuelson followed two seconds behind, one tick up on Gradus in fifth. Kristiansen was next, three minutes back.

That fall, Pippig went to Tokyo for the third edition of the World Championships, finishing sixth in the 10,000 meters. Then she went back to Berlin, where she increased her mileage to get ready for Boston in 1992. Pippig could now say for the first time that "things are so normal. Everything we wished for all these years, it has all come true. It's been such a very short time, sometimes I can't believe it." The sensitive Pippig did not forget all those left behind in the former East Germany who were too old to start out fresh and forge a new life as she and Dieter did. "Their lives are gone," she said. "They had plans too, and they couldn't make it."

Pippig divided her time between Berlin and Boulder, Colorado where she went for altitude training. Berlin grew after the reunification of Germany, with the streets crowded with construction projects and cars. But outside of the city "it is still very nice. You have lots and lots of forests and many lakes; it's really nice for training." Those government-owned forests remain Uta's favorite place to train. "There are 2-meter wide dirt trails," she says, holding out her hands. "There is no traffic at all, just a biker once in a while. It's good; you can go such a long while, and there are no fences." There were no fences around her racing career, either. She put in good training over the winter, getting ready for Boston and the Barcelona Olympics.

In April 1992, Pippig placed third at Boston for the second consecutive year, running 2:27:12 and finishing behind Russian Olga Markova (2:23:43) and Yoshiko Yamamoto of Japan (2:26:26). Commentator Katherine Switzer said at Boston that Pippig was part of the "new wave" of women runners. Uta would have been one of the favorites for a medal in the Barcelona Olympic Marathon, but she opted for the 10,000 instead. She did not want to run a marathon in the heat and pollution of Barcelona. Pippig placed 7th at the Olympics in 31:36.4.

Stuttgart Failure, Big Apple Success

In September 1993, Chinese women runners shocked the running world with their spate of mind-boggling world records at Beijing's National Games. Wang Junxia broke Ingrid Kristiansen's 10,000-meter record (30:13:74) with an unbelievable time of 29:31.7, and Qu Yunxia clocked 3:50.4 for 1,500 meters. Six different Chinese women ran under the previous world records 14 times. Questions arose about the possibility that the Chinese had used performance-enhancing substances, and after dominating the 1993 World Championships, the record setters seemed to drop out of sight.

Pippig focused on the World Championships in Stuttgart. She ran two road races and won them both, the Pittsburgh 10K and the Arturo Barrios Invitational, despite hard training weeks of over 100 miles before each race. At the Barrios Invitational, she broke the course record by 13 seconds, running 32:17 and beating Nadia Prasad and Olga Appell. She next won the Bix 7-miler in Davenport, getting pushed under the course record by Ann Marie Letko. (Uta likes running on the roads, saying she feels she had missed too many races before.) The next day Uta and Dieter left for Germany and its eight-hour time difference to get ready for the Stuttgart World Championships. She ran some track races in Europe, lowering her personal best in the 3,000 meters to 8:45 and then 8:40.

It seemed that Pippig was ready. But she had done "too much speed-work."

> I pushed too hard in training again, for one and half weeks, then
> I was tired. I was "overconcentrated." OK, Stuttgart is in my home
> country, so I have to be very good. [But] I pushed it too hard.

With tired legs, Pippig finished a disappointing ninth in the 10,000 meters, won by Junxia in 30:49.3

Uta took a short break after Stuttgart, and she began preparing for the New York City Marathon. Pippig, inspired by the Chinese, did the best training of her life, with total and complete dedication. She decided to postpone her premedical exams for a year, to give herself the opportunity to devote all her attention to running.

She and Dieter bought a new house in Boulder on a golf course in the rolling hills north of town. Her life was completely dedicated to training. She did not buy a television for their home because she felt it would take away from her training. "Watching TV can be stressful," she says. "Because I look at the political situation around the world, and this or that and mama mia, and think about my parents, I get very crazy, so I say forget it." In the evening, she would listen to the radio and study her textbooks. Her focus was so complete she did not even go shopping.

For the first time in her life, Uta had enough time to train, and she and Dieter were careful not to overdo it. "It is harder to make the same mistake we did before Stuttgart, because the training for the marathon is slower than for 10,000 meters," said Dieter. Uta had enough speed from her summer track training to run well at New York.

Two weeks before New York, she did her last hard workout—a 30-kilometer time trial in the mountains at 8,200-feet altitude, at 90 percent effort. She tapered the rest of the time before New York and finally allowed herself the time to shop for a sweater. While getting ready for her marathon, Pippig kept an eye on the Chinese women runners on the other side of the globe. At the October 31, 1993 IAAF World Cup Marathon in San Sebastián, Spain, Chinese women swept the top four places, with a winning time of 2:28:16, by Wang Junxia. Uta received several phone calls and faxed messages giving her the results. She breathed a sigh of relief: the 2:20 barrier was still there.

Pippig was confident she would run well at New York and was free from her wall of books. Training at the elite level while going to medical school was very difficult. "For the marathon, you have some very long runs, mostly up in the mountains. You have some very fast, endurance runs, and always you are very tired after these workouts, and you need to rest," says Dieter. "Then, because of the studying, your recovery needs much more time, and all these things. That is why this time, it was much better. Uta could train better."

Added Pippig, "I was pleased, because I was more relaxed after all the hard training. You finish the hardest part of the training, and you feel tired, and need a lot of time to recover." She ran well in road races before New York, clocking 31:52 at the Great Race 10K in Pittsburgh off a 160-mile plus week. Before heading to New York, Pippig declined to tell reporters what she was shooting for, but privately she wanted Katrin Dörre's German national record of 2:25.

New York was the race that propelled Pippig into the top ranks of world marathoners. Americans Kim Jones and Anne Marie Letko were to be her challengers. Letko had beaten Pippig in the 10,000 in the World Championships. New York was Letko's first marathon, and she let it be known beforehand that she was gunning for Pippig. In the opening miles, the American did look like she was ready to challenge for the win, but Letko fell behind by the eight-mile mark, and, by 15 miles, she was two minutes behind. Pippig was running only against the heat and the clock. Pippig's high mileage makes her stronger than any other marathoner, and she gets better as the race goes on. On this unseasonably hot and humid day, Letko was forced to drop out and was taken by ambulance to a local hospital, where she was treated for dehydration. Jones also was forced to drop out of the race. Pippig, taking only water, as she does in every marathon, had a shot at the course record of 2:24:40 set by Lisa Ondieki in 1992. Pippig was under course-record pace until 21 miles, before slowing but still winning easily in 2:26:24 in very hot conditions, more than 2 minutes and 30 seconds up on second place finisher Olga Appell of Mexico (now the United States). The race continued Pippig's streak of finishing in the top three in nine straight marathons since 1987, and it was her fourth win of a major marathon. "I'm happy with the race," she said, of her 41st-place overall performance. "I was surprised at how easy it was." She added

I like it when other girls run with me. But if they are going out too slow, then we can't run a very fast time near the end. And that's why you have to run your own race, but if possible, together with the other girls. Because if they come with you, you can run fast.

"Uta took New York City by storm," read one headline, and the media spotlight began to turn on running's newest star. "Look," says Dieter. "Anyone who knows the sport knows Uta would have run several minutes faster if the conditions were good." Pippig was satisfied; she had gotten the win she wanted in tough conditions. Now, she looked ahead to Boston 1994 and the chance to perhaps catch a flier on a good day on a fast course.

After taking a short break back in Boulder, Pippig returned to Berlin and rested. She took a break and cross-country skied regularly over the winter of 1993-1994, then began laying her basework in anticipation of Boston. "Heh, I'm having fun and training well," she said. "If things go well maybe I'll get a fast time." Dieter was confident that she would run her best race there. "Before Boston in 1990, 1991, and 1992, Uta was always tired," Hogen recalls. "There was no way to train correctly." Now by training correctly (with more recovery and more mileage), she had her sights set on becoming the first woman to break the magical 2:20 barrier in the marathon. She was still worried that a Chinese woman might do it first, after their out-of-this-world times. But the Chinese did not; they pulled out of the London Marathon and had "normal" performances during the next two years.

Can a woman run 2:20 for a marathon? "That's possible, for sure," says Pippig. "OK, when I heard about the Chinese for the first time, I tried to run like a madwoman," putting in even greater mileage. That did not last long, however.

But then I was tired. So many of us trained seriously for so many years; Ingrid Kristiansen, Liz McColgan, Lisa Ondieki, all trained so serious. Rosa Mota, all the great women, and they tried many things in training, all kinds of different training. And then some Chinese girls come . . . [she snaps her fingers] and they run under 30 minutes for 10K, they run near 8 minutes for 3,000 meters. It's not step-by-step.

Says Dieter, "They run 4:12 for one mile during the 3,000 meters; it's a world record." Adds Pippig,

If it is without drugs, then I take my hat off my head, and say oh, gosh, you are really great. Many people said it would be a *very* great thing, and the biggest goal for women in this century, to break 30 minutes [for 10,000 meters] and to break 2:20. And now, they did break 30 minutes, and everyone has a bad feeling. Instead of being something great I have a bad feeling about it.

Pippig says all she can do is wait and see what times the Chinese turn in. "I'll make my own training and try to push it very hard, because it's a good training system that we use."

Training: Fun and Hard Work

On the wall of the kitchen in Pippig's well-kept, frame and brick house in Boulder hangs a large calendar listing her training schedule, with the workouts color-coded; endurance workouts are in green, hard workouts are in red, and easy runs are in blue. It shows the basis of their training: rigorous, scientific workouts tempered by good humor. "The schedule is a way of keeping the training fun. When you do it for 20 years, it becomes second nature. . . . I like it. We do that because, if you have the whole year on one schedule, it's much easier to see mistakes," explains Dieter.

We have it from every year, and if you would like you can put 10 years on one wall, then you can see, after this training, we had this result. You can see a lot. And sometimes we saw mistakes this way. We like this kind of thing, if you go together through the schedule and see the different hard workouts. It's nice, and you should have fun when speaking about the training. If you don't have enough fun, I think it's stupid.

But keeping the hard work fun is not enough. "Fun and success, too," explains Dieter. "If you don't have success, you don't stay with it. All these workouts are hard, so if you have some success, then it's fun. And if you have very hard workouts, then you need to have easy days, too."

"It's like training, training, training, training hard, then you go easy," Uta says, her voice lowering.

Then you get a good feeling and you are able to stay with running. Because it's not easy to begin with running, and it's not easy to stay with running. That is why the schedule is so important. Very hard workouts, then very easy ones, just for fun. And for me, 3.8 meters per second [7 minutes a mile], that's fun pace.

Seven Kenyan runners, including Sammy Lelei (who ran a 2:07:02 marathon in 1995, the second-fastest ever), Lameck Aguta, and Simon Karori, train under Hogen, plus some other German runners. They call themselves "Team Magnolia," after Magnolia Road where they train in the mountains. Their training is measured in meters per second, the system used in the former East Germany. It is not common elsewhere, and Uta sometimes gets blank stares when she tries to explain the pace of her training runs.

"It's difficult to think in terms of miles," she says,

> because we measure everything in meters per second. If someone says, 4 minutes per kilometer, we say, oh, that's 4.17 meters per second. That was the old system in East Germany. For instance, your relaxing pace is around maybe 3.7 meters per second, then, if you go at a higher speed, it's 4.0 meters, and to go very fast, 5.0 meters per second.

Five meters per second is 32 minutes for 10 kilometers, 4.17 meters per second is 40 minutes for 10 kilometers, and 3.7 meters per second is 45 minutes for 10 kilometers. "We think in this system," Pippig says with a laugh. "It's a very clear system and very accepted system."

By whatever method you use to measure her speed, Pippig does some of the highest-mileage training ever of any woman, including Joan Benoit Samuelson. A typical training week for Pippig leading up to a marathon includes running three times each day, except when long runs are scheduled.

When training for the track, Pippig runs 15-20 400-meter intervals, the early ones in 75 seconds with the last ones in 66-69 seconds, with a minute recovery. Ten days before a track race, she will run 10 × 400 meters in 65-68 seconds. When training for the roads, she tries to run most of her workouts on hilly courses, because the courses she runs, like Boston, are hilly. Pippig usually trains through road races. "I can do that," she says, "because the depth in women's races isn't as great as for the men. But to win a race is tough for either men or women."

The average for 10 weeks leading up to a marathon is around 130 miles. The mileage the weeks before road races is lower, but still well over 100 miles. Her yearly schedule is one of peaks and valleys; some weeks Pippig runs up to 170-180 miles, followed by lower-mileage weeks. Hogen never counts the mileage Uta or his other runners put in. "I don't really care how many miles she does. For me, what's interesting are the workouts we did, the *quality* workouts. Uta can count the miles or not."

The first run is 3-5 miles at 6:30 A.M., followed by this schedule:

Sunday:	20 miles, 3.90 meters per second.
Monday:	A.M., easy. 10 miles (3.80 meters per second); P.M., 6 miles (3.80 meters per second); 15 strides; 45 minutes calisthenics.
Tuesday:	A.M., 6 × 1 mile in 5:15; 400-meter jog in 2 minutes for recovery; P.M., 6 miles.
Wednesday:	Same as Monday, except no strides.
Thursday:	A.M., 15 miles in "middle pace" (4.17 meters per second); P.M., 6 miles, strides.
Friday:	Same as Monday.
Saturday:	A.M., 6 miles (4.80 meters per second); P.M., 6 miles (3.70 meters per second).

Pippig rests up for major marathons or championship track races. Her highest mileage week was 180, followed by easy weeks. "But you know," Uta says with a laugh.

> I cannot go like the Chinese [runners]; I tried it. Over 160 miles a week is what the Chinese do every week! I was so tired, after 160-mile weeks. I was going to San Diego and was not so fresh. I couldn't run under 32 minutes [for 10K]; I could run just 32:17. You know, if you train very nicely, you can run much better.

Training "nicely" means hard days interspersed with "fun" recovery days. The Sunday long run is between 19 and 22 miles, at 8,500 feet. A few times a week Uta will run with some of the male runners Hogen is coaching. Having training partners is important, she says, because "sometimes it is nice to have someone one step in front of you."

Though she does much of her training at nearly 6,000 feet when in the United States, Pippig does not make a big deal about altitude. When they say altitude, they mean *altitude*, over 8,000 feet, where the effect of the diminished oxygen supply really is felt. Their times are slower than

Hogen's Coaching

Dieter Hogen coached middle-distance runners for eight years before taking on Uta and some other long-distance runners. The foundation of his philosophy of coaching is,

> If you want to go to the marathon, you have to be fast over 10,000 meters. If you want to go for 10,000 meters, you have to run fast over 3,000 meters. But always with endurance, not too much speed. Endurance is the key for everything. That was the way—I said to Uta, OK, your marathon is not bad, but first we see that you are faster for 10,000, 5,000, or 3,000 meters. Because if you want to run under 2:20 in the future, you can't do that with a best time of 34 minutes for 10,000 meters. That's why we wanted to go for much more road races, for more track races and so on.

Hogen is steeped in the East German running tradition. One influence was Czech great Emil Zatopek. "He was a crazy guy for his time. We were thinking about his training program; not so much high speed, but more repetitions. Zatopek's ideas are still part of our thinking and training." Later, Zatopek's ideas, which may be suitable for Nietzsche's *ubermensch*, were supplanted by those of Arthur Lydiard. "We were thinking about some guys in Germany, like Von Aken," the coach of Harald Norpoth, Germany's silver medalist in the Tokyo 5,000 meters.

Hogen continues building upon this legacy, keeping what has proven to work.

The bad news is that in the 1950s, they did too many intervals, with too high speed. And many runners got burned out, because of too intensive training. So we changed that a little bit, when they began studying Lydiard's ideas of more endurance. In 30 years, you learn a lot. And then you have to make your own ideas. And if you find the right way, especially with endurance and not so much speed, then you always have good runners.

Hogen says, Pippig's training falls somewhere in the middle of heavy interval training and the Lydiard over distance approach.

at sea level, but not much. For example, when training at over 7,000 feet, 1,000-meter repeats are typically done 5-10 seconds slower than at sea level. Pippig trains well in Boulder because she is comfortable there, and she blends in well in the athletic city. "It's very good there. The good thing for us is that so many people understand running and have a feeling for running. They know what it means. Surrounding yourself with a good atmosphere is key."

In February, 1994, Pippig clocked 67:59 in winning a half-marathon in Kyoto, Japan, 1 minute and 19 seconds off Ingrid Kristiansen's world best. That was such a good performance that some knowledgeable runners, when they heard the time, insisted it must be for 20 kilometers (12.4 miles) and not the 13.1-mile half-marathon distance. It was a time that showed Pippig was ready for a good marathon. She then came back to Boulder for some more high-altitude training. Uta upped her mileage to as much as 180 miles a week, followed by lower-mileage weeks, saying she was happy to start again with "serious training for six to eight [more] years."

A Run at the Record

The serious training resulted in some very serious racing. In April 1994, Pippig faced what was then being called the Boston Marathon's best women's field ever. Her main challengers were Olympic gold medalist Valentina Yegorova, two-time Boston winner Olga Markova, and South Africans Colleen De Reuck and Olympic 10,000-meter silver medalist Elana Meyer, who was running her first marathon. Pippig's training had been right on schedule, and she was prepared for anything that might come up—anything except for getting sick. "It's easier to get sick if you come in great shape," says Dieter, and that's what happened to Uta. She went for a run in the rain when she arrived in Boston the Tuesday before the race, and later that night she had "a little bit of a headache and a runny nose. On Wednesday it was bad and on Thursday and Friday it was *very* bad." On Friday, Hogen took Pippig to a local hospital, where she had a blood test. Sunday night, she took an easy run, and told Hogen she was ready to go. "I feel I'm in shape. I feel good; I have to go tomorrow and try. I'm in such good shape that even if I run with just one leg, I'll finish in the top three," she joked.

Says Dieter,

Uta is the kind of athlete who concentrates more and more on running, and it seems like everything is in her muscles. It seems like the body doesn't have enough power to fight against all these other things. You use *everything* for your shape. And then, you have to be much more careful than before.

Uta Pippig concentrates more and more on running.

Pippig was careful in the early going, running with a lead pack of Meyer, Markova, Yegorova, and De Reuck through the halfway mark. She was feeling good enough to run faster in the early going, but she held back until mile 15, when she threw in a 5:12 mile. Only Meyer could go with her, and, when the South African faded on the hills at 18 miles, Pippig was able to run in for the victory. Helped along by a favoring wind, she clocked 2:21:45, history's third-fastest time, after Kristiansen (2:21:06) and Benoit Samuelson (2:21:21). Yegorova was second in 2:23:33, followed by Meyer in 2:25:15.

"Sure, it was very good conditions and everything," said Hogen.

But Uta could say, if I didn't have this cold; if I didn't have this mental pressure, being nervous about finishing the race, then I can run 2 minutes faster. Then I'd have the same time as without the wind. That's why all this speculation about the wind . . . that's OK, but you shouldn't make too much of it. In the end, we really had luck that it was possible for Uta to race. Now she's happy that she beat the Olympic champion by two minutes.

Pippig was now a media star. She jogged with President Clinton and was a guest on the David Letterman Show ("he's a nice guy, but I couldn't understand all his jokes"). Pippig flew to Vienna to attend a trade show, took a train to Munich for appearances on German TV, then flew back across the Atlantic. "Uta gave a supreme effort in Boston," said Mark Plaatjes, the world marathon champ. "And then she just had so many things going on at once: interviews, running with the president, flying all around; all that eventually takes its toll."

The toll continued to mount through May, with interviews and photo shoots literally every day for weeks. Pippig, overwhelmed by all the attention, simply says, "It just got to be too much."

With Mota, Waitz, Kristiansen, and Benoit Samuelson out of the running spotlight by 1994, Uta was the biggest star in women's running. At the Bolder Boulder prerace press conference, Pippig was surrounded by TV cameras, photographers, and journalists. After 20 minutes of patiently answering questions such as "How does it feel to be an attractive woman runner?" Pippig suddenly says, "That's it, guys," and runs down the hallway, chased by several reporters, microphones in hand. Fortunately, none of the journalists was very fit, and Pippig easily got away from them, their cries of "One more question, Uta; Uta! Uta!" echoing in the empty hallway after her.

"Uta, Uta, Uta," was the cry Pippig and Dieter heard repeated with too much frequency in the months following her Boston win, and Hogen knew it was too much halfway through the Bolder Boulder, when Uta got dropped by eventual winner Nadia Prasad and finished second. It was her first loss since Stuttgart. The weary Pippig still blew kisses to the crowd when she finished (as she usually does when she wins a race)—the kisses just were not as big this time. Hogen then canceled not just the race planned for the following Saturday, but also *all* Pippig's races for the rest of 1994, passing up six-figures worth of appearance fees and prize money. He actually decided to end her season at the three-mile mark of the Bolder Boulder, when he saw how tired Uta looked. Pippig shrugged off discussions of how much money she was passing up. She learned early on to focus on the nonmaterial dimensions of life. "Money is not important," she said. "It's more important for me to have a vacation with Dieter." The only way to do that was to have a vacation from racing.

Taking a break is one of the fundamental tenets of Pippig's training, perhaps the main reason she has been running 2:30 marathons or faster for nearly 10 years and why she believes she will run the world record. Many runners are motivated to put in high-mileage weeks, but to do it for months and years as Pippig has done requires careful planning and staying mentally sharp.

> Here's a secret, that many runners don't know. If you have these breaks like Uta takes, your body can recover, and when you come back, you don't have to keep doing more mileage to get faster. And that's why you want to stay healthy for as long as you can, even if you don't race for six, seven or eight months. Then you can come back and do some great runs.

Taking a break gives the body a chance to renew itself and to feel that "the workouts are a new thing again," says Hogen. "It brings you to a new level."

If runners do not take breaks as Pippig does, very often the body takes its own rest, and the athlete either slows down, becomes injured, or gets burned out. Pippig avoids this by jogging for 3-4 weeks after a marathon and taking time off at the end of the year. "Then, we are in balance again," says Hogen. "Overtraining is one of the worst things you can do. You can get tired not just for several weeks, but maybe for the rest of your life."

This Age for Running

Something drives Pippig to continue looking for "great runs," so she decided to stop her studies for several years. "What I hear now is that so many runners are full-time runners. For me, I like to study, to read and to learn things. But not so tough like the last few years. It was crazy to do both." Pippig gets her work ethic from her parents. "They say work, work, work, because the job is the important thing. But now, I know I have this age for running. I like running so much and I'm having good results, and I'd like to improve my results, so I go for the sport now." In a 1995 interview with *Runner's World*, Pippig said

> Over the years, the desire for victory became more strongly ingrained in me. This seeps eventually into your flesh and bones. What for many people would be a horror—to complete this hard, daily training—is something totally positive, something that makes me happy.

Uta would have been Dr. Pippig and finished with her studying— and been able to turn to serious, or "professional running," sooner— except that the four years of university classes she took and passed in East Germany did not transfer to West Germany. "They said, 'Sorry, that's not our system. You have to start again.' Only physics transferred." Having to start her medical studies over is why Pippig needed so much time for schooling and why her life see-sawed between studying and running.

The discipline Pippig displays in whatever she does is the main ingredient to being a successful runner, says Hogen.

> That's maybe the most important part for endurance sports, like triathlon or running. Uta has the talent. You can't do that without talent. But the real big part is the very hard work, every day. Because it is not just running. We have a very, very strong schedule, for food, as well. For everything. What I mean is that Uta is doing everything around the sport.

That includes regular sauna, stretching, massage, and light weight lifting. "It's important to do everything you can to stay healthy and to relax, because the training is so very hard."

In the future, nutrition will play a bigger role in sports, says Uta.

> What you eat and what you do before and after the training is important too. Maybe the Chinese do know something. Maybe they have some better ideas on how to relax, so they are that much more fresh for their training. If I would train with them completely, every day for a year, from morning to 12 at night, eat with them, sleep with them, train with them, then we could know what they are doing.

But runners should not "just think of what the other girls are doing. That is not the key for your own success. You have to *think about your own self*," she says, enunciating the words. "Because it's a short time. Look, in 10 years, poof, it's over." So Uta keeps improving step-by-step. In the coming years, she plans to be even better. "There is always hope."

Hope is what kept Pippig going when she was in East Germany, and hope still fuels her, hope for a sub-2:20 marathon and for an Olympic gold medal, and hope for her country. But Pippig does not put a lot of pressure on herself.

I'm more relaxed for training, much more mentally strong, so I can train much harder. I have the mentality that I can train like a man, and it helps me a lot. So we'll go for fast times, and if it works, OK. If not, then we tried.

Going for 2:20

Pippig has the equanimity to take the vicissitudes of life in stride; that is why losing does not bother her. "Why should it? I'm just a normal person. I can lose a race." The way she races, win or lose, running in with a huge smile, blowing kisses, has endeared her to fans and the media. "Uta really likes her sport," Hogen says. "That's why she is very motivated to train harder than ever. And that's why I think she can increase her results a lot. I think she can run much faster than she ran in Boston."

So do others, including Frank Shorter, the 1972 Olympic Marathon gold medalist.

Dieter is smart about the way they are going about Uta's running, by trying to keep the pressure off of her. It's hard to break the world record, because everything has to be right on that day. It's not like a miler who can go to Europe and get several chances at a record. But of all the women running, Uta has the best shot at breaking the record. Physiologically, she has the potential to do it.

Psychologically, the fast times by the Chinese gave Pippig a sense of urgency to try to break the chimerical 2:20 barrier. "That is my second dream," Uta says, and she has devoted her life to it, living and training with total focus. Everything she does is geared to the 2:20 marathon. "I have been waiting for my record to go for years," said Ingrid Kristiansen, who set the record of 2:21:06 in London in 1985. But as 1995 wound down, she was still waiting. "It will be taken, but it depends so much on conditions, the course and the weather," Kristiansen told *Athletics Weekly*. "The women's scene seems to have stood still for years."

"One advantage Uta has is a coach who understands how to train," says Shorter. "She doesn't overrace. The main thing is you have to plan perfectly."

"Always, everyone is asking us about the world record," says Dieter. "Sure, you think about these times, but it's not the first thing you think about. Just you would like to do it. That's it. Also, you know to run 2:21 again is very hard. It's easy to go around saying things." Hogen agrees with Shorter and Kristiansen that conditions have to be right for Pippig to get the record. "Always you need two, three chances to break the record. If you have this shape, and you try it three or four times, maybe one time you can do it. In the marathon, you have to do everything very seriously, very carefully."

Pippig prepared very seriously for the 1995 Boston Marathon. Uta and Dieter had a new slogan for 1995—"Just do it." After 10 years with Adidas, the pair switched over to Nike for a reported $300,000 a year.

Pippig spent the winter cross-country skiing up to five or six hours a day at different Colorado resorts. In February, she fell on the ice while training, and she had to drop out of the Gasparilla 15K. It was the first time Pippig had pulled out of a race since 1984. Then she returned to Kyoto, Japan, and ran the half-marathon in 67:58, one second faster than 1994. "Maybe that means I can run my marathon at Boston one second faster," she joked.

It looked as if she may have to, as the field Pippig faced at Boston in 1995 was even deeper and faster than the previous year. Tecla Loroupe, the Kenyan who won New York (2:27:37) in the fall, was there, as well as Valentina Yegorova and Elana Meyer.

Pippig went to the front early, followed closely by her three main rivals. The winds were not favorable this year, buffeting the runners head-on, and Pippig knew she would be running for the win, not the record. The other runners let her break the wind, and she passed halfway in 1:11:23, looking back over her shoulder several times to see who was near her. It was always Yegorova and Meyer, and, at 19 miles, Loroupe joined the leaders. The race was shaping up to be a four-woman battle to the end, but Yegorova dropped off the pace and eventually dropped out.

Loroupe then took the lead from Pippig. But at the next water stop, at 20 miles, the two Africans, Meyer and Loroupe, lost ground while searching for their water bottles. Pippig picked out her bottle and opened up a gap. Meyer and Loroupe caught back up to Pippig, but, on Heartbreak Hill, the Kenyan fell back. "I run all the time in the mountains," Pippig said, "so Heartbreak Hill didn't bother me. But I don't want to say it's easy."

It was now Meyer and Pippig running together, with Pippig glancing over at her rival. But Meyer's leg started cramping, and she had to come to a complete stop to massage it. Pippig, despite being hampered by blisters, was able to run in for the 2:25:11 to 2:26:51 win; Loroupe dropped all the way down to ninth (2:33:10). Uta's second-consecutive Boston win was not as fast as the year before, but, in beating back the challenge of the world's top runners, Pippig showed she was the best women's marathoner in the world. She had the major marathon victories, the fast times—faster than Grete Waitz and Rosa Mota ever ran— the respect of her rivals, and the adoration of fans. She had everything but a major championship medal. And that, Pippig believes, would be coming in the next year.

In September 1995, Pippig won the Berlin Marathon for the third time, in 2:25:37. (Sammy Lelei, who does the same training as Pippig, only faster, won the men's race in 2:07:02.) Pippig had to come from behind after a tough battle with Kenyan Angelina Kanana, a postal worker from Nairobi.

"I've never met Uta; I've only heard of her. I'm trying to reach her level," Kanana said beforehand. The two didn't meet until 25 kilometers, as Kanana took off from the start, passing 5 kilometers in 16:46 and 10 kilometers in 33:26. Kanana, who had run 2:27:24 in her marathon debut in Hamburg earlier in 1995, was running with one man for company while the trailing Pippig was surrounded by a phalanx of males hoping to get on TV. When Pippig caught and passed Kanana, some of the men accidentally bumped the Kenyan. "After that, I was very unhappy," said Kanana. "I lost my interest in running [the marathon]."

"Look, it was a little crazy out there," said Pippig, who missed water bottles in the early going. "I was a little dehydrated, and had cramps in my right leg." Pippig was hoping to get the course record, but missed it by 26 seconds.

Berlin race director Horst Milde is a big believer in the arts, and commissioned a bust of Pippig, unveiled the day before the race. Instead of her trademark big smile, the bust has a slight "Mona Lisa smile." Chiseled on the back of the sculpture is the number 2:19:58, and Hogen says the 100th running of Boston is where Pippig might run that fast. "You can never say for sure if you can run a record, but we will try what we can at Boston."

Looking Ahead

Sitting on the porch of their home nestled in the rolling farmland north of Boulder one summer day before heading back to Germany, Hogen reflected on the hectic year and looked ahead. It is 11 in the morning, but Uta is still sleeping, finally getting some rest. "This is in the middle of our training courses," Hogen says, pointing to the nearby hills. It's a place where horses and cows are still more numerous than cars, and where a runner, if she wanted to, could run on dirt roads all the way to Wyoming.

The house looks similar to that of their neighbors (who include masters great Priscilla Welch), until you go to the downstairs work-out room. "When we moved in, we told the workers we had to have it done in three weeks. We changed the basement into a gymnasium suitable for a world record." The only trophy downstairs is a shoe Pippig wore on her first Boston win, now bronzed and mounted. There are weight machines, a sauna, and gym equipment. On the wall behind the treadmill are three posters of Pippig winning major marathons: Berlin in 1992, New York City in 1993, and Boston in 1994. There is space for another poster in the line—is it being saved for a world record? "That would be nice," says Hogen, "but it's not the kind of thing you can plan out." But, Hogen, lets on, "Training is perfect now. Even when the weather is bad, we can train very hard in here. And that's why Uta is *very* motivated to train harder than ever before to run these times."

World-record training involves more than putting in lots of mileage, says Hogen. "The running is just one part of our program. We spend a lot time making sure Uta stays healthy." That's done with the help of Dirk Schmidt, the physical therapist who travels with Pippig. He helps her with weight lifting, gymnastics, and stretching every day. He has been hired to stay with her for several years. "She must build up her body completely, not just the legs," Hogen says.

> Legs are just a part of it. Always at this level you are on a very small ledge, and just one step left or right, and you fall down. That's the problem, and that's why taking a break isn't such a bad idea. It gives her a chance to recover, mentally and physically.

Pippig's goals are winning the 100th running of Boston in April of 1996 and winning a medal in the 10,000 meters or marathon at the 1996 Atlanta Olympics. Hogen will know Uta is ready for what he calls "a big performance" by how she runs their standard workouts. One of those is the 40-kilometer long run on "special trails" up on Magnolia Road in Boulder at nearly 9,000 feet. "Let's say, it's in 7:30 [per-mile pace] and she can do it very easy, with a very low pulse rate, and she says, 'I have no problems at all until the last meters.' OK, that's the first thing."

The second aspect is fast tempo runs. "It's no secret; before Boston, Uta ran three workouts of 10 to 15K, with the last 10K faster than you have to run to win the Bolder Boulder [about 33:30]." Then there are the intervals, 8 or 10 × 1,000 meters or 6 × 1 mile with short recovery, in times that are 105 percent of the world-record pace for the marathon. Doing great workouts, however, is not enough, Hogen says. "Also, you need to look good, and your running style be very . . ." he pauses, "much one part. You need to be a smooth runner. That's the third part. And if you can do all these things together, and you can increase it week by week, until the last two or three weeks before the race, then you know, 'I can run this time.'"

> You see, it's all these things together; physical therapy, nutrition, very hard training, and a runner who wants everything. And who is not too . . . let's say, "I must have it!" [Hogen says, scrunching up his face.] A runner who has fun with it. Such a runner is much more free, a runner who can lose a race without problems, and say, "OK, I'll win another."

Seeing them together, it is clear that Pippig and Hogen are happy. They have a life far beyond what they ever imagined during the dark days of the late 1980s, living under a strict East German regime. "For us, it's unbelievable," says Hogen.

> Look, you must see the situation. In '89, we were perhaps not in a real prison, but a kind of prison. You *couldn't* leave it. Then the wall came down, and we had this little car and just three bags. We left everything behind us and we started with zero. And now . . .

He waves his hand, taking in the mountains, the lake full of fish, the house with its pine trees, flowers, birds, the neighbor's cat, the bucket of golf balls under the porch, and a sky as deep blue as Pippig's eyes. "And now we live in this house, and, we can travel around. It's . . . it's a change; an unbelievable change for us."

Great changes continue in Germany as well, as the country struggles to define itself. "It's a tough time at home, because it's so difficult to come together," Pippig says. "Unification is the biggest problem we have had in Germany." Pippig does her part to help her country move into its new era by being the best role model she can. She is one of the biggest heroines of the reunified Germany.

My biggest goal is to make the running nice, to make the sport more fun for the people. It's such an easy, nice and healthy sport; you need just some shoes; you need just a little trail, some friends, and a little time in the morning. You know, you *really* can be happy if you can run just a little bit.

Pippig is indeed running a lot, and the couple now spends all their time and energy trying to fulfill Uta's dream of running under 2:20. "Maybe we can do it," she says.

We have only one life to live, and it passes by very quickly. So we'll go for it, and maybe see if it's possible. And if we don't make it, at least we'll know we gave it our best effort. That's all any of us can do.

21

Noureddine Morceli

"Gifted by God"

Born February 28, 1970, Algeria

World records: 1-mile, 1,500, 2,000, and 3,000 meters

World-Championships gold, 1,500, 1991, 1993, 1995

World Indoor Championships gold, 1-mile, 1992

When Noureddine Morceli was a young boy growing up in the North African coastal city of Ténès, Algeria, his older brother, Abderrahmane, was Noureddine's role model. Abderrahmane was a top international runner who set the Algerian 1,500-meter record of 3:36.26 in 1977. Noureddine and another brother, Abdelkader, often tagged along to the track and bothered their older sibling for the T-shirts he brought back from the numerous races in which he competed. One afternoon, the exasperated Abderrahmane, tired of getting pestered by his younger brothers, told the two boys he would give a race T-shirt to whomever could win a race to the end of the street and back.

"It was a bit unfair really, because Abdelkader was nine and Noureddine was only five, and you know the sort of difference size can make," Abderrahmane told journalist Pat Butcher. But despite the age difference, Noureddine beat his brother that day, the first of what were to be many wins on his way to taking up Said Aouita's middle-distance crown and becoming the best runner of the 1990s.

While there are many similarities between Aouita and Morceli—both are from North Africa; they have similar builds and similar boundless confidence; they train extremely hard; they are fast over short distances yet able to win longer races; and they are prone to making brash predictions about their racing, which they then invariably back up—Morceli is no Aouita clone. Aouita was Morceli's hero while growing up, and Noureddine vowed to follow in the Moroccan's footsteps while forging an identity of his own.

Many view Morceli among the all-time best. "Noureddine is one of the three greatest runners ever," says Rich Castro.

"He's one of the greatest," agrees Benji Durden. "Who could believe he'd dominate the way he is? I don't think we've had something like that ever. He's been at the top for five years now. And if he moves up in distance to the 5,000 and 10,000, he could dominate there, too."

"We could be looking at the greatest middle-distance runner of all time," John Walker of New Zealand, the first man under 3:50 in the mile, told *Track & Field News*.

By the end of 1995, Morceli, only 25 years old, had been ranked number one in the world over 1,500 meters and the mile for *six* consecutive years. Morceli is the prime example of how talent and unflagging desire, nurtured by good family support and consistent, hard training, can make childhood dreams come true.

"Gifted by God"

Like Sebastian Coe, Morceli's career path was charted out at an early age. As a youngster, he had it ingrained in his mind that one day he would be the best runner in the world. Morceli was born a child of the sea, growing up a short sprint away from the Mediterranean in Ténès, Algeria. He liked fishing when he was a child, and running was always a part of his life. "My most vivid memory is of when I was seven, and watching on TV when my brother Abderrahmane placed fourth behind Steve Ovett in the 1977 World Cup 1,500 in Dusseldorf," Morceli told *Sports Illustrated*'s Kenny Moore.

Morceli's father, Abdallah, worked in a factory while his mother, Kamla, raised their nine children. The Morceli's are a devout Islamic family, Noureddine told Moore.

> All my family are very, very strong believers. I was always taught that good is from God and that he says, "*Move* if you want to get something. Don't wait and sit."
>
> I am gifted by God, and I prove it by working very hard. From age 11, I wanted to be world champion. I ran my first race at 12, four miles of cross-country on the beach. I sprinted too hard at the start and came in fourth, and afterward my chest burned, and I thought, "From now on I train seriously."

Morceli indeed became serious about training. When he was just 14, he and three friends went for a run and kept going, and going, and going. By the time they got home, they had been running for five hours.

When Morceli was 16, he ran 3:50.7 for 1,500 meters. But then he placed only sixth in the Algerian high school cross-country championships. "I got so upset that I trained three times a day," Morceli told Moore. "I was crazy. Two weeks later I beat all those guys in the Algerian youth championships and realized how good I could be." Afterwards, Moore relates, Morceli told reporters of his plan to become world champion.

He almost did a year later, finishing second to Kenya's Wilfred Kirochi in the 1,500 meters at the 1988 World Junior Championships. Later that year, he dropped his 1,500-meter time to 3:40.41, and he placed ninth in the World Junior Cross-Country Championships. Morceli attended Amarra Rachide College in Algeria, then enrolled at Riverside Community College in California on the advice of Julius Kariuki, the 1988 Olympic steeplechase gold medalist from Kenya.

Ironically, says Riverside coach Ted Banks, "Noureddine wasn't the guy I wanted to get. I had my eye on Kirochi."

Banks had heard about Morceli from Lotfi Khadila, a North African long jumper for Riverside, who also competed at the junior championships.

"You know the guy who's second?" Khadila asked Banks. "He's a pretty good prospect."

"Well, let's start working on him."

Khadila wrote to Morceli and, along with Kariuki, recommended Banks. Banks had been corresponding with Kariuki, who ran for Riverside in 1988, before winning the Olympic steeplechase gold. He was friends with Morceli and told him about Banks and Riverside.

"Working on" Morceli also meant keeping tabs on his brother, because it was Abderrahmane who encouraged Noureddine to come to school in the States. Abderrahmane's best finishes were a third in the World University Games and a fourth in the World Cup. He had wanted to attend a U.S. university, but his federation did not allow him. Instead, he stayed in Algeria and got hurt at the peak of his career. Though he was ranked as high as seventh in the world, Abderrahmane never reached his potential. That is the reason he wanted to do whatever he could to help Noureddine, and why he has taken care of Noureddine his entire career, just as Peter Coe took care of Sebastian Coe. "When Noureddine got good, his brother did everything he could to encourage him to go to the United States," says Banks, who offered Morceli a scholarship after Noureddine called him and read him his running resume over the phone, in broken English.

"It wasn't a gamble," Banks said at the time. "He was going to be good even if he didn't improve." Banks was glad he had Morceli once the Algerian arrived in Riverside, and he did indeed improve. "A couple of things impressed me about Noureddine," says Banks. "First of all, he is a great athlete. He has tremendous speed." Morceli could run 47-48 seconds for 400 meters without doing any speed training. "He has very good native speed," is how Banks puts it.

U.S. Olympic 1,500-meter runner Jeff Atkinson, who beat Morceli his first year at Riverside, said Morceli was always very polite. Even after he became a world-record holder, Morceli remembered his friends from his Riverside days. "He's always stayed a real friendly guy and is still soft-spoken and nice." says Atkinson.

Though he has the utmost faith in his ability and is given to some Aouita-like boastfulness, Morceli does not give any impression of cockiness in person. He is, writes Pat Butcher, "quiet to the point of silence, reticent to the point of self-effacement. His conversation over a meal is barely audible over the clink of cutlery."

Morceli's niceness, however, belies a tough inner character. Going to Riverside was a difficult adjustment, but Abderrahmane never doubted his brother would make it, saying, "We knew he'd survive. He has more strength of character than the rest of my athletes put together."

A Rookie at Riverside

Riverside is one of the oldest community colleges in California, about 60 miles east of Los Angeles and 100 miles north of San Diego. It is the center of the California naval orange industry and has a mild climate. Morceli did not know much English when he arrived after 33 straight hours of traveling, but he quickly took to the Southern California lifestyle. "The big advantage over Algeria was that I had all the facilities for training and treatment in one place," he said.

Morceli had not been doing much distance training when he arrived in California. "Noureddine doesn't like overdistance," says Banks. "He loves hard intervals on the track and would run some horrendous workouts" at Riverside, such as 20 × 400 meters in 64 seconds, with a short recovery.

Despite his quiet demeanor, Morceli won friends with a sharp sense of humor. When competing in his first track meets, Morceli insisted on wearing green shorts, Algeria's national color, instead of Riverside's black shorts. And it seems that Morceli knew just enough English to give Banks a scare. "He'd come up to me and say, 'Coach, I only have 10 units,' when he knows you need 12 to be eligible. He's learned enough about the system to joke about it," Banks told the *Riverside Press-Enterprise*. Morceli "tries to be a comedian," added sprinter John Crear. "He tells jokes. He's very friendly and easy to get along with."

The IOC offered Morceli a training grant in 1989, but he turned it down because it would have made him ineligible for collegiate competition. Morceli and his brother passed up the IOC grant to help his development, not just as a runner, but also as a person, because Morceli was forced to mature through adjusting to life in America. He worked on campus and enjoyed living like an American, doing things like going to the local Dairy Queen after practice.

In 1989, his first year at Riverside, Morceli ran a mile under 4 minutes for the first time, and at the Aztec Invitational also broke 14 minutes for 5,000 meters, also for the first time. Morceli was making steady progress, but he did suffer setbacks. "It was a tough experience for Noureddine as a freshman," says Banks.

In April, he went to the Mt. SAC relays, the best early-season track meet in the U.S. Runners know it as a place to get fast times, and the relays typically attract top fields. Morceli was entered with the big boys in the 5,000 meters. He had run 13:58 and was ready to run better.

But being ready often is not enough. Mt. SAC has huge fields in its distance races, sometimes up to 40 starters. Morceli was pushed around at the start of the 5,000 and knocked down. The runners were brought back, and the race was started again. Morceli went into the lead, but after forcing a hard pace, had to drop out. "He learned a good lesson, the hard way," said Banks. "It hurt like hell, for a guy with as much pride as Noureddine has, to have to drop out."

It was also hard for him during the holy month of Ramadan, when Morceli follows the dictates of Islam and abstains from eating or drinking from sunrise to sunset. (Some Muslim runners are extreme in their fasting, such as Abdi Bili, the Somalian miler, who can be seen going around spitting during Ramadan, because Muslims are not supposed to even swallow saliva during the fast.)

Ramadan, says Banks, "Really worried me, because Noureddine was training hard and he couldn't drink water or anything. But he was a tough guy, and never had a drop-off."

Banks has coached scores of world-class runners. He has coached nearly 40 years, starting at the high-school level and moving up through the ranks. He gained international renown as head coach of University of Texas at El Paso from 1973-1982. There, he won 16 NCAA titles and had 46 individual NCAA champions. Three times his teams swept the triple crown of collegiate running, winning cross-country, indoor, and outdoor titles. He brought many top African runners to the United States, including Tanzanian Olympians Suleiman Nyambui and Filbert Bayi. Morceli says, "Coach Banks makes a lot of athletes. Banks is a good coach. He has a lot of experience."

One thing that set Morceli apart from the other world-class runners that Banks coached was his early focus on becoming the best in the world. Continuing the theme that began when he was 11, Morceli told Banks of his championship dreams his first year at Riverside.

"Coach, can I break the world record?" Morceli would sometimes say while the two were sitting at a meet.

"You have the potential, Noureddine, but a lot of things are necessary to do that," Banks would invariably reply. "If you keep improving, you can do it."

Says Banks, "You not only have to have the ability, as Noureddine did, but you have to have focus, and keep it over time. It doesn't happen overnight. But Morceli was different in that he was thinking about the world record very early." Morceli was so serious that he did not even date when he first came to Riverside.

He had outstanding ability, good speed, and the early focus on breaking the world records. He was very determined and very tough. Noureddine is a tough-minded guy in anything he does. If he says he is going to go out at a certain pace during a race, he will, and he'll run that pace until he runs out of gas.

Like other top runners, Morceli had tremendous talent, coupled with an all-consuming work ethic. "It is almost an obsession with Noureddine," says Banks. "He didn't want to back off. He really ran some tremendous interval workouts. He just loves to run intervals on the track. We had to hold him back."

Early in Noureddine's career at Riverside, Banks and Morceli did not always agree on what workouts to do, which led to some conflicts between the two. Sometimes when they disagreed about workouts, Morceli would storm off, then come back and talk with an assistant coach, who smoothed things out. "He and I had our knockdown dragouts," said Banks. "Noureddine is very strong-willed."

The reason Banks is so insistent on his athletes following his schedule is that "I've had guys do secret workouts," he recalls. "They'll look great in practice and run terrible in races. I tell them, either do it my way, or don't do it at all with me. One of the things the guys understand— that I'm adamant about—is that they have to run my way."

Echoing the observation other top coaches and athletes have made, Banks says many runners run too hard on their easy days and too easy on their hard days. "I believe in easy days more and more, whether it's in basketball, football, or track," says Banks, who sums up the coaching philosophy he passed to Morceli this way: "You've got to be very easy on the easy days and the hard days have to be hard. You know what has to be done. This is the road you have to take. You have to do it."

The conflicts with Banks had Morceli considering leaving Riverside, especially after getting his first injury. But he stuck out the semester, and, after finishing final exams, Morceli left California to race on the European track circuit. His best time during the summer was 3:37 for 1,500 meters, and he lost only two races.

Wonder Boy

Morceli returned for his second year at Riverside in the fall, and, in February 1990, he set the national junior college mile record by running 3:55.83 at the *Los Angeles Times* indoor meet, placing second behind British Olympic silver medalist Peter Elliott.

On April 1, 1990, Morceli ran his 5,000-meter personal best and broke Julius Kariuki's junior college record by running 13:41.4. Morceli's breakthrough came three weeks later when he returned to Mt. SAC, a year older and a lot wiser than his 1989 DNF (Did Not Finish). Before the race, Banks told Morceli, still only 19 years old, to "stay back early and not spend too much energy." After sitting in the pack for the first 3,000, Morceli ran away from the field to finish in 13:25.2, a 16-second personal best. "I was feeling good," Morceli said. "I was hoping to get under 13:30." Two weeks later, he ran a 3:39.1(1,500) and 13:59.2 (5,000) double, prompting Banks to say, "He's in a class by himself."

It is common for top athletes in the U.S. system to run two or even three races every meet, and Morceli usually *won* two races per meet. At the junior-college state championships, Morceli, despite having a bad flu, won the 1,500 and the 5,000. In the 5,000 he jogged along in last before easily surging to the front and getting the win.

Banks said Morceli's improvement came not just physically—he was always talented and hardworking—but also "emotionally." In 1989, Banks said, Morceli was "immature. He didn't want to do some things, so we'd get into arguments and he'd leave. His second year, I didn't have any of that."

Given his talent and overwhelming superiority over U.S. college runners, Morceli could have developed a big ego, but he never did. Banks helped by not treating him as a superstar. His authoritarian approach to coaching was good for Morceli. At Riverside, Morceli was just a part of the 50-member team, traveling on the bus with the rest of the runners to meets. "He's a regular guy," said one track team member.

Still, Morceli's nickname among his Riverside teammates was "Wonder Boy," and he proved it by capping his Riverside career in 1990 with state junior-college titles in the 1,500, 5,000, and cross-country, along with Algerian records in the 1,500 and 5,000. He proved it again during the summer of 1990, going undefeated on the track in Europe and winning the IAFF Grand Prix 1,500-meter title.

Efficient Training

Morceli, says Atkinson, "is not a super-pretty runner like Seb Coe, but he is super-efficient. He has a little 'preying-mantis' motion with his arm." Adds Rich Castro, "He runs like a thoroughbred. The thing about Noureddine is his incredible leg turnover."

Some of this is natural, but Morceli works very hard on his speed, speed that allows him to win races from 800 meters through 5,000 meters. "One of the things you have to do in training is toughen yourself to the distance," Banks used to tell Morceli. Morceli does that by running quality intervals, getting used to running into oxygen debt by doing intervals faster than his race pace.

Morceli always takes a break at the end of his outdoor season, at the beginning of September, "to recharge his batteries," Banks says. He lifts weights during the off-season. When he resumes training, he runs basework, not a lot of mileage. When he starts doing intervals again, Morceli takes a longer recovery between repeats: for example, a quarter-mile jog when doing 400-meter intervals. Then he takes progressively shorter recoveries as the season progresses to gradually adapt to the stress. "Speed kills, and it takes a lot of reserve," says Banks.

The hard interval workouts Morceli loves to run are the centerpiece of his training. He shows up at the track with an entourage, including one or two pacemakers, his coach, and his advisor. "Noureddine is very likable, always smiling," says agent Luis Posso. He is smiling until he starts his workout; then he is all concentration. Even when running fast intervals, Morceli "is very relaxed, looking like he's walking," explains Posso. "It's like he's just jogging; he looks effortless." He's very focused during his workouts or races, with a look of concentration in his eyes as if he were running to Mecca.

A perhaps apocryphal story has Morceli running 12 × 400 meters in 51 seconds with a 20-second rest. Whether true or not, says Banks, "To put it bluntly, he is very talented."

Morceli did not like roads much when he came to Riverside, but he began incorporating solid, hour-long road runs into his schedule. Morceli had a good role model in 1988 Olympic steeplechase champion Kariuki, "who would just hammer road runs," says Banks. Morceli did not like to do that as much, preferring to train on the track, but he eventually learned the importance of running on the roads.

After all his road runs, Morceli always puts on his spikes and does some strides, a habit he learned at Riverside. "We wouldn't be concerned with speed or time, only changing gears and good mechanics," says Banks. "Noureddine concentrated on lowering his 110-race pace, dropping his arms, cutting down on the angle on the shoulder and the arms." The idea, says Banks, is "to bring his hands more up to his nose instead of parallel to the ground."

Morceli did not start running twice a day until 1990, his second year at Riverside. A typical week when getting ready for the 1990 track season included:

Sunday:	One hour, 15 minutes to one hour, 30 minutes at 6:30 per-mile pace.
Monday:	One hour hard on roads. Then change to spikes for easy strides, to work on his finish.
Tuesday:	One hour easy. How easy? As slow as 10-minute miles. "The hard days have to be hard, and the easy days have to be really easy," says Banks.
Wednesday:	Intervals such as 10-12 quarters with a short recovery. The recovery was often a 110-meter jog, but it could be as short as 55 meters when training for the 5,000 meters.
Thursday:	Very easy. Same as Tuesday.
Friday:	Fartlek striding and sprinting on golf course.
Saturday:	Easy.

Into the "Real" World

After finishing his eligibility at Riverside, Morceli moved back to Algeria, and his brother resumed being Morceli's coach while attorney Amar Brahmia, an ex-3:36.5 (1,500) runner, became his manager. "It's very nice to have someone from your family take care of you," Morceli told the *Los Angeles Times*. "It's very normal. This is our tradition."

Morceli set his sights on the 1991 indoor season, going after the mile and 1,500 records. He went to Mexico City in the winter of 1990-1991 for a training camp to prepare himself for an assault on Eamonn Coghlan's indoor mile record of 3:49.78 at the Millrose Games.

"When I was young runner, I always wanted to run in the front," he said in a *Los Angeles Times* interview before the race. "But it is not always wise to run in the front. It is not always the smartest strategy. I have learned now to do what I have to do to win. Now, I can run in the back and wait." The problem with that strategy is that already it was apparent that there were few runners around for Morceli to wait on if he wanted to get a record.

At the Wanamaker Mile at the Millrose Games in New York City on February 2, 1991, Morceli ran 3:53.5, turning back a late-race bid from Marcus O'Sullivan, the top indoor miler in the world. It was an exciting race, as Morceli took the lead on the fifth of the 11 laps. With a lap and a half to go, O'Sullivan came up on his shoulder, looking like he might go for his fourth Wanamaker win. But Morceli simply powered away to gain nearly 15 meters on the Irishman on the last lap.

That win made a believer out of O'Sullivan, who said afterwards that Morceli was not "ranked No. 1 in the world for nothing. He looked like he had a lot left. With two laps to go, I thought I was going to go by him." Morceli was not impressed with his time. "I can do better than 3:53," he said. "If a rabbit is faster, I can do 3:50. I will try."

Afterwards, he said that with a pacemaker taking him through a 1:54 first half-mile, he could have broken the record. He got a fast first half-mile a week later at the Meadowlands Invitational in New Jersey. After a half in 1:54.8, Morceli just missed the record, finishing in 3:50.81, the third-fastest indoor time. It was five seconds faster than Morceli had run in the same race the year before, and he crushed O'Sullivan, the two-time indoor world champion, by nearly six seconds. Sixth in the race was 1988 Olympic gold medalist Peter Rono in 4:03.2. Jeff Atkinson, who was fifth in the race in 4:00.26, explains Morceli's success by saying, "Noureddine has the right body type. He's the right size, has the right cardiovascular system and the right lungs. He is super-talented and works hard. He's got a gift, and he uses it. He's awesome."

Morceli next went for Coghlan's record at the U.S. National Championships on February 23 in Madison Square Garden. Morceli chased the record by himself, without the help of a pacemaker. Morceli was well known enough, even in the United States, to have a cheering section at the race, complete with banners; his fans chanted his name and clapped while he ran. Morceli was in the lead the whole way, and, after three-quarters of a mile, he looked like he was going to give his fans the record. But he slowed over the last quarter to finish in 3:52.99. Such was Morceli's dominance that second placer O'Sullivan was 5.1 seconds behind this time.

On February 28, 1991—his 21st birthday—running the 1,500 meters in the Placido Fernandez Viagas indoor meet at the Seville Sports Palace in Seville, Spain, Morceli followed rabbit Kevin Washington through a first 800 of 1:53.55, then came through to finish in 3:33.14. Because one of the clocks had malfunctioned, the time was officially recorded as 3:34.16, still good enough to break Peter Elliott's indoor world record. Second place was Fermin Cacho, a little-known Spaniard whom Morceli would get to know very well a year later.

A week after his first world record, Morceli won the 1,500 at the World Indoor Championships, also in Seville, clocking 3:41.57. That title was a springboard to a great 1991 European outdoor track season for Morceli, as he was ranked number one in the 1,500 meters. He continued to get closer to Aouita's seemingly untouchable 1,500 record by running 3:31.00 at Helsinki's World Games in June. Morceli said he was "very satisfied, but I could have run even faster if I had been pushed by another runner toward the end. And it was very windy out there."

Later that summer, he clocked a personal best of 3:31.2 to show he was ready for the World Championships at Tokyo. At the World Championships, the world saw a changing of the guard from middle-distance great Said Aouita to Morceli when the 21-year-old Algerian won the 1,500-meter title by the huge margin of two seconds in 3:32.84. Aouita, coming off an injury, was eleventh.

The victory made Morceli an Algerian hero. He was given the Algerian medal of honor, $80,000, and a new house. President Abdou Diouf of Senegal, a mostly Muslim country, threw a party for Morceli attended by diplomats from 60 nations. "It was something you can't imagine," Morceli said. All of Algeria rejoiced when Morceli was joined on the victory stand by Hassiba Boulmerka, who won the women's 1,500 meters. Boulmerka had earlier been rebuked by some in the fundamentalist Islamic movement in Algeria for wearing running shorts. She was called "shameful" and told to train and race in the traditional *hijab* and leggings.

Morceli was finished with 1991, a superb year that saw him go undefeated in 20 races over 800, 1,500 and 3,000 meters; he earned the world record he had been dreaming about for years. Banks was not surprised by Morceli's success, saying, Morceli "was really different, because of his background. He was very single-minded. He wanted to be the best, and he was very serious about it."

Failure and Redemption

In late 1991, Morceli went to Mexico for his winter training (just as Aouita used to do) and promptly became injured (also as Aouita used to do), resulting in an up and down 1992. Early in the summer, he lost Grand Prix meets to Italian Gennaro di Napoli and David Kibet of Kenya. The injury to his hip prevented Morceli from doing proper training, and only three weeks before the Olympics was he back to full strength.

Most people did not know about the injury, and, heading into the 1992 Olympics, expectations for Morceli were sky-high. He was the overwhelming favorite for the gold in the 1,500 at Barcelona, but in an Olympics of upsets, his was the biggest of them all, along with pole-vaulter Sergei Bubka, the multi-world-record holder who did not clear a height. After easily winning his heats, Morceli, still coached by brother Abderrahmane and running for the Mouloudia Sports Club, faltered in the final after being boxed in on the last lap.

According to whom you believe, Morceli was either boxed in by Kenyan team tactics, ran a poor race, or was not at full fitness because of the hip injury. It was probably a combination of those factors. Fermin Cacho of Spain thrilled the home-country fans with a 3:40.12 gold-medal win. Like Coe in the 1980 Olympic 800, Morceli has to shoulder the blame for running a poor tactical race, finishing a well-beaten seventh.

Morceli, like Coe, rebounded. Less than a month after Barcelona, he went for the 1,500-meter record on the fast track in Rieti, Italy. It was his last race of the 1992 season, and, this time, he had some fine pacemakers in David Kibet and William Kemei of Kenya. Morceli ran 13 seconds faster than he had in the Olympics and he broke Aouita's seven-year-old 1,500-meter world record of 3:29.46 by clocking 3:28.86. Concentrating on his finish, he did not know he had gotten the record until he heard the cheering from the fans; he told reporters after taking his victory lap, "I realized from the roar of the crowd that I had made it, and I devote this record to the Algerian and Italian people."

Two years earlier, Aouita had predicted that Morceli would be the one to break his record, and Noureddine proved him right.

More Gold, More Records

In 1993, Morceli solidified his claim as the world's best miler. He started the winter of 1993 by once more going for the elusive indoor-mile record. Still looking more like a high school senior than the best miler in the world, Morceli went for Coghlan's mark, but he came up short in winning the Millrose Games and Mobil 1-mile races. He then came very close in Birmingham, England, finishing in 3:50.7 after an opening half-mile of 1:53.0. He had missed Coghlan's record by one second. Afterwards, manager Amar Brahmia told *Track & Field News* that all Morceli needs "is somebody capable of chasing him and pushing him to the wall." Morceli added, in what has become the recurring motif of his career, "My problem is being by myself for the last half of my races. It's always best to have someone to push you." There were plenty of international stars capable of chasing him, but no one capable of pushing him. While Coe had Ovett and Cram pushing him, and Aouita had

Cram and several others at his level, "Morceli has only Morceli," one writer said.

After his indoor season, Morceli went to Albuquerque, New Mexico, for a period of high altitude training before heading to the track circuit in Europe. Like Zatopek and Aouita, Morceli's workouts have become shrouded in mystique. Luis Posso relates a workout Morceli did in Gainesville, of 12 × 400 in 56 seconds with a minute recovery. "No one else could do that," says Posso. O'Sullivan recalls that Morceli said that when he can run 16 fast quarters with a minute's rest, he's ready for the world record.

It did not look like Morceli would get any records in 1993, as his racing in Europe was plagued by poor weather. In Narbonne, France, Morceli crushed Olympic champ Cacho by more than three seconds in running 3:29.2, the second-fastest 1,500 ever, behind his own record. "As usual," wrote Track and Field News, "he was on his own after 1,000 meters." At his next race in Villenueve-d'Ascq, Morceli went for Coe's 1,000-meter record, but once again "the broken record replayed itself," as Morceli's only competition came from the windy and rainy weather.

Morceli has a reputation of wanting to race against the best. "Noureddine is well-coached and well-managed. He's not a prima donna. He doesn't duck anyone," says Atkinson. "Then again, he doesn't have to dodge anyone because there's no one for him to run against."

After a break for a training camp in the Swiss Alps, Morceli was ready to defend his World-Championships gold medal in August, but he almost did not go. Brahmia said Morceli would not compete in Stuttgart unless he was paid appearance money, as sprinter Carl Lewis supposedly received. Morceli's stand was that athletes should get prize and appearance money, because the IAAF receives lucrative advertising dollars from the meet.

Just before the championship started, the Algerian Federation said that yes, their star would run. He eventually ran, with some saying he was paid to compete. IAAF officials denied it (perhaps not wanting to set a precedent), but, if he was, he proved his point that runners deserved a share of the profits from championship meets. While the IAAF said it did not pay Morceli, he was quoted in Track & Field News as saying, "I don't want to go into details, but I got what I wanted."

Reports said Morceli paid a pacemaker to set a fast early pace. It did not matter, because on this day, nobody was going to beat Morceli, who hung near the leaders before sprinting an incredible last lap of 50.6 to easily win. His last 800 was 1:49.0.

Five days later in Berlin, Morceli went after the record he wanted: Steve Cram's eight-year-old mile mark of 3:46.32. Once again, Morceli was by himself after 2-1/2 laps. He still ran 3:46.78, just 0.4 from Cram's outdoor record. "The pace was exactly right," Morceli said afterwards. "Maybe I just wasn't tough enough at the end of the race." A week later in Brussels, he again missed the record, but he ran 3:47.3 in the cold and wind. Morceli told *Track & Field News* that "Cram, Coe and Aouita always had good rabbits in their fast times. But that's not the case for me."

As the season drew to a close on September 5, Morceli went to Rieti, where he had set his 1,500 mark the year before. Not facing any serious competition, Morceli was able to concentrate on the clock. He followed pacemakers through 400 meters in 54.3 and 800 meters (1:51.8), then he took the lead from Marcus O'Sullivan with a little over a lap to go. The chase for the mile record ended when Morceli powered home to finish in 3:44.39, the first sub-3:45 mile ever. Many track fans called it the greatest middle-distance performance ever.

Morceli's time was "absolutely scary," said O'Sullivan. Morceli's domination was such that Burundi's Vénuste Niyongabo, the most talented of the new milers coming up, placed second, more than *11 seconds* behind him. Morceli dedicated the race to the people of Italy and Algeria "and all those—like Cram, Coe and Ovett—who have beaten the mile record."

Afterwards, O'Sullivan echoed what most everyone who knows Morceli says: "He is a great athlete, yes, but he also is a genuinely amicable person. He always respects and has time for others. Morceli is one of very few athletes I would help any time to try to achieve what they want."

Ex-mile great John Walker was also impressed by Morceli's record. "The mile is the hardest and most respected record of all," Walker told *Track & Field News*. "It requires the speed of an 800 man and the strength of a 5,000 man. Morceli has both."

Morceli is "a tremendous worker," O'Sullivan told *Track & Field News*.

> He truly believes he can achieve things and he will do whatever work he feels is necessary to help him reach his goals. He really worked to improve his finish for this past season. He finished stronger than ever; nobody could approach him at the end of races.

Morceli ended his "all-conquering" year of 1993 with a win at the Grand Prix final in London to become the only miler ranked number one four years in a row; such greats as Ovett, Walker, and Peter Snell were all ranked number one three times in a row, and Cram was five times, but not in consecutive years. Morceli also led the rankings in the 1,000 meters and 3,000 meters, the first athlete to do that since Michel Jazy of France 31 years earlier. "Something close to legendary status is now coming Morceli's way," wrote *Track & Field News* in announcing its 1993 rankings. Morceli's only competition was with comparisons to past greats.

It had been quite a year for Morceli. He went undefeated in 16 races, won his second World-Championships gold medal, got revenge on Cacho, smashed Steve Cram's mile record, and was voted Athlete of the Year. Summing up 1993, Morceli told *Track & Field News* that "Perhaps I don't give the impression that I'm hurting out there on the track. But that is because I am animated by an interior force which covers my suffering. I believe in God. He is the secret of my success. He gives people talent."

It is more than talent, however, that makes Morceli perhaps the greatest middle-distance runner in history. What makes Morceli unique, mile great Eamonn Coghlan said in an interview, is that he "runs with no fear. Runners in the Western world have a tendency to create psychological barriers for themselves. Morceli runs with no inhibitions."

Morceli is anything but inhibited. After the mile record, he said, "I don't see anybody who can push me now."

Maintaining the Fire

Morceli had been setting a world record a year: 1991, the indoor 1,500; 1992, the 1,500; 1993, the mile. He showed he can be just as brash as Aouita was in his prime, saying early in 1994 that he wanted to set more records. This time he took aim at the 3,000-meter record, held by Kenya's Moses Kiptanui, who had broken Aouita's mark.

Morceli skipped the indoor-track circuit in 1994, saying he wanted to focus on the 3,000 and 5,000 meters in the outdoor season. In May, he attended the London gathering of the 14 living mile world-record holders on the 40th anniversary of Roger Bannister's breaking of the 4-minute-mile barrier. There, Morceli told *Track & Field News* that his goal was 7:26-7:27 for 3,000 and 12:54-12:56 for 5,000. "I feel I have to attempt these records while I am young. When I am older, it will be too late, and I will have regrets if I don't try."

Morceli's first try came a month later at Narbonne, France, where he opened his season with a 7:34.74 3,000 meters. Morceli did not run another 3,000 until August 2nd, in Monaco. Before then, he ran a 3:30.6 1,500 meters, defeating new mile sensation Niyongabo. He also clocked a 3:48.67 mile in winning the Goodwill Games.

"The only question with Noureddine is how much fire he can maintain. After you've beaten everyone and gotten world records, what's your motivation?" asks Atkinson.

In Monaco, on August 2, 1994, Morceli showed that the fire was still there when he took on a strong field in the 3,000 meters. He

Men's Mile World Record Progression

4:14.4	John Paul Jones (USA)	Cambridge	May 31, 1913
4:12.6	Norman Taber (USA)	Cambridge	July 16, 1915
4:10.4	Paavo Nurmi (FIN)	Stockholm	August 23, 1923
4:09.2	Jules Ladoumeque (FRA)	Paris	October 4, 1931
4:07.6	John E. Lovelock (NZL)	Princeton	July 15, 1933
4:06.8	Glenn Cunningham (USA)	Princeton	June 16, 1934
4:06.4	Sydney Wooderson (GBR)	London	August 28, 1937
4:06.2	Gunder Hägg (SWE)	Göteborg	July 1, 1942
4:06.2	Arne Andersson (SWE)	Stockholm	July 10, 1942
4:04.6	Gunder Hägg (SWE)	Stockholm	September 2, 1942
4:02.6	Arne Andersson (SWE)	Göteborg	July 1, 1943
4:01.6	Arne Andersson (SWE)	Malmo	July 18, 1944
4:01.4	Gunder Hägg (SWE)	Malmo	July 17, 1945
3:59.4	Roger Bannister (GBR)	Oxford	May 6, 1954
3:58.0	John Landy (AUS)	Turku	June 21, 1954
3:57.2	Derek Ibbotson (GBR)	London	July 19, 1957
3:54.5	Herbert Elliott (AUS)	Dublin	August 6, 1958
3:54.4	Peter Snell (NZL)	Wanganui	January 27, 1962
3:54.1	Peter Snell (NZL)	Auckland	November 17, 1964
3:53.6	Michel Jazy (FRA)	Rennes	June 9, 1965
3:51.3	James Ryun (USA)	Berkeley	July 17, 1966
3:51.1	James Ryun (USA)	Bakersfield	June 23, 1967
3:51.0	Filbert Bayi (TAN)	Kingston	May 17, 1975
3:49.4	John Walker (NZL)	Göteborg	August 12, 1975
3:49.0	Sebastian Coe (GBR)	Oslo	July 17, 1979
3:48.8	Steven Ovett (GBR)	Oslo	July 1, 1980
3:48.53	Sebastian Coe (GBR)	Zurich	August 19, 1981
3:48.40	Steven Ovett (GBR)	Koblenz	August 26, 1981
3:47.33	Sebastian Coe (GBR)	Brussels	August 28, 1981
3:46.32	Steve Cram (GBR)	Oslo	July 27, 1985
3:44.39	Noureddine Morceli (ALG)	Rieti	September 5, 1993

© Photo Run / Victah Sailer

Noureddine Morceli runs, seemingly unchallenged,
at the 1994 Goodwill Games.

faced Ethiopian 5,000-meter world-record holder Haile Gebrselassie in this race—it was the best miler in the world meeting the best 5,000-meter runner in the world, at a race in between their best events.

Morceli held back early, running with the Ethiopian through 2,000 meters in 5:01.4. They battled until Morceli ran away from Gebrselassie with a last 800 of 1:53.9, including a final lap of 55 seconds, to win in 7:25.11. That time cut Kiptanui's world record by nearly four seconds, and extrapolates to running two sub-4-minute miles back-to-back. The race was voted the "performance of the year" by track magazines, over Gebrselassie's 5,000 record of 12:55.30 and William Sigei's 10,000-meter world record of 26:52.23.

The 3,000 was Morceli's third outdoor world record, but it was still not enough. Two weeks later, he went for the 5,000 record at the Weltklasse meet in Zurich. World-record holder Gebrselassie was not there; Fita Bayesa of Ethiopia, Moroccan Khalid Skah, and William Sigei were. Morceli used a final 800 meters of 1:53.8 to get away from the field and win in 13:03.85. "Frankly speaking," Morceli told *Track & Field News* afterwards, "I need more experience over 5,000 meters. Now I realize there are two worlds: miling and running this long distance."

Four days later, Morceli ran to a third-place, 1:44.89 finish in the 800 meters. It was his first two-lap race in three years. American Danny Everett, wearing surfing shorts to illustrate his lack of a sponsor, won in 1:44.36. It was Morceli's only loss over any distance in nearly two years.

Morceli took one more shot at the 5,000 record in Rieti at the end of August, clocking 13:07.88. He then faced Niyongabo in the World Cup 1,500. Niyongabo, just 20, ran 1:45.13 for 800 meters, 3;30.66 for 1,500, and 3:48.94 for the mile, and he won 12 of 14 1,500s in 1994. But he could not keep pace with Morceli, who ended his season with a 3:34.7 World Cup 1,500 win. Morceli won by five seconds, his 22nd consecutive mile or 1,500 win. Morceli was again voted Athlete of the Year, only the fourth person to repeat; the others are Jim Ryun, Alberto Juantorena, and Carl Lewis.

Faster and Faster

The big race for Morceli in 1995 was the World Championships, where he would be going for his third consecutive gold medal inthe 1,500. Morceli showed that he was ready in July, when he took the last of Said Aouita's world records, setting a new 2,000-meter world record of 4:47.8, a time that shattered Aouita's eight-year record by three seconds. Morceli then took his record-breaking to a new level, breaking his own 1,500-meter mark with a time of 3:27.37 in the Nice Grand Prix meet.

Two weeks later, he clocked 3:27.5 in the Monte Carlo Grand Prix invitational, the second-fastest time in history. Morceli was on his own after 800 meters into the race, finishing nearly five seconds ahead of Steve Holman of the U.S.

Morceli's world records and medals are more than individual honors. They are also prizes for Algeria. The country has been racked by internal fighting since 1992, when the Algerian government canceled elections when it appeared that Islamic fundamentalists were going to win many seats in the National Assembly. The fundamentalists have waged a war of terrorism ever since, targeting Westerners and Algerian intellectuals, especially those educated in Europe. Estimates range as high as 30,000 killed by both the militants and the army, which backs the government.

Algeria "is living in the throes of war," a spokesman for Islamic Salvation Front, the party representing the fundamentalists, told the *Washington Post*. "Every human being on this patch of land is exposed to danger. Anybody can be killed."

With all the political problems, sports have taken on an even more important role in unifying the country, putting a great deal of pressure on Morceli. "Many people expect many things from me. It's a big responsibility. Everyone is looking at me. Everyone knows who I am. People look up to me," Morceli told the *Los Angeles Times*. "Some people don't understand. Some people expect too much." Referring to the situation in his country, Morceli adds, "I don't want to talk about politics. I am a sportsman, that is my job. I am not a politician. I follow politics, but I am not a political person."

"If you have your mind full of other things, you never run well," he said. "I have to concentrate on running. It's hard with the politics, but I always try to keep my mind clean."

Morceli has a twin sister who was a good runner before stopping training to go to college. Morceli's younger brother, Ali, is also very talented, having run 3:47 for 1,500 meters and a 1:48 800 meters when he was 19. Says Noureddine, "He's good, but he doesn't have the motivation."

It is a mystery why some athletes have the motivation, that "inner drive," to keep training year after year, which is what Morceli plans on doing. "It's important that an athlete not set just one record, then disappear," he told *Track & Field News*. "It's important for me to be at the top for many years. That is the mark of a true champion."

Like the great runners who have come before him, he also had that ineffable "aura of invincibility," says Frank Shorter. "Noureddine definitely has it. Nobody thinks they can beat him. *Nobody* does. Sure, he holds world records, but that's not as important as how other people view him." U.S. distance runner Todd Williams commented in 1995 to Dick Patrick of *USA Today*: "Morceli is the Michael Jordan of our sport. He can run a world record every time out. He's on another planet."

By any standard, Morceli is a true champion. By the end of 1995, the precocious Morceli had the mile, 1,500-, 2,000- and 3,000-meter world records, with an eye to holding *every* record from 800 through 5000 meters. He says he does not run for money, despite earning up to $40,000 per race. He wants to stake his claim as the best ever. "To really prove yourself in athletics nowadays, you have to stay 10 to 15 years. That's what I intend to do." He plans on winning a few more races along the way. "I can hold 10 world records. I personally believe I can run a mile in 3:34."

After what Noureddine Morceli has done thus far, who is going to doubt him?

AAU National Cross-Country Championships, 144
Abdesselem, Rhadi Ben, 50
Aerobic conditioning, Welch's, 86
The African Revolution (Ndoo), 61
Aiken, Andy, 157
All-African Games, Keino in, 48
Alvarez, Javiar, 183
Amateur rules and Zatopek, 26–27
Andersson, Arne, 26–27
Anentia, Arere, 39
Aouita, Said, 445–466
    early years, 447–449
    in Florence, 450–451
    Nikia Grand Prix, 451
    Seoul Olympics, 455–457
    as star, 453–455
    training, 457–461
    World Championships, 1991, 464–465
Arese, Francesco, 148
Association of Road Racing Athletes, 120, 276
Athletic Weekly, 176
Atkinson, Jeff, 552
Audain, Anne, 275, 276–277
Australian Institute of Sport, 399
Australian running tradition, 386
Bacheler, Jack, 140, 142
Baillie, Bill, 54
Bakke, Stefan, 229
Balcha, Kebede, 51
Banks, Ted, 551–555
Bannister, Roger, 16, 20, 386
Barcelona Olympics
    Moller at, 270–271, 281–287
    Morceli at, 560–561
Barrios, Arturo, 491–517
    early years, 492–495
    as marathoner, 509–513
    Mobil Grand Prix, 499–500
    training, 501–507
Bayi, Filbert, 408–410
Bedford, Dave, 177
Bednarksi, Tony, 245
Beijing's National Games, 530
Benoit, Joan. *See* Samuelson, Joan Benoit
Berlin Marathon, 1990, 529
Berlin Marathon, 1995, 545
Best Efforts (Moore), xii
Bikila, Abebe, 50–51
Bill Rodgers Running Center, 113
Bislett Games, Coe at, 305–306
Bjorklund, Garry, 173, 174, 189, 192, 197
    on Shorter, 155
    vs. de Castella, 376–377
    vs. Shorter, 114, 116–117

Blood doping suspicions of Viren, 193–195
BodyMind Connection, Moller, 281–287
Bolder Boulder, Pippig, 540–541
Bonnet, Francoise, 82
Boston Marathon, 1973, 106–108
Boston Marathon, 1975, 109–110
Boston Marathon, 1979
    Rodgers at, 121–123
    Samuelson at, 428–429
Boston Marathon, 1983, 431
Boston Marathon, 1987, 364–365
Boston Marathon, 1990, 417–420
Boston Marathon, 1991, 529
Boston Marathon, 1992, 530
Boston Marathon, 1994, 538–540
Bowerman, Bill, viii, 147
Breast cancer and Welch, 68
Brendan Foster (Foster), 194
Bright, Bob, 251
Brisbane Commonwealth Games, 1982, 377–
    379
British Amateur Athletic Board, 74
British navy, Welch in, 69–70
British running tradition, 294
Brown, Barry, 167
Budd, Zola, 332
Burfoot, Amby, 98, 100–102, 104–105, 115, 118
Burnout, Welch, 89–91
Campbell, Joseph, xiii
Campbell, Steve, 478
Cancer, Welch's, 91–94
Cascade Run-Off, Moller at, 276–278
Castro, Rich, 240
Cerutty, Percy, 384
Chataway, Chris, 20
Chicago Marathon, 1984, 251–255
Chicago Marathon, 1985
    de Castella at, 397–398
    Jones at, 258–261
    Seko at, 364
Christman, Paul, 73, 82–83
Cierpinski, Waldemar, 159
    vs. Seko, 357
Clarke, Ron, xii, 15, 29–30, 181, 386
    and Bikila, 50
    vs. Keino, 43, 52, 54–55, 58
    vs. Shorter, 143
Clayton, Derek, 145, 149, 150, 386
Clews, Gayelene, 374
Clohessy, Pat, 371–375, 384–388
    complex training, 372
Coe, Peter, 291–292
Coe, Sebastian, 61, 212, 289–324
    Bislett Games, 305–306
    early years, 290–295
    European Championships, 1986, 322–323
    Los Angeles Olympics, 318–322
    Moscow Olympics, 290, 309–314
    in politics, 323–324
    speed training, 295–296
    training, 319–322
    vs. Ovett, 296–298, 308–324

Commonwealth Games, 1962, 43
Commonwealth Games, 1966, 54
Commonwealth Games, 1970, 61
Complex training, 372
Coogan, Mark, 121, 504
Crawford, Mary, 436
Cuba, Alberto, 221
Cuban Track Federation, 218–222
Cyomex, 87
Davies, John, 275
Davis, Marc, xv
Debbagh, Aziz, 448
de Castella, Robert, xv, 369–402
    and Bjorklund, 376–377
    Boston Marathon 1986, 398
    Brisbane Commonwealth Games, 1982,
        377–379
    Chicago Marathon, 1985, 397–398
    and Clews, 374
    early years, 370–372
    Fukuoka Marathon, 377
    hill workouts, 388–389
    on Jones, 258, 260
    long runs, 391–394
    Los Angeles Olympics, 382–384
    marathons, 375–377
    Moscow Olympics, 376
    motivation, 394–395
    race preparation, 396–397
    recovery runs, 391
    retiring, 399–402
    track workouts, 390–391
    vs. Salazar, 380–381
    at Xavier College, 371–373
Densimo, Belayneh, 51
Dixler, John, 17, 32
Dixon, Rod, 147
Dunrossness Athletic Club, 73
Durden, Benji, 119, 120, 277–278
    on Benoit, 431
    on de Castella, 401
Edelen, Leonard, 154
800 meters/880 yards world records, 316
Elliott, Herb, iii
Ellwood, Kathy, 91
Emsley Carr Mile, 55
Enschede Marathon, 75
Ethiopian runners, 50–51
European Championships, 1978, 229
European Championships, 1982, 472–474
European Championships, 1986
    Coe at, 322–323
    Jones at, 262
Evans, Archie, 42–43
Federation Sportive Feminine International,
    228
5,000 meters world records, 185
Flying Finns, 172
The Flying Finns (Hannus), 176, 182
Forshaw, Joseph, 152
Foster, Brendan, 62, 160
    on Viren, 194

The Four-Minute Mile (Bannister), 16, 20
The Frank Shorter Story (Parker), 142
Froude, Derek, 260, 265, 384
Fukuoka Marathon
    de Castella at, 377
    Seko at, 360
    Shorter at, 153
Furukawa, Yoichi, 357
Galford, Chuck, 276
Gareau, Jacqueline, 336
Gebrselassie, Haile, 51
Geigengack, Bob, 138–139, 140
Gerschler, Woldemar, 7
Glasgow Marathon, Welch at, 74
Gomez, Rodolfo, 172
Grand Prix 1993, Morceli at, 563
Greater Boston Track Club, 107
Grelle, Jim, 53
Hägg, Gunder, 26
Haikkola, Rolf, 175, 176
Halberg, Murray, 272
Hannus, Martti, 176, 182
Hartmann, Kim, 288
Hayes, Johnny, 151
Heatly, Basil, 50
Heino, Viljo, 8, 9, 12, 27
Helsinki Olympics, Zatopek in, 15–24
Henderson, Joe, 114
Higdon, Hal, 236
Hill, Ron, 149
Hilton Hotels, 164
Hogen, Dieter, xiii, 32, 523–527, 537
Howard, John, 168
How They Train (Wilt), 14
Hunt, Brad, 323
Ignevova, Dana, 20–21
    marriage to Zatopek, 11
Ikangaa, Juma, 403–420
    Boston Marathon, 1990, 417–420
    early years, 404–406
    New York City Marathon, 1988, 411–412
    training, 413–417
Ikenaka, Yasuo, 358
International Amateur Athletic Federation
    (IAAF), 32, 228
International Cross-Country Champion-
    ships, 246–247
International Olympic Committee (IOC),
    149, 164
International Track Association, 63
Japanese marathoning tradition, 358
Jerome, John, 134
Jones, Steve, 83, 241–268
    Chicago Marathon, 1984, 251–255
    Chicago Marathon, 1985, 258–261
    early years, 242–246
    European Championships, 1986, 262
    father's death, 246
    injuries, 249–250
    International Cross-Country
        Championships, 246–247
    London Marathon, 1985, 256–257

Los Angeles Olympics, 250–251
    New York City Marathon, 1988, 263
    in the RAF, 256
    on Seko, 356
    training, 265–268
Juantorena, Alberto, 203–222
    at Cuban Track Federation, 218–222
    early career, 205–207
    injuries, 217–218
    Montreal Olympics, 210–214
    Moscow Olympics, 217–218
    Munich Olympics, 207–208
    training, 208–210
Kaggestad, Johan, 72, 232
Karvonen, Veikko, 172
Keino, Hezekiah Kipchoge, xv, 37–65, 154
    All-African Games, 48
    Commonwealth Games, 43
    death threat, 61
    early years, 39–40
    knee injury, 43–44
    Mexico City Olympics, 57–60
    Morley Mile, 48
    orphanage, 65
    police training, 41
    as professional, 63–65
    Tokoyo Olympics, 1964, 43–47
    training, 42–47
    vs. Clarke, 43, 47–48, 52, 54–55, 58
    vs. Ryun, 54, 55–56, 59–60
    and Whitfield, 44
    World Games in Helsinki, 47
Keino, Martin, 58, 63–64
Keino of Kenya (Noronha), 39
Kelly, John J., 102
Kenyan Amateur Athletic Association, 52
Kenyan Track Federation, 63
Kepka, Tadeusza, 495
Kristiansen, Ingrid, 325–344
    early years, 326–329
    London Marathon, 1985, 329–331
    New York City Marathon, 1989, 337
    training, 338–343
    vs. Samuelson, 437–438
    vs. Waitz, 328–330
    World Championships, 334–335
Landy, John, 386
Lebow, Fred, 78, 229
Lenton, Brian, 29, 373, 384
Leonard, Tommy, 114
Liquori, Marty, 48, 49, 60, 114
London Marathon
    1981, 74
    1984, 78–79
    1985, 329–331
    1987, 81–82
London Olympics, 9–11
The Lonely Breed (Clarke), xii, 30
Lopes, Carlos, 189
Los Angeles Olympics
    Coe at, 318–322
    de Castella at, 382–384

Jones at, 250–251
Seko at, 362–364
Waitz at, 236–238
Welch at, 79–81
Lovelock, Jack, 272
Lura, Lucas, 213
Lydiard, Arthur, 7, 65, 76, 176
"Manifesto of 2000 Words," 31
Marathoning (Rodgers), 102, 106
Martin, David, 292, 296
Martin, Lisa vs. Moller, 279
The Masks of God (Campbell), xiii
Masters running
    Rodgers, 129–131
    Shorter, 167–170
May, Jurgen, 52, 54
McDonald, Jack, 107, 112, 117
Melbourne Olympics, Zatopek at, 27–29
Men's marathon world records, 264
Men's mile world records, 565
Mexico City Olympics
    Keino at, 57–60
Michelsen, Albert, 154
Milde, Horst, 545
Miller, David, 291, 305
Mimoun, Alain, 28–29
Mobil Grand Prix, Barrios at, 499–500
Moller, Gordon, 274
Moller, Lorraine, 269–288
    Barcelona Olympics, 1992, 270–271, 281–287
    BodyMind Connection, 281–287
    Cascade Run-Off, 276–278
    early years, 271–275
    training, 281–287
    vs. Waitz, 278–279
Montreal Olympics
    Juantorena at, 210–214
    Rodgers at, 110–112
    Shorter at, 161–164
    Viren at, 188–193
    Waitz at, 227
Moore, Barbara, 387
Moore, Kenny, xii, 146–147, 151
    on Shorter, 135, 143
Morceli, Noureddine, xv, 549–568
    Barcelona Olympics, 560–561
    early years, 550–553
    Grand Prix 1993, 563
    at Riverside Community College, 553–558
    World Championships, 1995, 567
Morley Mile, 48
Moscow Olympics
    Coe at, 290, 309–314
    Juantorena at, 217–218
    and Rodgers, 124
    Viren at, 195–198
Mota, Rosa, 467–490
    early years, 468–470
    European Championships, 1982, 472–474
    injuries, 485–487

Seoul Olympics, 482–485
    training, 479–482
    vs. Samuelson, 477
    on Waitz, 240
Mukora, Charles, 59
Munich Olympics
    Juantorena at, 207–208
    Shorter at, 148–153
    Viren at, 178–184
    Waitz at, 226
Mutola, Maria, 219
Nakamura, Kiyoshi, 348–355
Ndoo, Philip, 61
Nebiolo, Primo, 32
Nelson, Cordner, 197
New York City Marathon, 1976, 112–113
New York City Marathon, 1978
    Waitz at, 229–231
    Welch at, 78–79
New York City Marathon, 1979
    Rodgers at, 123
    Waitz at, 231
New York City Marathon, 1987, 82
New York City Marathon, 1988
    Ikangaa at, 411–412
    Jones at, 263
New York City Marathon, 1989, 337
New York City Marathon, 1993, 531–532
New Zealand running tradition, 272–273
Nikia Grand Prix, 451
Nikolic, Dejan, xiii
Noronha, Francis, 39–40, 44–45, 49, 54, 56
Norpoth, Harald, 54
Nurmi, Paavo, 6, 13–14, 27, 186–187
O'Brien, Kerry, 55, 62
Off the Record (Lenton), 29
Okamoto, Hideshi, 351
Olsen, Eric, 164, 363
The Olympians (Coe), 61, 212
Olympic Gold (Shorter), 136, 146, 178
Olympic Heroes (Foster), 382
Olympics, women's running in, 228. *See also specific Olympics*
O'Rourke, Frank, 99
O'Rourke, Peggy, 71
Outside Magazine, 134
Ovett, Steve, 83, 299–300
    vs. Coe, 296–298, 308–324
Pan-American Games, 1971, 145–146
Pan-American Games, 1991, 221
Parker, John, 142, 144
Patrick, Dick, 568
Pedrosa, Jose, 470
Peters, Jim, 21–22
Pfeffer, Kirk, 123
Pietri, Dorando, 151
Pippig, Uta, 87, 170, 519–548
    Berlin Marathon, 1990, 529
    Berlin Marathon, 1995, 545
    Bolder Boulder, 540–541
    Boston Marathon, 1992, 530
    Boston Marathon, 1994, 538–540

Boston Marathon, 1995, 544–545
Boston Marathon, 1990, 1991, 529
early years, 521–522
leaving East Germany, 527–528
marathons, 524–527
New York City Marathon, 1993, 531–532
training, 534–538
Pitayo, Martin, 495
Plaatjes, Mark, 51
Prague Spring, Czechoslovakia, 31
Prefontaine, Steve, 159, 183
Putaruru Athletic Club, 274
Puttemans, Emiel, 143, 159
Quax, Dick, 145, 286
Quercetani, Roberto, 212
Quirot, Ana, 219
Reiff, Gaston, 11
Reilly, Brendan, 351
Reyes, Juan, xiii
Rinaldi, Robert, 475
Rochester, Joy, 497
Rodgers, Bill, viii, 97–131
    on Benoit, 428–429
    Boston Marathon, 1973, 106–108
    Boston Marathon, 1975, 109–110
    Boston Marathon, 1979, 121–123
    early years, 99–101
    masters running, 129–131
    Montreal Olympics, 110–112
    and Moscow Olympics, 124
    New York City Marathon, 1976, 112–113
    New York City Marathon, 1979, 123
    payment for races, 120
    on Shorter, 166
    training, 126–129
    on Viren, 195
    vs. Bjorklund, 114
    vs. Shorter, 99, 109-110, 114-115, 117-118, 125
    at Wesleyan, 101-103
Rome Olympic Marathon, 50
Romppanen, Eino, 173, 182, 190, 193
Rono, Henry, xv
The Runner (Olsen), 363
Runner's World, 89
Running Free (Miller), 291, 305
Running Stats, 529
Running Tide (Benoit), 423
Ryun, Jim, 54, 55-56
    vs. Keino, 59-60
Salazar, Alberto, 119
    vs. de Castella, 380–381
Salmininen, Ilmari, 172
Samuelson, Joan Benoit, viii-ix, 421–444
    Boston Marathon, 1979, 428–429
    Boston marathon, 1983, 431
    early years, 423-424
    high school running, 424–426
    Los Angeles Olympics, 431–436
    on Shorter, 166
    training, 438–441
    vs. Kristiansen, 437–438

vs. Moller, 279
vs. Mota, 477
and Welch, 80
Schlesinger, Dan, 356
Segal, Erich, 150, 152
Seko, Toshihiko, 345–368
    Boston Marathon, 1987, 364–365
    Chicago Marathon, 1985, 364
    as coach, 367–368
    early years, 347–349
    at Fukuoka, 360
    Los Angeles Olympics, 362–364
    marathoning, 349–352
    and Nakamura, 348–355
    Seoul Olympics, 365–367
    Tokyo Marathon, 1983, 359
    training, 360–362
    vs. Cierpinski, 357
    and Zen Buddhism, 353–354
Seoul Olympics
    Aouita at, 455–457
    Mota at, 482–485
    Seko at, 365–367
Sevene, Bob, 107
Shahanga, Gidamis, 378
Sheriff, Brian, 354–355
Shetland Islands, Welch at, 72–74
Shigematsu, Morio, 358
Shorter, Frank, viii, xii, 24, 133–170
    on Bikila, 50
    biking, 168
    early years, 136–139
    endorsements, 164
    Fukuoka Marathon, 153
    on Japan, 358
    on Keino, 49, 53, 55, 60
    masters running, 167–170
    Montreal Olympics, 161–164
    Munich Olympics, 134, 148–153
    Pan-American Games 1971, 145–146
    on Pippig, 543
    on training, 155–158
    on Viren, 178, 181, 192, 195
    vs. Bjorklund, 114, 116–117
    vs. Clarke, 143
    vs. Rodgers, 109–110, 114–115, 117–118, 125, 158, 167–168
    on Waitz, 33
    at Yale, 138–139
Simpson, Alan, 56
Singh, Sri Ram, 216
Snell, Peter, 56, 272
Son, Kitei, 358
Sotomayor, Javier, 220
Spedding, Charlie, 256–257
Speed training, 295–296
Sports Illustrated, 65, 143
Suzuki, Fusashige, 358
Taniguchi, Hiromi, 368
Tanui, Moses, 51
Temu, Naftali, 55
10K world records, 502

Terasawa, Toru, 358
Through the Tape (Lenton), 373, 384
Tokyo Marathon, 1983, 359
Tokyo Olympics, 364
    Keino at, 43–47
Track & Field News, 46, 210, 214
Training
    Aouita, 457–461
    Barrios, 501–507
    Coe, 319–322
    Ikangaa, 413–417
    Jones, 265–268
    Juantorena, 208–210
    Keino, 42–47
    Kristiansen, 338–343
    Moller, 281–287
    Mota, 479–482
    Pippig, 534–538
    Rodgers, 126–129
    Samuelson, 438–441
    Seko, 360–362
    Viren, 198–201
    Waitz, 233–235
    Welch, 75–77, 82–85
    Zatopek, 5–7
Training Distance Runners (Coe), 319
Tsuburaya, Kokichi, 50, 346
Tulu, Deratu, 51
Tuominen, Jaakko, 193, 201
Usami, Akio, 145
Väätäinen, Juha, 176
Vigil, Pablo, 157, 187–188
Viren, Lasse, 171–202
    blood doping suspicions, 193–195
    early years, 174–175
    injuries, 187–188
    Montreal Olympics, 188–193
    Moscow Olympics, 195–198
    Munich Olympics, 178–184
    training, 198–201
    vs. Shorter, 162
Wade, Michael, 42
Waitz, Grete, 223–240
    early years, 224–226
    European Championships, 1978, 229
    Los Angeles Olympics, 236–238
    Montreal Olympics, 227
    Munich Olympics, 226
    New York City Marathon, 1978, 229–231
    New York City Marathon, 1979, 231
    training, 233–235
    vs. Moller, 278–279
    World Cup, 1977, 229
Waitz, Jack, 229–231
Wallis, Bob, 245

Watman, Mal, 216
Welch, David, 70, 74–75, 83
    training method, 86
Welch, Priscilla, 67–96
    breast cancer, 68
    in British navy, 69–70
    burnout, 89–91
    cancer, 91–94
    and David Welch, 70
    Enschede Marathon, 75
    first marathon, 71–72
    Glasgow Marathon, 74
    London Marathon, 74, 78–79
    London Marathon 1987, 81–82
    Los Angeles Olympics, 79–81
    move to U.S., 80
    New York City Marathon, 1978, 78–79
    New York City Marathon, 1987, 82
    in Shetland Islands, 72–74
    training, 75–77, 82–85
Whitfield, Mal, 44, 46, 52, 60, 216–217
Wilson, Harry, 212
Wilt, Fred, 14
Wizards of the Middle Distance (Quercetani), 212
Wolde, Mamo, 51
Women's marathon world records, 330
Women's 5,000 meters world records, 333
Women's 10,000 meters world records, 334
Women's Olympics running, 228
World Championships, 1991, 464–465
World Championships, 1995, 567
World Class (Waitz), 225
World Cup, 1977, Waitz at, 229
World Games, Helsinki, Keino at, 47
Xavier College, de Castella at, 371–373
Yifter, Miruts, 51
Zabierzowski, Sigmunt, 206–207
Zatopek, Emil, iii–viii, 1–36
    amateur rules, 26–27
    black-listing, 31–32
    early life, 4–5
    first race, 4–5
    friendships, 29–31
    Helsinki Olympics, 15–24
    international experiences, 7–9
    London Olympics, 9–11
    marriage to Dana Ignevona, 11
    Melbourne Olympics, 27–29
    in military, 7–9
    retirement, 31–33
    at shoe factory, 4–5
    training, 5–7
Zavala, Luis, 493
Zen Buddhism of Seko, 353–354

© Charlie Johnson

Michael Sandrock, here (center) running with legends Rob de Castella (left) and Steve Jones (right), is an accomplished sports journalist with over 10 years of sportswriting experience. He's a two-time winner and two-time runner-up of the Colorado Press Association's Best Sports Story of the Year, and he has received the Colorado Society of Professional Journalists' award for sportswriting. Michael is currently sports editor of the *Colorado Daily* newspaper and a freelance writer for several running publications, including *Running Times, Runner's World, American Runner,* and *Footnotes.* He is a member of the Colorado Press Association and the Colorado Society of Professional Journalists.

An avid runner for 25 years, Michael is a training partner for many elite runners and holds personal bests of 2:24 marathon, 30:23 10K, and 14:48 5K. He earned varsity letters in track and cross-country, graduating with honors from the University of Colorado. He coached high-school track and cross-country and also coached track for the U.S. Information Agency in Africa.

Michael is the founder of the "Shoes for Africa" project in which runners donate new and used running shoes and clothing for underprivileged athletes in several countries, including the United States.

More Running Resources

Boston Marathon

The First Century of the World's Premier Running Event

Centennial Race Edition

Tom Derderian

Forewords by Joan Benoit Samuelson and Bill Rodgers

1996 • Paper • 664 pp • Item PDER0479
ISBN 0-88011-479-7 • $21.95 ($32.95 Canadian)

Lore of Running

(Third Edition)

Timothy D. Noakes, MD

Foreword by George Sheehan, MD

1991 • Paper • 832 pp • Item PNOA0438
ISBN 0-88011-438-X • $22.95 ($32.95 Canadian)

Better Runs

25 Years' Worth of Lessons for Running Faster and Farther

Joe Henderson

Foreword by Jeff Galloway

1996 • Paper • 264 pp • Item PHEN0866
ISBN 0-87322-866-9 • $14.95 ($19.95 Canadian)

To place an order: U.S. customers call **TOLL-FREE 1 800 747-4457**.
Customers outside of U.S. use the appropriate telephone number/
address shown in the front of this book.

Human Kinetics

*The Premier Publisher for
Sports & Fitness*
http://www.humankinetics.com

2335

Prices are subject to change.